THE APPLIED PSYCHOLOGY OF SUSTAINABILITY

Why doesn't everyone see sustainability as a priority? Why don't people think more carefully before making choices? What will it take for people to change? Examining the many psychological factors that lead to human behavioral effects on the environment, this book answers these questions definitively and provides practical guidance for approaches that have been used to successfully stimulate change.

The Applied Psychology of Sustainability provides an extensive, integrated definition of the processes that lead to climatic, ecological, and socio-economic *results*: It defines a Psychology of Sustainability. Each chapter applies elements from the core research areas of cognitive, social, and developmental psychology into the context of criteria specific to sustainability. Comprehensively updated to embrace great change in the field, this new edition expands on critical issues yet maintains its strong foundation that the psychology of decisions is the essential precursor to sustainability and that these decisions should be treated as the primary target of change.

Throughout the book, readers will find new ways of framing questions related to human adaptability and evolutionary psychology. *The Applied Psychology of Sustainability* is essential reading for students and professionals in a range of disciplines who wish to contribute to this crucial conversation.

Robert G. Jones is Emeritus Professor of Psychology at Missouri State University. He has consulted in organizational development and personnel decisions for over twenty-five years and has done public service work in community organizing for green space preservation and policy making for urban energy and growth management. His research and professional interests are in industrial and organizational psychology, and relate to management, prejudice, and ethical decision making.

"Are you a psychologist? Not a psychologist? This volume is for anyone who has an interest in sustainability, as well as for classes in related topics. Extremely well thought-out and accessible, Jones's volume is a unique contribution in applied psychology. It is a must for those involved in environmental policy—who are, after all, trying to change human behavior. Work for a sustainable product start-up? This book suggests your advertising campaign. While tempering our tendency to promote 'the answer,' Jones gives us a path toward changing what matters—ourselves—and argues persuasively for a greater role for applied psychology."

Lilias Jarding, Professor, Oglala Lakota College and
Director of Evaluation, Thunder Valley Community
Development Corporation, USA

"Incisive, honest, rigorous treatment of the psychological underpinnings of human decision-making and behavior. Essential reading for understanding, building, and promoting sustainable and regenerative interventions."

Elise L. Amel, Professor of Psychology and Chair,
Department of Earth, Environment and Society,
University of St. Thomas, USA

Praise for the first edition:

"In this brilliantly structured textbook, Robert Jones delves into the aspects of human psychology that underlie contemporary issues in sustainability. He couples his passion for improving the human condition with a deep understanding of the psyche, asking the crucial question: How can psychology help us understand and adapt to a rapidly changing world? I commend this text as an excellent introduction to the field of environmental psychology."

Neal Ashkanasy, Professor of Management,
University of Queensland, Australia

THE APPLIED PSYCHOLOGY OF SUSTAINABILITY

Second Edition

Robert G. Jones

NEW YORK AND LONDON

Second edition published 2020
by Routledge
52 Vanderbilt Avenue, New York, NY 10017

and by Routledge
2 Park Square, Milton Park, Abingdon, Oxon, OX14 4RN

Routledge is an imprint of the Taylor & Francis Group, an informa business

© 2020 Taylor & Francis

The right of Robert G. Jones to be identified as author of this work has been asserted by him in accordance with sections 77 and 78 of the Copyright, Designs and Patents Act 1988.

All rights reserved. No part of this book may be reprinted or reproduced or utilised in any form or by any electronic, mechanical, or other means, now known or hereafter invented, including photocopying and recording, or in any information storage or retrieval system, without permission in writing from the publishers.

Trademark notice: Product or corporate names may be trademarks or registered trademarks, and are used only for identification and explanation without intent to infringe.

First edition published by Routledge 2014

Library of Congress Cataloging-in-Publication Data
A catalog record has been requested for this book

ISBN: 978-1-138-59519-4 (hbk)
ISBN: 978-1-138-59524-8 (pbk)
ISBN: 978-0-429-48838-2 (ebk)

Typeset in Baskerville
by Swales & Willis, Exeter, Devon, UK

CONTENTS

1	Applied Psychology and The Environment: Promises and Assumptions	1
2	Applied Science and Sustainability: Some Basic Competencies	14
3	The Determinist in Us All	49
4	Differences Among People	70
5	Opening the Black Box	104
6	Social Contexts	131
7	Development, Identity Formation, and Motivation	166
8	Learning and Behavior Change	202
9	Processes in Applied Psychology	234
10	Broad Interventions	264
11	The Adaptive Capacity Scorecard	303
	References	326
	Index	410

1

APPLIED PSYCHOLOGY AND THE ENVIRONMENT
Promises and Assumptions

And shall we esteem it worthy the labour of a philosopher to give us a true system of the planets, and adjust the position and order of those remote bodies, while we affect to overlook those who, with so much success, delineate the parts of the mind, in which we are so intimately concerned?

David Hume in *An Enquiry Concerning Human Understanding*

Can we hold out hope that the scientific study of what goes on within us can help us to adapt to the natural world of which we are a part? It may seem obvious that basing our decisions on the results of careful scientific study will help us to adapt. But there are at least two ironies to this "common sense" belief. First, it is through such scientific results that we have wound up with many of our current problems. While dramatically improving the *individual* human experience, we have created *species-level* survival problems. Just in the past century, we have built very comfortable, fast, and safe transportation that billions of humans can and do use every day. But these same transportation machines that are so accommodating to *individual* needs also emit waste products that threaten the health of masses of human beings and contribute to the extinction of numerous *species* of living things.

This same trade off holds true for scientific psychology, as well. Psychology has dramatically enhanced our understanding of how we think and behave. During the same time that humans have developed our revolutionary transportation systems, applied psychologists have invented means to measure, explain, and successfully treat a host of *individual* problems, from common adjustment issues to complex neurological disorders that used to leave people dead or unable to function. At the same time, psychological science has been used quite successfully to incite overconsumption, mostly by circumventing our ability to make rational choices (Cialdini, 2007). This overconsumption is a major contributor to some of the *species* level problems in the news these days. So, the first irony of using science to solve problems is that it is a double-edged sword: The psychological tendencies and abilities

1

from which science springs have both saved us (as individuals) and led us into some of our worst difficulties as a species.

The second irony is that, to the extent that we are able to dispassionately explore the psychological bases for our success, we may find its limits. That is, through the scientific study of thinking and behavior, we may discover the limits of our species' ability to adapt. Put differently, we may become quite accurate at identifying the factors that will eventually make us extinct. These *limiting factors* will be explored in this book. The **promise** of this book is that, by understanding our psychological limitations, we will be able to realistically make the best of things, whether by successful adaptation or by preparation for extinction.

This exposes the first two **assumptions** of this book. The limiting factors we will explore include both our fundamental tendencies of thought and behavior and more complicated matters of individual and social conditions that place limits on our ability to think, learn, and change—in short, to adapt. We will start with the assumption that there are such individual and social psychological limits to our adaptive capacity: That we are not infinitely adaptable. A second assumption is that, although there is considerable science to support the idea that these factors affect our adaptability, there is an enormous amount we still have to learn in order to understand ourselves more accurately. And, finally, this book assumes some hope that, by honest and clear-eyed assessment of our strengths and shortcomings, we will be able to *use* our own limitations as leverage for enhancing the lives of those who will come after us. Like good parents, we will find ways to shield our offspring from the worst of our psychic warts. This paradox of using our limitations to manage the effects of these same limitations is at the heart of many applied psychological practices.

Why This Book?

It has become increasingly clear that there are substantial problems in our relationships with the intra-planetary systems of which we are a part. However, restating the list of sustainability problems confronting us is not a primary focus of this book. Rather, this book will focus on human decisions and actions, rather than the results of these decisions and actions. The next assumption follows from this: That human activities, especially during the past 200 years, are important causes of our sustainability woes.

For now, it is important to understand that any efforts to change the *results* of our activities—that is, to reduce sustainability problems—rely on understanding the *causes* of the *human activities* that contribute to them. In this book, human activities *themselves* will be the focus of inquiry, as well as the source of solutions. A way to think of this is that, if all the environmental outcomes that have been worrying scientists are the result of *human activities*, then the relationship between the psychological causes that lead to these environmental outcomes is entirely *mediated* by our activities. The mediated nature of this relationship is depicted in Figure 1.1.

APPLIED PSYCHOLOGY AND THE ENVIRONMENT

Human psycho-social processes → human activities → results of human activities

(A) **(B)** **(C)**

Figure 1.1 A mediated model of human effects on the environment

It may seem obvious that the logical targets for changing the *results* of our activities are (1) the activities themselves and (2) the human psycho-social processes that lead to these activities. But it is not so obvious as it first appears. The fact is that the vast majority of scientific inquiry and media attention has been on the *results* (global climate change, resource depletion, environmental toxification, species extinction, etc.), rather than on the *psycho-social causes* of relevant human activities. This book puts the scientific spotlight on the aspects of human thinking and behavior that are likely to lead to (un)sustainable *activities* and their results. The conclusions common in other scientific work on sustainability include such statements as, "Changes in XYZ are required," and, "We must endeavor to reduce this form of waste." The applied psychological approach will lead to advice about changing the human activities that are the actual causes of our problems. For example, "Reducing automotive emissions at the *individual* level relies partly on framing automotive advertising toward increased status for people at the conventional stage of moral development." This is the kind of direct advice emanating from applied psychology.

> The Nature Conservancy has a long and successful history of protecting sensitive ecosystems in North America and, more recently elsewhere. Here is a recent quote from their quarterly news magazine (Nature Conservancy, Fall 2018, italics added):
>
>> We must cut 30 gigatons a year of carbon emissions by 2030 if we are to keep global temperature increases well below 2 degrees Celsius. Nature can reduce more than one-third of the emissions needed to hit this goal *if countries invest* in carbon-storing forests, grasslands, wetlands, and farms.
>
> This illustrates the precision of basic earth sciences in describing and predicting climate change, as well as some of the potential ways to limit its destructive effects. The italicized part illustrates something that can be seen in most descriptions of environmental sustainability problems. Specifically, the main challenges involved in accomplishing this goal rely on changing human thinking and behavior—in this case getting entire countries to invest in protecting and restoring plant

> growth. The Nature Conservancy's mission encompasses a small but important part of this (buying sensitive lands for protection), but those who have tried to change the policies of entire countries know that this requires working with people to change how they make decisions. One phrase in one sentence, as in this example, gives short shrift to the changes required to realize sustainability goals.

Still, some may argue that the focus on environmental results has led to important solutions, without much reference to psycho-social causes. In fact, this is true, at least to some extent. First, we wouldn't have known about global climate change, water scarcity, and other environmental changes without climatologists, hydrologists, and other earth scientists. Second, some solutions proposed without psychologists or social scientists have been tried and have met with success. An important example is the wide success of single stream recycling programs to reduce solid waste, which has caught on in many larger municipalities. Here, the solid waste generated by municipalities has been significantly reduced through scientists identifying the problem, followed by decision makers identifying and proposing solutions, and implementing programs, usually without direct help from psychologists.

A closer examination of the change process leading to happy environmental *results* shows clearly that *psychological processes* are integral to these efforts. Waste in many forms, from household trash to large scale mining slag is (obviously) an important environmental *result* of human activity. Using sophisticated recycling programs to reduce waste starts with *predictions* of the amounts and sources of waste generated from human activities, then by attempts to *control* the waste stream by diversion to relatively productive ends. This diversion process relies on the *motivations* of many community members, which reflect the costs, profits, and convenience of the particular controls used in the recycling program. It also requires someone in the community having some *knowledge* of the ways to gather and interpret the data necessary to understand the waste problem. Notice that human activities, knowledge, and motivations are the primary concerns when trying to identify problems and implement solutions. Clearly, an understanding of these psychological functions (human activities, knowledge, and motivations) has played a role in communities where recycling has met with success.

Notice also that there are far fewer public programs dealing directly with the psycho-social *causes* of waste than with recycling existing waste. Following the household waste example back to its psycho-social causes quickly leads to questions about ways to reduce *consumption* of things like food, shopping bags, and food containers that are turned into "waste" in the first place. This seems not to have received as much attention, despite its obvious and perhaps greater potential impact. This is probably because the usual approach to controlling outcomes has focused on measuring *results*, rather than on the psycho-social causes of these results. The third assumption of this book is that programs that do gather information about these psycho-social causes are going to meet with even greater success.

Fresh water shortages provide another good example of the value of understanding the human causes of environmental results. The amount of accessible fresh water is a very small percentage of the total water on the planet, and supplies of it have been decreasing worldwide (National Geographic, 2018). Although some wealthy nations have increased supplies of water using sophisticated filtration systems that turn undrinkable water (sewage, salt water) into drinking water, they are neither universally available nor completely reliable (United States Geological Survey, 2018). Meanwhile, the widespread, lethal results of water shortages have begun to appear, partly because of the existing systems built to channel fresh water. A recent example in the U.S. comes from Flint, Michigan, where city drinking water was contaminated as a direct result of human mismanagement.

Some local governments in wealthy nations are also taking the further step of managing consumption—the human behaviors that have led to water shortages—by such means as taxing consumption, instituting fines for water consumption (i.e. fines for watering lawns on certain days of the week), and incentives for use of "gray water." While these may help in wealthy nations, more catastrophic problems of water quality and quantity seem to have been addressed by building refugee camps in places like Darfur, Syria, and other arid regions where large populations have been displaced due to fights over scarce resources. Focusing efforts on the *psycho-social causes* of water shortages (human water extraction and use, human contamination of water sources, human management of "waste" waters), though very challenging, is a more direct approach to controlling the *results* of these human activities. We will return to this example. For now, it should be clear that our assumptions that environmental issues are the result of human activities, and that these activities and their causes should be the primary focus of our efforts moving forward.

APPLIED PSYCHOLOGY AND THE ENVIRONMENT

Why an *Applied* Approach?

The urgency of scientific warnings argues for more than just working to *understand* the human activities that have caused our current planetary dilemmas. Many are convinced that we need to take action now, which requires *predicting and controlling* human activities, as well. The distinction between "describing and understanding" our world and "predicting and controlling" it are the emphases of "basic" and "applied" science, respectively. This book delves into both basic and applied fields, with the hope of providing support for the latter—for an *applied* psychology of sustainability. Thus, the need for action is urgent enough that prediction and control are required, in some cases before basic science has done much to describe or understand the human activities that cause environmental problems.

Put another way, we will assume that the scientific findings about the *results* of our activities convincingly show that recent environmental changes present us with urgent problems. Things are far enough along that we need to focus on controlling human activities, rather than taking the extra time to carefully describe their causes first, then take action. All science of course relies on description of phenomena, but applied psychologists rely on *adequate* description, rather than accurate, high fidelity description of human decisions. Applied psychologists are like travelers rather than (basic psychologist) cartographers: We rely on maps that are "good enough" to get from one place to another. High fidelity renderings of terrain and other physical features that are made by cartographers can be of value, but are rarely necessary for finding our way from town to town. Thus, applied science is expedient, in the sense that "good enough" description is all that is required for prediction and control of phenomena. We will return to discuss the potential for ethical quandaries that follow from this expedience.

This decision to focus on applied science may sound to some like a premature rush to action, to change the results of our activities. Ironically, this focus on *results* has dominated applied psychological work so far—with little reference to sustainability. Despite over a hundred years of scientific discovery in psychology, and over a hundred thousand applied psychologists who make good salaries by working to change human thinking and behavior, we know very little about how to sustain our species. Because applied psychologists do this work *for a living*, we are paid to address the concerns of our *clients*, rather than other interested parties. So predicting and controlling results such as mental health, workplace safety, personal adjustment to change, and corporate profits have all received extensive attention. At the same time, results that impact broader communities (such as sustainability, social justice, and community health) are generally not profitable, and have therefore received considerably less attention in applied psychology. Only where governments and large corporate clients have taken an interest in broader issues has there been income for applied psychologists in sustainability, and then only recently.

6

APPLIED PSYCHOLOGY AND THE ENVIRONMENT

The Ethics of Application

Hopefully, this call for immediate application of psychology to predicting and controlling people's thinking and behavior will have sounded ethical alarms for some readers. Ethics raise a set of philosophical issues that accompany all science—not just psychology. But philosophical questions play a particularly central role in applied psychological science. A quick examination of a few of these questions will help frame the ethical issues we will encounter throughout discussions of applied psychology of sustainability.

To start, much of the *basic* research in psychology directly tests philosophical ideas. For example, questions from the philosophical area of *aesthetics* have experienced a blossoming of tests under the heading of "Environmental Psychology." This basic research area is primarily concerned with how *perceptions* and *responses* to the natural and built world affect human behavior and well-being (Oskamp, 1995). In fact, the list of philosophical questions addressed by psychologists using scientific tests is quite long. Of particular relevance here, *moral philosophy* asks questions about how we decide what is "good" and "right," and it encompasses the applied area of *ethics*. There is some good news here: Basic research in *social psychology* has tested important questions about how and when people act morally. This area has yielded important research on altruism (Cialdini, 1988); prejudice and inclusion (Penner, Dovidio, Piliavin, & Schroeder, 2005); and self-regulation (Bandura, 2005) that has clarified the conditions under which we behave in self-interested versus pro-social ways. *Cognitive social psychology* in particular has advanced our understanding of the forces that support or hinder ethical behavior (Bandura, 2012). But this is basic research. It describes *how* things work rather than prescribing *how to* encourage pro-social behavior; and most of these descriptions are from labs—not from ordinary life.

In general, basic research areas have ignored the moral philosophy problems that arise when trying to *apply* their findings. And applied psychologists have tried for over a century now to integrate the answers found in basic research areas into *practice*. For example, basic research shows that monitoring of water consumption behaviors *can* reduce waste: Specifically, provision of real time feedback to people about their water consumption can reduce the amount of water they use. This is potentially very important to sustainability, but applied research first has to ask what processes psychology can ethically use to *control* water consumption with this knowledge. Finding practical ways to *implement* such a feedback system in an actual community relies heavily on a host of other social-psychological processes that are accompanied by serious ethical concerns. So, should applied psychologists influence a dictator in a country with heavy water consumption to create and enforce laws to try to force citizens to use such feedback systems? In more democratic settings, should social psychological tactics be used to manipulate public opinion without people's awareness or consent? How do we help to

7

deliberately manage the conflict that is inevitable in the policy decisions required to implement such a feedback system? These are just a few examples of questions applied psychologists ask when trying to translate basic research into deliberate change in individuals and organizations (Verdugo, 2006).

There is some good news here. Applying psychology to change people's thinking and behavior is not new. It has been successful in many endeavors, as will be outlined in this book. More good news is that an essential component of much of *applied psychology* is applied moral philosophy. Beyond the codes of ethics now guiding basic research, the largest applied domains (clinical, counseling, school, educational, and industrial-organizational psychology) have well-developed codes of ethics aimed at avoiding the kinds of breaches of trust that all sciences encounter as they become good at solving human problems. Many years of research about the efficacy of psychological applications has given practicing psychologists ethical tools for real change.

Until recently, these applied approaches have not been used to manage sustainable human behavior (Gifford, 2008; Koger & Winter, 2010; Ones & Dilchert, 2012; Oskamp, 1995; Vlek & Steg, 2007). Typical environmental psychology texts, for example, are concerned with understanding what makes people more or less comfortable, healthy, and effective in built and natural environments (Oskamp, 1995). Much less has been done to show how to control these outcomes in real settings, or how to balance current human comfort against future resource availability (e.g. clean water, healthy air, stable climate, etc.).

Since ethical issues become quite complex in applied areas, this poses a particular challenge to psychology of sustainability. Applied psychologists have successfully intervened to help manage a host of important problems in limited domains (i.e. mental health, learning in school, workplace effectiveness). But applied psychology of sustainability is new and addresses a very broad domain of human activity. The elaborate ethical codes of practice in established applied areas took considerable time to develop, and (as we will discuss later) deal with more limited domains. Because of these factors, diligence will be required as applied psychology of sustainability encounters ethical problems. In fact, working to "save the species" may be a very noble cause, but its urgency is likely to create moral and ethical pitfalls that less aggressive approaches rarely encounter. The final assumption here is that using psychology to advance sustainability will require very conscious monitoring of the processes brought forward as means to this end.

Assumptions

1   **Focus on social and psychological causes of human activities will increase sustainability or at least identify likely limitations of adaptability.**

APPLIED PSYCHOLOGY AND THE ENVIRONMENT

2 **Human activities are the initial source of *all* sustainability problems.**

3 **Although there is a large body of science about environmental sustainability, there are huge scientific gaps in understanding the causes of the human activities contributing to common sustainability concerns.**

4 **The urgency of scientific warnings about environmental degradation justifies an applied scientific approach to harnessing human strengths and shortcomings.**

5 **Urgency sometimes leads to ethical shortcuts, which means that applied psychological approaches to sustainability need to adhere to and monitor ethics.**

How Applied Psychology Works

In order to apply psychology to questions of sustainability, we first need to understand ethically constrained applied psychologists as *decision-making helpers*. What this means is that applied psychologists follow a process that engages stakeholders in defining problems, identifying, implementing, and evaluating potential solutions. Specifically, applied psychologists typically (1) assist decision makers in defining the "problem" and the outcomes they are seeking from an intervention; (2) administer appropriate assessments (and other fact-finding methods); (3) provide appropriately framed feedback from fact-finding; (4) assist in arriving at and implementing potentially effective means toward developing desired outcomes; (5) evaluate whether these outcomes have been actualized; and (6) provide feedback again. In order to do this, applied psychologists treat humans as both deliberate, individual actors (i.e., decision makers) and collective, constrained actors (i.e., susceptible to social and cultural influences). *Basic* research provides helpful descriptive frameworks that we will rely on in this book, remembering that this research helps to *describe and understand* human behavior, rather than predicting and controlling it the way *applied* psychology does.

Second, the expertise scientist-practitioner psychologists wield is not authoritarian: We are not usually quick to *prescribe* what people should or shouldn't do (Jones & Culbertson, 2011). This is at least partly because applied psychologists understand that different people often have very different views about the nature of problems. We seek to first understand how clients and other stakeholders *describe* problems *before* deciding actions. For many people who deal with everyday issues of sustainability, a key issue is working with both people who see sustainability as a "problem" and those who do not. So applied psychologists may see research on problem identification, decision making under uncertainty, group processes, and individual differences as very valuable tools for predicting people's choices. Some of

9

these have received very little attention from basic researchers interested in sustainable behaviors.

Third, and closely related to this, understanding how different individuals and groups define "success" is of central importance to practice. Different people see success in very different ways, following from their definitions of "the problem." For example, residents of Flint, Michigan and farmers in the Darfur region may see water quality and availability as a primary sustainability issue, while residents of Shanghai, China and Lagos, Nigeria are more likely to see air quality as their primary sustainability issue. This is sometimes referred to as *the criterion problem* and is at the heart of much applied psychological practice (Austin & Villanova, 1992; Ones & Dilchert, 2012). Thus, constructing stakeholders' various definitions of "the problem" and the associated "success" of solutions is a central component of practice for many applied psychologists.

Fourth, and perhaps most directly applicable to those who are interested in developing solutions with some hope of success, is the *assessment* of interventions. Only with clearly defined, multiple criteria for success, followed by rigorous evaluations of the effectiveness of interventions in achieving success, are we likely to arrive at changes in thought and behavior. Such "real world" evaluations have received some recent attention in psychology of sustainability. Because this text will take an applied approach, these will be important topical headings in later chapters of this book.

Organization of the Text

Applied psychology is primarily concerned with *defining criteria*, then finding precursor variables that can be manipulated and controlled to achieve desired ends. This textbook is structured accordingly. After defining basic terms and concepts, the second chapter addresses the essential task of developing applied psychological criteria, relying on a specific set of questions commonly posed in discussions about sustainability. The middle chapters are structured around a set of precursor variables. These psychological precursors are grouped roughly into basic research areas of psychology commonly found in introductory textbooks: cognitive, individual differences, social, developmental, motivation, and learning. The precursors of behavior will be framed as *fundamental tendencies*. These are:

1. Infallible causal inference and creeping determinism (from cognitive psychology; Chapter 3)
2. Differences in abilities and inclinations to think critically, learn, develop, and change (individual differences psychology; Chapter 4)
3. Differences in problem recognition and emotive responses (cognitive and motivation psychology; Chapter 5)
4. Social motives, inclusion, and group effected change (social psychology; Chapter 6)

APPLIED PSYCHOLOGY AND THE ENVIRONMENT

5. Identity formation, development, self-regulation, and change (developmental psychology; Chapter 7)
6. Behavior change: Developing, learning, altering self and environment (behavioral and cognitive learning psychology; Chapter 8)

Consideration of these fundamental tendencies will demonstrate to skeptics the importance of modern psychology to understanding many of the most complex and mysterious of the forces associated with our thought and behavior. This is why each fundamental tendency is used in its respective chapter to inform answers to the *five criterion questions* elaborated in Chapter 2. These are the following:

1. **What prompts people to think they have a problem (or not)?**
2. **What makes people think more or less carefully when they decide on an action?**
3. **What makes people change the way they think and behave?**
4. **When are people likely to take action?**
5. **What are the characteristics of change efforts that are likely to work?**

Only some of the precursors have been managed extensively in applied settings, and few have received attention with respect to these five general questions of sustainability. Therefore, no complete answer to the applied questions is available, but asking them—and trying to move toward answers—is likely to add value to the conversation. Also, consideration of our ability to manage "real world" problems of human-environment interactions based on this knowledge will often illuminate substantial gaps between what we know and what we think we need to know. This will help set the stage for future research.

The last few chapters will explore the applied areas that have attempted to predict and control various criteria associated with sustainability issues. These applied areas include consumer psychology, educational, industrial-organizational, clinical, human factors, community, and forensic areas of psychology. These areas will be introduced in Chapters 3 to 8, but specific interventions will receive attention in Chapters 9 and 10.

Chapter 11 will discuss whether precursor psychological *adaptive capacities* are likely to ultimately *be* adaptive. Presentation of this *adaptive capacity scorecard* will help develop priorities for action. This chapter will help to identify which of our fundamental tendencies are most influential on the five criterion questions, which tendencies are most amenable to change, and which are commonly used. This discussion will also provide tentative answers to the first questions posed in this chapter: Will we survive, and what are our greatest behavioral tendencies toward and away from extinction?

Most of the people reading this book have some desire to know whether psychological effects on thought and behavior will influence results that they believe matter. In the interest of addressing the question, "What can be done?" the last chapter will provide informed opinions about the likely results of efforts to manage psychological variables applied to sustainability.

Adaptive Capacity Scorecard

One of the major tools of applied psychology is assessment. Arguably the most important means for influencing change is to "hold up a mirror" to those who are trying to make decisions about their lives, work, organizations, public policies, and so on. For example, industrial-organizational psychologists often use an employee survey to get a clearer idea of how people in the organization are disposed toward the current management, work group, and organizational situations. When the results of the survey are revealed to organizational decision makers, they provide a data-based, empirical mirror of the organization's current state. When the empirical mirror is then considered in light of the outcome criteria that organizational stakeholders value, plans and priorities for action can be better informed.

Thus, the final promise of this book is to provide an initial sketch—not a high definition mirror—of the likely adaptive outcomes for our species. After addressing the five criterion questions, and comparing them with the fundamental tendencies described in each chapter, an *adaptive capacity scorecard* will be considered in the last chapter. It will provide some idea, in light of the fundamental tendencies described in the book, whether we are sustainable as a species. It will give a preliminary answer to the question of whether we can hope to indefinitely maintain our population at the quality of life we currently enjoy. The adaptive capacity scorecard at the end of the book will give preliminary answers to the following, more specific questions:

- *Are we likely to adapt? Are our fundamental tendencies likely to result in human extinction?*
- *Which stakeholders are likely to have "happy endings?"*
- *If it is changeable, how rapidly can important human behaviors be changed using each fundamental tendency?*
- *Should we (ethically) try to change behavior using these human tendencies?*

The answers that "experts" provide to these sorts of questions are often frustrating to those who ask. The answers this book will eventually provide are based on the thinking and research of such experts. Like Harry Truman's famous one-handed economist, for every answer "on one hand," there will usually be a trade off or possibility "on the other." This is because things happen "on average," with considerable variability, and in complex, multivariate fashion in applied science, and the relationship between behaviors and the results of behaviors are loosely coupled. Still, considering such possibilities is itself enough to aid us in decision making.

Intended Audience

Students and teachers interested in applying psychology to questions of sustainability, the environment, and social issues are the primary audience of this book. This book is not specifically intended for traditional environmental psychology courses, though it does cover some topics from this discipline, particularly in the later chapters dealing with approaches to change. Courses such as freshman seminar, upper-division elective and capstone courses in psychology (since most of the basic research areas are covered), and possibly graduate courses in sustainability and resource management are all potentially supported by this text. Some universities have begun to offer courses on "psychology of sustainability," for which this book should be most appropriate (as the title suggests).

The book is also intended to provide applied social scientists (management, public administration, recreation management, industrial-organizational psychology) and scientist-practitioners in various disciplines with an alternative framing of problems in and around human adaptability in the face of environmental change. Because the book will provide a somewhat new way of framing questions in applied evolutionary psychology, alternative directions for inquiry are also likely to emerge.

2

APPLIED SCIENCE AND SUSTAINABILITY

Some Basic Competencies

Applied psychology is defined by the use of current scientific methods and knowledge to predict and control outcomes that are valued by clients. Applied psychologists rely on psychological methods and theories to help guide clients' decision processes, based partly on a systematic assessment of the clients' circumstances. Later chapters will provide more substance about the valued outcomes addressed by different applications, how these valued outcomes are identified in practice, and other relevant aspects of applied psychology's sub-fields. In general, applied psychology is comparable in some regards to engineering, where scientific knowledge and methods are applied to practical problems like controlling water and traffic (important areas of civil engineering), energy generation and distribution (electrical and mechanical engineering), and so on.

Unlike traditional engineering, however, many areas of applied psychology are oriented toward a very systematic identification of client needs, and also managing ongoing relationships with clients. Chapter 10 will outline common steps involved in consultations with clients. As we have already seen, the ethical concerns of "rushing into" direct management of human problems through manipulation and control appear at every one of these steps. Because of this, and because this book takes a risky approach to questions of sustainability—to try to make change with only brief, ongoing description of the phenomena of interest—clarity about the fundamental issue of *competency* requires immediate attention.

A major risk associated with jumping into scientific action is the competence of the scientists taking action. There is an analogy with free climbing here—the kind of rock climbing where climbers use no ropes or anchoring devices. As with free climbing, *scientist-practitioners* (a term that many applied scientists apply to themselves) need to have a high degree of competence in order to avoid causing serious damage. In free climbing, the negative results of lower competence are obvious—falling off a cliff face. In the complex empirical world of applied science, the potential negative results are many, affect others than just the scientist-practitioner, and are not so obvious or immediate as falling off a cliff. This is especially true of a relatively new science like psychology, where the routes up the cliff face are still pretty sketchy and the consequences of inappropriate choices therefore unclear.

There are many examples of *premature applications of science* that have led to catastrophic consequences, even when the scientists involved were highly competent and generally behaved in an ethical fashion. Often, these consequences were imposed by powerful others who were threatened by the scientific worldviews put forward by the scientists. Galileo, who was imprisoned for suggesting that the Earth circled the sun, is often used as an example of this kind of unintended consequence. Other examples of catastrophic consequences of competent application come directly from the applications of science itself. For example, well-intentioned peacetime applications of nuclear energy have led to large scale threats to human well-being for generations to come (e.g. the reactor meltdowns at Chernobyl and Fukushima). In fact, even ethical efforts to try to change human thinking and behavior with respect to natural systems may have unexpected, damaging consequences unforeseen by scientist-practitioners.

Competency and Expertise

There are many examples that demonstrate the need for applied scientists to carefully consider the many possible consequences of their work. Such careful consideration relies on understanding both the likely and the unlikely consequences of various courses of action. Such *knowledge of complex contingencies* is one of the definitions of *expertise*. Expertise is a high degree of competence in a field of endeavor. The expert level of *competence* is founded on a thorough understanding of the connections between a set of actions and the *consequences* of these actions in a particular area of endeavor. *Competency* can be thought of as the initial framing that is required for development of a more thorough understanding of contingencies, and eventual expertise. Not surprisingly, explicit identification of the basic competencies of applied psychological science has been essential to formulating scientist-practitioner education and practice.

This chapter will briefly describe some of the most essential competencies of applied psychological science, interspersed with some of the core concepts that may serve as frameworks for eventual expertise in applied psychology of sustainability. The primary purpose of this chapter is to make would-be applied scientists aware of *core competencies* of this field, then provide descriptions of core competencies relevant to an applied psychology of sustainability. It is hoped that recognition, discussion, and management of these will support efforts to realize change ethically. To the extent that readers are familiar with applied science, some of this will be a refresher; but it is also a chance to integrate scientific inquiry into a framework for applying scientific psychology to sustainability.

APPLIED SCIENCE AND SUSTAINABILITY

Defining Terms

Psychology

A first step in science is to make time to consider definitions of basic terms and concepts. In this case, terms from the title of the book (sustainability, psychology) and related terms (ecology, behavior, systems, and adaptive capacity) will be discussed. Reaching a common understanding of these terms is sometimes difficult, but the discussion of their different definitions is important to the framing work of this chapter. In fact, constructive controversy about the definition of terms is often a solid basis for discovery and eventual agreement (Tjosvold, 2008). In practice, such discussion of "the problem" and of potential "solutions" as different people see them is a very important first step in applied science.

Many who are reading this will already know that psychology is the study of human behavior and the processes associated with these behaviors. *Behaviors* are observable actions, while *processes* are sequences of internal and external actions that affect behaviors. Processes are typically *inferred* from various measures, rather than directly *observed*. The *basic* research areas of psychology that will be discussed in this book have dealt with identifying these processes, and will be covered in the next several chapters. These include cognitive psychology (Chapter 3), individual differences (Chapter 4), emotive processes (Chapter 5), social and cross-cultural psychology (Chapter 6), developmental psychology (Chapter 7), and the psychology of learning (Chapter 8). Specific ideas for applied inquiry into sustainability will be suggested at the end of each of these basic research chapters. Eventually, this book will attempt to integrate these basic research areas with current *applied* areas (clinical and counseling psychology, forensic psychology, industrial-organizational psychology, and consumer psychology) to encompass major issues in sustainability (in Chapters 9–11). Throughout, the book will emphasize *prediction and control* of human behavior and decision processes for the emerging applied psychology of sustainability.

For those who are less familiar with psychology, there is often a need to clarify the scientific basis for psychological knowledge. Psychologists often are criticized for being pseudo-scientific. This tendency to dismiss psychological knowledge as non-scientific (or worse) may have numerous sources in popular and scientific discourse. Some dismiss psychology in reaction to their encounters with practitioners who claim psychological competencies, but behave otherwise. Other times people dismiss psychology because of their own lack of knowledge of the many scientific methods that have been devised to measure and manipulate psychological phenomena. It is well beyond the scope of this book to address even a few of these criticisms, some of which are more justified than others. For purposes of this book, every effort has been made to rely entirely on scientifically supported information, to provide appropriately narrow and clear conclusions, to criticize these conclusions based on contradictory rigorous evidence, and to avoid straying into areas that do not lend themselves to scientific scrutiny. These early chapters will help less familiar readers to identify the current limits of scientific methods for uncovering psychological phenomena. The extensive reference section is also provided so that readers who would like to track down sources can reach their own conclusions.

Ethics and the Precautionary Principle

The American Psychological Association (APA) and various other professional organizations in psychology have specific codes of ethics with respect to the gathering and use of scientific knowledge in both basic research and applied settings (APA, 2013a). Typically, these include protections based on participant informed consent and protection of privacy, as well as the researcher limits of competency discussed earlier, and "do-no-harm" boundaries (Rivlin, 2002). In general, ethics require a careful identification of potential *stakeholders* in decisions, and inclusion of these stakeholders' interests in these decisions (Doherty & Clayton, 2011; Phillips, 2003). For example, when we consider decisions to apply principles of psychological influence to get people to buy things, we need to consider the consequences of these consumption decisions. Many who are interested in sustainability would have us consider the interests of people who are not yet born, but who will end up living with the results of our current buying choices. We will return to this example in Chapter 10.

Put differently, ethical decisions about human influence on the environment are attempts to account for legitimate future stakeholders (Hansen, von Krauss, & Tickner, 2007a, 2007b; Kadak, 2000) using current scientific knowledge. If there is *any* potential harm to this group, codes of ethical conduct require careful consideration of ways to mitigate these potential harms. In psychological research, efforts to "do no harm" (Kadak, 2000; National Institute for Health, 1979) follow from this *precautionary principle*. Put simply, we won't usually *know* the effects of our actions, but we should always *consider* potential harm to others. In fact, this principle is an important basis for much of the popular concern over environmental *conservation* (Ehrlich, 2002)—because it's often very difficult to predict specific results of environmentally relevant choices, we take the "conservative" approach, trying to avoid future harm.

Professional codes of ethics sometimes include oversight from professional and legal communities of interest. These can include sanctions that have a big impact on professionals engaged in the practice of psychology. To date, there is no such oversight of the application of psychology to questions of sustainability (Lowman, 2013), including areas like consumer psychology and industrial-organizational (I-O) psychology that can have important environmental effects.

APPLIED SCIENCE AND SUSTAINABILITY

Competencies

Rather than providing the lists of competencies for all practice areas, Figure 2.1 describes the competencies of the Society for Industrial and Organizational (I-O) Psychology (SIOP, 2015). These were chosen because of the engagement of I-O psychologists in large scale change. Although there is overlap of these competencies with the competencies of psychologists providing service to individual and small group clients (i.e. clinical, school, and counseling psychology areas), the competencies of I-O psychology relate to organizational, institutional, and community-based clients who are more likely to have influence over decisions with very wide effects. For example, one individual client of a clinical psychologist may decide to buy a hybrid vehicle to reduce personal carbon emissions; one government agency client of an I-O psychologist may decide to purchase a fleet of hybrid cars for the 1,000 cars in their organizational fleet. Thus, I-O psychology competencies provide a potentially very sensitive framework around which to structure competencies for applied psychology of sustainability. We will return to the longer list of competencies in later chapters, attempting to elaborate on the

1. Ethical, Legal, Diversity, and International Issues
2. Fields of Psychology
3. History & Systems of Psychology
4. Professional Skills (Communication, Business/Research Proposal Development, Consulting, & Project Management Skills)
5. Research Methods
6. Statistical Methods/Data Analysis
7. Attitude Theory, Measurement, & Change
8. Career Development
9. Criterion Theory & Development
10. Groups & Teams
11. Human Performance
12. Individual Assessment
13. Individual Differences
14. Job Evaluation & Compensation
15. Job/Task/Work Analysis/Competency Modeling & Classifications
16. Judgment & Decision Making
17. Leadership & Management
18. Occupational Health and Safety
19. Organizational Development
20. Organization Theory
21. Performance Appraisal/Management
22. Personnel Recruitment, Selection, & Placement
23. Training: Theory, Program Design, & Evaluation
24. Work Motivation

Figure 2.1 Core competencies of Industrial and Organizational Psychologists (SIOP, 2015)

essential competencies for psychology of sustainability, and particularly integrating some of the "relationship" competencies needed for individual client practice.

The main point of reviewing these competencies is to realize that not "just anyone" is prepared to apply psychology ethically. This is a caution for readers who would get ahead of themselves based on a sense of urgency. Those who are urgently trying to change things are best advised to seek competency in at least some of these content domains through education and training under the supervision of credentialed scientist-practitioners.

A second reason for describing the competencies in Figure 2.1 is that, as this book progresses, these competencies will be fundamental to understanding the processes used in applied psychology. Put another way, this book provides initial education in these competencies. Of course, the first step for developing any competency is to define basic concepts, some of which follow here. This list of concepts will immediately add to the competencies in Figure 2.1, since psychology of sustainability encompasses human issues beyond individuals and organizations.

Adaptive Capacity

Darwin believed that each species changes in response to internal and external forces that combined to change the structures and behaviors of species over time. Among other errors, the internal changes relied entirely on *genetic* change—something that happens over considerable numbers of generations. Because natural selection of genetic changes is relatively slow, it is hard to imagine how it stands alone as the way that species adapt in the face of rapid environmental change (Bolhuis, Brown, Richardson, & Laland, 2011).

Darwin's cousin Francis Galton and his students helped us begin to understand that we may change more rapidly than this (Bolhuis et al., 2011; Hothersall, 1995). Galton's study of individual differences in human mental "adaptive capacities" (Hothersall, 1995) suggested that adaptation relies on genetics and natural selection, but that *individual differences* in mental abilities allowed for differential success in responding to the immediate challenges in our environment. Basically, Galton believed that "intelligent" people were better equipped for survival. Other researchers also showed that animals adapt through other means that occur more quickly than genetic change. Trial-and-error learning in a single organism's lifespan is one example of such adaptation, as is learning that occurs when other members of the species watch each others' trial and error (modeling), and complex learning that occurs through the development of general principles to guide actions (cognitive learning) and through rules and principles that are passed on generationally (culture). All of these forms of adaptation were left for later researchers to describe (De Waal, 2002). They will also be discussed later in the book.

Picture 2.1 Archaeopteryx is often used as a special example of genetic adaptation. The discovery of fossilized remains of this animal was the first proof that one of the branches of dinosaurs evolved into feathered birds. Although other dinosaurs were able to fly, this dinosaur's feathers made it better able to retain body heat than other dinosaurs. Thus, when global temperatures plummeted after a meteor impact, these were the dinosaurs that adapted to the changed conditions. We now call them birds

Perhaps most unique about our species is the set of mental and social adaptations that have given us science, culture, engineering, technology, organized economies, and self-government. Through these methods, we try to regulate our own behaviors using laws, customs, physical constraints (including buildings, fences, etc.), and education. However, these mental and social adaptations have also given us the power to alter the environment *to adapt it to our needs*, rather than adapting ourselves to the environment! These additions to the "adaptation" repertoire rely largely on our brain's *neocortex*— the thin layer of cells on the outside of the brain that make it possible for us to develop and test abstracted cause–effect hypotheses about our worlds. Rather than taking immediately consequential gambles—as occurs with trial and error learning, we develop general understandings about contingencies in the world, then act strategically toward some desired outcome. This remarkable ability not only allows for very rapid change, it makes it possible to alter our environments, sometimes drastically.

Adaptation therefore includes all of these processes: trial and error, modeling, cognitive learning, and changing our physical and social environments.

Adaptation is defined as these processes through which species and individuals change their forms and functions in ways that respond *effectively* to environmental changes. Various other definitions have been offered and discussed at length (Buss, Haselton, Shackelford, Bleske, & Wakefield, 1998; De Waal, 2002; Scher, 1999), but for our purposes, it is not just psychological changes that will be defined as adaptation, but those *changes that have given us advantages*. In some evolutionary theory, these advantages are ascribed to individuals, but can also be applied to our species as a whole. The distinction between the broad category of psychological "change" and the more narrow changes that help us to survive (adaptation) will be discussed at length at the end of this chapter. It is an essential distinction, particularly for applied psychology.

Adaptive capacity can be defined as the extent to which individuals, species, and broader systems are *capable* of successfully altering and maintaining structures and functions in the face of a changing environment (Kotrschal & Taborsky, 2010). Put another way, adaptive capacity is defined as the precursor to *viability*. At one extreme, very low levels of adaptive capacity result in death (at the individual level) and extinction (at the species level) when environments change. At the other extreme, some would suggest that adaptive capacity is the ongoing survival of a *species* with the optimal level of life quality of *individuals*. However, other evidence suggests that species may overwhelm their ecological niche, leading to extinction by overly successful adaptation. We will return to this in the definition of sustainability, where successful adaptation is defined by balancing the viability of individual, species, and eco-systems.

Returning to Darwin and Galton, a key basis for species level adaptive capacity is its reliance on *requisite variety*: The extent to which a species varies on characteristics relevant to survival (Ashby, 1956). Typically, characteristics with greater variability within a species provide the species with the ability to change over time in response to changes in the environment. So, for example, dinosaurs were thought to have become extinct due in part to their *invariant* characteristics (e.g. relative cold-bloodedness) in the face of a rapidly changing environment (drastic climatic cooling). Species where some individuals were able to vary body metabolism somewhat independently (i.e. warm-bloodedness) had an adaptive advantage in response to such climatic temperature changes.

Carrying Capacity and Levels of Analysis

A central problem in human viability has been referred to as the *tragedy of the commons* (Hardin, 1968), whereby individuals seeking their own individual best interests decrease the ability of the larger group to survive. The concept of *carrying capacity* is essential for understanding how the tragedy of the commons might play out in human activity. Carrying capacity is defined in terms of environmental resources necessary to sustain a given population indefinitely (Cohen, 1995; Meadows, Meadows, & Randers, 1992; Oskamp, 2000). For example, fresh water is an environmental resource necessary to human survival. Carrying capacity for fresh water involves calculating the amount of fresh water needed in order to support human populations indefinitely. There are other variables than just the amount of water itself or the number of people needing water, including such things as the resources needed to transport people to water or water to people, the political realities of resource ownership, and other complicating factors. But the general question of when and whether there will be enough water to support human populations is an example of carrying capacity.

In applied psychology, the problem of carrying capacity can be further articulated using the concept of *levels of analysis*. Because the same Francis Galton who invented individual differences psychology also worked with his students to invent inferential statistics, development of applied psychology has been intertwined with the development of statistics from its inception. The idea of levels of analysis comes directly from a very basic concept of statistical reasoning: the idea of N. When calculating averages (which most statistics are based on) in psychology, we start by considering the *number of people* from whom we gathered scores. This number of people is called the "N" of the sample—also called *sample size*.

In psychology, most samples consist of all of the scores from a set of people. Occasionally though, data will come from an "N" of decisions, where one person's choices across a set of options are analyzed. So, for example, a single student might be deciding which of a large group of classes to take. Here, the N would be the number of classes (or decisions about classes) made by the single student. The individual student's interests, preferences, and so on might be measured to identify why particular courses are chosen over others for this individual. Because this N is derived from a single person, it is considered a "lower" *level of analysis* than the N of students engaged in such decisions. Similarly, a "higher" level of analysis would occur when the behaviors of some number of *groups* of people are analyzed. For example, course choices made by students in different majors might be compared, making this a sample of N *majors*. In this instance, individuals are *aggregated* (combined mathematically), then analyzed at the higher (group) level of analysis.

The tragedy of the commons suggests that decisions at the individual level of analysis may affect outcomes across many individuals. It thus crosses levels of analysis in ways that are not yet fully understood. An applied psychological approach to understanding these "cross-level" effects might help to better articulate the nature of this concept.

The branch of psychology called *environmental psychology* deals with the degree to which both natural environments and our attempts to adapt the environment to our needs (i.e., *built environments*) affect individuals' experienced quality of life and ability to respond adaptively (e.g., cooperate socially, experience individual stress responses, work more efficiently, and so on). The *psychology of sustainability* is emerging from this field, but has a somewhat broader scope (Koger & Winter, 2010). As described in the introduction, this area deals with human decisions and behaviors (psychology) that are thought to affect variables associated with (mostly non-psychological, higher level) variables related to sustainability, such as resource use, consumption, land use, and related issues (Geller, 2002; Swim, Clayton, & Howard, 2011). Thus, the emphasis in environmental psychology is on *environmental precursors* to thought and behavior, while psychology of sustainability is focused more on the *decisions and behaviors that influence human and environmental sustainability.*

Both of these perspectives will be engaged in various parts of this book. However, where environmental psychology looks to the *physical precursors* of a wide range of behavioral and health responses, we will examine *psychological predictors* of environmentally relevant behaviors. These predictors have received more recent attention and include social, cognitive, developmental, and individual difference variables. Likewise, and unlike previous work in the psychology of sustainability, the outcomes considered relevant to sustainability will be elaborated and broadened here. Finally, different levels of analysis (individual, decision, and group) will be used to predict and manage human activities around environmental resources. These are all ways that this book is explicitly about an *applied* psychology of sustainability.

Environment and Systems

Wikipedia provides a definition of *environment* that will suffice for our purposes:

> In science and engineering, a system is the part of the universe that is being studied, while the **environment** is the remainder of the universe that lies outside the boundaries of the system. Depending on the type of system, it may interact with the environment by exchanging mass, energy (including heat and work) ... or other conserved properties. In some disciplines, such as information theory, information may also be exchanged. The environment is ignored in analysis of the system, except in regards to these interactions. The environmental systems are vital to the human race and to all living organisms. Without the systems in place and working, we would all cease to exist. Rivers and streams are an example; if this system fails, then the whole system would collapse.

The last part of this definition also touches on the *ecological perspective*: The idea that natural ecosystems are characterized by complex, sometimes non-obvious interdependencies. This perspective is based on the broader *open systems perspective*, which is a cornerstone of applied understandings of human decision making and behavior.

Open Systems Perspective

Meadows (2008) defines a *system* in terms of dynamically interrelated elements that interact within the constraints of some boundaries to transform inputs into outputs through an intervening process. Figure 2.2 provides a simplified depiction of a system. This figure will be used to organize discussions of systems in this book. Human systems (including individuals, groups, societies, political entities, economies, etc.) are considered *open systems*, meaning that the boundaries are permeable to the environment. Specifically, *contextual effects* have an influence through *feedback* mechanisms on inputs, processes, and outcomes, and the system itself also can have an impact on the context through all of these same feedback components.

Human behavior in a given context or environment is describable using the systems perspective (Gold, 1992; Lewin, 1951). We behave the way we behave based on both our traits and on the contexts within which we function. Behaviors (or lack thereof) are the "outputs" of (conscious and unconscious) decision processes. These are, in turn, influenced by both internal *inputs* (abilities, values, developmental stages, personality) and context (especially social and economic contexts). Not just behaviors, but both the mindful and the automatic processes (Kahneman, 2011) that precede behaviors, are important influences on outputs.

Taking this perspective on psychology will help at least to frame the book's discussions, and possibly our eventual ability to understand, predict, and control the choices that we constantly make within complex environmental and social systems (Maani & Maharaj, 2004).

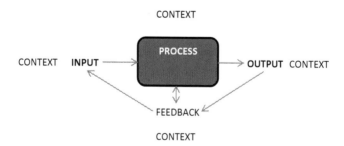

Figure 2.2 Simplified depiction of an open system

APPLIED SCIENCE AND SUSTAINABILITY

Sustainability

Sustainability is not a term with a scientific meaning in psychology. In fact, its definition is somewhat murky in general. The Environmental Protection Agency (EPA, n.d.) website defines it this way:

> Sustainability is based on a simple principle: Everything that we need for our survival and well-being depends, either directly or indirectly, on our natural environment. Sustainability creates and maintains the conditions under which humans and nature can exist in productive harmony, that permit fulfilling the social, economic and other requirements of present and future generations.

Perhaps a more applicable definition for our purposes comes from Oskamp (2000), who refers to sustainability as both species survival and well-being in this survival. This, with one addition and a qualification, is the definition used in this book. Sustainability can also be broadened to include the viability of the ecological context of individual and species level human systems. Harkening back to the definition of adaptive capacity, we can think of *sustainability* as the extent to which individuals, species, and broader systems successfully alter and maintain structures and functions in the face of change. This also qualifies sustainability as a definition that integrates multiple levels of analysis, including both individual and species level systems within an ecological system. It may even provide for something like an equation to describe sustainability, where optimal individual level comfort and survival are weighed with species level survival and earth system carrying capacity.

The reason that sustainability is in the title of this book is that we are interested in trying to provide a specific set of psychological variables that may help to predict and control the long term viability of both humans in the earth's ecosystems and of these ecosystems themselves. Viability is based on Oskamp's (2000) notion that well-being is an essential outcome. However, because this is a matter of considerable concern and controversy (Schouborg, 2001), and because there is not a large body of research on which to base this psychological definition, the framework provided here should be considered preliminary. This is consistent with the approach of some recent experts (esp. Klein & Huffman, 2013; Stern, 2000), who suggest that we provide relatively modest, exploratory definitions of scientific constructs.

A Scientific Approach

Two of the three authors of the U.S. Declaration of Independence were scientists (Jefferson and Franklin) and the third (Adams) a philosopher. When people were willing to follow their lead, they caused themselves all sorts of immediate heartache and sacrifice, but the long term result is nothing short of spectacular. Why is it, then, that only one or two of the subsequent U.S. presidents (after Jefferson) were scientists?

One answer to this is to see how governments have treated great thinkers and scientists through history. Many people have heard of what happened to Socrates, who was condemned for having taught young people how to use critical discourse. Fewer people are aware, perhaps, that some of the great scientists of the twentieth century were kicked out of Germany by the Nazi government. More examples include important early scientists and philosophers of science (Maya, Rhazes, Copernicus) who suffered (sometimes horribly) at the hands of powerful people who were threatened by what these scientists had found through careful observation of the real world (King, Viney, & Woody, 2009). So, although science has been at the center of some of the great changes in human history, it has not usually had a good relationship with political leadership. In the rare instances where it has (in the United States in 1776), amazing things have happened in the long term.

To further illustrate the politics of science, it has taken more than a century, and there is still a significant minority of American adults having trouble accepting the scientific discoveries around evolution (Newport, 2010). These discoveries are based in very solid evidence, have had a huge positive impact on our health and well-being, and continue to evolve (like good theories do); so why is it that we have such trouble accepting so wonderful a set of ideas?

Science and Certainty

How do scientists think about the world? People educated in science and philosophy of science know that scientific "discovery" is really just a *progress report* (Leahy, 2008). Furthermore, our explanations are not usually directly causal and certainly are not infallible. In fact, philosophers of science make a very basic distinction between what we *think* the world is like and what the world is *actually* like (Leahy, 2008). Furthermore, modern scientists generally acknowledge that the world is a *probabilistic* place. This section is about this basic concept in scientific thinking. It will also explain how this aspect of science is part of why people don't readily accept scientific findings (Krynski & Tenenbaum, 2007).

As described earlier, *epistemology* is the philosophical area concerned with how we come to know what we know. Philosophers have posited (and in some cases scientific psychologists have tested) various epistemologies. We will concern ourselves here with the epistemology of science—how science helps us to know what we know about reality.

APPLIED SCIENCE AND SUSTAINABILITY

Figure 2.3 provides a simplified model of the scientific process (Jones, 1997b). Before providing definitions of the components of this model, there are two important characteristics that need to be clearly understood.

The first is that the scientific process described in Figure 2.3 is *iterative*. A single scientific study addresses a valued outcome by stating a theory, creating a hypothesis, gathering data to test the hypothesis, evaluating the resulting data, and changing or retaining the original theory based on what was found. This single study represents just one "rotation" through the model here. What scientists do is move through this cycle *repeatedly*. This is the definition of an iterative process.

For example, you might want to know why people deny that there is global warming (a *value*). Your *theory* is that people's avoidant responses to climate change findings (B) are a result of emotionally aversive information about catastrophic change (A) that is often associated with information about global warming. So, your *hypothesis* would be that messages about global warming that include such "catastrophic" information are more likely to lead to aversive emotions, and therefore, people are more likely to try to find ways to avoid them.

You and your colleagues first might measure people's emotional responses to climate change information (a descriptive *research method*). Your measure is *scaled* (numbers are assigned to responses) and statistical analysis (*descriptive and inferential statistics* in Figure 2.3) shows that your measures of information and emotion are associated in this first study (sometimes called a pilot study). This result might move you to do a follow-up laboratory study (an experimental research method). In this second go-round (iteration), you are more

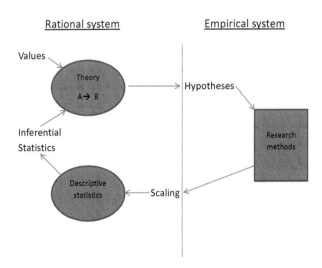

Figure 2.3 Iterative model of the scientific process

27

rigorous and randomly assign study participants to either hear a message about climate change that includes catastrophic information (experimental group) or not (control group). You then measure acceptance responses. The differences between the two groups' acceptance responses could then be compared using *inferential statistics*, and your initial theory altered or maintained. A third iteration could use a social marketing campaign (intervention study) to see whether adding a message about the advantages that may accrue to people who choose low carbon alternatives affects their purchase decisions. As you can see, this "cycling through" the scientific process is likely to create a fairly complicated picture of things fairly quickly.

A second important characteristic of the model in Figure 2.3 follows from this iterative approach. It is that science provides us with a *progress report*—not the "final word" about almost anything (Leahy, 2008; MacKay, 1988). Even when scientists are able to provide iterative evidence that rigorously tests a theory, all theories are subject to change. Furthermore, scientific research, as it is generally practiced, includes a critical review of all of the steps in Figure 2.3 by scientific peers. All reputable scientific publications subject their research articles to this sort of critical scrutiny, which, although it has its flaws, allows for meaningful dissent and (often) creative alterations in theories, methods, and analytical approaches. So, not only are reported studies "progress reports" about theories and methods, but science itself is a progress report on how to meaningfully approach problems of "knowing" and "value."

As we will see in the next chapter, humans do not like uncertainty! When the best source of information for making choices in life is framed as an uncertain *progress report*, it should come as no surprise that some people (especially the more risk averse amongst us) will respond unfavorably to science.

Defining the Divisions in Figure 2.3

The first, and most basic distinction in science is between the rational and empirical systems. The *rational system* is the system of thought that people apply to understanding the world. Some parts of the rational system include values, principles, commandments, laws, axioms, theorems, and (most importantly from the scientific perspective) theories. Notice, by the way, that all of these rationales for explaining things are *deterministic* in nature. That is, they are stated in terms of one thing *causing* another. For example, when we think of commandments and laws, we usually think of infallible rules that are meant to show people how one event (e.g., murder, adultery, stealing) causes an important outcome (e.g., damnation, execution, imprisonment). Theories are stated as somewhat more fallible causal ideas about how the real world works, and they are set up so that we can test them scientifically (MacKay, 1988).

The *empirical system* is the real world itself. For the sake of science, the empirical system has an existence apart from our particular experiences of it. In other words, science assumes that when a tree falls over in the forest and there is nobody there to hear it, it still sends out whatever it is that our senses and brains would interpret as a big noise. Though this may seem really obvious, it is surprising how important and controversial it can become when confronted with more deterministic epistemologies (e.g. dogmatic religious beliefs, totalitarian philosophies, strongly held traditions).

Science also approaches the empirical system using demonstrations that test our rational (usually overly deterministic) notions about the world (Greenwald, Pratkanis, Leippe, & Baumgardner, 1986). This is the first thing that makes science different from other epistemologies—that we test our notions in the bright light of critical scrutiny. We seek to *disconfirm* our dearly held deterministic notions (Greenwald et al., 1986).

Incidentally, this may help to explain why science has thrived historically in free societies—because we seek to test our ideas in the same way that entrepreneurs, explorers, and political activists take other sorts of risks. Free societies allow us to try our ideas out in the marketplace or the lab, whichever suits us. Authoritarian societies, and especially the leaders of such societies, do not like this "uncontrolled" activity, probably because it leads to fundamental questions about the adequacy of their authority.

So, here comes the biggest generalization in this book: The world is a *complex, multivariate, conditional,* and *probabilistic* place. Each of these terms will be defined in turn.

The world is complex. Most people would agree with this, though there are those who would argue that "everything you need to know is contained in___," then fill in the blank with their favorite authoritarian epistemology (Hathcoat & Barnes, 2010). *Authoritarian epistemologies* are not all bad, but they almost always suffer from some problems. First, they are defined as ways of knowing that require us to take someone else's word for what we believe to be true. This of course is fine, so long as the person whose word we are taking is relatively correct and well-meaning. If, however, we are taking the word of a seriously demented person or someone who wishes us ill, this is not such a good idea. And this is the first and perhaps most deadly aspect of authoritarian epistemologies: That "authority is not always right." Social psychologist Robert Cialdini (1988, 2007) (who we will hear from again in this book) has provided extensive discussion of this question in his now-famous books on social influence.

The second, and equally problematic part of authoritarian knowing is that it is often rigid. That is, it does not change even as circumstances demand change. If, for example we are to take biblical Old Testament rules as requirements for a moral life (a classic and fairly prevalent basis for authoritarian epistemology for three of the world's major religions), then we all should have sacrificed our goats this year. A more recent and highly dysfunctional example of this rigidity comes from World War II. The French high command after World War I assumed that warfare strategy would remain relatively constant, since that is what their (non-scientific) authority led them to believe. So, they spent huge amounts of treasure on the Maginot Line—a fortified line across eastern France. The German army simply ran around this line in their highly mobile tanks, overrunning France quite quickly and with relatively few German casualties. Thus, authority sometimes leads to rigid adherence to a course of action. If adaptation relies on variety in potential behaviors, such rigid adherence is often maladaptive.

Perhaps most important from the point of view of science is that authoritarian knowing is overly simplistic (Hathcoat & Barnes, 2010). Science's purpose is to *describe*, *predict*, and *control* what happens in the empirical world. Good science does this by carefully reviewing existing evidence, defining concepts, stating testable hypotheses, designing methods for testing hypotheses, and actually testing them in the empirical world. The data gathered are then summarized and reported, usually through the critical, peer review process. Science attempts to understand the world on its own terms—not according to our preconceived notions, however well-informed or authoritative they may appear.

What all of this leads to is a very complex and conditional "map" of the real world—our *scientific theory*. Think of it this way: When you first thought about how to get food as a baby, you probably cried loudly. Your simple "mental map" was that crying led to food. As people get older, we develop more sophisticated strategies for getting food, including everything from picking berries to shooting rabbits to shopping at the grocery store. What you also implicitly learned was that picking won't work when you are trying to get rabbits, that shooting at groceries probably won't get you food, and that crying at berries won't get them into your mouth. So, you learned the conditions under which certain causal relationships occurred: That crying only works when you are unable to get things from caregivers, that picking only works for bushes with berries, that shooting only works with rabbits, and that grocery shopping only works when you have money. In other words, you learned that these causal relationships are *conditional*. This simple example of the conditional nature of causal relationships extends to all sorts of aspects of the real world, most of them far more complex than getting food.

In addition, this very simple example can be extended to describe the probabilistic nature of these relationships. For example, unless you are extremely good and extremely lucky, you are not going to hit a rabbit every time you shoot at one, and you may not even see a rabbit every time you go out hunting for one. That is, the relationship between hunting and eating holds only some of the time. Even in the grocery store where money can buy you food, there will be times when you won't be able to get the particular food you are craving because it happens by chance to be out of stock when you are at the store. So, causal relationships in the empirical system are both conditional and probabilistic.

APPLIED SCIENCE AND SUSTAINABILITY

Trying to explain the multivariate nature of the real world is a bit of a challenge. One economist friend used to say that there is never a single problem, nor is there ever a single solution to any problem (T. Robert Circle, personal communication). What he meant is that, with anything worth understanding, there is usually more than one way of understanding it, more than one way of explaining it, and more than one approach to changing it.

Let's follow through with the earlier example of eating. Eating when you are hungry really appears to be a pretty simple relationship: Hunger leads to eating, and eating reduces hunger. The apparently single "problem" here is hunger and the single "solution" is to eat. Sadly, neither of these is really single. It turns out, for example, that our thirst receptors sometimes masquerade as hunger. It is also interesting that we tend to get hungry when we pass from the warm outdoors on a hot summer day into an air conditioned house. In this case, cooling leads to eating, with hunger as a sort of signal in between the two. Let's talk about eating, too. Eating could include all sorts of different foods with different properties that may or may not satisfy our particular nutritional needs of the moment. And then there's eating that occurs when we're not really hungry, which of course means that the "solution" (eating) occurs in the absence of the "problem" (hunger). So you can see that hunger is really not a single "problem" and that eating is really not a single "solution."

Instead, there are all sorts of other variables that affect our hunger and eating behaviors. *Variables* are factors that create differences in the things that happen around us. For example, temperature, humidity, and wind speed are variables used in describing and predicting the weather. Notice that these *vary* (are different) from one time or place to the next—hence the term variable. Most of the factors described by science are classified as variables—characteristics that differ, but can be described according to a single property.

Back to the eating example, there are variables that combine to signal hunger, and a whole host of different sorts of activities that can be described as eating. So, hunger and eating are part of a multivariate system, meaning that the system can only be adequately described according to more than one or two variables.

Finally, scientific ways of knowing have a frustrating (from the point of view of us poor determinists) habit of changing. Again, the critical scrutiny to which we hold our scientific findings leads to constant alterations in the various scientific "maps" we use to navigate our world. The only thing we can be sure of in science is that sometimes we will be wrong. And we hold hope that systematic, systems oriented approaches to understanding will advance our decisions in practice.

The Probabilist

Being probabilistic is perhaps the most important part of modern scientific understanding (Schum, 1994). Thinking about the probabilistic nature of the empirical system began at least as far back as the first and (as is typical of "first" scientists) greatly maligned political scientist: Nicolo Machiavelli. Machiavelli described fortune as a river that could be controlled by human efforts only about half of the time. Put in more modern terms, he argued that we can only control about half of what happens around us, and the rest is pretty much random. So, to answer the questions posed in this section, what scientists and philosophers of science know is that the world is a probabilistic place. And this, of course is what rubs us wrong—we are deterministic thinkers, but the world turns out not to confine itself to simple deterministic descriptions, much as we'd like it to.

Paradoxically, it is this desire for *understanding*, *predicting*, and *controlling* the complex and uncertain contingencies in the real world that motivates much of scientific inquiry. It's just that science has taken a long time, worked through more failures than successes, and come up only with a complex, spotty, and sometimes messy description of small pieces of the world at a time. This is unsatisfactory to many scientists, as well. It's just that we have come to accept it at some level, unlike many who seek simple, infallible causal explanations.

So, being a probabilist is at the heart of modern science, and some great philosophy (Schum, 1994). It means thinking in terms of the true complexity of our world, reminding ourselves about its ambiguities rather than trying to hide from them in authoritarian ways of knowing. Being a probabilist also means listening to science when we try to seek truth, recognizing that science itself provides us only with a progress report about an imperfect, conditional understanding of the world. And, perhaps most problematic, it requires a realistic, often difficult assessment of the various risks we are incurring when we apply scientific knowledge to our choices.

Applying Scientific Psychology

We have seen that predicting and controlling (or at least trying to influence) people's behavior is the purview of applied psychology. The probabilistic nature of the empirical world makes this a very risky enterprise, especially in the absence of thoroughly tested scientific theories. Since psychology is a relatively new science, there are few thoroughly tested theories to go by, making this risk greater than in some of the more mature sciences. Even so, this risk is often reduced by tried and tested practices that have shown positive results, with few or no obvious negative side effects. For example, in clinical psychology, cognitive behavioral therapies (CBTs) have shown positive results for treatment of depression, with no apparent side effects. In I-O psychology, several ability and personality tests have been used for most of the last century as effective tools to support hiring decisions, despite having little understanding of the psychological processes these measures tap. By accumulating scientific evidence of the ultimate effectiveness of such practices as CBT and employment testing, applied psychologists can have some confidence in their efforts, even without having a solid understanding of why these practices work.

But applying psychology to sustainability is particularly risky, since research specifically directed at predicting and controlling environmentally relevant behaviors has only recently begun (McKenzie-Mohr, 2000; Swim et al., 2011), and scientific theories around human environmental behavior have only begun to be discussed—never mind formulated. However, if we choose to take a deliberative approach to altering decision processes, then what else can we rely upon than the scarce evidence we have? Though people have a tendency to rely on unscientific bases for their decisions and actions, many of us would also like to rely on something derived from systematically derived, empirical evidence. But it does not change the difficult reality that applied scientists are gamblers, often with their clients' very consequential decisions. In the case of applied psychology of sustainability, species level survival may be one of the valued outcomes we are gambling.

We can see how complexity, probabilistic relationships, and ethical dilemmas take center stage in consequential decisions by returning to the example of the fresh water shortages that are currently facing many human populations. People need water both directly (drinking water for themselves) and indirectly (through agricultural use for cultivating plants and husbanding animals). This need for water is a fundamental human *motivation* which, when there is a shortage of water, generally makes other motivations (food, shelter, money) moot. Predicting and controlling water use has led to some valuable recent accomplishments in sustainability, but not without considerable complexity, uncertainty, and confronting some important ethical problems.

Perhaps the most exemplary of these projects is the Nature Conservancy's Colorado River Project (Nature Conservancy, 2018), which succeeded in restoring flow of the Colorado River all the way to its terminus in the Gulf of California for the first time in decades. This project relied on both basic science for *predicting* water flow and on *controlling* water flow upstream through various means—all of which relied on managing human choices.

Predicting how much of the Colorado River's waters—or any river's waters—will make it to their saltwater terminus has been accomplished fairly effectively by engineers using information from upstream water use, calculated evaporation rates and so on. These predictions are based on fairly reliable measurements of water inflow and diversion along the river's watershed, as well as well-supported estimates of evaporation and rain derived from basic research on physical properties of river systems. Much of the scientific basis for prediction can be derived from *models* of river behavior available in basic research literature.

But trying to *control* upstream water inflow and diversion has involved trying to manage human choices and behaviors. Attempting to control who gets scarce water, when they get it, and how much they consume for what purposes relies partly on *understanding* human motivations, choices, and behaviors to some extent, but relies even more on trying to change these choices and behaviors through various means. Such attempts to control people's choices and behaviors are fraught with complexity, uncertainty, and ethical dilemmas. Examples of successful efforts along these lines, such as the Colorado River Project, make this very clear.

In the Colorado River example, a concerted effort over more than a decade by the Nature Conservancy and various partners relied on a complex, flexible plan that persuaded people—several groups of people— to change upstream choices and behaviors. These included (1) persuading private land owners (especially farmers and ranchers) to alter economically important land use practices; (2) persuading private land owners to sell or donate their lands and to form land trusts to protect sensitive recharge areas; (3) persuading local, regional, and federal governments to change land and water practices on public lands; (4) persuading local and regional governments to enact land and water restrictions through complex political processes; and (5) persuading other conservation groups to join these efforts. Most of these efforts involved difficult ethical trade offs, and explicitly acknowledged the complexity and probabilistic nature of the changes that were proposed.

Applying this to other sustainability enterprises relies on managing the same complexity, ethical conflict, and uncertainty of human choices and behaviors. A further example, which is of particular importance to managing climate change, is the consumption of fossil fuels, particularly through the use of automotive transportation. Such transportation is of course a world wide practice, with enormous importance to the economies of most countries. The Colorado River Project's success at bringing the river's waters to the Gulf of California is a wonderful outcome, but is clearly dwarfed by any concerted efforts to appreciably reduce automotive carbon emissions. Imagine trying to convince tens of billions of auto owners, truck drivers, and heavy machinery operators to significantly change their daily behaviors—never mind trying to work with oil, auto manufacturing, and road construction industries to alter their economic models. Ordinance and enforcement have helped, as have international accords and resolutions. Yet the carbon cloud continues to grow after efforts through most of a century to reduce it.

Through this same period, there has been little or no mention of the deliberate application of psychology to these efforts toward sustainability, even in the few successful efforts like the Colorado River Project. In fact, as will be discussed in later chapters, some efforts in applied psychology have substantially *increased* problems of sustainability through the stimulation of consumption in the last century. It is the assumption of this book that such deliberate application of psychology toward sustainability will greatly enhance the probability of success in this enormous enterprise.

Why Not Determinism?

Deterministic thinking is thought to be a fundamental barrier at the heart of some of the problems we face in our lives together (Cialdini, 2007; Edwards, Wichman, & Weary, 2009). Those who would like the world to appear simple, deterministic, unconditional, and univariate are likely to be frustrated by realities and reminded of their frustration when scientists and scientific thinkers provide more complex explanations. Furthermore, being told that you are built to think too simplistically sounds a lot like an insult tossed by scientists at "lesser" thinkers. As we will see in the next chapter, it really isn't an insult at all. In fact, being aware of this tendency may actually help us (Maani & Maharaj, 2004; Weary, Jacobson, Edwards, & Tobin, 2001). And there do appear to be aspects of our thinking that are highly functional and more accurate than what scientific approaches have been able to achieve at this point. However, when we discuss these in Chapter 4, we will see that they are in surprising places where we would not expect to find "good thinking." In general, overly deterministic understandings tend to lead us into all sorts of traps (Cialdini, 1988, 2007) and may even create enduring problems. Reminding people of our simplification tendency may therefore be a major service.

So, why was there only one other scientist-president (Theodore Roosevelt) after Jefferson (Herbert Hoover was also a highly trained engineer, which probably classifies him as a scientist, as well)? Perhaps because complex thinking does not appeal to people the same way that simple, deterministic thinking does, and voting is often based on whomever is most appealing (Hart, Ottati, & Krumdick, 2011). The "simple" messages in political campaigns are probably good examples of this. Perhaps this is why Theodore Roosevelt was not initially elected president, but succeeded when McKinley was assassinated. It is also instructive to note that he had one of the longest peacetime presidencies, did much to develop the modern military, established the national parks and forest systems, invited a black man as his first guest to the White House (in 1901), and established laws that reduced the effects of wealthy elites on government, among other important accomplishments.

Basing policy making on a scientific approach appears to be a pretty good idea, if this historical evidence is any indication. So how can scientific psychology help to accomplish this?

The Utopian fallacy. Many of the early English settlers of the north-eastern United States sought to establish communities based on principles derived from Christian dogmas. Their notion was that if only people's social structures were arranged according to the religious law these settlers believed to be true, then they would live peaceably and in accordance with religious rules of conduct. Given the historical problems that occurred both within these communities and in their interactions with dissenters and other communities, it became clear that this utopian vision was not successful.

Further analysis suggests that although many people outside of these communities agreed with the overall criteria of establishing a peaceful and prosperous society, some of the more specific criteria for what was meant by these broad terms were quite different and even conflicted with the leadership of the communities. This probably occurred independently of the conflicts people had over the means to achieving a peaceful and prosperous society, some of which were acted upon in very problematic ways. For example, wars with indigenous communities, who often had dramatically different notions of what was "right" or "good," were rampant throughout this period, as were the development of dissenter communities. Ultimately, the utopian experiments failed (Molnar, 1967).

Where Is Applied Psychology?

There is still popular controversy about whether human *behavior* is the cause of rapid changes in the earth's ecosystems, despite strong scientific consensus about this question (Banerjee, 2012). Oddly, *behavioral scientists* have had little to say about this until the past couple of decades (Markowitz, Goldberg, Ashton, & Lee, 2012), and their voices are not typically among the most dominant or prominent in the discussions (Gifford, 2011; Swim et al., 2011). This is despite the broad application of psychological science to changing human behavior in recent history. While examples of this broad application may not be obvious, they are widespread and often appear to be quite successful, from consumer psychologists enhancing the effectiveness of advertising to therapeutic interventions that provide relief for people with disorders (Levy-Leboyer, 1979).

But perhaps the lack of obvious engagement of applied psychologists in questions of sustainability is not as odd as it may seem. For a start, making direct causal links between human behavior and physical and social outcomes is generally difficult, at least in applied settings (Borman & Smith,

APPLIED SCIENCE AND SUSTAINABILITY

2012; Campbell, 1990; Levy-Leboyer, 1979). This is partly because causal inference relies on direct manipulation—something that is often not possible or ethical in applied human science. Consider, for example, what it would take to deliberately manipulate whether some people are allowed to purchase and consume only organically grown foods, while others are allowed to use only processed foods, in order to see whether there are effects on their health and well-being. Although this might provide strong evidence for any such effects, the possibility of direct manipulation is both ethically unacceptable and practically unworkable (Gifford, 2007b).

Perhaps an even more powerful reason for lack of obvious engagement of applied psychologists is the inherent complexity of human thought and behavior. It is often difficult to explain one's understanding of such complexity, and even more difficult for non-scientists to listen to such complex explanations. This may help to explain the relative obscurity of applied psychologists in this politically charged discussion. Discussion of the sorts of emotions likely to engage "learning" instead of immediate responses will be discussed in later chapters, but even reducing complex ideas into simple language is unlikely to help people who are engaged in passionate discourse to stop and think.

Probabilistic approaches to problems also create ambiguities for ethical decision making. Thus, when we apply psychological principles to real world problems, we usually do so only with educated guesses. Ethics do not provide us with clear, unambiguous choices, as much as some of us would like them to (more on the psychology of this later, too). Accepted scientific knowledge will lead us to make good decisions more often than other sources of information—but only "on average." Often, it is just the best information we have available. Framed another way, if someone presents a "simple" ethical choice, they have probably not done an adequate job of defining the complexity and uncertainty of their moral dilemma.

This may also help explain why applied psychologists themselves are reluctant to venture into the controversy over human effects on the environment. Some psychologists know that the history of the field includes science based practices that have "contributed" to the problems of sustainable living. In fact, consumer psychology has probably had a substantial impact on the growth of the consumer economy, with its attendant lack of apparent sustainability. Before trying to increase sustainability—undoing these earlier efforts to support un-sustainable living—professionals may first need to acknowledge their error. Most of us do not like to say we were wrong, even in science.

Most importantly, psychology often moves in the opposite direction of the controversy: Rather than understanding *outcomes* of behavior, we seek to understand its *precursors* in human thought and social interactions. As we will see later, our natural tendency is to turn our attention to the possible *causes* of problems, rather than attending carefully, and first, to the behavioral *outcomes* that we would like to change. Even more frustrating to combatants in controversies, psychologists might ask questions that seem off-topic, like, "What are the factors that make people identify problems?" rather than questions about the apparent problems themselves. For the climate change/ sustainability controversy, people want to hear about the broad possible causes (overpopulation, resource depletion, and so on), rather than on trying to understand what leads some people to see climate change as a pressing problem (or not). It is not because psychologists are doubters about the need for considering questions around climate change, habitat loss, and so on— few scientists are. Rather, by understanding why some people see problems with ecosystems and some do not (Hornsey & Fielding, 2017), we are better able to identify and possibly change the thinking of "doubters." And this could be very powerful knowledge for those who would raise the alarm, as well as those who would try to calm people down. In other words, we look toward precursors when others tend to get very focused on the resulting environmental issue that is the source of controversy.

The Scientist-Practitioner Model

To reiterate, this book comes at questions of sustainability using scientific methods and knowledge of human behavior to manage "real-world" issues. Using this applied psychology approach, the book will develop around the question of whether the characteristics often seen as human adaptive capacities are likely to ultimately *be adaptive*. No complete answer to this question is even close to available, but asking it and trying to move toward an answer is likely to add value to the conversation.

The way applied psychologists often frame their approach is through the scientist-practitioner model (Hays-Thomas, 2006). The scientist-practitioner approach relies on empirical data gathered through generally accepted scientific processes in order to inform decision making. This model is applied in individual clinical settings, forensics (psychology applied to legal processes), educational, military, and industrial-organizational psychology (Hays-Thomas, 2006). The key notion here is not just that scientist-practitioners are informed by previous research findings, but also by scientific processes of framing and discovery.

In particular, applied interventions in work organizations typically follow the *ethics* of identifying important stakeholders and engaging them in structured processes of discovery. This stakeholder intervention process puts ethics into practice (Phillips, 2003) and is at the heart of scientist-practitioner approaches to applied problems.

A common first step in this process is to identify, with stakeholders, the outcomes they are interested in obtaining through a psychological intervention. For example, in organizational consulting about hiring programs, scientist-practitioners commonly start by discussing the primary objectives for instituting a hiring program, first with the organization's top leadership, followed by "task analysis" procedures engaging managers and position incumbents (Muchinsky, 2004). Some consultants also consider the interests of job applicants early in this process (Gilliland & Cherry, 2000), though it is not usually possible until later in the process to query job applicants directly. As we will see, this problem of representing absent stakeholders will be central to our discussion of stakeholder inclusion in decisions regarding sustainability.

The Criterion Problem

Perhaps the most crucial and difficult question in this process is referred to as *the criterion problem* (Austin & Villanova, 1992). *Criteria* are the standards that are used to decide whether objectives are being attained by some process. For example, a measure of subjective well-being is a common criterion to evaluate whether clinical psychology interventions have been successful. Criteria can be thought of as standards to judge the quality of "outputs" in the systems perspective.

Discussion

1. If you could change three things with respect to the future of our environment and species, what would these be?
2. What human behaviors or thinking would you change to make these happen (if you haven't already described human behaviors)?
3. Once you have generated your list, provide specific, agreed-upon definitions of key terms.
4. Some possibilities:

    a. Have people stop worrying about the environment
    b. Have people reduce the sizes and use of their cars
    c. Increase the amount of recycling that goes on
    d. Reduce the use of chemicals that degrade water and soil
    e. Increase the percentage of couples who have small families
    f. Encourage delay of gratification and altruism
    g. Have people take the long term interests of others into account in their decisions
    h. Develop more effective group decision making strategies for important decision making bodies

5. Probably, different factors will predict the outcomes on your lists, some are conflicting with each other, and there may not be agreement in the group about them.

> a. This is referred to in applied psychology as *the criterion problem*
> b. The "outcomes of interest" (*criteria*) are multiple, conflicting, and hard to predict
>
> 6. Identify at least one trade-off between two or more of the criteria identified.

It is readily apparent that there are often conflicts regarding the approaches that people take to deal with problems and arrive at desirable outcomes. For example, although we might all agree with the criterion (criterion is the singular of criteria) of "living happy lives," our understandings of how to reach this outcome often vary dramatically (Jayawickreme, Forgeard, & Seligman, 2012). Some believe that having lots of money is a means to happiness, while others might seek the company of friends to obtain the same end. This example is of course one that has been debated endlessly, but has received some empirical attention in recent work by *positive psychologists*, who are interested not in what troubles us psychologically, but by what makes us mentally healthy (Seligman & Csikszentmihalyi, 2000; Seligman, Steen, Park, & Peterson, 2005). The "causes" and facets of happiness (the primary criteria of positive psychology) do in fact vary and, consistent with the systems model, are multifaceted and somewhat complex (Jayawickreme et al., 2012).

What is less obvious is an even more fundamental problem in applied psychology: How can we identify other people's relevant criteria? In the case of public goods, such as electrical power, foods, other animals' interests, health care, and so on, different stakeholder groups may define desired outcomes very differently. Engaging stakeholder groups in developing *agreed-upon criteria* is itself rife with conflict, and generally involves multiple trade offs. However, identifying and engaging stakeholders is central to effective practice (Hansen et al., 2007b; Muchinsky, 2004; Teachout & Hall, 2002), as well as to moral philosophers' notions of ethics (Phillips, 2003).

For example, although citizens, CEOs of utility companies, and politicians may all agree about the need to survive as a species as a primary criterion, they may define "survive" in very different terms. Concerned citizens may define survival in terms of having clean air and water, beautiful recreational locations, and healthy foods. All of these may be compromised by various means of producing electrical power. Utilities CEOs may define survival in terms of having affordable and reliable services for their customers to be able to engage in basic activities required to sustain life, such as heating, potable water, and means for safely preparing foods. These may be compromised by spending disproportionate resources from a limited pool of resources on sustainability efforts. Politicians may define survival in terms of the viability of their political office for serving constituents' many needs. These could include needs that arise in the very short term (e.g., natural disasters that may fatally disrupt utility services), as well as the very long term (e.g., water in their political venue that is not fit for consumption). Politicians' ability to represent any of these interests may be compromised by expending political capital on one or the other problem, and jeopardizing popular acceptance of their regime. To complicate matters further, a very important stakeholder group in energy and water resources decisions is future human inhabitants of earth, who are not commonly involved in the process of developing policies. Clearly, these various criteria may be inherently conflicting in both their definition and the order of importance people assign to them, requiring significant trade offs among stakeholders' interests.

Never mind trying to come up with "solutions"—people have trouble even defining "the problem," as this example makes clear. Following from the utility example makes this very obvious: Reducing carbon emissions (important to sustainability advocates) is simply not the same outcome of interest providing cheap, reliable power to customers (important to utility CEOs). This may seem obvious, but people often leap to their favored solution before carefully understanding the criteria of interest to all stakeholders. One group's definition of "the problem," without explicit reference to other groups' definitions of their version of "the problem" is a common dilemma in applied science (see Austin & Villanova, 1992). Applied psychological processes often are simply aimed at arriving at an agreed upon list of criteria— which can be quite challenging.

Criteria for Psychology of Sustainability

Juxtaposing this process of stakeholder engagement with the criteria used in the research on environmental psychology helps to clarify this problem for a broader applied psychology of sustainability. Much of the sustainability research in environmental psychology (a *basic* research area, remember) relies on *pro-environmental behaviors* (PEBs; Siegfried, Tedeschi, & Cann, 1982) as the criteria of interest. PEBs are a class of individual, pro-social behaviors associated with consumption (Swim et al., 2011), altruism, citizenship, and concern for others' well-being (Bamberg & Möser, 2007; Cleveland, Kalamas, & Laroche, 2005; Cordano, Welcomer, Scherer, Pradenas, & Parada, 2011; Steg & Vlek, 2009). These include such things as reducing energy use, engaging in recycling, and personal implementation of new technologies associated with reduced environmental impact. Over 300 studies have used PEBs as the criterion variable, often in field studies (Bamberg & Möser, 2007; Hines, Hungerford, & Tomera, 1986; Ones & Dilchert, 2013; Osbaldiston & Schott, 2012). PEBs have been measured mostly using self-report inventories (Markowitz et al., 2012) that can be affected by changes in very specific physical features of the environment. For example, Rioux (2011) found individual difference predictors of elementary school students' battery recycling. A smaller group of studies has also looked at anti-environmental behaviors, such as breaking environmental protection laws (Hernández, Martín, Ruiz, & Hidalgo, 2010), choosing to use wood burning fireplaces (Hine, Marks, Nachreiner, Gifford, & Heath, 2007), and wasting water (Corral-Verdugo, Frias-Amenta, & Gonzalez-Lomelí, 2003). We will revisit some of these in later chapters.

While PEBs, attitudes toward sustainability, and related criteria (e.g., concern about the environment; Eiser, Reicher, & Podpadec, 1994) are important, there are other ways of defining criteria with respect to sustainability. An important example of this is people's *awareness* that there are significant environmental changes occurring (Hines et al., 1986). This gets to the problem that many people may not have formed attitudes regarding environmental issues, simply because they are not aware that such issues have been raised (Zheng, 2010). Similarly, there are those who do not see climate change, accumulation of waste, and other criteria coming from the environmentalist perspective as notable problems (Satterfield, Mertz, & Slovic, 2004; Yeager, Larson, Krosnick, & Tompson, 2011). Understanding how people arrive at the conclusion that environmental outcomes should not be considered *at all* is an important and generally ignored criterion (see Hornsey & Fielding, 2017).

Similarly, the concept of *place attachment* may be an important criterion for those who would like to preserve or maintain ecosystems and other environments (Bell, Greene, Fisher, & Baum, 2001; Scannell & Gifford, 2010a). There is still great diversity in its definition, including definitions relating to external characteristics of the place, the personal and shared meanings associated with a place, and individual evaluative dispositions toward a place. The first definition comes from traditional environmental psychology, but refers to external physical properties of a place, rather than psychological variables per se. The second definition—shared meanings of place, and the related notion of sense of place (Kudryavtsev, Stedman, & Krasny, 2012)—is mostly defined in terms of shared social constructions. Understanding the idiosyncratic meanings that different groups have for different places (Bell et al., 2001) may be exceptionally valuable for specific interventions, but are primarily predictors, rather than criteria. In Chapter 6, we will explore the "shared meaning" definition in terms of the effects of social context. However, because we will be working with attitudinal variables at length, the third definition—an evaluative disposition with perceptual, affective, and behavioral intention components—will be the definition we will explore more fully as a criterion variable. Finally, when we discuss identity development (Chapter 7), we will revisit place attachment using the earlier notion of place identity (Gifford, 2007a).

Doherty and Clayton (2011) include another criterion set that deserves attention. Following in the tradition of mainstream environmental psychology, these researchers would have us consider the effects of environmental changes on human health and well-being. From one perspective, this suggests that we simply prepare ourselves for the inevitable inconveniences (shortages, lost productivity) and potential catastrophes (e.g., increases in storm frequency and intensity) already set in motion by human activities. While these certainly matter, we will spend less time on issues of human responses to change (large and small) and more on the human behaviors thought to affect such changes. Still, questions of individual and collective responses to change will be considered in Chapters 10 and 11.

Finally, we tend to choose criteria in relation to only the outcomes that they view as most important to our interests. For example, the concept of the *triple bottom line* (people, profit, planet; Elkington, 1998; Hubbard, 2009) has become important within the context of businesses. Similarly, Klein and Huffman (2013) suggest that decision makers in work organizations focus primarily on problems of waste reduction and energy consumption, as opposed to criteria (e.g., habitat loss, climate change) that may have less relevance to organizational performance. Although these criteria are designed to narrowly serve the interests of the organizations that use them, the ideas behind these criteria are likely to have value beyond them. For example, organizations commonly assess whether their actions are seen as fair or just (Colquitt, 2001; Cropanzano & Greenberg, 1997). Assessing such perceptions of *procedural and distributive justice* may have important implications for problems of sustainability, and may therefore be of broader interest to stakeholders outside of a particular organization (Lima, 2006).

In sum, one of the more difficult and important steps in approaching interventions is *the choice of criteria*—the outcomes that are seen as important to various actors. Establishing criteria that are of importance often includes extensive discussion with a broad spectrum of stakeholders, supplemented by appropriate data gathering. Often, this data gathering provides a sort of "mirror" through which stakeholders are able to view the strengths, weaknesses, advantages, and roadblocks in steering toward various outcomes. In other words, clear-eyed definition of criteria as different stakeholders define them may help to identify the conditions under which criteria may be more or less attainable.

Treating sustainability as such a problem, composed of multiple criteria of different importance to different stakeholders, requires similar care, if we follow the scientist-practitioner approach. In particular, taking an empirical, stakeholder-driven approach to recognizing "what matters," proceeding with care in knowledge of what is likely to "work" or not, and, perhaps most importantly, acknowledging the assumption of error in our decisions are likely to provide us with clearer courses of action than other approaches.

APPLIED SCIENCE AND SUSTAINABILITY

Criteria Addressed in This Book

Unfortunately, for this book, as for most scientist-practitioner problems, we have very limited information from stakeholders on which to base criterion choices. In practice, criterion definition is based on data gathered from a particular situation. Chapters 10 and 11 provide an outline of this process. However, because sustainability has received lots of recent attention, some stakeholder interests have been addressed in public forums and in the environmental psychology literature. These will inform the choice of criteria for this book. Our sustainability criteria are based on issues that have been addressed by scientists, policy makers, activists, politicians, the news media, students, and ordinary people.

An important limit placed on the choice of criteria in this book is that they need to be *psychological*. This gets back to the distinction between behaviors and the results of behaviors (Borman, Bryant, & Dorio, 2010; Kane, 1997; Pulakos & O'Leary, 2010). The criteria we choose here are about people's decision making and behavior, *not the likely results* of these decisions and behaviors. For example, while we might be interested in carbon dioxide emissions, we would look to predict behaviors and decisions regarding such things as purchase and use of automobiles, since these involve choices and behaviors that influence emissions.

So, the criteria for this book are framed in terms of the following *five criterion questions* that address *psychological* outcomes of interest:

1) **What prompts people to think they have a problem (or not)?** There are those who argue that we don't and those who argue that we do. This question will be addressed by reference to research on precursors of *problem identification*. **What are the factors that lead us to think there is or is not a problem?** What happens when there is a problem and we ignore or otherwise deny its existence, and what are the signs that this is occurring? This is an obvious and central question in debates about climate change: Scientific consensus is very clear that this is occurring. So, what motivates such a large proportion even of relatively educated people to actively resist the very idea—never mind the strong evidence and scientific consensus? **When do we tend to see a problem when there really isn't one?** Ironically, some of the people who actively resist the idea of climate change also subscribe to conspiracy theory—that climate change is a giant hoax perpetrated by government to impose restrictions on our freedoms. Despite absence of evidence of such a conspiracy (in fact, better evidence of "conspiracy" against climate change science in public communications by oil industry executives), why do people see this "problem?" **Why do we continue to believe in things even after all evidence has shown that these beliefs have little or no basis?** An important early psychological study (Festinger, Riecken, & Schachter, 1964) described how

44

a doomsday cult that believed the world would end on a certain date were still deeply committed to the cult even after that date had passed with the world still intact. Understanding how, when, and why people do or don't identify problems will serve as the first psychological criterion for sustainability.

2) **What makes people think more or less carefully when they decide on an action?** People who are concerned with sustainability often ask why people don't think more carefully before they act. The growing body of psychological research on decision making suggests that careful thinking is more the exception than the rule. Almost all of the decisions we make in the course of the day may have started with some deliberation when we were first confronted with a choice, but have since been set in place by automatic processes. These same automatic processes tend to be over-generalized over time, where we apply an automatic decision rule formed in childhood (e.g. stranger = bad) to a broader class of situations later in life (e.g. all people who look different = bad). Psychological research on cognitive processes, individual differences, culture, emotion, moral development, and group processes will help to answer the question of deliberative thinking.

But it turns out that **deliberativeness** can also be addressed by reference to behaviors, rather than just cognitive processing. Foremost among these behavioral indicators are *pro-environmental behaviors* (PEBs; Siegfried et al., 1982) and *consumption* (Swim et al., 2011). For many PEBs, people need to be somewhat more deliberative at some point, since PEBs typically require conscious decisions, often to consider others' interests. However, consistent with the criterion problem, the basic research has not provided much consideration of practical means for identifying stakeholder differences in PEBs or for distinguishing between habitual and deliberate behavioral choices (Cleveland et al., 2005; Gregory & Di Leo, 2003).

Related to this, many PEBs have been identified and used in predictive studies (Cleveland et al., 2005; Siegfried et al., 1982). Efforts to empirically group PEBs have begun (Gifford, 2011; Levy-Leboyer, Bonnes, Chase, Ferreira-Marques, & Pawlik, 1996; Swami, Chamorro-Premuzic, Snelgar, & Furnham, 2010). But there does not yet appear to be a generally accepted typology, which makes specific predictions about certain types of behaviors tricky.

Because there are many questions remaining about how to define pro-environmental behaviors (Hubbard, 2009), we will take a very broad approach, borrowed from both cognitive (Kahneman, 2011) and health psychology (Cunningham, Galloway-Williams, & Geller, 2010; Hatfield & Soames, 2000). In particular, a variable related to deliberativeness in clinical and health psychology is *impulse control*: **When are**

people likely to control themselves? An understanding of concepts such as self-regulation, self-awareness, and emotive regulation will help to develop some ways to increase deliberativeness.

3) **What makes people change the way they think and behave?** For most people involved in efforts to promote sustainable living, this is a central question. Efforts to educate, to develop new relationships with the natural environment, and to persuade people of the merits of sustainability all are based on the idea that people can learn new ideas and ways of living.

Entire journals are dedicated to describing "environmental education" and the like. But this is an extremely broad question in psychology, which encompasses a much larger set of questions. Entire chapters of this book will deal with research on psychological change, covering various forms of individual **behavior change, learning, and development**, as well as some forays into change that occurs in social groups, organizations, and communities. As we will see, some of these have taken a decidedly applied direction, which will provide important bases for our adaptive capacity scorecard at the end of the book.

Recent research has begun to frame behavior change and cognitive learning as adaptive capacities, while social structures and their components (culture, norms, and morality) are generally not drawn in this light. Perhaps the most identifiable human characteristic—our inclination toward complex, deliberate, *social alteration of our physical environments*—has not received attention as a psychological "adaptive capacity," but will be introduced as such in this book. Virtually all of chapters 8 through 11 will be dedicated to identifying ways to predict and control human inclinations, thinking, and behavior. Many, important answers to this criterion question are available in psychology. Applying them to sustainability remains a central challenge.

4) **When are people likely to take action?** This question will be answered almost entirely with reference to social groups, rather than with reference to individuals. Although individual action can occasionally make a difference, most of the consequential actions in human affairs arise from social groups rather than individuals. Individuals may articulate ideas, but the path to actual change runs through social groups. This book provides a good example. Although I am able to articulate some ideas that may prove useful, it is through you, the reader, that these ideas find their way into action. And even the ideas articulated in this book are based heavily on the work of other individuals and small groups who have addressed specific psychological questions, making even a book with a sole author a group effort. So, several questions related to our social contexts fall under this general criterion. These include the following:

a) **What prompts people to consider and engage in collective action?**
b) **What makes people include or exclude other people from consideration when making decisions?**
c) **When are people likely to be altruistic?**

5) **What are the characteristics of change efforts that are likely to work?** There are those who would try to legislate our way out of environmental problems. Direct, centralized political control has actually been considered as a partial solution (see Bechtel, 1997, for a critique of the use of existing institutions as a solution for environmental issues). However, there are serious practical and ethical problems of, for example, establishing an "ecologically friendly" dictatorship. So, the ethical and practical implications of prediction and (especially) control of psychological variables will provide answers to this criterion question. The last few chapters will discuss "what works," based mostly on what has "worked" in the past.

In this context, advice about "what works" has at least two important boundaries. The first boundary relates to the ethics of "solutions." Ethical concerns (like advocating for eco-friendly dictatorships) will be addressed by reference to the structured, group processes through which success has been achieved in past efforts. It has been said that "process is everything," and processes through which people are given actual control over decisions that effect them are often messy; but "success" itself cannot be defined without reference to stakeholders. The second boundary relates to the idea of basing future actions on "past success." There is an inclination (discussed in Chapters 8 and 9) for us to "invent" "solutions" based on analyses of the *current* situation. The reason these terms are in quotations is that, often, our new inventions are not new at all. In fact, there is often previous evidence showing that others have tried these "new" approaches, only to find that they are also not "solutions" at all. Applied psychologists rely on *evidence-based practice*, where processes described in previous work can be retrofitted to the current circumstance with some knowledge of likely outcomes.

For applied psychologists, evidence based practice is the first answer to this criterion question.

The second answer is that initial, systematic assessment of some kind will help to understand what prior practices are likely to lead to which outcomes identified by stakeholders.

The "empirical mirror" sheds light on the nature of the decisions being made, and will be discussed using the concept of needs assessment in the applied chapters (8 to 11).

Psychology of Sustainability

It bears repeating that all five of these criterion questions are framed using psychological variables. These variables are all associated with thought, decisions, and behavior, rather than with the potential results of these thoughts, decisions, and behaviors. This is an important limitation of the perspective of applied psychology. Although applied psychologists are engaged in the management of human activities, the link between human activity and the results of these activities is "loosely coupled" (Orton & Weick, 1990).

For example, a politician may make exactly the same pitch for reducing energy consumption to two very similar groups of people and get quite different results. This scenario typically is a consequence of differences in contexts. So, following this example, prior to one of the speeches, the news may have reported an impending shortage of gasoline, while the other was preceded by a major uptick in the New York Stock Exchange. Impending shortages or future prosperity can make a difference in how people view the world on any given day.

The general point is that, although applied psychologists ultimately attempt to change *results* of people's decisions (e.g., reduction in energy consumption), we take the narrow assumption that it is only people's behaviors and decisions that we can directly influence. It also makes us very cautious about predicting how decisions and behavior will wind up affecting results. Put another way, we hope that our carefully devised criteria, systematic gathering of information, and conversations with decision makers will wind up having *adaptive* consequences. But we also assume we will miss the mark sometimes—just less often than other approaches taken to the same problem. We will discuss this problem of error (and management of error) next.

3

THE DETERMINIST IN US ALL

"Can you ever be sure of anything in this world?"
"Yes. One can be sure of being foolish."
Rafael Sabatini, in *Scaramouche*

Going all the way back to Roger Bacon, the thirteenth-century English friar, philosophers have been positing some serious problems with our thinking (King et al., 2009). The use of science to test Bacon's (and others') philosophical propositions had to wait 650 years, with the advent of cognitive science about fifty years ago (Kahneman, 2011). One of the general conclusions from these scientific tests is that Bacon's causes of error in human thinking are alive and well, long after the middle ages. Perhaps most important, this research also showed that one of our greatest assets—our ability to think in terms of cause and effect—may also be a major weakness in our everyday choices (Kahneman, 2011).

Put more precisely, our thinking is too *deterministic*. Deterministic thinking is the tendency to arrive at *directly causal, infallible* explanations for events (Austerweil & Griffiths, 2011). Such relationships are sometimes shown using the notation A → B. *Direct causality* means that we think in terms of one factor leading directly to another, such as sunshine making flowers grow. This direct causality means that we don't tend to think in terms of the many possible relationships that might occur between these two events. In the "sunshine → flower growing" example, photosynthesis occurs in between, so A → A1 → B. *Infallibility* means that we tend to think our explanations always work in all circumstances, that there are no conditions under which causal relationships will not hold.

It is much easier to demonstrate the tendency to be *causal* than it is to demonstrate the *infallibility* of our deterministic thinking, so let's start with the direct causal tendency. The following exercise is an excellent way to demonstrate this tendency.

Demonstration of Deterministic Thinking

Please take out a notepad to answer a couple of questions about three psychological findings from World War II. These three findings come from studies of U.S. war veterans. After each finding is presented, you will need to use your notepad to answer the following questions:

1. Does the finding come as a surprise to you? (Answer yes or no, please)
2. How do you explain either the finding or, if you were surprised, how do you explain your surprise?

Please record your answer to *each finding* first, then move on to the next finding. Here are the findings:

1) Better educated soldiers had more "psychoneurotic symptoms" than did less educated soldiers.
   Surprised? What is your explanation?
2) Soldiers from rural settings had fewer anxieties than soldiers from urban settings.
   Surprised? Explanation?
3) Before the war was over, fewer soldiers wanted to reenlist than after the war was over.
   Surprised? Explanation?

Before moving on, it is important to know that this exercise has been used extensively in psychology classrooms for over thirty years. It was originally used by a psychologist at a meeting of non-psychologists to demonstrate that "common sense" is an inadequate basis for understanding how things work (Ostrom, 1990). This is because, as we shall see, our "common sense" is often just plain wrong. The people who devised the exercise offer a scientific psychology that, however imperfect, bases our decisions on firmer ground than our benighted common sense. They argue that we should try to study our thinking and behavior in a systematic, scientific fashion, using large samples of people, and relying on statistical reasoning to understand from these samples what it is that makes us think and behave the ways we do.

More important to this book, this exercise demonstrates deterministic thinking. A first clue to this is that when people are asked to share their answers to the first question ("Does the finding come as a surprise to you?"), they almost always answer no. A small minority of people who have done this exercise are actually surprised by the finding that better educated soldiers had more psychoneurotic symptoms. Were you?

A second clue is that people come up with all sorts of remarkable and creative explanations for the three findings. Here are a few collected from explanations people have given just for this first finding:

1. Better educated soldiers tend to think too much about the consequences of their actions and are therefore paralyzed in times of emergency.
2. Less educated soldiers know to just follow orders without question, leading to success and survival.
3. Better educated soldiers tend to be from higher socioeconomic status and are therefore less able to deal with the privations of life on the march.
4. Better educated soldiers tend to ask lots of questions about their circumstances, which leads them to experience more stress.
5. Less educated soldiers have more "street sense" that allows them to adapt to changing events in combat conditions.

You may see themes emerging here, but the point is that there have been many varieties of direct, causal explanations offered for the findings.

Third, people's explanations come very quickly. In fact, this first part of the demonstration shows just how creative and quick we are at coming up with direct causal explanations for things we see, however briefly we may see them.

Think about your own response. How long did it take you to come up with your explanations for each of the three findings? If you are like most people, your explanation came almost automatically.

This shows how much we can pack into our causal explanations in a very short time. Although there is some disagreement (Sawa, 2009; Suddendorf & Whiten, 2001), evidence suggests that an understanding of means–ends reasoning, where one general set of events is followed by another, is a major characteristic that makes humans different from most other animals (Dore & Dumas, 1987; Penn, Holyoak, & Povinelli, 2008; Penn & Povinelli, 2007). It is thought to be based partly on the ability to rely on analogy—to readily apply rules from one circumstance to another (Biyalogorsky, Boulding, & Staelin, 2006; Flemming, Beran, Thompson, Kleider, & Washburn, 2008; Kahneman, 2011). Also, the generalization of relationships across specific events (*analogous thinking*) may help to explain our tendency to *persist* in our causal beliefs, even in the face of strong evidence to the contrary (Biyalogorsky et al., 2006; Kahneman, 2011).

From our example, in order to decide whether you were surprised, you probably relied on one entire set of variables (in this case, education) to decide whether it leads causally to a smaller set (stress, adjustment to new conditions). And you did it very quickly (Beuhner, 2003). We will return to the question of how different humans are from other animals in later discussions of sustainability. But for now, the point is that we are very quick and efficient in our causal thinking (Weary, 1985).

There's another, more subtle causality at work in this exercise, too: The "authority = right" *heuristic* (Cialdini, 1988). A heuristic is a simplification or *rule of thumb* that we use to guide our thinking and action (Kahneman, 2011). Heuristics are thought to be an important part of how we think and behave, particularly in uncertain circumstances. In our demonstration, when students hear the "expert" teacher telling them about important findings from psychology, they tend to believe the findings, even if they are surprised by them.

This is not always a good heuristic, as anyone knows who has seen an evil person take control of a country (e.g., Adolph Hitler). The authority = right heuristic can be deeply problematic, especially for people who are inclined to persist in their belief in the face of evidence to the contrary. It is also not a good heuristic to have used in our exercise, because this exercise is deliberately misleading (though not for any evil ends, I promise). In fact, all three of the findings in this demonstration are the *opposite* of what was actually reported in armed forces studies (Booth, Bucky, & Berry, 1978; Star, 1949a, 1949b; Stouffer, 1949). That is, better educated (Booth et al., 1978; Star, 1949b), urban (Stouffer, 1949) soldiers made *better* adjustments to wartime conditions, and soldiers were more inclined to reenlist *before* World War II was over than after (Star, 1949b). Take a moment to digest this: A textbook just lied to you!

This gives the demonstration added weight in a couple of ways. First, you now know that our ability to think in causal fashion has potentially serious shortcomings (making us believe the opposite of what is actually the case). Second, we tend to seek *confirming* explanations—few people are surprised by these findings, and we are not often surprised by events around us either. So, we rely on direct causal explanations to account for what we see, rather than looking for *disconfirming* cases. This *confirmation bias* (Hernandez & Preston, 2013; Munro & Stansbury, 2009) and its close relative *hindsight bias* (Fischhoff, 1975; Hoch & Loewenstein, 1989; Masnick & Zimmerman, 2009) have been explained in terms of *creeping determinism* (Nestler, Blank, & von Collani, 2008). This is the tendency we all have to remain certain of our choices and the heuristics that turn into "rules" over time.

To elaborate, imagine that, instead of asking whether you were surprised about the *outcome* of events, the exercise would have asked you to *predict* things in advance. So, for the three findings, you would be asked *before the war started* to predict the percentage of soldiers with college educations who would suffer posttraumatic stress disorder (PTSD) compared with the percentage of soldiers without high school diplomas. After the results were known (in this case, that higher education was associated with less PTSD), hindsight bias researchers would ask you to *recall* what you had predicted beforehand. In *hindsight bias* studies, participants consistently change their "memory" toward what actually happened (Fischhoff, 1975; Hoch & Loewenstein, 1989; Nestler et al., 2008). If you predicted 20% of college grads would have PTSD, but the actual number was 10%, you would tend to misremember your first guess in the direction of what actually happened—say 15%. This tendency occurs without people being aware that they are doing it, which is why it is labeled as creeping determinism or the tendency to think "I knew it all along" (Nestler et al., 2008).

A final lesson from this exercise is that even the relationships that *were* found could be explained using the counterargument explanations. For example, urban soldiers were better able to adjust to combat than their rural comrades, but urban upbringing is itself associated with greater stress (Lederbogen et al., 2011). So, we might explain the combat stress finding by suggesting that urban soldiers had learned better how to cope with stress, which in turn helped them adapt to stressful combat conditions. This sort of paradox is explained by reference to additional variables beyond the two that are described, as we will see later in this chapter. The thing to remember from Chapter 1 is that *it is a multivariate world.*

Heuristics, Biases, and Fallacies

Confirmation bias, hindsight bias, authority = right heuristic, and other heuristics, biases, and fallacies show that we often tend to rely on readily available, overly deterministic, and overly simplistic explanations (Kahneman, 2011). In this vein, Table 3.1 includes a partial list of some of the most notable heuristics, biases, and fallacies that have been uncovered by cognitive science. It should prove humbling for those of us who have been feeling pretty good about our brains. In this case, even humility won't help too much, but it may help to look back at this table now and then as a helpful reminder. All of these are examples of our broad tendency to oversimplify and to think deterministically.

We also tend to use *heuristics* when things are unclear (Edwards et al., 2009), and we have limited time or effort to spare (Pocheptsova, Amir, Dhar, & Baumeister, 2009; Todd & Gigerenzer, 2012). The use of deterministic explanations also allows us to maintain *the illusion of control*: Even though our explanations may be wrong, we want to feel that we can control our worlds (Koehler, Gibbs, & Hogarth, 1994) by reducing causal uncertainty (Edwards & Weary, 1998). So, rather than resulting just from lazy attempts to avoid spending time and effort using critical thinking (Kahneman, 2011; North & Fiske, 2012), heuristics and biases may be ways to readily adapt ourselves to changing circumstances.

Most of these heuristics are based on a fundamental tendency to rely on observed *association* as a basis for causal explanations (Kahneman, 2011). By using the "authority = right" heuristic, for example, we can rely uncritically on those who are in positions of power. This may come from a number of

THE DETERMINIST IN US ALL

Table 3.1 A short list of heuristics, biases, and fallacies with source citations

Individual decision effects	
Affect heuristic (Slovic & Peters, 2006)	Gambler's fallacy (Jarvik, 1951)
Anchoring and adjustment (Tversky & Kahneman, 1974)	Hindsight bias (Fischhoff, 1975)
Availability heuristic (Tversky & Kahneman, 1973)	Insufficient justification (Festinger & Carlsmith, 1959)
Confirmation bias (Nickerson, 1998)	Recognition bias (Rhodes & Anastasi, 2012)
Conjunction fallacy (Tversky & Kahneman, 1983)	Risk aversion (Kahneman & Tversky, 1984)
Socially referenced effects	
Attribution error (Weary, 1985)	Conformity (Asch, 1956)
Obedience to authority (Milgram, 1974)	Congeniality bias (Hart et al., 2009)
Expert = right heuristic (Cialdini, 1988)	Reciprocity (Cialdini et al., 1975)
Commitment and consistency (Cialdini, 1988)	Similar-to-me bias (Rand & Wexley, 1975)

motives, including the desire to believe in a trustworthy world. But, as most people know, a little critical thinking shows that this heuristic is often just plain wrong.

The list of psychological heuristics also includes *biases*, some of which you may have heard of before. However, the meaning of the term bias here is slightly different from some other common meanings. One way cognitive scientists think of biases is as *particular*, demonstrable tendencies associated with the *larger* tendency to optimize our limited mental resources (Kahneman, 2011). Using the language of a class of statistics called *factor analysis*, they are *surface* indicators of *underlying* factors, such as the tendency to seek the comfort of causal explanations (Edwards & Weary, 1998).

Most of the entries in the "individual decision" part of Table 3.1 rely on comparisons of how the world actually works (usually using mathematical models of reality) with how we take shortcuts to explain things (Kahneman, 2011). They are just *demonstrations* of the limits of our ability to think probabilistically. So far, however, there is not enough evidence to support one theory or another to help explain their commonalities and differences (Hilbert, 2012). The explanations that have been offered so far (illusion of control, associative learning, analogous thinking, creeping determinism, limited resources, etc.) are theories with a bit more evidence than "common sense" explanations for the demonstrated tendencies. But cognitive science is still

THE DETERMINIST IN US ALL

a new area, so deterministic thinking is really a straightforward observation rather than a theory. This is also true for the *socially referenced* heuristics, which demonstrate that, in most social circumstances, people look to other people to decide what to think and do (Cialdini, 2007). For our purposes, we will assume that association and *analogy* lead us to develop broad, causal principles (i.e., think too deterministically) and apply them as quick ways to answer the often difficult and ambiguous questions posed in everyday life.

A fairly comprehensive list of heuristics, biases, fallacies, and errors is in David McRaney's popular book, *You Are Not So Smart* (2011). His thorough and entertaining description of several of the biases listed in Table 3.1 is a helpful entrée to the more comprehensive treatments offered by psychologists Jonathan Baron (2007) and Daniel Kahneman (2011). Kahneman, who was instrumental in the discovery of heuristics and biases, won the Nobel Prize in economics in 2002 for his work with partner Amos Tversky (Nobel Prize, 2013). Among other things, this work convincingly refuted the "rational man" assumption in economics. This assumption—that people will make optimizing decisions in their economic transactions—was the primary assumption underlying the "invisible hand" theory of economics (Smith, 1776). It was also the basis for the popular theory that free market economies are self-correcting systems. Kahneman and Tversky not only convincingly refuted this assumption—they demonstrated some of the specific ways that we are irrational. Table 3.1 includes several of these.

As we will see, heuristics and biases have predictable relationships with the processes through which we arrive at decisions. In fact, they can be seen as *outputs* of common decision processes (Shah & Oppenheimer, 2009). At least three of these decision processes will be of particular importance to the applied questions in this book. In order of coverage, the first is the question of how we decide whether we have problems, also called *problem identification* (Moreland & Levine, 1991) and *threat appraisal* (Reser & Swim, 2011) processes. These will be covered in Chapter 5. Second, we will see how heuristics and biases are associated with (and often explain) the prejudices and stereotypes that guide our behavior toward others. The *fundamental attribution error* gets top billing as a cause for misidentifying the reasons for each other's behaviors. Our explanations for the results of behavior tend to be biased in terms of internal (abilities, motivations) versus external (situational) causes. Our tendency toward the use of heuristics extends to explanations about people. Chapter 6 will elaborate.

Infallible Causality

Now you have seen how ready we are to ascribe *causal* explanations to observed events and their outcomes. But this still leaves us with questions about the *infallibility* of our thinking. This is something that even scientists have problems with (Greenwald et al., 1986). It gets to the nature of "fact."

What scientists do is devise and execute tests of people's (sometimes religiously held) causal notions. While people may have a lot vested in their causal explanations, scientists sometimes have too much vested in their critiques of them, as well. So, scientists sometimes arrive at conclusions that they defend just as vehemently as any religionist, instead of thinking of their findings as conditional. Even scientists forget that things are probably not exactly as their studies suggest, due to conditions that have not yet been understood or accounted for (Greenwald et al., 1986).

A good example of this is the research finding that many managers and coaches rely on when trying to motivate others—*goal setting*. The basic notion in this research is that setting goals leads to greater effort and better performance. Of course, this sort of causal explanation is exactly the sort of thing that science is aimed at testing. In fact, a library search with "goal setting" as the search term found well over 3,000 peer-reviewed publications. Also, there are numerous quantitative reviews of goal setting, each combining results from many studies (Donovan & Radosevich, 1998; Klein, Wesson, Hollenbeck, & Alge, 1999; Kleingeld, van Mierlo, & Arends, 2011; Mento, Steel, & Karren, 1987; Tubbs, 1986).

So what's wrong with this finding? Well, it happens that there are all sorts of conditions that have been shown to be essential for the "goal setting effect" to occur: Commitment to goals, specificity of goals, moderate difficulty of goals, participation in setting goals, and the list goes on (Cummings, Schwab, & Rosen, 1971; Erez & Arad, 1986; Erez & Earley, 1987; Harris, Tetrick, & Tiegs, 1993; Latham, Erez, & Locke, 1988). In fact, it goes on to the point where other theories of motivation that predated the goal setting effect start to look like valid explanations for this effect (Chacko & McElroy, 1983; Garland, 1984, 1985; Garland & Adkinson, 1987; Quigley, Tesluk, Locke, & Bartol, 2007). Consistent with the idea that confirmation bias occurs in science (Greenwald et al., 1986), proponents of what was once called the "goal setting technique" (Helmstadter & Ellis, 1952) sometimes dismissed other viewpoints without empirical basis (Ordóñez, Schweitzer, Galinsky, & Bazerman, 2009) and promoted the goal → performance effect to the status of "goal setting theory" (Locke & Latham, 2006).

Perhaps the most damning condition put on the "infallible" goal setting effect is the finding that goal setting does not affect effort without "knowledge of results" (Erez, 1977; Neubert, 1998; Reber & Wallin, 1984). This is an essential condition that some would argue explains the effects of goal setting on motivation *better* than goals do (Garland & Adkinson, 1987). Think of it this way: *I want to do well on something because "it's a challenge"* (the "goal setting effect") versus *I want to do well on something because I anticipate a desired result* (the effect of "knowledge of results"). If you are like many scientist-practitioners, the latter proposition makes more "common sense" than the former. Feedback can also lead to performance improvement without any goals having been set (Kluger & DeNisi, 1996) and, some would argue, provides a simpler explanation.

Not surprisingly, then, there is some evidence that goals simply define what "doing well" means, so that we can get the results we desire. That is, goals alone are not what is motivating; they instead provide social guidance about the desired results of our actions (Erez & Arad, 1986; Garland & Adkinson, 1987). Defining standards and expectations is clearly associated with success in any endeavor, and makes goal setting a very important area of applied inquiry. In fact, there is considerable value to defining expectations, as we will see in later chapters (Osbaldiston & Schott, 2012). But the *causal explanations* for the effects of goals appear to have outstripped the evidence about their effects—they have taken on a sort of certainty that seems more like dogma than like science.

So, infallibility is a problem that even scientists struggle with. We seek "heuristics" that are well supported by evidence. In applied science, we seek these widely applicable rules of thumb because they can be used to make a difference in people's lives. The goal setting effect may help to improve people's work lives, whether or not we understand all of its mechanisms. We leave it to later, basic research to understand why this heuristic "works." But falling into the trap of infallibility can lead to over-extension of a practice and treatment of "goal setting" as an explanation rather than just the heuristic that it is.

As with causality, infallibility may give us the sense that things are simple and predictable, that there is nothing we cannot know, prepare for, or have a valid way to manage reality (Edwards & Weary, 1998; Koehler et al., 1994). In short, infallibility, like causality, looks a lot like the *illusion of control* at work. Unfortunately, this illusion of control is itself quite fallible (Koehler et al., 1994).

Having a complex understanding of the world can help to control it—at least to the extent that it can be controlled. This is borne out by the enormous advantages that scientific theories have given in many areas of life. In psychology, research on the systems perspective (Maani & Maharaj, 2004; Meadows, 2008), perspective taking (Hoever, Knippenberg, Ginkel, & Barkema, 2012), and expertise (Morrow, Leirer, Altiteri, & Fitzsimmons, 1994; Wu & Lin, 2006) support the idea that more complex and accurate understandings of the world often serve us well.

But there is also a counterargument to this. There is evidence that people with higher mental abilities simply arrive at effective heuristics more quickly, and that this explains why they can adapt better to their circumstances (Hertwig & Herzog, 2009). Consistent with this, heuristics can give clear advantages depending on the circumstances in which they are applied (Baron, 1990; Haug & Taleb, 2011; Lenton, Penke, Todd, & Fasolo, 2013; Merlo, Lukas, & Whitwell, 2008). In other words, in the right hands infallible causal thinking serves us well.

Ultimately, the paradox of objectivity, suggested by philosophers such as Hume and Comte (Petitmengin & Bitbol, 2009; Rosenberg, 1980) may place a limit on our ability to distinguish effective from ineffective heuristics. The question of objectivity is whether it is possible to *use* thinking to find the actual *limits* of thinking—a paradox. Certainly, the fact that scientists have recently been able to identify shortcomings in our objectivity—the heuristics, biases, fallacies, and errors described here. The ability to identifying these shows some promise that we can use our thinking to find the limits of our thinking. But the adaptiveness of such ways of thinking remains an important question we will address later.

This quote from Martin Hilbert (2012) of University of Southern California provides one point of view about the adaptive problems that may confront us on the basis of heuristics and biases:

The consistency of such systematic biases can be useful for predicting individual behavior and can also have disastrous large-scale consequences for society as a whole. If the mistakes in our judgments were random, the deviations would cancel each other out. For example, in a specific situation, some investors would overestimate and others underestimate risk. The overall result would be a self-regulating social system, indistinguishable from the one proposed by the efficient market hypothesis with its rational actors. Contrary to such views, however, our judgments are systematically biased toward one side or the other, and in specific situations, the large majority of investors will either over- or underestimate risk, not both. The worldwide economic crisis of 2008 delivered hard evidence for such dynamics (Ariely, 2008) and left many previous defenders of the rational and efficient market hypothesis in "shocked disbelief" (Greenspan, 2008, p. 16).

What is clear is that the study of biases, heuristics, and fallacies in human decision making provides important clues about the processes that can affect choices in all sorts of circumstances. Before going any further, it makes sense to have a closer look at some of the ways that psychologists and other scientists study decision making.

Models of Decision Making

Many researchers in applied psychology treat the individual person as the primary *unit of analysis* (Gifford, 2007b) in their research. By combining information from samples of individual responses, they hope to arrive at a more accurate description with which to attempt to predict and control people's behaviors and decisions. For example, on average, people with greater openness to experience may be more inclined to engage in pro-environmental behaviors than those with more narrow world views (Markowitz et al., 2012). A researcher would typically measure openness and pro-environmental behavior in a sample of individuals. Then, by *aggregating* individual responses to the openness and pro-environmental behavior measures into sample statistics, the researcher can identify whether there is some kind of relationship between the two. However, for an applied researcher, the actual question is whether it's possible to predict later *individual* behavior (not aggregated group behavior). This use of aggregated information to predict individual behavior is referred to as the *ecological fallacy* (Clancy, Berger, & Magliozzi, 2003; Cooper & Patall, 2009).

Applied psychologists have dealt with this problem mostly through analysis of errors (more on this later). However, there is also a smaller group of psychological researchers who, in addition to individuals, dig down and treat *decisions within* an individual as the primary unit of analysis. That is, researchers gather samples of decisions from single individuals and attempt to analyze these in much the same way that most researchers analyze data from samples of individuals (Bissing-Olson, Zacher, Fielding, & Iyer, 2012; Cooper & Patall, 2009). Such an approach has been used widely in economic psychology (Grønhøj & Thøgersen, 2012) and policy studies. It also bears a close resemblance to the *intra-individual* approach that has been suggested as a valuable means for understanding how people's environmental behaviors vary over time (Bissing-Olson et al., 2012).

One of the substantial advantages derived from this type of research is that people's decisions about how to behave with respect to their environments are often the primary basis for sustainable, and potentially less sustainable outcomes. For example, when you got up this morning, you may have gone to the bathroom and brushed your teeth with the water running or used the spigot to briefly wet your toothbrush before turning it off. The consequences of numerous individual decisions like this can dramatically affect the amount of fresh water that people consume. Understanding the factors that lead people to arrive at these different decisions can be potentially powerful, as many consumer psychologists have found in their work trying to increase consumption.

Another potential advantage of using the decision as a unit of analysis is that decisions are made by both *individuals* and by *groups* functioning in a more or less coordinated fashion (DeRue, Hollenbeck, Ilgen, & Feltz, 2010). By understanding the variables that influence individual decisions, researchers are more able to influence their outcomes. Applying more common aggregation of individual responses to group situations has posed some problems that can be managed by references to decision level analyses (Stenson, 1974).

THE DETERMINIST IN US ALL

What this means is that the use of decisions as the unit of analysis lends itself well to certain types of applied psychology, including the psychology of sustainability. In fact, an important program of applied research by Ilgen, Hollenbeck, and their collaborators (Davison, Hollenbeck, Barnes, Sleesman, & Ilgen, 2012; DeRue et al., 2010; Hollenbeck, Ellis, Humphrey, Garza, & Ilgen, 2011) has demonstrated ways to *simultaneously* evaluate the effects of decision processes, individual characteristics, and team characteristics on important outcomes. This research and the research on *group* heuristics and biases that effect our individual actions will be important touchstones in later chapters.

Since scientific psychology is applied extensively by advertisers, politicians, lawyers, salespeople, the press, and many employers to predict, control, and help make decisions, we will go beyond mainstream psychological research that uses individuals as the unit of analysis: We will rely on consideration of group and individual decisions as the units of analysis. In particular, much of what follows in this book will rely on a *systems perspective on the decision-making process*, described in Figure 3.1.

Some of the system *inputs* (causal variables) we will discuss in the next several chapters will include intelligences, situational expertise, motivation, personality, and various contextual variables. The effects of these inputs on various decision processes will be discussed as well, with particular emphasis on problem identification, optimizing and satisficing, and emotive appraisals

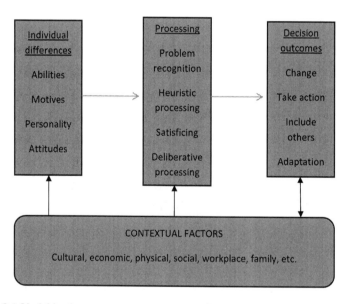

Figure 3.1 Variables in an open systems perspective on the human decision making process

and displays. As we will see, heuristics may actually be thought of as *processing* approaches that follow from the use of biases, fallacies, and errors. The outcomes of these inputs and processes for our particular outcomes of interest (criteria), and the effects of feedback and learning on potential change will be considered in later chapters.

Our Thin Neocortex

It would be easy to conclude from the long list of heuristics, fallacies, and biases in human thought that our hopes are slim for ever making decisions without considerable error. But this would be premature. During the early days of positive psychology, researchers began looking for what is "good" in our humanity (Kobau et al., 2011; Maier, Peterson, & Schwartz, 2000; Snyder & Lopez, 2002), rather than (among other things) the errors and biases in our thinking. This included closer examination of the factors that make us happy and healthy (as opposed to disordered and unhealthy), smarter and more pro-social. Given the basic cognitive research on errors, biases, and heuristics, it is not surprising that positive psychology, which came largely from clinical and counseling areas of applied psychology, was met with skepticism and some controversy (Snyder & Lopez, 2002). It was in this atmosphere that David Funder (1989) described the accuracy of our thinking as a dancing bear. The analogy suggests that, although our reasoning is error-prone and relies on shortcuts, it is still a remarkable evolutionary achievement. So, the bear dances poorly, but is remarkable in that it dances at all. Use of the (evolutionarily new) neocortex layer on the outside of our brains to make abstracted causal explanations, test them through a social network of scientists, and elaborately apply them to adapt our environments to ourselves is pretty amazing, despite the fact that it works only modestly well.

There is also a very important paradox to consider before arriving at conclusions. Our adaptive capacity—based on infallible causal reasoning—is influenced by our ability to understand and manage our tendencies toward errors. The *assumption of error* in science and formal statistics is part of what has led to remarkable advances in applied decision making. Understanding and adapting to the inherent imperfections in our neocortical functioning is testimony to its remarkable resilience. Objectivity is somehow preserved.

In Chapter 5, we will visit a human decision making system that appears to be better able to make accurate adaptive choices. Ironically, it is based in the emotive perception system that we have inherited as part of our mammalian endowment. The trick is that we apparently have the ability to integrate this more primitive (in evolutionary terms) system using our thin neocortex to assess others' motives (Dunbar, 2003). For now, however, we need to ask whether the infallible causal reasoning from our neocortical system is ultimately adaptive.

THE DETERMINIST IN US ALL

Picture 3.1 David Funder compared the human ability for abstract reasoning to a dancing bear. Our tendencies toward bias mean we don't always "dance" (think abstractly) very well. But the fact that we can "dance" (think abstractly) at all is remarkable

How This Fundamental Tendency May Relate to Our Decisions regarding Sustainability

Some interesting work relating specifically to pro-environmental behaviors has shown that *optimism bias* (Hatfield & Job, 2000) affects people's concerns over environmental degradation. This bias is defined as the tendency to believe that we are less likely to suffer ill effects from environmental degradation than our peers.

Unfortunately, much of the initial research demonstrating heuristics, fallacies, and biases occurred in laboratory conditions and often using well defined problems, unlike many problems people experience in applied settings. From an applied perspective, it is important to see how people outside of university psychology laboratories are affected by biases. Fortunately, there are more recent researchers who have shown how our biases can have effects in decisions made by individuals (Cialdini, 2007; Kahneman, 2011), groups (Cialdini, 2007; Pfeffer, Salancik, & Leblebici, 1976), and organizations (Salancik & Pfeffer, 1977; Takahashi, 1997) in applied settings.

Although these researchers do not target pro-environmental behaviors specifically, there is solid evidence to help answer the five criterion questions.

1. What prompts people to think they have a problem (or not)?

In this chapter, we have begun to explore a more nuanced version of this question: What prompts people to think they have a problem (or not)? As yet, the research covered so far only begins to provide actionable answers to this question when addressing problems of sustainability. However, it is clear that we tend toward irrationality in our typical decision making.

Furthermore, our tendency to be overly deterministic is pretty much *invariant* (Hilbert, 2012)! It may change a little between people and cultures (Pohl, Bender, & Lachmann, 2002), but it still remains a consistent effect, meaning that our efforts to change it are not likely to be effective. If there is much variety in our tendency to rely on heuristics, it is probably related to a very few factors, including (1) aspects of culture (Pohl et al., 2002; Schloss, 2000), (2) perhaps to metacognitive awareness of these tendencies toward error (Cialdini, 1988; Schloss, 2000), and (3) the presence of social oversight (Rogelberg, Barnes-Farrell, & Lowe, 1992). Cultural precursors are changeable, but not easily managed, since there are many sources of culture.

However, individual awareness may be enhanced through educational experiences, such as doing some further reading of the articles and books quoted in this chapter. For a recent example of basic research linking our ability to understand complexity and our tendency to rely on less simplistic responses, Maani and Maharaj (2004) established a link between *systems thinking* and complex decision making. An important question following from this is whether people who have studied philosophy, systems engineering, cognitive science, and applied psychology—have learned about the systems perspective—have a better sense of our intuitive tendencies. These experiences—and probably some others—typically expose people to the sort of probabilistic, error referenced thinking we have discussed. It may also be that the ability to educate *ourselves* relies on a broader perspective, which in turn promotes the ability to understand the effects of heuristics and biases. We will discuss this in later chapters.

Hearing other people's perspectives may also help us be more aware of our own biases. Direct group influences may alter the use of both socially referenced heuristics and individual biases. In particular, making choices as part of formal groups (scientists and philosophers) appears to have led us to develop the ability to adapt away from overreliance on biases and fallacies (Greenwald et al., 1986). Analysis of error, reliance on a scientific evidence, reliance on a community of scientists, and, perhaps most importantly, detailing the specifics of our biases and fallacies have given us some tools to potentially "bootstrap" away from some of their most destructive effects (Cialdini, 2007).

The irony of using our error prone thought systems to identify the specific errors to which these same systems succumb is promising in much the same way that technological solutions derived from physical sciences help us to adapt. Specifically, it is the public testing of our infallible causal explanations that has led to scientific knowing *and* to the understanding of error in decision making. So, our tendency toward infallible causal explanation is perhaps the least adaptive of our tendencies when not tested, but perhaps the most adaptive when tested in a critical community (i.e. subjected to scientific peer review) and assumed to be in error.

What is clear is that psychology can make a vital contribution to assisting in decision processes. Questions around the differences between what we see and what is "real" are old in psychology, going back to early psychophysicists (Hothersall, 1995). A favorite way of depicting this distinction in environmental psychology is the *Brunswik Lens Model* (Brunswik, 1952, 1955), which will be covered in depth in Chapter 5. Following from suggestive early work (Gifford, Ng, & Wilkinson, 1985; Stenson, 1974), some recent research uses the Brunswik Lens Model to predict decision making under conditions of uncertainty in applied settings (Hartwig & Bond, 2011; Zoogah & Peng, 2011). Interestingly, this more complex depiction of decision making under uncertainty also suggests some hope that human actors can make accurate judgments in real world settings.

For now, it needs to be recognized that our thinking can lead us to make a couple of general types of errors. Figure 3.2 depicts the simplest version of the analysis of error, derived from *Signal Detection Theory* (Baker & Schuck, 1975; Green & Swets, 1966; Kellen, Klauer, & Singmann, 2012). This approach demonstrates the outcomes of our infallible causal reasoning in the real world. By comparing our decisions with what is happening in the empirical system, we can see that we make both correct decisions and errors. Importantly, our heuristics and biases may lead us to correct decisions, even though they are not based on what is really happening. But heuristics can also make us (1) see problems when there aren't problems (false positives) or (2) ignore problems that are in fact there (false negatives).

Consider, for example, the two decisions that a soccer referee can make when she thinks she sees a soccer player commit a foul: To call the foul or not. If the referee calls a foul, she will have made one of two possible decisions: (1) If the foul actually occurred, the referee made a correct decision (a true positive or "hit") or, (2) if the foul actually did not occur, the referee made one kind of error—a false positive ("false alarm"). If the referee does not call a foul, then two other possibilities

THE DETERMINIST IN US ALL

	Decision made about some characteristic of the situation	
	Real	**Not real**
Real	True positive (hit)	False negative (miss)
Actual characteristic of the situation		
Not real	False positive (false alarm)	True negative (no call)

Figure 3.2 Basic analysis of error in decision making

exist: (1) If the foul actually occurred, a false negative ("miss") or, (2) if the foul did not occur, a true negative ("no call").

Applying this to a couple of heuristics and biases, the hindsight tendency to think we "knew it all along" means that we don't always see real problems when they confront us. This is perhaps part of the reason for "false negatives" (not seeing a problem when there is one). Alternatively, "false positives" (we think we have a problem when in fact we don't) may be predictable on the basis of our tendency toward risk aversion (Pachur, Hertwig, & Steinmann, 2012). The important thing to remember as a scientist-practitioner is that we can make both errors and correct decisions, even when we use heuristics.

The internal and contextual forces that lead to decisions errors, as well as some of the specific processes associated with particular errors, will be discussed in later chapters (particularly Chapters 5 through 8). For now, it is important to recognize that our tendencies to be irrational are "rationally" predictable and sometimes controllable, for better and for worse.

2. **What makes people think more or less carefully when they decide on an action?**

Put another way, when are people likely to be *deliberative* versus *expedient* in their decision processes? By definition, heuristic processes are shortcuts to making decisions. Therefore, if our criterion is to increase the deliberativeness of decisions with respect to our environment, our tendencies to be faulty thinkers are a primary target of this criterion.

As we have seen in the answer to question 1, there is both good and bad news about our ability to manage heuristics, biases, and so on.

Often, we are not able to directly affect outcomes or the decision processes that lead to them. Instead, trying to control factors that *influence* our decision processes is often our best hope for affecting these outcomes. As we will see later, there are also individual difference and social context factors that can be used to influence others' use of heuristics and biases. Some of these factors are quite accessible and some less so.

But one of the things that is becoming clear after the discussion of biases and heuristics is that, although they may be shortcuts, they often get us where we want to go (Åstebro & Elhedhli, 2006; Eubanks, Murphy, & Mumford, 2010; Kruglanski, & Gigerenzer, 2011; Nokes, Dole, & Hacker, 2007), and they can get us there more quickly than deliberative processes (Epstein, 2010). Striving for this criterion of deliberativeness may itself prove to be a mixed blessing (Eubanks et al., 2010).

3. What makes people change the way they think and behave?

It is unlikely that our neocortex will undergo substantial genetic change in the near term future (Bolhuis et al., 2011; Suddendorf & Whiten, 2001). But we can change how we make decisions as a result of the feedback we get when we have used a heuristic. It is likely that we "learn lessons" as a result of relying on heuristics, as in hindsight bias and creeping determinism: After seeing the result of an anticipated event, we change our thinking—without thinking about it! That is, we change our thinking *by relying* on heuristics (Masnick & Zimmerman, 2009; Reber & Wallin, 1984; Sawa, 2009).

We may also rely on various heuristics to convince ourselves of things (e.g., Gordijn, Postmes, & de Vries, 2001; Masnick & Zimmerman, 2009). For example, we might consider an argument for or against a belief based on who is making the argument (Schwenk & Cosier, 1980). If the argument is made by someone we think is similar to ourselves, we may change in one direction, and from someone different, in another (Gordijn et al., 2001). We choose who we watch heuristically, and we attend to things selectively based on heuristics when deciding whether to change. We will see more on this later.

Likewise, changes in culture, even during our short individual lives, may alter reliance on heuristics and biases. For example, recent research has found cultural differences in the degree to which people rely on hindsight bias (Pohl et al., 2002), suggesting that reliance on heuristics can be altered by changes in cultural traditions. More broadly, changes in thought and behavior will come from contextual effects (culture, laws, advertisements, politics, etc.) on our existing thinking. In other words, any change in the way that we think, as a general rule, will be based on how others manipulate (deliberately or not) how we think and behave on the basis of our strong tendency toward infallible casual reasoning.

It is also possible for individuals to deliberately try to change their reliance on infallible causal reasoning (Cialdini, 1988). For example, one way to create a careful decision making habit might be through in engagement with others in scientific and philosophical inquiry. Good conversations with smart, inquiring people can be highly valuable. But they also require education and time to spend on such thinking and conversation. Edwards, Weary, and their colleagues (Edwards & Weary, 1998) have shown that dispositional tendencies to be uncertain about the causes of events reduce reliance on certain types of heuristic processing. Chiesi, Primi, and Morsanyi (2011) have also found that certain characteristics lead people to develop more deliberative approaches over time.

We will see in the next chapter how people engage more readily in systemic (complex) thinking based on individual differences like education, expertise, and other fundamental characteristics. Later, the use of social and behavioral interventions will also be explored.

4. When are people likely to take action?

Individual action is often based on heuristics and biases. Gifford's (2011) list of seven psychological "dragons of inaction" includes several that are derived from the sort of non-deliberative heuristics we have discussed here. More specifically, inaccurate risk perceptions and discounting of expert advice may be important causes of *inaction*. But there are many questions that are less directly answered so far, including some of the core issues under this criterion.

For now, it is important to recognize that using heuristics to provoke collective action may work fairly well, on average. Also, following from the analysis of error (Figure 3.2), heuristics may even lead us to make correct decisions (hits and no calls) more often than not. But scientist-practitioners know that they can also lead to less effective decisions (false alarms and misses). A question that we will address later is whether being more careful and deliberate (not taking action) actually works better. For now, it is important to realize that taking action when it isn't warranted (false alarm) may be as much of a problem as not taking action when it is warranted (a true positive).

Of the many questions about the psychology of taking action, one that may be answerable based on heuristics is less obvious, and relates to the decision to take *collective* action. For most of us, there is a strong preference to work with others who are likeminded (defined in various ways). It follows that most collective action is taken by groups of like-minded people. But what makes us decide that we are similar to each other? What makes people include or exclude other people from their group?

Prejudices and stereotypes are often what we use to set people into "us" and "them" groups (Aboud, 2003; Fiske, 2002). And prejudice and

THE DETERMINIST IN US ALL

stereotyping are based on motivated heuristic processes (Fiske, 2004, 2012). The initial decision to include or exclude others from "likemindedness" is based on such heuristic processes (Hall, Matz, & Wood, 2010). But, even after we have formed "likeminded" groups, decisions to include other, outside stakeholders in our groups' later decisions can be based on prejudices, as well (Jackson, 2011). As we will see in some of the final chapters, creating an *inclusive* basis for action is likely to increase the effectiveness of the action.

Overcoming the tendencies toward prejudice and exclusion may require systematic, procedural interventions (to be discussed in several later chapters). For now, this problem can be framed in terms of using one set of motivational heuristics against another. In particular, heuristics based on social influences (e.g., authority, conformity, and reciprocity) may effectively overrule more individual biases and errors (e.g., attribution error, conjunction fallacy, and "similar to me" bias). We learn more about this approach when minority influences and perspective taking are discussed in Chapter 5.

Similarly, socially referenced heuristics (e.g., obedience to authority, beautiful = good) are likely ways to get people involved in collective action. But an important warning for those who would like to take leadership roles in collective actions is that there are important individual differences and skills that affect whether people can use these tactics effectively (Hogan, Curphy, & Hogan, 1994). Trying to take a leadership role typically requires specific, individual level characteristics (i.e., abilities, personality, motivations) that we will visit later. And those who choose to take on such leadership roles need to rely on more than just heuristic processing *themselves* in order to engage broad stakeholder groups in thoughtful decision processes.

5. What are the characteristics of change efforts that are likely to work?

Using people's heuristics, biases, and so on is far more practical and widespread than most of us are aware (Cialdini, 2007; Darke, Chattopadhyay, & Ashworth, 2006; Donoho & Swenson, 1996; Whittler, 1994). Furthermore, there is some good evidence about "how to use decision processes" to affect outcomes in applied areas like therapy, organizational change, and advertising. Clearly there is something practical about the use of our shortcuts to influence our behaviors.

A few examples of these have already been discussed in this chapter. We have seen that individual level biases are powerful, often practical ways to understand, predict, and control people's behaviors. But even putting them to work for the good of others involves serious ethical considerations, beyond their obvious practicality. We will see much more about this in Chapter 5, where socially referenced biases will be discussed.

68

Using Individual Level Biases to Affect Human–Environmental Interactions

As we have seen, the basis for many biases is association (Kahneman, 2011). This basic mechanism for behavioral learning comes from the coincidence in time and space of two events (Estes, 1960). We also know that even relatively simple organisms learn on the basis of association (Epstein, 2010; Rilling, 1996; Sahley, Boulis, & Schurman, 1994). More complex associative learning is also implicated in persuasion, attitude, and behavior change (Baumgardner, Leippe, Ronis, & Greenwald, 1983; Downing, Judd, & Brauer, 1992).

In practice, the associative principle has been used extensively in the branch of applied psychology called *consumer psychology*. Going back to John B. Watson, one of the founders of behaviorism, there have been examples of the use of the association principle in advertising. Here's how it works: The product appears alongside an attractive object. For example, a car brand is associated with beautiful mountain scenery. Yes, it is that simple, and it does work to some extent (for recent examples, see Lebens et al., 2011). Watch for examples of it in your favorite commercial media—you will see it in use every day.

However, effects of advertising on people's later buying behaviors are often fairly weak (Peterson, Albaum, & Beltramini, 1985) and the relationships, even with associative learning, are not simple (Baumgardner et al., 1983; Brown, Homer, & Inman, 1998; van Osselaer & Janiszewski, 2001). It is important to note that the research in consumer psychology is generally of the type where responses are aggregated across people, rather than across decisions. So it may have missed some factors that have a meaningful influence on buying (Totterdell & Holman, 2003).

Recent efforts to affect consumption (and other marketplace behaviors that are associated with sustainability) have also relied on the association principle (Lebens et al., 2011; Thøgersen, Jørgensen, & Sandager, 2012). For a couple of examples, how buying options are presented can be used to affect people's buying choices. Pichert and Katsikopoulos (2008) showed that the option that was offered as the *first* or "default" choice on electric bills led to it being chosen more often. This use of *anchoring* may affect the deliberativeness of people's later searches for alternatives and will be discussed in Chapter 5 under the heading of *satisficing*. Similarly, Thøgersen et al. (2012) showed how advertising a product as "green" led to the development of a "green" heuristic in later purchasing choices.

The evidence is fairly clear that we can apply some individual level heuristics and biases to influence people's eventual choices of purchase, health behaviors, and daily activities. However, several questions need to be considered before we can answer some of the criterion questions more fully. An important question that we will revisit is whether heuristics can be used to influence whether we see a problem in the first place. This will be discussed at length in Chapter 5. For now, we will turn to ways that differences among people can affect decisions—including differences in the ways that heuristics and biases are used.

4

DIFFERENCES AMONG PEOPLE

Much of the research in psychology—and in science in general—attempts to arrive at general principles. In the most developed sciences, these take on the stature of *laws*. So far, in psychology, there are very few of these principles that can be applied in all circumstances for all people. Part of the reason for this is that we have not yet accounted for the many underlying differences in our behavioral tendencies and ways that we think. Paradoxically, applied psychologists have found ways to rely on these differences themselves as a basis for making decisions, such as who to hire, how to sell different products and services, and how to approach therapeutic interventions.

Unlike other chapters in this book, this chapter will focus on these differences and their applications, rather than the general principles that tend to make us similar to one another. For example, the general tendency to be overly deterministic, which guides most people's thinking, may differ across people, based on critical reasoning skills related to mental abilities (Sternberg, 1997) and developed through educational experiences (Chiesi et al., 2011; Hatfield & Soames, 2000). In other words, the study of differences among people is not applied in the form of broad, general rules, like our tendency to be overly deterministic. Instead, we will explore the large group of characteristics, including intelligences, personality traits, attitudes, motives, and values that often differ dramatically among people. Despite their complicated interrelationships, this overview of the fundamental differences among us will reveal relationships between these and the five criteria for sustainability.

Differences among people along a set of empirically established, identifiable characteristics are the focus of research in an area of psychology called *individual differences*. Founded by Sir Francis Galton in the 1800s (Hothersall, 1995), individual differences research has explored whether there are *adaptive capacities* that differ among individuals (Eysenck, 1986). Galton and others found that measurable characteristics systematically differed based on *demographic* characteristics (e.g., gender, age, occupation, ethnicity), but they also began the process of digging beneath these more obvious differences among people to identify underlying psychological differences. Furthermore, he and his students developed the modern discipline of *applied statistics* to examine these relationships (Hothersall, 1995).

Although researchers continue to measure "boxcar demographics" like ethnicity, sex, age, and so on, the increasing sophistication of measures of our underlying, *psychological* characteristics has dramatically increased their use since Galton's time. References to the mental abilities, personality, attitudes, mental disorders, and other psychological variables invented by Galton's successors are now commonplace outside of scientific psychology. These characteristics vary between people (hence the term psychological *variable*) and are usually more highly correlated with important behaviors and outcomes than are demographic characteristics.

For our purposes, this chapter will limit discussion mostly to individual differences that are more or less stable over time—usually referred to as "abilities and other" *traits* (AOs). Knowledge and skill (KS) dimensions, which are thought of as more changeable, will be discussed to the extent that they mediate the effects of abilities and traits on decision making and behaviors. We will also return to the important question of just how *changeable* different individual differences are.

Applied Individual Differences Psychology

Individual difference *variables* have been particularly useful to scientist-practitioners, who use *individual difference measures* as the basis for many applied decisions. For example, standardized measures of differences in knowledge and ability have been applied to college admissions decisions almost universally for much of the last century. Basic psychological research on individual differences in personality has blazed other trails for applied researchers to follow, including the more recent use of personality measures for hiring and leadership development decisions. Personality measures have been so successful that they are often outside of psychology by corporate trainers trying to focus their clients on underlying differences in personality, rather than the boxcar demographic differences defined by group membership. The idea here is that awareness of these invisible differences will help to change people's thinking about interpersonal relationships. It is no surprise, then, that personality measurement has been used to predict sustainability, and that environmental psychologists have begun to acknowledge the importance of moving beyond boxcar demographics and situational features as predictors of various criteria (e.g., Gifford, 2007b; Ne'eman-Avramovich & Katz-Gerro, 2007).

There are many aspects of individual differences psychology that are quite fascinating to those who delve into them. Many college students, for example, are interested in criminal "profiling"—a forensic application of individual differences psychology. Perhaps the most important aspect of this area for our purposes is that individual differences are often *predictive* of individual and group behaviors. As students of *applied* psychology, we seek not just to *describe* and *understand*, but also to *predict* and *control* people's thinking and behavior with respect to sustainability. The potential implications of being able to account for systematic individual differences in our predictions are enormous and practical.

For example, applied forensic psychologists are sometimes asked to develop predictions about whether people who have been indicted for crimes are likely to try to flee or commit a similar crime in the future. Such predictions and similar predictions of "dangerousness" are used in court decisions to set bail and release people from prison (Greene, Heilbrun, Fortune, & Nietzel, 2007). Similar predictions have been developed recently for predicting who will or will not generally behave within the boundaries of social norms (Cordano et al., 2011). As we will see, this sort of profiling based on individual differences is also available for predicting who is likely to act against specific norms of conduct toward the natural environment (Armenta, Rodríguez, & Verdugo, 2009).

Understanding individual differences may also help to tailor interventions aimed at changing people's thinking and behaviors. In fact, accounting for individual differences when crafting persuasive messages has already proved valuable in fashioning persuasive messages, such as advertisements (Chatterjee & Hunt, 2005; Hirsh, Kang, & Bodenhausen, 2012; Petty & Wegener, 1998). Unfortunately, although there is a growing list of such predictive hypotheses for the five criteria outlined in Chapter 1, gathering data to test them has just begun.

Paradoxically, reaching large groups of people regardless of their differences has been attempted many times and in many settings, sometimes with the help of psychologists. As we have seen, *consumer behaviorists* (a group closely related to consumer psychologists) often target messages about products toward key demographic groups, with the hope that broader adoption of innovation will follow. However, these scientist-practitioners also look for individual differences that will assist in broader adoption (Blackwell, Miniard, & Engel, 2006). For example, Lee (2011) developed a set of six psychological variables that were predictive of green purchase behaviors in Hong Kong. Three of the six predictors were individual differences in knowledge and awareness.

Personnel psychology is a branch of industrial-organizational (I-O) psychology. Scientist-practitioners in this area are commonly employed in large organizations to assist with developing systematic procedures for selecting people for all kinds of jobs. The Society for Industrial and Organizational Psychology (SIOP) has grown dramatically over the past twenty-five years, due partly to the demonstrated value of such systematically derived selection procedures.

One of the newer applications in this specialty is team selection. Traditionally, psychologists develop and evaluate the accuracy of individual difference measures for predicting employees' job performance. Team selection procedures go further, using both the average across individuals' scores on these predictor measures, and the *variability* among individuals on these same measures to predict group performance. The results suggest that certain "combinations" of people will have greater success in achieving results. In particular, variability of certain aspects of personality across individuals relate to their later ability to work together and succeed (Jones, Stevens, & Fischer, 2000).

For organizations interested in selecting "group friendly" employees, this could prove to be quite helpful. But it is less help to sustainability scientist-practitioners who must work with groups that have already been constituted without such measures. There are two potential ways around this problem. First, if predictive individual differences are somewhat changeable (KS dimensions), knowing which ones are predictive may help to target individuals who need to change. Furthermore, practitioners sometimes provide developmental feedback to group members (including members with "group unfriendly" characteristics), with the hope that group members can learn to accommodate their own and each other's behaviors to account for their differences. This sort of "perspective taking" is showing promise for helping diverse groups work well together (Hoever et al., 2012).

A General Model for Predicting Behavior

Work performance research provides a broadly applicable set of variables for predicting people's behavior in applied settings. For our purposes, we will assume that it is fair to generalize predictors of effective work performance to other settings, including hobbies, social life, and other pursuits outside of the workplace. Thus, the applied model here will be assumed to predict people's actions outside of the workplace. The predictor variables have been grouped in various ways (Borman, 1992; Campbell, 1990; Campbell, McCloy, Oppler, & Sager, 1993; Morgeson, Delaney-Klinger, & Hemingway, 2005), but can be condensed for our purposes into a *non-compensatory* psychological model for predicting sustainability criteria. This model can be expressed as a simple Equation 4.1:

$$\text{Behavior} = f(\text{ability} \times \text{motivation} \times \text{knowledge of the situation}) \tag{4.1}$$

For our purposes, the *behaviors* of interest are quite broadly defined in terms of the five criteria described in Chapter 2. Among other things, we will address how ability, motivation, and situational knowledge may be associated with problem identification, awareness of issues, decision making processes, learning, collective action, inclusion, and pro-environmental behaviors.

These outcomes are a function of three factors, each of which will be discussed at length in this chapter. First, there is a list of psychological *abilities* that have accumulated a rich research and theoretical basis. These will be discussed in terms of their relationships with critical reasoning, learning, and social interaction. Second, there are numerous variables commonly associated with *motivation* that have been shown to predict awareness, decision processes, collective action, and social inclusion. These *personality*, *attitude*, and *values* variables have even been linked with people's pro-environmental behaviors in some recent research (e.g., Boer & Fischer, 2013). The third variable in this model is less cohesive, but includes people's awareness of the *social norms*, *role expectations*, and actual contingencies of actions in a given context. This might be thought of as *situational expertise*, which, unlike abilities and motivational variables, is not a commonly measured variable. Instead, measures of internalized norms, role ambiguity, and situational judgment are used for getting at situational expertise, often without reference to any broader construct.

This last set of variables points to an important warning about this model. It is primarily an organizing scheme, not a scientific theory. This means it is oversimplified and provides only general advice—not necessarily the type of advice applied scientists strive to provide when assessing situations and devising interventions. It does not closely reflect realities "on the ground," but it is used mainly as a scheme for organizing discussions about where to direct intervention efforts. So, for example, a fair number of ads have been aimed at *motivating* people to behave responsibly when drinking alcohol ("motivation" from Equation 4.1), when at the same time showing happy people drinking "without a care in the world." This visual communicates that the "norm" is for "good citizenship" ("situational knowledge" from Equation 4.1) is actually care free drinking, rather than responsible drinking. If consumption is the ads purpose (rather than necessarily *responsible* consumption), then having the "responsible" message (the motivation component) delivered in writing at the bottom of the screen, and the "consume" message delivered through depiction of attractive people having fun drinking (the "norm" component) makes sense. This is how Equation 4.1 can be applied, without necessary reference to particular scientific methods.

> Although it would sometimes be nice to just "go for it," acting on this impulse often leads to results very different from those which you anticipated. Think of a time when you "went for it." Tell a friend *your* story of how this "snap decision" happened. Reflect (and have your friend reflect honestly) about the factors that led to the eventual outcomes. Did you both agree? Were abilities and knowledge more important than effort? Did luck play into the outcomes?
>
> It is very hard to know what factors actually make the difference in people's stories. But people's *attributions* are fairly predictable. People tend to use different *causal explanations* for their outcomes, depending on their point of view. Equation 4.1 helps to try to sort out the possible reasons for our actions.

With this warning in mind, one aspect of this model that does represent a somewhat precise explanation lies in the way the three groups of predictors (ability, motivation, and situational knowledge) are described as non-compensatory. This is why Equation 4.1 is presented with multiplication signs, rather than addition signs. What this means is that the presence of one variable in large amounts does not make up for the absence of another. For example, a person living in poverty might care deeply about maintaining the health and integrity of the natural environment, but may not have the money to purchase "environmentally friendly" detergent for washing clothes. The absence of resources to take action here completely cancels the effects of motivation. Using the terms in the model, motivation does not predict behavior in the absence of ability.

Using another example, some people choose accumulation of wealth as their primary or even sole criterion of interest. If they succeed in accumulating wealth, they may be quite *able* to pay for expensive geothermal heating for their homes. However, unless there is financial gain to be realized from this choice (i.e., long term reduction in energy and system maintenance costs), their ability will be completely cancelled by their motivation to accumulate wealth as the basis for their purchasing behaviors. In the absence of motivation, this model posits that ability will not predict behavior.

Stated broadly, if either motivation or ability is set at zero, behavioral tendencies will be predicted to be zero, as well. When both motivation and ability are set greater than zero, alternatively, multiplicative effects increase the probability of behavior rapidly. So, using the two examples, just a little extra money or a little extra motivation will rapidly increase the predicted value of behavior.

Differences in Abilities and Inclination to Think Critically, Learn, Develop, and Change

Individual differences in abilities appear to predict the success of people's decisions across a host of circumstances (Judge, Higgins, Thoresen, & Barrick, 1999). Although basic research evaluating the relationship between intelligence test scores and the use of heuristics is rare (see Hertwig & Herzog, 2009), the idea that mental abilities have their effects on various outcomes *through* their influence on our thinking and learning is widely accepted. To think of this somewhat differently, Hertwig and Herzog (2009) suggest that intelligence is all about how well we develop situation relevant heuristics for everyday functioning.

One of the leading modern experts on intelligence has defined it this way:

> Intelligence comprises the mental abilities necessary for adaptation to, as well as shaping and selection of, any environmental context. According to this definition, intelligence is not just reactive to the environment but also active in forming it. It offers people an opportunity to respond flexibly to challenging situations.
>
> (Sternberg, 1997)

Applied psychologists do not typically refer to intelligence as adaptive capacity, but more often refer to it as *general mental ability*: "*g*." This framing is based on a mass of applied research showing that, among other things, scores on mental ability tests group around a single, underlying factor across circumstances (Schmidt & Hunter, 1993). This applied research has also shown that "*g*-loaded" measures are arguably the best predictor of performance across a very broad range of circumstances, including school and virtually all jobs, especially complex ones (Judge, Ilies, & Dimotakis, 2010).

An influential applied psychologist (Gottfredson, 1997) defines *g* as "[a] very general mental capacity that, among other things, involves the ability to reason, plan, solve problems, think abstractly, comprehend complex ideas, learn quickly, and learn from experience."

Though Geary (2005) argues that it is fundamental *motivations* that have led to the development of intelligences, intelligence remains a fundamental *ability* to change (adapt and learn)—not *motivation* to change. Sternberg (1997, 2004) also argues that social and cultural contexts are what define how we use intelligence to adapt our mental functioning. So, to the extent that we are motivated to adapt to our social and cultural contexts, the form our intelligences take will vary, sometimes widely. So far, however, the evidence suggests that common measures of *g* predict work performance across cultures (Salgado & Moscoso, 2002). However, most of this research used European and North American samples that, despite some level of ethnic

DIFFERENCES AMONG PEOPLE

diversity, are still defined by modern European and North American norms and cultural contexts.

Basic researchers, like Sternberg, acknowledge *g*, but still may embrace a more multifaceted and theoretically informed approach. For example, Carroll (1993) proposed a three stratum model that is hierarchically organized with *g* at the apex, broad abilities (i.e., auditory perception, verbal memory, analytical ability, production of ideas) just below *g*, and more specific factors that are determined by differences in individual "investment" in certain abilities (e.g., various musical abilities, knowledge of hydraulics) at the bottom of the hierarchy. Other basic research suggests that the relationships among component test scores are not as homogeneous as the *g* idea suggests (Guilford, 1972; Kaufman, DeYoung, Reis, & Gray, 2011; Major, Johnson, & Bouchard, 2011). This is consistent with Sternberg's notion that there are multiple intelligences, and is supported by several lines of applied research.

First, the relationship between mental abilities scores and various criteria are largely mediated by other, more specific factors (Judge et al., 2010; Schmidt, Hunter, & Outerbridge, 1986). The idea of such *mediation* is described in Chapter 1. Applied here, mental abilities predict job performance through their influence on job knowledge (Schmidt et al., 1986). Mental abilities predict well-being through their influence on health related habits (Judge et al., 2010). Mental abilities predict success at betting entirely through their relationship with situational expertise (Ceci & Liker, 1986). Figure 4.1 depicts how these *mediating variables* (job knowledge, healthy habits, situational expertise) translate mental abilities into different psychological outcomes.

This follows the *ability to learn* definition of general mental ability. That is, the *development* of specific skills is what is primarily predicted by general mental ability, followed by effects of this learning on performance and other psychological criteria (McDaniel, Morgeson, Finnegan, Campion, & Braverman, 2001). Put another way, the ability to learn things quickly and change our behaviors in response to situational demands is what is being predicted by intelligence measures, not the psychological criteria themselves.

Second, and adding to the complexity of the "ability to learn" explanation, separate measures of the specific abilities to make judgments about how to perform tasks are independent predictors of job performance (Chan & Schmitt, 2002; McDaniel & Whetzel, 2005). In other words, specific abilities are related to behaviors without reference to mental abilities. So, even people who learn more slowly (have lower scores on *g* tests) may still learn to

g → situational knowledge → performance

Figure 4.1 Depiction of the mediated relationship between general ability and performance

do jobs as well as people with high g scores—it just takes them longer. The use of *situational judgment tests* (SJT) helps to demonstrate this difference between "practical intelligence" (ability to do some complex task well) and general intelligence (ability to learn quickly). SJTs are devised to evaluate performance in specific work settings and require candidates for jobs to either describe or demonstrate what they would do in response to a specific set of circumstances. Consistent with partial mediation of the g–performance relationship, SJTs correlate significantly with g measures, but they also provide independent prediction of performance in actual work settings beyond what is predicted by g measures alone.

One way to think of this is that SJTs measure practical decision making based on what people have learned so far from their experiences in certain types of settings (Schmidt & Hunter, 1993). Here, learned knowledge and development of heuristics that apply to routine situations (Bröder, 2003; Hertwig & Herzog, 2009) fit well under the heading of situational expertise. So far, this suggests that situational judgment may be an important target for learning things outside of workplaces—they just take longer for some people to master. But, it turns out that general mental ability measures predict people's ability to learn heuristics that can be applied to later *novel* situations. This can be used to explain why mental abilities tests independently predict performance beyond what situational expertise predicts. Again, this means that mental ability has its own relationships with performance, apart from the specific skills of a given job. How quickly we learn a specific skill is predicted by general mental ability, but the direct application of these skills based on situational knowledge is independent of how quickly we learn them. Learning how to respond to repetitive situations is not as dependent on g as is learning how to respond to novel situations.

Consistent with this, there may be a reduction in the relationship between mental abilities test scores and performance over time, particularly for less complex tasks (Austin, Humphreys, & Hulin, 1989). For a job that doesn't change much, once someone has learned it, g measures only predict performance for a fairly short time. Once more, this argues for g explaining how quickly people can learn the contingencies of various situations—once learned, situational expertise is what matters. We will return to these questions later in the chapter when we discuss how to change people's knowledge of the situation.

Before we do this, however, we need to ask whether task performance is a fair proxy for the five criteria. Is the model in Equation 4.1 applicable to the five sustainability criteria? Can abilities and situational expertise predict effective decision making in the face of other uncertain, real world situations? The answer is not clear, but it is consistent with the idea that mental abilities predict how quickly and how well we learn to deal with a broad range of situations. It is clear that individuals who score higher on mental abilities tests have greater success (variously defined) across the life span

DIFFERENCES AMONG PEOPLE

(Judge et al., 1999). Whether such individual success is good for species level adaptation remains an important, unanswered question (Hardin, 2007). We will return to it, particularly in light of Sternberg's notion that intelligence is associated with how people deliberately change their environments.

Multiple Intelligences

Again, prominent basic researchers (notably Sternberg, 1997) have criticized the idea of a singular intelligence on the basis that it is not a theoretically meaningful construct. This is echoed in applied research regarding the concept of *emotional intelligence* (EI). Basic researchers (Mayer, Salovey, & Caruso, 2004) defined EI and provided an initial demonstration of the nature of this complex concept. It is defined as an independent trait consisting of four dimensions: (1) Awareness of one's own emotions; (2) ability to manage one's own emotions; (3) awareness of others' emotions; and (4) ability to manage others' emotional responses.

Many tests of the various measures of EI have yielded mixed results. First, the four factors defined in the original concept have received limited support (Maul, 2011). Second, it has been established that EI is empirically distinct from personality (Law, Wong, & Song, 2004) and g (Fox & Spector, 2000). Third, some (but not all) measures of EI have been shown to predict various criteria (Fox & Spector, 2000; Jordan, Dasborough, Daus, & Ashkanasy, 2010), including general well-being (Kotsou, Nelis, Grégoire, & Mikolajczak, 2011) and success in certain types of jobs (Joseph & Newman, 2010; O'Boyle, Humphrey, Pollack, Hawver, & Story, 2011). There are also studies that show relationships between EI and good citizenship (Carmeli & Josman, 2006; Charbonneau & Nicol, 2002). As of yet, however, there is little research on EI that can be directly applied to the five criterion questions.

As we will see, one theory suggests that EI is another, potentially important type of situational expertise (Jones, Levesque, & Masuda, 2003; Jones & Rittman, 2002; Jordan et al., 2010; Joseph & Newman, 2010). In particular, like situational judgment, it provides incremental prediction above and beyond general intelligence (O'Boyle et al., 2011).

Situational Expertise and Complex Mental Representation

Ceci and Liker (1986) studied people who had greater and less success betting at the races. The study showed that successful betters (1) had more complex "mental maps" of the horse race prediction problem and (2) were no more intelligent than less successful betters. This once again suggests a meaningful distinction in real world settings between people's situational expertise and their general ability to learn about situations. But does the structure of the horse race prediction problem require betters to change the ways they make choices after their

> successful "mental map" is in place? If such learning is necessary, then general mental ability should be predictive. It follows that horse racing doesn't change much.

Differences in Inclinations and Motivations

Apart from abilities, there are a number of systematic areas of inquiry in psychology that help us to understand how people differ in the ways we adapt to the world (Buss, 2012). The most prominent of these individual difference approaches use *personality* and *attitude* variables to explain our (mal) adaptive behaviors.

Personality

Providing a comprehensive definition for the notion of personality is well beyond the scope of this text (see Hogan, 1998; Mayer, 1998). For the sake of simplicity, we will rely on a definition that tells what personality is not. First, it is not singular. That is, personality is an overarching term for a *set* of characteristic ways in which people think about themselves and others (Hogan, 1998). Second, personality characteristics are generally classified as reasonably stable individual differences (Costa & McCrae, 1988). That is, personality does not change readily, but is classified as a set of *traits*. Third, although personality is occasionally related to skills and abilities, it is defined not in terms of competence, but rather in terms of tendencies of thought and behavior that describe our characteristic or habitual ways of relating to ourselves and others, how we typically view the world around us, and how we approach our day-to-day tasks of living (Hogan, 1998). In summary, personality consists mostly of stable individual psychological characteristics that are related to our conscious and unconscious motivations, relations to self and others, and development in response to the contexts in which we commonly function (Hogan, 1998).

The *Five Factor Model* (FFM) is a widely accepted approach to classifying normal range personality (Barrick & Mount, 2012; Costa & McCrae, 1988, 1989; Digman, 1997; Widiger & Trull, 1997). Most of the well researched measures of personality that have been developed over the past half century or so have been shown to fit reasonably well into the Big Five taxonomy (John & Naumann, 2010). A *taxonomy* is an empirically derived organizing scheme. In the case of the FFM, data have been drawn from a very large sample of people over considerable time in both basic and applied settings (Costa & McCrae, 1989). These data have been analyzed and combined using statistical techniques, yielding five prominent factors. These five factors have been broken into various sub-categories and separated from other, less prominent groups of characteristics.

The main statistical techniques used here fall under the heading of *factor analysis*—whence the five *factor* model. In the case of the FFM, factor analysis is used to find commonalities underlying the correlations between people's descriptions of themselves and others. Five point Likert response scales are used for the items in most personality inventories. These yield more finely grained distributions of scores than the *dichotomies* (either/or categories) that are often used in popularly available personality measures. This means that classifying someone as (for example) introvert/extrovert is not an either/or proposition, but a matter of degree, with most people falling toward the middle of this continuum (Buss, 2012).

Definitions of Big Five personality factors with Costa and McCrae's subfacets

Neuroticism / emotional stability

Definition: Tendency to experience negative arousal or mood, be labile and impulsive.

Subfacets: Anxiety, angry hostility, depression, self-consciousness, impulsiveness, vulnerability.

Extroversion / introversion

Definition: Tendency to seek external stimulation, be energetic, and assert presence and wishes socially, including talkativeness; also called surgency.

Subfacets: Warmth, gregarious, assertive, activity, excitement seeking, positive emotion.

Experiential openness

Definition: Intellectually and experientially curious, seeking new aesthetics, adventures, and discoveries, and varieties of experience. Sometimes called intellectance.

Subfacets: Fantasy, aesthetics, feelings, actions, ideas, values.

Agreeableness / tough-mindedness

Definition: A tendency to "go along to get along" socially, be cooperative and trusting rather than antagonistic toward others.

Subfacets: Trust, straightforwardness, altruism, compliance, modesty, tender-mindedness.

Conscientiousness

Definition: Tendency to be planful and organized in approach to life tasks.

Subfacets: Competence, order, dutifulness, achievement striving, self-discipline, deliberation.

The Big Five are fairly broad groupings of these responses, with more specific "facets" of personality composed of smaller sub-groups of items. The five factors are typically presented in the order of largest to least "covariance." What this means is that, taking all of the correlations among all of the items into account, the largest cluster of response covariance is extracted as the first factor in factor analysis, followed by the next largest, and so on. The box of the Big Five describes a common grouping of the FFM in applied psychology.

Class activity. Complete and self-score a reputable personality inventory. Students should be the only people to view their own, individual reports. Discuss the nature of the questions asked (self-focused, Likert scale, and so on). Is this a good indication of "who you are?" Is it a mirror of how you see yourself?

Applied Measurement of Individual Differences

We have seen already that measurement of intelligence is a very widespread application of psychology. The FFM is also commonly used to inform decisions regarding hiring (Judge et al., 1999; Ones, Dilchert, Viswesvaran, & Judge, 2007) and has received increased use in selecting college students (Komarraju, Karau, Schmeck, & Avdic, 2011; Richardson, Abraham, & Bond, 2012). Some dimensions of the FFM predict behavior only in certain situations (e.g., people high in extroversion often make good salespeople). However, one factor predicts criminal activity in various settings (Blickle, Schlegel, Fassbender, & Klein, 2006; Hogan & Brinkmeyer, 1997; Ones & Viswesvaran, 2001; Wiebe, 2004), performance and compliance across most jobs (Ones et al., 2007), and performance in academic settings (Poropat, 2009). *Conscientiousness* (C) is partly defined in terms of persistence toward goals and an organized approach to tasks, so its relationship with performance and good citizenship should not come as a surprise.

If we consider job performance as one indication of people's tendencies to make good decisions generally, conscientiousness is a good candidate for a predictor of careful decision making. In fact, it is mostly defined in terms of self-regulation (orderliness, self-discipline, deliberativeness) and deference to others' standards (sense of responsibility, dutifulness, competence, and achievement striving). This combination of self-regulation and conformity may make conscientiousness a double edged sword, since rigid adherence to a course of action and conformity may make it difficult for people high in C to learn and change (DeYoung, Peterson, & Higgins, 2002).

Only *openness* (O) and its close cousin *need for cognition* are correlated with mental abilities test scores (Cacioppo, Petty, Feinstein, Jarvis, & Blair, 1996). Associated with more effortful mental activities, openness can perhaps be thought of as willingness or desire to learn and change. It therefore falls under the heading of "motivation" in Equation 4.1. As we will see, there is some recent reason to believe that *openness* predicts people's approach to the natural environment, as well.

There is also growing agreement that *extroversion* (E) and *neuroticism* (N) have strong relationships with life satisfaction and well-being. Not surprisingly, neuroticism is associated negatively with subjective well-being and other health related outcomes. Extroversion is correlated positively with many positive life outcomes and generally relates to happiness (Steel, Schmidt, & Shultz, 2008). However, the causality of this is by no means clear, as pain and other problems in life may actually lead people to report less emotional stability (Thayer, 1996), and success may increase the tendency to be socially dominant and sociable (two of the extroversion subscales; Costa & McCrae, 1989).

The FFM can also be grouped together in various ways, in the same way that intelligence is clumped under *g* to simplify prediction (Digman, 1997). Just looking at the Big Five box suggests a couple of possible "meta-traits" where the five factors can be reduced into fewer traits. For example, FFM traits might be combined in terms of their *intra-individual* versus *social* orientation. Specifically, neuroticism and openness are associated with intra-individual motivations to be reactive and to try new things, respectively. Agreeableness and conscientiousness, though they have internal aspects, are somewhat related to social conformity and concern for the interests of others. Similarly, recent research about such "meta-trait" groupings of the Big Five suggests that they may also fit well into *plasticity* (E + O) and *stability* (N + A + C) super-dimensions (DeYoung et al., 2002; Hirsh, DeYoung, & Peterson, 2009), which relate to specific neurological systems. In practice, subfacets of the FFM are often combined in idiosyncratic ways to predict performance in particular jobs (Hogan & Hogan, 2007). Such convenient *composite* groupings of FFM subfacets and factors may have important applications for predicting sustainability criteria, as well (Milfont & Sibley, 2012; Wiseman & Bogner, 2003).

Error in Application

As with all psychology, there is an assumption of error in the use of individual differences measures to make selection decisions. In Chapter 3, we visited the fourfold table of errors derived from Signal Detection Theory (Figure 3.2). This reasoning about error has a long history of use in selection. Figure 4.2 describes the application of this approach to the problem of predicting of later behavior based on a known

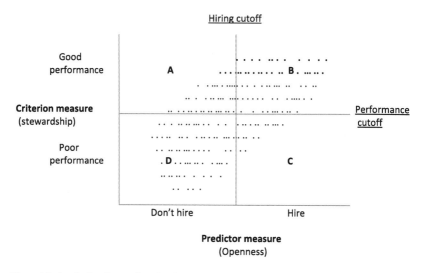

Figure 4.2 Analysis of error in selection using individual difference measures

correlation between the same type of behavior and an individual difference measure.

As an example, in a recent study, Markowitz et al. (2012) showed that openness and environmental stewardship were moderately, positively correlated (r = .39). This is the sort of evidence that is commonly used to validate the use of a measure of openness for hiring decisions. So, suppose that applied psychologists wanted to predict stewardship behaviors in an envirocompany startup using this information. Figure 4.2 provides a way to analyze the outcomes of this approach to hiring decisions.

One way of depicting this correlation between a predictor measure (in this case openness) and a criterion measure (in this case stewardship) is the *scatterplot* in Figure 4.2. When we set the cutoff score for hire/don't hire decisions on the openness scale (*x* axis), we are likely to make two types of errors. To understand these errors, we also need to establish a cutoff for acceptable/unacceptable levels of stewardship (on the *y* axis); this would be the "good performance/poor performance" cutoff in our example. In quadrant A, there are *false negatives*: People who demonstrated acceptable levels of stewardship, but who were excluded from employment based on their openness scores. They were screened out by the predictor measure, even though they would have done a good job. Quadrant B includes the *true positives* (*hits* in Figure 3.2). These are the people who made the predictor cutoff score and are good stewards. *False positives* (Quadrant C) are the people who made the predictor cut, but failed to live up to predictions—they didn't exhibit adequate stewardship. Finally, Quadrant D includes the *true negatives* who were correctly predicted to not be good stewards and were screened out.

This analysis of error points to three important things. First, the enviro-company is trying to maximize its true positives—people who will do the job well. This is usually managed by setting hire/don't hire cutoff scores on openness to do just this. Second, applicants for the enviro-company job would usually like to minimize their chances of being in the false negative group. Third, and perhaps most important for our purposes, although there will be errors, even when there are substantial correlations between predictors and correlations, there are fewer errors when there is a relationship between predictors and criteria than when there are not. In other words, although there is error here, it is less error than some of the alternatives. For example, we could simply hire people for our enviro-company based on their family membership with other people in the company. So it is very important to note that, while the decisions may lead to error sometimes, error is less likely than when hiring is made without this systematic, measurement based approach.

An exercise in analysis of error. The death penalty is applied based on assessments made by juries. Forensic psychologists are among those who apply analysis of error to these jury predictions. Substitute actual guilt/innocence as the cutoff on the y axis in Figure 4.2. Substitute the cutoff of guilty/not guilty on the x axis. Now, assume that the correlation between jury judgments of guilt and actual guilt of the defendant in death penalty cases is quite high (r = .90), so there are very few errors for every correct decision. Notice that this still relies on the assumption that jury predictions of guilt and innocence include errors, as recent examples of DNA exoneration indicate.

Whose interest is served by each type of error? What are the societal interests served by over versus under applying the death penalty?

Now apply the same logic to more or less stringent enforcement (predictor cutoffs) of environmental regulations. More stringent cutoffs would mean tighter enforcement, sometimes even when people have not violated these regulations (plotted as a guilty/not guilty cutoff on the y axis). Is the societal interest in sustainable behavior enough to allow for more stringent enforcement of environmental laws? Should we weigh problems of false positives or false negatives more heavily?

The application of analysis of error is an example of the sort of ethical approach that applied psychologists take. The "humble assumption of error" limits the claims of effectiveness that reputable scientist-practitioners can make about the interventions they use. But it also provides clear, empirically based assessments of relevant characteristics, rather than relying on hunches and heuristics.

Also, there are ways to account for the limitations of one predictor (e.g., an intelligence measure). Applied psychologists often add more independent measures in order to enhance predictive accuracy and reduce the chances of error. For example, in addition to an intelligence measure, we might also include a measure of conscientiousness that independently predicts later behavior.

Following the Markowitz et al. (2012) example from Figure 4.2, adding additional variables uncovered a mediated relationship between personality and pro-environmental behavior—described in the box below.

Which would you guess is more predictive of pro-environmental behaviors: Altruistic aspects of personality (agreeableness) or aesthetic aspects (openness)? Before you read further, write down your guess, and an explanation.

There is some research (Ewing, 2001) suggesting that individual differences associated with altruism are important predictors of pro-environmental behavior. However, more recent research has shown that the tendency to be sympathetic is less predictive in some situations than in others (Stürmer, Snyder, & Omoto, 2005). Also, research using more commonly accepted measures (Markowitz et al., 2012) shows that conforming and altruistic personality dimensions (agreeableness and conscientiousness) *were not related* to pro-environmental behaviors. By contrast, aesthetic interest, creativity, and inquisitiveness (components of openness) were. This has been explained by the idea that people who are willing to consider the world around them in broad terms (so-called universalist perspective; Guagnano, Dietz, & Stern, 1994) are more likely to consider adopting new ways of doing things in the interest of keeping the world they experience in their daily lives more pleasant. Thus, the relationship between openness and pro-environmental behavior may be mediated by people's sense of attachment to nature. If people feel pleasure from nature, then their openness leads them to treat it well.

Other Trait Like Characteristics That May Be Important

As mentioned at the beginning of discussions about personality, this is a very complex, multifaceted area of both theory and research. Despite some controversy, we have seen that personality measures have led to significant advances in several applied areas. And the controversy itself has led to some potentially valuable additions to the FFM that deserve attention. These additions present some future avenues for scientist-practitioners to approach our five criteria. Some of these candidates for individual differences will be considered at greater length in discussions of identity and development in Chapter 6. But two deserve attention here, since they already appear to have achieved status as stable individual differences that can be separated from the Big Five.

Authoritarian Personality

The first of these is *authoritarian personality*. Most researchers in the field credit Altemeyer (2004) with the origin of the construct, though there were earlier researchers working on similar tracks (Elms & Milgram, 1966). Altemeyer's primary interest is an unabashed desire to identify people who are likely to be threats to a free society (Altemeyer, 2004). He has since argued, with considerable research support, that authoritarianism comes in both *submissive* and *socially dominant* forms. Socially dominant authoritarian personalities are seen as the most dangerous in societies that value freedom. They are:

> among the most prejudiced persons in society. Furthermore, they seem to combine the worst elements of each kind of personality, being power-hungry, unsupportive of equality, manipulative, and amoral, as social dominators are in general, while also being religiously ethnocentric and dogmatic, as right wing authoritarians tend to be.
>
> (Altemeyer, 2004)

The original concept of authoritarian personality was based on the notion that some people are more likely than others to rigidly adhere to dogmatic, religiously ethnocentric views. Later research has shown a host of correlates with authoritarianism, including tendency toward prejudice (Arvaniti et al., 2009; Jost, Glaser, Kruglanski, & Sulloway, 2003); discrimination and harassment of people in subordinate positions (Begany & Milburn, 2002; Knapp, 1976; Petersen & Dietz, 2008); belief in the idea that people in less powerful positions deserve their situations (Cozzarelli, Wilkinson, & Tagler, 2001); and adherence to culturally stereotyped gender roles (Peterson & Zurbriggen, 2010). Perhaps most interestingly, authoritarianism is negatively correlated with mental abilities (Davids, 1955; Heaven, Ciarrochi, & Leeson, 2011; Jacobson & Rettig, 1959; Leeson, Heaven, & Ciarrochi, 2012; O'Connor, 1952) and positively with various kinds of anxiety (Davids, 1955; Jost et al., 2003; O'Connor, 1952; Oesterreich, 2005; Singer & Feshbach, 1959).

Following from this, authoritarianism has been defined is in terms of an *authoritarian reaction* (Oesterreich, 2005). Authoritarian reaction is flight to apparent relief in the face of uncertainty. Those who feel unable to develop their own coping strategies in the face of their initial, anxious reaction to an uncertain world may find habitual comfort in the apparent certainty of authoritarian beliefs. Hence the authoritarian personality comes to be. This sort of flight in the face of anxiety and the inherent uncertainty of science may help to explain some responses to scientific information about environmental degradation.

Although authoritarianism correlates with other personality and ability dimensions, these are relatively small correlations, so it probably does stand alone as an individual difference (Jost et al., 2003). However, some also suggest that it is an ideology or value system, rather than a personality characteristic (Heaven et al., 2011; Jost et al., 2003). Considering the evidence of its persistence across generations (Williams, Ciarrochi, & Heaven, 2012) with possible genetic components (McCourt, Bouchard, Lykken, Tellegen, & Keyes, 1999), this seems unlikely. Nevertheless, we will wait to integrate more of the large literature on authoritarianism in Chapter 6, when we consider the development of moral reasoning.

Applied Authoritarianism?

The clear political overlay to research on authoritarianism may help explain the lack of broad application of this very large research literature when compared with the FFM. Most applied psychology relies heavily on the ability of scientist-practitioners to relate effectively to a broad range of stakeholders, often with very different political views. Trying to apply what is clearly a politically charged notion in circumstances where consensus is sought is likely to prove risky. However, some studies have examined applications of authoritarianism in forensic (Fodor, Wick, Hartsen, & Preve, 2008; Ray & Subich, 1998), clinical (Martinez & Forgatch, 2001; Reitman et al., 2001), educational (Bogacki, Armstrong, & Weiss, 2005; Tom, Cooper, & McGraw, 1984), and work psychology (Ezekiel, 1968; Laguna, Linn, Ward, & Rupslaukyte, 2010; Marks & MacDougall, 1959; Nicol, Charbonneau, & Boies, 2007; Rubinstein, 2006; Tosi, 1973). Results of these studies appear to lend some equivocal support to the predictive power of authoritarianism (Jost et al., 2003), at least in certain types of settings (e.g., police and military samples).

Understanding the various correlates of authoritarianism, and particularly submissive authoritarianism, may help scientist-practitioners looking for ways to ethically integrate the interests of diverse stakeholders. If authoritarian reaction is a common response to scientific alarm regarding environmental issues, finding ways to reassure people with authoritarian tendencies may be a very valuable tool. We will return to this in the final section of this chapter.

Self-Regulation and Attitude toward Self

The second of the "other" individual differences we will discuss is *causal uncertainty* (CU; Weary & Edwards, 1994). This is one of several candidates for additional "big" personality factors because of its low correlation with the FFM dimensions (Edwards, Weary, & Reich, 1998). CU is defined as a stable individual difference in people's self-perceived ability to detect cause and effect relationships in the social world (Edwards et al., 2009; Jacobson, Weary, & Lin, 2008). Higher CU has been associated with increased effort in tasks and decision processes (Jacobson et al., 2008; Weary & Jacobson, 1997), reduced prejudice (Tobin, Weary, Brunner, Gonzalez, & Han, 2009; Weary et al., 2001), increased persuasive capacity (Tobin & Weary, 2008), and increased depression and anxiety (Edwards & Weary, 1998; Jacobson, 2007). Although its relationship with the use of specific heuristics is not established, its relationship with decision effort more generally may prove helpful in applied research. An important question still to be answered is whether it is possible to change our beliefs about our own sense making abilities.

The evidence coming from self-regulatory literature suggests they may be. CU is at least partly a belief about one's own abilities. Such beliefs are referred to as *self-efficacy beliefs* (Bandura, 1982; Hackett & Betz, 1989). *Self-efficacy* is defined as people's beliefs about their own abilities in a particular enterprise (Betz & Wolfe, 2005). Some researchers have also offered the idea of a *generalized* self-efficacy: The general belief about one's own competency in a host of situations (Betz & Klein, 1996). Hartman and Betz (2007) have shown that conscientiousness and extroversion correlate positively, and neuroticism negatively with generalized self-efficacy, suggesting its coherence with the "super-dimensions" of the FFM.

Bandura argues that we learn self-efficacy through trial and error, modeling from others, and persuasion (in order of effectiveness). We also learn to focus our self-regulation toward tasks that we have had success with in the past. This is where self-regulation comes into Bandura's theory. Knowing what it is you are aiming at (a goal) is learned through feedback we receive about what is expected in a given context. We will return to this in Chapter 5 when we discuss cultural contexts and Chapter 6 when we discuss development. But for now it is important to note that, unlike personality, self-efficacy may be changed in applied efforts to motivate action.

Bandura's original conception of self-efficacy linked it with effort toward outcomes—one way of defining motivation. If you believe you are incapable of something, you are less likely to try to do it than if you think you can master it. For example, if I don't think I can stand living with less heat in my home, I am less likely to try. This also points out that some part of motivation lies in the belief that one is able do something. In particular, beliefs about one's ability to change have shown to be important predictors in applied settings (Ferris et al., 2011; Hackett & Betz, 1989; Stajkovic & Luthans, 1998; Wu & Griffin, 2012). This puts self-efficacy squarely under the heading of self-regulation: I will try to regulate my actions only if I think myself capable of doing so. It is also for this reason that goal setting research has become increasingly integrated with work on self-regulation (Bandura & Locke, 2003).

However, several of the individual differences we have discussed so far also relate to self-regulation. Conscientiousness is partly defined by habitual impulse control and neuroticism by habitual lability (mood swings). Emotional intelligence, sometimes referred to as emotional maturity (Anderson & Jones, 2000), is also associated with self-regulation (Mayer et al., 2004). It is still unclear how such dispositions of self-regulation may relate to people's beliefs about their own abilities to control themselves and their environments. But it is generally accepted that these beliefs about one's self influence effort and motivation (Bandura, 1982).

Perhaps the relationship between dispositional self-regulation and situational self-efficacy is similar to the relationship between mental abilities and situational expertise. For example, if I have higher trait anxiety (neuroticism), I may be less likely to feel efficacious in situations where anxiety is easily aroused. Findings from Wu and Griffin (2012) support the notion that we change at least our self-beliefs as a result of such experiences, if not our understandings of situations.

Applied Self-Regulation

Self-efficacy interventions have been applied successfully in career counseling (Hackett & Betz, 1989) and personnel selection (Judge, 2009). Goal setting interventions, which are designed to promote greater self-regulation, are widely touted and have received strong experimental support (Bandura & Locke, 2003), with slightly less support in applied settings (Pulakos & O'Leary, 2010; Tubbs, 1986). This may be because of the misconception that goals are purely influencing motivation (Bandura & Locke, 2003), rather than defining behavioral expectations or standards in a given situation (Bobko & Colella, 1994; Erez & Arad, 1986). Following from the model of performance at the beginning of this chapter, self-efficacy is a non-compensatory motivational factor, while goal setting is primarily a means to develop an understanding of the expectations for a situation and the means to meeting them (Bandura & Locke, 2003)—a form of situational expertise. Regardless, in combination with feedback, and given adequate knowledge, skills, abilities, and other characteristics (KSAOs), self-efficacy and goals are likely to prove powerful as ways to change behavior (Bandura & Locke, 2003; Burnette, O'Boyle, VanEpps, Pollack, & Finkel, 2013).

But there is a further step between personality, self-regulation, and eventual behavior. A recent meta-analysis suggests that self-regulation mediates the relationship between personality and attitude (Lanaj, Chang, & Johnson, 2012). Put in the form of a flow chart, and using the example of predicting pro-environmental behaviors:

Openness → regulatory focus on learning about nature
→ attitude toward the environment → behaviors

Meta-analysis uses statistical techniques to combine many single studies. What this meta-analysis shows is that our stable tendencies (e.g., toward curiosity) only affect our evaluations of various outcomes (attitudes) through the filter of what we think we can control in ourselves (self-regulatory focus). Another recent meta-analysis demonstrated a very similar complex relationship has emerged in research on workplace behaviors. Thomas, Whitman, and Viswesvaran (2010) showed that employee proactivity (a set of behavioral outcomes associated with good citizenship) is predicted by personality, but that this relationship is similarly mediated by the attitudes of job satisfaction and organizational commitment:

Personality → attitudes toward job and organization → proactive behaviors

These large scale meta-analyses both suggest that our eventual actions result from personality only through the filters of self-regulation and attitudes. We will consider attitudes next.

Activity and Discussion

1. Complete and self-score a reputable questionnaire or attitude scale.
2. Have self-feedback of this by students privately.
3. How does this questionnaire differ from a personality inventory?
4. Is it a good indication of all of your views on environmental issues (problem of sufficiency)?

A common problem with all kinds of psychological measures (mental abilities, personality, attitudes, tests for classes, etc.) is that they do not ask for responses on every aspect of the concept of interest. For example, a typical paper and pencil mental abilities measure may not measure ability to apply thinking in "real world" situations. This missing of important information is called the *problem of sufficiency*: Whether the measure measures every aspect of what it is designed to measure.

5) Did you have to think twice about questions or were they totally clear to you (problem of contamination)?

Sometimes the questions in psychological tests and inventories are unclear or have more than one meaning to different people. This means that they are likely to gather information about things that are not intended: The problem of *test contamination*.

6) An assumption of ethical test development is that there will be errors of sufficiency and contamination in any measure. So, why are these imperfect tests used?

One answer is that such systematically developed tests will usually do a better job of helping make decisions than will more heuristic or unstructured approaches. And the evidence generally supports this. So, even though Figure 3.2 shows false positives and false negatives, there are fewer of these *errors* than there are *correct decisions* using this type of measure.

Attitudes

Like personality, there is considerable controversy about the finer points of what constitutes an attitude (Eagly & Chaiken, 2007). Most definitions include reference to *evaluative dispositions* with respect to various *attitude objects*, including other people (Ajzen & Fishbein, 1980), the environment (Maloney & Ward, 1973; Nigbur, Lyons, & Uzzell, 2010; Schultz & Oskamp, 1996), and sustainability initiatives in general (de Barcellos, Krystallis, de Melo Saab, Kügler, & Grunert, 2011). Eagly and Chaiken (2007) attempt to reconcile the different definitions of attitude has led to a definition that separates *evaluative disposition* from the *behavior intentions* that correlate with attitudes (Vallerand, Deshaies, Cuerrier, Pelletier, & Mongeau, 1992). Behavioral intentions were included as part of the definition of attitude for many years (Vallerand et al., 1992), but were often not highly correlated with evaluative dispositions. This newer approach (without behavioral intentions) defines an attitude as "a psychological tendency that is expressed by evaluating a particular entity with some degree of favor or disfavor" (Eagly & Chaiken, 2007). For example, someone might think the sustainability movement (attitude object) misguided (evaluation), while others see it as imperative on the same continuum (degree of favor or disfavor).

Although the relationship between attitudes and behavioral intentions is often high (Vallerand et al., 1992), the relationship between attitudes and actual behavior is dependent on a host of other factors (Crano & Prislin,

1995; Glasman & Albarracín, 2006). These include such things as the specificity of the attitude object, the strength of the attitude, and the norms or values from which they arise (Vallerand et al., 1992). In general, the relationship between attitudes and actual behavior is mediated by people's intentions (Ajzen, 1991; Lee, 2011).

There are strong similarities between attitude and personality. Both are commonly measured by agreement with statements: "To what extent do you agree with the following statements?" Both typically ask for evaluations along a Likert scale. Perhaps the most important difference is that personality inventories ask people to describe and evaluate themselves, while the content of attitude items usually ask for evaluations of aspects of the external world. Even so, personality measures occasionally do ask for evaluations of external factors ("Parties are fun"), and some attitude questions refer to the person responding ("I like wild animals").

So what is the distinction between attitude and personality? Perhaps it is that attitudes are assumed to be transitory and malleable (i.e., can be changed) and personality more stable and difficult to change. As we saw with mental abilities, personality probably sets the stage for attitude formation and change with respect to specific circumstances. We have dispositional tendencies (personalities) that set us up to construe things a certain way, but our notions about appropriate action (attitudes) are formed by our changing understandings of circumstances.

Applied Attitudes

Although much of the basic research and theory relating to attitudes is important and helpful for predicting and controlling factors associated with our five sustainability criteria (Nigbur et al., 2010), we will treat attitudes almost entirely from the applied perspective. There are three reasons for this. First, attitude measurement is widely used to predict and control human behavior in a host of real world settings (cf. Baldinger & Rubinson, 1996; Becker & Gibson, 1998; Brett & Reilly, 1988; Corrigan & Miller, 2004; Tziner & Murphy, 1999). Second, there is a growing literature on attitude measurement in environmental psychology. Starting with Maloney and Ward (1973), attitudes toward the environment have been measured, sometimes using samples outside of university settings (e.g., Cleveland et al., 2005; Hansla, Gamble, Juliusson, & Gärling, 2008). This work has been extended to other attitudes (e.g., commitment to the environment; Davis, Le, & Coy, 2011) and a fairly broad range of behavioral outcomes (Cleveland et al., 2005; Milfont & Duckitt, 2010). Third, while it has also experienced some refinement, there has been less concern in this literature for finer points of definition or for developing an "attitude theory." Efforts instead are directed at understanding the ways people represent questions of sustainability (Hansla et al., 2008; Milfont & Duckitt, 2010). Theoretical problems are often not addressed in applied settings. This emphasis on the dependent variable, rather than with processes or precursors, is typical of applied research (Klimoski & Jones, 2008).

Consistent with this, some applied researchers use attitude surveys as means to get a quick, practical measure of people's motivational tendencies at a given point in time. If a political pollster is trying to predict people's voting behaviors a few weeks from now, there is probably less concern with where the behavior comes from (e.g., personality, abilities, norms, values) than "what will work"—that is, what will predict actual voting behavior in two weeks. Political surveys, consumer preference surveys, organizational climate surveys, and so on are typically canted toward this "what will work" perspective. These are used as current snapshots of what the target group is thinking and feeling. This information is used, in turn, to predict short term behavior, to target change efforts, and to tailor other interventions.

Values

Although values are occasionally invoked in applied psychology, particularly when defining cultural variables, their application is sparse, compared to the large basic research literature on this topic (Schwartz et al., 2012). In general parlance, values are "[i]mportant and lasting beliefs or ideals shared by the members of a culture about what is ... desirable or undesirable. Values have major influence on a person's behavior and attitude" (Business Dictionary, 2013). Since values are nested in contexts (esp. cultural contexts), they are only partly *individual* differences. We will see much more about them in Chapter 5. But, their importance to motivation deserves consideration here, as well.

Chan (2010) argues that values are actually complex "process" variables in decision making. Values are part of the ongoing application of implicit cultural expectations and beliefs to various situations. So, we might choose to buy organic lettuce rather than non-organic lettuce because the value of organic agriculture comes up in our thinking while we are making the buying choice. If we have not incorporated the "buy organic" value, we might see organic lettuce as simply expensive—not having the additional value associated with its higher cost.

Following from this, values can be seen as boundaries for our behaviors. That is, we don't always know when our values are influencing us to *do* certain things, but they are invoked more consciously (and socially) to *stop us from doing* certain things. We might think of values as *internalized* rules of conduct. This is consistent with the idea that we don't even think when we invoke values. They are mostly determined by culture and family and often learned in childhood. So, values become *habitual* (as opposed to deliberative) ways of thinking and behaving early in life.

Bowing and shaking hands are examples of rules of behavior when we meet a new person in Japanese and Western European cultures, respectively. These are typical habits, sometimes called *norms*, rather than carefully considered actions under many circumstances. However, deciding not to shake someone's hand or bow—to break the rule of conduct—might be based on more deliberate invocation of certain values. Specifically, if the person proffering a bow or hand shake has committed some breach of conduct, then the (very deliberate) response might be to withhold the "traditional" response. Similarly, someone from Japan might have to consciously change the rule of bowing and deliberately shake hands with someone when in a Western culture. This will get a longer discussion in Chapter 5, when norms and social aspects of emotive perception are discussed. Suffice for now to say that the trappings of values and traditions are a strong way to signal group inclusion and exclusion (Greenberg, 1988; Tracy, Shariff, Zhao, & Henrich, 2013).

Summary of Motivational Variables

Motives are the internal forces that direct and modulate our activities. Following from the non-compensatory equation at the beginning of this chapter, motives are sort of valves. Without motives being "open," abilities are not used. In fact, there is some evidence that, without motives, people will not even develop abilities and skills (Von Stumm & Ackerman, 2013). It is only if having an ability *matters* to me that will I spend the time and effort to learn it. Anyone who has taken up an instrument or learned a sport understands that motive is necessary for learning. The absence of motive means abilities will not be applied to performing behaviors. Similarly, following from the valve analogy, all the motivation in the world will not make up for a lack of ability.

Some personality measures are fairly good proxies for long term motivational tendencies. They suggest when people will be more or less inclined to self-regulate in given circumstances, and sometimes more broadly (i.e., conscientiousness). Likewise, self-efficacy sets limits on our tendencies to exert effort toward various ends and may be more malleable than personality. Attitude measures provide a more immediate idea of motivational direction and strength and sometimes give those who would like to change individuals' motives a ready target. Values set strong situational constraints on motivated behaviors.

Applying Individual Differences to Sustainability Criteria

Intelligences, personality traits, values, attitudes, and motivations may go a long way to explaining why people see and behave differently around our five criteria.

DIFFERENCES AMONG PEOPLE

1. What prompts people to think they have a problem (or not)?

It will become increasingly obvious that there are at least two major questions within this one. In order to believe that there is a problem, people must first be made *aware* of the situation that might be construed as a problem and only then *appraise* whether there is a threat to existing or future goods. Being aware of the situation around us is at least partly a function of intelligence and openness. We have seen, in particular, that the acquisition of knowledge happens more rapidly on average for people high in intelligence and openness.

Appeals to people lower in these stable traits would therefore need to address easy to understand issues and be directed toward broad communications (e.g., ads on popular TV shows), rather than more complicated and obscure sources. Much of the information about sustainability for many years seemed to have been concentrated in outlets such as public television and scientific journals. This appears to have changed, but appeals to mass audiences are still sometimes "preaching to the choir" in terms of the complexity of information provided (Pinazo & Agut, 2008).

Remembering that situational expertise is also part of what makes intelligence functional, it may be important to realize that even some highly intelligent people need to be made aware of circumstances. In fact, such awareness of the existence of discrepancies has been used to distinguish experts from novices (Mehrez & Steinberg, 1998). We will learn more about this in Chapter 7.

Once awareness has been achieved, people higher in trait anxiety (e.g., neuroticism) are more ready to identify the existence of a "problem," almost by definition. The effects of this recognition on their decision to treat things as problematic, however, may depend on trait causal uncertainty and authoritarian reaction, both of which relate to anxiety. High causal uncertainty, which gives people the urge to try to learn more and withhold judgment, may lead to willingness to accept that there is a problem, if enough of their sources of information support this conclusion. But CU is also associated with depression, which may mean that people high in CU will be "helpless" in terms of taking action. Similarly, authoritarianism may lead people to seek "authorities" to reassure themselves in the face of anxiety producing information. Since many people choose authorities who appear "certain" of their knowledge, it is far less likely that authoritarians will fall under the influence of probabilistic scientists.

Alternatively, people low in trait anxiety may be fully aware that the scientific community has raised concerns, but be less likely to be alarmed. Reaching these individuals' "set point" for concern (to be discussed in the next chapter) may be quite challenging.

DIFFERENCES AMONG PEOPLE

2. What makes people think more or less carefully when they decide on an action?

The answer to this appears fairly straightforward. A candidate for "highly deliberative decision maker" would be someone who is smart, high in causal uncertainty, and highly self-regulatory (i.e., low neuroticism, high conscientiousness, high emotional maturity, and high self-efficacy). Being deliberative about larger sustainability issues has in fact been shown to relate to emotional stability and conscientiousness, among other variables (Swami et al., 2010). People high in openness are also likely to put stock in exploration of issues that they find interesting or challenging, but the direction of their curiosity may be an issue. Understanding the direction of attitudes may help to predict this (Cleveland et al., 2005), and cultural tendencies toward long term thinking and altruism might also prove to be predictive. Authoritarianism is almost by definition non-deliberative, by contrast.

Deliberation with respect to the effects of one's actions on others—altruism—is predictable on the basis of intelligence and openness, as well. We have seen that agreeableness is not predictive of altruism, while openness is (Chochola, 2010; Markowitz et al., 2012). But intelligence presents an interesting conundrum in its relationship with altruism. Counterproductive behaviors have been positively predicted by mental abilities in work situations (Marcus, Wagner, Poole, Powell, & Carswell, 2009). This suggests that people higher in intelligence may tend to be "defectors" in terms of helping the group do better. In terms of altruism more generally, and despite common stereotypes to the contrary (Mõttus, Allik, Konstabel, Kangro, & Pullmann, 2008), intelligence has been shown to correlate positively with "unconditional altruism" (Millet & Dewitte, 2007). This is an important puzzle, since mental abilities are conceptualized as individual adaptive capacities and correlate with a host of positive individual outcomes, including life success. These recent findings suggest that the willingness to "give it up for the good of others" is a part of smart thinking—but so is the inclination to defect from the group.

Similarly, authoritarianism (which is associated with lower intelligence) is associated with less altruism (e.g., Lefcourt & Shepherd, 1995) and less inclination toward pro-environmental behavior (Arbuthnot, 1977). But recent research also suggests that authoritarianism can be associated with pro-environmental attitudes, as well. Reese (2012) showed that, in a country (Germany) where pro-environmental laws have been in place for some time, certain aspects of authoritarianism predicted positive attitudes toward pro-environmental behavior. We will see how the social context may interact with individual characteristics in this way in Chapter 5.

3. What makes people change the way they think and behave?

Most of the traits discussed in this chapter are just that—stable traits. Richardson et al. (2012) provide an example of this view:

> Many studies have assessed the role of personality in academic performance. Dispositional personality traits are assumed, like intelligence, to exert a constant influence over performance across situations. Such traits are, in part, genetically mediated and remain relatively stable over time.

Yet, this generally accepted view continues to receive challenges on several grounds. Nisbett et al. (2012) provide convincing evidence that mental abilities are at least partly affected by culture and other contextual factors and are thus to some extent changeable. Certainly education itself is aimed at increasing people's mental abilities. But Woodley and Meisenberg (2012) show that such change may be a slow, perhaps even generational process. The gradual increase in mental abilities scores and the narrowing of the gaps between various cultural groups over the past several decades (Wonderlic, Inc., 2007) support this contention. Other researchers have also shown that motivation may play an essential role in developing ability over time (Von Stumm & Ackerman, 2013).

Specific to personality, several lines of research (Branje, Van Lieshout, & Gerris, 2007; Maiden, Peterson, Caya, & Hayslip, 2003; Roberts, Walton, & Viechtbauer, 2006) provide evidence that some personality characteristics can be altered over time, though this tends to vary from trait to trait. For example, emotional stability is at least partly a function of health habits (Maiden et al., 2003; Thayer, 1996). Specifically, general physical health and associated exercise, diet, and the use of mood altering substances may all influence the extent to which people or more or less labile (have changeable moods)—a defining characteristic of neuroticism. It is particularly interesting to note that early psychological therapies were often aimed at "neurotic" symptoms. Presumably, the idea was to deliberately change these. And, given the efficacy of clinical psychological interventions for mood disorders (Cuijpers, van Straten, Andersson, & van Oppen, 2008), it seems likely that applied psychologists have identified ways to manipulate some of the mechanisms of neuroticism.

However, as mentioned a little earlier, neuroticism is associated with a lower "set point" for deciding that we have a problem. If the intention of interventions is to increase the likelihood that people will see "a problem" in the environment, then mental health services may run counter to such efforts. This is another example where the pursuit of a good for an individual (i.e., therapy) may run counter to species level adaptation.

Alternatively, being lower on neuroticism may lead people to see hope for their efforts to make change. So-called self-determination (Ng, Chan, & Hui,

2012) is something of an amalgamation of N, E, and generalized self-efficacy. Like self-efficacy, self-determinism predicts the tendencies to take independent action. Pelletier and colleagues (Pelletier, 2002; Pelletier, Tuson, Green-Demers, Noels, & Beaton, 1998) were the first to establish a link between self-determination and pro-environmental behaviors, in particular. Similarly, Harland, Staats, and Wilke (2007) found that, in addition to other predictors of pro-environmental behavior, efficacy, ability, and personality all predicted people's tendency to take action.

We will also see in Chapter 5 that many of the mechanisms for changing people's minds (and behaviors) rely on social pressures to conform. DeYoung et al. (2002) showed that personality predicts such conformity. Using both university and community samples, they applied a higher order, two dimensional taxonomy to the prediction of conformity. Dimension one, called *stability* (emotional stability, agreeableness, and conscientiousness) positively predicted conformity but, at the same time, was associated with rigid adherence and poor adjustment to change. The second dimension, called *plasticity* (extroversion and openness) was negatively associated with conformity. Applying this further, it seems likely that authoritarianism, which is defined in terms of conformity to authority, makes people more pliable to others' invocation of norms, and less inclined to follow their own deliberative paths.

Finally, by virtue of their malleability, attitudes and self-efficacy expectancies often pro-vide readily available sources for change. The ways we define ourselves, both accurately and inaccurately, are sometimes called *identity*. Personality, self-efficacy, and attitudes toward self are often considered components of identity. To the extent that people's beliefs about themselves can be altered by feedback, these may be good entries to fundamental change. However, their shortcomings as entry points for intervention include their complex links with behaviors and the very changeability that makes some of them ready sources of change. If they can be changed by one party, they probably can be changed by others.

In Chapter 5, we will switch focus from internal, more or less stable characteristics to the situational features that can influence people's thinking and behaviors. The complex interplay of traits and situations will provide a somewhat clearer idea of how identity translates into action, particularly through the activation of *norms*—"expected" ways of thinking and behaving in different circumstances, depending on identity variables.

Understanding that personality, efficacy, and attitudes are to some extent internalized aspects of our social, cultural, and developmental contexts may be particularly important for change. But these may be very challenging avenues for change, as well. For now, it is important to emphasize again the complexity of the relationships among the many variables related to motivation (personality, self-regulation, attitudes, and values), and their importance to making us who we are.

DIFFERENCES AMONG PEOPLE

4. When are people likely to take action?

Awareness can be a precursor to change (Anderson, Romani, Phillips, Wentzel, & Tlabela, 2007; Hansla et al., 2008; Scott, 2009). But taking action often occurs without any great awareness. Chapter 2 described the many ways that shortcuts lead to action, and Chapters 4 and 5 will demonstrate even more powerful preconscious motivators of action. For the purpose of applying individual differences to answering this criterion question at the individual level, it is necessary to limit "action" to deliberate action. Then we will turn to how individual differences may affect collective action, both with and without deliberation.

At the individual level, some primary problems of taking deliberate action relate to altruism and inclusiveness. Specifically, both the inclination and the ability to take action are almost certainly related to mental abilities. We have already seen that people higher in mental abilities are typically more altruistic. This means that mental abilities are associated with taking action for the common good. In addition, intelligence is negatively associated with authoritarianism (Davids, 1955; Heaven et al., 2011; Jacobson & Rettig, 1959; Leeson et al., 2012) and prejudice (Hodson & Busseri, 2012). So, it is highly likely that people with higher levels of mental abilities are also more inclined to be inclusive in their approaches to problems. Inclusiveness—including other stakeholders in our decision making process—is often a defining characteristic of deliberate action.

However, it is also likely that anxiety may charge authoritarians toward action, as well. History suggests that creating a high level of anxiety (fear mongering) can move authoritarians to take action. However, recent analysis of the relationship between authoritarianism and anxiety (Oesterreich, 2005) suggests that it is not likely to be deliberate, individual action, but rather mob reaction.

Developing contextual knowledge in a variety of different social, cultural, and natural environments may also increase people's tendency to take action. In fact, learning about the world around us is a focus of many interventions and relates to people's tendency to take action (Amel, Manning, & Scott, 2009; Anderson et al., 2007). Even learning about the specific viewpoints of other individuals can lead to different actions in social situations (Gilin, Maddux, Carpenter, & Galinsky, 2013). Since intelligences (g and EI) have been defined in terms of "learned knowledge and development of heuristics that apply" to situations (Hertwig & Herzog, 2009), it is therefore likely that intelligences lead to action, as well.

But situational expertise may be the conduit through which intelligence flows into action: A mediating variable. As we have seen, situational expertise is an internalized understanding of our context that leads to better decisions. To the extent that people have such situational

100

expertise, they are likely to have better outcomes for their decisions—a primary predictor of self-efficacy (Bandura, 1982). It is likely then, that self-efficacy will be higher in a well-learned situation. Evidence linking core self-efficacy with job performance (Chang, Ferris, Johnson, Rosen, & Tan, 2012), and job knowledge with performance suggests this.

In any case, if you believe that you can do something (high self-efficacy), you are more likely to try to do it. Self-efficacy is itself an important motivator of action.

Individual differences may also help to predict and control deliberate *collective* action. First, there is a large literature in I-O and educational psychology on leadership. The definition of leadership is messy, but the prediction of effective leadership is well established across a broad class of situations (Hogan et al., 1994; Thornton & Rupp, 2006). People higher in intelligence, certain personality traits, and situational expertise tend to elicit better outcomes for their groups (Hogan et al., 1994).

Second, there is a small but important literature on individual differences as they play out in groups. Effective collective action requires some consideration of both the level of certain individual differences across group members and the variability in these characteristics (Jones et al., 2000). In particular, agreeableness, social dominance, and authoritarianism all have shown effects on group performance. Similarly, shared situational expertise may influence group action (Coovert & McNelis, 1992; Klimoski & Mohammed, 1994) similarly to its effect at the individual level. We will learn more about precursors of group action in Chapter 6.

The problem of *inaction* has been a major concern for advocates of action on environmental issues. Most notably, some of Gifford's (2011) psychological "dragons of inaction" relate to the individual differences we have discussed in this section. Understanding these as potential levers for creating action is consistent with the applied approach advocated in this book. However, understanding inaction remains essential to developing effective action, as we will see in Chapters 5 and 6.

5. **What are the characteristics of change efforts that are likely to work?**

This question of practicality appears fairly straightforward based on our answers to questions three and four. If we want to know what we can actually do to make changes using individual differences, we need to know more about the stability of the individual differences we would like to target. We have seen that attitudes may be fairly straightforward ways to change a broad range of behavioral intentions, but may work only for a short period of time. Values and intelligences, by contrast, are likely to be costly and time consuming targets of change. Self-efficacy and situational awareness may be both important and practical targets for change, both because of their malleability and their relative permanence.

However, there are at least three very fundamental problems with focusing on individual differences as the sole basis for change. First, and paradoxically, we have a tendency to bias when it comes to deciding what is and is not changeable. The *fundamental attribution error* (introduced in Chapter 2) shows our tendency to believe in stable individual characteristics as the basis for most *other* people's negative experiences. For example, there is a tendency to attribute the experiences of rape victims to their stupidity ("they should know better than to walk around late at night in attractive clothing") rather than to conditions over which they had little control (their ride home left without them). The idea that there is something the victim could have done about their situation also demonstrates hindsight bias, and both this and attribution error help to establish the illusion of control. For example, blaming a victim of environmental disaster based on internal attributions, you yourself would "know better" than to "build your house in a hurricane-prone area."

Second, just as we tend to overestimate stable internal characteristics (AO individual differences) for explaining behavior, so we also tend to underestimate the power of the situation. As we will see in Chapter 5, there are mounds of evidence that the situation, and especially the social situation, can have a more powerful effect on behavior than internal characteristics (Mahn & John-Steiner, 2013).

Third, this complexity is not yet well represented in applied research (Klimoski & Jones, 2008). Ongoing research on person-by-situation interactions continues to emphasize this problem (Hanges, Schneider, & Niles, 1990; Jones & Parameswaran, 2005).

Our discussion of how people *internalize* their situation may help to shed light on this issue. Specifically, the behavior prediction model at the beginning of the chapter provides a means for understanding the relationship between stable individual characteristics and situational variables. Recall that this model described non-compensatory prediction of behavior on the basis of *ability* × *motivation* × *situational expertise*. But, developing situational expertise takes time and effort. If you are motivated to understand the situation, this should lead to greater situational expertise than if you don't care much about the situation. Thus, it may be that situational expertise is an indicator of long term motivation.

An example of this will help to illustrate. Think of the effects of choosing to do certain tasks over time on later performance of these tasks, versus tasks that you did not choose to do. For example, you might enjoy building a composting container for trash. So you work on perfecting this skill over time. Such motivated effort would tend to give you expertise in this specific task over time, so that you might end up helping friends build composters. Alternatively, learning about climate science may not particularly excite you, so you

DIFFERENCES AMONG PEOPLE

don't learn much about it, but instead rely on others for your information. When someone asks you to explain climate science, you defer to your expert source. These motivated experiences (building composters and reading books) may have profound effects on the development of situational knowledge, separate of the effects of stable characteristics like mental abilities.

Similarly, think of how your family situation affected your choices to do certain kinds of things outside the family. Although you yourself may not have been motivated initially, your family experiences led you to see things as valuable and other things as less valuable. For example, your family may have highly valued trips to the library and reading good books. You learned a little about how to use libraries, read books, and enjoyed these experiences. By contrast, your family took little interest in camping. These "values" have led to you now knowing less about camping than about how to use a library.

As a practical matter, individual differences are used as predictors of many behaviors across a wide range of practice settings. Regardless of the complex theories and explanations that help to drive our understanding of their nature and development, applications continue to yield valuable results. Individual difference measures are highly practical, even if we don't entirely understand why they are.

5

OPENING THE BLACK BOX

Reverend Dr. Martin Luther King, Jr. made a beautifully succinct statement of our criterion two, when he said, "Rarely do we find men who willingly engage in hard, solid thinking. There is an almost universal quest for easy answers and half-baked solutions. Nothing pains some people more than having to think." In this chapter, we will consider the current scientific evidence about human thinking and decision making. Reviewing this research will make it very clear that our thinking leads to many errors, some of which Dr. King may have correctly identified in this quote. We will also see that psychological researchers are very cautious in their own applications of science, having learned that error is part of all human decisions—including their own.

A case in point is the reluctance of psychologists to sound an alarm about environmental sustainability. Environmental psychologists have only recently sounded the alarm that many climate and biological scientists have been sounding for some time (Gifford, 2008; Koger & Winter, 2010; Ones & Dilchert, 2012; Swim et al., 2011; Vlek & Steg, 2007). Several of these calls to action acknowledge that psychology has been a bit slow in responding. One explanation for the apparent slow response is that other natural scientists have not recognized either the value of psychology or its culpability in dealing with issues of sustainability.

But another reason for this slow response may reflect how basic researchers in psychology approach error in *decision making processes*. Applied psychologists know that predicting the future is a very risky gamble, especially with the complexity of human thinking and behavior involved. Basic psychologists have defined this more specifically in at least two large research literatures. First, these are the same people who helped develop our current understanding of human biases, including our tendency toward *risk aversion*. This demonstrated tendency to sound the alarm too quickly (Kahneman, 2011) is known to both basic and applied researchers, as is the analysis of error. Psychologists are also trained to mind the gap between *perceptions* arising from our *rational systems* and physical characteristics of *empirical systems*. Thus, we assume that our own decisions are sometimes wrong, including the decision to sound the alarm.

OPENING THE BLACK BOX

The first step in decision making, though, is believing that we have a problem or opportunity that deserves attention—our criterion question one. Back to the applied psychologists' problem: Forensic psychology provides a good recent example of the problem scientist-practitioners have when they make predictions about "when we have a problem" (Edens, Buffington-Vollum, Keilen, Roskamp, & Anthony, 2005). Some clinical forensic psychologists provide opinions about future dangerousness of people convicted in capital murder trials. That is, they provide expert opinions about whether society at large "has a problem" with a particular convicted murderer. This practice goes on despite many years of research calling such clinical judgments into question, to the point that some professional societies have come out against the practice entirely!

Given all of this, it is quite notable that basic researchers in psychology have called attention to the problem of climate change—and asked applied psychologists to get involved (Gifford et al., 2009)! It suggests that the evidence is strong enough that psychologists need to develop science based practices to help deal with this and related issues—despite the high likelihood of errors.

Decision Processes

There are some very important similarities between applied psychologists and some of the physical scientists who have sounded the alarm. Many applied *sciences* are grouped under the heading of engineering. So far, only one field of applied *psychology* has been grouped this way explicitly (human factors engineering), even though the principle interests of engineering and applied psychology (predicting and controlling empirical systems) are the same. It is not surprising, then, that applied psychology has integrated similar approaches to those used in other engineering fields. For example, we have seen that applied psychologists have integrated the systems perspective into science-based practice. This has led inevitably to a concern with the *processes* that are of primary interest to all engineering disciplines. What happens between the *inputs* into a system and the *outputs* that we observe?

The *processes* of interest in applied psychology relate to the way we make decisions and do (or do not) behave as a result. Once we know something about how, for example, mental abilities (inputs in Figure 5.1) lead to performance (an output), we have begun to unravel the process problem. In this chapter, we will rely on four approaches to understanding what goes on inside the "black box" of human decision processes. The first is *control theory*, which is an offshoot of the systems perspective and borrows heavily from *cybernetic systems* in other engineering disciplines. Control theory has proven particularly helpful for understanding how people decide there is a problem, and when the problem has or has not been resolved (Carver & Scheier, 2012b). The second, related approach is the emotive perception model

105

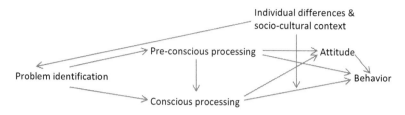

Figure 5.1 A thumbnail description of the decision making process

(Jones & Rittman, 2002). This model focuses on the emotive components of control theory, but is based more specifically on *appraisal theories* of emotion. It is used to explain people's preconscious emotive processing of observed events and how these are predictive of both fixed action responses and, to a lesser extent, deliberate behavioral responses.

The third and fourth approaches—*Signal Detection Theory* and the *Brunswik Lens Model*—take us beyond traditional engineering, however. The success of engineering has generally relied on physical laws, to the extent that we understand them. Better engineering solutions simply "work" in the empirical system, usually within some bounds of tolerance. However, predicting the behavior of human systems is much like predicting the weather—an important similarity between applied psychology and another area of applied science—meteorology. Both humans and the weather (1) are typically quite complex, (2) have only become objects of scientific study during the relatively recent past, and (3) seem to allow only for highly probabilistic, uncertain predictions and manipulations. It is interesting to note that applied meteorologists do not pretend to the engineer label either. To the point: *Psychological engineering* needs to be understood in terms of an "error-prone" framework. Our psychological engineering solutions are quite imperfect, and we need to clearly incorporate this understanding into both our practices and how we communicate what we do for various stakeholders.

> *Government spending.* Are we doing enough to curb global climate change? Most people who listen to the scientific consensus would probably say no. However, the *Wall Street Journal* (January 28, 2013, "As Temperatures Keep Rising, Geoengineering Gets a Closer Look" by Paul Basken) recently reported that the U.S. government "spends $2.6-billion a year on climate science, distributed through 13 different agencies, mostly aimed at cutting carbon emissions." The report also points out that this is more than is spent by any other government but is still far less than what was spent to clean up after Hurricane Sandy—a storm that has been partly attributed to the effects of global climate change. This article also describes a growing

> interest in geo-engineering—deliberately altering climates in order to attempt to avert some of the worst effects of climate change. This could involve massive efforts costing enormous amounts of resources on further changing of the earth's ecosystems—for a somewhat uncertain end.

But incorporation of error into applied science does not rely on just description of the errors in decision outcomes discussed in Chapter 3. It also requires careful consideration of psychological processes that lead individuals and groups toward different decisions. So, although Signal Detection Theory and Kahneman's work provide initial frames for error in the outcomes of applied psychology, more complex models are required for understanding the processes through which errors (and correct decisions) occur. The Brunswik Lens Model moves in this direction by explaining how the process we are interested in—decision making—actually works to predict our choices.

We will discuss these perspectives in turn in this chapter, describing important applied research findings about decision processes along the way. *Threat-rigidity*, *satisficing*, and *escalation of commitment* will be used as prominent examples of how heuristics, control theory, and the Brunswik Lens play out in real world decision processes.

Problem Identification and the Discrepancy Test

Although there are many models of decision making in basic research (Beach, 2009; Marewski & Mehlhorn, 2011), most begin with *discrepancy tests*. These are based on the notion that we selectively attend to things that matter in the world around us. On one hand, we have expectations about how things *should* play out in the world. For example, you might expect your friend to say hi to you when you meet at the student union. On the other hand, things don't always play out as we expect. So, what happens when you see your friend at the student union, and there is no smile or hello for you today?

If there was a smile and hello, you would perceive no *discrepancy* between what was expected and what happened and would pay it no mind (direct no additional attention to the situation). But not getting a smile and hello means that there is a discrepancy between *expected* and *perceived* events. This is an example of a negative discrepancy—something good that was expected, but didn't happen. Discrepancies can be both positive and negative: A big hug from your friend might also be discrepant, but positive.

Cybernetic models are often used to frame this problem and are commonly referred to under the heading of control theory (Carver & Scheier, 2012b). These models have found many applications in *artificial intelligence* systems (an area that applies psychological concepts to systems engineering; Hammond,

1996), consumer psychology (Lee, Sudhir, & Steckel, 2002), classroom performance (Eccles & Wigfield, 2002), health promotion (Scheier & Carver, 2003), therapy (Carver & Scheier, 1999; Cullin, 2005), and job performance (Lord, Diefendorff, Schmidt, & Hall, 2010). Cybernetic models frame discrepancies between "ideal state" and "perceived state" in terms of a discrepancy threshold—usually called a *set point*. The set point is used to tell a system when to change its processes (start/stop/modulate) in response to its environment.

Usually, a system changes its *input* in order to maintain some state within the system's boundaries (e.g., homeostasis). For example, when the temperature in a room reaches the set point determined by a thermostat, the heating system starts or stops. When the heater turns on, it requires more energy from the power sources that create heat (e.g., gas, electric inputs). In our interpersonal example, if your friend didn't smile and say hello, you might put forth a little more energy to get their attention or find out what the problem is.

But discrepancies can also change the set point itself. So, following from the example of meeting your friend, the "big hug" response might lead you to change how you define an "expected state" from this friend. From now on, your set point is not triggered by a hug. You now *expect* a hug instead of just a smile, and anything less will be a slight negative discrepancy. Thus, your set point for discrepancy has changed.

Open systems of all sorts are governed by this sort of "built-in decider" in response to *feedback* from the environment. Applying the temperature control problem to human physiological systems, our brain's hypothalamus is sensitive to heat and cold (Katz & Meiri, 2006; Ranson, 1939). When it detects that a certain temperature threshold (set point) in our physical environment has been reached, it switches various nervous system actions on or off. For example, if we feel cold enough (reach our low temperature set point), we start shivering—an automatic behavioral process. We may also seek warm shelter, don more clothes, or fumble for the thermostat—all of which are more deliberate behavioral responses. All of these actions (automatic and choice) consume more energy inputs.

In human decision making models, reaching a set point is referred to variously as problem identification (Moreland & Levine, 1991), threat/opportunity perception (Billings, Milburn, & Schaalman, 1980; Jackson & Dutton, 1988), perceived risk (Ma & Wang, 2009), or discrepancy test (Beach, 2009). Because discrepancies can both increase (positive feedback) and stop (negative feedback) action, we will generally use the terms *discrepancy test* and *threat/opportunity*, rather than the more one-sided "problem" or "risk" framing (Beach, 2009; Carver & Scheier, 2012b).

Of course, this description of cybernetic models is the simplest case, and research on highly complex human systems is relatively new. We will see, for example, that there are multiple set points for multiple arousal systems when we experience emotions (Carver & Scheier, 2012a) and when we make more deliberate decisions as individuals and groups (Lee et al., 2002). Further, set points are often modulated by different internal variables (e.g., neuroticism may affect when we see a problem).

It is also important to note from here on that decision processes occur with both individuals *and groups*. When it comes to group decision processes, we need to understand that different people in a decision making group may have different set points (Lee et al., 2002). This is one reason for the criterion problem: The same events in the world may strike some people as *threats*, others as *opportunities*, and still others see no meaningful discrepancy at all. It is also why the systems perspective is helpful—it can be applied to both individuals and groups.

Why, after an average of ten mass murder incidents involving automatic weapons each year in the United States, has the Newtown atrocity led more people to see that we "have a problem?" There are many possible explanations for why people now see a problem, when before they didn't. Can you think of some possibilities? There are several, of course. First, there is the tendency to "blame the victim," which comes from research about the fundamental attribution error. In other recent mass murder cases, the victims were adults, whose choices might be used to explain why they were murdered. Some of the possible "blame the victim" explanations include (1) they chose to go to violent movies at night, (2) they chose not to carry a weapon to protect themselves, and (3) they should know not to go to shopping malls. Such explanations help us to *think* we have some deterministic control—we can find ways to deliberately avoid risk. But they don't readily apply to children, and most of the Newtown victims were young children. Children generally do not have as much control over their lives and decisions as adults do and cannot be expected to competently protect themselves.

Another answer might be that, although some people do see a problem, others still do not. For example, a Gaiean (someone who believes that the Earth is itself a self-correcting system) sees such events as "acts of nature" that serve to reduce human populations. Others might frame the problem differently *after* the fact by altering the set point for "problem." For example, they might make the specific instance less troubling by comparing it to people who are experiencing terror on a daily basis (e.g., the suffering citizens of a war torn country). This change of the set point might make the Newtown atrocity appear to be a smaller problem because of reframing.

Decision processes may be more or less emotive and deliberative, depending on both individual differences (from the previous chapter) and social contexts (discussed in the next chapter). The *internal* response processes that follow from the appraisal may be more or less conscious and more or less emotive (*hot versus cold* cognition). Shortly, the *emotive perception model* will be used to describe preconscious "hot" cognition. If the response is more conscious, the processes that follow may also be more or less deliberative, conscious, and effortful. To the extent that decision processes are both conscious and effortful, they are sometimes referred to as *substantive processing* (Forgas, 1995). As we will see, automatic preconscious processes are often fairly predictable (Katz & Meiri, 2006), but conscious processes are somewhat less predictable.

A thumbnail of these relationships is presented in Figure 5.1. This is by no means a representation of the more elaborate (and often more accurate) models of decision making. Instead, it is used to organize the concepts discussed here.

Applying the thumbnail model to sustainability, we may decide that there is a problem with environmental air quality (a *threat*). If this appraisal is preconscious (e.g., we awake with trouble breathing in an air pollution event), we are likely to experience an emotive response prior to any behavioral or more deliberative response (Heath, 2012; Norton, Bogart, Cecil, & Pinkerton, 2005). In this instance, components of our behavioral responses may be *fixed action patterns*—responses to environmental stimuli that are preconscious and often hard-wired (Cialdini, 1988). Following our example, we may sit up quickly and gasp for breath.

Another possible behavioral response comes *after* this emotive episode. Later in the day, we deliberately go to a store and purchase an air cleaner for our bedroom. Thereafter, even though we don't have any particular emotive arousal, we habitually turn on the air cleaner in our bedroom before going to bed. This is a heuristic response that may involve very little conscious processing after it has been learned. In fact, this behavioral response may require no discrepancy or problem identification once it is learned. Just a reminder that the air cleaner isn't on would be enough of a discrepancy to take action—no problem breathing or emotive response would be required.

Alternatively, we may have become accustomed to not noticing air quality issues through the process of *habituation* (Lima, 2006). After several years reading articles about deteriorating air quality in the local newspaper, we very consciously decide that there is a discrepancy between actual and preferred air quality. Our *conscious* behavioral responses in this instance might be anything from business as usual to fairly drastic individual action, depending on a host of other predictor variables. We might decide we are now in danger (*threat framing*) and move away from the city. Or, we might frame this as an *opportunity* to get involved in improving the quality of life in the community and set about organizing an action group.

It should be noted that threat and opportunity framing are not mutually exclusive (Carver & Scheier, 2012a; Lord et al., 2010). We could see a threat, but *reframe* it as an opportunity. Also, this deliberative process may lead us to change our set point and (1) decide very consciously that there really is no problem after all (heighten our set point) or (2) lower our set point to the extent that we have emotive responses every time we read more news about air quality. How and when we alter set points is an important question (Katz & Meiri, 2006), especially for many people interested in raising awareness about issues of sustainability. Evidence on hindsight and other biases suggest we change set points fairly easily under some circumstances (Hazan, Agarwal, & Kale, 2007; Oudejans, 2008).

Individual differences are part of what determines set points (Smith & Kirby, 2009) and our responses to discrepancies (in Figure 5.1). For example, we have seen how differences in neuroticism and causal uncertainty can make us more or less likely to identify problems. Similarly, these same individual differences may help to determine the extent to which our responses are more or less deliberative (e.g., conscientiousness). Since intelligence affects how quickly we learn heuristic responses, it may reduce perceived novelty of situations over time. This learning about the situation might reduce the number of situations that elicit perceived discrepancy. Learning that we are *able* to control our circumstances (i.e., high self-efficacy) may also reduce threat perceptions. As we saw in Chapter 3, however, we do not know much about such processes that translate stable individual differences into behavior.

We also saw how individual differences may affect the extent to which we seek collective action. We will see in Chapter 6 that social context (e.g., the local newspaper) and cultural context may direct the extent to which we seek collective action (e.g., working with a group of concerned citizens for stricter car emission standards).

Applied Problem Identification

Consumer psychologists have employed the discrepancy test approach in various guises (Arts, Frambach, & Bijmolt, 2011; Bruner, 1986; Lee et al., 2002), mainly to predict and manipulate buying decisions. Anyone who has watched TV advertisements knows this approach. Often the first part of the commercial loudly proclaims that there is a problem that needs to be rectified or an opportunity to exploit. It goes something like this: Your "usual" expectation (about a car, health, personal hygiene) is really a *problem*—and it can be solved by product X! Or the price we would usually pay for a product is now much lower—it's on sale! Both of these use discrepancy tests to stimulate changes in process—in this case buying decisions.

Organizational psychologists and their colleagues have also developed applications that target problem identification (Keil, Depledge, & Rai, 2007; Leidner & Elam, 1995). One example of this is the literature on *escalation of commitment* to a losing course of action. Also called the "sunk costs" problem, there is a tendency for decision makers who have invested in a course of action to ignore, discount, and otherwise attempt to avoid discrepancy test information when their course of action is failing (Staw, 1997). There are recent demonstrations of this tendency toward denial of problems in environmental psychology (Feygina, Goldsmith, & Jost, 2010), and for people confronted with disconfirming scientific evidence (Munro, 2010) as well. Attempts to counter such resistance include development of situational expertise (Keil et al., 2007), self and group regulatory interventions (Heath, 1995; Schott, Scherer, & Lambert, 2011; Schultze, Pfeiffer, & Schulz-Hardt, 2012), and accountabilities to authority, all of which have been shown to reduce escalation of commitment (Keil et al., 2007; Schott et al., 2011).

Until very recently, the discrepancy approaches described here have not taken individual differences into account. In the case of advertisement, everyone watching a particular show gets the same "discrepancy message" and "solution," so that a twenty-five year old learns about the advantages of a drug that helps with Alzheimer's disease (extremely uncommon in twenty-five year olds) and a seventy year old watching the same show may see much more importance to this "threat and solution" message. Often, advertisers use such demographic differences (age, gender, social class) as surrogates for psychological individual differences.

This broad approach has been replaced in many cases by *psychographics* in recent years. Psychographics are patterns of behavior that are obtained by the use of "cookies" that are downloaded by advertisers and other interested organizations onto computers and personal electronic devices. These cookies track the behaviors (including buying preferences) of users on their private devices, which can then be analyzed statistically to group them into behavioral patterns. Psychographic analysis appears to be a powerful tool for developing advertisements that are targeted based not on demography, but on actual behavioral patterns.

Decision Process Applied to Sustainability

Some of the strongest recent applications offered by research in environmental psychology relate to the factors that determine people's problem identification (Hornsey & Fielding, 2017). Islam, Barnes, & Toma, 2013; Reser & Swim, 2011). In particular, the escalation problem has found its way into environmental behaviors through issues of threat and resource set points (Homburg & Wagner, 2007). Threat appraisals involve comparison of our situation with set points that are "bad enough" to constitute a threat. Following the thermostat example, this is when the temperature reaches a low enough point that the heater gets activated. *Resource set points* are used in discrepancy tests of whether we have what is needed to adequately cope with potential threats. This is like checking to see that there is enough wood to light the fire place if the temperature does reach a low level. Such resource set points show that people make plans based on causal reasoning. Not surprisingly, then, related studies in applied settings show that both immediate appraisal *and* awareness of contingencies are precursors to environmental action (Feygina, Jost, & Goldsmith, 2010; Gifford et al., 2009).

Martin, Bender, and Raish (2007) provide another good example of how to incorporate the set point and discrepancy test concepts into applied environmental behavior research. Their work demonstrated how decisions about responses to environmental concerns rely on *threat appraisals*. Threat appraisals are a subset of discrepancy testing where the set point is related to a problem reaching some threshold requiring action. Their study asked homeowners in wildfire prone areas what would determine their decisions to move or stay. Differences in knowledge about residential wildfire risk predicted the kind of information homeowners relied on. Less knowledgeable people were inclined to worry about their vulnerability (rather than the severity of the risk) and to look to their neighbors in order to decide whether to move. That is, less informed people put things into yes/no (vulnerable/not vulnerable) categories, then relied on social conformity heuristic as their basis for action. Better informed residents were more likely to directly assess their own resources, rather than their immediate vulnerability, when arriving at decisions. That is, better informed people considered specifics of the situation, rather than simple either/or categories, and also considered future contingencies before taking action.

Using Figure 5.1 to interpret this, less informed residents relied on immediate, pre-conscious *appraisal* (fear or not fear), then fell back on social context to make their choices. Better informed residents focused more on a deliberative consideration of the resources at their disposal to meet future contingencies.

Gifford et al.'s (2009) large, multinational study used an approach somewhat more consistent with the more general discrepancy test than with the specific threat appraisal approach. First, people appraised the discrepancy between current and future environmental conditions in their country. Second, respondents appraised the extent to which their country's conditions were better than conditions in other countries (a form of social comparison). Results showed that people's appraisals of future conditions in their countries were (1) accurate when compared with independent assessments and (2) pessimistic (threat appraisal). Appraisals of their own country in comparison to others were more optimistic (positive discrepancy), despite general pessimism about the future. Although there were problems with framing of the research question (future appraisals were framed as likely *negative* discrepancies versus discrepancies in either direction), the results remained convincing—a large percentage of people in many countries see environmental changes as a threat.

Another way that discrepancy tests are subtly incorporated into environmental behavior research is through the social dilemma framework (Dawes, 1980; Gifford, 2007a; Gupta & Ogden, 2009; Botelho, Dinar, Pinto, & Rapoport, 2014). This is derived from heuristic and bias research (Kahneman, 2011) and is not directly looking at processes such as discrepancy testing. However, there is a discrepancy comparison at the heart of the framework. Specifically, we compare likely *personal* consequences of self-interested behavior with the likely *social* consequences of this behavior on *others'* well-being. This can be described as a discrepancy test comparing one's own actions with "ideal" actions regarding broader social goods. Individual's perceptions of discrepancies between their attitudes and behaviors (Gupta & Ogden, 2009), norms and behaviors (Biel & Thøgersen, 2007; Mulder & Nelissen, 2010), and social contexts and behavioral intentions (Sen, Gürhan-Canli, & Morwitz, 2001; Botelho et al., 2014) have all been shown to predict aspects of our five criteria. Following from Figure 5.1, norms and social dilemmas may create a second discrepancy test, affecting the relationship between initial discrepancy and action (Thøgersen, 2008). This and other influences of social context will be covered at greater length in Chapter 5.

A central question for this chapter (and also criterion question two) relates to differences between more and less conscious, deliberative responses to discrepancies (Grasmück & Scholz, 2005; Martin et al., 2007). Framed another way, we need to know when people are likely *not* to think before acting—what has been called *limited processing* (Dawes, 1980; Perowne & Mansell, 2002). We are just beginning to understand how to use social comparisons to get people to stop and think before acting.

Time and Social Dilemmas

It turns out that awareness of what our neighbors are up to may have a very different place in decisions when people are thinking ahead. Botelho et al. (2014) showed that, when resources are limited and multiple actors are using them, decisions may follow a more complex pattern than previous studies have suggested. Specifically, when two, competing actors consider the limits of resource extraction over time, both parties will tend to modulate their decisions to try to maintain resources for longer periods. If this holds true in actual decision situations, it could be very good news for sustainability.

Appraisal Theories of Emotion

Emotive responses are important when we are deciding whether we have a problem, and sometimes what action we take (Carrus, Passafaro, &

Bonnes, 2008; Simunich, 2009; Swim & Bloodhart, 2013). So, where do emotions come from? Following from William James' first psychology book on the topic (James, 1890), Peter Lang provides a good description of the widely accepted appraisal theories of emotion (Lang, 1995). Specifically, our preconscious mind is constantly (1) appraising the various stimuli in the world around us, looking for potential threats and opportunities. If some stimulus reaches our set point, we (2) pre-consciously decide there are positive (*approach*) or negative (*avoidance*) outcomes related to the stimulus, and (3) experience autonomic arousal consistent with this appraisal (Nerb, 2007; Shimojo, Simion, Shimojo, & Scheier, 2003). These emotional *episodes* (Weiss & Cropanzano, 1996) serve a *motive readiness* function (Lang, 1995), preparing us to take action to approach what we want and avoid what we don't want (Elliot, Eder, & Harmon-Jones, 2013). Figure 5.2 illustrates this theory.

Thus, *emotion* is a broad term used to denote arousal states that prepare us for motivated responding (Lang, 1995). Two examples help to illustrate how emotions serve as motive readiness responses. First, if someone you are attracted to smiles at you, you are likely to feel various sorts of arousal, depending to some extent on your gender. Regardless of your gender, the *limbic system* in your brain prepares you to approach this person. Also, for androgen sensitive (male type) brains, the *amygdala* is heavily activated (Hamann, Herman, Nolan, & Wallen, 2004; Stoléru, Fonteille, Cornélis, Joyal, & Moulier, 2012). This appendage to the limbic system is sometimes called the "hot button," which prepares you for fight or flight by stimulating the *sympathetic nervous system* (Stoléru et al., 2012). Thus, seeing someone attractive smile at you may make you feel both pleasantly excited, and if you have an androgen sensitive brain, you may freeze, break out in a sweat, and feel like running away. Freezing and sweating are both examples of *fixed action patterns*, and running away is a behavioral correlate to these fixed patterns—that doesn't always happen.

Alternatively, if you catch a glimpse of a growling dog running toward you while you are riding your bicycle, you are likely to experience a somewhat different type of arousal. Your amygdala is likely to activate, but you are not likely to feel simultaneous urges to approach the stimulus—just to run (or in this case ride) away. Unlike the smiling potential mate, the behavioral response in this circumstance may be more predictable across people. We will return to this under the heading of *situational strength*: the consequences of having the dog catch you are pretty obvious (a *strong situation*), unlike the smiling mate example.

Figure 5.2 Summary of the motive readiness theories of emotion episodes

In both these approach and avoidance examples, the cybernetic model would describe your responses as determined by a set point. That is, even though a smiling potential mate might not be considered a "threat," the cybernetic model would use the same *discrepancy test* framing as for the growling dog. The specific sort of set point at work would determine whether this is a threat appraisal, opportunity appraisal, or both.

It is also important to note that, in both the smiling other and growling dog situations, whether you acknowledge having experienced emotions or not, neurological measurement systems would most likely show your arousal system was active (Hamann et al., 2004). The point is that some of us don't recognize such arousal as an emotion (Frewen, Dozois, Neufeld, & Lanius, 2008). But it is how psychologists define many emotions—as *motive readiness responses*. In our examples, we might call these sexual excitement and fear, respectively. Table 5.1 provides a description of basic emotional arousals.

Class discussion. An oil exploration and development company holds rights to a property in a western state. It happens that someone has built a home on one of the places where these preemptive mineral rights are held (a so-called Split Estate). The company decides to drill literally into their backyard. Beyond an initial response of surprise, disbelief, and anger, people may also experience a sense of betrayal and helplessness that persists over time. These emotive responses still have episodic components when similar stimuli are presented at other times. How might such event based, learned emotions be used to influence public opinion? Give an example of how you might develop a media program or advertising campaign to change the way people process information based on emotion.

The *scripts* that people have—their expectations for social situations (Abelson, 1981)—vary substantially from group to group and (especially) culture to culture. This means that, although the emotive responses themselves are consistent and similar from person to person, the triggering of a discrepancy can be quite different from person to person and culture to culture. We will

Table 5.1 A typology of motive readiness responses

Appraisal	Type of outcome	
	Desired	Aversive
Approaching	Pleasure	Fear, disgust, sadness (?)
Avoiding/Missing	Frustration, anger, sadness	Relief, humor

learn more about the effects of norms and culture in the next chapter. For now, it is important to recognize that, although emotional responses may be fairly consistent across cultures, the triggers of emotions can vary widely (Roseman, Dhawan, Rettek, Naidu, & Thapa, 1995).

Basic and Social Emotions

Frijda (Frijda, Kuipers, & Ter Schure, 1989), Smith and Lazarus (1993), and Ekman (1992) are among the most prominent proponents of appraisal theories of emotion. Ekman's research, which can be found in many introductory psychology texts, shows that people understand visual emotive displays across cultures. This suggests that emotive perception is a part of our genetic endowment, since parts of it are invariant across language, norms, and other aspects of communication that vary across cultures. These basic emotions include anger, fear, pleasure, sadness, disgust, and surprise (Ekman, 1992).

However, there is some variance in emotional expression, display, and understanding across groups (Matsumoto & Ekman, 1989; Roseman et al., 1995; Russell, 1994). We will see in the next chapter that there are both basic and "self-conscious" or *social emotions* that help to explain these group differences (Jones et al., 2003). Still, the general point remains: *Visual indicators* of our internal fixed action responses may communicate to others whether you see "threat or opportunity" in much the same way as some other large social mammals communicate these.

Emotion and Mood

Emotion can also be distinguished to some extent from mood. Moods are states associated with the amount of energy we have available to respond to situational stimuli (Thayer, 1996). If you haven't had enough sleep or food, chances are good that you will feel less able to respond to the challenges that occur around you. Another way of saying this is that you will be in a "bad mood." Moods are not aroused by stimuli in our immediate environment—they are not directly motivated responses (Perrott & Bodenhausen, 2002). Instead, they are *internal signals* from our bodies to signal readiness in case a threat or opportunity presents itself. Moods may also predispose us to appraise things more as threats (low energy/bad mood) or opportunities (high energy/good mood). In other words, they control our set points.

Emotions, by contrast, are *episodic* (Forgas, 1995; Perrott & Bodenhausen, 2002; Weiss & Cropanzano, 1996). That is, they are responses to identified stimuli (attractive people, scary dogs, and so on), while moods are not based on such appraisals (Perrott & Bodenhausen, 2002). Moods do predispose us toward different appraisals, but they are distinct from the arousal that occurs after. Such emotional arousal is usually short lived, since it relies on the limited resources our bodies have available to deal with a threat or opportunity.

This may explain why strong emotive arousal is often followed by exhaustion and a period of recovery. This emotion–exhaustion effect can be used to explain the tradition across cultures of serving food after a funeral. People who have just experienced strong emotions (in the case of a funeral, sadness) have drained their resources, meaning that their mood is likely to signal low resources. Following Thayer's (1996) description of mood, a "bad" mood would be predicted, leading to a need to either rest or replenish resources through such things as eating food. Hence, to avert even worse sadness and trouble after a funeral, food is served!

Finally, emotional arousal can be relived by imagined reference to the original arousing stimuli. You might feel a little shiver when you think of that attractive potential mate—or the scary dog—long after they are gone. But such arousal based on memory is still episodic. See the following box for more on this.

Can our fixed action patterns be harnessed to sustainable behaviors?

You may remember John B. Watson from the discussion of how psychologists have worked to stimulate purchasing behavior (Chapter 3). Arguably the most famous research by Watson was his ethically questionable work with a child known only as "Little Albert." Watson and his research assistant would present Albert with a "cute" bunny and watch him try to approach it. Then, they would make a loud noise behind Albert's back that elicited a fear response along with the bunny. After a short time, Albert learned to associate the bunny with a (pre-conscious) fear response. Instead of trying to approach it, he would try to crawl away—to avoid it.

This early research on associative learning between neutral stimuli and some response (in this case fear) has been used to successfully cure phobias. It can also be applied to getting people to approach things that are otherwise neutral, such as a product for sale. Pro-environmental behaviors are not usually preconscious. However, there may be effective ways to make them so using emotive responses, which might help to establish them as habits in our daily lives.

Choose a pro- or anti-environmental behavior and come up with a way to (1) associate it with a preconscious approach or avoidance response and (2) increase or reduce its occurrence. What are factors that might make pro-environmental behaviors "habits?"

Applied Emotion

Is there anything about emotive responses that has been used in applied settings? As central as emotion is to the human experience, and as important as emotion has been to basic psychology, some areas of applied psychology have only recently begun incorporating emotion into decision making (Bornstein & Wiener, 2010). The exception to this—clinical psychology—has a rich research literature directed toward understanding emotive responses (David, Ghinea, Macavei, & Eva, 2005; Lazarus, 1995) and mood related disorders (Naragon-Gainey, 2010; Olatunji & Wolitzky-Taylor, 2009). But there is still a great deal to learn about how to predict and control emotional responses in the workplace, courtroom, classroom, and marketplace (Ashkanasy, Härtel, & Daus, 2002). The application of emotive responding and decision processes to sustainability is also quite recent (Blomfield, Troth, & Jordan, 2016), but provides some of the most promising work to date.

The large question is how to apply research on emotion to predicting and controlling people's tendency to engage in more deliberative responses. One answer comes from forensic psychology. Ask and Granhag (2007) showed that anger and sadness exerted very different influences on the substantive processing of criminal investigators. Anger (*sympathetic arousal*) led to narrower, heuristic focus on a few decision variables. Sadness broadened the set of relevant variables used in investigators' decisions.

Organizational psychology has incorporated emotive discrepancy tests to group decision making as well. For example, Chattopadhyay, Glick, and Huber (2001) showed that organizational decision processes sometimes conform to the sympathetic arousal pattern found in individuals—we narrow our search (Ask & Granhag, 2007). This so-called *threat-rigidity hypothesis* is characterized by a tendency to reduce search and revert to "tried and true" heuristics under stress (Gladstein & Reilly, 1985).

Research on individual decisions has also enhanced prediction of substantive processing in organizations (e.g., Fisher, 2002; Louis & Sutton, 1991; Ma & Wang, 2009). For example, industrial-organizational (I-O) psychologist Cynthia Fisher (2002) demonstrated how emotional events relate to momentary job satisfaction, but only predicted behavioral intention through their effects on attitudes. That is, eventual evaluations of our general job situation (job attitudes) are based on deliberative processing, rather than immediate emotive responding. Individual differences also played important roles in predicting who intended to stay in their organizations in this study.

There is also research connecting affect with consumption (Watson & Spence, 2007; Wang, Seidler, Hall, & Preston, 2012; Valor, Antonetti, and Carrero, 2018), responses to environmental risks (Lefevre, de Bruin, Taylor, Dessai, Kovats, & Fischhoff, 2015), and pro-environmental behaviors

(Raudsepp, 2005; Venhoeven, Bolderdijk, & Steg, 2016). *Affect* is a term used loosely to describe mood, emotion, and components of attitudes, so this research cannot be directly linked with discrete episodic emotions. However, it has shown that affect often trumps other, more substantive processes when deciding about environmental behaviors (Halpenny, 2010; Hinds & Sparks, 2008; Raudsepp, 2005) and about people's views of themselves (Venhoeven et al., 2016). We will return to this last point in the next chapter.

The Brunswik Lens and "Error"

The past twenty years has seen increasing awareness of the interconnectedness of emotive, approach/avoidance responses with all sorts of decision processes (Forgas, 1995; Kruglanski et al., 2012). However, for the purposes of predicting decision outcomes and for direct interventions aimed at changing "cold" (deliberative) processing, it still helps to work backward from decision *outcomes* to the *processes* that lead to them. The *Brunswik Lens Model* (Brunswik, 1955; Hammond, 1996) provides one way for understanding decision processes from this direction. Consistent with applied psychology, the focus in this model is on the criteria (outcomes of decisions) as a first step to effective prediction and control.

In Chapter 3 we discussed Kahneman's (2011) use of comparisons between "known" characteristics of the world around us (specifically, statistical relationships) and our everyday decisions. This "error detection" approach is based on the correspondence between "actual" and "judged" outcomes (Hammond, 1996; Kruglanski, 1989). The Brunswik Lens Model (hereinafter, BLM) takes a somewhat different approach to "error" (Hammond, 1996). While human judgments are sometimes clearly wrong in light of the empirical system (Kahneman, 2011), on average these "wrong" judgments may serve important, adaptive functions. For example, the deterministic thinking described in Chapter 3 may actually be a very functional response to changing circumstances, even though it may be "error" or "bias" in the moment.

To understand this, it helps to understand the idea of *creeping determinism* (Nestler et al., 2008). Recall that hindsight bias is the tendency to think we "knew it all along" when we see things that actually did differ from our prior expectations. Using the Signal Detection Theory (SDT) model of error, hindsight bias can be framed as a tendency to think you had no "misses" or "false alarms" in past decisions. Evidence regarding hindsight bias (see Chapter 3) shows that this tendency to think we "knew it all along"—even though we were actually wrong in our initial decision, seems to be deeply ingrained our thinking (Nestler et al., 2008). So how is this adaptive? One answer is that, in order to adapt to changing realities, we often need to change our understandings of the world around us *without* a lot of energy being wasted on second guessing our earlier (erroneous) decision.

This way, rather than basing our future decisions on previous, error prone ones, we "start from where we are now." This is consistent with some social cognitive researchers (e.g., Funder, 1989; Kruglanski, 1989) who suggest that "errors" (in the Kahneman sense) are not always "mistakes" (Murphy & Cleveland, 1995; Oaksford & Chater, 1992). That is, *thinking* that appears to be incorrect in comparison with "real" circumstances may in fact be highly functional for learning to deal with problems in our daily life through a sort of free flowing trial and error. Put another way, we efficiently learn—and change—the heuristics that "work" for our circumstances.

The BLM (depicted in Figure 5.3) gets to some of the specifics of this sort of learning. Perhaps the best way to explain the BLM is through an example (see Figure 5.4). Suppose that you are planning to buy a new car. You might be especially interested in the following set of factors (*cues* in Figure 5.3): price, gas mileage, durability, and cargo space. You are considering purchasing one of six models of car (*options*). The BLM would predict your purchase decision by using the *weights* you set on each cue (upper left of Figure 5.3) when you make decisions about each car. The mathematical approach to combining weights—called regression—can be used to derive weights based on your decisions about a large enough set of options. This use of regression, which is called *policy capturing*, gives psychologists an idea of which dimensions are most important (most heavily *weighted* across options) in your buying decisions. So, back to our example, as a student you may weigh price as most important in your choice of car. As someone interested in sustainability, you may weigh gas mileage as next most important, and as someone who likes to go camping, you may weigh cargo space and durability roughly equally, but third in line after price and gas mileage.

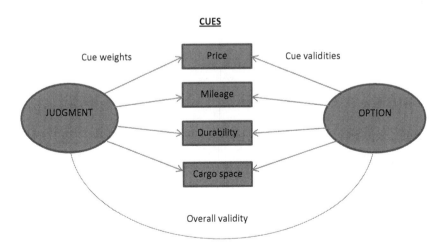

Figure 5.3 Application of the Brunswik Lens Model to car choice

OPENING THE BLACK BOX

CUES

OPTIONS (car models)	Cost ($)	Gas mileage (average mpg)	Expected life (yrs.)	Cargo space (cubic feet)
Car A	$ 5000	38 mpg	4	64
Car B	$ 4500	32 mpg	3	62
Car C	$ 4700	36 mpg	4	67
Car D	$ 5100	34 mpg	6	65
Car E	$ 5500	40 mpg	6	71

Figure 5.4 A car buying decision matrix

To the extent that you apply all cues equally to each option, the BLM would be able to compare your weighting and overall decision accuracy against an *optimized* model. That is, the "correctness" of your decision could be assessed in three different ways. First, the weights you assign to each cue (on the left side of Figure 5.3) could be compared to the actual weight for each cue (cue validities) on each option in the real world (on the right side of Figure 5.3). For example, your notion about prices of cars would be compared to actual car prices. Second, the BLM could also be used to compare your combined weights across options to the optimal combination of the cues (real world "accuracy" of your weights, ala Kahneman). Third, the SDT comparison of your overall choice versus the "optimal" choice could be made using the BLM. It is important to notice here that, even though you did not weigh or combine the cues optimally, your overall decision may have been "correct" using the SDT approach. For example, even though option B has higher gas efficiency and cargo space than you think (your weights are incorrect), you correctly choose it as your overall favorite (a *hit* or *true positive* in SDT terms). Using the language of heuristics and biases, you used an error to make the "right" choice!

From another perspective, rather than describing how we make incorrect decisions, the BLM describes how we make decisions, period. Also, instead of trying to describe errors in decision making outcomes, the BLM provides an early description of the decision process. Some of the concepts that have arisen from this approach shed important light on how processing differences lead to errors. Perhaps most importantly, the BLM and its descendants provide many opportunities for those who would *predict and control* decision processes. Although there may be higher fidelity models for describing general decision processes (e.g., Kruglanski et al., 2012), the BLM provides a usable framework (criterion five).

Applied Brunswik Lens

Analyses of error (Hansen et al., 2007a) and the BLM (Hammond, 1996) have found applications in numerous settings. Epidemiologists (Graham & Wiener, 2008), risk analysts (Hansen et al., 2007a), forensic psychologists (Hartwig & Bond, 2011; MacLaren, 2001), educational psychologists (Davis & Plas, 1983; Permut, 1973; Pleskac, Keeney, Merritt, Schmitt, & Oswald, 2011), and I-O psychologists (Aguinis & Smith, 2007; Hitt & Barr, 1989) have all integrated analysis of error into their work. But much of this applies SDT rather than BLM approaches. Not surprisingly, the concern of applied science is often with the outcomes of decisions (signal detection), rather than with the processes through which decisions are reached (Brunswik Lens).

The BLM presents a major twist in applications, because of this difference from signal detection. Instead of being directed at outcomes (criteria) alone, the Brunswik Lens can be used to manipulate and control decision processes in applied settings. Because the BLM helps to understand how we *arrive* at "errors" and "correct decisions," it also allows for some control over the things that lead to decision outcomes. For example, people who rely on lies to achieve their ends may try to keep cues scarce (Hartwig & Bond, 2011), creating a need for I-O and forensic psychologists to identify these tell-tale cue manipulations. For another example, rigid adherence to a dogmatic approach while ignoring other possible cues may dramatically increase the number of false positives. Using a BLM approach, clinicians can address the underlying cue errors (cue validity) of the beliefs that lead to rigid adherence, rather than attacking the "wrong final decision" of the rigid adherent. In more general terms, having the BLM framework as a way to demonstrate and feed back specific cue and cue combination processes to people is a powerful approach to learning, as we will see in Chapter 8.

Tying together the inputs (appraisal processes) and outcomes (errors/correct choices) using the process approach of the BLM helps to explain other important applied decision making problems. We have already discussed the threat-rigidity problem and *escalation of commitment*. The BLM provides a way to understand how distorted discrepancy tests affect outcomes, in a process called *satisficing*. Recall that using all cues (e.g., cost, gas mileage) on all decision options (brands of cars) is called *optimizing*. Satisficing occurs when, rather than optimizing, we go through only as many options as we need to until we find an option that meets the minimal requirements for all cues. In the car purchase example, suppose that the third option isn't over your budget, gets decent gas mileage, and has just enough cargo space. In other words, it passes these discrepancy test set points. There may well be an option further down the list that exceeds these set points and has higher values on these three cues. But, rather than completing an exhaustive search through all options, you stop the search and purchase this option because it is just "good enough." This abbreviated search based on a "good enough" set point is the definition of satisficing.

Affect and Satisficing

Now, recall that emotive appraisals at the beginning of the decision making process affect the extent to which we are likely to search for alternatives. In the case of sadness, we tend to look further through the cues available (using BLM language), while sympathetic arousal (anger, fear, frustration) is more associated with threat-rigidity—a reduction in search for information. It should come as no surprise that the reduced search for information seen in threat-rigidity and escalation (Keil et al., 2007) is associated with such arousal (O'Neill, 2009). Anticipation of pleasant emotions (Harvey & Victor-avich, 2009) and avoidance of unpleasant emotions (Ku, 2008; Ng, Wong, & Fai, 2008) also help to predict escalation.

There is some confounding of this by lack of separation of "negative affect" (an unclear admixture of sadness, anger, neuroticism, and anticipated regret) with specific emotional episodes, and this has led to some contradictory findings (Wong, Yik, & Kwong, 2006). But this does not change the general finding that threat-rigidity and sympathetic arousal have been suggested as a basis for explaining *escalation of commitment* (Tsai & Young, 2010) and exclusion of potentially important cues in decision making (Hart et al., 2009). Thus, affect can frame BLM persuasion, learning, and cognitive change.

Applying the Five Criteria

1. **What prompts people to think they have a problem (or not)?**
   The decision of basic psychologists to sound the alarm about climate change to the broader community of psychologists was a major departure from the usual, guarded approach to making error prone decisions about discrepancies (Cox, 2007; Hansen et al., 2007b). And it creates a particularly difficult quandary for scientist-practitioners.

   As we have seen, a first step in ethical application of psychology is the consideration of the criteria for success of multiple stakeholder groups. Even when these stakeholders are present to provide input, this is a delicate affair. Consider for example the therapist providing therapy to someone who is considering separation from a spouse who is seen as abusive. Does the therapist directly seek the view of the alleged abuser?

While this is a delicate problem, imagine now trying to ask the eight year old daughter of this couple about her view on the problem.

This inclusion of silent future stakeholders in our error prone decisions is at the core of the sustainability issue. Should we deliberately manipulate the behavior of living people in the interest of trying to possibly preserve something we think is a "good?" As of now, we have only a sketchy idea of which of the nearly infinite consequences of human activities might occur. Does our ethical code provide for deliberately, sometimes without consent, altering human behavior on a massive scale?

Class discussion. In the 2006 documentary *An Inconvenient Truth,* former U.S. Vice President Al Gore set forward a well illustrated case for why people should *see a problem* with global climate change. Survey results showed that most of the people who saw the film said they were affected by it (nz.Neilsen.com). But many staunch climate change "deniers" remained skeptical, even after seeing the film, and movement toward curbing carbon emissions remains slow.

What about this movie kept it from reaching deniers? Think about the sources of the message (Al Gore and a Hollywood film), the framing (e.g., the emotional tone of the documentary), and the timing of the movie's release (at the beginning of a presidential campaign). What attributions were denier viewers able to make based on your answers to these questions? How might their decision processes, and especially the emotions elicited by the movie, help to explain their continuing denial?

One way to deal with people's cautious approach to deciding that there is a problem is to reframe it. Given what we now know about the cybernetic model, in fact, we can expand the definition of this criterion question. Instead of framing things only in terms of "problem identification" or "risk assessment," the cybernetic model suggests that any discrepancy between what is expected and what is observed can be considered as a threat or *an opportunity*. Using this "discrepancy test" approach, it is possible to predict when, whether, and how people will decide to take action, at least to a point.

Gadenne, Kennedy, and McKeiver (2009) helped to demonstrate this idea of reframing in an applied setting. They showed that organizational decision makers can be encouraged to frame environmental "problems" as potential opportunities when laws are changed to support sustainable decision making. This reframing is a key aspect of some of the interventions we will discuss in the last few chapters.

The fact that environmental discrepancies are commonly seen as threats may belie our human tendency to overweight risks (risk aversion) versus gains (Kahneman, 2011); and, as we have seen with sympathetic arousal (anger, fear), threat framing increases the chances that we will revert to rigid, uncreative responses. Thus, applying what we know about emotion to discrepancy testing also informs our answer to this criterion question.

One recent study (Schaffner, Demarmels, & Juettner, 2015) supported the predictive power of both emotive responses and the focus on decision processes addressed by the BLM. These authors found that persuasive messages were seen as more favorable when they relied on "approach" emotions (i.e. positive discrepancies) and provided procedural ideas for making choices. The criterion variable here was just people's judgements of message favorability, but the application of emotive and procedural information provides a good starting place.

Assessing things as threats versus opportunities is also highlighted in analysis of error. Scientist-practitioners, working on the probabilist assumption of error—provide further reason to be suspicious of our tendency to incorrectly appraise things as "problems." Our analysis of emotive appraisal shows that even "opportunity" appraisals can include a "problem" component: Recall the tendency toward sympathetic arousal ("threat" arousal) even when seeing a potential mate smile. Recent work (Delton, Nemirow, Robertson, Cimino, & Cosmides, 2013) suggests that, when observers suspect that others will engage in problematic behavior, there is a tendency to moralize. This tendency to find fault where there is none is likely to engender real problems where there were none before.

2. **What makes people think more or less carefully when they decide on an action?**

This chapter has focused primarily on answers to this question. Understanding the process through which we arrive at the decision that there is a discrepancy provides help with predicting and controlling the quality of our thinking (Keil et al., 2007). How we frame the situation affects how we approach decision making and, to a lesser extent, how we arrive at decisions to act.

The BLM suggests that "hard, solid thinking" (from the M. L. King quote at the beginning of the chapter) be defined in terms of the extent to which we gather adequate information about cues and use substantive processing to combine them in valid ways. This starts with the individual inputs into our decision processes. Sure enough, and consistent with this definition of "hard, solid thinking," Chapter 3 showed that people higher in conscientiousness and causal uncertainty tended to make somewhat better choices, regardless of their level of intelligence.

OPENING THE BLACK BOX

But Chapter 3 also showed that individual differences in intelligence predict success in decision outcomes through their effects on how quickly people learn situation specific *shortcuts* (heuristics)! Consistent with this, satisficing has been shown to lead to better decisions under some circumstances (Güth, Levati, & Ploner, 2010). Even more interesting, there is BLM research (Langhe, de van Osselaer, & Wierenga, 2011) showing that intelligence and "configural thinking" (akin to openness) made a difference in decision outcomes, regardless of situational accountabilities to be thorough. Put simply, intelligence appears to have trumped thoroughness, at least in complicated decisions. And, more importantly, it appears that "hard, solid thinking" may not always lead to the best decisions (Hogarth, 2010; Louis & Sutton, 1991), especially when emotions are involved (Jones et al., 2003).

This is echoed in work on the trade off between individual advantage and social goods—the *social dilemma* frame. Welsch and Kühling (2010) framed social dilemmas in terms of errors. They showed that pro-environmental behavior, not "rational" decision making, can direct people's buying choices. They also showed that, although people are likely to gain few obvious advantages from altruism, the increase in well-being apparently made this sacrifice worth it. This has been supported in more recent work on the effects of "recalled emotions" on sustainable choices (Rowe, Wilson, Dimitriu, Charnley, & Lastrucci, 2019).

Alternatively, Valor et al (2018) demonstrated that emotions can sometimes reduce the tendency to make sustainable choices. Consumers who are unable to sustain an eco-friendly lifestyle, even due to circumstances beyond their control, can experience aversive emotions. Enough experience of negative discrepancy between expectations and perceived behavioral options can change thinking and behavior about sustainability over time. For example, if consumers wish to recycle plastics, living in a community that doesn't offer this option may lead to repeated experiences of frustration. Following from basic behavioral research on aversive emotive responding, this can lead to "giving up on" living an eco-friendly lifestyle.

These studies have helped to understand the "gray areas" between deliberative decision making and decision making based entirely on habits and heuristics. They demonstrate that emotions may effect decisions in either of these directions. However, more generally, the tendency to be thorough about our decisions appears to be more the exception than the rule. We rely heavily on heuristics, are affected by initial emotional appraisals, and tend not to go through all the options before arriving at decisions. As we have seen over and again, applied psychologists rely on this when trying to predict and control the "human weather."

Perhaps the greatest challenge of thinking is not to get people to "think hard:" It is to get us to "think long." When do people "take the long view?" How can we increase the chances of this through applied psychology? These are key questions for future research (Corral-Verdugo & Pinheiro, 2006).

The Matsushita Corporation in Japan uses a 100-year strategic plan. This requires decision makers to consider the consequences of their actions well beyond their own life times. Similar thinking may occur in some family businesses (Muchinsky, 2013). However, shorter term strategic plans are more common. This has been suggested as a major issue in corporate governance—a lack of foresight that leads to self-serving decisions (Fellner, Güth, & Maciejovsky, 2009; Güth et al., 2010).

---

3. What makes people change the way they think and behave?

This chapter offers a few answers to this question. The primary lesson learned is that we can measure change in terms of changing behavior, changing set points, and changing expectations or scripts. There will be much more to go on in the next chapter, using the concepts of *cognitive dissonance* and *norms*. Cognitive dissonance relies to some extent on a discrepancy test, but almost always includes a social context as the basis for changing behavior and scripts.

For changing set points, by contrast, we have seen that both people's expectations and the results of past discrepancy tests can influence future expectations. Going backward from decision outcomes all the way to initial discrepancy tests is a bit of a stretch. But evidence suggests that set points are an important target for change. Advertisers often rely on this approach, as have a few recent efforts to increase pro-environmental behavior (Elgaaied, 2012). Creating apparent discrepancies by framing threats and opportunities may be important starting points. There is also evidence that the *focus* of our discrepancy test is what persuades us to think substantively and change behaviors. Focusing our attention toward things that are new or different may be what instigates "hard, solid thinking." For example, Hernandez and Preston (2013) successfully reduced the tendency to seek confirming evidence (confirmation bias) and discount disconfirming evidence (one of the aspects of sunk costs). In one of the conditions in their experiment, participants had to read a persuasive message that used lots of big words. This created "disfluency" in reading and increased careful processing. It also successfully changed people's attitudes by increasing their attention to views different from their own. Just making us stop and look may get us to think.

We have seen how similar *emotional* disfluency may also affect the tendency for people to attend to broader sets of cues and make better decisions. In terms of changing people's thinking processes, sympathetic arousal (anger and fear) reduces processing (threat-rigidity) and sadness and pleasure increase it (Ask & Granhag, 2007; Keil et al., 2007). In terms of changing people's views, however, evidence about threat and sadness is inconclusive (Keil et al., 2007; Munro & Stansbury, 2009). We need to know more about the effects of arousal on deliberation if we are to manage the emotional issues of sustainability (de Hoog, Stroebe, & de Wit, 2007). We will return to this in Chapter 10.

Process models have begun to find their way into explaining pro-environmental behavior (PEB; Harland et al., 2007; Story & Forsyth, 2008b). While it is still quite early to draw strong conclusions, these models suggest that *awareness* of situational factors, *discrepancy tests*, and a decision about personal responsibility (in this order) predict the tendency toward altruism and taking action (Story & Forsyth, 2008b). What is clear is that the literature on persuasion is broad and potentially helpful (de Hoog et al., 2007; Johnson & Eagly, 1989; Kumkale & Albarracín, 2004) and that we have only begun to apply it to sustainability in this chapter. We will learn more in Chapters 5 and 10.

4. When are people likely to take action?

Clearly, there are at least two general types of action in Figure 5.1. The first is impulsive responding based on emotive appraisals. Targeting this process as a means for stimulating action may be successful, but may also lead to major mistakes. For example, much criminal behavior is based on impulsive responding (Stanford & Felthous, 2008). Instead of "acting on our guts," deliberative, substantive processing may lead to more effective action. Individual differences (e.g., conscientiousness, uncertainty avoidance, emotional intelligence) and factors in the social context (e.g., norms, cultural variables, authority, and conformity) may change the way we arrive at decisions to take action.

Social and cultural contexts are the main topics of the next chapter. It is important to recognize that there may be substantial differences in the aspects of the world around us that will elicit emotive responses and substantive decision processing.

5. What are the characteristics of change efforts that are likely to work?

As in all questions about intervention, we start with the criterion question. In this chapter, we have seen how discrepancy tests are the bases for individual and group decision processes. Understanding various stakeholders' expectations, their set point levels, and the kinds of responses they habitually use are all important targets as we try to define criteria in applied settings. What is the "expected" course of events for different stakeholders? Based on individual differences, motives, values, and other determinants of set points, how likely is each stakeholder to see a problem (or not)? What are the initial emotive reactions of stakeholders during decisions? What are likely responses based on their sympathetic and parasympathetic arousal levels? How do we frame discrepancies based on these?

Collective action is essential to most change efforts. Questions about deliberative versus impulsive action in groups need to be considered as we introduce information that may hit set points in some but not in others. Similarly, stakeholders may be more able to work together when they understand and address each other's set points. In practice, helping groups manage discrepancies, emotions, and the decision processes that follow matters. We have seen how repeated exposure to discrepancies may change set points, how emotive responses can be elicited when people discover new information, and how emotional responses may also change as set points change. Knowing something about how to manage these variables in complex human decision processes is highly practical.

6

SOCIAL CONTEXTS

> A wee little worm in a hickory nut
> Sang, happy as he could be,
> "Oh, I live in the heart of the whole round world,
> And it all belongs to me!"
> > "It" by James Whitcomb Riley

In Chapter 3, we learned how individual differences in abilities, motivations, and situational expertise can be used to predict people's later behaviors. Applied psychologists use such predictions to make decisions about how to treat people with disorders, who to select for jobs, schools, and juries, and how to approach behavior change. For example, openness and environmental stewardship are positively correlated, such that stewardship behaviors can be predicted from measures of openness. We could use this information to select people high in openness as future employees for our enviro-company startup.

But we have also learned that there are serious errors likely when we make decisions—all kinds of decisions, including selection and treatment in applied settings. Chapters 2 and 3 showed in particular how we tend to attribute observed behavior to stable, internal characteristics, rather than to the situational factors that may be more responsible for those behaviors—the *attribution error*. Making our selection decisions based on stable individual differences (like openness) tends to overestimate the importance of such stable characteristics.

Thinking of this another way, we take the *effects of the situation on behavior* as "background" when we observe each other, rather than as a primary causes of behavior. Stable traits are overestimated as explanations of others' behaviors, and situations underestimated (Gigerenzer, 2011). The end result is that we tend to understand behaviors without reference to the boundaries of the situation in which we observe them. These *situational boundaries* are the "hickory nut" in the James Whitcomb Riley poem, above.

The problem with living in a hickory nut is that the interaction between person and situation is often a complicated and, sometimes, very powerful way to predict thinking and behavior. By missing or ignoring situational effects, we may miss powerful options when trying to manage important decisions. In this chapter, we will first consider how our social context is a *direct input* that causes behavior. Second, when we stop noticing our situational boundaries, it is often because we have *internalized* our contexts through the effects of norms, social identity, and culture. We take for granted what we expect to have happen in social situations, even though other people may have entirely different expectations than ours for "normal" behavior. Our third approach will describe how the situation *interacts* with people's *individual differences* to affect thinking and behavior. Specifically, situational boundaries often *moderate* the effects of individual differences on behavioral outcomes like pro-environmental behaviors. Applications of these three approaches to context—direct input, internalization, and interaction with individual differences—help to predict and control behavior in real world settings.

The Power of the Situation

We are social animals. Our neurophysiology, developmental patterns in families, and, most obviously, the fact that we have lived near other humans throughout our history are all testimony to this. However, scientific study of how this social context affects individual psychology is a fairly recent phenomenon, with an explosion of research starting in the middle of the twentieth century. Although psychology generally concerns itself with individuals as the unit of analysis, *social psychologists* have taken a leadership role among scientists who are trying to understand how social context influences behavior. The understanding of social behavior as an essential component of human adaptation is even more recent (Cacioppo & Hawkley, 2012; Cialdini, 1988; Wilson, 2012).

Much of the early research has helped us to understand how social context serves as a *direct input* (independent variable) that leads to behavioral outcomes. In a very short time, we have accumulated convincing evidence about the behavioral effects of authority, small social groups, crowds, minorities, and a host of other social contextual variables (Aronson, 2004; Cialdini, 1988, 2007). Not surprisingly, it turns out that our behavior and thinking are often very strongly influenced by social inputs. Such outcomes as helping, inclusion, discrimination, obedience and conformity, persuasion, and learning are all decisively affected by differences in social contexts (Aronson, 2004; Cialdini, 2007).

The evolution of social psychological research has also illuminated *process* variables. *Social cognition* and *person perception* developed as important areas of research after the research that treated context as an *input* (Ostrom,

SOCIAL CONTEXTS

Carpenter, Sedikides, & Li, 1993; Skowronski & Ostrom, 1992). *Attitude formation*, differences between *minority and majority influence*, and processes that lead to *prejudice* and *inclusion* are relevant examples we will discuss in this chapter.

Problems with Applying Context

Applied psychologists have also been quick to integrate what basic research has revealed about social behavior and cognition. *Manipulations* of social context are fairly common in applied psychology, particularly in *consumer psychology*, *leadership*, and *group dynamics*. But, venturing this way has also revealed ethical problems associated with deliberately manipulating social situations without the consent of those who are targeted for manipulation (Cialdini, 1988; Sieber, 2010).

Short of manipulation, *controlling* for situation variables can help to reduce error in prediction. This is often the most that can be accomplished within ethical boundaries. Nevertheless, the powerful effects of social, cultural, and organizational contexts on our thinking and behavior can at least be accounted for. For example, if you can identify whether there is powerful political figure telling people to behave a certain way, you can control for some of the effects of authority. Combining this authority identifier with measures of relevant personality characteristics provides for more predictive power than accounting for either authority or individual differences alone. Figure 6.1 provides a *Venn diagram* to illustrate this kind of direct prediction. If you add together the areas in the "authority" circle and the "personality" circle that overlap with behavior, you will account for more of the area in the "behavior" circle.

Following from this simple approach, we will now turn to an examination of how social contexts are defined in both basic and applied research, and how they have immediate, direct effects on behavior.

Figure 6.1 A Venn diagram describing prediction using two input variables (person and situation)

SOCIAL CONTEXTS

Direct Social Influences

As with most science, if we seek to understand differences in outputs, we first define variables that characterize inputs. In the case of situational inputs, one approach has been to describe them in terms of situational strength (Mischel, 1977; Mullins & Cummings, 1999). *Situational strength* is defined as the extent to which contingencies of behavior are more or less clear, based on situational cues and normative expectations. A *strong situation* has obvious contingencies (sets of possible outcomes) and expected ways of responding. A few examples of strong situations include combat drills, traditional classrooms, religious observances, and fast food restaurants. In the case of drills, behaviors are determined by well learned rules that have been very clearly defined by an *authority* and are often clearly associated with life and death *contingencies*. Although there are not life and death contingencies in traditional classrooms, people learn from authorities and conformity which behaviors are expected and which are forbidden. Behaviors in religious observances are generally learned through *culture*, often in the form of rituals to which people learn quickly to *conform* by watching others' behavior (*social referencing*). Even fast food restaurants have *norms* that are quickly learned, also through social referencing and conformity.

Weak situations have unclear or ambiguous expectations for behavior. First dates, new jobs, seminar classrooms, and actual combat conditions are all examples of weak situations. Following these examples, most adults have experienced the sense of uncertainty and ambiguity on first dates and new jobs. There are potentially very desirable and undesirable contingencies of behavior (love, marriage, and success versus rejection and humiliation) in these weak situations. But the means through which we might arrive at one or more of these outcomes are usually quite obscure, and there is rarely a set "*script*" that one can follow to arrive at the desirable outcomes. Similarly, seminar classrooms are often unsettling to students who are new to them, and actual combat (unlike drills) is chaotic—defined by uncertain relationships between behaviors and outcomes.

Considerable research suggests that individual differences are better predictors in weak situations (de Kwaadsteniet, van Dijk, Wit, & de Cremer, 2006; Jones & Parameswaran, 2005; McDonald & Donnellan, 2012; Mullins & Cummings, 1999; Suls & David, 1996; Webster & Crysel, 2012). For example, in the absence of an authority figure, authoritarianism is predictive of sexually harassing behavior (Pryor, LaVite, & Stoller, 1993). But, when an authority figure makes clear statements about the negative contingencies of such behaviors (i.e., punishment, ostracism), individual differences in authoritarianism are no longer predictive of these behaviors (Pryor et al., 1993). Generally, the *situation* is more predictive of behavior than are *individual differences* when cues are clear—in strong situations (de Kwaadsteniet et al., 2006; McDonald & Donnellan, 2012; Meyer & Dalal, 2009; Weiss & Adler, 1984).

SOCIAL CONTEXTS

In fact, the idea that individual tendencies bow to situational pressures is almost a truism in social psychology (Galinsky, Magee, Gruenfeld, Whitson, & Liljenquist, 2008), despite a few exceptions (Van Cappellen, Corneille, Cols, & Saroglou, 2011). We will return to this idea in the section on person–situation interactions.

But first, we will examine the direct effects of situations on behavior. Authority, conformity, and normative influences are all well researched examples of such situational effects: They are some of the most famous ways of operationally defining situations (Cialdini, 2012; Mischel, 1977). We will examine examples of each of these. The social heuristics in Table 2.1 often exert powerful effects on both behavioral outcomes, and on the decision processes that may intervene *between* people's perception of the situation and their behaviors.

The Social Situation

It bears repeating that most of the contexts in which we make decisions are in some way social. From infancy, we interact socially with people every day, sometimes for the vast majority of the day. So it should come as no surprise that we often rely on social information to decide whether we have a problem. This is the basis for conformity and authority effects on behavior. *Social referencing* is defined as observation of others' actions when choosing our own behavioral responses in ambiguous situations (Kim & Kwak, 2011). Social referencing is generally associated with early childhood, though the choice to mimic what others do is also seen in effects like *modeling* and *conformity*.

The influences of authority and conformity are profound, as demonstrated in early social psychological experiments by Stanley Milgram (1974) and Solomon Asch (1956), respectively. Milgram's famous studies demonstrated that the majority of people will follow a designated leader over a figurative cliff and will shock an innocent stranger to death. Asch's study showed that people will discard what they see with their own eyes when enough of the people around them say they don't see the same thing.

And these dramatic examples are mirrored in more ordinary, everyday events. For example, you probably did what your professor asked at least once during class this week without really thinking why you should or shouldn't have done it. You may also have remained silent on an elevator, simply because the people around you (even your friends) also did so. The point is the same: Authority and conformity predict behavior in social contexts (Cialdini, 2007).

An important part of the effects of social pressures comes from research on groups, more generally (Levine & Moreland, 2012). *Norms* are used to explain why people behave consistently in many social situations—not just when there is pressure for conformity and obedience. Norms are shared expectations for behaviors in particular social contexts and roles. A famous study of students who were randomly assigned to take on the roles of prisoners and prison guards at Stanford University showed the powerful effects of these expectations on people's behaviors (White, 2012). There are also many examples from everyday life where people take on social roles and then behave in ways consistent with their roles in particular social circumstances. For example, your decisions to enter a classroom at a socially designated time, sit in a particular chair, and attend when the instructor begins talking are all examples of the norms of being a student. We will see later how powerful norms can be for explaining and changing the ways that people behave with respect to natural environments (Bamberg & Möser, 2007; Cialdini, 2012).

Part of the power of norms is that they can easily become cultural *values*. What is "normal" often turns into what is morally "right." This can be seen in religious observances, where the rituals passed down through authority and conformity are vested with mystical importance. Such importance is usually associated with *culture*—defined partly in terms of the values people use to explain traditions, and the behaviors that follow from these traditions. Seen this way, culture need not really be separated from the norms that are learned through conformity and authority and that are associated with such things as religious observances. But we will also see later that there is more to culture than just norms that have been internalized through conformity and authority.

Applying Social Context

Most decisions are made in weak situations—under conditions of uncertainty (de Kwaadsteniet et al., 2006; Kahneman, 2011). The complex contingencies and uncertainties of the weak situations we encounter every day may help to explain why applied researchers rely heavily on individual difference predictors, rather than social context predictors of various outcomes. Interestingly, the basic research area of environmental psychology has advanced our understanding of *physical* (as opposed to *social*) contexts enormously (Gifford, 2007b). Perhaps the most important message about context from much of this work is that the effects of physical contexts rely on both their *actual* characteristics (e.g., population density) and people's *perceptions* of them (e.g., perceived crowding).

Still, broad, theoretical definitions of context are sparse in most applied areas of psychology (Meyer & Dalal, 2009; Tett & Burnett, 2003). This is perhaps because applied psychology relies on initial assessment of *specific* contexts through methods such as job analysis (Sanchez & Levine, 2012), behavior analysis (Fagerstrøm & Arntzen, 2013; Lewin & Donthu, 2005), and climate surveys (de Beuckelaer, Lievens, & Swinnen, 2007). The concept of *situation specificity* means that scientist-practitioners carefully consider the

SOCIAL CONTEXTS

particular social contexts of jobs, families, classrooms, courtrooms, and so on (Austin et al., 1989; Tett & Burnett, 2003). In this way, applied psychologists attempt to simply report situational boundaries when using individual difference and attitude measures, rather than directly measuring or manipulating situational effects on behavior.

However, there is also substantial research on direct manipulations of context through such things as leader and group development, family therapy, consumer marketing, classroom activities, and space design. But manipulation of contexts raises important concerns, and not just because the variables that distinguish between situations are not well defined. When teachers, therapists, urban designers, consumer psychologists, and industrial-organizational (I-O) psychologists deliberately alter situations without the people affected knowing it, they risk unintended consequences. Because the targeted people may not be aware of what is being done to try to alter their behavior, they have no reason to prepare in case of adverse consequences. This is the problem of *informed consent* to participate in research.

I-O psychologists routinely deal with this problem by gathering people's *perceptions* of the organization in order to simply measure (rather than manipulate) situational characteristics (de Beuckelaer et al., 2007). This is not as common in other applied areas and provides a potential frontier for scientist-practitioners interested in managing sustainable behaviors. The use of direct measurement of perceived situational characteristics allows researchers to account for situational effects without the moral ambiguity of trying to manipulate people without their knowledge or consent. Even with this, prediction and control of behavior through broad contextual variables should be evaluated using an ethical lens.

We will also see in Chapter 8 how standard educational interventions, such as classroom experiences, training, and therapy can be aimed at developing an *awareness* of the influences of social contexts. Such standard interventions are generally treated as exempt from close ethical review. Since people deliberately choose to experience learning and change in these settings, there is less concern with informed consent.

Internalized Context I: Culture

One recent and very promising approach to the problem of managing context is the use of *cultural differences* as a basis for predicting behavior. "Culture represents a set of shared knowledge and implicit theories about the world including beliefs, values, attitudes, and other constructs needed to interpret and navigate various environments" (Hong et al., 2000, in Sharma, 2010). Culture sets an important boundary on how individual differences affect behavior in different situations. Although culture is partly defined by difference in social contexts, recent research has successfully used it as a determinant of individual thinking and behavior—a psychological variable

137

SOCIAL CONTEXTS

(Fischer & Poortinga, 2012; Morling & Lamoreaux, 2008; Schwartz, 2007). Notice that knowledge, values, and attitudes are all included in this definition, and all are also individual difference characteristics discussed in Chapter 3.

Hofstede (1980, 2012) and others (Forsyth, O'Boyle, & McDaniel, 2008; Lu, 1998; Piron, 2006; Schwartz, 2007; Sharma, 2010; Sinha & Verma, 2006; Stelzl & Seligman, 2009) have suggested several psychological dimensions that vary across cultures. These values and habitual views of social interaction are psychological, but can be thought of as *internalized, strong situational* characteristics that vary across cultures. In the absence of *external* strong situational cues, people can rely heavily on cultural norms and values to guide behaviors (Fischer & Poortinga, 2012). A partial list of the proposed psychological dimensions of culture follows:

1. *Power distance* is the degree to which people expect power to be unequally shared. It is not closely related to authoritarianism but is more a question of relative acceptance of social stratification.
2. *Societal collectivism* is defined as the degree to which a society as a whole rewards collective versus individual behavior.
3. *In-group collectivism* is the degree to which people express loyalty within their family and other close social groups (e.g., work groups, community groups, clubs).
4. *Uncertainty avoidance* is defined as the degree to which individuals want to avoid uncertainty. This is presumably related to stress coping responses that may differ across cultures (Frone, 1990).
5. *Gender egalitarianism* is the extent to which gender roles are minimized or accentuated in a culture. Some cultures tend to emphasize gender dimorphism, while some are more likely to minimize naturally occurring average differences between genders.
6. *Assertiveness* is the degree to which people are accepting of assertive individual behaviors in social relationships.
7. *Performance orientation* is the extent to which individuals and groups value the achievement of desired outcomes.
8. *Future orientation* is variability in behaviors such as planning, saving, and consideration of future consequences of current actions.
9. *Humane orientation* is the degree to which individuals value generosity, friendship, and caring.
10. *Benevolence*, closely related to humane orientation, and also called Yi or Shu, is the degree to which people are oriented to behaving morally or righteously.
11. *Universalism* is defined by Schwartz (2007) as "the breadth of the community to which people apply moral values and rules of fairness." This dimension looks at whether people differ in their tendency to define their "in-group" within more or less broad boundaries.

SOCIAL CONTEXTS

While the use of various combinations of these dimensions has grown dramatically since they were originally proposed, there are substantial problems with their measurement (Spector, Cooper, & Sparks, 2001). With the exception of future orientation, many of the scales used to try to identify differences in culture have demonstrated poor internal consistency and factor structure. Nevertheless, the search for ways to identify systematic psychological differences across cultures continues (Forsyth et al., 2008; Schwartz, 2007; Taras, Kirkman, & Steel, 2010).

While it is problematic to make broad generalizations based on culture, researchers have noted some dramatic cultural contrasts between Native and European cultures in North America. Native people in the United States often considered land as community property, to the point where individual ownership was a new notion introduced in the Americas by Europeans. This *in-group collectivism* extended to a tradition of land use based on respect for resources. Tribes often moved seasonally to where resources were occurring, rather than altering land to produce commodities. In some tribal groups, all things were shared. Even today, there are social norms against any one person owning too much in some tribes (e.g., among the Lakota of South Dakota).

In terms of *future orientation*, there were several examples of extreme future orientation among native peoples. According to Ben Franklin, the Iroquois Nation followed a "seven generation rule" going back at least to initial European contact: Decisions took into account the interests of seven generations into the future. This may also have demonstrated a more *universalist* perspective, since unborn humans were included as people with similar moral rights to those currently living. Allowing for regeneration of lands was considered important, versus the purely consumptive use of land and natural resources more common among certain groups of European settlers. This tendency toward future orientation was also demonstrated in the spiritual (values based) attachment that many native people express with respect to their traditional lands today. The concept of *place attachment* is defined in terms of the special connection people have with some part of their physical environment (Gifford, 2007a; Raymond, Brown, & Robinson, 2011). For many native people there is a strong sense that we are part of the earth in general; we may use the earth's resources, but using them up would be analogous to dying.

While some European settlers certainly formed strong attachments to the land, the attachment often involved a sense of individual ownership, with rights to use the land as one pleased. Individual pursuit of happiness found its way into many famous events in North American history, including land and gold rushes, wars over the definition of individual property (i.e., the U.S. Civil War), and an economy driven by rapid consumption of resources. Even today, corporations dominated by this same European cultural mindset have only three or five year plans for the future—far less than seven generations.

These fundamental differences in understandings about the nature of personhood, our attachment to the land, and obligations to future humans provide good explanations for the violent conflicts between these cultures historically. Alternatively, many from both cultures expressed admiration for the independence (low societal collectivism), egalitarianism (low power distance), and courage (high tolerance for uncertainty) that European and Native cultures generally shared.

We have seen that individual differences may be "trumped" by strong situations. However, there is recent evidence that this may not be the case for culture (Chen et al., 2006; Gelfand, 2012). This research evidence shows that people's compliance with situational expectations may actually vary depending on their culture. While this is still an emerging area of research, it is consistent with the idea that our internalized cultural contexts exert strong influences on our actions.

Applied Culture

With increased interactions across cultures in the recent past, there is a growing applied literature evaluating the relationship between culture and a host of applied criteria, including mental health (Aguilera, Garza, & Muñoz, 2010; Scaini, Battaglia, Beidel, & Ogliari, 2012; Wildes & Emery, 2001), buying behavior (Morling & Lamoreaux, 2008), marital satisfaction (Dillon & Beechler, 2010), safety (Li, Harris, & Chen, 2007), organizational commitment (Meyer et al., 2012; Taras et al., 2010), and test performance (Born, Bleichrodt, & Van der Flier, 1987; van de Vijver, 1997). We will start with a few studies on the relationship between pro-environmental behavior and culture, then apply other studies looking at culture to the five criteria in the last section of the chapter.

A central aspect of culture is shared *values* (Schwartz, 2007). These are defined as shared notions of what is good, right, or desirable, and can be thought of as fundamental to *shared motives*. Pro-environmental behaviors (PEBs) have been grouped according to three value sets that appear to differ to some extent across people (Hansla et al., 2008; Scannell & Gifford,

2010b): (1) *egotistical values* (concern for how environmental issues affect our own interests); (2) *social-altruistic* and *civic values* (concern for the well-being of other humans); and (3) *biospheric values* (concern for the broader natural world). These, in turn, are related to some of the broader value types that differ across cultures: power, benevolence, and universalism.

There is a small, but growing, literature on how these psycho-cultural characteristics affect environmental sustainability criteria. First, three studies (Cordano et al., 2011; Levy-Leboyer et al., 1996; Zheng, 2010) demonstrated that cross-cultural differences in norms are reflected in people's broad attitudes and inclinations regarding environmentally responsible behavior. Parbooteah and his colleagues have approached pro-environmental behavior and cultural values from the narrower perspective of organizational ethics (Parboteeah, Addae, & Cullen, 2012; Parboteeah, Bronson, & Cullen, 2005). One of these studies used a very large dataset from the GLOBE study (House, Javidan, Hanges, & Dorfman, 2001) to see whether *support for sustainability* differed on several psycho-cultural dimensions. Findings were generally consistent with expectations, such that assertiveness was negatively associated with support for sustainability, and collectivism, future orientation, and humane orientation were positively associated with it.

> Why are there so few lawns in Japan? It is not just land scarcity, since many people do own land around their homes. The use of the land usually includes growing produce and other crops, as well as the famous ornamental gardens often seen in Japan. One plausible explanation is the *value* that people in this traditionally animistic culture put on the land. Having a lawn that is neither productive nor aimed at a considered aesthetic is simply not part of the cultural tradition.
>
> Another is that Americans, following from the British tradition of "greens" and enclosure see lawns as "normal"—even though most of the rest of the world does not. Seeing land ownership and land having value in itself, apart from any utilitarian use, is part of the Western culture and value structure. One answer to the question of why there are few lawns in Japan is actually, "Why do we have lawns in the United States?"

Several other studies offer tantalizing glimpses into the many issues associated with culture that may affect sustainability. Soyez (2012) showed that people from individualistic cultures (United States, Australia, Canada, and Germany) tended to take an ecocentric values perspective (similar to biospheric values), while people from the more collectivist Russian culture took a more anthropocentric (social-altruistic) view when making decisions about

SOCIAL CONTEXTS

consumption. Although Berenguer, Corraliza, and Martín (2005) looked at underlying values rather than culture, their results showed that urbanites were less likely to translate their pro-environmental values into behavioral intentions than were people from rural settings. Eom, Kim, Sherman, and Ishii (2016) found that concern for the environment translated into support for action more in individualistic cultures, while conformity predicted support for action in a collectivist cultures. Relating to these last two studies, a meta-analysis of sixty-six articles provided a couple of potentially very valuable conclusions about the relationship between culture and the psychology of sustainability (Morren & Grinstein, 2016). The main finding was that cultural differences do make a difference in whether intentions translate into action. In developed, individualistic countries, people are more likely to act on their intentions.

Internalized Context II: Theories of Social Identity and Life Space

In order to understand what part of context is being internalized, it is important to understand the very permeable boundaries between the individual and the social world around us (Gold, 1992). Social and environmental psychologists have used two main theories to understand these boundaries between people and their social context. The first of these is Lewin's (1951) *Field Theory*. At its core, Field Theory argues that people's life tasks (purposes, hopes, fears, and other motivational forces) create a force field of approach and avoidance motivations (Higgins, 2012) that define the ways that what is "inside" us is affected by what we see "outside" us. For example, the emotive responses we discussed in Chapter 4 are based on Field Theory. "Positive" emotions are defined as motive readiness for approaching desired aspects of our environment, and "negative" emotions prepare us to avoid or remove undesirable aspects of our environment.

In addition to explaining our choices of action, Field Theory also helps explain how our personal boundaries develop and change in response to feedback from events that happen as we try to approach the things we desire and avoid the things we fear. Field Theory is largely used, then, to define what lies inside our boundaries of self and how these boundaries are formed and changed through experiences with what is outside of them. The core concept here is that social events, and our attempts to approach and avoid them, are likely to change our internal selves.

Social Identity Theory (SIT; Tajfel, 1982) takes a different approach, by defining boundaries in terms of the social groups we embrace or reject. SIT is a powerful means for explaining which norms we follow, how cultures define "self," and outcomes such as prejudice, inclusion, helping behaviors, harassment, and aggression. The processes through which these boundaries between "self" and "other" are developed and change are perhaps less well understood.

Application of Boundary Theories

The decision to include or exclude others from our moral group is clearly an important one. The large research literatures trying to understand the basis for exclusion, inclusion, prejudice, aggression, and universalism are testimony to this (Crandall, Eshleman, & O'Brien, 2002; Fiske, 2002, 2004; Jackson, 2011). Trying to affect people's decisions about who to help, who to drop bombs on, how to treat the natural environment, and a host of other highly consequential decisions may rely on this underlying choice to include or exclude. In fact, some argue that the choice to treat other people as being equally entitled to the goods of life on earth is the primary basis for adaptation and sustainability (Gifford Pinchot, 2011, personal communication; Schwartz, 2007).

Not surprisingly, there is some research showing that social identity is related to environmental activism (Dono, Webb, & Richardson, 2010) and green buying (Gupta & Ogden, 2009). These findings suggest that social identity leads people to see themselves as good environmental citizens, which in turn may affect activism. What is less clear is how to change social identity. We will return to this question in Chapter 6, when we discuss the development of the social self.

Internalized Context III: Situational Expertise

The important message from environmental psychology—that both the *actual* and the *perceived* situation affect behavior—has an analogue in applied research. Internalizing the situation may not just include norms, culture, and values. It may also include accurate perceptions of social contexts—situational expertise. We visited both basic and applied research in Chapter 3 showing how intelligence translated into positive outcomes, partly through its effects on how quickly people learn about their contexts (McDaniel & Whetzel, 2005; Sternberg, 1997; Zhang, 2002). Following from this, applied interventions to increase knowledge of the contingencies of a situation have been shown to influence the effectiveness of people's responses (Higgins, 1990; Maurer, Solamon, Andrews, & Troxtel, 2001; Speekenbrink & Shanks, 2010). With respect to sustainability, for example, increasing people's awareness of environmental concerns may increase the chances of pro-environmental behaviors (Bamberg & Möser, 2007; Kollmuss & Agyeman, 2002).

Like other situational variables, knowledge of the situation is often ignored when people try to explain each other's behaviors. For example, people are often inclined to use ability and motivational explanations for behavior and underestimate people's understanding of the situation in arriving at conclusions. For example, being stuck behind a driver going twenty miles per hour under the posted speed limit on a clear road might lead us to ascribe their behavior to stupidity or lack of effort attending to the road conditions (perhaps using four letter words). If we see that their license plate is from a distant state and that there are many commercial billboards obscuring official road signs, we might change our explanation for their behavior—they don't know where they are going! But notice that this last explanation is likely to come *after* the individual ability and motivation explanations.

In terms of perceived *social* contexts, not much is known about situational expertise. *Person perception* research has led to important insights into the processes underlying our understandings of the social situation. Perhaps the most important product of this basic research over the years is *attribution theory*, which we discussed briefly in Chapters 2 and 3. The *actor–observer difference* is particularly important as a way to understand the difference between the *perception* of the causes of other people's actions versus the *actual* abilities, motives, and situational pressures that influence their behaviors (Schlenker, Hallam, & McCown, 1983). In simplified form (Robins, Spranca, & Mendelsohn, 1996), it has been shown that people tend to explain others' "happy" outcomes to luck, and their unhappy outcomes to internal causes (especially abilities and motives). Alternatively, we switch this when we are explaining our own outcomes (and the outcomes of those close to us). That is, we tend to ascribe our own happy outcomes to internal stable causes (effort and ability), and our unhappy outcomes to the situation and to luck. We will see later how attributional tendencies play out.

Another attempt to address expertise in social contexts comes from person perception research aimed at understanding how people make sense of each other's emotional displays. We have seen that emotions are motive readiness responses (Lang, 1995) based on appraisals of perceived threat and opportunity. Many introductory textbooks in psychology cite the *universal recognition* of facial emotional displays across cultures (Ekman, 1993, 1994; Izard, 1994; Russell, 1994). The argument here goes back to Darwin (Frijda, 1953): Our mammalian endowment prepares us to recognize and understand some shared meaning in emotional displays.

The content of this shared meaning has not been explained, particularly in light of the apparent ability of humans to regulate emotional displays in order to manipulate others' construal of social meanings. So, how do we become "experts" about emotion displays and, by extension, about social contexts?

First, we need to understand why we *display* emotions. Instead of just experiencing arousal and acting on it, we have a strong tendency to express emotions, especially in our highly visible facial displays. Why don't we just save energy and act on arousal responses? For example, if we experience fear (sympathetic arousal), why don't we just run away? Why do we also feel the urge to show fear in our faces? What compels us to express emotions, particularly in a way that others can so readily see? An obvious answer is social: We want to communicate our state of arousal to others.

An important critique of the research on universal emotional displays (Russell, 1995) opened up some very interesting and important questions about the exact nature of our knowledge of one another. Russell posed important distinctions between people's *experience* of emotion, their display of emotion, and the *construal* of emotion by those observing displays. Some view facial displays as "pure signals" of underlying emotional states. Others, like Russell (1995) and emotional labor researchers (Ashforth & Humphrey, 1993) regard facial displays as "social tools." In both cases, emotional displays serve *signaling functions*, but the latter view treats these as susceptible to self-regulation, as well. For example, poker players often deliberately try to hide their emotional displays.

Second, to become experts, we need to understand more precisely what it is that emotional displays are signaling. This is where the *construal* of emotional signals comes in. For psychologists, whatever is being *signaled* also needs to be *understood* in terms of the meaning ascribed by the observer. It is not just the emotive response that the person making the display is feeling that matters. To be social experts, we need to understand what the message is in "the eyes of the beholder." This leaves the question open: "What, exactly, do emotions communicate?"

The *Emotive Perception* model (EPM) addresses this question. EPM posits that the display (non-display) of emotions serves an *external* signaling function for both "basic" (Jones & Rittman, 2002) and "self-conscious" (Jones et al., 2003) emotional displays. Reviewing from Chapter 2, we follow four steps in arriving at emotional arousal, internally. First, our motives direct our attention. Second, we appraise things using a discrepancy test between expected and perceived events. Third, we experience emotive arousal. Fourth, we may (or may not) behave according to our arousal state. More specifically, we may display or hide our emotive responses, based on our understanding of the situation.

Observers rely on perceptions of actor emotional displays to arrive at evaluations of actor *motive*, going back up through the same mechanisms as those followed by the internal signaling function. Actors probably (1) observe actor emotions, (2) appraise situations in terms of threats and opportunities, and (3) arrive at an attribution of actor motivation with respect to the situational (see Figure 6.2). Displays (deliberate or otherwise) thus signal to observers the actor's motives in a given context.

For example, suppose we see a stranger at the airport watching a news report about the passage of a new international accord to reduce carbon emissions. If the person smiles widely at this, most of us would take this as a clear indication that the person appraised the news as a positive outcome. It seems very obvious that among this stranger's motives is a desire for

Figure 6.2 Simplified summary of observer motive attributions

increased sustainability. The *communicative* function of the person's delight is to let others know that he or she is so motivated. Being social animals, we can communicate our motives just this simply.

Less obvious, perhaps, is how naturally we as observers *use* others' emotive displays to infer their motives. The fact that most of the people reading this probably think this is so obvious as to be elementary is yet more evidence that we take such emotive displays as "built-in" components of our situations—our hickory nut. Consider, for example, that many other, less social animals have far fewer ways to display emotions and the motives behind them. Cats, for example, have very few facial expressions with which to try to communicate their motives.

Starting with "simple" situations, like this one, research has demonstrated that observers rely on actor emotional displays in order to assess the actor's effort level (Jones, Chomiak, Rittman, & Green, 2006). More importantly, the observers' assessments of effort are highly accurate, at least in these simple circumstances. This research used stimulus materials where actors with different levels of motivation were observed performing a simple block building task. The contingencies of such a task (building a tall tower with wooden blocks without them falling down) should be quite obvious to observers who have themselves worked on this task.

Not surprisingly, emotional observations by people watching these actors were highly accurate. This is consistent with the "universal recognition" research. Two other findings significantly extended our understanding of why people display emotions for others to see. First, observers' motive inferences were also highly accurate. Using a signal detection theory approach, there was unusually low error in these inferences. Second, and even more telling, observers based these very accurate estimates of actor effort levels on the emotions they observed, consistent with the EMP. In other words, people base attributions about motivation levels on the emotional displays we observe.

Even this may seem obvious—perhaps because it is so intuitively plausible. Far less obvious is how we incorporate our knowledge of the contingencies of the social context (situational expertise) into this type of inference. Again, because we have few measures of social-psychological context, it remains very empirically challenging to understand the construal of emotional displays in more complex situations, such as those we encounter every day. In weak situations, observers probably need background knowledge about the situation in order to arrive at accurate attributions about the target's motives.

Put differently, we first try to use appraisals to understand emotive displays, and only then do we rely on attributions (León & Hernández, 1998; Smith, Haynes, Lazarus, & Pope, 1993). However, there is still much to learn about how people arrive at motive attributions in weak situations. Situational expertise, particularly with respect to the motivating contingences of the situation, may help to explain this.

Motive Sharing

By contrast, the EMP model does provide guidance on the purpose of construal—*motive sharing*. First, consistent with recent findings, the model posits that observer construal of actor display serves an important purpose for the observer (Mumenthaler & Sander, 2012). Specifically, observers try to decide whether the actor *shares their motives* in the given context where the emotion is displayed. Following from Wharton and Erickson's (1993) work, motive messages from emotive displays signal social inclusion. Second, consistent with Russell's (1994) critique, the model separates internal "positive and negative" responses from external emotional displays. Specifically, *integrating* displays send a message that "all is well" socially—that we are safe with one another because we share motives. *Differentiating* displays, however, signal that we do not share motives—that we are in potential conflict with one another (Bechtoldt, Beersma, Rohrmann, & Sanchez-Burks, 2013). Thus, others' emotive displays serve as discrepancy tests to which we differentially attend (Roesch, Sander, Mumenthaler, Kerzel, & Scherer, 2010) and that steer us toward or away from one another.

One of the important implications of this is that actor displays may also be deliberately altered or hidden in order to signal this same "motive sharing" message (Jones et al., 2003). For example, an actor may display a "self-conscious" emotion (e.g., pride or shame) that signals social inclusion (motive sharing), even though there is no underlying acceptance or rejection of the observer. Similarly, in complex social contexts, emotive perception itself may be inaccurate. In particular, motive inferences may be based on variables other than accurate construal of emotional displays. Poker players often rely on this.

So, where do group members get their notions about the emotions displayed by others, if not from the other's emotions themselves? One possibility is that internalized situational expectations "trump" actual actor motives when observers try to make sense of emotional displays in weak situations. In particular, *display rules* (Allen, Pugh, Grandey, & Groth, 2010) may be the bases for motive inferences (Ashforth & Humphrey, 1993; Jones, 1997a; Mann, 2007). Display rules are norms for emotional displays in stronger, scripted situations, such as service interactions in restaurants. We expect

Figure 6.3 Emotive Perception model in complex contexts

others to display emotions in the situations where we know the display rules (Mann, 2007; Rafaeli & Sutton, 1987).

One way to think of this is that, once display rules are internalized, people carry a strong situation around with them. Norms provide clearer expectations for how people are "supposed to" behave, based on our own understanding of the situation. And emotional display norms tell us a lot about who to approach and who to avoid in everyday, weak situations.

It is important to note here that it is not the emotions alone that give people cues about motive. It is people's construal of the situation that may lead to (1) their expectations about emotional displays (display rules) and (2) their inferences about others' emotions. Figure 6.3 describes this idea that people use their own appraisals of situations to make sense of the emotions they see in others. This suggests that situation contingencies may lead to "ghost" observations of actor emotions that the actor did not in fact experience or try to display. Observers may go "back up the inference chain" only as far as the social context to make inferences about motives expected, ignoring emotions observed in certain circumstances (e.g., where motives and situations are complex and the observer is unacquainted with the actor). This is consistent with studies of leadership perceptions, where schema consistent information is remembered and embellished (Cronshaw & Lord, 1987; Nathan & Lord, 1983), and schema inconsistent information is simply not noticed.

So, in weak social situations, it may be very difficult to develop accurate understandings of others' motives without expertise about both the situational contingencies and the person being observed. This sort of social situation expertise may be at the basis of the idea of emotional intelligence. Its practical applications are only now being explored.

> Poker players (and other people involved in competitive gambling) go to great lengths to try to mask emotional arousal. Why would this be? The answer may seem obvious to those who have done this sort of gambling, but try answering it for yourself! Now try to "hide" your own emotional displays to others in a group. Ask your group members to tell you what they think you are trying to hide. It's not easy either to hide or to see emotions sometimes. What are the characteristics of the person having the emotion (and trying to

> hide it) and the observer that might affect how well you hide and make sense of emotions? Are certain emotions harder to hide than others? Are there situations where it might be harder to "fake" or hide emotions?

Application of Internalized Motivational Contexts

Emotional display rules have received very limited attention, even though they were brought to light in applied research (Brotheridge & Grandey, 2002; Rafaeli & Sutton, 1987). Still, these may have important applications for people directly involved in efforts to alter decisions. Perhaps the most obvious implication is that particular emotional displays may be expected in a given situation. This should not come as a surprise to those who had held service roles, except that it may only occur with unacquainted observer–actor pairs. Knowing how to get people to feel "part of the group" or "ostracized" can be a powerful tool for change.

A less obvious implication is that, if we wish to influence emotions experienced by observers (e.g., investors, students, voters), managing perceptions of the social context itself may create some important (1) expectations about emotions and (2) attributions about motives. The broader idea is that, when unacquainted individuals interact in motivated circumstances, it may be important to consider aspects of the context (e.g., problem definitions and motivational contingencies) that define expectations of stakeholders. The display of appropriate emotions represents expertise about norms *in a specific situation*.

This is certainly consistent with the popular notion that "appearances matter" in social contexts and that much of leadership is actually theater—setting the stage is essential. What may be more surprising is that the expectations that are set by a particular stage may be defined in terms of expectations about emotions to be displayed, rather than the expected motives, which are internalized by cultures and scripts. Going a step further, if we know how to display unexpected emotions, we may send a powerful message without a word being said (Jones & Parameswaran, 2005). If we are trying to change motives, we may be able to do so directly, through emotive displays.

A second application following from the EPM is that, in order to influence social interactions (e.g., to enhance motive sharing), it may help simply to manage emotional display norms among group members. This is consistent with evidence in the literature on prejudice and attitude change (e.g., Crandall et al., 2002), where strongly expressed norms affected inclusion and exclusion.

At a deeper level, structuring group interaction in such a way that they get to know each other's actual motives, apart from inferences from emotive displays, may be valuable. Discussion itself has been shown to influence group effectiveness (Samuelson & Watrous-Rodriguez, 2010). Similarly,

Libby, Trotman, and Zimmer (1987) found that group members' recognition of expertise among themselves enhanced group performance. Finally, and consistent with considerable management literature, clearly stating motivational contingencies in complex situations may help to reduce misunderstandings, as when leaders articulate task structure (Burke et al., 2006) or articulate strategic contingencies (Robinson, Lloyd, & Rowe, 2008).

Applied psychology has also provided effective ways to get at internalized contexts, particularly in I-O psychology. We saw in Chapter 3 how situational judgment tests and emotional intelligence are applied ways to measure internalized understandings of social contexts. An important method for developing an understanding of behavior in context is through direct behavioral simulations and experiences. The *assessment center method* is a particularly relevant example of these (Thornton & Rupp, 2006). In assessment centers, situational experts observe candidates for selection, promotion, and development engage in a series of job related (context specific) simulations. Participants' behaviors are then evaluated by the situational experts, and feedback is provided to participants.

Even though they are based on very flawed human judgments, assessor predictions have been shown to out-predict almost any other predictor measure (Schmitt, Gooding, Noe, & Kirsch, 1984), often over considerable time spans (Howard & Bray, 1988). Future job promotion and success, life satisfaction, and efforts to develop relevant knowledge have all been successfully predicted by assessment center ratings. One prominent explanation for this is that assessors incorporate their complex understandings of social contexts (like the ones being simulated) when they make judgments about the effectiveness of individual behavior in a simulation of the social context (Jones & Born, 2008; Klimoski & Brickner, 1987). Evidence partially supports this, since assessment centers appear to predict outcomes above and beyond predictions made by intelligence and personality measures (Thornton & Rupp, 2006).

Research on emotional intelligence (Salovey, Caruso, & Mayer, 2004) provides another promising approach to applying social context expertise. Jordan et al. (2010) were among the first applied psychologists to call for an understanding of how we internalize social contexts through emotional intelligence. Similar to the assessment center research, some measures of emotional intelligence add explanatory power to measures of intelligence and personality alone (O'Boyle et al., 2011).

Although the applied research on effects of internalized social context are not well organized, the broad and fairly advanced work on the use of norms and values in basic environmental and social psychology provides guidance. In particular, persuasion research provides effective means for directly manipulating behavior using social context. Again, this carries significant problems in terms of ethical science based practice. However, existing training and development methods may also educate people about the social contexts of schools, organizations, and other social entities—though this is not always what they are explicitly aimed at doing. We will see more about

Decision Processes

Consensus is still evolving among social cognition researchers regarding the processes through which authority, conformity, norms, culture, and emotive perception affect behavior. Much of the research in this area suggests, consistent with the heuristic explanations in Chapter 2, that we rely on various fundamental rules to save ourselves from effort under conditions of ambiguity, and when there are time and resource constraints. Researchers who subscribe to this explanation argue that we follow simplifying rules (Cialdini, 2012; Goldstein, Cialdini, & Griskevicius, 2008, 2011; Goldstein, Griskevicius, & Cialdini, 2011) to guide our behavioral choices. Among these are the rules of *reciprocity, commitment and consistency*, and *social proof.*

Social proof relies on the broad heuristic that, if we simply behave like the people around us, we will generally make the correct behavioral decision. This social referencing heuristic is used to explain authority and conformity effects. Reciprocity is a basic social rule that requires us to return in kind what others have given to us. Cialdini argues that reciprocity is fundamental social glue (see Cacioppo & Hawkley, 2012). If you give me something of value, I am obligated to repay you. It can be applied to things as simple as a smile: If you smile at me, I feel an obligation to smile back at you. But this approach has also been used specifically to increase pro-environmental behaviors (Goldstein et al., 2008).

Once we have reciprocated, the *commitment and consistency* rule takes a place in social cognitive processes. This is the idea that we "keep our word" to others, but goes considerably deeper, and is more generalized than just verbal commitments. In simplified terms, once you have made a commitment—explicit or subtle—it is expected that you will reliably (consistently) conform to it in general—not just in the situation where you made the commitment. For example, Cialdini (1988) showed that, if you could get people to put a "don't litter" sticker in their home's front window, they were more likely later to agree to larger pro-social gestures in order to remain consistent with their initial commitment. In fact, research suggests that this social cognitive process may even lead us to broadly define our actions around such commitments (Cialdini, 1988; Reno, Cialdini, & Kallgren, 1993).

There is considerable evidence to support these social-cognitive process explanations. There is also a more recent explanation that is compelling and particularly worthy of note in the quest for increasing pro-environmental behavior. Reicher, Haslam, and Smith (2012) have shown that decisions to follow authorities and to conform to group pressures may be a result of *social identification* with the group (or leader). To the extent that we see ourselves as belonging with a group or a leader, we will be more likely to conform and obey (Reicher et al., 2012). This is consistent with the very old notion that we seek to belong—to be connected with others similar to ourselves (Walton, Cohen, Cwir, & Spencer, 2012).

It is also consistent with the repeated finding in social cognition that attributional tendencies rely on the groups to which a person belongs. If we are watching someone who is "one of us," we tend not to make internal, stable attributions for undesirable outcomes quite the way we would for strangers (Finney & Helm, 1982; Kassin & Baron, 1985; Robins et al., 1996). Alternatively, our tendency to disparage ability and character is consistent and strong for those who we see as members of "the other group" (Kassin & Baron, 1985).

But social identification is a double edged sword. When it comes to effective group decision making, identifying with a group may lead to dysfunctional *conformity*, *social loafing*, and *process loss*. We have already seen how social referencing and conformity can lead to silence in elevators. Social loafing also occurs in ambiguous group situations where people make less effort toward tasks than they do when the group is absent (Albanese & Van Fleet, 1985; Karau & Williams, 1993). Other potential problems of group decisions include *risky shift* (the tendency of cohesive groups to polarize toward extreme positions) and *groupthink* (the tendency of group members to self-censor dissenting views). These are more controversial than conformity effects (Aldag & Fuller, 1993; Belovicz & Finch, 1971; Isenberg, 1986; Mullen, Anthony, Salas, & Driskell, 1994; Watson, Michaelsen, & Sharp, 1991). But certain kinds of group *process loss* phenomena can sometimes lead to poorer decisions than decisions made by the best individual in the group alone (Aldag & Fuller, 1993; Henry, Kmet, Desrosiers, & Landa, 2002; Miner, 1984; Mullen & Copper, 1994).

Applied Group Decision Processes

There is a growing literature that attempts to counter the process losses brought about by social interactions. Interventions such as the stepladder technique (Rogelberg, O'Connor, & Sederburg, 2002), assigning a devil's advocate (Greitemeyer, Schulz-Hardt, & Frey, 2009; Valacich & Schwenk, 1995), recognition of expertise (Henry et al., 2002; Henry, Strickland, Yorges, & Ladd, 1996; Libby et al., 1987), group salience (van Dick, Stellmacher, Wagner, Lemmer, & Tissington, 2009), and perspective taking (Galinsky, Maddux, Gilin, & White, 2008; Hoever et al., 2012) have all shown promise as ways to decrease process loss in applied settings. Most of these rely on basic research showing that (1) face to face discussions increase effectiveness (Samuelson & Watrous-Rodriguez, 2010) and (2) giving voice to minority views changes the way people think (Galinsky & Moskowitz, 2000; Greitemeyer et al., 2009). After discussing these underlying processes from the basic research, we will see how they function as applied approaches to group decisions.

The last century has shown quite clearly how social *minorities* can make deep and lasting change (David & Turner, 1996; Wood, Lundgren, Ouellette, Busceme, & Blackstone, 1994). Research on *minority influence* has shown that minorities influence majorities in two general ways: *Conforming* and *normative* effects. We have already discussed conforming influence. In the case of minorities, conforming influences typically make reference to existing norms (Maass & Clark, 1983). For example, Reverend Dr. Martin Luther King, Jr. appealed to Christian ideals and norms in his call for equal rights for African Americans. If you believe in the first commandment of traditional Western religions ("Love thy neighbor as thyself"), and define "neighbor" as other people in general, then conforming Christians should treat African Americans equally. Jim Crow laws were obvious examples of unequal treatment for many white Southern Christians—hence a conforming minority influence affected many people to change behaviors and, ultimately, laws regulating these behaviors. Using psychological concepts, these new laws translated conformity (shared values) to authority influences (laws).

Normative minority influence occurs when consistent and relatively extreme minorities change people's underlying attitudes and behavioral intentions (Downing et al., 1992; Martin, Martin, Smith, & Hewstone, 2007; Wood et al., 1994). Early in the U.S. civil rights movement, Reverend Elijah Mohammed founded the Nation of Islam, which took a consistent and extreme position toward discrimination of the white majority that exerted control in the United States. The "Black Muslims" (as the Nation of Islam is sometimes called) argued, for example, that all white people are the devil to be shunned based on their skin color. The clear message to those who were exposed to this worldview was that hatred based on skin color is a foolish notion—one that pervaded U.S. society at the time that the Nation of Islam was founded. Arguably the most famous Black Muslim was Malcolm X, who is still considered a hero by many.

Class exploration. Greenpeace and the Nature Conservancy are examples of groups dedicated to preservation of natural environmental resources. Greenpeace has famously taken action in the Pacific by attempting to directly intervene to stop nuclear tests by the U.S. and French governments. By sailing ships to sites of nuclear tests before these occur, Greenpeace activists disrupt governmental attempts to destroy ecosystems. Their attempts culminated with an explosion that sank their ship, the *Rainbow Warrior*, and implicated the French government in the explosion.

The Nature Conservancy uses private funds and partnerships to acquire environmentally sensitive land in attempts to preserve and protect various species and ecosystems for posterity. Their success as an organization has been recognized by many awards and has a rapidly growing endowment. This group operates under the assumption that choices about how to use land are the sole right of land owners.

> How do the approaches of these two organizations relate to norma-
> tive and conforming minority influences? Can you identify evidence of
> behavioral or attitude changes as a result of their efforts? Use the web
> to help answer this question. How strong is the evidence of their
> success?

The basic research has shown some of the processes through which minority influences occur (Moskowitz & Chaiken, 2001; Wood et al., 1994). Based on this research, situational strength and individual differences both have demonstrated effects (Bettenhausen & Murnighan, 1985; Richeson & Ambady, 2003), with much left to know about both. However, applied scientists working toward sustainability (or any other practical outcome) need to consider ways to internalize norms. Having one's own "compass" (internalized norms) in the face of weak situations may make a difference in people's ethical behaviors. It bears repeating that norms strongly predict behavior (Bamberg & Möser, 2007; Cialdini, 2003; Harland et al., 2007). They are internalized social inputs that affect behavior and thinking. This important lesson for applying social psychology to problems of sustainability will be revisited in the final section of this chapter.

It is also important to notice that these effects rely on the power of the group. It should come as no surprise then that efforts to deliberately give minority views a voice through group pressures have a positive overall effect on group decisions. The interventions mentioned above (i.e., devil's advocacy, recognition of expertise) try to give minorities a voice, but they may also be altering norms in two ways. First, they are ways to deliberately establish a group norm for giving all members a voice. Second, because they give minorities a voice, there is a greater chance for subsequent minority (normative) influence to occur.

So, how do we develop norms that support sustainability (within ethical boundaries)? It will require the remainder of this chapter and both of the next two to try to answer this applied question. An important starting place is to frame the question based on a clear eyed understanding of current psychological science. Specifically, the relationship between social context and behavior is complex. In the simplest terms, the effect of context on behavior is *moderated* by individual inputs (i.e., individual differences in knowledge, skills, abilities, attitudes, and motives). This is referred to as the "person by situation" interaction.

Person by Situation Interaction

In Chapter 3, we saw how the individual differences that people bring with them to situations can affect their actions. In this chapter, we have discussed the direct effects of situation on behavior through such things as conformity, authority, and norms. So, we return to the question of which of these—individual traits or situational pressures—has the larger effect when trying to predict behavior? Do situations trump individual differences or will our traits find ways of expressing themselves, regardless of the situations in which we find ourselves?

The various answers to this question come mostly from basic personality and social psychology research (see Mischel, Shoda, & Mendoza-Denton, 2002; Sherman, Nave, & Funder, 2012, for recent examples). The complexity of the answers is mirrored in the many ways that scientist-practitioners develop interventions to enhance well-being and effectiveness in all parts of our lives. One area of applied psychology is particularly illustrative of the importance of this distinction: The combined effect of person and situation on behavior is the main reason that industrial and organizational (I-O) psychology has both I and O components in its title. The I side is concerned with changing individual behaviors in jobs (through selection on the basis of traits, training of skills, etc.) and the O side with changing the situation (through leadership, motivational interventions, team building, etc.). In fact, I-O psychology is sometimes considered a branch of *applied social psychology*.

Returning to basic research, the first answer to the person–situation question comes from the idea of an *interaction effect*. Interaction effects are used to describe the combined effects of two variables on an outcome of interest. Interactions occur when the effects of one variable (A) on another (B) are changed by the level of a third variable (C). This third variable (C) is called a *moderator*, and interaction effects are sometimes referred to *moderated relationships*. Figure 6.4 describes this set of relationships.

Using the systems perspective, interactions are analogous to valves and switches in engineering. Without the intervention of a valve, water flows down a pipe between points A and B in Figure 6.4. When the valve intervenes (closes), the connection between A and B is stopped. Similarly, with an electronic switch, electrical current flows from A to B when the switch is on, but not when it is off.

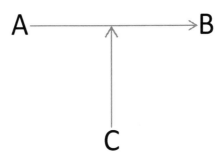

Figure 6.4 Depiction of an interaction effect, also known as a moderated relationship

SOCIAL CONTEXTS

Following from what we have discussed already in this chapter, the effects of individual differences (A) on behavior (B) are moderated by the degree to which a situation (C) is high or low on some characteristic. In our ongoing example, situation strength is a similar valve or switch: Open the valve (weak situation) and individual differences (A) affect behavior (B). When the valve is closed (strong situations), the relationship between individual differences and behaviors is "shut off:" The effects of the situation trump the effects of the individual differences that the person brings to the situation (de Kwaadsteniet et al., 2006; Galinsky et al., 2008; Sherman et al., 2012).

Moderated relationships and interaction effects have a long history in psychological research. They started with the relatively simple notion in early social psychology that personality affects behavior when the situation allows it. For example, people higher in openness are more likely to try new foods when the foods are available. However, most experimental examples are probably oversimplifications, due to the actual complexity of both individual difference and situation effects on behavior.

Attitudes

Basic research on the formation of attitudes provides a somewhat more complex view of the interaction processes through which individual and situation combine to affect decisions and behavior (Petty, Wheeler, & Tormala, 2013). Attitude change has been studied extensively, mostly under the heading of *persuasion*. As we discovered in Chapter 4, attitudes fit uncomfortably under the heading of *individual differences*. Like skills and knowledge, they are more malleable than personality, values, and abilities (Petty et al., 2013). But the process through which we are persuaded show that attitudes can be changed relatively permanently—and are thus similar to individual differences—when we are persuaded through substantive processing. But, situational forces can also change attitudes fairly quickly without our careful processing, as well.

Most of us think of behaviors following from attitudes: We carry an attitude with us and behave accordingly. This deterministic understanding is not surprising, given what we learned in Chapter 3. But, it turns out that there are times when we behave first, which then results in a change in our attitude: Behavior precedes attitudes. This is explained using several processes under the heading of *cognitive dissonance* (Festinger, 1957; Gawronski, 2012).

The primary basis for cognitive dissonance is *cognitive inconsistency* (Gawronski, 2012). Most of the time, our actions are consistent with how we see ourselves. For example, you see yourself as environmentally aware and you generally behave accordingly. But what happens when we behave in ways that do not conform with our notions of self? For example, you generally recycle and try to ride your bike, rather than driving to work. But, one day you get angry at someone cutting you off in traffic and deliberately

156

toss a can out the window of your car. Now, your behavior is inconsistent with how you see yourself.

For many people, this inconsistency between your notion of who you are and how you behave leads to cognitive dissonance, where your actions are inconsistent with your attitudes. Evidence is good that, in many circumstances, inconsistency and cognitive dissonance cause changes in how we feel about things—our attitudes. In the case of angry can throwing, you might decide that you are more worried about injustices in the world than about the environment.

Another example of cognitive dissonance is used as a way to get people to form strong commitments to causes (a type of attitude). *Insufficient justification of effort* (Cialdini, 1988) occurs when people put forth effort for a cause without proportionate reward. For example, hazing often produces this attitude change. A new recruit, who has volunteered for the armed forces, goes through a very stressful and exhausting basic training. After the experience, the recruit reports far greater commitment to the cause of this branch of the military than before joining.

Cognitive dissonance uses the social cognition of the recruit to illuminate this attitude change. The realization that the stressful social situation was chosen (i.e., a behavioral choice), without sufficient justification, requires an explanation. Deterministic thinking provides this explanation: The recruit concludes that he or she must really care deeply about the country and this branch of the armed services. Perhaps it is not a surprise that among the most rigorous of the armed forces basic training is the Marines—whose motto is "*Semper Fidelis*," meaning "forever faithful." What started as a more or less instrumental choice (i.e., getting paid, having a place to stay, and food to eat in return for joining) turns into a deep moral commitment—a value.

Deciding to be part of a group—to take on a *social identity*—often involves similar cognitive dissonance effects, where behavior is followed by attitude change. The ultimate effect is typically the internalization of a group's norms, values, and display rules.

Applied Person–situation Complexity

Using cognitive dissonance to change attitudes is fairly common (Cialdini, 1988). However, scientist-practitioners may be cautious about relying on deliberate manipulation rather than measurement. The *trait activation* approach provides one such measurement based approach. Trait activation (Mischel et al., 2002; Tett & Burnett, 2003) provides arguably the most complex applied description of person–situation interactions. It may ultimately prove useful in a wide range of applied settings.

Tett and his colleagues (Tett & Burnett, 2003; Tett & Guterman, 2000) suggest that measureable characteristics of the social environment determine which personality traits are likely to be manifest and how they are manifested. Following from earlier work by Robert Hogan (Hogan & Roberts, 2000; Hogan & Shelton, 1998), Tett and Burnett (2003, p. 502) define personality as both "intraindividual consistencies and interindividual uniquenesses in propensities to behave in identifiable ways in light of situational demands." This means that personality is not strictly a set of internal traits, but also tendencies that are perceived by other people in various social situations.

Trait activation involves the sorts of direct (input) effects of both traits and situations we have already discussed. In addition, trait activation proposes specific "situational demands" that can be measured and used to characterize work situations. These include (1) job demands—expectations regarding more or less rewarded traits (e.g., the duties listed in a job description); (2) distractors—situational features that divert people toward expressing unrewarded traits (e.g., time spent socializing apart from work demands); (3) constraints—features that reduce the ability to express traits (e.g., limited opportunities for social interaction); (4) releasers—discrete events that allow for the expression of otherwise constrained traits (e.g., a work retreat); and (5) facilitators—events that make information that already exists in a given situation more likely to elicit traits (e.g., telling someone that they have great social skills in a certain social situation).

Job demands include many of the internalized characteristics we have discussed so far, including norms. Job demands are also a way to "lump" situational strength under a single heading. Specifically, the reward contingencies of job demands may be obvious (e.g., getting fired for displaying certain traits) or quite subtle (e.g., being socially ostracized by certain members of the work group by violating implicit norms). The obvious contingencies define "strong" situations, and the more subtle ones "weak" situations. However, the other four characteristics provide some new ways to measure, manipulate, and control situational contexts.

Another way to understand trait activation is through what we have already learned about how abilities can interact with situations through internalized expertise. Application of trait activation to these non-personality traits appears fairly straightforward. Specifically, the intelligence–performance relationship tends to lose some power after a fairly short time, in strong situations (i.e., in relatively straightforward tasks). Although mental abilities do appear to be stable themselves, recall that they are defined partly in terms of how readily people learn about their situations (Sternberg, 1997). Thus, people higher in mental abilities are more able to change behavior to adapt to contexts. So, paradoxically, it is not how changeable individual differences are across an individual's lifespan that may matter. Rather, it is whether, over time, they help us to adapt and change. This is consistent with an interaction of situational demands and ability to meet these demands—consistent with a person–situation interaction.

Tett and Burnett provide an impressive list of evidence suggesting the value of applying personality trait activation hypotheses across many work situations, including assessment, hiring, training, team building, and situational analyses. It is beyond the scope of this chapter to go into detail, since use of trait activation in applied settings is fairly recent (Shaffer & Postlethwaite, 2012). Readers interested in applying some of these ideas to the five criteria are encouraged to read more about this approach and its potential applications (Tett & Burnett, 2003).

It is also important to note that the internalized aspects of context we have discussed (situational expertise, norms, culture, values, attitudes, and social identity) appear to be missing from trait activation. However, some of these (especially norms and values) are commonly assumed to be part of the basis for personality (Hogan, 1998); some are just not explicitly discussed in the trait activation model. Nevertheless, trait activation is used to explain the complex effects of personality and motivation, not abilities or learned expertise.

Applying the Interactionist Perspective to Sustainable Behavior

As mentioned earlier, there is evidence that norms are important for predicting pro-environmental behaviors (Cialdini, 2003; Robertson & Barling, 2013; Smith et al., 2012). In fact, when it comes to PEBs, there is considerably more research on these inputs from the social situation than on inputs like individual differences, learning, or culture. This represents a major disconnect with traditional applied psychology, where individual differences, situational learning, and culture are mainstream areas for intervention. The relationships between these interventions and norms are there, but norms are not the focus of interventions, even in group and leadership interventions (Robertson & Barling, 2013).

There is, however, a growing list of applied interventions that influence pro-environmental behaviors. A recent meta-analysis concluded that it is too early to be definitive, but that "treatments that included cognitive dissonance, goal setting, and social modeling" were the most effective (Osbaldiston & Schott, 2012). All three treatments are means to *internalize* situational characteristics. We have already seen how cognitive dissonance does this. Similarly, we saw in previous chapters how goal setting is based on the notion that people learn the contingencies of their situation and self-regulate accordingly. Social modeling is an application of the social referencing we have already discussed.

It should also be noted that the authors of this study were clear that different outcomes were differentially affected by different interventions and that sample sizes were too small to allow for strong prescriptions. It is also unclear how these internalized contextual inputs may combine with individual characteristics, following from the interactionist perspective. Nevertheless, this is an important first step for applying what we know about person–situation combinations to PEBs.

Even with ongoing work on trait activation, direct application of interactionist psychology to sustainability and many other criteria has been slow in coming. Again, this might simply be because the situation tends to overwhelm the effects of individual characteristics on behavior. However, there are a few notable exceptions. The first of these is *power* (Galinsky et al., 2008). People who possess greater power (perceived ability to control situations) are somewhat less likely to succumb to situational pressures—they tend to conform to their own inclinations. The other, which we have already seen, is culture (Boer & Fischer, 2013; Chen et al., 2006; Grinstein & Nisan, 2009), which can exert greater influence than the situation depending on characteristics of both person and situation. Boer and Fischer in particular showed the complex interplay of various aspects of context (economic, ecological, and cultural) with values and attitudes toward pro-social behaviors. Finally, Nigbur et al. (2010) showed that individual characteristics and social norms in a neighborhood combined to influence curbside recycling.

Application of group process research has also been slow in coming, despite its widespread use in applied settings. However, Velden, Ten Beersma, and De Dreu (2007) showed how decision rule effects on decision outcomes are moderated by pro-social motivations of group participants. Similarly, Wade-Benzoni, Tenbrunsel, and Bazerman (1996) showed how group discussion could reduce the effects of egocentrism when people make choices in an environmental resource dilemma. While only a first study along these lines, these are consistent with the other work incorporating the interactionist perspective into predicting PEB (above).

Given these findings (Chen et al., 2006; Grinstein & Nisan, 2009; Nigbur et al., 2010; Osbaldiston & Schott, 2012; Velden et al., 2007)—that internalized aspects of context have powerful effects on PEBs—a promising approach is to consider other internalized aspects of context, as well. When do values, social identity, and situational knowledge influence our tendency to think and behave in ways that take into account multiple stakeholders in a distant future?

Social context, Social boundaries, and Predicting the Five Criteria

1. **What prompts people to think they have a problem (or not)?**
   Values, norms, culture, social identity, and other internalized aspects of social context can influence PEBs (Cialdini, 2003; Tracey, 2005)—but only when people see that there is a problem (Nordlund & Garvill, 2002). Paradoxically, we tend to rely on social information to decide whether we have a problem: People who identify with the people

communicating the "we have a problem" message are more likely to see the problem as "real" than those who do not identify with the source of the message (Langner, Hennigs, & Wiedmann, 2013). At the very least, social models we observe can influence our behavior, whether we see a problem or not (Langner et al., 2013).

In fact, the power of the social situation on behavior need not rely on any answer to the "do we have a problem" question at all. For example, Tyler, Orwin, and Schurer (1982) showed that people were less "susceptible to norm-based messages about energy consumption when the personal costs were lower than when they were higher." When PEBs got expensive, people found "reasons" for not seeing a problem. Whether people continued to act in an environmentally friendly fashion was left unmeasured in this study, but the message is clear: We will succumb to situational pressures, even when our norms direct us otherwise. This is an example of a person–situation interaction used to explain the perception of a problem.

Direct inputs from social contexts (authority, conformity, and norms) are undeniably important. But they are also problematic for any scientist-practitioner psychologists interested in ethical decision making. Deliberate, direct manipulations of powerful contextual inputs without informed consent of the targets of these manipulations should be considered extremely carefully, and with the engagement of all legitimate stakeholders. Anything less than this holds potential for ethical breach. Social psychologists who venture into applied settings intending to apply such tools (i.e., consumer psychologists) need to take their cue from ethical codes of other scientist practitioner fields, such as educational psychology, clinical psychology, and I-O psychology, among others.

As a case in point, Cialdini (2003) has warned against the use of purely descriptive norms for trying to communicate that there is a problem. When people are informed that there are many others who are polluting, this suggests that it is the norm—it is OK to pollute. He argues that, "Only by aligning descriptive norms (what people typically do) with injunctive norms (what people typically approve or disapprove) can one optimize the power of normative appeals." Processes for identifying injunctive norms provide an excellent opportunity for engaging stakeholders. In other words, it is a good idea to ask people what they think before you act.

Turning this question another way, perhaps it is important for people to understand that there are powerful, ethically questionable attempts to persuade us daily. Basic social psychological research has contributed enormously to the variety and power of persuasion techniques available (see Knowles & Linn, 2004). But, when advertisers, talk shows, and politicians deliberately employ social-psychological manipulations without our informed consent, perhaps we need to see a problem where we didn't see one before. The type and number of persuasion attempts directed at consumers every day suggests that such an increase in awareness is warranted. We will discuss this further in Chapter 10.

Some of the more promising interventions discussed in this chapter are aimed at processes that alter problem identification. Group process interventions such as devil's advocacy require one member of the group to deliberately identify possible problems with a course of action. Perspective taking (Galinsky & Moskowitz, 2000) is an example of an individual level attempt to consider flaws in one's own approach to a situation. Similarly, making people aware of their own vulnerability to social persuasion manipulations may help reduce the effects of these manipulations (Sagarin, Cialdini, Rice, & Serna, 2002). Other ways of developing such deliberate problem identification processes at the individual level will be discussed in Chapter 7 when we consider self-regulation. Mindfulness (Scott, 2009), feedback (Steg & Vlek, 2009), double-loop learning (Argyris, 2002), and other applied interventions will also be discussed in later chapters.

2. **What makes people think more or less carefully when they decide on an action?**

Such process interventions also increase decision processing time at both the individual and group levels. It is clear, however, that situational pressures as *inputs* can directly reduce decision processing. Strong situations elicit heuristic processing, in the absence of clarifying cues. A famous example of this is from the Kitty Genovese murder, where over thirty people watched the brutal murder of a young woman in New York City. However, later research suggested that having one person who identified that there is a real problem and established another individual as responsible tended to reduce this effect (Cialdini, 1988).

Consistent with the applied research we reviewed earlier, well managed processes can enhance decisions, where strong situational inputs can impair them. For example, in Chapter 4, we saw the conditions under which homeowners would move from their homes in wildfire prone areas. Differences in knowledge about risk directly predicted the information people relied on in this relatively strong situation. Specifically, less knowledgeable residents succumbed to social pressures, consistent with a strong situation. Conformity trumped individual inclinations. Better informed residents were more likely to be deliberative in both their thinking and their actions.

Framing group processes in terms of situational knowledge provides parallel findings that support the power of *internalized* contexts. For example, groups that have knowledge of one another's areas of expertise are perhaps more likely to get complete information about situations before making decisions. Similarly, well-managed group conflict may accomplish a similar increase in integration of perspectives (Samuelson & Watrous-Rodriguez, 2010; Tjosvold, 2008). Presumably, differences in group knowledge sharing increase deliberative processing and lead to better decision outcomes. Thus, knowledge of the situation may reduce situational strength effects, as we saw in the discussion of internalized situational knowledge (Libby et al., 1987).

Finding ways to assess people's situational expertise may be a good place to start *before* trying to apply situational pressures. We have now visited the assessment center method, which is used for selection and development in many organizations (Thornton & Rupp, 2006). If emotive perception is the dancing bear behind assessment centers, then methods for honing our emotive perception skills should help size things up before we try to intervene. In the last few chapters, we will see how important it is to assess what the people around us do and don't know about their situation before we step in.

3. What makes people change the way they think and behave?

In addition to managed group processes that lead to learning based change, group effects that elicit heuristics can also change attitudes through cognitive dissonance. Similar to the double edged effects of norms (Cialdini, 2003), change and learning effects may have unintended or even deliberate negative consequences. So it is sensible to realize at this point that learning and change are neither positive nor negative in themselves, but can be used in both ways, or even be neutral in effect.

Two things are fairly clear, however. The first is that some things are readily changeable (as we have discussed under this criterion before) and some are not. Developing a social identity, openness, intelligence, and culture/values are mostly the purview of parenting and education. We will discuss these "slow changing" variables in Chapter 7. The second sensible suggestion, which is new to this chapter, is that greater awareness can sometimes trump even the effects of culture and conformity. Helping people successfully navigate the contingencies of their contexts may itself be a powerful aim of social-contextual interventions. Chapter 8 will describe some ways to develop situational expertise.

If our social contexts make the importance of the natural environment more readily apparent, then the internalization of the norms of this social context may have profound and fairly immediate effects on behavior. Given this, it is not surprising that norms have received so much attention as predictors of pro-environmental behavior. One important study (Chen, Lupi, He, & Liu, 2009) has already demonstrated the effectiveness of social norms for influencing sustainable farming practices when coupled with monetary rewards.

But this does not solve the problems of finding ethically viable ways of internalizing social norms. Inviting stakeholder engagement, including informed consent, and assessing current situational knowledge should reinforce deliberate efforts to change people. Educational experiences may work better once these initial steps are implemented. The chapters on interventions (9 and 10) will deal with some ways to internalize norms.

What is apparent again from this chapter is that inclusion and the conflicts that sometimes accompany integration across social identities can lead to change under some circumstances. Realizing effective, ethical change will rely on managing conflicts between social identities. Identifying and managing potential conflict through the group processes discussed earlier are some of the ways to affect change.

4. When are people likely to take action?

It should be clear from this chapter that most people need to belong to a group. This is a powerful source for collective action. As one successful social activist put it, people may join an action group based upon emotive episodes and cognitive discrepancy tests, but they stay because of attachment and the sense of belonging that comes with membership in a group. This is born out in studies of what motivates people to get involved in environmental action (Cornelissen, Dewitte, Warlop, & Vzerbyt, 2007; McDougle, Greenspan, & Handy, 2011)—being a member of a social group is the best predictor.

But work with social groups requires managing emotive and decision processes, based on an understanding of people's distinct motivations. We have reviewed ground breaking work in this chapter on the management of social contexts to influence behaviors that conserve natural resources. But it is clear that this excellent work on how to use social information to influence sustainable behaviors is just a starting point. Just tapping people's motivation does not ensure sustained, directed, or effective action. In fact, it should come as no surprise that motivating people to take action can be a double edged sword (Cialdini, 2003) sometimes leading to very undesirable outcomes. For example, the need of people with dogmatic authoritarian tendencies to enforce existing norms (Kessler & Cohrs, 2008) can lead to troublesome, conflict laden sorts of action. Gang enforcers do just this sort of "norm enforcement," often using lethal violence.

"Collective narcissism" (de Zavala, Cichocka, Eidelson, & Jayawickreme, 2009) may also be an important source of dysfunctional collective action. Collective narcissism is defined as "an emotional investment in an unrealistic belief about the in-group's greatness" (de Zavala et al., 2009). It is associated with low private esteem, but high public esteem for the group. And it predicts aggression against other groups, independent of authoritarianism. Efforts to alter group members' private beliefs about their group's ability to deal with perceived threats may be one way of reducing the tendency toward collective narcissism.

SOCIAL CONTEXTS

Also, given the answer to criterion question two (deliberative decision making), conformity and authority may work in a given place and time. Internalizing norms, culture, values, and identities so that people acting alone will behave "as if someone is watching" are important "action" objectives of social influence. Perhaps even creating a norm of critical reasoning (Sagarin et al., 2002) is one way to accomplish this.

However, existing culture and norms can lead to very different outcomes, even when the same social influence attempts are applied. For example, Grinstein and Nisan (2009) showed that a deconsumption campaign in Israel worked better for the majority Jewish than for Arab, Orthodox, and other minorities. Being aware of culture and minority status can make a big difference in collective action.

Returning to the point made at the beginning of this chapter, the complex interactions among person and situation variables make applied interventions highly *context dependent*. Going back to the way that applied psychologists often take context into account—by trying to define the specific situation within which interventions are being discussed—is a very practical approach. Broader definitions of context—both external and internalized—remain important. But, as a practical matter, it probably helps to understand the constraints of the particular context within which we are trying to take action. We will return to this problem in the chapters on interventions.

5. **What are the characteristics of change efforts that are likely to work?**
   Such realistic assessments of the contingencies of our social environment are a core part of much applied psychology. Taking things "as they are" and moving forward from there seems obvious, but, as a practical matter creates challenges. For a start, getting our *own* action group to agree to situational assessments—or any course of action for that matter—requires many of the same sorts of influence we have seen in this chapter. Bringing such actions to the community is often even more challenging.

Summary

In this chapter, we have seen how situational constraints can influence action in both "strong" and "weak" ways. Individual differences work better in weak situations, and strong situations are hard to resist. Internalized norms, culture, and expertise may substitute for strong situations, but they vary in the degree to which they are amenable to ethical manipulation. At the very least, applied psychologists have methods for evaluating situational variables before developing interventions. Interventions for problem identification, behavior change, and taking action all require an understanding of effects of the situation, the person, and the interaction of person and situation.

7

DEVELOPMENT, IDENTITY FORMATION, AND MOTIVATION

The Development of Human Systems

The human ecosystem is highly complex. We might even think of ourselves as central structures in a sort of above ground coral reef system, with symbiotic, parasitic, and commensurate relationships with millions of living organisms on a daily basis. While we may not readily recognize our complexity or our interdependence, many living things are decidedly dependent on us, for better (e.g., bacteria that break down waste in our guts) and worse (e.g., cold viruses). And we are also dependent on many of them as a species and as individuals. Modern theories of development are increasingly based on this understanding: We are ourselves complex, natural ecosystems that develop and change around basic structures, as we continuously adapt to our contexts.

We can also think of ourselves as being like many other complex natural structures: We gradually develop inherent asymmetries over time. We have seen hints of these asymmetries in individual difference profiles and in preconscious influences on thought and behavior. Also, like other complex structures, the course of our asymmetrical development is heavily influenced by our attempts to adapt to the contexts in which we have grown and developed. Thus, understanding why we behave in a certain way today relies to a large extent on understanding how our motives in a context have led us to reliably behave this way over substantial periods of time—one way of defining *development*.

In this chapter, we will consider the development and trajectory of human psychological systems. We will first discuss essential principles of the dynamic development of complex human systems. Cognitive, social-emotional, and moral development will be described using dynamic and stage theories, and applications considered along the way. The next section will introduce the concept of identity and its relationship with motivation. As in all of the other chapters dealing with our fundamental tendencies, we will return to the five criteria at chapter's end.

Throughout, we will see how developmental *processes* occur at the *boundaries* of ourselves and our contexts. Examining these person–context boundaries from a developmental perspective will uncover new ways of looking at the motivations that are key to our stable formation—and to the ways we change. Ultimately, we will consider how our asymmetrical development can, in turn, affect natural and social contexts, and how deliberate efforts to influence development and motivation might be used to help us to adapt as a species.

Key Issues in Developmental Psychology

Most of the applications of developmental psychology are in educational (e.g., Fox & Riconscente, 2008; McDonough, 2005; Suggate, 2010), clinical and counseling (e.g., Carthy, Horesh, Apter, & Gross, 2010; Lent & Hackett, 1994), and forensic psychology (e.g., Kuppens, Laurent, Heyvaert, & Onghena, 2012). These applications, like most, are concerned more with "what works" than with "why things work."

This is a particular problem for developmental psychology, for at least three reasons. First, the majority of developmental research has historically focused on children, adolescents, and older adults—not so much on young and middle adulthood, which combined is the largest group in the human population. Common approaches to development look at the individual, familial, educational, and cultural variables that affect development of mental, social, and moral systems through childhood and adolescence (e.g., Pachur, Mata, & Schooler, 2009). Much of this work suggests that, unlike learning, development is characterized by qualitative changes that occur as dramatic shifts, especially in childhood and later life (Crain, 2000).

In some ways, this is good news for efforts to influence sustainable human thinking and behavior: There are interventions in childhood and adolescence that can exert powerful influences. There are also interventions that can affect fairly dramatic shifts at any age. But the focus on times of dramatic life changes *does* create problems in terms of the *sorts of motivations* that are more or less common in middle adulthood versus childhood and later life (Erikson, 1968; Heckhausen, 1997; Heckhausen, Wrosch, & Schulz, 2010; Kanfer & Ackerman, 2000; Shanahan, Hill, Roberts, Eccles, & Friedman, 2012). Motivations play a key role in dynamic development (Bandura, 2012; Dweck & Leggett, 1988), which is why motivation will be covered at length in this chapter.

A second application issue is that basic research in developmental psychology is concerned with the social and cognitive *processes* through which we *become*, rather than with simply how we *are*. Basic research in developmental psychology is focused on how and why things change over (sometimes extensive) periods of time, not how we can use current circumstances to effect change in the short run. Since much applied psychology is directed at relatively short term effects, the best we can often do is take development into account, rather than trying to significantly alter its trajectories, at least in adults.

Still, this being versus becoming distinction can be helpful when applied psychologists help to develop and implement *interventions*—deliberate efforts to change how people think and behave. First, taking the *long view* is often necessary in practice. Understanding in advance that change can be unpredictable, iterative, slow much of the time, and sudden at others can help to keep efforts on track in the face of frustration. Second, we have seen that scientifically based interventions often rely on an understanding of the system *dynamics* through which people *change*. In this chapter, we will define dynamic change in terms of (1) how people develop through the lifespan; (2) how to characterize and (where possible) measure people's current developmental trajectory; and (3) what common issues are important to people as a result (boundaries, relationships, and self-regulation).

Interventions that take the long view try to account for *dynamism*, and target developmentally appropriate motivations may be more likely to effect change. But application is often more expedient. That is, what "works" in an intervention may occur "on average," and despite any careful description of where people are in their development and motivational tasks (Baumeister, 1989). Because this book is about applied psychology, we therefore run the risk of short changing developmental processes, mainly by concerning ourselves more with how things *are* at a point in time than with how they are evolving.

In order to integrate developmental *becoming* with current states of *being*, we will rely on several expedients. In particular, the development of self-regulation, mindfulness, and identity will provide much of what we need to know for applications—"on average" and at a given state of being. We will also focus on the areas that relate to these: Emotive, cognitive, and social development. Motor development is less relevant to our applications.

The third problem for applying basic research is the proliferation of theory in developmental psychology (Haase, Heckhausen, & Wrosch, 2013; Rutjens, van Harreveld, van der Pligt, Kreemers, & Noordewier, 2013). We will deal with this by relying mostly on dynamic theories, consistent with the systems perspective taken throughout the book. Stage theories will be discussed, but we will start by understanding the dynamics of *ontogenesis*.

Ontogenesis

Most textbooks on developmental psychology use the "nature versus nurture" debate to frame human development, and separate development into *stages* based on common sensory-motor, cognitive, socio-emotional, and moral milestones. While the nature–nurture debates have led to substantial advances in basic research (cf. Hastings, Zahn-Waxler, & McShane, 2006),

DEVELOPMENT AND MOTIVATIONAL SYSTEMS

they have somewhat less value from an applied perspective. Scientist-practitioners typically manage without close consideration of nature–nurture explanations.

Stages are to some extent another story. Werner's principle of ontogenetic development (Werner, 1957), along with later, related theorists (Dawis & Lofquist, 1976; Thelen, 1995; van Geert, 2000) can be used to describe and understand development *without* reference to concrete milestones (stages) or nature/nurture dualism. Stages of development are sometimes used to categorize people for applied purposes, so we will learn about them, as well. But Werner and other dynamic theorists provide a broadly applicable, flexible approach to understanding the ongoing development of human systems through the entire lifespan (Franklin, 2000; Nsamenang, 2006; Siegler & Chen, 2008). This is why we will rely on ontogenetic processes.

Ontogeny and *ontogenesis* are terms that are broadly applied to the origins and development of human systems. According to Werner, ontogenesis occurs through the engagement of two underlying processes: *Differentiation and integration* (Werner, 1957). Differentiation is the process that occurs as thinking, emotive responses, and moral reasoning move from *simple and clustered* to more *complex and specialized* forms. Integration occurs as these systems are grouped together into well defined, complex systems. These two processes merge into a unified process of change that can occur, often unpredictably, through the course of development (cf. Thelen, 1995; van Geert, 2000). Recent work suggests that these complex, fluid dynamics can be used to describe human development in terms of *self-organizing systems* (Jones & Parameswaran, 2005; Thelen, 1995; van Geert, 2000). In simplified terms, we develop asymmetries and specific behavioral tendencies through the interactions among internal elements (especially abilities and motives) and external events.

Hard work versus innate talent? Introductions to developmental psychology often rely on the nature–nurture dialectic. However, there is a natural tendency to attribute ability versus motivation when we try to explain the causes of great accomplishments. In the arts, sports, business, and science we can all think of examples of people who have reached the top of their fields.

Think of an example of a person in your favorite art, sport, or other area of endeavor, then try to answer the following questions:

1. Why is this person great at what he or she does? Now think about the *process* through which this person became *great* and *continued* to be

> (or not). How did this person become great? Share your explanations with each other in a small group.
>
> 2. Did your explanations for why your chosen individuals *are* great (question one) differ from your explanation for how they *became* great (question two)? Did ability or motivation enter into your explanations?
>
> 3. Was there a tendency in your group to attribute success to ability in *why* they are great and to motivation in *how* they got that way? If so, then you are thinking of this person in terms of an ontogenetic, self-organizing system. In particular, this approach starts with some "basic" ability that was developed and maintained because of motivations.

Cognitive development provides some good illustrations of the ontogenetic principle (Siegler & Chen, 2008; Tideman & Gustafsson, 2004; van der Maas & Straatemeier, 2008). The idea of the "naive scientist" has been used to illustrate this. People use their experiences over time to develop differentiated mental understandings of the external world (Clary & Tesser, 1983; Kuhn, Cheney, & Weinstock, 2000), in much the same way that science itself progresses (Figure 1.2). As we come to understand cause and effect relationships in the contexts within which we operate (Beilin, 1996), we develop an increasingly complex, specific understanding of the contingencies of behavior there.

Differentiation and integration can also be used as simplifying explanations for social development (Werner & Kaplan, 1963). Early in social development, individual behavior is based on simple interactions and varies little across situations. Infants cry at their caregivers when they are hungry, regardless of their social context. As we reach an understanding of the simple contingencies of contexts, we begin to differentiate behavior. As we grow into later childhood, we learn to conform to the conventions of the context through social referencing. This means that our social behaviors are hard to separate from the context in which they occur (see Cole & Wertsch, 1996). However, Werner and Kaplan (1963) argued that *distancing* also occurs as people develop into adulthood: We establish and define a separate, *individual identity* (Dweck & Leggett, 1988; Kulik, Sledge, & Mahler, 1986; Markus & Wurf, 1987). In addition, as we learn the contingencies of multiple contexts, we may even further differentiate our social behaviors based on our knowledge of a social context (Jones & Rittman, 2002). Again, ontogenesis occurs: We integrate context *into* our identity (Arnocky, Stroink, & De Cicco, 2007; Markus & Cross, 1990; Markus & Kitayama, 2010), while differentiating behavior by social context.

Stages of Cognitive Development

Piaget's *stage* approach to cognitive development (Piaget, 1970) adds valuable content to the ontogenetic approach. Piaget used children's errors in thinking to demonstrate how thinking develops as children grow. Key changes in the types of errors children made were used as milestones to distinguish *stages of cognitive development*. Piaget's stages start with *preoperational* cognitive development in early infancy, where children are largely unable to separate what they *perceive* from what is actually *present* in the world around them. The most famous example of this *undifferentiated* world view comes from Piaget's demonstration of object permanence. When an object is hidden from an infant, the infant no longer recognizes its existence—the infant has no *mental representation* of the object. Predictably, children learn to mentally represent objects in memory when trying to manipulate and explain events. Piaget labeled this ability to *differentiate* between perceived and actual objects *concrete operations*. Once the child was able to integrate groups of objects and events into clusters of contingent relationships (what Piaget called assimilation), people have reached the stage of *formal operations*. The hallmarks of formal operational thinking are the abilities to think in analogy and use abstract reasoning—both of which are *integrative* processes (using Werner's ontogenetic term).

But formal operations probably continue to develop after childhood, which may explain why we teach and practice critical reasoning in colleges (Dunn, Halonen, & Smith, 2008; Kuhn et al., 2000). In fact, complex mental representations of the outside world are a defining feature of *expertise* (Ganzach, 1994; Kaplan, 1990). First, expertise relies on a highly developed, differentiated view of the complex empirical system. Experts demonstrate the ability to accurately recognize particular situational contingencies (Ganzach, 1994; Linhares, 2005), and to accurately predict and manipulate outcomes based on these contingencies (Linhares, 2005): Experts know "what leads to what" in the empirical world. Experts are also better at clustering aspects of the situation appropriately (Ganzach, 1994)—to *integrate* characteristics common across situations (Gobet & Simon, 1998; Linhares, 2005).

> We have seen that people are often not inclined to rely on scientific expertise. This appears to run counter to the "expert = right" heuristic. One possible explanation for this is that we often seek expert advice when our heuristics are not working. And experts have a highly differentiated view of the empirical system—a view that most people do not share or understand. If we go beyond heuristic processing and ask experts for their advice, we often face this differentiated understanding head on. So, instead of getting strong, causal advice from experts, we often receive complex, highly conditional information to

help with our decisions. We may want to hear a simple set of contingencies: "If you do A, you will get B infallibly." Instead of giving us a new (preferably simple) rule to guide our decisions, experts tell us that "If we do A, we may get B *if the circumstances are such and so.*" Put another way, experts try to explain their complex, differentiated view. Unless we have a somewhat differentiated view of things ourselves, accepting and following expert advice may not seem to conform to the "common sense" heuristics we often start with.

There have been important critiques of Piaget's and others' stage theories (Brainerd, 1978; Lourenço, 2012; Rutjens et al., 2013). But the evidence for stages of *cognitive* development is relatively strong (Barry, 1978; Dudek & Dyer, 1972) and consistent enough with the principles of ontogenesis to add important content to the systems approach.

Applied Cognitive Development

Development of formal operations and advanced systems thinking is part of the reason for higher education (Davies, 2011; Kuhn, 2011; Songer, Kelcey, & Gotwals, 2009). It is almost certainly part of the reason that you are reading this book, for example. Trying to apply what you have learned about basic research areas of psychology to issues in your own life requires the ability to "abstract" the concepts and principles here with the specific problems you are dealing with in life. However, the fact that we are assumed to need many years of formal education is testimony to the presumed stability of cognitive stages. Once we have reached concrete operations, for example, it may be quite some time before we are able to move to formal operations, if we are able to do so at all. This presents a significant problem for interventions aimed at advancing development.

The ability to abstract—to operate formally through differentiation and integration—is also an essential skill for most professional areas of endeavor. This may explain why we need even more formal training to become applied psychologists, health providers, lawyers, and members of other professions. Professional training often includes entire classes on ethical reasoning, presumably to enhance our moral reasoning, as well. Such reasoning, as you know, is not always easy or fun and often requires difficult trade offs in professional practice.

One application of cognitive development is not obvious. It connects to the early work of Jean Piaget, who is arguably the most influential developmental psychologist to date. Piaget's interest in the development of

> reasoning in children was preceded by an early applied psychologist, of whom Piaget was aware (Smith, 1994). Alfred Binet had won a contract with the French government to devise a test to place children in the appropriate school grade. Using an interview not unlike Piaget's method for determining cognitive development, Binet did just that. Although it was altered dramatically by later applied researchers, his test became the first mental abilities measure (Hothersall, 1995).

From another viewpoint, professional education might be thought of as an attempt to develop situational expertise (cf. Moore, 2004). We learn the complex contingencies of the situations we will likely encounter in practice. But even from this perspective, there is an assumption of some prior level of cognitive development before we are able to develop such expertise (Kanfer & Ackerman, 2000). The elaborate processes employed to screen students for most professional training programs is testimony to this assumption: It takes a long time to learn, so schools only accept those applicants who are most likely to learn essential expertise in the relatively short time available.

Again, this treatment of development as a trait is commonplace. In the case of cognitive development, even early in education, stages of development are used as preconditions for different learning experiences. As you can see in the box above, mental abilities tests were originally devised to manage this problem for children in the education system. Early in life, interventions to increase mental abilities do make a difference (e.g., Protzko, Aronson, & Blair, 2013); later, these abilities are much more stable (Deary, Whalley, Lemmon, Crawford, & Starr, 2000). The conventional view is that intelligence can be altered only through genetics or by teaching parents to create a stimulating early childhood environment (Devlin, Daniels, & Roeder, 1997; Protzko et al., 2013).

Modern applications of mental abilities follow from this assumption of stability, as we saw in Chapter 4. Such testing is widely used for selecting and placing students and employees (Farr & Tippins, 2010; Ones, Viswesvaran, & Dilchert, 2005), for reaching decisions about defendants and inmates (Diamond, Morris, & Barnes, 2012), and for draft pick numbers in major league sports (Herring, 2012).

In addition to the long term interventions we group under the broad heading of education, there are still attempts to influence mental ability after early childhood. Several recent studies (Ackerman & Kanfer, 2004; Ackerman, Kanfer, & Beier, 2013; Von Stumm & Ackerman, 2013) suggest that intellectual abilities are at least partly a result of *motivated investment* in developing component abilities and skills. People who have reasons to develop their abilities do so. These researchers have demonstrated the relationships between motivational variables and mental abilities scores (Duckworth, Quinn, Lynam, Loeber, & Stouthamer-Loeber, 2011; Rich & Woolever, 1988). They have also shown how the combination of abilities and investment measures are predictive of success (Ackerman et al., 2013).

One of the more influential notions in recent educational research also relates the development of cognitive abilities through motivation. Learners need to see what they are learning as meaningful to current or future life tasks (Kuhn, 1990; Noe, Tews, & Dachner, 2010). For example, you may not care to learn about sustainable development unless you see that it matters to your own interests. You need a reason to develop expertise. Again, the contention that we can (and do) develop mental abilities over time, *based on our desire to do so* runs counter to the generally accepted view of intelligence as a very stable trait (Deary et al., 2000). Not surprisingly, short term interventions to change general mental abilities are not common after early childhood.

Development of Other Cognitive Traits

Applications to other aspects of cognitive development are perhaps more common, particularly in clinical and health psychology. Recent techniques have targeted the development of *metacognition* through clinical interventions (Wells, 2009). In particular, techniques derived from meditation (Eberth & Sedlmeier, 2012) are used to reduce trait anxiety (Chiesa & Serretti, 2009), depression (Piet & Hougaard, 2011), and pain (Igna, 2011). Although these interventions are aimed at emotive outcomes (Chiesa & Serretti, 2009), their approach is an attempt to bring people to higher levels of perspective on their own thinking. For now, we will focus on their use for cognitive development, then see how they are applied to socio-emotional development in the next section.

In fact, cognitive development is defined partly by the ability to take *perspective* on lower levels of developmental functioning (Wenar & Curtis, 1991). Metacognitive methods (such as *mindfulness* and *acceptance* therapies) are based on efforts to "develop enhanced awareness of moment-to-moment experience of perceptible mental processes" (Igna, 2011). Given what we know about the apparent stability of cognitive abilities, the development of this cognitive ability through relatively short therapy seems unlikely. But, the results of this approach are quite impressive (Galante, Iribarren, & Pearce, 2013; Piet & Hougaard, 2011; Veehof, Oskam, Schreurs, & Bohlmeijer, 2011).

Perhaps the most dominant intervention in all of psychology for the past few decades has been Cognitive Behavioral Therapy (CBT; Cristea, Montgomery, Szamoskozi, & David, 2013; Mitte, 2005). This highly effective therapeutic approach alters the way that distressed people of all ages think

DEVELOPMENT AND MOTIVATIONAL SYSTEMS

about their own emotional responses, motivations, and behaviors (e.g., Kowalik, Weller, Venter, & Drachman, 2011; Piet, Würtzen, & Zachariae, 2012). From a developmental perspective, CBT attempts to alter cognitions about *self* through (among other things) metacognitive awareness of the factors that affect one's emotional responses (Mischel, 2004).

The CBT approach is consistent with two important lessons learned from developmental psychology. First, there is a complex interplay among cognitive, social, emotional, and moral development (Kennedy, Felner, Cauce, & Primavera, 1988). These act as a single system, and effective interventions need to consider the interrelations involved. Second, despite using a relatively short intervention period, CBT relies on developing metacognitive perspectives and self-regulatory changes. This attempt to get people out of the "hickory nut" of their "normal" state may explain why CBT has a powerful influence on people's well-being. Essentially, CBT helps people to learn to relate to *themselves* differently.

Although CBT is widely used for therapeutic interventions, mindfulness and perspective taking remain frontiers for applied sustainability research (Amel, Manning, & Scott, 2009; Reysen & Katzarska-Miller, 2013). One possibility here is that people's ability to take perspective on themselves (e.g., emotional intelligence) provides the same tools as those required to take perspectives on broader issues (Reysen & Katzarska-Miller, 2013), such as their relation to future people and the natural environment. We will return to this idea when we discuss identity and motivation.

Socio-Emotional Development

The case for stage theories is quite problematic in socio-emotional development (Decety, Michalska, & Kinzler, 2012; Winefield & Harvey, 1996). This makes the concepts of differentiation and integration perhaps most applicable for predicting development of these systems. In fact, dynamic theories have been the focus of much recent research (Bandura, 2012; Markus & Cross, 1990; Olson & Dweck, 2009). These tend to be fairly complex (Pratkanis & Greenwald, 1985), so we will begin with a straightforward analysis of *emotional development*.

Srofe and Waters (1976) articulated the case for understanding emotional development as one part of cognitive development. As infants, behavioral responses to emotions appear to come directly from our mammalian brain (i.e., the limbic system). They are not filtered, or mediated, by the inhibitory functions that develop over time in parts of the cerebral (outer) brain (Decety et al., 2012). As we mature, we learn that the contingencies of our emotional expressions are not so simple. For example, infants often get what they want by smiling and crying—simple emotional displays. But, once our caregivers see us as able to use words and move around on our own, these simple displays may not always get us what we want. Instead, we learn to

DEVELOPMENT AND MOTIVATIONAL SYSTEMS

try to *control* emotive displays to get what we want (Spinrad, Stifter, Done-lan-McCall, & Turner, 2004). We recognize these social-emotional relationships at a very early age (Johnson et al., 2010).

The development of such emotional *self-regulation* may depend on the circumstances in which we are operating (Eisenberg, Duckworth, Spinrad, & Valiente, 2012), again suggesting that we can differentiate our thinking and behavior according to contexts (Jones & Parameswaran, 2005). Even though emotional self-regulation may have a strong dispositional component (Järvenoja, Volet, & Järvelä, 2013), it can be learned, particularly early in life (Kanfer & Ackerman, 1996; Zelazo & Lyons, 2011). The large number of clinical interventions aimed at affecting it attest to this (e.g., Zimmerman, 2008).

It may be that what continues to develop as we experiment with self-regulation is our understanding of context. We discover "what works" based on emotional displays in a context and attempt to change our behavior accordingly (Järvenoja et al., 2013; Lamm & Lewis, 2010). This is consistent with the idea of internalizing contexts from Chapter 5—a complex *integration* of self with context (Markus & Cross, 1990; Markus & Kitayama, 2010). This process is partly learning rather than development, so we will return to it in Chapter 8. But it is also related to the more gradual development of identity, and we will learn much more about it soon.

An example at the highly differentiated end of socio-emotional development is the career diplomat. This job requires knowledge of the social and emotional protocols (norms) for multiple, complex social situations in different cultures, and differentiation of behavior accordingly. Thus, *situational expertise* is again definable through ontogenesis.

To elaborate further, social development can be defined in terms of the *motivated* development of personal and social identity (Dweck & Leggett, 1988; Markus & Cross, 1990; Mohr, 1978). Recall that some of the elements we internalize in the formation of identity are the norms, values, and culture of our social context. But identity researchers go beyond these social components of identity to include the elements we use to define our personal identity, as well. These include a host of variables, including beliefs about our own competence (Bandura, 1978), the goals or life tasks we pursue (Baumeister, 1989; Dweck & Leggett, 1988), categorizations of self—who we are and who we are not (Markus, 1977; Pratkanis & Greenwald, 1985), and future expectations of self (Markus & Nurius, 1986).

Again, internalization of social context guides the *direction and effort* we place toward self-regulation (Heckhausen & Schulz, 1999). In other words, our *motives* help define identity in much the same way they help us learn to walk. We learn to control our behaviors based on feedback we get in different situations (Bandura, 1978; Carver & Scheier, 2012a; Pratkanis & Greenwald, 1985). This behavioral control in turn helps us to get what we want and avoid what we don't want for ourselves and for others (Zimmerman &

Moylan, 2009). How we "typically" behave is often the basis for self-definition—for identity. Thus, the ongoing formation of identity is driven by motivations through life.

The finding that motivation often changes through the lifespan (Heckhausen, 1997; Heckhausen et al., 2010; Markus & Kitayama, 2010; Shanahan et al., 2012) may be important in practice. The capacity for motivational change at all ages suggests that social development, and particularly identity development, is a promising target for intervention. It is generally understood that harnessing motive is a vital component for changing people's outward behavior. But it is also an important basis for deeper changes in identity. When we address the problem of defining motivation later in the chapter, we will see that harnessing motive can be very tricky (Dweck & Leggett, 1988; Kulik et al., 1986; Markus & Kunda, 1986).

The development of healthy adult identity also involves the differentiation of self from context—the development of *boundaries* between ourselves and others (Burris & Rempel, 2004; Fisher, 1985; Levin & Unsworth, 2013). However, much of the research on social development refers less to the formation of boundaries than to the obverse—the formation of attachments (Fearon, Bakermans-Kranenburg, van Ijzendoorn, Lapsley, & Roisman, 2010; Van Ijzendoorn & Kroonenberg, 1988). Patterns of *secure, avoidant,* and *ambivalent* social attachment appear to be formed early in life, based on patterns of parent–child attachments and to be remarkably consistent across time and social relationships (Roisman & Grohl, 2011; Schneider, Atkinson, & Tardif, 2001; Stroebe & Archer, 2013).

This finding that patterns of attachment are consistent across long periods and across relationships suggests that there is not much developmental change in attachment after childhood. Even criticisms of the evidence on attachment patterns (see Roisman & Grohl, 2011; Schneider et al., 2001) suggest applications simply try to control for this relatively stable characteristic. Perhaps this explains why adult disorders of attachment and boundaries (i.e., personality disorders) tend to be difficult to change through most current clinical interventions (O'Connor, Spagnola, & Byrne, 2012).

Despite the stability of *attachment patterns,* however, there are interventions aimed at changing how people manage the social components of their individual identities. To the extent that people require themselves to conform to unrealistic expectations that were originally imposed by families and other important social groups, they may experience serious, lifelong difficulties (Portes, Sandhu, & Longwell-Grice, 2002). We will discuss interventions that affect such *internalization* problems shortly, when we consider clinical applications of development.

Applied Socio-Emotional Development

Applications in socio-emotional development include many of the same interventions derived from cognitive development. Direct interventions to advance development (especially in clinical and counseling) and to manage adjustment through stages (e.g., in grief counseling) are common practices. Less direct interventions, such as measures of individual differences, are also widely used, as we have seen. These measures define levels of development in order to simply treat them as limiting factors in more direct efforts to change (e.g., professional education, job training).

Again, some of the most important of the direct interventions come from clinical and forensic psychology and aim to develop and manage *self-regulatory* processes. Many of the developmental successes and quandaries we experience result from attempts to maintain control of our social world (Bailie, Kuyken, & Sonnenberg, 2012; Carver, La Voie, Kuhl, & Ganellen, 1988; Zimmerman, 2008). On the one hand, the emotional problems people experience (especially depression and anxiety) may result from self-regulation. People tend to set high standards for their own and others' behavior (Carver et al., 1988). These unrealistically high standards are typically internalized from childhood experiences (Klassen, Tze, & Hannok, 2013) and are associated with anxieties about the consequences of not meeting them (Cole, Peeke, Martin, Truglio, & Seroczynski, 1998; Sportel, Nauta, de Hullu, & de Jong, 2013). Failure to meet sometimes unrealistically high standards is associated with a negative view of oneself and resulting depression (Portes et al., 2002; Sowislo & Orth, 2013). Once again, clinical interventions (especially CBT and mindfulness) have shown considerable success in managing these problems (Roemer et al., 2009).

On the other hand, many problems of social development come from inadequate self-regulation. Framed variously as *self-control, impulse control, delay of gratification*, and *self-regulation* (the term we have been using), these are defined mostly in terms of motivation and behavior (Burnette et al., 2013; Duckworth & Kern, 2011; Lanaj et al., 2012). For purposes of application, the usual interest here is in increasing the tendency of people to be deliberative about the way they act on impulses—what we have framed as criterion question two.

Once again, training and therapy that target mindfulness have shown impressive results (Orme-Johnson, 2000). Starting in childhood, caregivers can help children develop metacognitive skills, including empathy (Miller & Eisenberg, 1988) and mindfulness (Zelazo & Lyons, 2011), as means to enhance self-regulation. Along similar lines, training caregivers themselves to engage in mindfulness while interacting with children can lead to healthier forms of attachment (Snyder, Shapiro, & Treleaven, 2012). In schools, contextual features that motivate self-motivated learning are an essential challenge (Gaeta, Teruel, & Orejudo, 2012). Mindfulness interventions here aim to get students to choose to do their own, self-regulated learning based on personal goals (Gaeta et al., 2012; Harris, 1990). Interventions also use mindfulness to enhance self-regulation over violent behavior (Gillespie, Mitchell, Fisher, & Beech, 2012), anxiety (Roemer et al., 2009), and general stress responses (Brown & Ryan, 2003; Zelazo & Lyons, 2011).

DEVELOPMENT AND MOTIVATIONAL SYSTEMS

The success of these interventions for increasing effective self-regulation is mostly with children. Important aspects of self-regulation are learned early in life (Razza & Raymond, 2013) and persist across the lifespan (Mischel et al., 2011). Once again, such stability suggests that we treat certain parts of self-regulation as individual differences when we address criteria two (deliberativeness) and four (taking action).

Clearly, self-regulatory applications have important implications for moral as well as social development. Self-regulation often makes it easier to get what we want (and to avoid what we don't) as *individuals*; it is instrumental rather than altruistic. But self-regulation is also part of altruistic action (Loizzo, 2012) and moral behavior (Gillespie et al., 2012; Mischel & Mischel, 1994; Vallerand et al., 1992). As we will see when we consider motivation, altruism is defined at least partly by how we regulate our social behavior to meet others' interests, as well as our own.

Socio-Emotional Applications in Non-Clinical Populations

We saw in Chapter 3 that selection on the basis of people's socio-emotional development has taken on greater importance in recent years. The application of measures of emotional intelligence and personality are often directed at controlling social behavior in schools and workplaces.

More direct attempts to alter socio-emotional development rely heavily on a *facilitated approach* (Buenaver, McGuire, & Haythornthwaite, 2006; Košir, 2005; Kuk, 2000; Orme-Johnson, 2000; Shibbal-Champagne & Lipinska-Stachow, 1985). Facilitation involves more than just the presentation of topical material accompanied by practice and feedback. It relies on the presence and monitoring of a professional, often with expertise about both the change processes being used and the empirical research pertaining to such processes. Furthermore, most facilitated experiences take time.

A prominent example of a facilitated intervention with particular relevance to criteria three and four comes from work on *intercultural development*. *Intercultural sensitivity* is defined as differences in people's "orientations toward cultural difference" (Hammer, Bennett, & Wiseman, 2003). Lower levels of intercultural development are defined in terms of three *ethnocentric orientations*, where people define their reality entirely in terms of their own cultural experiences. Higher level intercultural development is defined using three *ethnorelative orientations*. Ultimately, ethnorelative orientation involves meaningful integration of other cultures with one's own—inclusion under criterion four.

Interventions aimed at advancing from ethnocentric to ethnorelative social development have shown some success (DeJaeghere & Cao, 2009; Endicott, Bock, & Narvaez, 2003). Facilitated processes appear to work better than unfacilitated experiences for these (Pedersen, 2010). Less obvious is that facilitation shares a core aspect of many successful interventions. We will see in Chapter 8 how *assessments* are used for *feedback*, both about people's initial state and about their changes.

For now, it is also important to recognize the role of stage theories in such facilitated interventions. In particular, *stage norms* can also be used to help clients (1) define where they are heading in the change process (goals and criteria); (2) recognize the progress they are making (through feedback); and (3) provide strategies and develop habits for future self-regulation. For example, the feedback you get from tests and quizzes does just this. This should make it clear that facilitated self-regulation interventions more generally are a means to develop metacognitive approaches to behaviors and choices.

An Application of Attachment

There is evidence that *place attachment* (Halpenny, 2010; Kudryavtsev et al., 2012; Scannell & Gifford, 2010b) may provide an important avenue for applications (Hixson, McCabe, & Brown, 2011; Wolsko & Lindberg, 2013), as well. We have seen that early parent–child attachment patterns are quite stable across later relationships. While these patterns have never been tested with respect to secure, insecure, and ambivalent attachments to *place* (Minami, 2009), it is clear that people form attachments with places (Hernández, Hidalgo, Salazar-Laplace, & Hess, 2007; Scannell & Gifford, 2010a), including defining their own identity partly by reference to places (Chow & Healey, 2008; Prochansky, Fabian, & Kaminoff, 1983; Scannell & Gifford, 2010b).

Most of the research on place attachment and place identification has implicitly taken the individual differences approach: It is measured as an attitude or trait (Lewicka, 2011; Liu & Sibley, 2004). It appears to include several dimensions, and various researchers have taken different approaches to its definition (Chow & Healey, 2008; Hernández et al., 2007; Hixson et al., 2011; Raymond, Brown, & Weber, 2010; Scannell & Gifford, 2010b). It has also been correlated with other traits (e.g., openness, Wolsko & Lindberg, 2013; ecocentrism, Needham & Little, 2013) and recent research has shown that it predicts intentions with respect to the environment (López-Mosquera & Sánchez, 2013; Raymond et al., 2011; Scannell & Gifford, 2013), independent of more general *altruistic* intentions or identity (Hinds & Sparks, 2008).

However, measures of place attachment appear to behave more like attitude measures than more stable individual differences (Jorgensen & Stedman, 2001; Scannell & Gifford, 2010a). Specifically, place attachment may be less predictive of *behavior* than it is indicative of current *intentions* (Mishra, Mazumdar, & Suar, 2010; Raymond et al., 2011) and reactions (Devine-Wright, 2011; Devine-Wright & Howes, 2010; Vorkinn & Riese, 2001). In fact, anti-environmental behaviors appear to occur *regardless* of attachment or identification with place (Hernández et al., 2010). Although there have been no meta-analyses published to date, it appears that people's desire to remain near a place (*proximity maintaining*) in order to do the things they wish to do (*purpose fulfillment*) are the clearest behavioral correlates of place attachment and identity. So, like other attitudes, place attachment may actually be a surrogate for motivation.

On the one hand, treating place attachment as an attitude may explain why there has been less interest in the variables that lead to its development (Hay, 1998; Mazumdar & Mazumdar, 2004; Morgan, 2010). Assuming that we are looking for points of entry that may help to influence attachments and their outcomes, this may pose a problem for scientist-practitioners. Several studies have shown variables that may serve as developmental predictors of attachment. These include having spent more time in a place (Devine-Wright, 2011; Filo, Chen, King, & Funk, 2013), enjoying time there (Chow & Healey, 2008; Hixson et al., 2011), being a place of origin versus later arrival (Hay, 1998; Hernández et al., 2007), and various forms of social connectedness (Fried, 2000; Hidalgo & Hernández, 2002; Mazumdar & Mazumdar, 2004; Rollero & De Piccoli, 2010; Uzzell, Pol, & Badenas, 2002). Figure 7.1 provides a heuristic view of some of these variables.

Figure 7.1 Socio-emotional variables affecting and affected by place attachment

> *Discussion.* Many people who have had wilderness experiences will attest to the powerful effects of their experiences on well-being and personal outlook. Share personal experiences you have had in the wilderness and discuss some or all of the following questions:
>
> 1. What was a particular highlight of your experience—something you still remember really well?
> 2. What emotions did you experience during this experience?
> 3. Were you primitive camping (tent without amenities)?
> 4. Were you there with a group? If so, was it family, friends, strangers, or some mix of these?
> 5. How long were you in the wilderness?

DEVELOPMENT AND MOTIVATIONAL SYSTEMS

6. How did you feel when you came back to "civilization?"
7. Did you feel that this experience has changed your view of "civilized" life? For example, are you as picky about the comfort of your body and personal surroundings as you were before the experience?

Often, when you ask someone when the experience occurred, it was during a break from the routines of their everyday lives (Korpela, Hartig, Kaiser, & Fuhrer, 2001). Could this contrast and the removal from ordinary activities account for the effects (Stedman, 2006)? Also, the intense engagement with other people in these environments may be an important part of the experience.

Evidence suggests that people who are permanent residents of a place are more likely to feel attached to it (Kelly & Hosking, 2008; Nielsen-Pincus, Hall, Force, & Wulfhorst, 2010), especially when they have social connections (Fried, 2000; Uzzell et al., 2002). So the effects of such interventions may be short lived. Alternatively, longer times spent in natural places may subtly change the nature of this attachment (Kyle, Graefe, Manning, & Bacon, 2004b), so the effects of time may not be so obvious.

Although there are now useful ways to measure place attachment, place identity, and aspects of context, this still begs an important applied question: How do we deliberately intervene to increase people's attachment to place? If place attachment can be treated as an attitude, it may be possible to alter it using relatively short term interventions.

Tourism research provides some clues for answering this question, as the box above might suggest. For a start, individual differences in biocentrism may predict both place attachment in natural settings and inclination to participate in outdoor experiences (Needham & Little, 2013). So, participants in such experiences are likely to be (1) higher in biocentrism to begin with and (2) "ready" to accept the developmental change that may occur in these experiences.

Second, it appears that such experiences may just lead people to feel good (White, 2012), especially when they are mindful of what is happening during the experience (Moscardo, 1988). So, although there is a "feel good" experience involved in nature, this may simply be an emotive episode (Weiss & Cropanzano, 1996), rather than permanent change.

On the other hand, we have already seen how mindfulness can change cognition and emotive responses, so it may hold promise for longer term interventions aimed to increase (or reduce) place attachment (Vitt. rso, Vorkinn, & Vistad, 2001). Research on place attachment in service environments shows some promise for developing place attachment in fairly short time periods, as well. Social support can enhance attachment to place, at least for people who are feeling isolated in their daily lives (Rosenbaum, Ward, Walker, & Ostrom, 2007). Having a familiar, friendly face may be an important part of guided wilderness experiences, for example.

Findings in educational research bring us back to the idea that *long* experiences in controlled contexts (e.g., semester-long classes) may prove effective as socio-emotional interventions (Semken & Freeman, 2008). Unfortunately, until quite recently, much of the educational research on interventions aimed at increasing place attachment and pro-environmental behavior has relied on case studies (Barth & Thomas, 2012). Such work provides good information about ways that such efforts are developed and implemented, but does not provide as much value for evaluating "what works" in applied settings (including in classrooms). New work is moving toward a better understanding of "how to" enhance place attachment and environmental behavior in classroom settings (Fielding & Head, 2012; Kudryavtsev et al., 2012).

Elaborating briefly about the links in Figure 7.1, however, suggests that current predictors are not readily changeable. Social connectedness (Fried, 2000: Uzzell et al., 2002), the amount of rewarding time spent in a place (Devine-Wright & Howes, 2010; Gifford, 2007b), and whether it is a person's place of origin (Hernández et al., 2007) may not be easy to develop in short time frames. The attachments that form with place may even be intergenerational (Mazumdar & Mazumdar, 2004) and lead to decisions to stay in places that are not seen as highly viable for human habitation (Phillips, Stukes, & Jenkins, 2012). So, while the components of place attachment in Figure 7.1 provide guidance, current efforts at direct intervention are likely to be *context specific*, trying to measure rather than trying to change it (Bonaiuto, Carrus, Martorella, & Bonnes, 2002).

Still, some environmental psychology researchers are taking an unusually applied approach by treating place attachment as a changeable attitude. This reflects the concern for "what works" (versus deep explanation) common in applied research (criterion five). But, we need more research about systematic intervention strategies that can change people's place attachment and identification. Such interventions are important, not just because of their potential to change place attachment, but because they may open new ways for achieving behavior change. For now, we are able to rely on existing place attachment measures to evaluate people's status and devise and monitor change efforts. We will return to this question when we discuss wilderness experiences in Chapter 8.

Moral Development

Moral development is perhaps the most theoretical area of research in developmental psychology. Although there is still some controversy, there is considerable evidence supporting the validity of stage models (Cohn &

Westenberg, 2004; Dawson, 2002; Killen & Smetana, 2006; Walker, Gustafson, & Hennig, 2001; Walker & Hennig, 1997). More importantly for our purposes, the dynamic approach has not been widely used to describe moral development (Kim & Sankey, 2009; Sherblom, 2015).

This is problematic for applied psychology of sustainability for at least a couple of reasons. First, not having a dynamic theory means that applied scientists are faced with "gambling" that they have identified the correct stages and contexts as the basis for action. In many circumstances, measures of stages are problematic (Krebs & Denton, 2006; Van Vugt et al., 2011). Identifying the developmental basis for people's thinking about a situation may therefore be quite challenging. When combined with the larger problem of defining psychological contexts (Chapter 5), trying to effect behavior *in a given circumstance* is complicated.

Second, as we shall see, among the areas of development, questions of moral choice are among the most important to our criteria. Decisions about how to treat others (including future people), how to behave when faced with trade offs and dilemmas, and when to take action in the interest of principles, all rely on moral judgments. Even trying to predict when people will make such choices in a real world setting can be highly controversial (Sackett, Burris, & Callahan, 1989), never mind trying to manipulate others' moral choice processes.

We will fall back on three ways to manage this quandary. First, we will fold moral development into cognitive development using a well supported and commonly referenced approach—Kohlberg's stage model (Colby, Kohlberg, Gibbs, & Lieberman, 1983). Second, dynamic, ontogenetic ideas will be suggested that may help for purposes of application, if not for purposes of future theoretical development. Third, we rely on the common approach taken by applied psychologists—using individual differences to predict and control for moral development.

Kohlberg's Stages

For some time now, Kohlberg's stage model of moral development has been the touchstone to which other models refer. It has received very substantial support (Cohn & Westenberg, 2004; Walker et al., 2001), despite its critics. It follows Piaget's stage model of cognitive developmental (Crain, 2000) and is associated with other cognitive indictors (Colby et al., 1983). The stages in Kohlberg's model are as follows.

Level 1, called *preconventional morality*, bases moral reasoning first on what others (especially authorities) say is right (Stage 1), and later on the trading of behaviors for outcomes (Stage 2). The underlying assumptions of people (mostly children) at this level of moral reasoning can be broken down into the following: What is good for me is "good," what is punished is "bad,"

DEVELOPMENT AND MOTIVATIONAL SYSTEMS

and all I need to do is get others to accept my choices (including through bribery and coercion). Moral good is based on power.

Conventional morality (Level 2) follows the conventions, first of one's identified social group (Stage 3) and then of broader society (Stage 4). The basis for morality in these stages is the maintenance of good relationships. Using concepts from Chapter 5, morality is divined by social referencing and accomplished by conformity. Moral good at this stage is defined by norms—the way things are "normally" is the way things *ought* to be.

Kohlberg called the third level of moral reasoning *postconventional morality*. People who have reached this level of moral reasoning are concerned with principles that balance individual rights against the needs of civil society (Stage 5). In Stage 6, moral reasoning, people seek universal principles that can be used to balance the interests of multiple stakeholders. Stage 6 moral reasoning follows from modern moral philosophy and the principles that guide the ethical practice of psychology.

There have been numerous critiques of Kohlberg's stage theory. Prominent among these is Gilligan's (Gilligan, 1982; Woods, 1996) early critique, which was based on the finding that Kohlberg's method for measuring moral development tended to differ on the basis of gender. She argued that the measurement system that Kohlberg used to assess moral development failed to account for the tendency to orient higher level moral choices toward maintenance of relationships with others, rather than purely abstracted principles. More recently, some have argued that, although people's self-reports of moral reasoning may conform to Kohlberg's stages, their actual behavior is only loosely related to these self-reports (Fearon et al., 2010; Krebs & Denton, 2006). Kohlberg himself has offered modifications based on these critiques (Kohlberg, Levine, & Hewer, 1994).

Class discussion. We now know about heuristics and biases (Chapter 2) and the idea that we have some trouble "seeing beyond ourselves." Developmental stage models pose a similar quandary: How do you know that you are in a given stage without having already passed through it? Have you ever heard someone say something like, "You can't really understand what it's like to [fill in the blank here] until you have actually experienced it?" Try answering the following questions to understand this idea.

Question 1: Think about this from the point of view of moral development. How would you know that you have arrived at a conventional or postconventional stage of moral development?

Comment: In Chapter 4, we saw (following from the Brunswik Lens) how people can arrive at effective decisions pretty much by accident. Think about a time when you did something that others told

DEVELOPMENT AND MOTIVATIONAL SYSTEMS

you was brave or even heroic, but you really weren't aware that you were being brave at the time.

Question 2: Was this a conscious choice or something you did more by impulse or instinct? How did you find out that you were doing something morally good—was it just that others told you so? Did you really agree with them deep down after they told you?

Comment: Now think about how you figured out that this was (or was not) a morally correct or brave thing to do. Presumably, it was at least partly because another person or group reflected back to you that they thought what you did was morally good. Group processes—like this—can provide a mirror like this.

Question 3: Who were the "other people" who let you know that you did something good, even though you may not have recognized it before they mentioned it? Do you suppose this is the way that children also rely on others to help them to recognize what is "good" or "morally right?" If they are at the preconventional level of moral reasoning, what is the basis for deciding another person's notion is correct?

Comment: When you reach conventional moral reasoning, you tend to look at what others are doing, and not necessarily what they are saying, when you decide what's the right thing to do. In other words, you are no longer relying on the word of people with power over you to decide what is right.

Question 4: After watching people in your main social group (the family or other group whose norms you followed as a child) for a time, did you decide than what they are doing was not "right?" If they told you that you did something "brave" or "heroic" would you necessarily believe them?

Question 5: At what age do people usually start to question the wisdom of their elders' and groups' actions? How does this relate to the development of postconventional reasoning? Are adolescents really more moral than their elders? Are young adults more moral than their teenage friends?

Comment: You can see from this discussion that the process of development through moral stages relies on the same sorts of group processes that can lead people to make better decisions than we tend to make based on our own heuristics and biases. You can also see, perhaps, how difficult it may be for people to break away from the power of their caregivers and social groups. It may require taking the viewpoint of another group for a while in order to learn to be critical thinkers. Where might this happen?

DEVELOPMENT AND MOTIVATIONAL SYSTEMS

One of the most difficult quandaries for trying to deliberately increase moral awareness is the finding that people who are at lower levels of moral reasoning don't realize that they are (Gabenesch & Hunt, 1971). This gets back to the "hickory nut" at the beginning of Chapter 5, and the problem of immersion in a normative context (Hammer et al., 2003). "What is normal" is also what people using conventional moral reasoning see as "what is right."

This qualitative difference in understanding is further evidence that moral development does follow a stage sequence, with people in earlier stages by definition unable to understand or behave on the basis of later stages. Because of its association with rigid thinking, social, and psychological problems (McCleary & Williams, 2009; Schultz & Searleman, 2002), trying to get people with authoritarian inclinations to recognize these tendencies in themselves is an important problem (Black & Phillips, 1982).

There are two additional reasons to suspect that, at least in the short term, attempts to change people's moral reasoning may be quite difficult. First, earlier stages of moral development are associated with lower mental abilities (Cohn & Westenberg, 2004; Colby et al., 1983; Heaven et al., 2011; Jacobson & Rettig, 1959; O'Connor, 1952; Songer et al., 2009). As we have seen, learning occurs more slowly for people lower in mental ability (Austin et al., 1989; Gottfredson, 1997). Thus, helping people to function at higher levels of moral reasoning is likely to take longer for the very people who are likely to have problems, when compared to those who develop such reasoning more quickly.

Second, the probable effects of childhood experiences make change less likely. As we have seen, development of our approaches to the world often occur early in life, and they tend to remain stable (Eisenberg, Hofer, Sulik, & Liew, 2013). In the case of moral development, there is some evidence that we tend toward authoritarianism (lower levels of moral reasoning) as a result of punitive and authoritarian parenting (Devereux, 1972; Richardson, Foster, & McAdams, 1998). Bu contrast, altruistic behavior (higher level moral action) appears to be based on affectionate and empathic parenting (Hoffman, 1975). Such powerful early experiences may make later change difficult.

Moral Development as an Individual Difference Variable

Once again, treating moral development as an individual difference helps deal with these problems and avoids the theoretical issues with stage versus dynamic models. We have seen several standards that are commonly applied to individual difference variables, including stability and common use in applied settings. In addition to its relative stability (Eisenberg et al., 2013; Kennedy et al., 1988) and relationships with several applied individual differences measures (Ashton, Paunonen, Helmes, & Jackson, 1998; Cohn & Westenberg, 2004; FeldmanHall, Dalgleish, & Mobbs, 2013; Hilbig, Zettler,

Leist, & Heydasch, 2013; Jacobson & Rettig, 1959), moral development meets an additional standard. Moral reasoning indicators appear to yield normally distributed data (Cohn & Westenberg, 2004; Cummings, Maddux, Cladianos, & Richmond, 2010; Rossano, 2008). That is, there are a few people on one end of the distribution who think only of their own interests, and a few people on the other end whose behaviors are driven by a principled consideration of the common good. This leaves most people trending around the middle level of moral development, where socially referenced (conforming) morality is the basis for behavior. Given these features of moral development, applied researchers may treat moral development as an individual difference (e.g., Johnson, Hogan, Zonderman, Callens, & Rogolsky, 1981; Kennedy et al., 1988).

> *Conformity, authority, and morality.* Given the normal distribution of moral development (as in Figure 7.2), an essential part of moral compass for most people comes from their own circumscribed group. "How things are, is how they are supposed to be" for many people at this stage. The idea of loyalty is one way of describing this—you are morally obliged to help those who are in your group and less so to those outside of it. So, for example, there are numerous stories of otherwise ruthless promulgators of a group's identity paradoxically behaving in a highly chivalrous fashion—toward those who are in their own group, but not to those "outside" their own group (Stürmer et al., 2005).
>
>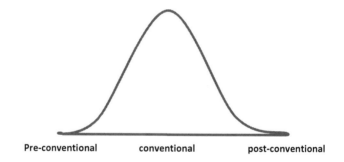
>
> *Figure 7.2* The normal distribution of moral development
>
> For example, the court of Genghis Kahn appears to have been a beacon of tolerance and enlightenment. His many wives practiced their own various religions with impunity, and there was little or no overt violence in his court (Weatherford, 2004). But his reputation in warfare was legendary for its brutality and lack of conscience. When

trying to subjugate other tribes and kingdoms, he followed a very different moral code than he did within his selected group.

A moral compass for people at the lower end of the distribution is their revered authorities—people who are presumed to have reached a "higher level" of moral development. As explained in Chapter 3, authoritarianism may be explained partly in terms of reverence for a "safe" authority and lower level development of moral reasoning. Who we choose to revere, however, may have an enormous effect on our willingness to behave altruistically. Some moral leaders show themselves to be tolerant only to select people, while others model tolerance for those *outside* of their own, circumscribed group.

Altruism as a Dependent Variable

Perhaps the most important aspect of moral development for our purposes is how it motivates people to different sorts of moral behavior. Such behavior is commonly defined in terms of altruism—the willingness to help others (including broader society) at one's own expense and without expectation of return (Khalil, 2004; Yamamoto, 2010). Basic research has provided much to go on when it comes to moral, ethical, and constructive behaviors, including literatures on pro-environmental behavior (PEB) (Markowitz et al., 2012; Story & Forsyth, 2008b), helping and cooperation (Hilbig et al., 2013), forgiveness (Antonuccio & Jackson, 2009), and altruism per se (Miller, Kozu, & Davis, 2001; Snyder & Dwyer, 2013). The important issue for practice is how self-reported behavioral tendencies (like PEBs) are translated into altruistic behaviors (Ewing, 2001; Markowitz et al., 2012).

Altruism appears to increase in childhood (Evans, Athenstaedt, & Krueger, 2013), which suggests that it is a component of moral development (Hastings et al., 2006). This suggests that early "critical periods" are important target periods for interventions to develop altruism. If self-reported PEBs are primarily indicators of stable moral development, then trying to change them may be as challenging as changing some other aspects of development.

Applications of Moral Development

Applied psychology is often more concerned with what people do *in a particular context*, as well. Rather than relying on evidence of broad relationships between self-reported altruism and various predictors, practitioners are faced with idiosyncrasies of a given context. Forensic psychology is particularly rife with examples of the predictors of immoral, unethical, and destructive behaviors (Van Vugt et al., 2011) in the specific contexts of the criminal justice system. Similarly, educational applications are often aimed at predicting and influencing pro-social behaviors (e.g., Samson, Ojanen, & Hollo, 2012) in classrooms. Industrial-organizational (I-O) research also deals with moral, ethical, and pro-social behavior in work contexts (Chiaburu, Oh, Berry, Li, & Gardner, 2011).

Many of the interventions for socio-emotional and cognitive development impact moral development. For example, when people's impulses are illegal or damaging to others (i.e., immoral), effective self-regulation interventions may reduce the tendency for these impulses to translate into action (e.g., Gillespie et al., 2012; Martin, Dorken, Wamboldt, & Wootten, 2012). Similarly, educational interventions for cognitive development may help to bring people from conventional to more principled consideration of other stakeholders (Schlaefli, Rest, & Thoma, 1985).

Moral Education

Given what we've learned so far about perspective taking and stability, it should not be surprising that getting people to think in terms of others' legitimate interests (rather than just their own interests or the norms of their own cultural and social groups) is challenging (Feng, 2012; Feng & Newton, 2012). This has not stopped educational practitioners from intervening to advance moral reasoning (Schlaefli et al., 1985). In fact, this is a point of public controversy (McDonough, 2005; Molnar, 1997). But, Kohlberg's stages are associated with level of education (Dawson, 2002) and ethical reasoning does change through relatively short interventions (Ketefian, 2001; Schlaefli et al., 1985; Tichy, Johnson, Johnson, & Roseth, 2010), so education may already increase moral reasoning without really intending to.

It is important to remember, again, that educational interventions also rely on relatively long periods of exposure in fairly controlled settings. Understanding the *contextual factors* at work here may be particularly important to developing interventions that work outside of the relatively controlled context of a classroom. Given this, an important recent innovation in educational psychology is the attempt to directly measure the *contextual factors* that influence moral reasoning (Maeda, Thoma, & Bebeau, 2009). What is different about measuring moral context is that it attempts to identify specific contextual characteristics that support or impede moral development.

As a practical matter, screening and selecting people for roles where moral reasoning is important may be more cost effective than trying to train people once they are invested in complex contexts (i.e., schools, work organizations, family systems). In fact, interventions that subtly screen for moral development are common (Connelly, Lilienfeld, & Schmeelk, 2006; Sackett & Wanek, 1996). Workplace *integrity testing* is an effective practice for many kinds of employment decisions (Ones & Viswesvaran, 2001). Similar assessments are often used to select people for sensitive and critical jobs on the basis of factors related to moral reasoning (e.g., mental abilities, conflict management skills, integrity, and narcissism). Educational leaders (Schmitt, Schneider, & Cohen, 1990), athletes (Bolter & Weiss, 2013), government and industry personnel (Hogan et al., 1994; Wu & Lebreton, 2011), and security personnel (Bloom, 1993) are sometimes selected based on measures of integrity and moral reasoning.

Many applied psychologists have an overarching concern for moral development. Ethical and effective application of psychology relies on practitioners understanding postconventional morality. Specifically, most areas of applied psychology require ethical consideration of legitimate stakeholders' interests. Effective practice typically starts by identifying stakeholders, then considering their interests through the entire process of intervention. For example, educational psychologists consider the interests of both the schools and school systems they serve, as well as the interests of students and their families. This awareness of the various interests of legitimate stakeholders is a type of *differentiation*. The applied psychologist develops *situational expertise*, often through well established research methods (e.g., clinical interviews, standardized measures of satisfaction, and so on).

Ethical and effective practice also requires skillful *integration* of the interests of different stakeholders. Rather than thinking in terms of "good and bad" and "winners and losers," this involves careful consideration of potential outcomes of decisions. For example, when the client of a clinical psychologist discloses their intent to commit a serious crime, the clinician has a professional responsibility to notify law enforcement authorities (representatives of societal stakeholders), outweighing their responsibility to maintain the confidentiality of the client. If the client commits a crime and the clinician has notified authorities, the clinician's own interest in continuing to provide licensed services is protected. This example has fairly straightforward, legal (versus moral) grounds. More often, principled weighing of stakeholder interests requires creative and nuanced solutions: Principled moral reasoning is thus essential to effective, ethical applied psychology.

Forensic Psychology and Moral Development

As you might expect, scientist-practitioners in the legal system intervene to manage problems of moral reasoning. This may be difficult for certain kinds of criminals, but efforts to enhance self-regulation have shown promise for certain types of offenders (Gillespie et al., 2012). However, in forensic settings, psychologists are faced with the dilemma we discussed early in this chapter. Developmental change is slow, but many of the decisions made by law enforcement, attorneys, judges, and prison personnel need to be made quickly. For most practical purposes, applications assume that moral development is more or less set in adulthood. Thus, the aim is not to alter people's level of moral reasoning, but to set laws and policies given the current level of moral reasoning in the target groups (especially defendants, convicts, and juries). Following laws and internalizing norms are not the same as postconventional moral reasoning. Getting people to *behave* ethically is their aim.

As we have seen, such behavior is often a result of external factors, including enforced laws, norms, and policies. Hence there is a broader interest in managing public policy and law in the interest of enforcing moral behavior using psychological principles. Forensic psychologists have taken on important roles in this venue, as well. In particular, their research has helped policy makers, law enforcement, and other government decision makers make informed policy level decisions. For example, forensic psychology has provided important evidence regarding the effects of legal punishment (Cheatwood, 1993; Gromet & Darley, 2009; Martin et al., 2012). Does it actually deter crime (affect the moral thinking of other, similar criminals)? Does it reduce the suffering of the victims and their families? Does it help to rehabilitate offenders who may be able to make positive contributions, given the right sorts of incarceration experiences? These questions of moral reasoning have sometimes played a prominent role in discussions of criminal justice policies.

Applications of Moral Reasoning for Sustainability

There is a growing research literature on applications of moral development and sustainability (Feng & Newton, 2012; Karpiak & Baril, 2008). Perhaps the strongest evidence in this area is consistent with what we have already seen about moral development: We base moral reasoning (and behavior) on what we see and learn in our families of origin (2012; Thøgersen, 2009). Also, higher levels of moral reasoning are associated with principled reasoning about broader social groups than our families and other immediate social groups (Kahn & Lourenço, 2002).

Consistent with this stable view (Karpiak & Baril, 2008), willingness to accept a broader group as "our own" has also led to the development of individual difference measures. For example, *Affinity toward diversity* (ATD; Corral-Verdugo et al., 2009) has been shown to correlate with PEBs and altruistic intentions. People who are concerned about sustainable future are by definition treating future inhabitants of the planet as part of their moral circle. Put differently, future people are given a voice as stakeholders, consistent with postconventional moral development. Similarly, people at higher levels of moral development tend to score higher on *ecocentrism* (concern for the environment). Ecocentric orientation has even been shown to relate to actual pro-environmental action (Thompson & Barton, 1994).

Otherwise, there is conflicting evidence about PEB. Various self-reported measures of altruism and moral development have shown robust correlations with similar *self-reported* behavioral intentions. However, as with other sorts of intention behavior links (e.g., Vallerand et al., 1992), when actual pro-environmental behaviors are measured, convenience, cost, and other contextual features tend to take precedence over altruistic intentions (Ewing, 2001; Gifford, 2011). This tends to contradict the notion that people with pro-social inclinations are more likely to treat the natural environment well. It also means that treating moral development as an individual difference may not be so helpful for managing criterion four, since these inclinations predict intentions, but not necessarily actions.

Still, recent innovations in the measurement of predictors of social and moral behavior suggest that this approach may still hold promise. *Conditional reasoning* measures (Boardley & Kavussanu, 2008; James & LeBreton, 2012; Stanger, Kavussanu, Boardley, & Ring, 2013) have shown potential for predicting actual altruistic and anti-social behaviors (Lievens & De Soete, 2011). These identify certain types of self-delusional reasoning that are more common in people who habitually engage in anti-social aggression. They also correlate more highly with behaviors than do self-report measures.

But, some of the findings from the applications of moral reasoning to sustainability fly in the face of the accepted notion that moral reasoning is relatively stable. Several researchers have shown how interventions can be used to change moral reasoning quickly. Berenguer (2007, 2010) has demonstrated that empathy manipulations can increase moral reasoning about the natural environment. This research is based on Batson's negative state relief hypothesis of altruism (Batson et al., 1989). Similar interventions have been used to change moral reasoning (Bratanova, Loughnan, & Gatersleben, 2012) and acceptance across cultures (Hammer et al., 2003).

Mindfulness interventions outside of schools and therapeutic settings may also hold promise for developing principled moral action with respect to the environment (Loizzo, 2012). The evidence here is only suggestive (Amel et al., 2009; Moscardo & Pearce, 1986), showing meaningful relationships between mindfulness, environmental awareness, and well-being in selective samples. This research also suffers from several problems, including small, unrepresentative samples and self-reported outcomes (Amel et al., 2009). But mindfulness interventions may have an effect on altruism in general (Orme-Johnson, 2000), so effectiveness with respect to the natural environment seems likely.

DEVELOPMENT AND MOTIVATIONAL SYSTEMS

Motivation and Development

Ontogenetic development relies on attempts to adapt to circumstances in order to realize our motives. But motivation is often described in terms of specific situations. This sort of *situational specificity* can be applied to motivations in socio-emotional (e.g., learning to control smiles and frowns for a sales job); cognitive (e.g., learning to read in order to please elders); and moral development (e.g., learning ethical codes as part of advanced professional training). These examples reflect forces that most people can intuitively understand as motives. Most of us seek to "get something" as a result of our behaviors.

It should come as no surprise, then, that motivation has no single meaning. What is generally agreed is that motivation both *directs behaviors* and *affects the effort* or energy we expend. We have already discussed the *approach* and *avoidance arousals* that control emotive responding. This theory of motivation relies on underlying *arousal systems* (Kagan, 2012) that are evoked by internal, subcortical feedback (hunger, thirst); internal learned feedback (associative memory); external stimuli (smells, sounds); and external learned stimuli.

Heckhausen and his colleagues (Heckhausen et al., 2010) state that "a central feature of adaptive capacity is the regulation of motivation. An individual's developmental potential is won or lost by mastering the challenges of regulating motivational processes." But self-regulation leads to adaptation at least partly by how it affects our relationships with others. To manage these, an essential motivation for many adults is trying to make sense of how our own behaviors, aspirations, fears, and preferences affect the people around us. We are motivated to try to see ourselves as others see us, so we construct *self-schemas* (Markus, 1977), often referred to as (our old friend) identity.

Identity evolves as we attempt to adapt—as we try to gain what we want and avoid what we fear in the world (Markus & Nurius, 1986). Particularly in socio-emotional development, differentiation and integration are put to the task of developing a separate but integrated identity. We have visited this idea in several places already. What is different about the approach taken here is that motivation is treated as a central component of identity development. Most textbooks on the topic of motivation do not include it under the heading of development. But, identity and motive are both part of an evolving, interdependent, and dynamic process—a system (Dweck & Leggett, 1988; Lewin, 1935; Markus, 1977; Markus & Kitayama, 2010; Markus & Nurius, 1986; Markus & Wurf, 1987; McArthur & Baron, 1983).

Dweck (2012) argues that a core component of our identity is the *implicit theory* we hold about whether people can change. This belief about the stability or changeability of ourselves and others can limit or advance development, as well. Our beliefs about whether we can develop and change are akin to self-efficacy expectancies posited by Dweck's Stanford colleague, Bandura (1978). Evidence strongly suggests that implicit theories affect our motives (Burnette et al., 2013; Sevincer, Kluge, & Oettingen, 2014), identities, and future orientation (Sevincer et al., 2014).

Applied Motivation and Identity

In terms of sustainability, we have already discussed at length the possibilities for place attachment interventions having effects on identity. It is clear that identifying with a place can incline us to treat it differently (Arnocky et al., 2007). There is also evidence to suggest that place attachment itself is a protection against identity problems during developmental transitions (see Hay, 1998). So, having a place to "hang on to" can make change a bit easier.

> Some people are deeply committed to the preservation of a natural setting, but do not consider themselves as "environmentalists." Consider, for example, a farm owner whose family attachment to a place goes back many generations and includes a "stewardship" identity. Now, imagine an "expert environmentalist" providing advice about how to structure the farm operations. It should come as no surprise that many people in rural settings resist such controlling messages.

Crompton and Kasser (2009) have made the beginnings of a case for identity based sustainability interventions (Scott, 2009). They provide a short, initial list of possible approaches to integrating sustainable thinking and behavior into people's self-definitions. From our applied perspective, the book suffers from several shortcomings. First, it defines identity negatively—by what is *not* environmentally friendly. Second, it lacks empirical support in many instances (Scott, 2009). Third, it takes a predictor centered approach, instead of the applied, criterion centric approach described here. While it lacks practical value as a result of these flaws, it provides a very important insight about identity.

One of the most successful examples of identity based applications comes from I-O psychology. *Perspective taking* is at the crux of *leadership development* interventions. These typically start by gathering the perceptions of stakeholders in management and executive decisions (including executive assessors, peers, and subordinates) using standard measures, then providing feedback to the target person in a facilitated setting. Feedback typically engages target leaders in discussions about the specific effects they have on others within and across contexts. These provide differentiating information (e.g., how people in different contexts see the leader differently) and integrating information (e.g., how the leader affects people regardless of context). Such engagement of various stakeholders is also at the heart of ethical decision making (Phillips, 2003), which makes these moral development interventions. This approach is starting to reach sustainability management development (Tang, Robinson, & Harvey, 2011).

Educational interventions can also be framed in terms of identity development. Children often learn "the rules" for their social world through experiences in school and other educational experiences (e.g., summer camps, ballet classes). Work by Jason Chen and his colleagues (Chen & Pajares, 2010; Chen & Usher, 2013) has shown that students' notions about whether they themselves can change and grow have a significant impact on their achievement in school. In fact, this research suggests that such beliefs about self are fundamental to whether students will try to learn in the first place. Implicit theories and self-efficacy set developmental limits on students' identities.

Using Readiness to Support Intervention

Trying to make change without reference to such developmental limits is a fundamental challenge of application. There is a middle ground between direct attempts to *change* development and simply *measuring* development as an individual difference. We have seen that some interventions (e.g., early childhood education, training, and therapy) attempt to directly alter development, usually under controlled conditions (classrooms, therapists' offices) and over significant periods of time. Other interventions simply screen out those who are not seen as easily changeable. The concept of *readiness* uses an interactionist perspective to integrate these approaches. Effective developmental interventions often target people who are "ready" to make the leap either by virtue of their development or having them vested in an advantageous context (e.g., colleges, religious training, wilderness experiences). If the targets of change are "ready," then desired change may occur.

One step beyond these efforts to control or select for readiness are direct interventions to change readiness itself. For example, Yeager, Trzesniewski, and Dweck (2013) have shown that relatively short term interventions can alter the implicit theories that place limits on readiness. It may be that such efforts to affect readiness work more for children in classrooms than adults in complex environments.

Applying the Five Criteria

1. **What prompts people to think they have a problem (or not)?**
   Using developmental psychology to answer this question inevitably runs up against the problem of perspective taking. People who are at earlier stages of development are unable to take perspective on their own stage and do not recognize this limitation in themselves or others. If our aim

is to help people discern a problem or be reassured about it, it makes sense to address the concerns and motives of their *current* stage. For someone at a conventional stage of moral and cognitive development, it makes sense to address common norms of their social groups—a discrepancy would be defined in relation to these accepted social norms. Others' set points may be determined partially by egocentric concerns (early stages of moral development) or by broader moral circles (post-conventional reasoning). For most people, addressing conventional values and identities within people's groups will probably have greater success than addressing principles or the interests of other stakeholders outside their social sphere.

This is not to say that moral and cognitive developmental stages are set in stone. It may be that educational experiences have an effect on concern for climate change (Cummings et al., 2010; Twenge, Campbell, & Freeman, 2012). But such educational interventions require political will (Scott, 2009) and persistence over time.

A question raised by place attachment research is how people's dependence on place and identification with place affect the set points for when they see a "problem" (Kyle et al., 2004b). For those who are simply dependent on a place for their resources, there may be less of a problem with degradation than for people who are attached to a place by their identities. What this means is that, if people identify with a place, they may be more sensitive to changes occurring in the place (Kyle et al., 2004b). Finding ways to develop identification with place may therefore be an important lever for raising concerns.

But being attached to a place may also change the system to which they apply a set point. Consider the case of a person whose family has been attached to a place for many generations. When an "outsider" arrives and announces that there is a need to change the way that this land is managed, the discrepancy test is aimed not at the set point for the external environmental system, but at the person's own identity system. If the person sees himself or herself as a "good steward" of the land (a common phrase in agricultural communities), and the outsider hasn't established this, then the identity discrepancy may lead to rejection, even though the person is motivated to be a good steward! This is akin to being told to sweep the floor by a parent in the other room who doesn't know you have just done this, unbidden. Messages about the need for change need to account for identity systems—not just external environmental systems (Crompton & Kasser, 2009; Whitmarsh & O'Neill, 2010).

2. What makes people think more or less carefully when they decide on an action?

Development places limits on people's tendency to think deliberatively, as well. Social and moral development may be particularly important in this regard. If we would like to see people think more carefully before they act, it is probably important to know who they are taking their cues from. For most people, it is probably not an internal, mindful process so much as social referencing that leads them to be careful. If their norm group is visibly behaving one way, it is not likely that they will take the time to carefully consider acting another way.

This does not change the enormous amount of work done by clinical and educational psychologists to enhance metacognition through mindfulness and CBT. The purpose of such therapies is mostly to help people be more deliberative about the social and moral consequences of their decision processes. It may not enhance cognitive development, but it inclines people both to use deliberative thinking and, ultimately, to arrive at new ways to act in non-deliberative ways—on the basis of new habits.

A final note for this criterion: People in developmental transitions may be more inclined to seek help with decisions. The people to whom they turn for help often include professionals who are educated, complex, deliberative thinkers. Some decision making professionals are given thorough training in decision processes, and in the case of many applied psychologists, they are also trained as ethical facilitators. This is a central argument for why this book may make a difference: People who are knowledgeable about applied psychology may be more effective, deliberative decision helpers.

3. **What makes people change the way they think and behave?**
This chapter is largely concerned with the problem of distinguishing things that are changeable from those that are not. Developmental change is defined as change that occurs only when people reach a point where they are both able and willing to change (Baldwin, 1895; Thelen, 1995). Efforts to directly change developmental trajectory and stage may therefore be slow and arduous.

Still, taking developmental stage into account through measurement and prediction is common and can be used to target change efforts. Recent work has begun this sort of developmental measurement in research on environmental behaviors (Levin & Unsworth, 2013). Similarly, certain aspects of development may be altered by following a few lessons learned here: (1) Framing situations to establish readiness; (2) tailoring interventions to address unique aspects of an individual's current identity and motives; and (3) developing perspective taking through mindful, well conceived, facilitated feedback. These may be costly and "one person at a time."

It also may help to think of developmental change in terms of *punctuated equilibrium* (Dziengel, 2010; Gersick, 1991). Evidence has shown that therapeutic change sometimes occurs in the form of "sudden gains," where people experience deep, altering insights into themselves and others (Aderka, Nickerson, Bøe, & Hofmann, 2012). Punctuated equilibrium theory provides an elegant and intuitively sensible explanation for this. The theory argues that development is generally slow, but that "critical exchanges" can lead to quite dramatic change.

For example, conflicts and other emotional episodes that clarify motives in groups often lead to very different sorts of relationships after the episode (Chang, Bordia, & Duck, 2003). Imagine that you are used to going on long weekend hikes with an old friend. On one of these hikes, the friend shows signs of anxiety. When you prompt, the friend self-discloses serious financial hardships as a result of your weekend trips. This leads to a change in your relationship from a reciprocal (or mutualist) relationship to an altruistic relationship, where you help pay for your friend to come on these trips during hard times.

There are no scientist-practitioner applications of this approach to change in the sphere of sustainability to date. However, this theory is consistent with the dynamic systems perspective that has led to successful interventions in other areas. It also argues for a very clear and specific assessment of the context within which change is sought. We have already seen repeatedly how analyses of people's *current* preferences, fears, and hopes can be used to aid in change. Similarly, integrating people's views of context is fairly common in practical assessment. Such perceptions and motivations within a context serve as essential starting points for systemic change. Chapters 8 through 10 will clarify this.

We have also framed motivated social and moral development using the concepts of attachment and identity. Identity change may involve dropping some of the norms of behavior we learned in childhood in favor of social norms we learn through other social and cultural experiences later in life. Besides changing our conventional behaviors to suit a new social environment, learning new norms through such things as living abroad may lead to metacognitive development. Given that these changes can and do occur throughout life (Shanahan et al., 2012), and that there are ways to deliberately make such change, identity development may be a critical target for change (Crompton & Kasser, 2009).

Still, developmental change occurs rapidly and, in some cases, more easily early in life. Asymmetries in the development of personality, intelligence, and culture are often the result of parenting and childhood education. Among these early life developments, implicit theories that people have about whether we are able to change are arguably the most potent predictor of change. Simply put: If we learn to believe that people can change, then we will be more likely to try to change (ourselves and others). Among the aspects of development that we probably learn early, implicit theories may place the most powerful limits on the extent to which people will be willing to try to change.

DEVELOPMENT AND MOTIVATIONAL SYSTEMS

Parents, teachers, and cultures that act on implicit theories that assume the possibility of change may be at significant advantages in terms of adaptation, not just because they will actually try, and occasionally succeed at making change (Smetana, Jambon, Conry-Murray, & Sturge-Apple, 2012). They are also at an advantage in terms of the more optimistic outlook implied in this belief. We will return to the advantages of optimism in the last chapter.

4. **When are people likely to take action?**

On one end of the continuum, people with *entity* implicit theories ("We are who we are") are less likely to take action. Identifying those with such theories is one way to evaluate people's readiness for action (Silverberg, Betis, Huebner, & Cota-Robles, 1996). Given the right circumstances, and by taking other developmental variables into account, it may be possible even to get these reluctant souls to act. This again gets to the question of how to motivate people toward change, given their identities, attachments, and socio-emotional and moral development.

What is different under this criterion is the importance of group processes for action we discussed in Chapter 5. Choosing to work with others to take action is commonly based on common norms and group memberships. As we have seen, most people are probably at a conventional stage of moral reasoning. So, it may seem obvious, but it often helps to catch whole groups of people at conventions. (Be mindful of where you have seen the root of this word in developmental stages.) The broader point is that people at different stages of moral development will take action for very different reasons.

Taking action also involves more than just changing the way we think and behave as individuals. Kyle, Graefe, Manning, and Bacon (2004a) findings are suggestive that people's tendency to further invest in a place (e.g., by taking action) relates to the extent to which they identify with the place and see it as being crowded. This suggests that, as populations rise and crowding increases, people may be more likely to take action. Again, understanding how context affects people differently based on their developmental asymmetries may prove a critical lever for action. Catching people in the right place at the right time can make a big difference if we are trying to get them to think about or try something new.

5. **What are the characteristics of change efforts that are likely to work?**

If we substitute "hereditary intelligence" with "adaptive capacity," it becomes clear from this chapter that we have made much progress toward understanding the many influences that interact to influence adaptive capacity since Lippmann wrote these words. It is equally clear that thinking of anything (including intelligence) as a stable characteristic may be problematic. Instead, we have seen how human characteristics, including our ability to change—sometimes adaptively.

DEVELOPMENT AND MOTIVATIONAL SYSTEMS

Still, from an applied perspective, it also became clear in this chapter that some things should be treated as if they don't change. The best we can hope to do sometimes is to measure development and treat people accordingly. For example, it may not help much to discuss the interests of future humans if we are conversing with someone who has a history of ambivalent attachments. The uncertainties of relating to others may overwhelm even good intentions for someone with this tendency. Similarly, it may be very hard to convince donors to allocate resources to efforts to affect change when their implicit theories assign us to unchangeable boxes. Sometimes we have to take people as they are, rather than trying to change their thinking—in this case their identities and social motives.

There are some changeable aspects of development, but they often involve long term interventions in controlled environments (e.g., classrooms, clinicians' offices, prisons). Stage theories start with the assumption that development involves major, qualitative change, so these long term efforts may have profound effects. Harnessing such powerful forces in therapy and other facilitated "punctuated equilibrium" experiences seems very promising. At very least, the old idea of "getting them while they're young" is at work in schools and homes every day. This may explain why there is an entire journal of *Environmental Education*. We will return to this in several later chapters.

To clarify further, practicality is partly defined by what is already being done: Once someone has shown something is "doable," others may try it. In this light, scientist-practitioners have a long history of trying to affect aspects of development through long term interventions. Both therapy and education have shown impressive effects on socio-emotional and cognitive development. The fact that these often take time makes them less practical, but no less valuable, given the good probability for substantial change. Developing more complex understandings about a situation are even examples of short term changes that appear to affect fairly difficult targets for change. We will see more about this in the next chapter.

Nevertheless, for some time now, psychologists interested in sustainability have focused on what appear to be more changeable targets than developmentally complex constructs like attachment, identity, and motivation: They have focused on observable behaviors. Instead of trying to go at the more profound determinants of our emotive responses, thinking, and actions, these psychologists have been working every day to get people to act the way the psychologists—and hopefully the targets of change themselves want to act. We will learn more about these efforts in the next chapter.

8

LEARNING AND BEHAVIOR CHANGE

Human history becomes more and more a race between education and catastrophe.

H. G. Wells, 1951

Until now, we have looked at things that do not change much (heuristics and biases) or change slowly after childhood (personality, mental abilities, motivations). In this chapter, we will learn more about the relatively quick kinds of change we all know as *learning*. Learning is defined in various ways by different authors and researchers. We will define it as two general kinds of change: Behavioral and cognitive. These reflect a fundamental split in the research on learning, as we shall see. But, both kinds of leaning occur as a result of motivated interactions with our context and involve the integration of new information (Gluck & Myers, 2001; Schacter, Gilbert, & Wegner, 2009).

Behavioral learning includes relatively permanent behavioral change. Strong situational influences (Chapter 5) may alter behaviors, but may not change how we think—or even how we behave in similar circumstances later. Such situationally determined changes in behavior may *lead* to more permanent learning, as we will learn. But behavior change in itself does not qualify as learning, in our definition. The second kind is change in thinking or skills, mostly associated with changes in memory.

Learning can occur quite quickly if we are in the right place, with the right motivation, and under conditions of developmental readiness. Furthermore, learning can have deep, lasting impacts on our ways of thinking, as well as behaving. In fact, this is why we have defined learning as relatively permanent (Schacter et al., 2009). Even some of the less changeable characteristics, as we have seen, are still susceptible to long term, socially incited influences (the therapeutic and facilitated interactions discussed in Chapter 6). However, the ease with which we *can* learn strongly suggests that we learn new ways of thinking quite quickly (Bouton, Todd, & León, 2013; Neumann, 2007). Developmental change does not appear to be as quick, and so it places limits on the kinds of psychological change that occur through learning interventions.

Still, learning is like development in its reliance on *motivation* and *context* (Blume, Ford, Baldwin, & Huang, 2010; Dekker & Fischer, 2008; Kim, Kim, & Svinicki, 2012; Volet & Kimmel, 2012). The things that appear relevant to us in a context are what affect our actions and thinking, and sometimes change them. We will assume that we learn because we need or want to and that this is incited by our context.

Several systems have been proposed over the almost century and a half that psychologists have systematically studied learning (Hothersall, 1995). Most introductory psychology textbooks start chapters on learning with a consideration of *associative learning*. This sort of learning is an important basis for learning in all sorts of organisms, from the relatively simple to highly complex (Myers, 2009). We will start with a brief consideration of associative learning, including learning processes that involve *behavioral learning, connectionism*, and *neurocognitive* systems (Gluck & Myers, 2001). This will lead to some criticisms and applications of *associationist* research and an in depth consideration of the third criterion. If we want to change people's thinking (criterion three), then we need to know where to focus our efforts. Figure 8.1 provides an initial answer to this question.

The chapter will then move quickly to problems of application. There are two main reasons for this break from our usual rhythm. First, basic research on learning has grown up fairly independently of much of the applied research (Gagné, 1962). Consequently, the second section of the chapter will consider the scientist-practitioner approaches that have expanded the field of *cognitive* learning. The second reason for moving directly to application is that the gap between traditional environmental psychology and an applied psychology of sustainability is very apparent in their divergent approaches to learning. Environmental psychology has taken a strong associationist, laboratory based approach until fairly recently (Giuliani & Scopelliti, 2009), while a host of applied problems have required scientist-practitioners to take a variety of other approaches. In order to understand these differences, it will help to first review the evolution of learning theories.

Very stable, unchangeable				Very changeable
Biases	*Mental abilities*	*Cognitive & moral reasoning*	*Social Identity*	*Cognitive learning*
Heuristics	*Personality*	*Personal identity*	*Socio-emotional regulation*	*Behavioral learning*

Figure 8.1 The continuum of changeability in fundamental characteristics

Learning Theories

Tolman proposed the idea of "cognitive maps" in the 1940s (Tolman, 1948). Research of his time, and much of the basic research moving forward, was dominated by the *behaviorist perspective*, making his ideas fairly radical in comparison. But, the behaviorist perspective set learning research on solid scientific footing, relying only on *observed behaviors* and *controlled contextual variables* (Thorndike, 1933). Behaviorism was also the basis for some of the ground breaking research that demonstrated how learning *can* occur by association (Hothersall, 1995; Thorndike, 1933; Watson, 1914, 1998). But the difficult questions around motivation and readiness to learn were largely left to others (Nevin, 1999).

Instead, through several decades of research, behaviorists focused almost entirely on a single question: How does behavior change? The primary answer to the question, in behaviorism, is to change the stimuli that trigger behavioral responses. In other words, behaviorists approached change by deliberately altering the observed physical environment, in order to alter observed behaviors. Their approach was to closely control contextual *stimuli*, through such means as the "Skinner Box" used by animal researchers. Stimuli that *reinforced* a behavior were defined (circularly) as those that increased the likelihood of the behavior recurring (Hill, 1997).

There is strong evidence supporting the associative learning approaches to behavior change that have come from behaviorism and its offshoots (Gluck & Myers, 2001). At its most basic, learning relies on having two events occur close to one another in time and space, which leads to the learning of an *association* between these two events (Boring, 1933; Hill, 1997). For example, we saw in Chapter 4 how John B. Watson (who coined the term behaviorism) and his assistant famously presented a white rabbit to a young child, immediately followed by a loud noise (two wooden planks hitting each other right behind the child). Having these two events (a rabbit and a loud noise) occur at about the same time led the child to form an *association* between the two. That is, the child learned that the rabbit meant trouble, even when the noise was not presented. While such associative learning appears quite simplistic to modern eyes, the basic notion of associative learning has, to some extent, stood the test of time.

Perhaps more importantly for our purposes, the behaviors the child exhibited as a *result* of this association were emotive—he cried (appealed to caregivers) and attempted to move away from (avoid) the rabbit. This is consistent with the idea that stimulus events lead to responses that are *motivated* attempts to alter the stimulus environment. This is sometimes called *operant learning*. The general model is that a *stimulus* event (S^D) leads to a *behavioral response* (R), which in turn leads to change in the *stimulus environment* (S^R) (Cone & Hayes, 1980). Such *conditional learning* occurs when the circumstances present the "right" sorts of stimuli.

Among the most obvious problems with this early approach is that *motivationally relevant* stimuli are essential to forming associations. That is, if the child had been presented with a piece of paper (instead of a cute rabbit) and something that did not arouse his sympathetic nervous system (like a loud noise would tend to do), he probably would not have formed a strong association or a behavioral response. The experimenters in this study did little to consider systematic, underlying differences in stimuli that influence emotive responses. Definition of the psychological variables underlying the effects of *reinforcement* and *feedback* were left to others.

But it is something that Watson's colleagues in his later career in advertising understood *in practice*. Advertisers' approach to getting people to buy things was to present a *motivation arousing* stimulus (not a neutral stimulus) along with their product (Adams, 1916; Buckley, 1982; Kreshel, 1990). By pairing of *emotive* stimuli with an advertising message, consumers learn to associate the product with this arousal, making it more likely that they will remember the product when it comes time to buy. Such attempts to associate a product with some fear or desire is still used by advertisers today (e.g., Lewis, Watson, & White, 2008); however the psychological processes addressed in advertising have expanded considerably (Walden, 2012; Weilbacher, 2003).

Problems with Associative Learning

This sort of targeting based on motivation shows one of the ways that associative learning is somewhat limited in practice. In order to get people to learn and behave, we must first understand and appeal to their motives, as with other sorts of approaches to changing thinking and behavior. But we also need some control of context. We have seen how this problem of situational specificity and generalization applies to all areas of practice—it goes back to the roots of behaviorism. It is partly dealt with by more cognitive learning approaches, where we learn sets of rules (e.g., norms of behavior) that we rely on across stimulus situations (Cox, 1997; Goldstein & Ford, 2002). But the problem remains: How do we control the stimuli in a situation in *just* the way required to cause change?

This problem relates to the final of our five criteria: Practicality. Although it would be nice to be able to directly alter the conditional stimuli that lead people to behave in various ways, this is often not possible. Among other things, this implies enormous control over the many contexts within which people live and work. For example, if we want to get people to take public transport more often, we might need to reduce the use of other modes of transport. In the case of the single occupancy automobile—a very common modern alternative to public transport—we might seek to reduce the number of roads available, increase the cost of gas, and increase the tax on ownership and operation. The time, effort, and resources needed to accomplish these changes would be quite high. Efforts to accomplish such change have met with some success, as we will see in Chapter 9, but behavioral learning has only been part of the approach taken (Cone & Hayes, 1980; Koh & Wong, 2013).

The broader problem, then, is to find ways to alter people's behaviors across a host of situations, and regardless of the particular emotive responses they may be experiencing at the time. We will return to this problem when we consider *transfer of training* (Blume et al., 2010; Cox, 1997; Ford, 1997) and applied *cognitive learning* (Colquitt, LePine, & Noe, 2000; Rotter, 1966).

Another problem with behaviorist interventions is that they may not last and do not constitute learning by our definition. Precisely because of the demonstrated ease of making behavior change in well controlled stimulus environments (Bouton et al., 2013), one change may easily be trumped by another. Behaviorists have shown how to extinguish, shape, and suppress behaviors that have been learned previously. But, differences between contexts explain these differences in behavior.

Recent Associationist Research on Memory

Since the time when Tolman (1948) popularized the idea of a "cognitive" approach to learning, there have been important changes in the field. But associationist research has continued and has led to important strides toward understanding the fundamental systems of learning. Recent *neuroscience* research has crossed increasingly sophisticated physiological evidence with mathematical models, largely using a *connectionist* framework derived from behaviorism (Taatgen, 2013). This has led to a revolution in our understanding of how *memories* are formed, retrieved, and are lost, among other important discoveries (Anderson, 2007; Taatgen, 2013).

Neural processes of associative learning appear to work through several areas of the brain. Signals from perceptions are sent to the emotive systems of the brain (*midbrain* and *amygdala*), whose effects appears to "sort" stimuli into rewarding and aversive categories (Gruber & McDonald, 2012; Murty, LaBar, & Adcock, 2012; Petrovich, 2011). That is, consistent with the appraisal theories of emotive responding, our brains decide whether stimuli "matter." In particular, stimuli that are novel lead us to activate memory processes (Daselaar, Veltman, & Witter, 2004). Put in terms of *discrepancy testing* and *control theory*, we make an *emotive appraisal* and direct our attentions accordingly. In particular, we tend to allocate more attention to stimuli that signal loss over those that signal gain (Yechiam & Hochman, 2013). As with heuristics, we tend to be risk averse (Kahneman, 2011) and weigh negative information more heavily (Skowronski & Carlston, 1992).

Next in our learning and memory process is a set of structures at the base of our outer brain called (collectively) the *hippocampus* (Gluck & Myers, 2001). After stimulating the part of the brain associated with the

LEARNING AND BEHAVIOR CHANGE

hippocampus, electrical signals evoked by contextual stimuli are moved in two other, general directions. Some go to the *cerebellum*—an area of the brain that manages many motor functions. Association of this sort is consolidated into *procedural memory*—sometimes called "motor memory" (Gluck & Myers, 2001). This sort of learning often occurs without much conscious awareness or regulation (Reas & Brewer, 2013). Other learning goes into parts of the *cerebrum* (the top part of the brain) to form *declarative memory*—what is usually called "remembering." This part of memory accounts for the ability to label, store, and retrieve information, such as words, faces, events, and places.

Effort, Motivation, and Associative Learning

Like decision processes, learning processes tend to be more or less deliberative, depending on such things as the emotive arousal people experience beforehand. As we saw in Figure 5.1, certain emotive responses can trump substantive processes when we are deciding how to behave (Norton et al., 2005). Likewise, with *learning*, the hippocampus often "takes over" and does its encoding quite quickly (Reas & Brewer, 2013). An aroused amygdala can lead to quick responding, and procedural learning—without much conscious mediation (Reas & Brewer, 2013). Such "fear" arousal can also suppress certain aspects of learning and memory (Petrovich, Ross, Mody, Holland, & Gallagher, 2009).

Emergencies are strong situations. Almost anyone would see a threat, not an opportunity, for example, when a tsunami is expected to strike a nearby shoreline. So, how do people learn to respond to disaster? For most of us, anyway, our amygdala sends strong warning messages, leading to procedural (as opposed to more deliberative) responses.

"Drills" are used for this very reason. We learn and continuously practice a very clear set of procedures to follow when disaster strikes. This sort of learning under stress is probably qualitatively different from learning (and behavior) that occurs when we are not under stress and have time to explore and consolidate things into memory.

But some aspects of learning may require more than such automatic processing. In fact, considerable, persistent effort is often required to deliberately learn or retrieve complex information (Abney, McBride, & Petrella, 2013; Taatgen, 2013). Anyone who has tried to learn complex information knows this well. In terms of arousal, "interest" or "exploration" types of arousal (Gluck & Myers, 2001) involve more conscious effort and may be controlled by other areas of the brain—the amygdala is not in charge (Gluck & Myers, 2001). Thus, deliberate, effortful learning may be more likely when we feel safe or, using others' terms, "relaxed" (Blume et al., 2010; Cassaday, Bloomfield, & Hayward, 2002). There is evidence that this is when cognitive learning is at work, as well (Gluck & Myers, 2001; Thomas, Laurance, Nadel, & Jacobs, 2010). We will return to this when we consider the types of motives that are involved in different sorts of learning.

For now, it is important to recognize that the *content* of learning may follow from motivational variables, as well. In particular, some research suggests that we are busy learning about the *contingencies* of behavior from infancy (Strickland, 1989; Thiessen, Kronstein, & Hufnagle, 2013). That is, we are trying to represent in memory not just those things that *happen together* (associated events), but those events that *follow from* other events (Kalechstein & Nowicki, 1997; Thiessen et al., 2013). Thorndike (1927) famously labeled this the *Law of Effect*. In addition to remembering individual instances in a situation to guide our actions, we also generalize aspects of the situation to other situations that look similar (Taatgen, 2013). From this perspective, when we learn, we are broadly representing how our motives are (and are not) met by different *classes* of behaviors and *types* of situations (Blume et al., 2010; Hattie, Biggs, & Purdie, 1996).

Durable Change and Decay

Although associationist research is among the most convincing in the study of human thinking and behavior, its aim is very much description and explanation—not *control* or *prediction*. We have already seen how control over the motivational value of stimuli sets important limits on the application of associationist findings. It is a challenge, for example, to control stimulus arrays with humans in the same way that they are controlled for animals in a Skinner Box. However, we will see exactly how this is accomplished when we discuss the use of electronic media in Chapter 10.

Still, there is limited evidence about what sorts of learning are likely to be durable across time. In other words, what are the sorts and conditions of learning that establish *predictable* change over time? Basic research evidence about the *decay* of associative learning sheds light on this, at least in controlled settings. First, decay appears to happen more readily for aversive stimuli (Duvarci, Nader, & LeDoux, 2008; Nakatani et al., 2009) and in contexts that are substantially different from the original context of behavior change (Blume et al., 2010; Hattie et al., 1996; Neumann, 2007). Further, associations may be more *durable* when incoming information is associated with "old" associations, rather than when it is classified in our processing as "new" (Han & Dobbins, 2008). In other words, it may be easier to remember things that are consistent with our previous, broader understandings of the contingencies of situations (Taatgen, 2013; Thiessen et al., 2013). Finally, the phenomenon of *spontaneous recovery* shows that associations that have been *extinguished* (apparently unlearned) often reappear when the situation is close

LEARNING AND BEHAVIOR CHANGE

enough to the original learning situation (Thanellou & Green, 2011). Understanding how learning generalizes to broader contexts is particularly important for applied learning, as we will see.

Applications of Behavioral Learning

Some of the early voices for using psychology to change the impact of human activities on the natural environment were rooted in the behaviorist perspective (Cone & Hayes, 1980; Steg & Vlek, 2009; Stokols, 1978). Application of behavioral learning to pro-environmental behavior is where traditional environmental psychology shines. Until fairly recently, environmental psychologists were concerned almost entirely with the effects of contextual factors on human behavior (Cone & Hayes, 1980; Giuliani & Scopelliti, 2009). In fact, early efforts to explicitly define the criteria for psychological sustainability came directly from this perspective and targeted environmentally protective and destructive behaviors (Cone & Hayes, 1980). These eventually morphed into the long list of pro-environmental behaviors that are now used widely in environmental psychology.

Not surprisingly, behavioral interventions in environmental psychology rely on altering the *physical stimuli* and *reinforcement* characteristics of situations (Oskamp, 1995)—what we have referred to in more general terms as the *context*. Many examples of possible interventions have been suggested in urban planning, architecture, and workplace design (Gifford, 2007a; Giuliani & Scopelliti, 2009; Sundstrom, Bell, Busby, & Asmus, 1996). Recent examples include *urban design* interventions for reducing crime (Marzbali, Abdullah, Razak, & Maghsoodi Tilaki, 2012), increasing traffic safety (Lewis et al., 2008), increasing bicycle and pedestrian commuting (Koh & Wong, 2013), and increasing children's quality of life (Broberg, Kyttä, & Fagerholm, 2013). Beyond just behavioral outcomes, research into the experience of *restoration* in natural settings has been evaluated in terms of the experiences of various stimuli, such as noises (Mace, Corser, Zitting, & Denison, 2013), temperatures (Hipp & Ogunseitan, 2011), and the geographic features of the environment (White, Pahl, Ashbullby, Herbert, & Depledge, 2013). The general approach of these studies is to compare differences in situational stimuli or directly manipulate them in order to assess their effects on behavioral outcomes (Giuliani & Scopelliti, 2009).

Similarly, behavioral interventions rely on the Law of Effect—the idea that behavior follows from its past consequences (Thorndike, 1927). Various incentive programs have been suggested and tried in environmental psychology, with some success (Abrahamse, Steg, Vlek, & Rothengatter, 2005; Oskamp, 1995; Winkler & Winett, 1982). For example, several rebate programs have shown success at reducing water consumption (Winkler & Winett, 1982). Feedback interventions, where people receive information about the results of their behaviors, also have features that are derived from associationist learning (Woodward, 1982). We will cover these under cognitive interventions, however, since there are specific cognitive differences that arise from different sorts of feedback. Related to this, we will see other ways that purely associationist interventions are limited by a number of factors, not the least of which is the problem of tapping different people's different motives (Abrahamse et al., 2005; Schultz & Oskamp, 1996; Steg & Vlek, 2009; Thøgersen, 2006).

Some Problems of Application for Sustainability

If our interest is in advancing the application of psychology to sustainability, a larger question is why, after thirty years of basic research, these interventions are not yet widespread (Gifford, 2008; Giuliani & Scopelliti, 2009). There are several possibilities, most of which are discernible from an applied perspective.

First, environmental behavior interventions do not always assume input from stakeholders. The assumption that psychologists should be able to "convince" people of the "rightness" of their ideas (Altus & Morris, 2009; Cohen-Cole, 2005; O'Donohue & Ferguson, 2001) often flies in the face of political realities—these are often highly charged political processes. For example, interventions to change urban landscapes require working with neighborhoods and city governments. Many cities are under great economic and demographic pressure, and the voices of "experts" are at least drowned out and often deliberately ignored in the interest of people's initial, emotive impulses (Chapter 4). As testimony to this, we have already seen many examples of people's unwillingness to rely on expert opinions in the realm of sustainability (Gifford, 2011; Martin et al., 2007).

Second, this begs the question of how to affect change. In the mainstream, behaviorist approach of traditional environmental psychology, this appears to be left to chance. We shall see in later chapters how scientist-practitioners attempt to manage complex change processes. The success of these approaches is not easy to demonstrate. But, it may be time to put these other approaches to the test in questions of sustainability, given the potential importance of behaviorist applications.

Third, putting this another way, our behavioral focus has led to neglect of *criterion definition*. For many environmental psychologists, the outcome of interest is assumed to be reduction in negative outcomes of human behavior (Abrahamse et al., 2005; Geller, 1992). But, even by *seeming* to ignore how other people define problems (Pfeffer, 2010), we set ourselves up to be ignored in turn. We will see in the applied chapters how the relationship between psychologist and client is essential to applications.

Fourth, and closely related to this, the criterion problem looms large in environmental psychology. The associationist approach has concerned itself mostly with changing *observable behaviors*, rather than any kind of deeper

LEARNING AND BEHAVIOR CHANGE

cognitive changes, including the changes in identity, motivations, decision processes, and development we have discussed. Put in terms of our five criteria, this perspective has concerned itself mostly with one part of criterion three: What makes people change the way they behave (Steg & Vlek, 2009)? Other criteria (e.g., when do people decide they have a problem?) are rarely addressed.

Pro-environmental behavior (PEB) measures encompass a long list of behaviors that are thought to affect sustainability. As we have seen, these can be thought of as altruistic or "good" behaviors. There has been debate about whether more restrictive laws are the appropriate basis for altering such "moral" behavior. Environmental psychologists are ready with a list of ways to alter contexts that may be enacted through such laws. For a few examples, municipalities could include bike lanes on all streets, fund efficient public transportation, and require recycling, among other things. All of these would tend to increase the likelihood of behaviors that are thought to be more sustainable.

However, it is left to others to find ways to arrive at the enactment of such laws. Changing people's notions about sustainability (criterion one), trying to increase thinking about related issues (criterion two), helping people to develop and learn new ways of thinking (criterion three), and inciting people to act on what they think (criterion four) are, as we have seen, all activities in which scientist-practitioner psychologists have engaged.

Finally, we know very little about the long term effects of behavioral interventions (e.g., Abrahamse et al., 2005; Nakatani et al., 2009; Neumann, 2007; Thanellou & Green, 2011). If behavior is readily learned through association, can it be "unlearned" quickly, as well? Does a mere change in context affect whether people will maintain behaviors? Sadly, we have only a handful of studies to rely on for long term learning in applied settings, even though the question was posed by scientist-practitioners many years ago (e.g., Gagné, 1984). We will return to this issue later in this chapter.

Questions and criticisms aside, at least we know a good bit about how to set the stage for behavior change. By carefully defining contexts, identifying motives, engaging people in such a way that they freely consent to change attempts, and then managing the change process, behavioral interventions may be among our most powerful tools. The behaviorist perspective has provided the beginnings of important psychological solutions, if only by demonstrating how differences in physical settings and reinforcement can influence behaviors (Sundstrom et al., 1996).

LEARNING AND BEHAVIOR CHANGE

Associative Learning and Consumer Behavior

Behavioral psychologists have been involved in marketplace interventions since the early days of the "consumer revolution" (Kreshel, 1990). We will learn in Chapter 10 about some of the interventions aimed at getting people to buy and consume (Blackwell et al., 2006). Now that we know of the many trade offs associated with overconsumption (including waste management, pollution, health problems, etc.), such interventions appear to be canted toward the interest of shareholder profit over other stakeholder interests (Smith & Cooper-Martin, 1997).

Still, early psychologists had every reason to believe that their involvement in stimulating consumption was, in general, a societal good. In fact, until Kahneman (2011) and other psychologists debunked the fundamental assumption of "free market" economics, psychologists who were engaged in *consumer behavior* appeared to be justified in the assumption that the marketplace would sort the interests of different stakeholders. The assumption that people make optimal (i.e., highly rational, deliberative) decisions in the marketplace, meant that the sellers of goods and services should do what they wanted (short of lying) in order to sell their products (Smith, 1776). This *caveat emptor* ("buyer beware") doctrine led some psychologists to comfortably fit in with the development of the consumer culture of the middle of the twentieth century.

Frank Stanton's career in broadcasting is an illustration of how behaviorism met limits in practice. As a graduate student in psychology at the Ohio State University, Stanton started by measuring behavior. However, his long, successful career as president of CBS also allowed him many chances to apply *targeted* advertising (Cahill, 1997). Target marketing uses stimuli that are commonly arousing to people in various demographic groups (e.g., Aaker, Brumbaugh, & Grier, 2000). To the extent that demographics such as gender, age, income, and level of education represent differences in motivation, targeting could be thought of as taking a more cognitive approach to behavior change. The significant motivational differences between genders (e.g., Hamann et al., 2004), ages (Heckhausen et al., 2010), and levels of education (Gegenfurtner & Vauras, 2012) are just a few examples of how demographics reflect motivations. Rather than leave it to chance or assume that everyone will find a particular stimulus arousing, it is now common practice to use stimuli that are motivating to the people to whom advertisers are trying to sell a product or service (Aaker et al., 2000; Cahill, 1997).

Many people concerned with sustainability see the consumer culture as a large part of the reason for current problems (Ehrenfeld, 2008; Grant, 2010; Winter, 2004). Scientific knowledge has moved well beyond the laissez-faire (free market) doctrine, with its assumption of rational choice in the marketplace and *caveat emptor* doctrine. Modern scientist-practitioners should be well aware that deliberate attempts to (1) alter the associative context and (2) target emotive responses to "shortcut" more deliberative processes (see Chapter 4) may cross important ethical boundaries (Ringold, 1995).

This calls to light perhaps the most difficult problem with applying behaviorist environmental and consumer psychology. This approach would have us deliberately alter contexts, in order to change *selected behaviors*. A fundamental question from the viewpoint of application is this: Who selects the "desired" behaviors? The authoritarian approach is that "experts" have the "correct" answer. This is quite contrary to modern philosophy of science (Viney, 2001) and to effective scientist-practitioner approaches (Highhouse, 2008; Jones & Culbertson, 2011). As a practical matter, convincing stakeholders to place limits on the actions of other stakeholders (and perhaps themselves) is a difficult process.

In the next few chapters, we will deal at greater length with the changes that are created by deliberate psychological interventions. Promising new work on the effects of consumer interventions that target both behaviors and *deliberate decisions* regarding sustainability (e.g., Hanss & Böhm, 2013; Scott, 2009) will be discussed at length.

Applied Cognitive Learning

Psychologists at the time of World War II were given the daunting task of helping the U.S. military to train millions of new recruits in a long list of jobs and specialties. Researchers such as Robert Gagné (1962, 1996)) were among those assigned to this work. Rather than following a theoretical perspective derived from the associationist laboratory research of the time, these psychologists took a decidedly pragmatic approach. In fact, Gagné's work is among the most obvious examples of an almost purely applied approach to the psychology of learning.

Applied learning theorists since this time have certainly integrated aspects of behavioral learning into interventions (e.g., Wickens, Hutchins, Carolan, & Cumming, 2013). This has been paralleled in recent decades by an explosion in basic research as part of the *cognitive revolution*; but, much of this recent research has been done in laboratories and has addressed aspects of learning that are not obviously relevant to sustainability applications (e.g., Coutanche & Thompson-Schill, 2012). For the most part, cognitive learning has dealt far less with the theoretical bases for learning (Kalechstein & Nowicki, 1997) than with *how to* get people to learn (Stricker, 1997). These researchers are among the most *criterion* driven of scientist-practitioners—their clients want to know the evidence about "what works" (sometimes called *efficacy research*), rather than evidence about *why* things may work (e.g., Steenbergen-Hu & Cooper, 2013). The motto is, "If it works, use it."

Also consistent with this strong applied bent, learning interventions are often preceded by a systematic analysis of context (Goldstein & Ford, 2002; Surface, 2012; Wickens et al., 2013). Rather than trying to develop broadly applicable learning interventions, scientist-practitioners rely on an understanding of the contingencies of a particular situation that may limit or facilitate learning. Once the situational contingencies are accounted for, learning interventions can be tailored accordingly. While this reflects the stimulus-response approach of associationist science, it typically takes a very broad approach to *measure* components of context, rather than the close *control* used in behavior analysis (Malone, 2004).

We shall also see that, because of the applied nature of much of the cognitive learning research, scientist-practitioners have time and again run up against the central issue of what makes people *want to* learn (Colquitt et al., 2000; Goldstein & Ford, 2002; Noe, 1986). Applied approaches have evolved in ways that appear to increasingly address this issue (Noe et al., 2010). But it remains an important challenge for both science and practice.

Cognitive and Social-Cognitive Learning

Cognitive and social-cognitive approaches to learning have been around for some time and take many forms (Meredith, 1927; Rotter, 1990; Tryon, 2010). Rather than provide a comprehensive discussion of the many forms of cognitive and social-cognitive learning, we will have a look at a few examples that have been evaluated enough times to warrant meta-analytic reviews in major journals. In broad terms, all of these approaches are attempts to change the way that people *think* as a means to change the way they behave (Tryon, 2010). This focus on thinking is what classifies them as cognitive approaches to learning. Integration of evidence regarding *feeling* (emotive responding) is included under the "cognitive" heading as well (Colquitt et al., 2000).

Because we have already discussed goal setting and the Brunswik Lens Model in other chapters, we will start with these as examples of cognitive approaches to learning. Goal setting applications revolve around the explicit development and description of *learning outcomes*. These outcomes are the stated aims of learning in classroom (Rolland, 2012) and worker training (Goldstein & Ford, 2002) experiences. Goal setting has been shown to help people learn the *contingencies* of behaviors in a given context (Erez & Arad, 1986), both through clarification before behavior and (especially) through the effects of feedback about results of behaviors (Erez, 1977). In other words, goal setting helps people to set up a "theory" about how things work before they try a new approach, then provides "evidence" after they try new behaviors.

In classroom applications, efficacy evidence suggests that goal setting may reduce learning (Rolland, 2012), except under certain conditions. The first condition is that teachers need to be seen as supportive. This condition has been demonstrated in workplace settings, with supervisor supportiveness, as well (Smither & London, 2009). One explanation for this is that lack of supervisor support is associated with anxiety (Kirmeyer & Dougherty, 1988), and anxiety, in turn, reduces learning (Colquitt et al., 2000). Thus, it is likely that a supportive context leads people to experience less anxiety and learn more declarative information.

Another explanation following from this is that goals are typically set by teachers, school boards, and legislators, rather than by learners themselves. Learners are venturing into situations where the contingencies are defined by others, rather than by themselves. This may make them more hesitant to test situational contingencies. But it may also make goals seem more *controlling*, depending on the way they are framed (Osman, 2012; Rawsthorne & Elliot, 1999; Tanes & Cho, 2013) and internalized (Hollenbeck, Williams, & Klein, 1989; Kumar & Jagacinski, 2011). Thus, the second condition for goals not exerting a negative effect on learning is that they be accepted by the learners themselves (Osman, 2012; Rawsthorne & Elliot, 1999).

Workplace and classroom intervention evidence shows a host of additional conditions (Goldstein & Ford, 2002; Osman, 2012) that help to determine whether goal setting will affect behaviors and learning. But, as we have seen in Chapter 1, the key aspect of goal based interventions in general is the provision of feedback (Erez, 1977). It is no surprise then that feedback interventions have also grown up alongside goal setting interventions.

Multiple cue probability learning (MCPL; Hammond, 1996) is sometimes used as a basis for such *feedback based* learning. This approach is derived from the Brunswik Lens Model and has many applications outside of formal classroom settings (Balzer, Doherty, & O'Connor, 1989). The idea behind it is to provide people with feedback about the contingencies of their decisions. Such feedback can take three forms: Task information, cognitive information, and functional information. Using Figure 5.3, task feedback provides information about individual cue validity, cognitive feedback captures the cue weights that people are using for decisions, and functional information provides overall validity information about decisions.

Balzer and his colleagues (Balzer et al., 1989, 1994; Balzer, Sulsky, Hammer, & Sumner, 1992; Dalal, Diab, Balzer, & Doherty, 2010) have provided strong evidence about the types of feedback that do and do not enhance learning. They have shown repeatedly that giving people feedback about (1) how they make their decisions (cognitive feedback) and (2) the overall effectiveness of their decisions (functional information) are less likely to positively influence learning than feedback about (3) the *actual contingencies of individual tasks* (task information). That is, information about the actual relationships between each cue, and the real relationships of these with the situation, positively affects learning (Balzer et al., 1989). This finding has been replicated in another meta-analysis, as well (Kluger & DeNisi, 1996).

Following our example from Figure 5.3, feedback about *how you are using* price, gas mileage, durability, and cargo space to arrive at your decision to buy a car is not likely to affect your future thinking. Telling you that *you perceive* gas mileage as most important, price as next most important, durability as least important, and cargo space not at all important is not likely to affect your decision. Nor is information about *the overall validity* of your decision ("You got the 'right' car"). Instead, feedback about the relationship between *actual* prices, gas mileage, durability, and cargo space and *the optimal choice* for you can change your thinking. That is, information about specific outcome contingencies is the information that you want to learn.

The lesson from this is research is that confronting people with the invalidity of either their *approach* to making decisions (*cognitive feedback*) or their final choice (*functional feedback*) is not likely to affect their learning. Specific information about optimal choices on each dimension—about contingencies—does have a learning effect. Using the cognitive maps analogy, learning about the *actual territory* we are trying to navigate is more helpful than information about the errors in *our own representations of that territory*. Thus, Brunswik Lens Model learning is an attempt to alter people's maps to conform to the territory they are trying to navigate.

This is consistent with goal setting research in recent decades, as well. Hierarchical goal structures have been used to demonstrate how people represent the contingencies of a situation in memory. Applied research along these lines has shown that people use such structures as "cognitive maps" to navigate the contingencies of their actions in classrooms (McInerney & Ali, 2006), virtual environments (Jung & Kang, 2010), economic choices (Canova, Rattazzi, & Webley, 2005; Lawson, 1997), and executive suites (Bateman, O'Neill, & Kenworthy-U'Ren, 2002; Reger & Palmer, 1996).

Most of the motivational differences we have discussed are not directly addressed in the MCPL approach. However, work following closely from it (Kluger & DeNisi, 1996) poses important motivational questions, based on integrations with control theory and research on arousal. In particular, Kluger and DeNisi (1996) suggest that wide discrepancies between feedback and desired states lead to greater arousal and allocation of more attentional resources. When things look really discrepant, we attend! This is consistent both with what we have seen about the physiology of learning processes and what we saw in Chapter 4 about emotive responses in decision processes.

However, the Feedback Intervention Theory (FIT) posed by Kluger and DeNisi does not integrate some of the *other* important motivational systems we have discussed. That is, there is still no strong theoretical integration in these applied literatures to explain how motivational variables like approach/avoidance, identity, culture, and personality relate to the learning that follows from feedback.

Nevertheless, motivation, in one or more of its forms (set points, traits, self-efficacy, identity, etc.) probably does play an important role in cognitive learning (Colquitt et al., 2000). For example, our "readiness" to learn can be affected by individual differences in *neuroticism* (He, Cassaday, Bonardi, & Bibby, 2013; Witmer & Gotlib, 2013). Put in terms of control theory, people with lower set points for amygdala arousal (higher neuroticism) may experience greater anxiety and find fewer opportunities to explore (Gluck & Myers, 2001). These set short term limits on the kind of learning we do.

Imagine that you are trying to talk to someone who is skeptical about global climate change. Use what we know about emotion in learning and the use of cognitive feedback, functional feedback, and contingency feedback to develop a persuasive strategy. Remember that telling someone that their thinking about the environment is wrong or that their overall decisions are wrong is not as likely to get them to learn as feedback about actual contingencies that matter *positively* to them.

Other findings suggest that it is not just immediate emotive responses that influence what and how we learn. To the extent that cognitive learning addresses "higher order" learning (associated with life tasks and identity), we might expect more integration with stable, motivational inclinations (cf. Kluger & DeNisi, 1996, 1998; Murayama, Pekrun, Lichtenfeld, & Vom Hofe, 2013). Using the language of memory researchers, representations of *ourselves* in memory can influence the extent to which we are motivated to attend and learn (Prebble, Addis, & Tippett, 2013). This is consistent with the evidence that *self-efficacy* is important for learning (Prebble et al., 2013; Richardson et al., 2012).

As with behavioral learning, the problem of durability is a problem in cognitive learning, too. Although longitudinal studies are few (Leutwyler, 2009; Murayama et al., 2013; Roberson, Kulik, & Pepper, 2009), there are clues in these that suggest durability may follow from stable traits like neuroticism and identity (Noe et al., 2010). To the extent that these motivations are fairly stable over time, people's greater or lesser motivation to *learn* may be quite stable, as well (Goldstein & Ford, 2002; Von Stumm & Ackerman, 2013). Also, given such stability of motive, lasting change may result from higher order learning. As researchers delve further into the motivational *whys* of cognitive learning, it is likely that this problem will be dealt with more extensively in applied settings, as well.

Social Learning and Problem-Based Learning

Social learning theory is quite consistent with these other approaches and provides additional clues to explain cognitive learning. Social learning is based on the premise that we learn the reinforcement contingencies of situations through observation of our own and others' behavioral outcomes (Rotter, 1966, 1990). We observe the feedback resulting from behaviors (our own and others), then use these observations to arrive at understandings of situational contingencies (Bandura & Walters, 1963; Woodward, 1982). There has been controversy over the idea of modeling, where we use observations of others as the basis for learning (Cowan, Longer, Heavenrich, & Nathanson, 1969). But what is clear is that we learn more and more quickly in the presence of others (Cowan et al., 1969; Durlak, Weissberg, Dymnicki, Taylor, & Schellinger, 2011; Lou, Abrami, & d'Apollonia, 2001).

Although social learning has been part of practice for a long time (cf. Meredith, 1927; Woodward, 1982), recent approaches were developed partly to address the even older problem of motivation in learning (Burke et al., 2011; Hughes, 2012). For a start, applications of social learning in classrooms suggest that students are focused on different aspects of the learning situation at different stages of development (Kalechstein & Nowicki, 1997; Kuppens et al., 2012). For example, early teens are often more focused on the approval of their peers than that of their teachers (Hughes, 2012). Thus, social development places limits on the *sources* of information to whom we attend; so practitioners have found ways to embed learning in motivationally relevant social contexts (Kuppens et al., 2012). Such developmental "readiness" is a frontier of applied learning research (Beier & Kanfer, 2010; Kanfer, Beier, & Ackerman, 2013).

Problem based learning has proven to be a particularly successful approach that incorporates both cognitive and social learning in adult learners (Gijbels, Dochy, Van den Bossche, & Segers, 2005; Koh, Khoo, & Wong, 2008; Schmidt, van der Molen, Te Winkel, & Wijnen, 2009). It appears to have started in medical school education and has expanded substantially since its beginnings in the 1970s (Schmidt et al., 2009; Vernon & Blake, 1993). Problem based learning engages supervised teams of learners in the steps of decision making about topical problem, often over extended periods of time (Schmidt et al., 2009). Its efficacy has been demonstrated in workplaces (Koh et al., 2008), as well as enough educational settings to warrant multiple meta-analytic reviews (Dochy, Segers, Van den Bossche, & Gijbels, 2003; Gijbels et al., 2005; Schmidt et al., 2009; Vernon & Blake, 1993).

Several reasons have been offered for the remarkable success of such social learning interventions. First, social learning appears to give people convincing reasons to believe that their learning will lead to increasingly specific, desirable outcomes (Kalechstein & Nowicki, 1997). In their recent meta-analysis of problem based learning in medical schools, Schmidt et al. (2009) summarized the evidence succinctly:

> The results suggest that students and graduates from the particular curriculum perform much better in the area of interpersonal skills,

and with regard to practical medical skills. In addition, they consistently rate the quality of the curriculum as higher. Moreover, fewer students drop out, and those surviving need less time to graduate. Differences with respect to medical knowledge and diagnostic reasoning were on average positive but small.

This assessment of social learning in education goes for similar sorts of learning in social groups outside of school settings, as well (Tannenbaum & Cerasoli, 2013).

The effectiveness of social learning is consistent with the two conditions of learning that we have already seen. The first is that learning alongside other learners may provide a very *supportive* learning situation. Peers are likely to be concerned with some of the same *motivational contingencies*, providing for the possibility of the *shared motives* discussed in Chapter 4. They may also "share the load" and thus reduce anxieties over workload, at least in the sort of highly motivated learners described by Schmidt et al. (2009). The second is that *feedback* from these group members is likely to relate closely to these motivating *situational contingencies* (Conway, Amel, & Gerwien, 2009). One way of thinking of this is that social learners are building a *shared mental model* (Mohammed & Dumville, 2001; Salas & Cannon-Bowers, 2001) of their tasks in a situation. Finally, knowing about the tendencies of others in your learning group may provide clarity about the contingencies of *their* social behaviors. The increase in interpersonal skills among problem based learners is perhaps testimony to this (Schmidt et al., 2009).

The popularity of *cohort* learning programs in other postgraduate professional education (Schmidt et al., 2009) may be rooted in an understanding of the effects of social learning, as well. In addition to cognitive and interpersonal skill changes, social learning in these programs may help people to *internalize* professional *norms and culture*, and develop a professional *social identity* (Collin, 2009; Mann, 2011; Meijers, 1998). To the extent that these carry over beyond educational experiences, the mental models following from social learning are likely to operate in workplace environments, as well. Even beyond this, when we bring learning groups with us to experiences outside of training and therapy, we may be able to continue to apply shared mental models as we work together. We will see how this may be highly valuable to people engaged in collective action (criterion four).

The Problem of Transfer of Training

In this way, social learning may be one answer to the problem of *transfer of training*. Transfer of training is defined as the extent to which learning that occurs in one context (e.g., classrooms, therapy, job site) is later applied in other, relevant contexts (Ford, 1997). This implies at least two dimensions: Transfer *across time* and transfer *across contexts* (Blume et al., 2010). It also relies on the question of relevance: Do the skills learned in one context actually apply in another (Ford, 1997; Kozlowski et al., 2001)?

The CEO of a large insurance carrier budgeted a million dollars to bring in customer service training for all headquarters employees who had direct customer contact. There was little effort to define the nature of the "problem" that the CEO saw with customer service—what psychologists call needs assessment. He had heard some customer complaints and seen a presentation by the training program's vendor, and this was enough information for him to institute training.

As the actual bill for the training approached two million dollars, an industrial-organizational (I-O) psychologist was asked to perform a rigorous, experimental design evaluation of the efficacy of this program. To almost no one's surprise, the customer service training was having little effect on either the employee's workplace behavior or the number of customer complaints. Instead, and despite the massive investment in a learning "solution," many of the trainees (most of who were women) reported that they were using what they had learned on their families—not at work. The CEO was replaced soon after.

Transfer of training has been defined as the *ultimate criterion* for learning interventions (Ford, 1997). The quest for transfer has led to some of the most insightful applied research on how to incite and maintain learning. Working toward a better understanding of conditions that facilitate and reduce transfer has also led to valuable insights into the precursors of learning (Blume et al., 2010; Kozlowski et al., 2001), and to the development of some interventions that have shown considerable success (Boyle & Lutzker, 2011; Burke & Hutchins, 2007). Although rare in other areas of applied research, there is even *longitudinal* research about what leads people to take what they have learned in one context and try it in another (e.g., Korunka, Dudak, Molnar, & Hoonakker, 2010).

Evidence about the conditions that affect transfer point to three general factors: (1) Individual differences in learners, (2) characteristics of training design and delivery, and (3) characteristics of the situation where the training is to be applied. Individual differences in mental abilities and motivation (including conscientiousness) have shown robust effects on training transfer (Blume et al., 2010). As we have seen in job performance, differences in mental abilities may affect how quickly and well people learn situational contingencies (Bereiter, 1995; McDaniel & Whetzel, 2005). Closely related evidence suggests that the development of cognitive representations (variously referred to as mental maps, mental models, and knowledge structures) lead to greater transfer (Schuelke et al., 2009). Learner motivation is consistently associated with transfer, as well (Blume et al., 2010). Self-efficacy (Kozlowski et al., 2001), conscientiousness (Blume et al., 2010), identity (Kane, 2010; Pidd, 2004), and numerous other motivational variables affect learning across types of training and learning contexts (cf. Abney et al., 2013; Noe et al., 2010).

We have seen how other characteristics both of the delivery of learning interventions and of the learning versus transfer contexts can affect transfer. Linking behavioral information to contingencies (Balzer et al., 1989; Neumann, 2007), including through social learning (Conway et al., 2009), and providing a situation that is not anxiety inducing (Colquitt et al., 2000; Kirmeyer & Dougherty, 1988) can affect transfer.

Many other innovations in training delivery address cognitive aspects of the learning experience and have shed light on transfer, as well. For example, varying behavior outcome contingencies in training may not always lead to better performance in identical work situations. But deliberate, minor shifts made in the contingencies of training tasks can lead to greater generalization across similar tasks in the real world (Madhavan & Gonzalez, 2010). This research suggests that transfer is enhanced when the training environment to some extent mimics the *uncertainties* of the real world.

Clearly, and despite considerable strides, the problem of transfer remains an important focus of applied research (Ford, Smith, Weissbein, Gully, & Salas, 1998). Its importance to several of the five criteria will be clarified.

Self-Regulatory Approaches

Self-regulatory approaches to learning have been developed specifically to address the transfer problem (Blume et al., 2010; Ford, 1997). Rather than relying on a facilitator, teacher, or trainer to set up a favorable learning context, a self-regulatory approach aims to help learners to develop their own metacognitive learning strategies and structures (Bandura, 2005; Ford et al., 1998). Effectively, self-regulated learners carry a learning map around in their own heads, with less need for contextual factors to stimulate learning and enhance transfer. This should sound familiar, as we discussed internalized context in Chapters 5 and 6. In self-regulated learning, the learning process itself is ultimately identified and "owned" by the learner.

Ultimately, self-regulated learning provides the learner with the final choice over both the subjects learned and the approach taken. Several "experimental" approaches to learning in the United States in the 1960s started with this assumption. For example, St. Olaf College initiated the Paracollege program in 1969 (Brown, 1989) based on this approach. After passing a series of general topic examinations, students

designed and pursued their own courses of study without any require-
ment of completing courses or receiving grades.

The efficacy of this approach was assessed only twice but showed that
completion of graduate study after college among Paracollege students
was 40% (Brown, 1989). That is, after completing undergraduate study,
they entered graduate programs (at such places as Cambridge University,
University of Chicago, Ohio State, and other prestigious institutions),
then *completed* their graduate courses of study. This completion rate for
graduate study is high, given that only about 10% of the U.S. population
has graduate degrees (according to the 2011 U.S. Census).

The self-regulatory approach also integrates behaviorist and social-cognitive
perspectives using a central motivational assumption: People generally learn
what they think they *need or want* to learn and apply it when they think it
matters. In effect, self-regulatory learning interventions teach the learner to
define the motivational context for themselves in such a way that they will
increase the behaviors *they* desire. By recognizing the realities of their contexts and of their own needs, learning strategies emerge.

Efficacy and practicality of self-regulatory interventions are supported
across numerous *single case studies* (Perry, Albeg, & Tung, 2012). These studies
come out of the behaviorist tradition, as well, following changes in one individual's behaviors over time. Despite this relationship with behaviorism,
however, self-regulatory interventions rely on metacognitive strategies,
including reminders of the relationship between learners' own motives and
the actual outcomes of their behaviors (Balzer et al., 1989; Kluger & DeNisi,
1996). So, self-regulatory learning effectively blends approaches in order to
enhance transfer of training (Alberto & Troutman, 2008; Ford, 1997; Perry
et al., 2012).

For example, counseling interventions rely on an analysis of how individuals' motivations are played out in their daily lives (Little & Chambers,
2004). Once valued outcomes (personal criteria) are identified, counselors
can discuss how a client's actions "fit" with these outcomes. Based on these
discussions, clients can develop realistic notions about the *contingencies* of their
daily actions in a context, as these relate to their desired (and avoided) outcomes. Development of self-regulatory strategies can then help to better
align behaviors with desired outcomes (Little & Chambers, 2004). Relapse
prevention strategies can be used to maintain self-regulation after training
(Hutchins & Burke, 2006).

Another way of thinking of this is that self-regulation internalizes contextual contingencies (Ford, 1997; Ford et al., 1998; Schmidt et al., 2009). The
effect of this is to help learners to determine where different behaviors may

apply or not apply, depending on contextual cues. That is, it focuses on the transfer of learning across contexts by way of self-feedback about *cue validity*. To the extent that feedback suggests that our initial assessments about the "correct" behavioral responses were good ones, we will likely repeat both the initial assessments of the situation and the pursuant behavior in the future (Kluger & DeNisi, 1998).

In fact, Ford (1997) defines transfer of training itself partly in terms of acquisition of *adaptive expertise*—an understanding of when and where to apply learned behavioral contingencies. Developing adaptive expertise has been the focus of some very effective training (Kozlowski et al., 2001; Sterman, 2006). Using ideas we have built on since Chapter 1, effective cognitive learning helps people recognize the complexity and uncertainty of their contexts using something akin to a systems perspective. Developing this kind of expertise about environmental issues or any other complex system takes not just time, but intelligence, supportive feedback, and conscientious effort.

We also saw in Chapter 6 how our understandings of context affected our ability to understand others. We discover which emotional displays "work" in a context and learn new behaviors (and contingencies) accordingly (Järvenoja et al., 2013; Lamm & Lewis, 2010). Further, in emotive perception, we may learn how to "read" *each other's* motivations through the development of this sort of expertise about stimulus behavior contingencies. Such meta-emotive cognition may serve change agents well, as we will see.

In educational settings, formative assessment applies some of these same approaches in order to develop a learner's own, self-regulatory strategies (Clark, 2012; Kingston & Nash, 2011). Evidence generally supports the careful development of feedback mechanisms that address the particular interests of individual learners. Such assessment may appear expensive and time consuming in practice, but its cost may be offset by the potential for sustained learning across the lifespan (Nicol, 2007). In any case, helping people "learn to learn" has been the basis for a host of effective interventions (Brown, 1989; Kingston & Nash, 2011; Sitzmann & Ely, 2011).

It is important to note that individual differences and developmental trajectories may place important limits on self-regulatory approaches (Little & Chambers, 2004). For example, we saw in Chapter 4 how self-regulatory capacity may vary depending on conscientiousness. Similarly, Chapter 6 clarified the effects of social, cognitive, and moral development on both our motivations and our self-regulatory capacities. These may not be easily affected by interventions and may place stubborn limits on our ability to self-regulate. Alternatively, adaptive learning may be quite easy and fun for people who know how to manage their own behaviors in the service of their motives.

As we have seen, differences in transfer may also be based on an interaction of the complexity of the situation and the expertise of the learner. Using a workplace example, in job specific training, learners are often expert about the job in other ways, and are simply adding material to their already complex cognitive maps (Sun, Zimmer, & Fu, 2011). Novices have the more difficult task of learning about a complex situation (Blume et al., 2010; Jones & Parameswaran, 2005; Kozlowski et al., 2001; Sun et al., 2011). Thus, there may be greater effort involved for novices than for experts. Knowing that there is a lot of work involved in learning may be enough to scare some less motivated people off.

In fact, an even more profound type of change may follow from meta-cognitive interventions. By clarifying people's stated motives at the beginning of the intervention, metacognitive reflection may effectively *change the motives themselves*. Most readers will know a college student who discovered, after trying some of the specific activities involved in a career, that they really didn't want to follow a career path after all. Evidence on *realistic previews* shows that initial information about situational contingencies can lead people to reduce their strivings toward a particular career or job (Premack & Wanous, 1985; Saks, Wiesner, & Summers, 1994). This contingency information may serve as a "gut check"—"Here's what it's like to do this: Do you really want it?" Thus, the initial discussion of motivations and aspirations used in some interventions may help people *self-select* into or out of learning experiences, based on identity and motivation (Saks et al., 1994).

Cognitive Learning and Sustainability

We have seen that most of the potential applications of traditional environmental psychology come from a behaviorist perspective. Considerably less empirical attention has been paid either to cognitively mediated learning (Hanss & Böhm, 2013; Haq & Zimring, 2003; Pelletier, Lavergne, & Sharp, 2008; Winkel, Saegert, & Evans, 2009) or to the long term effects of contextually specific learning (Abrahamse et al., 2005; Winkel et al., 2009) to sustainability criteria.

Much of the scholarship related to education about sustainability issues has focused on developing ideas for learning interventions. Given the tradition of application in learning, it is ironic that there is less quantitative, psychologically based evidence regarding the efficacy of these approaches (cf. Hanss & Böhm, 2013; Læssøe & Ohman, 2010). Studies that do report quantitative evaluations of interventions have also tended to have methodological problems (Hornik, Cherian, Madansky, & Narayana, 1995; Zelezny, 1999). One way of thinking of this is that educational scholarship has dealt with context specific descriptions of what "might work" instead of broad evaluations of what "will work" for learning interventions. Contextually narrow approaches are, as we have seen, an important part of application. But efficacy evidence about transfer of sustainability learning interventions is still developing.

That being said, there were a number of early researchers in sustainability who tried to incorporate both the systems perspective and motivational issues into interventions. Granted, this research, which was meta-analyzed by Winkler and Winett (1982), was concerned with behavior, rather than learning outcomes. But it did look at the motivational components of change in water consumption behaviors.

Very recent applied work has also taken more of a systems approach (Ginns, Martin, & Marsh, 2013; Hine, Bhullar, Marks, Kelly, & Scott, 2011). In fact, promising new studies have looked at the effects of interventions on psychological variables related to sustainability. In children, *environmental education* has been shown to influence beliefs and affect, in addition to behavior (Collado, Staats, & Corraliza, 2013). Interventions with adults to create awareness of purchasing choices (e.g., Hanss & Böhm, 2013) have also taken a systems approach.

Applied Cognitive Maps

Environmental psychologists were also the first to attempt to apply the concept of cognitive maps outside of laboratories (Gifford, 2007a,b; Heft, 2013; Kitchin, 1994). Their work has been used to design signage to help people find their way around. The problem of *wayfinding* can be effectively managed through developing external stimuli that will catch people's attention and help them to learn fairly complex visual–spatial relationships. Like other learning, individual differences place a limit on transfer (Hund & Nazarczuk, 2009; Rodrigues, Sauzéon, Wallet, & N'Kaoua, 2010; Woollett & Maguire, 2010).

Research on how people learn to find their way around has also led environmental psychology research into the cognitive learning domain (Haq & Zimring, 2003). People learn a physical area by starting with nearby features (concrete operations) and rapidly form more abstracted (differentiated and integrated) representations of the relationships in a larger space (Haq & Zimring, 2003). What is perhaps more interesting is the speed with which learning of these spatial relationships occurs (Haq & Zimring, 2003; Murray, Brasted, & Wise, 2002). This suggests that wayfinding involves procedural learning, rather than more cognitively mediated, declarative learning.

Once again, however, motivation is begged in much of this work. Wayfinding, for example, may only matter to novices who are looking for a particular place that has importance to them. We still need to understand what gets people to *want to* form cognitive maps if we are looking for effective, durable change. Living in physical locations where there are problems getting around may provide such motivation, at least for some (Grasmück & Scholz, 2005; Martin et al., 2007).

There have been two recent applications of the cognitive mapping approach to problem based learning about sustainability issues. One (Rye, Landenberger, & Warner, 2013) demonstrated the use of concept mapping in teacher training about watersheds. The other (Truelove & Parks, 2012) asked people involved in environmental action about the contingencies of various actions. This study showed that even people who are motivated to take action have cognitive misrepresentations of contingent relationships when compared to actual relationships—much like bias and heuristic research (Kahneman, 2011). Neither study provided evidence about the efficacy of their problem based learning interventions, demonstrating again that much remains to be done to address the five criteria.

The broader applications of cognitive learning are still exploring the roles that motivation, identity, and development may play in transfer of training (Blume et al., 2010; Noe et al., 2010). Here, applied sustainability research has an opportunity to take the lead. In fact, there are a few examples of applied work in sustainability that incorporate motivational variables into interventions.

For example, an educational intervention with the Spanish hospitality industry (Cegarra-Navarro, Eldridge, & Martinez-Martinez, 2010) has recently integrated both contingency learning and social-emotive issues we have discussed. Applied psychologists here discovered that a large scale sustainability training intervention was successful partly because there was clear communication that old ways of doing things could be "unlearned" *without* incurring problems. As in other cognitive learning, the emotive concerns of learners in a social context appear to have played an important role in the success of this training process. In addition, feedback about actual contingencies, consistent with feedback interventions, appears to have been the primary mechanism for this intervention.

We have also seen that reducing people's stress is an important way to set the stage for deliberative learning (Gluck & Myers, 2001; Petrovich et al., 2009). Given this, *restorative* experiences in natural environments may provide such a learning platform (Hartig & Staats, 2003). Some of the activities involved in outdoor learning experiences are actually quite stressful (Bunting, Tolson, Kuhn, Suarez, & Williams, 2000; Priest, 1992), so choosing activities based on their stress reducing properties is likely to be necessary if cognitive learning is the goal. This is also an important platform for research, given the popularity of outdoor experiences in learning and therapy (e.g., Priest, 1992; Wolf & Mehl, 2011).

Research on *cognitive consistency* and *cognitive dissonance* also provide important clues for applications of feedback in order to increase PEBs. Recall that this approach pits what people *say* they believe against how they *act*: "Here is what you did when you made this choice, but here are your (inconsistent) values statements." Such interventions (also known as "hypocrisy" interventions) have shown effects on water consumption (Dickerson, Thibodeau, Aronson, & Miller, 1992; Kantola, Syme, & Nesdale, 1983) and energy conservation behaviors (Kantola, Syme, & Campbell, 1984). It is not clear whether cognitive or behavioral feedback is responsible for their effect. Based on what we have learned (Balzer et al., 1992), the behavioral feedback

("Here's what you did"), not the cognitive feedback ("Here's what you said you believe"), is what affected behavior change (Harmon-Jones & Harmon-Jones, 2019). Transfer is not addressed in these studies, but they have shown the potential importance of identity in learning.

Safety Training as Analogue

If we consider hazardous outcomes as one way of operationalizing the risks that can be incurred by human activities in the environment, then *safety training* is addressing important criteria for purposes of sustainability. Evidence from applied safety training *does* delve into the KSAOs (knowledge, skills, abilities, and other characteristics) and motivations behind learning and behavior change. For example, recent meta-analyses show fairly conclusively that having actually been exposed to hazards made certain kinds of safety training more effective (Burke et al., 2006, 2011). If you have experienced a safety hazard, high quality training is likely to make a difference in your later behavior. If you have not experienced problems, then training effects may be less pronounced. By substituting "a safety hazard" with "an environmental disaster," we can infer that people who have experienced environmental problems are more "ready" to listen to engaging learning experiences.

> Although popular wisdom may be that people only "wake up" when they actually have experienced a disaster, it is not entirely clear that such motivated learning in fact occurs on its own (Le Coze, 2013). Instead, it appears that the experience of a disaster has less to do with this sort of learning than it does with the *motivation* to learn when learning opportunities are presented (Burke et al., 2006, 2011).

Another important finding from these studies is the comparison of underlying, psychological aspects of learning interventions. Cognitive learning interventions (e.g., lectures, readings, and video based training) may not be as *engaging* as others (e.g., modeling, simulations, and hands-on experiences). The finding that "engagement" is associated with differences in transfer once again supports the idea that motivation precedes and needs to be maintained by learning (Burke et al., 2006; Noe et al., 2010).

Innovation, Creativity, and Learning

We change as a result of our immediate surroundings through behavioral, cognitive, social, and self-regulating mechanisms. Some of these sorts of learning involve behaviors that alter the context, usually in a reactive fashion. That is, we respond to the context by changing the context, with little thought. For example, we may swat at a mosquito that is approaching us. Sometimes, however, we attempt to change the world around us in a more deliberate fashion, usually in order to try to make it conform to our needs (Heft, 2013).

Such altering of context could even be considered a hallmark of our species. There are of course other animals that alter their natural environs, usually in order to mate and raise offspring: Think birds' nests, ant hills, and beehives. Other large primates even use tools to "bring the environment into conformity" with their needs; and a silverback gorilla's fitful ripping up of undergrowth may bear a resemblance to (mostly male) humans mowing their lawns on the weekend. But humans have done this sort of alteration of empirical systems to conform to our rational systems in unprecedented, sometimes remarkable, and sometimes catastrophic ways.

Our adaptation does not rely on learning itself, as it does with other animals. It relies on very deliberate *application* of what we have learned in order to alter the world around us. For a few obvious examples, chances are that you have been reading this in a building that keeps you away from predators, maintains some temperature to keep you warmer or cooler than you would be outside the building, and controls light sources so that you can do your activities at any time of the day or night. These adaptations all relied on humans who learned to manipulate environmental materials to form structures, alter temperatures, and produce artificial light sources.

As with other adaptations (genetic and behavioral), some of the alterations we make do turn out to be adaptive (by chance or design) and some do not. But, changing the world around us only "works" sometimes. First, the deliberate changes we make to our contexts are generally based on our cognitive maps of them. To the extent that the changes we make are novel, psychologists refer to them as *creative* (Hunter, Bedell, & Mumford, 2007; Kim, 2008). To the extent that these novel approaches are *effective*, we refer to them as *innovative* (Hunter et al., 2007). Creativity relies on our individual abilities to transfer ideas from one context to another (Hunter et al., 2007; Kim, 2008). Presumably, innovation relies on these same individual differences, but also relies to some extent on the needs of the moment in our context, and the accuracy of our cognitive map of the context.

Some of the evidence so far is consistent with cognitive learning research. People are more creative when they are less stressed (Byron, Khazanchi, & Nazarian, 2010; Davis, 2009) and feel as though they have greater control over situational contingencies (Byron & Khazanchi, 2012). Although mental abilities are slightly related to creativity overall (Kim, 2008), differences in people's ability to deconstruct situational contingencies (called divergent thinking) is more related (Kim, 2008). This is quite consistent with the idea that situational expertise is what predicts our ability to operate creatively (Jones & Parameswaran, 2005; Rauch & Frese, 2007). Finally, there is some evidence that openness is related to creativity (Hammond, Neff, Farr, Schwall, & Zhao, 2011).

Learning to be creative or innovative sounds like a wonderful thing, but it is also a big part of the environmental issues with which we are concerned. We have altered our environments so substantially that we may no longer be able to adapt to them. That is, we have problems because we learn to alter our environments without adequate consideration of the eventual contingencies of these changes. But, paradoxically, being creative requires a transfer of contingencies (Strickland, 1989). In fact, how we learn enough about the situation to change it in *innovative* ways remains an important area of research.

It is what motivates us to innovate and the direction of our innovation that perhaps matters most. Here, we are faced again with the question of not just cognitive, but also moral development. Some complexity in our representations of an empirical environment is probably essential to innovative change. But volition with respect to the direction of change we make is guided by fairly unpredictable personal inclinations (Jones & Parameswaran, 2005). So, we might choose to innovate in ways to kill other life forms, extract resources, or set barriers against other legitimate interests. Alternatively, we might try to find ways to reduce the harm we cause, support our common life and interests, and break down barriers. Innovation is not inherently good or bad—*volition* in those with situational expertise is.

Applying the Five Criteria

1. **What prompts people to think they have a problem (or not)?**
   Stimulating a fear response reduces our ability to learn complex information. If we see things as "a problem," and especially an anxiety arousing problem, we tend to revert to procedural responses that we have already learned. This can be very helpful when we are facing a major threat.

   But framing things as a threat or problem will tend to reduce our openness to learning new things and being creative (Byron et al., 2010; Witmer & Gotlib, 2013). Instead, if a discrepancy is framed as an *opportunity*, and we have time to consider various potential consequences, we may come up with some very creative, even innovative responses. Being with a group, where we can share feedback and workloads may help with this. Perhaps most importantly, having a "perspective," such as self-regulation and social learning allow, may even reduce our tendency to frame things as threats in the first place.

   Motivation and development may also place limits on problem versus non-problem framing. How hard does it appear to be to engage in unsustainable versus sustainable actions (called *green efficacy*)? If I identify myself as wanting to "go green," but it looks really hard to do, I may change to a less "green" motivation (Kantola et al., 1983). By the same token, if the expense and trouble of buying and maintaining a gas-guzzler is made salient at the start of the decision making process, people may choose other alternatives. Self-efficacy, like most things, can work for or against our particular aims. So, framing things as threats (e.g., gas-guzzlers are hard to maintain—a problem) may not always be advantageous. It helps to think these issues through before framing messages.

But what we know about people's understanding of sustainability issues strongly suggests that we do have a problem that learning may be able to help manage. Many people do not see any problems with environmental change (Leiserowitz, Smith, & Marlon, 2011; Maibach, Leiserowitz, Roser-Renouf, & Mertz, 2011), which constitutes a huge opportunity for scientist-practitioners to develop learning interventions that work. We will see more about "what works" shortly.

2. **What makes people think more or less carefully when they decide on an action?**

Clearly, the answer to the first criterion question helps to answer this one. The emotions that follow from motivations can have considerable effects on learning, in much the same ways emotions affect deliberative decision making. We have seen that people who are afraid or angry are less likely to make the considerable effort needed to learn more complex information about the world around them. We are more likely to learn things we care about—but not if we care about it to the point of anxiety.

This and earlier chapters have also made it clear that self-regulation is one way of defining deliberative decision processes. In this chapter, we have seen good evidence that we can learn to be more self-regulatory (Little & Chambers, 2004). In fact, there is important recent work showing that learning to be aware of our choices can have an impact on pro-environmental behavior (Amel et al., 2009). The broader research on how people learn self-regulation is quite considerable and presents some solid recommendations for "how to" do this (Blume et al., 2010). These include a supportive social environment, learning that addresses our developmental concerns, contingency relevant feedback, and processes that involve the development of maps toward learning itself.

People with greater expertise about the situation are (1) more likely to have had the opportunity to learn through the "explore" (rather than "react") mode; (2) better able to integrate what they see into their more accurate mental models of the world; and (3) paradoxically, have less need to be deliberative because what they already know makes it possible for them to act adaptively without as much deliberation (they have developed better cognitively mediated heuristics).

People who deliberate about how their own motives relate to their learning are also able to transfer what they have learned more effectively (Blume et al., 2010). Put another way, understanding how identity and behavior are linked may help people to be who they want to be across situations. It may also help people to make realistic decisions about who they are *not*—what they thought they wanted to do, but, upon discovery of realities, decide they don't.

3. **What makes people change the way they think and behave?**
    We do so every day. Among the important questions for our purposes are (1) how to incite this change in others, (2) how to maintain changes once they are made, (3) how to help people manage their own learning, and (4) how to direct this durable, self-directed change in ways that makes it more versus less adaptive to both the individual and the species.

    Associative learning (aka behavioral learning) has been the "go to" approach in environmental psychology and consumer behavior for some time. Carefully controlling the stimulus environment—essentially putting people into elaborate Skinner Boxes—has shown some impressive results and has found a powerful medium in smartphones and social media, both of which can control the stimulus context. Treated as a singular construct, feedback has also had effects on various kinds of sustainable behaviors, though, once again, the conditions under which this operates are not at all clear (Karlin, Zinger, & Ford, 2015). So, the associative approach has very substantial limits, particularly in terms of durable, deliberative, and self-directed change across stimulus situations. We can get people to act the way we want them to, at least for a short time, and under very specific conditions using associationist methods, but fundamental questions remain, including whether behavior change is actually "learning" at all. Durable change is likely to be elusive when the "learning" situation doesn't match the more consequential contexts where change is desired, and when the feedback is not related closely to the motives behind people's behavioral choices.

    Cognitive approaches have opened important frontiers, and scientist-practitioners have developed quite successful means for more generalized, deliberative, and self-regulated learning as a result. People in classrooms, training facilities, and in a broad range of less controlled learning environments are given the means to navigate the contingencies of their situations, decide which principles apply in what circumstances, and figure out how to learn what they want to learn for themselves. This empowering approach to learning is likely to have far reaching, even life long effects on both the way we think and even on the things we are motivated to do. Personal identity and motivations, particularly in the form of self-efficacy, can be changed by such learning (Bandura, 1978). Less empowering circumstances relegate us to reactive, often fear based sorts of rote behavioral change.

    Cognitive learning itself may lead to creative new behaviors, as well, with potential for resulting innovation. This is one of the places where moral development may place an important limit on our adaptive capacity. To the extent that we learn things that are likely to reduce species level adaption, all the glories we have discovered in cognitive learning may lead us drastically astray. Thus, the idea posed by H. G. Wells in the initial quote for this chapter isn't always true: By advancing education, we may give monsters wings.

This speaks directly to what the factors that motivate people to learn: (1) Control over what and how we learn; (2) a supportive, non-stressful learning environment; (3) focus on specific, actual contingencies of action (developing situational expertise); (4) a chance to receive specific, contingent feedback that helps to develop new self-regulatory strategies; and (5) social and individual reflection on what has happened through the learning experience. To the extent that these variables are well managed, there are even chances to advance moral development (Bandura, 1969). Particularly in social learning, these steps will often include consideration of the needs of other learners, and the social and altruistic contingencies of one's actions. This knowledge often has great practical value for effective action and learning; so focusing on the needs of *others* is often quite adaptive for the *individual*.

Nevertheless, even in social learning there is a need to allow for aspects of development that cannot be readily changed, at least in short term learning experiences. *Adaptive education* (Waxman, Wang, Anderson, & Walberg, 1985) is largely defined by this problem: Different learning approaches are used, depending on individual differences in children. This is not so much a particular set of "steps" or best practices in learning as it is a careful assessment, followed by targeting of learning experiences based on individual differences. We may not always have the luxury of standardized assessments outside of classroom and therapeutic settings. But, as we shall see, addressing the particular motives and developmental trajectories of our audiences, then targeting our messages to them, can be quite effective (Waxman et al., 1985).

Perhaps the most important question for this criterion is, "What makes people *maintain and generalize* new ways of thinking and behaving?" Scientist-practitioners in sustainability have important opportunities to apply what we know so far about how to enhance transfer and, by extension, to innovate.

4. When are people likely to take action?

As a general rule, people need to understand the situation in order to take effective action. At the beginning of the learning process, we need to know the situation well enough to decide whether discrepancies are real. Later in the process, as we gain social expertise, astute learners come to understand the contingencies faced by *other* stakeholders. Needs assessment is a way to gather exactly this kind of information about others' needs, barriers, and the contingencies they see in their choices.

Helping individuals to learn the situation and learn to self-regulate are important parts of this. But they are only part. We have seen again that effective action relies on groups. In fact, we might even define another dimension of "training transfer" that is particularly important to this criterion question. When will people transfer learning to those around them? How do we help groups to learn differences in knowledge and expertise among their members? What is the group level analogue to self-regulation that allows groups to effectively learn from one another? Guiding groups to *shared mental models* may be an important answer to this criterion question. The effects of social learning on collective action require more consideration in applied research on sustainability.

5. **What are the characteristics of change efforts that are likely to work?**

Efficacy research about learning interventions has provided a wealth of good answers to this question. We have only briefly reviewed the extensive research on conditions that help to increase the likelihood of behavioral and cognitive learning and transfer. What has received less attention in the applied research is the extent to which stakeholder engagement plays a role in any of this. The closest we have come to accounting for this is through the use of needs assessment—where multiple stakeholders are engaged in the interest of defining the situational contingencies (Goldstein & Ford, 2002). This sort of "collective learning" may prove to be a highly practical, if time consuming and difficult aspect of change.

9

PROCESSES IN APPLIED PSYCHOLOGY

In 1962, Rachel Carson issued a call to action. She directed our attention toward controlling *ourselves*, rather than controlling the *external* environment. Scientists have not answered this call. Despite the tremendous development of applied psychological methods, science continues to focus on *external* environmental changes, rather than on controlling the *human activities* that cause these changes. Worse, applied psychology has taken a central role in stimulating these human activities, mostly by contributing to organizational and consumer decisions with major environmental consequences. Despite having the methods for controlling human activities, Carson's call seems to have been largely ignored by the people most able to answer it.

In this chapter, we will continue our exploration of some of the more prominent and effective of these *methods*, with an eye to applying each in service of the five criteria. Because there are large research literatures in each applied area, we will explore applied psychology in two chapters. After a general introduction, this chapter will cover applications from human factors engineering (HFE), educational, clinical, and forensic psychology. Chapter 10 will consider applications of industrial-organizational (I-O) and consumer psychology (CP) in market and community interactions, respectively. Current and potential applications in the service of the five criteria will be considered for each area.

Many of these applications are common—used on a daily basis. Their widespread use is testimony to their practicality, so criterion five is to some extent assumed. But, for most, there are also limitations to their practical use outside of certain contexts. For example, clinical interventions usually start and end in a private office with a skilled practitioner. They are often impractical in other settings. And, just because interventions are practical and commonly used does not mean that they are effective, even in the circumstances for which they were designed. We have much to learn about the efficacy of some, and new interventions have yet to be developed and evaluated.

One indication of the importance of applied approaches can be gathered from a look at Table 9.1. Most of the leading causes of death in the U.S. are directly addressed by applied psychologists. Accidental death is

Table 9.1 Ten leading causes of death by age group, adults, United States—2010

Rank	Age group 15–24	25–34	35–44	45–54	55–64	65+	Total
1	Accident 12,341	Accident 14,573	Accident 14,792	Cancers 50,211	Cancers 109,501	Heart disease 477,338	**Heart disease 597,689**
2	Homicide 4,678	Suicide 5,735	Cancers 11,809	Heart disease 36,729	Heart disease 68,077	Cancers 396,670	**Cancers 574,743**
3	Suicide 4,600	Homicide 4,258	Heart disease 10,594	Accident 19,667	Respiratory disease 14,242	Respiratory disease 118,031	**Respiratory disease 138,080**
4	Cancers 1,604	Cancers 3,619	Suicide 6,571	Suicide 8,799	Accident 14,023	Stroke 109,990	**Stroke 129,476**
5	Heart disease 1,028	Heart disease 3,222	Homicide 2,473	Liver disease 8,651	Diabetes 11,677	Alzheimer's disease 82,616	**Alzheimer's disease 120,859**

Source: Adapted from National Vital Statistics System, National Center for Health Statistics, CDC: Office of Statistics and Programming, National Center for Injury Prevention and Control, CDC.

addressed by HFE, suicide and stress-related illnesses (cancers and heart disease) are addressed by clinical psychology, and several are addressed by public campaigns, which are informed by consumer and educational psychology research.

The list of practical, effective psychological interventions with potential applications in the service of the five sustainability criteria is also long. Although only relatively few have received tests specific to the five criteria, there are many opportunities for interested scientist-practitioners to give them a try.

An Overview of the Areas of Applied Psychology

How They Differ From Basic Research Areas

There are several factors that set the major areas of applied psychology apart from the basic subdisciplines we have discussed so far. The first is that they are generally accepted as being applied, as opposed to *basic* areas (DeLeon, Bullock, & Catania, 2013; Proctor & Vu, 2011). Part of what this means is that they are defined more by the scientific processes followed in practice than by the theories that describe their phenomena of interest. As discussed in Chapter 2, scientist-practitioners are focused on solving the problems they confront, and are less concerned with complex explanatory frameworks. Basic research is also carried out mostly by academic researchers and more often occurs in laboratories.

Second, although the explanatory frameworks of basic research can be very helpful in practice (DeLeon et al., 2013; Lévy-Leboyer, 1988), their primary purpose is to describe and understand *causes* of behavior. Applied research, by contrast, is aimed at managing *outcomes* of psychological processes through measurement, prediction, feedback, and direct intervention. As we will see, the *identification of important outcomes* is itself an important process in applied psychology.

Third, most scientist-practitioners in the applied disciplines are employed full time outside academia. For example, there are approximately 85,000 licensed clinical psychologists in the United States alone (American Psychological Association, 2013b). I-O psychology has experienced dramatic growth over the past twenty years (Rogelberg & Gill, 2004; Society for Industrial and Organizational Psychology, 2013b), and over 70% of this group is employed outside academia (Khanna, Medsker, & Ginter, 2012).

Aside from being "not" basic psychology, what do these areas share in common? First, applied psychologists function as *decision helpers*, rather than as teachers and researchers. A common misconception about this is that they simply provide expert advice: A client presents *a problem*, and the "expert" provides *a solution*. We will see that applied psychologists support all aspects of clients' decisions using science based processes. We will also see

PROCESSES IN APPLIED PSYCHOLOGY

that it is rare to identify a *single* problem with a *single* solution. Second, and quite obviously, applied psychologists *have* clients. At the heart of the decision making process is the *relationship* between the psychological service provider and the people asking for advice (de Haan, Duckworth, Birch, & Jones, 2013; Gehrie, 1999; Hedge & Borman, 2008; Imel, Hubbard, Rutter, & Simon, 2013). Third, and perhaps most important, is the common approach taken to discovery and feedback.

Intervention process used in applied psychology

1. Identify and gather information from stakeholders
2. Assess and statistically analyze relevant variables
3. Provide initial feedback to appropriate stakeholders
4. Design and implementation interventions
5. Assess and provide feedback to appropriate stakeholders to evaluate interventions

---

The box is an overview of the procedures followed by most of the subdisciplines of applied psychology. It shows that applied psychology interventions follow a process that is designed to support decision making in every step, from identifying problems to evaluating the outcomes of the interventions that have been designed to address these problems. Like the scientific process in Figure 1.3, it is also an *iterative* process of discussion, discovery, feedback, discussion, discovery, feedback … To briefly elaborate, most subdisciplines start with initial interviews with primary stakeholders, in order to arrive at some agreement about the nature of the client–psychologist relationship (Church & Waclawski, 2008; Lévy-Leboyer, 1988; Morrison, 1993). Depending on the area of practice, there is greater or less structure, and more or less research literature to guide these initial interactions (Bengtsson & Agerfalk, 2011; Church & Waclawski, 2008; Lévy-Leboyer, 1988; Morrison, 1993). Initial discussions are also an opportunity to begin to define the criteria for desired outcomes of the relationship.

Step two in the box is common to all the scientist-practitioner approaches (APA, 2013b; Lowman, 1998; Morrison, 1993; Nelson, Hoelzle, Sweet, Arbisi, & Demakis, 2010; Poropat, 2009; Walters, 2003). This *assessment* step can provide many kinds of information about the empirical system in which scientist-practitioners are operating. Although these vary among specialties, assessments provide initial information about inputs (e.g. individual differences), processes (e.g. group characteristics), and outcomes (i.e. criteria) in the situation. Initial assessment also provides a *baseline* measure that can be compared when the assessments are repeated later (i.e., after interventions have been attempted). By comparing later assessments (step five) with baseline assessment, decision makers are able to discover whether changes have occurred.

Statistical analysis of the results of these initial assessments serves the same sort of diagnostic purpose as thermometers, MRIs, and other technologies provide to medical practitioners. However, in addition to serving as passive diagnostic tools for professional decision making, clients of psychological services often take a more active role in evaluating the evidence from these assessments. Instead of "informing" clients about their strengths and problems, results of assessments are used to provide *feedback*—step three in the process in the box. This feedback is a starting point for ongoing discussion and reflection about underlying issues (Jones & Lindley, 1998; Lillie, 2007; Poston & Hanson, 2010).

One way of thinking of such feedback is that it provides a sort of "mirror" to clients. Sometimes we may see things that we like, sometimes not, and sometimes we are surprised by the discrepancies between assessment results and our previous notions about ourselves and our circumstances. In short, assessment based feedback is used as a metacognitive aid in decision making with clients.

Conversations with people whose jobs involve sustainability often do not include "quick fixes," such as changing laws through political action (Albee, 1979). In fact, they often touch on the same processes that scientist-practitioners follow on a more formal basis (Table 9.2).

A good example is the James River Basin Partnership (2020), or JRBP. This group has successfully implemented broad change in individual thinking and practices at the top of a large watershed—in a historically very politically conservative area. Their successes have involved no change in public policies or enforcement mechanisms. They have relied entirely on (1) multiple stakeholder engagement (through executive board composition, donor bases, and individual landowners); (2) various sorts of funded investigations (chemical, biological, and psychological) to identify water quality concerns and issues; (3) feedback and discussion of evidence with stakeholders (board and community); (4) careful design and implementation of (highly successful) solutions; and (5) ongoing evaluation research and feedback.

Listening to longtime employees of the JRBP is almost like listening to successful scientist-practitioners in psychology. Their *how to* includes such things as (1) listening without judging; (2) seeking to understand stakeholders' concerns; (3) discussing practical, potentially valuable new approaches; (4) providing assessments and feedback of information relevant to specific stakeholder interests; and (5) following up to

PROCESSES IN APPLIED PSYCHOLOGY

> find out about further concerns. A big part of what they are trying to accomplish is to reach people who are resistant to government and environmentalists with scientifically based ways to manage their farms, streams, lawns, and beloved places—in ways that are also good for others "downstream."

For clients of all sorts of psychological services, a key point in the intervention process is step four: Decision making about change. Some initial assessments may show that there is little value to be gained by further efforts to change thinking and behavior. Assessment feedback discussions may indicate that "all is well" or, possibly, that change attempts simply would require too many resources of various sorts. However, if discussions about initial assessments suggest that changes are practical and likely to advance client's purposes, then the design and implementation process has begun. It is during intervention design that the client is usually gaining a better understanding of what the entire process is likely to do. In fact, discussion of what is being discerned though the "mirror" of feedback often leads to important insights and changes without further intervention: The first three steps are interventions themselves.

Step five is often a repeat of step one. But, follow-up data gathering and feedback is somewhat less common than the previous steps (Fischer, Moeller, Cress, & Nuerk, 2013; Goldstein & Ford, 2002). Using a medical analogy, surgeons don't commonly go back immediately after the surgery to do the same tests used in diagnosis. Instead, as in many psychological interventions, a client's reports about their satisfaction are enough.

Still, there are plenty of situations where comparisons are made between "preintervention" and "postintervention" assessments. These can take a number of forms (Cook & Campbell, 1979; Goldstein & Ford, 2002), all of which fall under the general definition of *evaluation research* (Wortman, 1983). Such research may be required by funding agencies, insurance companies, and policy making bodies. In fact, evaluation research is quite common in applied psychology: Most of the meta-analyses reported in this book are accomplished by combining a large number of evaluations of single interventions. But evaluation research is less common than are initial assessments. Almost all scientist-practitioners rely on step two—initial assessments—while many fewer do full blown evaluations of the efficacy of the interventions they have used (Goldstein & Ford, 2002; Grove & Ostroff, 1991; Ployhart & Weekley, 2010).

There are several possible reasons for this (Grove & Ostroff, 1991). First, evaluation research is more feasible in the subdisciplines that deal with large samples of individuals (i.e., educational and I-O psychology), than for those that provide services one person at a time (i.e., HFE and clinical psychology). The second is cost. After spending considerable resources on initial assessments and systematic interventions, clients may be reluctant to spend additional resources, especially if they have already have formed clear notions of how things have turned out. Like surgeons, if the client is happy, scientist-practitioners are often just as happy to leave such research and feedback alone. A third is the delicacy of providing feedback from such research. This can often be very conflict laden, and is often avoided for this reason (Goldstein & Ford, 2002; Grove & Ostroff, 1991). The people who paid the psychologist to help may have little desire to know whether the resources they spent were unjustified by the outcome. These are some of the ethical issues associated with step five.

Beyond the process in the box detailing the five steps, the similarities among subdisciplines are not so universal or obvious. In fact, one way to find underlying similarities—sometimes shared only by one or two areas—is to understand their *differences*. We will discuss several ways of distinguishing the subdisciplines: The first of these is *level of analysis*.

Level of Analysis

The concept of levels of analysis derives from statistical reasoning. When statisticians reach conclusions, they do not usually do so on the basis of single cases, but on *samples* composed of numerous cases. If the cases being analyzed are characteristics of individual people, then *individuals* are the level of analysis (Hollenbeck et al., 1995). For example, individual differences measures use samples of individuals as their level of analysis. If analyses are being done on a sample of *decisions or behaviors* displayed by a single individual, then decisions or behaviors are the level of analysis (Noell et al., 2013). Table 9.2 describes the levels of analysis used in applied areas.

Human factors engineering is mostly aimed at affecting decisions and behaviors at the individual and (to a lesser extent) group levels of analysis. Educational psychology is focused primarily at individual level differences in classrooms (sometimes at the *group* level of analysis), with less research on broader (*organizational* and *community*) levels. Likewise, clinical and counseling subdisciplines address individual decision making, behavior, and development, typically imbedded in a small social context. Forensic psychology is concerned with everything from jury decision making (at the group and decision levels) to policy level decisions made by law makers and court systems. I-O psychology and related management disciplines deal primarily with the individual (selection and training) and group levels of analysis (i.e., leadership, work groups). But, I-O psychology is also involved in organization level decision making, as well. Consumer psychology addresses individual decisions of target groups in larger *market* contexts. Like I-O and clinical psychology, research on the influences of *culture* on decisions is also emerging in consumer psychology.

PROCESSES IN APPLIED PSYCHOLOGY

Table 9.2 Primary levels of analysis associated with applied subdiscipline areas

	Decision/ behavior	Individual	Group	Organization	Social systems	Culture
Area of application						
Human factors	X		X			
Educational		X	X			
Clinical/counseling	X	X	X			X
Forensic	X	X	X		X	
Industrial-organizational		X	X	X		X
Consumer behavior	X	X	X	X	X	X

By looking at the number of "x"s for each subdiscipline in Table 9.2, we can also get some idea of the extent to which they are practiced in the broader psychological contexts of organizations, legal systems, markets, and cultures. After considering a few more factors that distinguish them, the subfields will be discussed in the order they are listed in Table 9.2. We will start with subareas that focus on decision and behavioral levels of analysis, then move toward broader, more contextualized approaches. Ultimately, an applied psychology of sustainability needs to consider *all* of these levels of analysis.

Different Views of the Psychologist's Role

These issues with evaluation research demonstrate some of the complexities of the psychologist's role as a change agent. It is also part of the reason that most applied subdisciplines subscribe to the *scientist-practitioner model,* as we discussed in Chapter 2. This approach relies on scientific knowledge and methods, and on applications that are based on scientific evidence (American Psychological Association, 2013b; Lowman, 1998). Clearly, and as we have repeatedly seen, the scientist-practitioner model integrates ethical caution into this process as well. But the ethical codes of subdisciplines emphasize different components of the procedures in Table 9.2 (Dekker, Hancock, & Wilkin, 2013; Lowman, 1998). For example, clinical psychologists are explicitly constrained from engaging in certain types of *dual relationships* with clients (e.g., having a business relationship with a current therapeutic client). But, this sort of constraint on the relationship established in step one of Table 9.2 is not as carefully delineated in other areas. For example, it is quite common for scientist-practitioners in I-O psychology to be both employees and consultants to an organization (sometimes called *internal consultants*). This dual relationship often requires skills and methods for managing conflicting interests between the goals of the organization and those of the individual managers who these psychologists serve (Lowman, 1998; Schippmann & Newson, 2008).

241

Another important difference in psychologists' roles relates to the criteria addressed in step one. In very general terms, some subspecialties emphasize criteria associated with risk and others deal more with opportunity for gain. HFE is generally a *risk management* approach, often with a narrow focus on safety and the costs associated with employee health (Burke et al., 2011). Similarly, practitioners in the subspecialty of forensic psychology are sometimes engaged in assessments of the "dangerousness" of people indicted for crimes (Edens et al., 2005) and of faking of mental illness (Greene et al., 2007). Similarly, clinical psychologists have taken the lead in scientifically based assessment of pathology and its attendant risks. Finally, some I-O psychologists are engaged in helping to avoid legal challenges to personnel decisions (Jones & Wilson, 2013; Sharf & Jones, 2000).

The recent *positive psychology* movement (Kobau et al., 2011) helped to increase attention to an "opportunity" framing. Psychologists take this approach in counseling, educational, and I-O psychology by addressing positive criteria, including subjective well-being, self-directed learning, and career satisfaction, respectively. Positive psychology is a school of thought, rather than a subspecialty, but its message is clear to many scientist-practitioners: We are helping improve people's lives, not just avoiding risks.

The framing of the psychologist's role also plays a part in other steps in Table 9.2. Similar to the traditional medical model, the *expert only model* (Kehoe & Murphy, 2010; Muchinsky, 2004) effectively includes only two of the steps in Table 9.2: Assess and intervene. Although there may be initial conversations with clients, these tend to be fairly straightforward, followed by diagnosis, brief consultation about the results of diagnostic assessments, and an "expert" recommendation for intervention. Evaluation of results is often left to the person doing the intervention, with minimal feedback. Only if "the problem" persists is there a need for further assessment and intervention—often by another "expert."

The process in Table 9.2 includes steps that may "send a message" about this to the stakeholders involved in intervention processes. Using an example from I-O or HFE, step one can explicitly include stakeholders from different parts of an organization in the decision process, rather than just the management team. Using this approach may create a greater chance for stakeholder *voice* (Cawley, Keeping, & Levy, 1998) and broader engagement in implementation efforts (Cawley et al., 1998; Dul et al., 2012; Kehoe, Mol, & Anderson, 2010; Muchinsky, 2004).

In many cases, the goal of scientist-practitioners is not so much to hand people a "solution" as it is to help them arrive at their own, ongoing methods to effectively address problems and opportunities. We saw an example of this in the last chapter: Rather than relying entirely on designated "teaching" contexts for learning, methods that develop self-directed, self-regulated learning are often the aim of educational interventions (Clark, 2012; Gaeta et al., 2012; Sitzmann & Ely, 2011). We will revisit this later.

PROCESSES IN APPLIED PSYCHOLOGY

Implied in many of these differences is the greater or lesser reliance on a systems perspective with respect to human psychology. Researchers in HFE and CP do not commonly take the systems perspective; they do not typically place human behavior in its broader social contexts (Challenger, Clegg, & Shepherd, 2013; Salmon, McClure, & Stanton, 2012). HFE does take a systems perspective when considering the human–machine interface in some research (Kontogiannis, 2011; Salmon et al., 2012). But this is more an engineering system analogy than a broader view of the organizational context in which HFE practitioners are trying to affect change (Challenger et al., 2013; Salmon et al., 2012).

Human Factors Engineering

Human factors engineering (also called *ergonomics*) is a subdiscipline of both psychology and engineering that is described as "the fit between the human being and those inanimate things, especially machines, with which he or she interacts" (Dainoff, Mark, & Gardner, 1999). Of the applied disciplines, it is the most closely affiliated with basic research in environmental psychology (Bell et al., 2001; Sundstrom et al., 1996), though it is grouped under the heading of I-O psychology by some researchers (Bell et al., 2001). It is safe to say that HFE is focused more on the decision level of analysis than any of the other applied subdisciplines (Hollenbeck et al., 1995; Kaempf & Orasanu, 1997). This is because its prominent applications are aimed at the problem of human error in our interactions with machines.

Safety and *usability* are the primary criteria of HFE applications (Thatcher, 2013). Applications of HFE have been so successful in developing safe decision making in aviation (Kaempf & Orasanu, 1997) and driving (Morgan & Hancock, 2011), that interest in applying what we know from HFE to other high stakes activities has grown in recent years. In particular, health care applications are being developed (Carayon, 2010; Durso & Drews, 2010) in the interest of reducing medical errors.

Ergonomists have also begun to consider sustainability; but it is safe to say that this has not been an explicit focus of the field (Martin, Legg, & Brown, 2013; Thatcher & Yeow, 2016). However, much HFE work is quite relevant to the five criterion questions (cf. Haslam & Waterson, 2013). For example, work in engineered solutions related to human motor abilities have provided *decision level* sustainability solutions (Nadadur & Parkinson, 2013).

A more dramatic application of HFE to sustainability comes from the long history of environmental damage as a result of human error (Chiles, 2001). Helping people to avoid the sorts of industrial accidents that have proved devastating for the natural environment is clearly of value. And HFE may already have had important, positive effects on sustainability criteria related to this. Interestingly, the traditional HFE approach often tries to build this into the technological system, so that operator behavior is more or

243

less automatic within the workspace. This actually suggests that criterion two (deliberative thinking) is unnecessary, in the interest of this type of environmental risk. Other research has taken the opposite approach, using the idea of situational awareness.

However, criterion one (recognizing when there is a problem) and criterion four (taking action) have received extensive attention. A recurring theme in analyses of disaster (Chiles, 2001; Dekker, 2011) is that these occur when there is no single individual who understands the entire system well enough to quickly diagnose and appropriately act. Developing technologies to do this has not always worked, so these criteria remain quite important in HFE (e.g., Bisantz & Pritchett, 2003).

We have already seen how many of the principles from HFE can be applied to built environments outside of workstations. For example, there is a growing initiative to increase neighborhood "walkability" by people interested in reducing carbon footprints (e.g., Werner, Brown, & Gallimore, 2010). While they have not been applied to sustainability criteria (Hanson, 2013), the design principles used in HFE have been used to accomplish similar ends. For a few examples, *habit formation* has been shown to affect water consumption (Gregory & Di Leo, 2003), energy consumption (Stedmon, Winslow, & Langley, 2013), recycling (Hanson, 2013), and other aspects of un-deliberative behavior (Friedrichsmeier, Matthies, & Klöckner, 2013; Verplanken & Wood, 2006). Similarly, *affordances* have shown significant effects on recycling (Best & Kneip, 2011; Duffy & Verges, 2009). This involves designing things to reduce *behavioral cost*— in this case making recycling more convenient.

HFE interventions sometimes include *feedback systems*, as well (Reagan, Bliss, Van Houten, & Hilton, 2013). Feedback systems often provide real time warnings to operators when they reach certain set points (e.g., driving speed) and are typically used to increase safety (Reagan et al., 2013). These innovations have become increasingly sophisticated since their early consideration (Weber, 1980). Recent research suggests that such systems hold promise for reducing consumption of energy, water, and other resources (Grønhøj & Thøgersen, 2011; Fang & Sun, 2016). However, cognitive issues may limit the ability of feedback systems to sustain changes (Abrahamse et al., 2005).

> Energy monitoring systems have become popular means to provide feedback in homes and cars. Which of the five criteria do these systems target? Based on what we know about learning and behavior change, what would tend to make these systems more or less effective?

In addition to changing behaviors based on space design, HFE research has also taken a more cognitive turn in recent years (Hollnagel & Woods, 1999). Notable examples of this are *situation awareness* (Morgan, 2010; Wickens,

PROCESSES IN APPLIED PSYCHOLOGY

2008) and *cognitive load* (Hutchins, Wickens, Carolan, & Cumming, 2013) research. Like some other successful applied constructs, both of these are defined more by effective measurement than by a well developed theory (Charlton, 2002; Sarter & Woods, 1991). Essentially, situational awareness applies the idea of metacognition to the problem of attention choice we discussed in Chapter 5 (Rousseau, Tremblay, Banbury, Breton, & Guitouni, 2010). Enhancing people's control over their attention (criterion two) has value in high stakes environments, reducing the chances of spills, nuclear accidents, and other disasters, at least in specific situations (Stanton, Salmon, Walker, Salas, & Hancock, 2017).

Ultimately, when there is an emergency, averting catastrophe may rely on the abilities of operators to make sense of the complexities of their situation. Even with highly sophisticated systems, catastrophes have been avoided by having one operator who fully understood the entire system (Chiles, 2001). Designing "fool proof" systems may be unattainable.

In his book, *To Save Everything, Click Here*, Evgeny Morozov argues that technological "solutionism" is the latest utopian fallacy. Although there are many examples of amazing innovations, technology can be used for all sorts of ends—from humanitarian to despotic. And technologies are rarely complete solutions in complex empirical systems.

Recent interest in applying HFE to issues of sustainability has led to a remarkable integration of stakeholder criteria using a broader systems perspective (Meshkati, Tabibzadeh, Farshid, Rahimi, & Alhanaee, 2016). What makes this work even more remarkable is that it is being developed in a strategically sensitive region, making this an even greater challenge for practice.

Problems with the Practice of HFE

Overall, though, there are several issues that remain in HFE. Firm roots in the behaviorist tradition make some HFE interventions susceptible to the same criticisms we saw in Chapter 8. These include (1) lack of broad systems approach (Carayon, 2010; Challenger et al., 2013); (2) no processes for multiple stakeholder criterion development (Ryan & Wilson, 2013); and (3) the "expert only" intervention assumption, with its attendant ethical issues. Human factors engineers often come in as "experts" and assume that clients will use the methods provided, regardless of other stakeholder criteria, broader systems constraints (Dekker et al., 2013), and individual consent (Lowman, 1998). Put in terms of Table 9.3, there is very little HFE research dealing with broader contexts (Dul et al., 2012).

245

PROCESSES IN APPLIED PSYCHOLOGY

HFE is also the clearest example of a *risk management* approach to practice and intervention. Creativity and innovation may prove to be very important to developing solutions related to the five criteria. Because of this framing, current HFE interventions may have less of an impact on innovation than other approaches. This may relate to the narrow application of HFE to a short list of criteria, defined by the field itself (Dekker et al., 2013), as well as to the field's strong risk-aversion orientation (Lukersmith & Burgess-Limerick, 2013). A broader systems approach and greater stakeholder engagement may increase the likelihood of innovative solutions (Mueller, Rosenbusch, & Bausch, 2013). Using such approaches in concert with HFE to address the five criteria presents a creative frontier.

Educational Psychology

We had a glimpse in the last chapter at the contributions that have emerged from educational psychology. We currently live in a period with unprecedented levels of literacy, productivity, and innovation worldwide. Many believe that this is largely the result of educational systems that promote cognitive complexity, moral development, and democratic cultures (Rindermann, 2008). The particular role of educational psychology in this is hard to discern, in light of the many other factors at work. What is fairly clear is that this subdiscipline has led psychology in advancing our understandings of how to change the way people develop, reason (morally and otherwise), and act in educational settings.

The American Psychological Association (APA; 2013c), Division 15 website describes educational psychology in this way: "members' work is concerned with theory, methodology and applications to a broad spectrum of teaching, training and learning issues." However, the vast majority of the membership of Division 15's American Educational Research Association (AERA) is employed in academic institutions (2013). This is appropriate, since formal learning mostly occurs in schools, and much of the research done occurs with school groups (Zelezny, 1999) rather than with less controlled learning contexts (Erdogan, Uşak, & Bahar, 2013; Hattie, Marsh, Neill, & Richards, 1997). But the focus of the field is almost entirely on *theoretical formulation* and *empirical evaluation* of potential new approaches, rather than their practical *development and implementation*.

In terms of sustainability, there are entire scholarly journals (i.e., *Environmental Education Research, Journal of Environmental Education, International Journal of Environmental and Science Education*) dedicated to development and evaluation of educational interventions addressing most of the five criteria. Although these publications include academic authors from many disciplines—mostly not from educational psychology—it would be fair to say that many of the articles in these journals are informed by educational psychology, and many articles explicitly address psychological variables (especially awareness,

246

knowledge, and attitudes). People looking for potential means to affect learning based change have a deep and wide resource on which to draw, thanks to this subdiscipline.

What works in environmental education? Zelezny's (1999) meta-analysis showed that *classroom interventions* in 4th–8th grades and in college worked better to increase pro-environmental behaviors (PEBs) than did interventions with other age groups and in other settings. She also critiqued the quality of many studies, and the heavy reliance on self-reported, rather than observed behaviors. Also, few of the interventions in these studies concerned themselves with changes in deliberative thinking, taking action, or engagement of other stakeholders. Ten years later, another smaller review (Erdogan et al., 2013) showed that the same criticisms still seemed to apply (Barth & Thomas, 2012; Zelezny, 1999).

In fact, a 2013 search of the primary journals of AERA and APA, Division 15 showed no articles with the combination of "educational psychology" and issues related to sustainability criteria (i.e., "sustainability," "environmental," "green"). Educational psychologists provide many of the rigorous evaluations of learning interventions, which suggests a very wide range of possibilities for psychological research on criterion three. Until now, though, they have missed sustainability applications, particularly in science education (Erdogan et al., 2013).

This lack of direct attention is problematic, especially given the kinds of profound change that prolonged learning experiences can affect. In Chapter 7, we found that there is not a great deal of educational psychology research addressing this question of developmental change (Barth & Thomas, 2012; O'Donoghue, 2006). There is some evidence that distinguishes the educational experiences that lead to such change (e.g., Kudryavtsev et al., 2012), but the few longitudinal evaluations of educational effects on the five criteria generally look at attitudinal rather than developmental changes. One of these in particular (Stern, Powell, & Ardoin, 2008) found that some changes in beliefs and awareness persisted over a few months, while others "faded." We saw in Chapter 4 that attitudinal measures may not capture persistent change and thus not tap into the profound developmental and motivational changes that some would like to see for criterion three.

However, in terms of short term learning, educational interventions have received a good bit of attention. The effects of outdoor experiences on attitude change have received several evaluations (e.g., Hattie et al., 1997; Smith-Sebasto & Cavern, 2006; Stern et al., 2008). As a rule, these have shown positive effects on attitude and awareness outcomes (Stern et al., 2008), such as connection with nature, stewardship, knowledge of biodiversity, and concern for the environment.

Another, related avenue of research comes from studies of *inclusion* of other people in one's moral circle (Schwartz, 2007). Remembering that sustainability concerns often involve an understanding of the effects of our actions on others, research on educational interventions that lead people to be more inclusive may have value for interventions in sustainability. The evidence is fairly strong that such classroom experiences have small but significant (Bowman, 2010) and lasting effects (Bowman, Brandenberger, Hill, & Lapsley, 2011). Helping people to develop broader identities (Schachter & Rich, 2011) and the metacognitive skills to consider others in their decision making (Smith, 2002; Yoon, Langrehr, & Ong, 2011) are frontiers in educational psychology that have potential applications to sustainability. We will see more about some of these soon (e.g., Yoon et al., 2011).

Learning or development? There is a remarkable example of rapid, large scale attitude change in the United States during the past fifteen years or so (Baunach, 2012). Efforts to increase acceptance of sexual and gender minorities provide an example of how broadly disseminated social action may have powerful effects. Among other things, strong advocacy coalitions, large scale collective action, and engagement with many stakeholders appear to have been involved in the changes in attitudes and laws relating to LGBT rights (Frank, 2013). Regardless of its various causes, some psychologists actually point to the events of the 1990s and 2000s as an example of massive developmental change (e.g., Dziengel, 2010).

An important question, which has yet to be answered, is whether these changes will persist: Is this a more or less permanent change? If so, then it may be possible to affect other massive developmental changes through similar actions. If not, it may be that we have just seen a temporary switch in attitudes.

Alternatively, there is research that suggests potential problems with environmental education. Activities that are not well founded in what we know about how people learn and change may not lead to desirable outcomes. For example, Sellmann and Bogner (2013) showed that one day *environmental education* experiences may actually reduce students' concern for environmental problems. Other research has also demonstrated some of the variables that may place limits on these short term experiences (e.g., Smith-Sebasto & Obenchain, 2009). Finally, while such change in attitudes and beliefs may have important short term effects, it bears repeating that they do not necessarily lead to differences in moral action (e.g., Smith-Sebasto & Obenchain, 2009; Stern et al., 2008).

The need remains: Educational psychologists can play an important role in rigorously evaluating "what works" for affecting the five criteria in applied settings (in and outside of classrooms). Further research can

PROCESSES IN APPLIED PSYCHOLOGY

provide practice based evidence about variables that support or hinder such learning and developmental interventions (e.g., Hattie et al., 1997; Perry et al., 2012). Perhaps the most important is this: The "captive audiences" in school classrooms create opportunities for educational psychologists to manage contextual features in such a way that students develop their own, self-regulated learning, based on their individual motives and identities (Gaeta et al., 2012). Longitudinal research will be necessary to discover whether moral development changes as a result of these efforts.

Even without their direct involvement, there are efforts to apply what psychologists have demonstrated about "what works" in learning to most sustainability criteria—not just PEBs. There are successful examples of the use of problem based learning (Oluk & Özalp, 2007) and other innovations (Zelezny, 1999) in classrooms, as well as with adult learners outside of classrooms. As an example, Nguyen, Graham, Ross, Maani, and Bosch (2012) applied a host of innovations to a learning experience for professionals involved in biosphere management. This involved,

> learning as a group of professionals, with senior organisational support and commitment to apply systems approaches in the workplace; enjoyable adult learning approaches tailored to the needs of participants; complementing teaching of systems thinking and techniques with participatory methods for working with the participants in developing solutions to their sustainability issues; and building in evaluation at every stage, through participatory methods taught in the course.

In Chapter 8 we saw how social learning with professional cohorts through *engaging, motivationally targeted, problem based approaches* that include ongoing assessment are all features that work. While this example did not include any final evaluation of the efficacy of their approach, it did demonstrate how educational psychology can have an impact.

Elder hostels and eco-tours have become increasingly popular with adult learners. These are groups of people who have the time and money for such experiences and are motivated enough to spend both. The extent to which principles from educational psychology are applied to these is not clear, at least from the current literature in this important field. But the growth in this segment of the population in much of the world suggests tremendous human resources can be marshalled from this group.

Since Zelezny's (1999) findings regarding sustainability education, discussion of sustainability in business education has grown (Wright & Bennett, 2011). The effects of work organizations on our five criteria can be enormous, and business education has to some extent taken this seriously (Bamburg & Rowledge, 2009). With a few exceptions, however, these initiatives do not employ interventions based on educational psychology research. Instead, they rely on conventional models of learning (Thomas & Cornuel, 2012; von der Heidt & Lamberton, 2011; Wright & Bennett, 2011), and do not include rigorous evaluation research.

Approaches to Intervention

Educational psychologists tend to focus heavily on steps two and five from Table 9.2. Entire journals in this area are focused on the problems of initial assessment and eventual evaluation. In fact, until fairly recently, there has been little stakeholder engagement in the development and implementation of interventions—steps one and four in Table 9.2. These steps are of considerable importance to many educators (Norcini et al., 2011). Regarding step one, the development of *stakeholder engagement* appears to have been on the periphery of science, but often at the heart of practices that are informed by the subdisciplines of applied psychology (Davies, 2011; Langley, DeCarlo Santiago, Rodríguez, & Zelaya, 2013; Murphy et al., 2005; Teachout & Hall, 2002). While multidisciplinary stakeholder engagement has found its way into educational *practices* for sustainability (Murphy, Bruce, & Eva, 2008; Uiterkamp & Vlek, 2007), psychologists appear not to have been involved.

A few educational psychologists have called for greater attention to the measurement of context and gathering information from a broader stakeholder group as part of initial *needs assessment* (Birnbaum & Deutsch, 1996; Goldring & Berends, 2009; Norwich, 1988), but professional educators appear to have taken the lead on this. Educational needs assessment is used to identify potential targets of individual and classroom change and to establish baselines of learning or development (step two in Table 9.2). It should not be "news" at this point that scientist-practitioners who wish to address the five criteria will need to have a careful eye on stakeholders in the broader context (Delicado, 2012; Dunsmuir & Kratochwill, 2013; Læssøe & Ohman, 2010) as they implement step two.

Step three (feedback) in Table 9.2 is also relatively neglected, in comparison to steps two and five. Although the effects of feedback on individual learners are well documented (e.g., Kluger & DeNisi, 1996), feedback to other stakeholders (teachers, administrators, parents, policymakers) is not. Again, there is a need for more research on stakeholder reactions to feedback, since educators and applied psychologists work in communities with multiple, often conflicting constituent groups. Applying the considerable sophistication of educational psychology to evaluating stakeholder feedback systems (Upreti, Liaupsin, & Koonce, 2010) remains a critical need.

There are a few examples where *both* steps one and three have been explicitly addressed together in the research literature. The first interventions that have explicitly engaged multiple stakeholders in discussion and feedback have done so in the physical design of school spaces (Krasner & Richards, 1976; Pivik, 2010). In other words, *environmental* psychologists have engaged students, teachers, and administrators in the physical design of schools. Second, a few modern educational psychologists have taken a more dynamic approach than even Table 9.3 describes. The concept of *formative assessment* has become an important and somewhat controversial approach to educational intervention (Kingston & Nash, 2011). It treats criterion definition as an ongoing process, often tailored to the needs of individual learners, and reliant upon ongoing assessment and feedback. In a way, formative assessment is an attempt to metacognitively regulate the learning process through the adjustment of the context to the individual—rather than the other way around. Methods are targeted at (1) the current status of the individual learner, teacher, and classroom; (2) outcomes that are particularly relevant to the learner's motives; and (3) learning methods that are practical in these particular circumstances (Clark, 2012; Kingston & Nash, 2011). Finally, administrators and classroom teachers are integral to the feedback process (Schneider & Andrade, 2013). In short, formative assessment takes a systems approach to learning.

The use of formative assessment by environmental educators is promising (Erdogan & Tuncer, 2009; Jenkins, 2010), but there is still much to know about when and where to apply it (Kingston & Nash, 2011). Using it to develop criteria may be one important frontier. For example, asking different stakeholders to evaluate ("grade") multiple ideas for addressing a local environmental issue may help them to arrive at shared standards for such judgments.

Current Limitations

Scientist-practitioners are limited by several gaps in the research regarding applications of education for sustainability. In terms of our five sustainability criteria, very few studies have looked at criterion one. In fact, little research has addressed the fact that some learners do not recognize environmental degradation as an issue, and even see it as politically manufactured (Feygina et al., 2010; Hornsey & Fielding, 2017). More importantly, it highlights again questions about developmental limitations on learning. If people are motivated to protect the status quo (Feygina et al., 2010), then they are arguably at the conventional stage of moral reasoning—"How things are is how they ought to be." However, using place attachment to affect set points

(Kyle et al., 2004a) may hold promise, since these may occur within the bounds of current development.

The problems we saw in Chapter 8 also can be repeated here: Educational psychologists have neglected some important issues. But environmental education scholarship outside of psychology has problems of its own. Some researchers suggest that the work on intervention efficacy focuses on faddish solutions (Thomas & Cornuel, 2012; von der Heidt & Lamberton, 2011; Wright & Bennett, 2011), lacks rigor (Parker, Jordan, Kirk, Aspiranti, & Bain, 2010; Zelezny, 1999), and is narrowly focused on criteria of the researchers' choice. Still, the possibilities presented by this research are broad and sometimes quite creative. Applying a psychological perspective should help develop these innovations.

Perhaps the biggest issue confronting educational psychology is one that has been posed before in other areas of applied psychology: *Transfer of training* (Ford, 1997; Stern et al., 2008). Most educational psychology is applied with children in classes—even for outdoor education (cf. Stern et al., 2008). Effects of policy, organization, culture, and social contexts on learning are recognized, but research has not moved to these higher levels of analysis (Dunsmuir & Kratochwill, 2013). The generalization of what we have learned from educational psychology to marketing, public forums, and elsewhere is a natural "next step."

Humor is an important part of everyday life for many people. However, it has fallen into something of a "crack" between areas of applied psychology. Educational psychology has adopted it as an adjunct area (Oluk & Özalp, 2007), and clinical psychologists have recognized its value as a mindfulness tool (Kaplan, 2013; Zhang & Zuo, 2008). Clearly, taking a positive perspective on things that threaten our security can be helpful if we are to move forward in challenging situations. Humor can be a very creative and mindful way to do this (Thorkildsen, 2006). But how can psychologists harness this potentially powerful tool in the interest of sustainability? Educational settings may provide one answer.

Clinical Psychology and Related Subdisciplines

Clinical psychology interventions are commonly accomplished through assessment, followed by interventions. For most adults, these interventions are mutually agreed upon as part of ethical practice (American Psychological Association, 2013b), and are aimed at enhanced well-being (Baby, 2012). Well-being is defined in terms of metacognitive and developmental change, learning new forms of self-regulation, improving social relationships, and managing emotions

PROCESSES IN APPLIED PSYCHOLOGY

(Böcker & Breuer, 1980). Although behavior changes are often desired consequences (DeLeon et al., 2013), broader psychological systems—including the *processes* and *contexts* of motivation, development, cognition, emotion, and identity—are primary targets of change (Cordova, 2001; Stackert & Bursik, 2006).

Clinical interventions are far more than just ordinary conversations between two people. In fact, it would be hard to find more extraordinary interactions in all of human relationships. One way of thinking of this is that clinical psychologists are working to help clients more effectively manage their *internal environments*. Therapies attempt to change internal contexts by curing or alleviating the effects of mental illnesses (Mitte, 2005; Stackert & Bursik, 2006), managing impulses (Sher, Winograd, & Haeny, 2013), and developing healthy boundaries and identity (Cash, 2005; Gehrie, 1999). Even when helping people to manage their social contexts, clinicians often direct people toward changing their *internal* responses to external events.

Ways of managing internal contexts have been treated at length in the very large literature in this applied discipline. Virtually all of the interventions (often called *treatments*) involve the management of decision processes (Maddi, 1998) through interactions with a professionally trained and licensed facilitator. Very similar intervention practices are central to subdisciplines closely related to clinical psychology, including *counseling psychology* (American Psychological Association Division 17), *school psychology* (APA Division 16), *consulting psychology* (APA Division 13), and *forensic psychology* (APA Division 41), along with a few other specialty areas. Although there are substantial differences among these areas, for the sake of shorthand, we will lump them under the clinical psychology heading here. Since our concern is with outcomes rather than disciplinary boundaries, research findings from all of these areas are incorporated into the discussions that follow.

This broad research addresses many elements that are relevant to the five criteria. We have seen (Chapter 7) that clinical interventions are often aimed at durable, developmental, and metacognitive change. Given this aim, science based clinical practice to some extent assumes *transfer of learning* as a defining characteristic. What is learned in the confines of a clinician's office is intended to be developed and used outside of that office, in order for desired outcomes to occur. The focus on this question is arguably one of the greatest strengths (Kazantzis, Whittington, & Dattilio, 2010; Latham & Heslin, 2003) that clinical psychology can bring to sustainability criteria. We will learn more about how change in therapy is transferred into action when we consider criterion four, below.

1. **Criterion one: discrepancy testing**

    Clinical applications rely heavily on initial recognition of the need to change. An old joke gets to this point well: Question: "How many clinical psychologists does it take to change a light bulb?" Answer: "Only one: But the light bulb has to want to change." Helping people to be

253

"ready" for change is a central issue for clinicians (Norcross, Krebs, & Prochaska, 2011).

However, criterion one poses a dilemma for clinical practitioners aiming to "raise the alarm." Many clinicians address clients' anxieties, with the primary purpose of helping them to reduce or eliminate them. Deliberately alarming people about environmental problems (see Fritsche, Jonas, Kayser, & Koranyi, 2010) clearly runs counter to this therapeutic criterion.

However, in some contexts, this aim is congruent with criterion one. As catastrophic environmental events continue to escalate, the need to help manage responses to these events will continue to grow (Boin & McConnell, 2007; Cox, 2012). Dealing with *anxieties* about such changes in our natural environments can be framed as problems of *coping* with *stress* (Adams & Adams, 1984; VandenBos & Bryant, 1987). Beyond just coping, *anxiety disorders*—particularly *posttraumatic stress disorder* (PTSD)—can result from catastrophic environmental events (Adams & Adams, 1984). Strong evidence supports applied methods for coping with threatening circumstances, both before and after catastrophic change (Benish, Imel, & Wampold, 2008; Cherry, 2009).

There are a number of effective methods developed in clinical subdisciplines for managing criterion one (establishing when a problem exists) and criterion four (taking action). Methods for managing people's responses to threats have a long history in these subdisciplines. These include coping strategies for *non-therapeutic* settings, including relaxation techniques (Kraag, Zeegers, Kok, Hosman, & Abu-Saad, 2006), social adjustment (Kraag et al., 2006), humor (Mesmer-Magnus, Glew, & Viswesvaran, 2012), certain types of religious involvements (Ano & Vasconcelles, 2005), and self-regulation (Gaudreau, Carraro, & Miranda, 2012). Effective *therapeutic* approaches to helping with traumatic change (Nemeth, Hamilton, & Kuriansky, 2012) include mindfulness (Grossman, Niemann, Schmidt, & Walach, 2004), self-efficacy (Luszczynska, Benight, & Cieslak, 2009), and preparatory coping (Saile, Burgmeier, & Schmidt, 1988) interventions. The stress coping literature has even specifically addressed applications in responses to major environmental and manmade catastrophes (e.g., Adams & Adams, 1984; Nemeth et al., 2012; VandenBos & Bryant, 1987).

Once we decide we have a problem, clinicians can help us to deal with both the *perception* and the *realities* of this belief. If the perception is just that (not a reality), then clinicians can help manage "reality tests" and techniques for dealing with irrational fears (Wells, 2003). If the perceptions of threat coincide with realities, clinicians can apply the methods mentioned above to help cope with stress and maintain the ability to creatively adapt (Baas, De Dreu, & Nijstad, 2008). Other methods available outside of the care of a clinical psychologist include exercise (Hamer, Taylor, & Steptoe, 2006; Thayer, 1996), diet (Long & Benton, 2013), relaxation techniques (Richardson & Rothstein, 2008), and other everyday stress management tools. As we have seen, anxieties, even in the face of real threats, sometimes make us less able to be deliberate (Ask & Granhag, 2007; Perowne & Mansell, 2002) or be creative (Baas et al., 2008), both of which are often important to facing life's real challenges.

Is it possible that environmental toxicity affects mental disorders? It may be that clinicians and their cousin subdisciplines may have been working with the *results* of environmental toxins for many years. So-called *environmental insults* have been implicated in at least three of the major psychological disorders of the past hundred years: autism, attention deficit/hyperactivity disorder (ADHD), and schizophrenia.

Although the causes of autism and ADHD are not yet known, some evidence suggests that toxins in the environment may be responsible for the enormous growth in both of these disorders (Dietrich, 2010; Koger, Schettler, & Weiss, 2005; Swanson et al., 2007). As a result, psychologists trained in *behavior analysis* therapies are in high demand, due to the success they have had in managing both disorders (Fabiano et al., 2009; Virués-Ortega, 2010). Give the prevalence of toxic chemicals released into the environment over the past century, there may be challenging work for clinical psychologists in years to come.

Perhaps the greatest contribution that clinical psychology has to offer for criterion one is related to a problem that many clinicians confront—resistance to change (Beutler, Harwood, Michelson, Song, & Holman, 2011). *Resistance* (also called *reactance*) is a tendency for people to respond negatively to others' attempts at persuasion (Brehm & Brehm, 1981). Meta-analytic findings suggest that *directive* approaches work well for clients low in resistance. But resistant clients are more inclined to change in response to *non-directive* approaches (Beutler et al., 2011). Non-directive approaches consider possible outcome contingencies with clients, including "reverse psychology"—suggesting alternatives that are not likely to be effective (Thorkildsen, 2006). The potential value of knowing this about reactance may help with criteria one, but it relies on the ability of persuaders to recognize resistance when they see it. Competent professionals are prepared for this.

2. **Criteria two and three: learning to exercise deliberative choice**
   Helping people to be deliberative in their courses of action is a central criterion for much of clinical practice (American Psychological Association, 2013b; Baby, 2012; Böcker & Breuer, 1980). Many therapies are heavily

PROCESSES IN APPLIED PSYCHOLOGY

canted toward this end (Mischel, 2004; Wells, 2003). As we saw in Chapter 7, some therapies are aimed at *reducing* self-regulation (in *internalizing* disorders; Klassen et al., 2013; Sportel et al., 2013), and some at *increasing* self-regulation for problems associated with impulse control (Burnette et al., 2013). Cognitive Behavioral Therapy (CBT) and mindfulness interventions (Orme-Johnson, 2000; Zelazo & Lyons, 2011) have been quite successful for internalizing issues (Orme-Johnson, 2000; Piet et al., 2012; Regehr, Glancy, & Pitts, 2013; Roemer et al., 2009).

There is enormous evidence of problems with overconsumption in affluent societies. At the decision level, people make destructive choices at alarming rates. Some of these are more problematic for the individual, as is the case with obesity, which has grown dramatically in recent decades (McMichael & Butler, 2011; Sturm, 2008). Other impulse mismanagement may have deleterious consequences for others, as in the cases of crime, deliberate wasting of scarce resources, and damage to resources that are shared with others.

All of us can think of examples of the frustrations associated with such misdeeds, but finding practical ways to manage them are seldom easily at hand. For example, even when there are laws against impulse driven behaviors, these are not effectual in every case and may have little preventive effect. Instead, they may cause a brief reduction in individual misbehavior, followed by a return to baselines.

Psychologists offer many methods for both preventing and reducing waste and criminal behavior. But most involve interventions in fairly controlled circumstances (i.e., clinician's offices, classrooms, workstations, and criminal justice venues), rather than in those circumstances where such misdeeds are most likely to occur (e.g., in bar rooms, private homes, and parking lots). Dealing with misbehavior in *uncontrolled settings* is arguably the greatest challenge for increasing deliberative behaviors.

However, for criterion two, the challenge often lies in increasing (rather than decreasing) people's tendency to stop and think before acting on destructive habits or impulses. Clinical psychologists follow several approaches to try to meet this difficult challenge. Starting in childhood, clinicians work with caregivers (Miller & Eisenberg, 1988; Zelazo & Lyons, 2011) and educators (Gaeta et al., 2012) to help children develop metacognitive skills, self-regulation, empathy, and mindfulness. CBTs have also been applied successfully for self-regulation of violent impulses

256

PROCESSES IN APPLIED PSYCHOLOGY

(Gillespie et al., 2012) and treatment of addictions (Hendershot, Witkiewitz, George, & Marlatt, 2011).

The problem of durable, generalized change (the *transfer* problem) has taken center stage for clinical psychologists involved in brief therapy. Giving clients the ability to solve their own problems after a few short sessions is a challenge. But, mindful clinical approaches can establish robust effects in a fairly short time (Gingerich, Kim, Stams, & Macdonald, 2012; Poston & Hanson, 2010). These innovations may hold promise for addressing sustainability criteria two (deliberation), three (learning and change), and four (taking action).

We have also seen that, for some stubborn disorders (borderline, anti-social, and other personality disorders), managing the boundaries between ourselves and our contexts is a challenge that cannot be met without significant changes in contexts. Institutional treatment, incarceration, halfway houses, and management of social support systems all may help to create firmer boundaries and feedback in order to delimit behavioral responses to impulses. For example, addiction counseling often includes such a systems approach (e.g., Liddle, Dakof, Turner, Henderson, & Greenbaum, 2008). This is why the group level of analysis is included for clinical practices in Table 9.2. But these are of limited value for the five criteria.

Since CBT and mindfulness are effective for the management of deliberative processes, finding ways to apply them more widely to the management of *impulsive consumption* could prove to be very helpful for sustainability efforts. Unfortunately, there are at least two problems that need to be considered with any such efforts. First, there are stakeholders with enormous vested interests in consumption, particularly for profit. There are obvious examples of profitable enterprises aimed at reducing impulsivity (e.g., weight loss plans, saving on energy costs, treating addictions). But, there are also examples of major, policy based efforts to overcome impulsive consumption. These include such efforts as the "War on Drugs," lawsuits against cigarette companies (Oreskes & Conway, 2010), and the "Let's Move!" campaign to reduce obesity (Let's Move, 2013). We will see more about these in Chapter 10.

Second, the practical and ethical application of clinical approaches outside of intimate therapeutic settings may be quite limited. Managing human behavior in uncontrolled settings is already difficult. Ethically, people in therapy generally provide voluntary consent to therapies aimed at changing their consumption behaviors. In fact, finding ethical and effective ways to apply what we know about self-management *outside* therapy is perhaps the next great challenge of human history. The good news is evidence showing that confronting people appropriately can increase the tendency toward deliberative action (Swim & Bloodhart, 2013).

Some initial efforts to examine the role of mindfulness and other metacognition for sustainability have been descriptive, rather than applied. Findings suggest that people who are mindful about the consequences of their behaviors on the environment have greater well-being (Jacob, Jovic, & Brinkerhoff, 2009), tend to be quasi-religious, rather than "churchgoing" (Brinkerhoff & Jacob, 1999), and are focused more on their actions than on their impulses when deciding whether to engage in PEBs (Amel, Manning, & Scott, 2009). If we count such things as cognitive dissonance, goal setting, and the use of reminders as metacognitive strategies, then the picture is more complete. Osbaldiston and Schott (2012) meta-analysis of eighty-seven experimental studies showed that these types of interventions have significant effects on actual (versus self-reported) pro-environmental behaviors. Although these were not facilitated interactions with licensed psychologists, the results are encouraging for broader use of metacognitive approaches.

3. **Criteria four and five: the impracticality of taking action**

A clinical psychologist often helps a client to take action. Such action is commonly defined by the context that matters most to that individual—with a spouse, parent, child, boss, or other important social situation. There are also effective tools to aid in this *transfer* of insights from therapeutic to other settings. Among the most studied, and arguably most effective, are a set of techniques that are generally grouped under the heading of *homework* (Kazantzis, Whittington, & Dattilio, 2010; Sánchez-Meca, Rosa-Alcázar, Marín-Martínez, & Gómez-Conesa, 2010). These include behavioral experiments (Wells, 2003), monitoring of dreams (Kazantzis et al., 2016), and other sorts of actions outside of the clinical setting.

Getting people to "do good" in broader social contexts may not be a common objective, however (Maddux, 2008). Ironically, it may be a primary aim only for clients who are facing incarceration, suffering from addictions, or otherwise compelled to change. However, people who have learned to manage or overcome a disorder may lead more mindful lives, which may also make it possible for them to take a greater interest in broader contexts and generally have a more positive effect on those around them.

We have already seen that mindfulness is associated with both PEB and subjective well-being. However, research about whether mindfulness translates into altruistic action is more equivocal. To the extent that clinicians successfully treat anxiety, they may already contribute to the tendency of people to focus on broader issues than their own. Although the relationship between anxieties and altruism may be complex (Fujiwara, 2007; Wu, Tang, & Yogo, 2013), altruistic homework activities may both help clients to manage anxieties and "do good." Thus, clinicians may be able to address criterion one (reducing problem framing) by integrating it with criterion four (altruistic action).

There is good reason to believe that treatments for depression may increase the likelihood that people will take action, as well. Evidence has shown that environmental stressors (Baum, Fleming, Israel, & O'Keeffe, 1992) and anxiety about environmental problems (Pelletier, Dion, Tuson, & Green-Demers, 1999) may lead to depression (Klassen et al., 2013). The helplessness that often accompanies depression may reduce people's inclination to take action (Evans & Stecker, 2004; Parker & McDonough, 1999; Pelletier et al., 1999). Common, effective psychotherapies for depression and anxiety (Mitte, 2005; Piet et al., 2012) may therefore increase the likelihood that people will take action.

Use of restorative therapies in outdoor settings. Enhanced mindfulness and stress reduction are sometimes associated with experiences in natural environments (Hattie et al., 1997). Enhancing mindfulness and reducing stress also have long histories in therapies for people with certain clinical disorders, as we have already learned. *Restorative therapy* gives people with disorders an opportunity to experience the beauties of nature, in the hope that these same mindfulness and stress reduction dynamics will help with disorders.

Unfortunately, evidence about restorative therapy is currently inconclusive (Kamioka et al., 2012). One important concern is whether the anxieties that some people are experiencing *about* the natural environment (Pelletier et al., 1999) may negate the positive effects of restorative therapy. Reminding already depressed and anxious clients about looming environmental problems may not be efficacious for these groups as they are for the general population (Hattie et al., 1997). Finding ways to control for this problem may aid in the further development of restorative therapy.

Model for Intervention

Clinical interventions follow the first four of the five steps in Table 9.2 fairly closely (American Psychological Association, 2013b; Sharp, Williams, Rhyner, & Ilardi, 2013). The practice of clinical psychology, however, takes a more finely grained approach to the first step in Table 9.2. We have seen that reactance may require different approaches (Beutler et al., 2011; Thorkildsen, 2006). So, clinicians are challenged to find out what is motivating a person to seek help. In fact, the common difficulties clinicians experience when trying to find out what a particular client wants have led to an entire line of research concerned with *establishing rapport* (Fontes, 2008; Giordano, 1997) and development of *therapeutic alliance* (Flückiger, Del Re, Wampold, Symonds, & Horvath, 2012; Imel et al., 2013). The maintenance of this alliance through the process of therapy is even used as one definition of therapeutic effectiveness (Imel et al., 2013; McLeod, 2011).

The ability to build such alliances may also be essential for scientist-practitioners in sustainability. We could all learn from clinical research about how to create an interpersonal context where criteria are defined jointly, feedback is based on good evidence, conflicts are resolved appropriately, and solutions devised ethically. Although clinical methods have limitations outside of the therapeutic setting (Chang, Lee, & Hargreaves, 2008), some have been part of effective teaching (Koch, 2004) and management (Rhoades & Eisenberger, 2002) for some time. Understanding the extraordinary nature of the therapeutic relationship may extend to well-being in broader contexts (Ng et al., 2008).

Forensic Psychology

There are people who, through their actions and decisions, deprive others of future goods. In some cases, these actions and decisions are classified as crimes. In others, the law is relatively mute. But other stakeholders, including ethically driven psychologists, have an interest in preventing such behaviors through science based practice. The ethics of clinical psychology require attention to the broader good (American Psychological Association, 2013b), and the mission of Division 41 (American Psychology—Law Society; American Psychological Association, 2013d) provides service under the broad umbrella of the legal system.

Forensic psychology is a subdiscipline that supports decisions about people in the legal system. Most forensic psychologists are clinicians who provide feedback based on individual assessments of people's state of mind, mostly in wealthy countries. Rather than relying on "gut reactions" (as is often portrayed in the popular media), forensic psychologists make extensive use of standardized inventories and protocols, to help make decisions about intelligence, psychosis, "faking," and disorders (Greene et al., 2007; Nicholson & Norwood, 2000). This information can be used to help decide whether defendants knew what they were doing when they committed a crime or have any idea of why they are being punished (Greene et al., 2007). Assessment based feedback is also used to determine dangerousness for both bond hearings and parole decisions (Greene et al., 2007).

Perhaps such individual assessments can be used to predict when people are likely to behave altruistically and take sustainable action. Additionally, more basic research about the causes of criminal tendencies, including such things as identity and attachment, may help to develop assessments that can inform these efforts. For example, understanding how anger plays into people's tendency to view destructive behaviors more favorably (Anderson, Cooper, & Okamura, 1997) may help to reduce anti-environmental behavior. Similarly, finding ways to allay the anxiety caused by such anger (Carré,

PROCESSES IN APPLIED PSYCHOLOGY

Fisher, Manuck, & Hariri, 2012) may prove helpful in attempts to take action. Sometimes, though, behaviors that are illegal also turn out to be aimed at the greater good. Developing an empirical basis for understanding why and when people will take action "for the greater good," even when this may lead to their incarceration could be an important avenue for research, as well.

> Several of the recent mass murders in the United States have been committed by people who were later classified as psychotic—meaning they were completely out of touch with reality when they committed their heinous crimes. Forensic psychologists have become indispensable to legal decision making partly because of these cases. Such essential involvement in institutional decision making is one of the ways that scientist-practitioners are becoming involved in decisions about sustainability, as well.

By a conservative estimate, at least 17% of people who are arrested in the United States have some form of serious mental disorder, which is higher than the rates in the population at large (Steadman, Osher, Robbins, Case, & Samuels, 2009). Given this, it is not surprising that forensic psychology has taken on an increasingly important role in decisions about individual defendants (Greene et al., 2007). But, the general success of feedback from individual assessments has led to broader engagement in other common decisions in the criminal justice system. This engagement includes such things as trying to identify perpetrators (Greene et al., 2007), understanding the nature of eyewitness memory (Heaton-Armstrong, Shepherd, Gudjonsson, & Wolchover, 2006), and understanding how children respond to different phrasing of questions when they provide testimony (Goodman & Melinder, 2007).

Forensic psychologists have also been involved in the development of court ordered programs for treatment of addiction, spousal abuse, and other interventions. For example, *mandated community treatment programs* typically engage people who have important stakes in the lives of people convicted of crimes (Cheon, 2008). These programs have shown potential for reducing future criminal behaviors (Hough & O'Brien, 2005). The engagement of *multiple stakeholders* appears to have important role in their success (Cheon, 2008).

In fact, forensic psychology is given separate attention here because it addresses the higher *levels of analysis* in Table 9.3. By engaging stakeholders in broader social networks, forensic clinical psychologists have demonstrated some means to successfully, and ethically apply the systems perspective. At the group level of analysis, forensic psychologists have been employed in jury selection (Devine, Clayton, Dunford, Seying, & Pryce, 2001; Lieberman,

261

2011). At an even broader level of analysis, forensic psychologists have provided evaluation research to assist policy makers' decisions. For example, research about the deterrent effects of punishment (Andrews & Bonta, 2010), the conditions under which people are likely to return to criminal behavior (Langevin et al., 2004), and the effectiveness of programs to prevent crime (Hollin, 2013) have all been addressed. Again, these demonstrate the importance of applied psychology to decision making at several levels of analysis.

By engaging in this type of research, forensic psychologists have taken on the many questions raised by the stakeholders in the criminal justice systems. Defendants, juries, witnesses, victims, jails and prisons, and society at large have all received answers to questions that address societal "goods." Similar indirect and, where possible, direct engagement of stakeholders is important to the ethical practice of sustainability psychology (Ter Mors, Weenig, Ellemers, & Daamen, 2010).

Forensic Psychology and the Five Criteria

Forensic psychology also demonstrates the direct involvement that applied psychology can take in determining avenues toward effecting the five criteria. First among these is their direct engagement in law making. Applying what has been learned about engaging law makers may be the most direct influences of psychology in government. In addition to lobbying efforts at the Ffderal level, the American Psychological Association has presented formal statements to government bodies (called *amicus* briefs). Forensic psychology has been involved in all levels of government, albeit to answer limited criminal justice questions.

Furthermore, when some of the questions they have addressed are grouped under the five criteria, it is easy to see a pattern emerge. First, predicting criminal behavior in various settings (especially for police on the streets, in community trends, for probation hearings) is clearly concerned with identifying future problems. The "Do we have a problem?" question (criterion one) is being addressed very directly. Second, and often as part of the prediction problem, clinical psychologists focus some assessments on self-regulation. Depending on a prisoner's issues in this area, then their ability to be deliberative (criterion two) and "learn their lesson" from prison experiences (criterion three) can be evaluated. Drug courts are another way that self-regulation is addressed through intervention. These help people be more deliberative in their approach to problems. Third, the training of police officers, rehabilitation of prisoners, and educating judges and juries about the nature of criminal behaviors all address criterion three (learning and change).

Of course, these three criteria have been addressed by other applied areas, but specific lessons learned from criminal justice may be very helpful. For example, evaluating legal interventions that are most likely to deter would-be polluters is exactly the sort of problem that forensic psychologists have successfully taken on in other criminal justice settings.

However, there are no other applied areas except possibly I-O psychology that have taken collective action and been so successful at intervening on all levels of analysis. Practical action (criteria five and four, respectively) is a hallmark of forensic psychology. Applying what we know about this subdiscipline to sustainability is likely to be very fruitful.

Summary

The success of science based practices relies on many of the variables we have discussed in this chapter. As change agents (Hedge & Borman, 2008; Schippmann & Newson, 2008), we face complex, conflict laden, and ethically sensitive decisions. At the beginning of this chapter, we saw how consideration of a few important issues can help to define and manage this change process. First, a fairly straightforward consideration of the scope of the systemic changes we are addressing (Table 9.3) provides an analytical framework. Next, thinking through the processes we may need to apply (Table 9.2) provides a temporal framework. Flexibility is important to application of these steps; to the extent that they are practical and ethical, we may choose to give them greater or less weight. Because the subdisciplines concentrate efforts on particular steps in Table 9.2, flexibility can be built into the intervention process using the lessons learned from each. By studying clinical psychology and its related subdisciplines, sustainability psychologists can establish and maintain lasting, durable relationships with our stakeholders. Creating *client* relationships in itself may be an initial goal of the intervention process for psychology of sustainability. Following from forensic psychology, careful consideration of the people and groups with stakes in our decisions, and developing clear relationships with these stakeholders, may play key roles in the success of our efforts. Educational psychology accentuates the importance of working with motivated groups in relatively controlled settings as part of the action and learning criteria. We will see in the next chapter how broad based assessments and well managed feedback in workplaces, and strong persuasive messages in controlled media, can have profound effects. I-O and consumer psychology both function at broad levels of analysis (sometimes called "real world" settings) with effective ways to promote strong, flexible interventions.

10

BROAD INTERVENTIONS

Just as clinical and educational psychology have had big effects on people's quality of life in their immediate social contexts, so *industrial-organizational* (I-O) *psychology* and *consumer psychology* (CP) have had effects in other contexts. Applications of psychology in broader systems has helped to enhance practical decisions, serve individual ends, and assist with group decisions in ways that are not prevalent in other subdisciplines. There is enormous potential for *scientist-practitioners* working in I-O and CP to affect the five criteria in work organizations, in the marketplace, and beyond.

In addition to their demonstrated effectiveness, this potential comes from the extensive, current engagement of these scientist-practitioners in work organizations. The saying that "80% of success is showing up" (attributed to Woody Allen) may help to explain this. Just by virtue of being involved in organizational decision processes, these subdisciplines already have a place at the table. They have been involved in some important decisions about the relationship between people and the planet for some time (Klein & Huffman, 2013).

There is a problem with this: The effectiveness of I-O and CP has often been measured against the financial bottom line, rather than other criteria (Cascio & Fogli, 2010; Lefkowitz, 2008). By putting their expertise to work in the service of criteria other than obvious, concrete indicators of *organizational effectiveness* (OE), these psychologists may jeopardize their positions as valued organizational partners in some organizations (Cialdini, Goldstein, & Griskevicius, 2011). This may help to explain why many professionals in these disciplines have only recently started to openly address questions of sustainability in their professional roles (Muchinsky, 2013). Many psychologists, practicing ethically, have been waiting for the opportunity to present itself, often quietly pushing efforts forward from the background and in their home communities. But, for many, it has been their clients' decisions that have given them the ethical opportunity to take up sustainability issues. And, there has been growth in scientist-practitioner work on these topics (Campbell, Provolt, & Campbell, 2013; Huffman & Klein, 2013; Lombardo, Schneider, & Bryan, 2013; Ones & Dilchert, 2012).

In this chapter, we will see how effective practices in I-O and CP have found their way into work organizations around the globe. We will explore ways to enhance existing practices by applying principles and methods from I-O and CP. Further, there are many ways that I-O and CP can be applied in service of the five criteria that have not widely known. Explorations of these new approaches will inevitably raise questions about the need to redefine the scientist-practitioner model (Hakel, 2013; Lefkowitz, 2008, 2013). But first, it is important to understand how both I-O and CP are engaged as organizational partners in many work organizations—public and private, for-profit, and governmental. The integration of applied psychology to decisions in organizations is deep and broad.

Work Organizations as Contexts for Applied Psychology

It would be very safe to say that we are organizational mammals (Wilson, 2012). "Organization" is broadly defined here to mean that humans are disposed toward formation of groups with *explicit* aims and purposes (Katz & Kahn, 1978). Even though families are often at the core of organizations, they are excluded from this definition, since they are generally organized around more *implicit* needs. We form organizations, and often join them in the first place, because we believe that we share common aims (He & Brown, 2013; Jones et al., 2003; Randsley de Moura, Abrams, Retter, Gunnarsdottir, & Ando, 2009). There is reciprocity to this, as well: Organizations of various sorts (including work organizations, religious groups, clubs, professional societies, and political groups) can help to define, reinforce, and change the frames through which we understand ourselves (Hakel, 2013; Hartman & Weber, 2009). For example, this book is being read by students—members of organizations which are explicitly aimed at changing the way students view the world.

Identity class activity. A straightforward way to illustrate the importance of group membership to personal identity is to ask a few friends to describe themselves. Try answering the following prompts:

1. How would you describe yourself?
2. Describe your current situation.
3. What are you currently trying to accomplish with your life?

Chances are good that memberships in organized groups (schools, professions, workplaces) with explicit, shared purposes will come up in many of their answers.

BROAD INTERVENTIONS

Because *identities* are entwined with organizations in this way, decision makers in organizations may exert profound effects on motives, decisions, and actions (DeRue & Ashford, 2010). To the extent that psychologists are able to influence the decision processes of leaders and others in and around an organization, we have an opportunity to affect broadly defined motivations and the actions that follow from them (Cialdini et al., 2011; Lombardo et al., 2013). The power of the changes that can be affected by these applied areas is sometimes underestimated. Some CP applications directly encourage, create, and maintain *brand identities*, some of which may have shown up in the exercise above. As with clinical psychology, I-O psychology may elicit *developmental* change. As we have seen, these are sometimes very profound, lasting changes. But change is not always easy.

Psychology Applied in Organizations

Applied psychologists work in several areas of work organizations, but most can be found in human resource, training and development, research, and marketing functions. Figure 10.1 uses the systems perspective (DeShon, 2013) to show where applied psychology functions in organizations. Consumer psychologists typically work to develop and manage the organization's relationships with people *outside* of the organization, including customers and the public. From the systems perspective, these professionals concern themselves with what the organization offers (*output*) to the people who provide

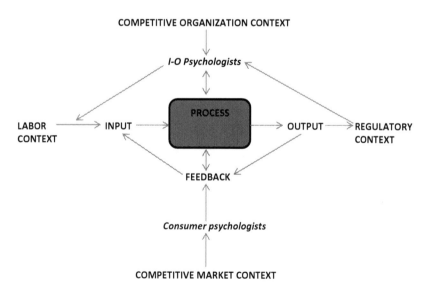

Figure 10.1 Common applied psychology functions in the organizational system

essential *inputs* (customers and potential customers). They are integral to the *feedback* received from the market about such things as consumer preferences, market shifts, and competitor strategies. I-O psychologists work to manage inputs (e.g., personnel selection) and processes (e.g., training and development systems). This involves managing the organization's relationships with people entering or already inside its boundaries (i.e., recruits, applicants, and employees). External factors affecting these decisions include both labor markets and regulatory aspects of the organizational context.

Both groups function as *decision facilitators*. A common misconception about this is that applied psychologists simply provide expert input about alternative solutions to problems. Although this is part of what they do, it often comes toward the end of the decision process. As we saw in Chapter 9, applied psychologists provide support for all aspects of the decision process, from identifying shared (and conflicting) stakeholder aims (Clulow, 2005; Lombardo et al., 2013; Finlay-Robinson, 2009) to evaluating effectiveness of solutions. They are thus defined as facilitators of the decision process.

Industrial and Organizational Psychology

About two-thirds of the approximately 8,000 members of the Society for Industrial-Organizational Psychology (2013c) are employed in work organizations outside of universities. I-O psychologists work in several areas of work organizations, but most can be found in human resource, training and development, research, and marketing functions.

I-O psychologists facilitate decisions about how to manage human thinking and behavior through two general approaches. *I-side* (industrial-side) practices support changes in the ways that *individuals* in the work context think and behave (Vinchur & Koppes, 2011). I-side practices support decisions about recruitment, selection, training, performance evaluation and feedback, and reductions in force, all of which are aimed to alter behavior by changing individuals. *O-side* (organizational-side) practices help to manage the psychological *context* of work, including job design, role clarification, and social relationship development (i.e., manager, co-worker, subordinate, and customer relations). Organizational psychology takes a more *interventionist* approach, directly helping leaders, managers, and groups through their decision processes, often targeting motivational factors (Latham, 2007; Vinchur & Koppes, 2011). However, O-side interventions often involve selection, training, and feedback (especially for leaders and groups), and I-side practices are interventions, as well (Muchinsky, 2004; Tippins, 2002): I-O psychology is thus a single field.

An underlying difference in I-O psychology interventions is the extent to which they assume people can be changed (see Figure 8.1). Approaches like training, development, and structured feedback try to change the thinking and behavior of *current* people in the organization. Personnel selection, by contrast, relies on aspects of people that are more difficult to change. Rather than directing scarce resources toward developing intelligence or extroversion, selection systems rely on the stability of these individual differences, and manage who is included in organizations using these and other stable traits.

Criteria for I-O psychology interventions are often aimed at *stability*. Although the idea of *organizational change* is highly touted (McFillen, O'Neil, Balzer, & Varney, 2013), stakeholders are often quite consistent about what they are hoping to get from their investment (Salancik & Pfeffer, 1977; Sørensen, 2002). For starters, most stakeholders have a basic, shared interest in the continued survival of the organization in which they are employed or otherwise invested. Beyond this, in very general terms, they are concerned with *organizational effectiveness*. Instability (and the desire for change) may be more a result of OE being defined in many ways, by different stakeholders (Cyert, Dill, & March, 1958; Katz & Kahn, 1978).

Table 10.1 provides a few examples of the different definitions that these stakeholder groups may bring to decision making in organizations (see

Table 10.1 Example grid of stakeholder definitions of organizational effectiveness

	Stakeholder groups				
	Policy makers	Executives	Managers	Employees	Customers
Avoidance definitions					
Survival	X	X	X	X	
Stability	X	X	X	X	X
Demand fulfillment		X	X		X
Cost containment	X	X	X		X
Lawsuit avoidance	X	X	X		
Regulatory compliance	X	X	X		
Work–family balance			X	X	
Sustainability	X	X			X
Approach definitions					
Growth	X	X			
Mission accomplishment	X	X			
Return on investment	X	X			
Quality		X	X	X	X
Job performance			X	X	X
Employee engagement		X	X	X	X
Equity			X	X	X
Sustainability	X	X	X	X	X
Well-being	X	X	X	X	X

Koocher & Keith-Spiegel, 2008). For a start, *executives* and *policy makers* (i.e., boards and ownership interests) in almost any kind of organization are likely to be interested in such things as growth, fulfilling demand for services, and mission accomplishment (Ambec & Lanoie, 2008). *Managers* and *supervisors* are often concerned with *maintaining* employee performance, avoiding lawsuits, and minimizing costs. For many companies, both managers and executives are concerned with *employee engagement.* Engagement can include such things as commitment, retention, and citizenship (Macey & Schneider, 2008; Organ, Podsakoff, & Podsakoff, 2011). These criteria often have fairly *immediate* financial consequences, such as turnover, which can be very costly for organizations with highly trained workforces. They may also have expensive longer term outcomes, such as quality problems due to haphazard work. Potential and current *employees* themselves are often interested in work–family balance (Cleveland & Colella, 2010; Masuda & Visio, 2012), equitable rewards for work (Donovan, 2002), and satisfaction (Thierry, 1998).

As with criteria for sustainability, Table 10.1 makes it clear that the *criterion problem* is an essential focus of I-O psychology in practice: Different stakeholders have different, sometimes conflicting ideas about what they are expecting to get from the organization. Understanding how organizational stakeholders weigh these criteria is an important part of effective interventions (DuBois, Astakhova, & DuBois, 2013; Vinten, 2000). When there is conflict, managing the conflict process is also important for developing broader understandings and a lasting solution (Johnson, Johnson, & Tjosvold, 2000). It is essential to applying the five criteria, as well.

The Five Criteria and the Five Step Approach to Intervention

The place that I-O psychologists already have in organizational decision making creates many opportunities for increasing organizational sustainability. The intervention process described in Chapter 9 provides opportunities at every step for integrating sustainability into organizational decisions. As in other applied areas, I-O psychology involves systematic assessment and feedback, both about criteria and about the variables that are likely to affect these criteria. The development and use of these assessments (called *psychometrics*) is a core scientific *competency* of the ethical practice of I-O psychology (Aguinas & Glavas, 2013; Society for Industrial and Organizational Psychology, 2013a). As experts in this, I-O psychologists can carefully choose assessments that will address sustainability and add value at every step in the intervention process, and for all of the five criteria.

In fact, a broad assessment of organizational conditions—referred to as *needs assessment*—is a common first step in most organizational interventions. *Needs assessment* is an attempt to develop an empirically founded understanding of the "readiness for change" of the people in and around an organization (Aguinis & Kraiger, 2009; Goldstein & Ford, 2002). The types of information that are commonly gathered in needs assessment follow closely from the steps in the intervention process:

BROAD INTERVENTIONS

1) *Outcomes* (criteria) that stakeholders believe are important for organizational effectiveness;
2) Behavioral and attitudinal *measures* thought to be associated with these outcomes;
3) Type of *feedback* stakeholders seek from baseline assessments;
4) Specific information about the types of *potential interventions* seen as likely to help;
5) *Evaluation* of intervention effectiveness based on baseline and criterion measures.

In practice, needs assessment can also be thought of as an attempt to "control for" the situation. Rather than trying to *manipulate* the many situational variables at work in a complicated social system, *measuring* these variables allows for "targeting" interventions within the particular organizational context. It also defines limits on ethical and practical intervention (criterion five), given the many, often complex person–situation dynamics at work. This, in turn, helps to identify which parts of the situation are (and are not) likely to be alterable, as a practical matter.

Needs assessment is not widely recognized as an intervention method by itself. While it is correctly seen as situational fact finding, it explicitly engages multiple stakeholders in the development of an understanding of the organizational system—criteria and all. As such, it is clearly an intervention which stimulates discussion and sometimes conflict about the mission and methods of the current organization, prior to more deliberate and designed interventions. Furthermore, providing feedback from assessment results is clearly an intervention in itself, as well. Unfortunately, I-O psychologists are generally not as well trained to provide metacognitive guidance from feedback, as are their colleagues in some other areas. The emergence of sustainability as an organizational aspiration, with its broader inclusion of stakeholders, argues for more formal development of such skills in I-O. Fortunately, recent applied research provides guidance for *meta-emotive facilitation* of the conflicts inherent in interventions (Järvenoja et al., 2013; Li, Ahlstrom, & Ashkanasy, 2010).

Although current approaches will not provide all of the tools needed to increase sustainable action, history suggests that I-O psychology can make important contributions with them, as well as developing effectual new approaches. I-O psychology can be highly effectual when dealing with many challenges faced by groups of people organized to make change happen.

Applying Needs Assessment to Sustainability Criteria

Applying needs assessment to sustainability more specifically is challenging, depending on which criterion, and which aspect of needs assessment is being addressed. Table 10.2 crosses the steps in needs assessment with four of the five sustainability criteria. The "practicality" criterion (five) is a "given" in

BROAD INTERVENTIONS

Table 10.2 Some needs assessment methods for sustainability criteria

	Criteria			
	Discrepancy test	Deliberativeness	Learning	Action
Steps in needs assessment				
1. Outcome identification	Strategic planning Subject matter expert discussions	Consistency and quality measures Job perform-ance observation Organizational culture artifacts	Awareness indicators Environmental knowledge	Current investments Triple bottom line use Political Investment
2. Baseline measurement	Behavioral measures	Cognitive measures	Knowledge measures	Self-report and behavioral measures
3. Initial feedback	From all meas-ures in step 2	Action planning from feedback	Skip to step 5, below	From all meas-ures in step 2
4. Potential interventions	Feedback of observation Creativity interventions Stepladder technique	Werner's group technique Selection (mental abilities, conscientious-ness, neuroti-cism openness, dogmatism)	Hypocrisy feedback Enriched training Development Coaching exercises Outdoor experiences	Organize work-ing group Work redesign Organizational development Start time for intervention
5. Assess-ment and feedback	Same as step 2	Progress since steps 1 and 4 Same as step 2	Same as step 2	Progress since steps 1 and 4 Same as step 2

this analysis, since the primary concern of needs assessment is just that—what will work in this situation? It is important to understand that this is a *criterion centric approach*: We start with where we are trying to go, then try to map a practical approach to get there (Bartram, 2005).

Criterion One: Discrepancy Testing

Central to pretty much every organizational intervention is awareness of some threat or opportunity in the organization's context (Gallagher, Joseph, & Park, 2002; Zemke, 1994) and some effort to define desired outcomes arising from these. Discrepancies in organizational systems (criterion one) can appear without much warning, or may be identified through deliberate processes, as in the case of *strategic planning* (Schweiger, Sandberg, & Ragan, 1986). Strategic planning attempts to systematically consider how to exploit future opportunities and avoid future threats.

But, discrepancies are often found somewhere between "sudden" discoveries and formal strategic planning. In particular, criterion definition that goes on as part of step one (Table 10.2) is a common source for identifying discrepancies. Here, I-O psychologists start by asking organizational *subject matter experts* (SMEs) some carefully devised questions (Goldstein & Ford, 2002; Ryan & Wilson, 2013). These SME interviews are a clear opportunity to identify sustainability issues, as well. For example, asking the right questions may help to get an initial idea of how aware stakeholders are about such things as waste, hazards, pro-social behaviors, and other sustainability issues.

In addition to such conversations, scientist-practitioners can use less obtrusive sources of initial information about the five criteria. These may help guide efforts to define the situation, and to formulate the more comprehensive assessments that follow. For one example, some organizations keep quality records, which may provide evidence about long term thinking. Lower quality may indicate a "sell and ship" approach, while higher quality may indicate more of an interest in customer retention for the future. For a second example, information about the organization's current investments, accounting practices (e.g., use of triple bottom line), and budget for political lobbying provide valuable information about action inclinations (criterion four). In more general terms, these are artifacts that provide important information about the *culture*, and especially the entrenched *values* of the organization (Ashkanasy & Jackson, 2002; Pulakos & Hedge, 2002).

Criterion Two: Baseline Measurement as Formalized Deliberation

A core component of needs assessment is the systematic *measurement* of aspects of the organizational system that may be relevant to desired outcomes (Goldstein & Ford, 2002). These measures include indicators of the current status of valued outcomes (e.g., performance, organizational commitment), as well as inputs and process that are hypothesized (by SMEs and other stakeholders) to have an impact on these outcomes (Jones & Lindley, 1998). Needs assessment typically gathers measurements of *person* (knowledge, skills, abilities, etc.) and *situation* (e.g., measures of employee engagement, perceived justice) factors, in order to predict important outcomes. Although needs assessment data are often grouped according to levels of analysis, this *person analysis* (individual level knowledge, skills, abilities, and other characteristics or KSAOs) and *situational analysis* (work, group, and organizational context levels of analysis), follows readily from the social psychological analysis we saw in Chapter 6. The resulting data provide a simpler framework for decision makers in later steps.

BROAD INTERVENTIONS

Individual behavior→group process→organizational output→ market output→environmental outcomes

Figure 10.2 A model of organizational precursors to environment outcomes

Ultimately, needs assessments are attempts to address stakeholder interests and criteria (step one in Table 10.2). In practice, how carefully these are defined and how well they are measured may have profound effects in later steps (Teachout & Hall, 2002). Similarly, in order to clearly communicate the approach being taken and the variables involved, a *thumbnail model* of how variables are thought to relate to one another can also be helpful during needs assessment. Figure 10.2 describes a simple example of such a model, derived from the *systems approach* (Katz & Kahn, 1978; Surface, 2012).

Unfortunately, there are many examples of failure, and even catastrophe, when organizational decisions fail to account for important realities and constraints of their systems and contexts (Chiles, 2001). Some of these "missed" variables were difficult to foresee. Others were ignored or undervalued, even when decision makers had been made aware of their potential importance (Clark & Eddy, 2017). More stakeholder engagement and better feedback processes may help to alleviate both of these problems (Ramanujam, Venkatraman, & Camillus, 1986).

Criterion Three: Feedback as Organizational Learning

Done well, step two provides credible *feedback*, both immediately after baseline and in later waves of measurement (step five). Such feedback is one of the most powerful forms of organizational intervention (Church, Margiloff, & Coruzzi, 1995; Gallagher et al., 2002; Hinrichs, 1991). At the individual level, we have already seen how carefully devised feedback can affect people's learning about the circumstances in which they operate (Balzer et al., 1992). At the organization level, entire *consortia* of for-profit and government organizations are built around organizational survey feedback (Mayflower Group, 2013; Office of Personnel Management, 2013). Consortia are groups of organizations that share common resources, such as industry standards, certification processes, and survey results. A member organization can compare its results with other organizations in the consortium (see Gifford, 2011 for uses of consortium feedback for sustainability).

Feedback may sometimes be delivered through a *facilitated process*, guided by psychologists. Given the very sensitive nature of feedback in some cases, and its potential for affecting learning (Church et al., 1995; Gallagher et al., 2002), it may deserve very careful handling (see Balzer et al., 1992; London, 1997; Stone-Romero & Stone, 2002). Carefully constructed *plans of action* are often the final products of feedback.

Letting people know when they are "doing wrong" may provide a certain satisfaction. *Confrontation* (Swim, 2013; Swim & Bloodhart, 2013) may even change people's behavior for the better. So far, however, there is no evidence about how long the results may last or about when confrontation might backfire!

Consider the following example: A person drops a lit cigarette butt out of their window as they step out of a parked car. What is wrong with this action? Under what circumstances might it be likely to have a greater or lesser impact? The answers are several, and include the following: (1) They are contributing to a major source of litter; (2) they are potentially causing water pollution; and (3) they may be starting a fire, if conditions are right.

Now think about how you might provide feedback to this perpetrator. First, consider what you would like to say. Second, think about the decision process model in Chapter 5: Would it be better to be more or less deliberative? How might emotive responses—yours and the other person's—affect the outcome of this encounter? Third, think about the types of feedback that are likely to lead to learning and behavior change (Chapter 8). What kinds of feedback might lead to violent reactions?

Now, imagine that you are a member of the local police, so it is your responsibility to say something. What exactly would you say? Depending on whether you feel that it is "safe," your success in changing this person's future behavior probably relies on your ability to reflect on the *behavior you saw* (not a characteristic of the person) and inform the person about the external consequences of that behavior. For example, you might say, "Cigarette butts cause forest fires" or "Did you know that cigarette butts are a major source of water pollution?"

Criterion Four: Design and Implementation of Interventions

The information derived from needs assessment and feedback is often critically important to deciding what interventions are likely to work. It is common for organizational decisions to be based on inadequate or inaccurate information about "the problem" when arriving at choices about "the solution" (Bonaccio, Dalal, Highhouse, Ilgen, Mohammed, & Slaughter, 2010; Cohen, March, & Olsen, 1972; Hinrichs, 1991; Jones & Wilson, 2013). Investments into intervention may turn out well, even when they

BROAD INTERVENTIONS

are haphazard. But more careful consideration yields feedback about the actual contingencies of a situation, which are the basis of learning (Chapter 8). In general terms, understanding the idiosyncrasies of the situation and the people in it is an important part of effective intervention (Goldstein & Ford, 2002). Put in person–situation terms, identifying ideas for *both* I-side (person) and O-side (situational) interventions can be devised based on needs assessment and feedback information.

Intervention choices generally follow this I versus O distinction. To the extent that the targets of intervention are malleable (i.e., knowledge, preferences, skills, attitudes), interventions can target *current* employees, managers, and executives. To the extent that stable individual differences (abilities, personality, identity) are associated with important processes and outcomes, interventions can target *future* hiring and firing.

"Engineering" naturally occurring human systems: The case for nepotism

Some people suggest that nepotic behavior—provision of privilege on the basis of family membership—can be observed in all human groups. In organizations, parents pass family businesses to their children, husbands and wives share privileged information outside of their work groups, and the examples go on.

Many attempts have been made to reduce the possibility of such events occurring, from celibacy in Catholic priests to employing eunuchs in the Chinese civil service. In modern times, many organizations have anti-nepotism policies that many well intentioned people applaud—even though these policies may not actually do what they are intended to do.

Such *interventions* to "manage" natural *human* systems may be analogous to attempts by civil engineers to reduce flooding in a natural *river* system by building dams. While some stakeholders applaud such efforts, others may strongly oppose this sort of intervention. People who want cheap, relatively low carbon electrical power, for example, may want to see more dams built; people who live in the river valley above the proposed dam may not.

In the case of nepotism, blanket anti-nepotism policies may have very negative effects. For a start, these may exclude highly *capable* family members from participation in organizations in which they share a vital stake. This sort of trade off is a concern when we attempt to manage elements of any organizational system. The assumption that our criteria are the same as others or are the only valuable criteria is naïve, and also violates ethical principles for professional conduct. "Waging war" on behaviors that appear to be unsustainable, without first giving significant consideration to and, when possible, engagement of legitimate stakeholders, is neither ethical nor sustainable itself. Following our nepotic example, an argument has been made that family businesses are, in fact, "greener" (Huang, Ding, & Kao, 2009). This argument is based on the notion that family firms are likely to consider a broader cast of stakeholders than other firms: Future, as yet voiceless family members are considered when decisions are made.

Interventions generally rely on decisions at different points in the employment relationship process (see Figure 10.3). Historically, I-side psychologists developed recruitment, selection, training, development, and evaluation systems. As the O-side took hold, there was increasing interest in managing the *relationship* between organization and employee, more generally. Understanding how people become aware of organizations (Farr & Tippins, 2010), make choices to join (Van Hooft, Born, Taris, & Van der Flier, 2006), decide to stay and engage (Bretz & Judge, 1998), and leave employment (Sablynski, Lee, Mitchell, Burton, & Holtom, 2002) have all become important targets for intervention.

Moving an organization toward sustainability criteria may rely on interventions at one or more of these steps in the relationship process. In terms of recruitment, this suggests that communicating the organization's stance on the five criteria may increase the chances of attracting like minded applicants (Gully, Phillips, Castellano, Han, & Kim, 2013). For selection, *structured interviews* (Roth & Huffcutt, 2013) that include questions aimed at the five criteria may help base organizational membership on sustainability values, and have the advantage of being job related in other ways, as well.

Organization: Recruitment → Screening → Training & → Evaluation → Retention or
& Selection Development Severance

Individual: Awareness → Job choice → Entry & → Engagement → Withdrawal
Socialization

Figure 10.3 Analysis of the employment relationship as a process

> You are the head of hiring for Company G, a large company that produces and markets low impact gardening products to individuals and commercial landscaping companies. Company G is in an environmentally progressive region and attracts customers and employees who subscribe to an ecocentric ethos. The company's founder and managers have a long history of expressing this same ethos as part of their strategy.
>
> Company G uses a "values inventory" as part of its selection process. Applicants who do not strongly endorse an ecocentric value orientation are not hired. Unfortunately, the environmental values measure used for this purpose leads to hiring a disproportionate number of women (Sahin, Ertepinar, & Teksoz, 2012). It also asks questions about people's deeply held values (Duus, 2010).
>
> A male applicant who was not hired on the basis of this inventory brings a complaint to the state Equal Employment Opportunity (EEO) board, arguing that the values inventory is discriminating on the basis of gender and religion—both of which are protected classes under this law. His complaint is upheld, given the actual hiring proportions and the sensitivity of questions asked. It is now up to Company G to show that, even though this selection device discriminated, it is defensible on the basis that it is job related. What can Company G do to demonstrate the job relatedness of the values inventory for its business?

Because client organizations are typically concerned with their own, core criteria (profit, constituent service, fundraising), psychologists helping develop sustainability need to respond to these criteria first, as an ethical matter. In I-O psychology, this relies on establishing the job relatedness of assessments and interventions, and avoiding unfair discrimination on the basis of various demographic groups (age, gender, ethnicity, and others). Several methods can be used to establish job relatedness. One of the most common is *work analysis* (Pearlman & Sanchez, 2010), which is (conveniently) a core part of needs assessment. The strongest case for job relatedness is often made by demonstrating empirically that a selection measure or training experience *correlates* with important job performance measures in the target job. Sustainability outcome measures can be included in this kind of evaluation study, as well.

Even better, the widespread use of certain well established selection measures may already have contributed to sustainability, without measuring sustainability outcomes. We saw in Chapter 4 that *mental abilities measures* correlate positively with several aspects of the five criteria, including deliberative thinking, learning, practical knowledge, and altruism (Millet &

Dewitte, 2007). Mental abilities measures have also shown high correlations with various *performance measures*, and are commonly used in personnel selection (Judge et al., 2010). If pro-environmental behavior (PEB) and other sustainability measures are also related to mental abilities, it is quite likely that *intelligent organizations* (Pinchot, 1996) already employ people who are inclined toward sustainable action. The point here is that these processes are *already in place* to test commonly used predictors: Good sustainability outcome measurement is what is lacking.

One recent concern about job relatedness has to do with age discrimination. Although there is a common stereotype that older adults are less concerned with sustainability than younger adults, the evidence is the opposite (Wiernik, Dilchert, & Ones, 2016). Older employees, on average, tend to be more concerned with sustainability (Wiernik et al., 2016).

Interventions aimed at changeable characteristics fall under the heading of socialization, training and development, and motivation. Once people are hired, the most common formal learning experiences are orientation (Waung, 1995) and training (Goldstein & Ford, 2002). We have already learned in Chapters 8 and 9 about how to design enriched learning and will spend no more time on these issues here. Suffice to say that enriched, social, motivationally relevant experiences are more likely to elicit intended decisions and behaviors.

However, *transfer of training* across time and circumstances is probably more relevant in organizational learning than in other settings (Ford, 1997). In the workplace, training is often quite brief and people often will be returning to work circumstances that are quite different from the training context (Goldstein & Ford, 2002). Developing training that manages these issues poses a challenge for interventions encouraging people toward sustainable action (Arthur, Bennett, Stanush, & McNelly, 1998; Witherspoon, Bergner, Cockrell, & Stone, 2013). This means two things in practice. First, "one size fits all" training is unlikely to have broad effects across circumstances. For example, outdoor experiential learning can backfire, given more or less stressful experiences (Bunting et al., 2000). Second, effective needs assessments needs to match training to specific work settings. Being able to account for interpersonal support, conflict, individual capacities, and motivation can be essential to transfer (Blume et al., 2010). This may be especially so with self-regulation of conservation behaviors (e.g. recycling paper, turning off lights).

However, this situation specificity may not be as true for *team training* as it is for training that is aimed at individual learning. Team training effects tend to generalize across criteria (Salas et al., 2008) and in some cases across situations—a one size fits all approach may be justified. In particular, training aimed at *coordination* of group functions and *adaptation* to changing circumstances may have utility across different groups and circumstances (Salas, Nichols, & Driskell, 2007). Specifically, groups that are able to recognize their own members' expertise are better able to adapt to changing circumstances (Salas, Rosen, Burke, & Goodwin, 2009). This *recognition of expertise* at the group level resembles metacognition in individuals. The good news here is that, as we saw in the previous chapter, metacognition (framed as "mindfulness") is already known to relate to sustainability criteria.

Longer term interventions may also be especially useful for sustainable action. These include *coaching*, *multisource feedback*, and *developmental assessment*. Developmental interventions resemble clinical interventions, since they are often aimed at self-insight. Because this doesn't come quickly sometimes, development takes the "long view" and is sometimes integrated into *succession planning* (Dowell, 2002), which identifies internal talent to fill vacancies in the organization as they occur. Because they take the long view, succession and development may be particularly consistent with deliberative attempts to enhance sustainability.

As people move into positions with more people in their supervision, developmental exercises start to resemble O-side interventions. The decisions and actions of executives, for example, usually affect a larger number of people than the decisions of others. In this way, managers and executives *become* the situation for those affected. Changing who is in the top executive job is effectively changing the context for the majority of the individuals in the organization. This relationship is described in Figure 10.4.

In fact, the most important part of the organizational context for most people is their immediate social context (Hinsz, 2008). Who we work with (and for) can have far reaching effects on our motivations and decisions: Choosing to join an organization, perceiving discrepancies in our contexts, thinking before acting, learning, and taking appropriate action may all have relationships with variables in this social context. Given this, it is not surprising that most O-side interventions involve changes in the structures and processes of leadership and work groups (Muchinsky, 2000). While larger

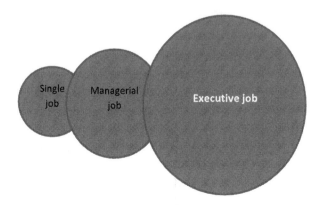

Figure 10.4 How person becomes context

organizational systems are often changed (e.g., the compensation system), and may have effects on behavior, these effects are usually mediated through group processes (e.g., how line managers implement such changes).

Assessing potential leaders is therefore a very powerful instrument for those who are interested in changing organizational decision processes. As with other selection decisions, *executive selection* relies partly on stable traits. For example, there has been renewed interest in recent years in the problem of screening leaders for their *moral development* (Kaiser, Hogan, & Craig, 2008; London, 2002), and especially their ability to genuinely empathize with others. Early research screened for authoritarian dogmatism (Tosi, 1973) and more recent work has centered on screening out people with narcissistic tendencies (Kaiser et al., 2008). However, consistent with what we have seen in developmental interventions, selection devices can also account for the ways that prospective executives manage the effects they have on others. The degree of self-insight is recognized as an important component of leadership effectiveness (London, 2002). It is not a great leap to suggest that potential executives' awareness of their effects on others extend to awareness of the effects of their decisions on future stakeholders.

Ultimately, executives manage the organization's relationships in the weak situations *outside* its boundaries (Cross, Ernst, & Pasmore, 2013). Predicting how people in these *boundary spanning roles* will respond to stress (Voydanoff, 2005), then helping them to "cognitively map" their situations (Hustad & Bechina, 2012), are frontiers for intervention. Boundary spanning effectiveness may prove to be an essential challenge for environmental sustainability, since the links between behaviors and environmental outcomes are indirect and engage many stakeholders. In fact, organizations may provide the most powerful "launching pads" for broader community and societal change. More on this later.

Apart from altering social contexts, other interventions alter the structure and design of work contexts. We have seen how human factors engineering alters the physical design of work in order to optimize workload, situation awareness, and behavior. Other contextual changes include job redesign, compensation system management, and restructuring the organization (i.e., changing the organizational "chart"). With a few exceptions (Oldham & Hackman, 2010), evidence suggests that such interventions can affect the thinking and behavior of people in the organization (Morgeson, Garza, & Campion, 2013), often in unanticipated ways. Evidence also shows that such contextual changes are more likely to be successful when they do take psychological precursors into account—and particularly the "match" between context and motive (Morgeson et al., 2013; Neuman, Edwards, & Raju, 1989). There may be few substitutes for addressing people's individual motives (e.g., identity, developmental stage, self-efficacy) when designing for sustainability.

BROAD INTERVENTIONS

Criterion Five: Evaluation Research as a Reality Check

Step five in the intervention process—evaluation—is an attempt to determine whether interventions have accomplished their intended purposes. Put in terms of our five criteria, evaluation is aimed at criterion five: Practicality. But, developing ways to rigorously test practicality is often too costly to be easily justified (Cascio & Fogli, 2010). Evaluation itself may be impractical.

As we have seen in other applied areas, there is reluctance to do evaluations, often for some very good reasons. Deciding (1) whether investments in interventions were worthwhile and (2) what "next steps" might be helpful are primary reasons for doing evaluations. So, to the extent that these are important, evaluation is more likely to be required. For example, evaluation may be demanded if the organization spent millions on an intervention. If it was accomplished without major expense, then the expense of evaluation itself may not be worth the effort.

It also bears mentioning that needs assessment is often iterative. As in our original model of science (Figure 1.2), scientist-practitioners assume that they do not have all the answers and, in fact, may have chosen inadequate interventions (McFillen et al., 2013). It therefore makes practical sense to treat interventions as *incremental* (Sørensen, 2002). Managing organizational decisions takes sustained effort (Schwab, 2007) and careful attention to people's motivations along the way. This is because, consistent with the quote at the beginning of this chapter, people tend to resist even changes that yield very happy results.

Consumer Psychology

Framed in systems perspective terms (Figure 10.1), consumer psychologists work to develop and manage the organization's relationships with people *outside* of the organization, including customers and the public. These professionals concern themselves with what the organization offers (*output*) to the people who provide essential *inputs* (customers and potential customers). They are therefore integral to the *feedback* received from the market about such things as consumer preferences, market shifts, and competitor strategies.

In this section, we will consider the role of psychology in this process and in the consumer economy more broadly. We will see how some of the tools of applied psychology play a role in the relationships that are formed between organizations and the people in markets, and how these relationships exert influence on decisions made by both. Then, we will consider how psychologists can use these tools to lend a hand in broader community and political activities. These are frontiers for sustainability and therefore raise a number of practical and ethical questions. The final section will consider the ethical role of applied psychologists in these efforts to *sell sustainability*.

> Many of us learned at a fairly early age that "selling" our ideas is an important part of life as a social being. Sometimes it would be nice to just go for what you want. And in individualist cultures, the myth of making it "on your own" is reinforced, making it more likely that people will act on this impulse. The results are often very different from what was expected. Among other things, there are usually social factors and random events that play roles in the outcomes of our efforts—intended and otherwise.
>
> Reflect again on the story you told a friend in Chapter 4: The time when you "went for it" and succeeded in getting what you were after. Were there other people whose actions (or lack of action) had an effect on the eventual outcome of your story? Did you have to talk to others to try to explain *why* you were doing the things you were doing, before you did them? If you did, you were revealing your *motives* to the other people. We saw in the emotive perception discussion how this allowed them to make decisions about whether they shared motives with you.
>
> Did you have to explain how your actions and their potential outcomes would affect *them*? If so, you were engaging in one of the fundamental aspects of selling.

The American Psychological Association (APA), Division 23 (Society for Consumer Psychology, 2013) describes CP as "the study of human responses to product and service related information and experiences." The "information and experiences" include everything from advertisements to word of mouth. But the general focus of CP is quite narrow: "consumer responses to product and service related information" (Society for Consumer Psychology, 2013). This subdiscipline relies heavily on the person–situation approach we saw in Chapter 6, using individual differences, situational variables, and the interaction of these two to predict people's responses. The systems approach has received less attention in CP.

Two things narrow the person–situation approach in CP even further. First, as a rule, the *person* variables in CP center around motivations, rather than knowledge, skills, or abilities. Second, *situational* variables are often *manipulated* by using social stimuli in communications about the product. These manipulative stimuli are increasingly being built into the product itself. We will see how media, such as smartphones, even build the *situation* into the product.

Unlike some of the other applied subdisciplines, this division of APA does not have a separate code of ethics available through their website (Society for

BROAD INTERVENTIONS

Consumer Psychology, 2013). Nevertheless, consumer psychology researchers have been exploring both ethics problems (Cialdini, 1999; Smith & Cooper-Martin, 1997) and approaches to reducing overconsumption (Etzioni, 1998; 2004; Heath & Chatzidakis, 2012). In fact, some cutting edge efforts to increase pro-environmental behaviors (PEBs) have come from CP (e.g., White & Simpson, 2013). We will return to some of these sustainability applications soon.

Approaches to Intervention

Like other areas of practice, it makes sense to think of CP as a way of managing decisions about relationships. In some ways, these decisions are similar to the decisions made in an employment relationship. CP is helping to manage the relationship between an organization's decision makers and people in its market (Figure 10.1). Unlike I-O, though, the decision makers in the *market* generally wield a different sort of power than the people who work in the *organization*. Consumers wield power over basic *inputs* into the organizational system. The organization also has very little reciprocal power with buyers: Once the consumer has paid for a product or service, the buyer–seller relationship is mostly at the discretion of the consumer. Employees wield power over other *inputs* —the KSAOs and behaviors they use in exchange for rewards, usually for a longer time than consumers. In additional to this reciprocal, usually daily relationship, employees contribute to the *processes* in the organizational system, rather than just inputs. This more complex and multifaceted relationship may help to explain why there are more I-O than CP practitioners.

Many retail firms in the United States have added moneylending functions since the banking deregulation of the 1980s. Incentives to finance a purchase based on a formal loan from the company that sold you the product did not used to be as common a practice. This creates not one, but two relationships between the organization and the consumer. On one hand, there is the ancient buyer–seller relationship. On the other, there is the borrower–lender relationship.

On what psychological variables might this dual relationship have an effect? Might it increase or decrease consumer awareness of the organization's products and services? How about its potential effects on deliberativeness, learning, identity, and future action? Does it make one or the other of these relationships take on greater practicality for the consumer? How about for the organization?

| Organization: | Strategy → Development → Point of purchase → Service → Word of mouth → Recapture & advertisement |
| Individual: | Motivation → Awareness → Purchasing choice → Brand identification → Defection & deliberation |

Figure 10.5 Process analysis of the consumer–organization relationship

Because organizational decisions about their relationships with consumers generally occur in the marketing research, product development, sales, and advertising functions, applied psychologists can be found in these functions (Society for Consumer Psychology, 2013). Consumers take part in this relationship from the point when they become aware of the organization's offerings (Srinivasan, Vanhuele, & Pauwels, 2010); through their buying decisions and experiences (Srinivasan et al., 2010; Wright & MacRae, 2007); their evaluations of satisfaction with what they get when they buy (Gelbrich & Roschk, 2011; Szymanski & Henard, 2001); their loyalty (Eisend, 2006; Eisend & Stokburger-Sauer, 2013; Toufaily, Ricard, & Perrien, 2013); and their defection (Singh, Hansen, & Blattberg, 2006). CP research is organized accordingly (see Figure 10.5).

Like all human relationships, there are examples of all sorts of consumer–organization relationships, including everything from strong, mutually beneficial relationships to abusive and exploitative ones. In general, though, there is a tendency for those of us who are concerned with sustainability to see consumerism in a very negative light, and to see marketing as exploitative (Heath & Chatzidakis, 2012). Unrestricted growth in markets is seen as a central driver of sustainability problems (Thompson, Marks, & Jackson, 2013; Zovanyi, 2013), and organizations that constantly clamor for our money are pervasive in modern Western societies. It's not hard to make a connection between the two, especially given the power of large organizations over individual consumers in many consumer economies (Hastings, 2013; Rotfeld, 2004).

There are some good reasons for mistrusting professionals involved in fueling consumer demand. Nevertheless, many of these same professionals *within* work organizations share the hopes and concerns of people outside their organizations. For a particularly important example, there are often people working in organizations who are deliberately trying to change things from within (Pinchot, 1999). Even more than this, the ability of marketers to influence others often relies heavily on their responsiveness to the hopes and demands of their customers and markets. Trying to create and maintain a good relationship with people in the market is, after all, a central purpose of their work. To the extent that organizations base their survival on *consumer demands*, the relationship may be more to blame for hyper-consumption than are either of the parties to it. There is plenty of blame to go around.

BROAD INTERVENTIONS

Looking forward, in order to understand the *ethics of consumption*, we need to consider both *our* decisions to *buy* (or not) and organizations' approaches to *getting us to buy*. In order to understand our decisions in this relationship, it will help to understand the strategies CP takes to organizational decisions about their relationships with *us*—the consumers.

There are many strategies that organizations take. We will focus on three of the more prominent ones here: *Target marketing, branding*, and *market creation*. These approaches try to influence *purchasing choices* and *loyalty*—common CP criteria. It would be a bit of a stretch to refer to these strategies as *interventions*, since CP is often reliant on a very small portion of the people in a market deciding to purchase their client organizations' products and services. Instead of dealing with a "captive audience" of students, therapeutic clients, participants in legal proceedings, and employees, CP is often trying to influence decisions across a very large group in very heterogeneous contexts.

Put another way, *transfer of learning* and *situational specificity* are even more problematic to CP than they are to other applied areas (Cheon, Cho, & Sutherland, 2007). Helping people to recognize the value of a product or service *in its particular context* is perhaps the greatest initial challenge for establishing a relationship between organization and customer. Imagine learning about a shampoo (used in the shower) on the radio in your car on the way to work. Here, "matching" the learning situation (your car) with the situation where the seller would like you to use the product (your shower) is quite a stretch. Finding a way to sell you this shampoo with an electronic device (radio) while you are actually in the shower can be quite a challenge, as well.

Targeting

One way to manage this situational heterogeneity is to largely ignore it, giving attention instead to central "person" variables. *Target marketing* does just this. It relies on identifying and exploiting motivations that are particularly salient to a targeted group. The logic of target marketing is almost identical to the logic of selection in I-O psychology: It uses individual differences to predict later behaviors. For example, the desire of many young people to find love (an individual difference in motivation) is exploited by advertisements that include rich images of sex, love, glamour, and marriage. The end result is to encourage purchase of the organization's product (e.g., cologne, clothing, car, etc.) by young people.

Traditionally, target marketing has been based on demographics, rather than being directly linked with psychological variables. However, there are examples of targeting that cross this divide, such as targeting based on cultural orientation (Lee & Choi, 2005), gender roles, and stereotypes (Royo-Vela, Aldas-Manzano, Küster, & Vila, 2008). The advent of "cookies" in

285

BROAD INTERVENTIONS

computers and smartphones has also made targeting considerably more accurate, since cookies are based on previous viewing and buying *behaviors*.

In fact, behavioral targeting is another way to deal with lack of situational control. Although this is a very situationally specific approach (Weilbacher, 2003), the focus on observable behaviors has led to some interesting effects. Point of purchase displays and associationist approaches to advertising (see Chapter 8) have both led to some successful interventions. For example, research has assessed the conditions under which people are *willing to pay* for things at the point of purchase (Wertenbroch & Skiera, 2002). This is how inexpensive *impulse buy* items became available where the lines form at checkout counters. These effects rely on a very specific situation, with very limited contingencies, and they are often effective within these circumstances.

Branding and Identity

Branding is another way to manage the effects of situational differences. Recall from Chapters 6 and 7 that *internalizing* of norms, values, and culture are ways to get people to carry the context around with them. In Chapter 8, we also saw how generalized learning, through declarative memory, makes it easier to apply contingencies across multiple situations. Branding is an attempt to create both a generalized memory of the product (Bock & Izquierdo, 2006) and, more often, to get people to *identify* themselves with the community around a company, product or service (Cornelissen, Christensen, & Kinuthia, 2012; Marzocchi, Morandin, & Bergami, 2013). In effect, branding directs *motivational* resources toward "belonging" to a brand group—a *social identity* (Alsem & Kostelijk, 2008; Cornelissen et al., 2012)—and understanding the world through a learned brand lens (Bock & Izquierdo, 2006).

Although research in the psychology of brand identity is fairly recent (Marzocchi et al., 2013; Plassmann, Ramsøy, & Milosavljevic, 2012), it is likely that this sort of product identification strongly dictates behaviors. For example, the "brand" of many sports teams has a strong effect on behaviors in sports venues. People attend carefully, yell loudly, and even cry based on their identification with a particular team. In addition, and like other social identities, branding is carried around with us to many circumstances, effectively managing the *situation specificity* problem by internalizing the "brand" situation. Following from this, if people have consistent, positive experiences with a brand (e.g., they associate themselves with a winning team), their behavior may be quite consistent across time and contexts (Bonnici, 2006). Again, following from the sports brand example, many people wear cherished old clothing with their sports identity emblazoned across it. In short, effective branding creates a mobile psychological context (Bonnici, 2006).

BROAD INTERVENTIONS

Using Psychology to Create New Markets

At its most effective, marketing can create entirely new markets. This generally starts with *product development* (Blackwell et al., 2006). Psychologists are sometimes involved in this, usually helping to identify consumer motivations that will be addressed by the new product or service (Rosa & Spanjol, 2005; Schifferstein, 2010; Society for Consumer Psychology, 2013; Søndergaard & Harmsen, 2007). Product development has been compared to a seduction process, through which the organization uses a multitude of cues to lure the consumer to their product (Schifferstein, 2010). Ethical questions abound here, and we will return to them later. Fortunately, attempts at seduction often fail (Penny, 2009).

A recent trend in product development is the direct involvement of consumers from the start of the process (Mann, 2007; Nishikawa, Schreier, & Ogawa, 2013). Treating consumers as partners in product development is a direct acknowledgment of the fact that CP is primarily about a healthy (and ethical) consumer–organization relationship. This approach has also met with considerable success from the organization's viewpoint (Nishikawa et al., 2013). And, to the extent that it engages consumers who care about sustainability, it may be an opportunity to instill sustainable features into new products and services from the start of the marketing process (Lee & Kim, 2011; Mann, 2007).

Once the product is developed, the extensive research on *diffusion of innovation* (Overstreet, Cegielski, & Hall, 2013) provides some clues about how to manage the process of marketing the new product. The creation of new markets has been compared to a life cycle, with early adopters leading to broader adoption, mature markets, laggard adoption, and eventual decline (Blackwell et al., 2006; Mahajan, Muller, & Bass, 1990). Following a simple mediated model (Figure 10.6), it is clear that creating a new market relies on early adopters.

There is a substantial psychological research literature explicitly aimed at understanding *adoption* (Arts et al., 2011). Generalizations can be made about individual differences of early adopters (de Mooij & Hofstede, 2011; Tellis, Stremersch, & Yin, 2003). Early adopters tend to have greater uncertainty avoidance, have a more individualist cultural perspective (Arts et al., 2011; de Mooij & Hofstede, 2011), and see greater advantages in the new innovation than non-adopters (Arts et al., 2011). Potential early adopters may also see greater complexity in an innovation, and are more likely to *intend* to adopt it, but less likely to actually do so than actual adopters, who see less complexity (Arts et al., 2011).

Early adoption→middle adoption → mature market →laggard adoption→decline

Figure 10.6 Mediated model of diffusion of innovation over time

> Are you an early adopter? Think about your choices regarding purchasing, consumption, and waste. What has led you to make consumption choices in the past? Do you think these will change as you learn more about how to make such decisions more deliberately?

CP and Sustainability in Historical Perspective

Consumers are generally trying to enhance their well-being through their decisions in the marketplace. Ultimately, ethical questions may affect these decisions only to the extent that consumers are made aware of them, whether they bring moral reasoning into the process or not. But, people in the marketplace are often not made aware of the ethical implications of these decisions. To complicate matters, we saw in Chapter 7 that principled moral reasoning is exercised only by a minority of the population. This means that ethics are considered only by some consumers. For example, young children often make choices entirely on impulse. Thus, many consumers do not consider their own error-proneness, act deliberately, or take eventual responsibility for their actions.

Given this, it falls to organizational decision makers to consider the five criteria. In fact, there has been concern for some time about ways that marketing and advertising rely on people's awareness and diligence—or lack thereof (Belk, 1975; Cialdini, 2007; Patrick & Hagtvedt, 2012). Thus, an important question for CP is how to manage the decisions of *both* parties to the market relationship.

We have already seen, in Chapter 5, how our decisions can be more or less deliberative and wind up with more or less error. In Chapter 3, we also saw how we are a bit blinded by our tendency to believe that our decisions will always get the expected result. Ethical decision making demands that we consider these factors: (1) *Awareness of our own fallibility* (Cialdini, 2007; Ji & Wood, 2007; Wallach, 2010) and (2) *deliberation in the face of uncertainty* (Clegg, Kornberger, & Rhodes, 2007; Matthews, 2011). Ethical consumer choice can also rely on the ability to see beyond our initial, emotive reactions, as we saw in Chapter 5. Once we have made decisions and seen their outcomes, ethics also require that we take time to (3) *learn from both our deliberations* and the *results of our choices* and (4) *take appropriate future action*, (5) when *practical* (Campbell, Vasquez, Behnke, & Kinscherff, 2010). These should look very familiar: They are the five criteria.

CP holds great promise for devising interventions to affect such ethical decision making. Unfortunately, applications in *marketing* and *advertising* have a somewhat checkered past. Historically, these endeavors have included attempts to get people to (1) ignore otherwise obvious problems (e.g.,

BROAD INTERVENTIONS

cigarette company campaigns); (2) rely on heuristic and emotive processing rather than more careful consideration (see Cialdini, 2007; Darke et al., 2006); and (3) retain ways of thinking and behaving that are potentially maladaptive (e.g., ads to buy high fat content foods). Chapter 3 introduced the *rational man* approach to economics that spawned these sorts of applications.

By contrast, it was psychological research that refuted the "buyer beware" practices spawned by the rational man model. The 2002 Nobel Prize winner for economics (Nobel Prize, 2013), psychologist Daniel Kahneman, showed quite convincingly that the free market assumption of *rational choice* is not well founded (Kahneman, 2011). This move toward greater concern for the ethics of the organization–market relationship has been supported by many consumer psychologists, and particularly with respect to questions about "trickster" marketing (Cialdini, 2007) and overconsumption (Alexander & Ussher, 2012; Cherrier, 2009; de Barcellos et al., 2011; Dickinson, Crain, Yalowitz, & Cherry, 2013; Etzioni, 1998; Heath & Chatzidakis, 2012; Huneke, 2005; Jain & Kaur, 2006; Ji & Wood, 2007; Knussen & Yule, 2008; Kotler, 2011).

In terms of the five criteria, a major issue in advertising is to get people to attend to a discrepancy (Grewal, Kavanoor, Fern, Costley, & Barnes, 1997). The result has been that research on criteria two (deliberate attention), three (learning), and four (eventual action, i.e., to spend effort and money on a product or service) all depends on first attending to discrepancies (Figure 5.1).

Automobile Dependency

It would be hard to overstate the enormity of the effects of automobiles on our physical environments. The effects are sometimes fairly obvious: Since the introduction of the first cars about 100 years ago, personal automobiles have dislocated local neighborhoods and ecosystems, supported sprawling metroplexes, and cost trillions of tax dollars to build and maintain infrastructure. Less obviously, billions of tons of liquid, solid, and gaseous carbon has been dispersed from mines and oil deposits underground into atmospheric gas. Even those who dispute climate science have not disputed this. Most people also do not realize that cars are a top cause of death by accident (see Table 9.1). All of this occurs, even though there are healthier, safer, more efficient, less costly, and more sociable forms of transport available, such as walking, biking, trains, buses, and ferries.

So why is it that some people love their automobiles to the point of obsession (Reser, 1980)? Is it a coincidence that, for many years, by far the largest share of the advertising dollars spent in the United

States has been spent trying to get people to buy cars (TVB, 2013)? For example, in 2012, more than twice as much was spent on TV advertising for automobiles (over $925 million) than for telecommunications—the next highest sector total (TVB, 2013). Although the relation between ad dollars and car purchasing does not indicate causal relationships, people choose to travel, vote, pay taxes, and even fight wars to support their desire for cars. It is clear that much more than money is spent on cars.

A question for CP innovators is whether there are similar ways to influence people and organizations to use alternative forms of transportation. The evidence so far shows that people's intentions to choose more sustainable transportation than cars do not translate into action (Lanzini, & Khan, 2017). Applying psychology to narrow this intention–behavior gap is an important frontier.

A major example of this comes from consumption associated with the automobile, which has permeated virtually every aspect of modern life in many countries. Did applied psychology have an effect on the burgeoning use of the automobile? The answer is, "Probably." Consumer psychology goes back a long way (Barry, 1987). We have seen in Chapter 8 how Frank Stanton and John B. Watson put their doctorates in psychology to work helping to get people to buy things; and a lot of buying occurs in relationship to cars. What is certain is that I-O psychologists had a hand in the human resource, research, and training functions in many of the major oil, steel, automobile, and government organizations that pushed for and supported the growth of the automobile economy.

CP Strategies for Sustainability

Targeting and Branding

Early marketing research targeting sustainability developed the notion of a *conservation ethic* to distinguish people's motivation toward sustainability (Belk, 1975; Painter, Semenik, & Belk, 1983). These efforts did not appear to have gone very far (Russell & Mehrabian, 1976), but targeting has gained traction in recent years, with the appearance of a new wave of research trying to tackle sustainability questions (de Barcellos et al., 2011; Ehrenfeld, 2008; Hanss & Böhm, 2013; Hines et al., 1986; Maibach et al., 2011; Soyez, 2012; Winter, 2004). Some examples of these more recent efforts include assessment of characteristics that distinguish people who are likely to pollute (Hine et al., 2007), reduce household waste (Tobias, Brügger, & Mosler, 2009), and respond favorably to green advertisement (Aaker et al., 2000; Jain & Kaur, 2006).

These have targeted both *predictor* and *mediator* variables. For example, a large scale study in Australia directly assessed a host of psychological variables that are likely candidates for targeting PEB, including *environmental values, trust in authorities, risk perceptions*, and several other potentially important *predictor* variables (Hine et al., 2013). Lee (2008) has also assessed the relative importance of a group of *mediator* variables relevant to the five criteria. Adolescents' decisions to *take responsibility* for their choices and to *take action* were predicted more by *peer influences* than by personal attitudes and beliefs.

Used in the interest of sustainability, the behavioral approach can also have very meaningful effects, again in specific circumstances (Do Paço, Alves, Shiel, & Filho, 2013; McKenzie-Mohr, 2000). For a few examples, researchers have evaluated actual consumer habits in household recycling (Knussen & Yule, 2008), laundry cleaning (Laitala, Boks, & Klepp, 2011; Laitala, Klepp, & Boks, 2012; Richter, 2011), coffee mug purchase and use (Ryoo, Hyun, & Sung, 2017), and household water consumption (Gregory & Di Leo, 2003). McKenzie-Mohr (2000) has also demonstrated how to work through a systematic *behavior analysis* process with key community partners, in order to increase sustainable behaviors within specific circumstances. However, as we saw in Chapter 8, behavioral approaches are double edged, mostly because established behaviors often trump intentions in specific circumstances (Ji & Wood, 2007; Lanzini & Khan, 2017).

Targeting and behavioral research also bear a close resemblance to research on how people treat their *internal environments*, that is, their *health habits* (Cunningham et al., 2010). If research on health outcomes is an indication, much more can be done, so long as it is understood that the contexts of behavioral research are narrowly defined by contexts. In any case, there are more than just research methods in common between psychology of sustainability and *health psychology* (Taylor, Poston, Jones, & Kraft, 2006). There is some intriguing evidence that healthy behavior and sustainable behavior go together rather nicely (Farmer, Breazeale, Stevens, & Waites, 2017).

The applications of branding to sustainability are a bit complicated and may require some very creative thinking (Rowe, Wilson, Dimitriu, Charnley, & Lastrucci, 2019; Mena, Hult, Ferrell, & Zhang, 2019). There are examples of potential "sustainability brands," such as *fair trade* (Brinkmann & Peattie, 2008) and *voluntary simplicity* (Etzioni, 1998, 2004). Using the voluntary simplicity example, there are features of a successful brand in this idea (Cherrier, 2009). It is at heart a values based *social identification* that is associated with deliberate reduction in the consumption of goods (Cherrier, 2009; Shama & Wisenblit, 1984; Thompson & Sinha, 2008), and sustainability research has recognized the effectiveness of social norms as precursors of PEB (Alexander & Ussher, 2012; Goldstein et al., 2008; Oates et al., 2008).

There is a need for research on the efficacy of voluntary simplicity and similar sustainability identities as branding strategies.

> There are organizations whose leadership rejects the notion of sustainability and much of its associated science, but whose actual products promote such things as reducing environmental impact (e.g., some economy cars), recycling (e.g., motor remanufacturing firms), and reusing (e.g., car parts retailers). Their brands may not acknowledge "reduce, reuse, recycle" values, but their effectiveness relies heavily on just these values. Similarly, some brands may reflect sustainability, but the organization's internal and marketplace actions send a different message. Applied psychologists try to base interventions on an understanding of both actual values and the "match" between values and actions.

Sustainability Adoption

Starting with what we already know about adoption of innovation, we can confidently answer a few questions about what makes people more or less willing to pay for public goods (Trapero-Bertran, Mistry, Shen, & Fox-Rushby, 2013), more likely to see personal value in pro-environmental consumer choices at different points in the adoption cycle (Welsch & Kühling, 2010), and be more mindful in purchasing choices (Sheth, Sethia, & Srinivas, 2011). For those who have already adopted certain innovations, there are even some ways to create affordances in the buying situation that help them to make more informed choices (Atkinson, 2013).

Overcoming resistance to new ideas is part of getting people to adopt them. One way to think of this is that the new idea needs to be discrepant enough from existing experiences to elicit attention in the first place. Once noticed, adoption may rely next on the emotion attached to it. Forty years of sustainability targeting shows that *avoidance framing*—eliciting fear and uncertainty—has dominated sustainability advertising (Bortree, Ahern, Dou, & Smith, 2012). There is controversy about the effectiveness of avoidance framing, with researchers arguing whether it is more (Newman, Howlett, Burton, Kozup, & Tangari, 2012), or less effective than *approach framing* (Bortree et al., 2012). One recent study suggests that sustainable choice is more likely when its immediate positive consequences are emphasized (van der Wal, van Horen, & Grinstein, 2018). Otherwise, uncertainty appears more likely to reduce sustainable choices.

There is probably value to remembering (from Chapter 6) that *motive sharing* is the question people ask as they view emotive messages. Research about

BROAD INTERVENTIONS

targeting people who are likely adopters hints at this. Avoidant affect (Bortree et al., 2012), perception of positive motive sharing (Welsch & Kühling, 2010), and framing of advertisements (Eisend, 2006; Rucker, Petty, & Briñol, 2008; Steg, Dreijerink, & Abrahamse, 2006) may all affect adoption. Similarly, research about the trust people have in advertisers (i.e., the extent to which they "share motive") may also have an impact on adoption (Do Paço & Reis, 2012). What this means for practice is not that emotion itself is having an effect, but rather that the motive sharing message sent by the emotion makes the difference. Emotive appeals may need to send a "you're one of us" message for most purposes.

> The use of humor in television advertising (Gulas & Weinberger, 2006) suggests that organizations have realized the importance of positive affect for getting people to attend to and remember messages (Janssens & De Pelsmacker, 2005). However, humor may work better when advertisers are trying to get people to be more deliberative, rather than when the humor is designed to just make people "feel good" (Janssens & De Pelsmacker, 2005). There are also cultural differences in people's responsiveness to different forms of humor (Hatzithomas, Zotos, & Boutsouki, 2011).

Media and Sustainability Interventions

Arguably the most powerful intervention tools in history can be classified under the heading of visual-audio media (VAM). VAM provides powerful means to control the contexts that affect behavior. They do so by dominating the context, by grabbing and keeping people's attention. For example, if we are trying to get people to learn about sustainability, situations outside of schools and workplace training are quite complex, making learning difficult to manage. But, VAM creates its own situation—a specific, highly controllable situation, once people are attending to it (Montgomery & Chester, 2009). As such, VAM has become a very rich platform for leaning interventions.

> VAM use is so pervasive in many societies that it is extremely challenging to try to describe the psychological variables involved in its effects (Lim & Kim, 2007). For our purposes, it is important to note that the use of VAM in the interest of sustainability is not a new idea (Syme, Seligman, Kantola, & MacPherson, 1987). Targeting (Lee, 2008) and persuasion (Greitemeyer, 2013; Lee, 2011; Syme et al., 1987) have been examined

so far, with branding research yet to come. Some evidence suggests, however, that media coverage of green issues has given more time to "anti-green" than to "pro-green" advertisers (Thøgersen, 2006). The success of these efforts has been gauged in very few studies (Ostman & Parker, 1986; Syme et al., 1987; Taddicken, 2013), so more evaluation research will be needed before arriving at broad conclusions. Almost certainly, effects will be limited by target motivations and contextual factors.

Current VAM technologies have gone a step further. Widely used social networking systems have created new markets in real time, based almost entirely on customer choices (Atkinson, 2013; Sheth et al., 2011). The genius of *social marketing* is that it doesn't use previously existing marketing channels, but rather creates channels as a marketing message is spread—like word of mouth, only on a massive, electronic scale. This revolution in marketing has grown up alongside and, in some cases, highly integrated with popular movements toward sustainability.

Not surprisingly, some innovative researchers have been part of these co-movements, and have found some ways to integrate psychology into online social networks and sustainability. While this research is fairly new in both marketing and sustainability (Kotler, 2011; Kozinets, Belz, & McDonagh, 2012), there are a few promising studies. For example, one study has looked at factors that differentiated people's involvement in both social networks and PEBs across countries (Minton, Lee, Orth, Kim, & Kahle, 2012). Another has shown that social networks may rely on the same approach and avoidance framing that influences sustainability messages (Krishen, Berezan, & Raab, 2019). It is worth noting that online interactions and social networks are themselves ways to reduce the costs associated with personal interactions.

The Five Criteria

Criteria One and Two: Discrepancy tests, impulse, and Deliberation

Much of the research we have discussed deals with ways to influence the consumer decision making process. But, before returning to this research, we will first review the product development research. Although there is little for sustainability researchers to go on at this first step, there are a couple of important innovations that deserve attention. As we have seen, product development often relies on satisfying unmet needs in the marketplace. Starting with consumer motivations, organizations seek *discrepancies* between these motivations and what is currently in the market. Devising new products and markets to reduce these discrepancies can even be the starting point for creating entirely new markets.

An example of a successful new "product" that is associated with sustainability is *ecotourism* (Buckley, 2012; Jaafar & Maideen, 2012). The idea here is to exploit tourists' desire to experience the beauty and diversity of pristine natural systems, with an eye to profit. Obviously, there are substantial concerns with having untrained crowds bumbling around in delicate ecosystems (Buckley, 2012; Takahashi, Veríssimo, MacMillan, & Godbole, 2012). Nevertheless, such tourism may have at least two important pro-environmental effects. First, learning about and coming to appreciate the delicacy of such ecosystems may help to alert people to important problems (Gibson, Dodds, Joppe, & Jamieson, 2003). Well designed ecotourism experiences along these lines may have powerful, even developmental effects (Gibson et al., 2003; Lee, Lawton, & Weaver, 2013; Weaver, 2005). Second, because ecotourism often occurs in fairly remote regions, the human populations there may receive substantial benefits (Jaafar & Maideen, 2012; Takahashi et al., 2012). This has implications for environmental justice, which we will return to later.

Much of the literature in CP deals with the sorts of decision processes we saw in Chapter 5. Such things as the reflex to attend and appraise (Heath, Brandt, & Nairn, 2006), emotive and deliberative responses (Heath, 2012), and social effects on decision processes (Goldstein et al., 2008; Ryoo et al., 2017) are very important to sustainability. But, the primary outcomes of interest in CP revolve around emotional responses to a product, followed by the choices to act in various ways (criterion four), and to adopt its brand identity. These outcomes may be even more important to the psychology of sustainability.

In terms of discrepancy testing, we have already seen how advertisements use emotive triggers to get people's attention. Loud noises, highly attractive people, evocative scenery, and a host of other approaches have been used simply to turn people's attention toward an ad (Heath, 2012). Perhaps the most interesting part of this research is that *conscious* attention (what we have called deliberativeness) actually can *reduce* the impact of evocative messages (Heath et al., 2006). Following from Figure 10.7, the less thinking we do, the more likely the emotive message will have a direct effect on our choices.

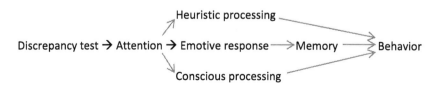

Figure 10.7 A thumbnail model of the consumer decision making process

BROAD INTERVENTIONS

Emotive appraisals and deliberation have also received some attention in the research on message framing. The avoidance and approach concepts from Chapter 5 (Bortree et al., 2012; Newman et al., 2012; Steg et al., 2006; Krishen et al., 2019) have wide application, but have not yet been used to frame sustainability messages. One possibility, based on the emotive perception of people hearing sustainability messages, is that trust (shared motives) may override message framing effects.

In addition to deciding whether we can trust the source (Do Paço & Reis, 2012), recipients also need to decide whether they can do anything about problems and opportunities. For example, if messages about the effects of climate change are aimed at *preventing* their negative effects on the people watching, they are less likely to have an impact than when they include relatively easy things people can do *promote* sustainability in the "world out there." Dickinson et al. (2013) showed not just that avoidance framing tended to reduce people's reliance on deliberative processes. They also showed that, by describing contingent relationships in the empirical system, people learned about what they *can* actually do.

In sales, things are rarely presented as "scary" unless a "solution" to the fear is immediately in the offing. For example, life insurance commercials are aimed at selling you insurance that will cover your family when you die (a scary event for many people). But, these commercials tend to frame things in terms of being "good to your family," with images that elicit positive affect. Rather than trying to prevent a bad thing from happening (especially something that is inevitable), the commercials aim at promoting a good.

This may explain why scaring people may not always sell them on the idea of sustainability. If the purpose of commercial messages is to learn, remember, and eventually act in a broad set of circumstances, then influence attempts should probably be canted away from anxiety, and toward metacognitive learning. But, being "rational" is not likely to work for many people who are "deniers" either—they are often just scared and respond to avoidance messages by "avoiding" (Newman et al., 2012; Hornsey & Fielding, 2017).

Since neither fear nor rationality may have the desired effect on any given individual, what are some approaches that are likely to increase attention, learning, and adoption? Does initial assessment matter?

Research that directly addresses these facets of the consumer psychology of sustainability is fairly recent, so conclusions are tentative. Still, several findings deserve attention. First, we know more about what may lead consumers to see goods and services as sustainable (Albinsson & Perera, 2012; Hanss & Böhm, 2013). Following the process in Figure 10.7, consumers' initial attention to "green" advertising often relies on its apparent sincerity—that "green" is not just a sales tool (Carrete, Castaño, Felix, Centeno, & González, 2012; Do Paço & Reis, 2012; Hartlieb & Jones, 2009). In terms of product features, we have already seen that engagement of consumers in product development may lead to desirable, situation specific features associated with sustainable products (Lee & Kim, 2011; Mann, 2007). This includes production that follows fair trade practices and low energy consumption, which consumers see as components of sustainability (Bradu, Orquin, & Thøgersen, 2013; Hanss & Böhm, 2013). Actual purchasing is seen as green when it is community based (Albinsson & Perera, 2012). After consumption, recyclable packaging is seen as an important feature of sustainable marketing (Hanss & Böhm, 2013).

Second, and regardless of these specific perceptions of sustainability in marketing, there is evidence that all can be collapsed into a single, underlying dimension—identity (Strizhakova & Coulter, 2013; van Dam & van Trijp, 2011). In other words, people may have specific, concrete ways of defining sustainability, but these rely on an underlying, motivated evaluation of self as a sustainable consumer (Thøgersen, 1999; 2009; Han & Stoel, 2017; Venhoeven, Bolderdijk, & Steg, 2016). Once again, carrying context around in our heads is probably more important than the labels used by CP and environmental psychology.

Third, although our identity may motivate us to make a difference, sometimes the situation interacts with such person variables (Aqueveque, 2006; Cleveland et al., 2005; McDonald & Oates, 2006; Thøgersen, 1999; Thøgersen & Ölander, 2006). For example, cost (Thøgersen & Ölander, 2006), the amount of effort required (McDonald & Oates, 2006), scarcity (Nichols, 2012), and other trade offs (Thøgersen & Ölander, 2003) can reduce the chance that we will act on our sustainable inclinations. Perhaps most problematic is "licensing" behavior, where consumers consume more on their next purchase because they were "green" in their first (Meijers, Noordewier, Verlegh, Willems, & Smit, 2019).

This and other gaps between motive and realization can be a major hurdle (Cleveland et al., 2005). Fortunately, it is this sort of discrepancy that marketing functions often address, through pricing, logistics, point of sale, and other approaches (Blackwell et al., 2006). Thus, finding ways to make it "easier to be green" is an important direction for future CP research (Cleveland et al., 2005; Dilling & Farhar, 2007). One approach to this is to create incentives, through such things as preferred customer programs (Nollet,

Rebolledo, & Popel, 2012), prize lotteries (Lee & Qiu, 2009), and discounts for sustainable practices (Ryoo et al., 2017).

Another approach to increasing deliberative consumption harkens back to some of the metacognitive and self-regulatory approaches discussed in Chapters 7 and 9. Simply helping people to learn to say no to consumer pleas may be a good place to start (Patrick & Hagtvedt, 2012). Other researchers, as we have seen, argue that we need to start with an identity, then apply mindful approaches to consumption choices (Sheth et al., 2011). This approach targets a healthy awareness of different interests (our own, the environment, and holistic) in consumption decisions, which may rely on differences in developmental stage.

Criterion Three: Watching and Learning versus Trying and Learning

Learning research has found its way into CP mostly in the advertising product choice step in the consumer–organization relationship (Figure 10.5). Although some CP research has treated advertising as a way to help consumers learn about product features (van de Wetering, Bernstein, & Loftus, 2005), modern research does not typically frame consumer outcomes in terms of expertise about product contingencies. Rather, the concern is more with whether people remember advertisements (Finlay, Marmurek, & Morton, 2005; Gontijo & Zhang, 2007), products (Bock & Izquierdo, 2006; Malaviya, Kisielius, & Sternthal, 1996), and brands (Bonnici, 2006; Weilbacher, 2003), and whether these memories are more or less favorable (Malaviya et al., 1996). In terms of learning, the concern here is with episodic memory and attitudes resulting from social information.

Learning as a result of direct product experiences has received attention, as well (Bradley & Sparks, 2012). Often framed in terms of *customer loyalty* (Toufaily et al., 2013), this research again confounds attitudes (i.e., customer product evaluations) with learning contingencies through experience.

Consumer sustainability research has only begun to apply learning, but it has done so in some interesting ways. At the point of product development, we have seen how complex, group level learning has been harnessed to enhance sustainable features of products (Mann, 2007). In terms of procedural learning, we have also seen how immediate feedback has been used to increase sustainable buying habits (Grønhøj & Thøgersen, 2011; Karlin et al., 2015). And, old fashioned learning about the contingency features of sustainable products has also been examined in social marketing (Robelia, Greenhow, & Burton, 2011).

However, there are many opportunities for CP to address learning, as well as to advance our understanding of behaviors in market relationships through the learning lens. One area in particular is the "learning by trying" approach to understanding sustainable choices. It would be hard to find a more deliberative, emotionally meaningful way to learn than through feedback about the actual consequences of sustainable choices.

BROAD INTERVENTIONS

Criterion Four: Taking Action

CP has spent most of its efforts trying to understand, predict, and control a very limited set of variables that are associated with the relationship between customers and organizations. Decisions to purchase and to come back and purchase again are examples of actions, but have less to do with the sorts of collective, altruistic, and sometimes risky actions that confront people involved in broader efforts to change, outside of an exchange relationship.

Sustainability research has an important role to play here. Among the most important variables associated with risk taking in consumer choice is the *cost of switching* (Kim & Gupta, 2012). One way to approach this cost is to determine how much people are *willing to pay* for a new product. Willingness to pay has found its way into the research on non-profit spending (Koschate-Fisther, Stefan, & Hoyer, 2012), as well as to sustainability choices (Clark, Kotchen, & Moore, 2003).

Arguably the most important variable for predicting people's willingness to take action is, once again, social identity (Alsem & Kostelijk, 2008; Cornelissen et al., 2012; Dacin & Brown, 2006). Developing brand identities for sustainability is an important frontier for the CP research that is aimed at individual and collective action. To the extent that people intent on change can create brands that help people identify and carry contexts with them, there may be greater likelihood of "right living" and positive action for both the good of the individual and of the species (Sheth et al., 2011).

Another frontier lies in efforts to make consumers more than just passive recipients in the organization–consumer relationship. We will return to the idea of organizing consumers to take action to directly influence organizational decisions. We have seen that some ethical marketing practitioners have already learned to include consumers as equal partners in product development. Similar efforts at active consumer engagement may have value through other phases of the relationship, as we have seen with recent social network marketing. "Buy local" efforts certainly allow for direct consumer action, as well, since direct, ongoing, personal relationships are integral to local community exchanges. We will return to these in discussions of community and political engagement in the next chapter. Recall also that practicality (criterion five) is assumed in applied psychology, since the areas we discuss here are already applied practically in many situations.

A New Ethical Frame for Applied Psychology in Organizations

Several prominent I-O and consumer psychologists (Belk, 1975; Etzioni, 1998; Hakel, 2013; Lefkowitz, 2013; Lowman, 2013; Pfeffer, 2010) have called for new conversations about the ethical practice of psychology in organizations and communities. Further impetus for considering ethics in practice also comes from the call for consideration of ethics with respect to psychology's role in addressing sustainability (Lowman, 2013; Pfeffer, 2010; Schouborg, 2001; Swim et al., 2011).

Some organizational scholars argue that the practice of applied psychology already aligns well with principles and criteria of sustainability (e.g., Geller, 1995; Scully-Russ, 2012). As a practical matter, psychological facilitation often engages multiple constituents and a principled approach. Similarly, psychologists often serve the "conscience" role, following from the humanist tradition of psychology (Berry et al., 2011; Lefkowitz, 2013). Adding future planetary inhabitants to the discussion will only serve to enhance the effectiveness of our practices, in this view (Scully-Russ, 2012).

On the other end of the spectrum are those who argue that applied psychologists need to start with a very fundamental discussion of the ethics of science based practice (Hakel, 2013; Hays-Thomas, 2006; Lefkowitz, 2013). This position is based on the belief that current practice is so entwined with competitive, for-profit economic values (Hakel, 2013; Tencati & Zsolnai, 2009) that it can only be improved by radical reconsideration of the basis for the ethical codes. Some have even argued that sanctions and enforcement mechanisms should be considered in any new ethical codes.

Various positions have been taken toward the center of this debate. Some moderate voices would start with additions to current ethical codes (Lowman, 2013), in order to be more explicit about the relationship between current principles and sustainability in practice. This centrist position is likely to deal with the tension between corporate *embeddedness* and the independent, ethical practice of professionals. Taking steps to include principles of sustainability in professional practice raises the possibility that scientist-practitioners may jeopardize their status for facilitating other important decisions. They may have to consider whether, by advocating sustainability, they will lose, maintain, or further integrate their status as valued partners in decision making. In many cases, the greatest good may be served by allowing professionals to "choose their organizational battles," based on ethical and practical priorities. Setting enforceable limits based on universal principles may conflict with this.

We have seen that organizational decision making is often very situationally specific. If, as professions, organizational scientists decide to include the interests of unborn stakeholders in our ethical codes, then this situation specificity needs to be considered carefully. There are organizations that are *currently* seeking our help in developing a more sustainable approach, on one hand, and those whose entrenched approaches may make change a slow, painful process, on the other hand. I-O and CP may have small roles or more deeply embedded roles in these organizations. Figure 10.8 depicts this tension. Perhaps the greatest opportunities for further engagement are in quadrant A, where psychologists are currently tangential partners in change,

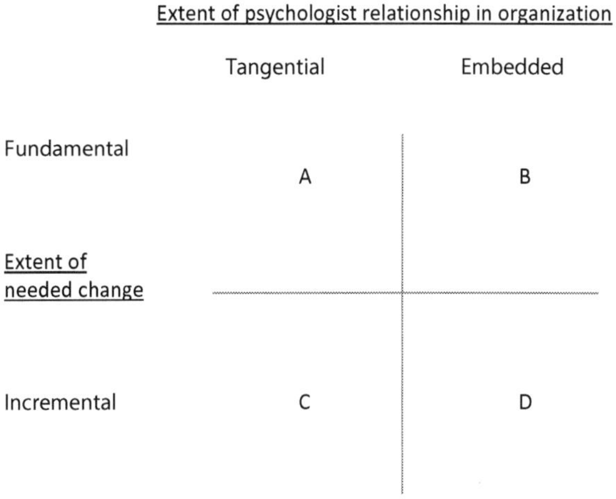

BROAD INTERVENTIONS

Extent of psychologist relationship in organization

	Tangential	Embedded
Fundamental	A	B
Extent of needed change		
Incremental	C	D

Figure 10.8 Tension between situational embeddedness and change efforts

but where dramatic changes are sought. Being deeply embedded partners in radical change efforts are perhaps the most risky for ongoing relationships, since failure sometimes carries great cost (e.g., organizational death). But practitioners in this quadrant (B) often have much to lose in any case. There are great opportunities, with perhaps less risk in quadrants C and D, where explicit ethical principles might provide considerable support and guidance.

Community Based Ethics

For psychologists who choose to become involved in community action, there is little help in current ethical codes. For these applied scientists, there is a clear need to integrate basic philosophical principles into ethical practice. It is beyond the scope of this book to elaborate at length on modern moral philosophy as it is applied to community action. In a nutshell, ethical decision making is based on identification of legitimate stakeholders (Miller, Effron, & Zak, 2010), and inclusion of their interests in an agreed upon *process* of decision making (Phillips, 2003). Sustainability itself relies on this sort of inclusion (Corral-Verdugo et al., 2009; Heft & Chawla, 2006), and successful applications rely on such inclusive processes.

Psychologists who are intent on community action for sustainability at least need to ask whether it is *right* to use the considerable power of psychological science in their cause. Understanding that imposing our will for "the good" is just as troublesome as imposing it to get people to buy things, waste energy, and so on. For example, even the use of psychology to increase green consumption has ethical problems. People don't always know that someone is deliberately trying to manipulate them, and there is no "debrief" once they have been exposed to manipulations. This breaks a fundamental tenet of ethical scientific research and practice: *Informed consent* of the people who are being subjected to psychological interventions. If targets of consumer influence are not informed about being subjected to such attempts, then they are not able to provide informed consent. The ethical principle here is that people have a right to decide for themselves whether they want to be subjected to psychological interventions. In the case of providing research data, they also have a right to know that this is happening before handing over private information.

Social marketing and word of mouth bring up remarkably complex ethical questions. For example, when one person sends a marketing message along to another person, does the choice by the second person to open the message constitute informed consent? When the message starts with someone who stands to gain from people's responses to the message, is there an ethical dilemma? How do free speech rights, enshrined in some nations' constitutions, run counter to this?

Thus, engagement with community and government action requires careful consideration, with all stakeholders represented in each step of the decision process (Clulow, 2005; Epstein & Widener, 2011). But, because sustainability is addressing the interests of an unknown future, we need to acknowledge that ethical choice is based on an ever imperfect telling of the future—it necessarily relies on theory, not evidence (Heft & Chawla, 2006). But, it is at least based on science, not blind guesswork or wishful thinking.

11

THE ADAPTIVE CAPACITY
SCORECARD

> Man prompted by his conscience, will through long habit
> acquire such perfect self-command, that his desires and
> passions will at last yield instantly and without a struggle to
> his social sympathies and instincts, including his feeling for
> the judgment of his fellows.
>
> Charles Darwin, *The Descent of Man*

We now know that Darwin's view of our ability to perfect self-regulation is quite optimistic. Evidence about persistent biases and heuristics, stable individual differences in impulse control and deliberativeness, powerful influences from our social and cultural contexts, developmental stumbling blocks, and failure to transfer learning all suggest, in fact, that we may be in deep trouble.

From the perspective of modern science, he also had a naïve understanding of the biology of humans: We do not adapt purely through habit and genetic mutation. Like many other animals, large and small, we instinctively change the environment around us in order to facilitate our activities. Like some of the other large primates, we even tear up the undergrowth to make things seem safer. But our adaptations are also considerably different from other species. We follow our amazing neocortex into very *deliberately* changing the environment *and ourselves* drastically, and in innovative ways. We have done so for a long time and are likely to continue to do so: This strong inclination to very deliberately organize and alter our internal and external environments is not likely to change.

The scorecard presented in this chapter will put Darwin's optimistic notion to rest by reference to each of the fundamental psychological characteristics covered in Chapters 3 through 8. In support of Darwin's assessment, we can do much to make ourselves more adaptable through the interventions in Chapters 9 and 10.

303

A Murky Crystal Ball

Although psychologists are inclined to concern ourselves with *individual* adaptive capacity, our close colleagues in the other branches of biological science operate on the principle that adaptation occurs at the *species level*. The things we do as individuals, groups, and organizations all tend to influence the chances that our *species* will successfully adapt to both the manufactured and relatively unabridged world. But it is important (and perhaps a bit terrifying) to realize that any given individual, group, organization, or society may persist or disappear in the interest of species level survival. And, frankly, the forces that shape the success or failure of our species through our own actions are poorly understood at this point. As we have seen, even arriving at firm conclusions about the success of individuals based on their differences is error prone and contextually bound.

Therefore, a few points need to be highlighted before we proceed. First, we cannot know exactly what the future will hold. This point may be very obvious to many of us, but there are those who, in their zeal, believe that they know exactly what will happen next. There are those who "know" that our way of life is coming to an end, as well as those who are equally certain that we have no sustainability problems worth mentioning (Maibach et al., 2011). There are various shades of imperfect understanding in between these extremes. All of us are almost certainly wrong, as has been made clear from mountains of applied evidence presented in this book. And, most importantly from the viewpoint of psychology, it is clear that we are not especially rational, even in science sometimes. Again, this is one reason why, in applied science, we assume an uncertain future.

Our crystal ball also needs to be very carefully handled for another, related reason: We make errors in decisions about more than just what we think the future holds. Even if we are completely correct about whether there is a problem in our future (criterion question one), we will still make errors about the other four criteria. Whether we need to be deliberative, how we need to change, whether we should take action, and how practical our course of action may be are all error prone decisions themselves. They are also important points for debate and research, even if we accept a problematic future. We have seen this in biases and decision processes, individual differences, social contexts, and all of the applied areas.

In a recent description of the *matching law* of choice, McDowell (2013) put it this way: "Adaptive behavior is behavior that occasionally results in the acquisition of resources, or the escape from or avoidance of threats." In other words, survival relies on our choices being correct "often enough." We can behave in ways that have no adaptive meaning in a context, and we can even indulge in maladaptive behaviors sometimes. It is just "on balance" that these need to be adaptive. This law probably holds for scientific decisions, as well. So, at best, we can expect the scorecard presented here to provide plenty to debate, with more adaptive answers emerging through ongoing scientific inquiry.

The Criterion Problem and Then Some

Second, even if we make all the right choices on the five criteria and wind up taking action that "works," we face the criterion problem. It follows from two "facts of life" in applied science. The first is that there are many different, sometimes conflicting criteria for different stakeholders, meaning that not everyone will see the results of interventions as happy endings. For example, if we incite people to take collective action and successfully change things "for the better" (as defined by the folks who took action), chances are that we will upset other people in the process. Other stakeholders may have very different notions of happy endings and of what "for the better" means. This is why successful interventions generally take as many stakeholders' interests into account as possible before acting.

The second "fact of life" is that our interventions can only change some of the variables involved in our perceived problems, and only partially change even these, if we are lucky. The idea that applied psychology "controls" variables is an overstatement—we may be able to *influence* things a little, but persistence will almost always be required. Accepting this means accepting that interventions are iterative, ongoing processes, often without any clear or immediate results.

This is one explanation for why, although many environmental laws have been passed to keep water, air, and soil intact and available to many people, there are plenty of things left to do, and probably always will be. People who believe that there will eventually be no more need to improve things are probably deluding themselves, if history is any indication. Put a little differently, given the uncertainty about future possibilities, it is important to realize that adaptation will *always* be required both of ourselves and of our species.

Psychology and Only Psychology

Third, changes *in human thinking and behavior* are assumed to be the primary basis for adaptation in this book. We have not concerned ourselves with technological innovation, genetic change, or even much of the current scientific evidence about our planetary environment. There are plenty of books showing the likely importance of these. But the primary assumption of this book is that having "the facts" about these is not especially relevant to the sorts of *psychological* variables that can be marshaled to affect change. Well considered, coordinated action in homes, schools, therapies, legal proceedings, organizations, markets, and polities need to be as firmly based as possible on "the facts" about applied human psychology. We are the current key species, and we need to use what we know about *ourselves* if we wish to manage our behavior.

Finally, previous work in basic environmental and social psychology has directed our attention toward social and physical variables that can be manipulated in the interest of changing the behaviors that are thought to be associated with species level adaptation. These have helped us to understand ways that attitudes and behaviors *can* change to fit the *experimenters'* notions of what *ought* to be changed. But how do we use psychology to manage the fundamental natural *impulse to change* things that *even these scientists are indulging*? Again, we are instinctively inclined to think causally and act systematically on our thinking. This is why we tear up the undergrowth, build walls and rooves, devise heating and cooling systems, develop smart phones, and try to create more sustainable systems. It is not a question of our ability to do these "adaptive" things—it is a question of how we direct these inclinations toward the greater good.

This is similar to the blind application of technologies without careful consideration of (1) the needs and interests of stakeholders affected by the technology, (2) the actual purposes to which new technologies can be put, or (3) the actual efficacy of technologies. Such technological "solutionism" (Morozov, 2013) has found its way into psychological research on learning, with new technologies being evaluated as learning aids without reference to the needs of learners or facilitators, learning outcomes sought, or side effects of having large, expensive technologies in small, poor classrooms—often with poor results. Technological solutionism has even found its way into psychology of sustainability, despite its early stage of development. A recent meta-analysis showed that "eco-innovation" is driven almost entirely by technology, rather than actual needs in the market, regulations, or firm-specific needs (Zubeltzu, Erauskin, & Heras, 2018). The effectiveness of the "eco-solutions" was neither measured nor reported.

Worse, because of our tendency to rely unquestioningly on our impulse to build "solutions," technologists appear to have little interest in the ethical codes that constrain scientists in other applied disciplines. As a result, these are questions that ethical scientist-practitioners need to ask of all interventions, including technological ones: Why are you trying to change a particular set of behaviors or attitudes? How did you choose these behaviors? If the answers do not make reference to criteria as defined by stakeholders in the "solution," then it's time to go back to the drawing board. Questions about what we *will* try to change and *why* are far more difficult to answer than what we *can* change. This is a very practical matter, if we have some hope of lasting efficacy and actual adaptation. Decision making helpers need to be very deliberative about this, since others are not.

What Is The Question?

In his book, *The Hitchhiker's Guide to the Galaxy* (1986), Douglas Adams' main character, Arthur Dent, wrestled with a problem similar to the one we have tangled with in this book. He discovered early in the story that the answer to the eternal question was forty-two. But he did not learn what the eternal

THE ADAPTIVE CAPACITY SCORECARD

question *was* until the end of the story: "What is 6 times 8?" The apparent solution was clear, but the problem not defined.

At the beginning of this book, we posed a short set of questions as the basis for the *adaptive capacity scorecard*. These are ways of posing the general question of *adaptation* without knowing exactly what adaptation will mean for our species and planet:

- *Are we likely to adapt? Which fundamental tendencies are likely to result in human extinction?*
- *Which stakeholders are likely to have "happy endings" in the event that we do adapt?*
- *If it is changeable, how rapidly can human behavior be changed using each fundamental tendency?*
- *Should we (ethically) try to change behavior using each tendency?*

Notice that most of these are questions about the fundamental tendencies we have covered in the book: *heuristics, individual differences, decision processes, social influences, development, and learning.* By breaking things down this way, we have simultaneously made the adaptive capacity question more manageable and the answers more complex. In fact, these are all *predictor* variables and, as applied psychologists, a *criterion centric* approach is essential. This is why we posed the five *criterion* questions, which address various aspects of the "eternal" question: Will we adapt?

> Alien invasions, a meteor hitting the Earth, and zombie plagues are all examples of life threatening changes to human survival and adaptation. The fact that movies dealing with such catastrophes sell is evidence that most people really do care about whether we will be able to adapt. Given the happy endings of most of these, many people believe the answer is, "Yes!"

Our Grades on the Five Criteria

What follows is the promised scorecard on the five criteria. It is a rating of the likelihood of our species surviving based on analyses through the lens of applied psychology. But it is also a scorecard for applied psychologists, who are in essential positions to address Rachel Carson's call to action at the beginning of Chapter 9: How do we change ourselves? The fundamental tendencies presented in Chapters 3 through 8 provide us with some answers to her question—some viable avenues for change. This does not mean we will actually use these avenues to create a more sustainable future, which is why this is framed as adaptive capacity (rather than, say adaptive "likelihood"). Our crystal ball would have to be extraordinarily prescient for us to know whether the tools of applied psychology will actually be used toward the goal of sustainability.

307

THE ADAPTIVE CAPACITY SCORECARD

1. ***Discrepancy testing and willingness to see a problem***

Although developmental frame and certain individual differences (especially intelligences and anxiety) place a limit on people's ability to see problems in our collective future, it is more *willingness* than ability that appears to constrain discrepancy testing. Specifically, we have seen how dogmatism, immediate emotional responses, social contexts, moral development, identity, and learning are all motivationally driven variables. How to find or create a moment in people's lives when they are "ready" to see a problem is perhaps one of the greatest challenges in applied sustainability. Since the first edition of this book, scientists are starting to understand why people deny science (Hornsey & Fielding, 2017) and how to persuade them to behave more sustainably (Palomo-Vélez, Tybur, & van Vugt, 2018; Taufik, 2018). Not surprisingly, *emotive* variables play a central role in "seeing the problem" (Onwezen, Reinders, & Sijtsema, 2017; Palomo-Vélez, et al., 2018) or not (Lefevre, de Bruin, Taylor, Dessai, Kovats, & Fischhoff, 2015).

In his book, *Inviting Disaster* (2001, p. 141), Jim Chiles put it well: "We can harbor our fantasies for a long time, even a full lifetime, as long as nothing occurs to upset them." This is a major vulnerability for human adaptation, particularly since some of our greatest resources for innovation—innovative scientists and inventors—have not addressed it much. Our innovative resources need to be oriented toward more than just technological and situation specific behavioral solutions: The problems they address need to be defined by more than just scientists in their particular social and professional context and inventors and entrepreneurs in the marketplace. Put another way, innovation for sustainability needs to be understood from the perspective of broad, applied psychological systems.

Science in general has a big problem. Important voices for sustainability have called for a multidisciplinary approach to manage environmental issues (e.g., Feng, 2012; Meadows, 2004; Pelletier et al., 2008). But, there has been very little discussion of a core element of our planetary environmental system—*our own thinking and action.* Psychology is arguably the most interdisciplinary of all sciences (Swim et al., 2011). We can be found teaching in most of the health related fields (medical schools, public health, physical therapy, other behavioral medicine), most management and marketing departments, under the guise of cognitive neuroscience in natural and applied sciences, and of course as part of the social sciences and liberal arts curriculum. Applied psychologists work in every aspect of our lives, from prenatal care through the lifespan, and in virtually every context: Families, schools, workplaces, and even in our sleep. Yet applied psychology has rarely been invited into conversations about sustainability.

THE ADAPTIVE CAPACITY SCORECARD

Psychological science also has a problem. With the possible exceptions of (mostly basic) environmental psychology research and a recent interest in industrial-organizational (I-O) psychology and consumer psychology (CP), we have done little to marshal our own innovative resources toward managing change. Until recently (Kilbourne & Mittelstaedt, 2012; Ones & Dilchert, 2012), we have seen sustainability as largely an academic issue, through which we can voice "expert" opinions, rather than work with many stakeholders to help to manage decisions made by people outside the university.

Worse, the innovations that have occurred with respect to altering human consumptive thinking and behavior appear to have moved us toward overconsumption, rather than toward more sustainable behaviors. Thus, efforts to manage our "urge to build" do "have a problem"—and a big one. And the problem is with the very group in whom many people are placing their trust for a more sustainable future—applied scientists. Our capacity for altering the course of human behavior has been successful in getting people to consume, to perform well at work, and so on. But these professionals seem to have forgotten future stakeholders until very recently.

To the extent that key decision makers do recognize this ethical imperative, our capacity for directing our unthinking urge to build things can be directed, perhaps adaptively. To the extent that we are able to integrate psychological innovations into broader systems, the future seems bright. But currently, as a species, we get a D on this dimension. The fact that a large portion of the human population appears not to know, care, or believe that the changes we have made in our shared natural system is problematic. The fact that people engaged in "getting out the word" and the people who are "expert" in changing human thinking are not working together or not especially involved is also a major problem. The only reason this is not an F is the dawning realization among people who are able to make change that we do, indeed, have a problem.

2. ***Deliberative decision processes***

Many people interested in sustainable adaptation believe that we should try to get people to be more careful or thoughtful. Based on what we have learned here, it turns out that this only makes a difference some of the time. And, although it would be nice for some of us to see many more intelligent, socially adept, morally developed, open and creative people in our daily lives, the fact is that there are plenty who lack one or more of these character traits—and are not likely to develop them any time soon. Instead, we should probably be relying on people who do have these traits to help engage in collective action—to create the context for sustainable behaviors; but that's for later discussion.

An underlying assumption of many environmentalists appears to have been that, by providing alarming evidence, we should increase people's thoughtfulness (Bortree et al., 2012). As it turns out, our preconscious neurological processes tend to send "alarm" messages in exactly the opposite direction—away from deliberative processes (Gluck & Myers, 2001). So, it is not surprising that such "alarming" environmental messages have met with very limited success in moving people toward more pro-environmental behavior (PEB). Until we address sustainable adaptive thinking through appropriate *emotive* channels, we are likely to continue to have problems. Sustainability messages that come from trustworthy members of people's identity groups are likely to help here. Also, giving people a sense that they *can affect* meaningful change (Levy & Zint, 2013) and providing some of the ways they can do it *in their own interest* (e.g. Ryoo et al., 2017) is likely to meet with greater deliberation.

Even though many of us may *want* to be pro-environmental (Siegfried et al., 1982) and reduce consumption (Swim et al., 2011), PEBs typically require conscious decisions and trade offs. Not surprisingly, our best intentions are often moderated by more immediate, situational pressures that are not easily altered (Thøgersen & Ölander, 2006).

Getting people to consider the interests of people outside of their own identified group is even more problematic. Various facilitated experiences, leadership, and other forms of minority influence have shown promise for doing this. Campaigns like the ones that have advanced the rights and interests of historically disadvantaged groups (e.g., Dziengel, 2010) often rely on these social, collective influences. Here again, we are venturing into criterion four.

However, these social psychological approaches quickly raise the question of whether it is ethical to affect change by *relying* on people's undeliberative, habitual, and emotional responses. Many environmental psychologists and consumer psychologists have been operating on this behavioral basis for a long time, with quite variable success. Consumer psychology has had some success getting even thoughtful people to buy impulsively. But environmental psychologists, who have generally relied on institutional and individual permission, have had almost no impact beyond changing specific behaviors in very specific contexts. Many scientist-practitioners interested in the common good argue that we need to revisit these ethical questions.

If we base our grade purely on people's fundamental tendencies to be more or less deliberative, we are again faced with close to a failing grade (let's say a *D*). There may be a fair percentage of people who exercise deliberative choice, but these are probably a minority. To the extent that basic scientists have had success demonstrating how to change behavior despite this, we are also in the *D* range, since these efforts have been extremely circumscribed, for the most part. Add to this the history of scientist-practitioners deliberately relying on undeliberative decisions in the market, and we have a very clear *F*. However, the fact that these ethical and practical issues have been raised and discussed over the past decade or so is a major step forward. A compromise grade, then, is probably a *D*+.

THE ADAPTIVE CAPACITY SCORECARD

3. *Deliberately changing the way we think and behave*

Helping people to *change* the way they view the world, make decisions, control impulses, and relate to others have drawn on all of the subdisciplines in psychology. Although the forces that influence development and learning can send people in many directions (for better and for worse to themselves and the planet), learning is one of the greatest adaptive capacities in nature. The cognitive learning that is made possible by the neocortex is even more remarkable, as it has led to innovations that dramatically effect individual well-being.

Whether we have the capacity to direct our impulse to change toward the good of our species and planetary home is a central question. If we base our answer on the changes we have made so far, it would be hard to give anything less than an *A*. Likewise, if we look at the largely unrecognized role that psychologists have played in contributing to the huge changes in the past century, it is clear that psychology gets at least a *B* on this criterion. We know far more about how people learn than we did a century ago and have applied what we know about learning and development in many venues, generally for the greater good. Other scientific disciplines and their engineering adjuncts obviously deserve high grades on this, as well, but not because the changes we have made are all good—just because we have demonstrated the *capacity* to make learning based change. We sure can change, and we can do it really quickly when we're so motivated.

The problem is, of course, with motivation—not ability. For this reason, the answer to this criterion question relies on the answer to the first criterion question. If we see enough of a problem (or opportunity), then we get motivated and, once motivated, have a good chance of making necessary changes. This means that the grades on these two questions are non-compensatory. So, even though we get a *B+* on criterion three, our overall grade still remains a *D+* at this point.

4. *Taking action*

Most of us take action toward some purpose or other almost every day. Once again, motivation is essential to this, which means we have the same non-compensatory problem when we combine the grade from this criterion with the grade from criterion one. But, this non-compensatory relationship goes both ways. If people decide to take action, the influence they have on others is often related to criterion one. We saw in social psychology (Chapter 6) that minority influence sometimes gets people to understand discrepancies where they didn't see them before. If those of us who are deliberative, emotionally competent, and morally advanced take action, sometimes we will boost our (collective) grade on criterion one. This is especially so when we create context by taking leadership roles.

Collective action is also essential to the kinds of large scale, high impact changes that many people see as necessary for sustainable adaptation. We have already seen how psychologists get involved in all kinds of group interactions (clinical facilitation, classroom learning, organizational and political leadership, courtroom dialectic and advocacy) and establish special relationships (clinical, consumer, employment) that can have substantial, systematic, and even carefully managed influences on the parties to them. These interactions are among the most powerful venues for people to learn about problems and opportunities, deliberate about decisions, develop and change their thinking and behavior. In fact, many psychologists would argue that we have only seen a small fraction of the possibilities for positive change that would occur with an expansion of these kinds of relationships, both in number and kind.

Compared to some other forms of relation based change (e.g., coercion, deception, conformity), psychologists offer ethical approaches that make these changes not only more efficacious, but more likely to result in positive outcomes for all stakeholders. Clearly, the "free market" approach is empirically and morally bankrupt. Apart from its very inequitable consequences, its individualistic decision making process lacks both efficacy and ethics. But, ethical scientist-practitioners have shown the efficacy of their alternative approaches in many venues with many hundreds of thousands—perhaps millions of people. Organizations have "discovered" the value of applied psychology in the marketplace and have stimulated a very busy labor market for scientist-practitioners.

Clearly, other sciences have also had enormous effects on individual and species wellbeing, usually in that order. But ethical processes are not usually built into the process of, for example, electrical engineering and metallurgy. If you were to ask a meteorologist, engineer, or physicist what ethical procedures they were required to conform to in order to have their research approved, you would probably get a quizzical look. Ask even *basic* researchers in psychology and neuroscience the same question, and they would tell you a story. Applied researchers often have many stories to tell about ethical trade offs.

Partly for this reason, applied psychologists are uniquely qualified to take part in collective action. Skilled scientist-practitioners know how to make things happen and they know how to apply ethics to the process. Unfortunately, this hasn't happened much in service of sustainability. Prompting people to engage in collective community and political action and providing ethical facilitation to such action is a frontier for applied psychology (Huppert, 2009). In fact, there are enormous opportunities for sustainable adaptation through education, organizations, communities, and the media. The box below provides a short list of the host of possible interventions available for consideration. Notice that these are roughly organized along the developmental continuum and from the individual through the broad market level of analysis.

THE ADAPTIVE CAPACITY SCORECARD

Targets of collective action to promote psychological criteria for sustainable adaption

- Early childhood interventions in the media that enhance cognitive, social, and moral development.
- Motivating and enabling parents and teachers to provide stimulating, secure early environments that increase formal operational, postconventional reasoning, reduce dogmatism and anxiety, strengthen attachments with others and with places, and increase openness.
- Provide earlier education to increase awareness of essential components of psychology, including scientific reasoning, the vulnerabilities and strengths of heuristics and biases, the nature of development and individual differences, dynamics of social inclusion and exclusion, and the metacognitive and meta-emotive components of learning.
- Address conventional moral reasoning by promoting identification (especially in teens) with attractive social models who call attention to discrepancies with "approach" affect, behave deliberatively, visibly learn and change toward sustainable behaviors, and take positive collective action.
- Explicitly address postconventional moral reasoning, metacognition, foresight, and inclusive identity in clinical interventions.
- Apply needs assessment processes that include sustainability criteria and precursor measures to interventions, particularly in schools, organizations, and communities.
- Use education, organizational, and marketing interventions to increase careful deliberation in high impact decisions, such as large, high impact purchases.
- Use organizational policies and practices that develop individual identity and corporate cultures of stakeholder inclusion.
- Affect community and political change based on principles of psychology, such as space design at the decision level, cognitive and moral development at the individual level, effective advocacy at the group level, and stakeholder engagement processes at the community level.
- Use disaster preparedness for inevitable natural disasters, raise awareness of institutional commitment to sustainable adaptation, and intervene at the identity level after events have occurred.

THE ADAPTIVE CAPACITY SCORECARD

Collective action provides opportunities to demonstrate the efficacy of inclusion, and the positive individual and community consequences of altruistic action. And, unlike economic definitions of well-being, empirical psychology clearly shows the positive contributions of cooperation (Balliet & Van Lange, 2013), altruism (Gilbert, 2010; Schwartz, Meisenhelder, Ma, & Reed, 2003; Yang, 2013), and collective identity (Dimitrova, Chasiotis, Bender, & van de Vijver, 2013) to individual well-being. Thus, collective action is often efficacious and, when it is efficacious, is self-motivating (Tabernero & Hernández, 2011). It may also help people recognize discrepancies, then provide them with private, social, and principled motives to do something to help change things (van Zomeren & Spears, 2009).

Our adaptive capacity score on this is an *A*, as individuals, species, and scientific psychologists. We have certainly not lived up to this capacity yet. But there are many opportunities to do so.

5. **Practicality and ethicality**
This criterion has already been addressed in the previous one. But two other points need to be made. First, in addition to the many current applications that give psychologists a "place at the table," questions about the ethicality of broader applications still need to be addressed. Engaging many stakeholders should enhance both the process and outcomes of ethical discussions *prior* to the application of psychology in community and political action. These discussions should take place very soon, as a practical matter.

Second, the enormous stakes in such issues as climate change mean that there will likely be a tendency toward "winner" and "loser" groups (Thomas & Twyman, 2005). The psychological mechanisms at work here are beyond the scope of this book (see Balliet & Van Lange, 2013, for an initial discussion). But the ethical issues of eventual inequities deserve careful consideration when scientist-practitioners sit down to discuss the ethics of adaptive sustainability.

The crystal ball in this book says that there will be plenty of demand soon for applied psychology in the interest of future stakeholders. Our capacity to make good things happen earns a *B* in a probabilistic, multivariate world with only a murky crystal ball.

Addressing the Five Criteria and Adding a Sixth: How to Get a Better Grade Next Time

As we have seen, applied discussion of the psychology of sustainability and adaptation are fairly recent (Aaker et al., 2000; Hine et al., 2007; Jain & Kaur, 2006; Klein & Huffman, 2013; Ones & Dilchert, 2012; Tobias et al., 2009). As a very general statement, these initial discussions center around what scientist-practitioners can do, looking forward, to directly reduce the

314

THE ADAPTIVE CAPACITY SCORECARD

impact of human activity on climate, energy use, and waste management. These early discussions appear to assume that everyone sees that we "have a problem" (criterion one), but have not yet addressed the five psychological criteria extensively—and almost not at all from an applied perspective.

Basic researchers in environmental and social psychology have led the way in understanding how people are more or less deliberative (criterion two) and more or less likely to change their attitudes and behaviors (parts of criterion three). Again, with few exceptions (Cialdini, 2007), getting people to see the need for change (criterion one) and to take deliberate action (criterion four) have not entered into these discussions. Consequently, our discussions of broad interventions are limited by lack of applied evidence and a potential overreliance on basic research with unknown practical value.

Fortunately, there are a few studies of broad applications to go on for each criterion, but coverage will be uneven, to say the least. Also, the fifth criterion—practicality—is implicit in virtually all of these applied areas. One essential avenue for practical interventions has been missed, however: Political and community based action.

Political and Community Based Interventions

Direct psychological intervention in the public sphere has been very slow in coming (Rupp, Williams, & Aguilera, 2010). There are many ethical reasons for this, not least that psychologists are constrained first by the interests of our clients, under most circumstances, with broader social interests as lower priorities. For example, there are sometimes conflicts between ethical principles and the laws that govern clinical practice, as when a clinician is required to report a client who is threatening violence. Here, the ethics of confidentiality can be outweighed by broader social interests. But the circumstances are often ambiguous, and the client–psychologist relationship is central to such decisions.

Currently, there are few ethical discussions about the use of *broad applications* in psychological practice, particularly in the interest of the five criteria. Some psychologists are to the point where the interests of *future stakeholders* take precedence over the interests of clients, and even over some of the cherished principles of science based practice. Put into marketing terms, these are early adopters, but they are probably still a minority. The problem of conflicting stakeholder interests looms large for scientist-practitioners who practice in organizational settings, especially for those at the latter stages of moral development.

In this section, we will review the potentially relevant research on minority influence (Chapter 6) and leadership (Chapter 10), as well as a few broad applications. We will also see that current government and not for profit organizations have established avenues that may not be obvious, but hold considerable promise for realizing the aims of sustainable futures. I hope to

THE ADAPTIVE CAPACITY SCORECARD

provide the beginnings of an agenda for future action. Although direct questions about ethical codes were addressed in the last section of Chapter 10, so will not be repeated here, ethical questions remain integral to this discussion, as well.

Criterion One: Getting People to see a Problem

Awareness of potential problems (Hines et al., 1986), discrepancy testing (Eiser et al., 1994), and initial emotive responses to information about environmental change (Cho, Martens, Kim, & Rodrigue, 2011; Satterfield et al., 2004; Yeager et al., 2011) are the central variables at work in criterion one. Clearly, applied efforts at increasing awareness alone have not been enough to reach many people. It should also be clear by now that awareness is only the first in a chain of variables, and may not always be necessary to incite action (Heath et al., 2006).

Instead, given people's tendency to conclude that we do not have environmental problems, it may be more fruitful to develop means to manage the emotive responses that go with discrepancy testing. We have several places to look for help with this. The first is the feedback literature (Balzer et al., 1992; Kluger & DeNisi, 1996; London, 1997). This research makes it clear that feedback needs to be directed toward what people can *actually do* to enhance their lives. As we saw in Chapter 8, feedback about *personal characteristics* and about *overall decision validity* are not likely to affect people's views. Translated, this means *not* telling people that they are wrong-headed or have made a bad decision. Persuading people that there is a problem may rely heavily on feedback about how things are likely to affect their personal lives.

For some portion of people, concern with justice and fairness may be an important means for establishing discrepancies, as well. Stakeholder theory may be lost on people at earlier stages of moral development, but appeals to existing, conventional, and authoritarian values may work for many. Whether our current behaviors have negative effects on unborn people may be a "hot button" for selling sustainability to conventional reasoners.

In addition to the type of feedback provided, managing the *credibility* of information sources is important, as well. Both CP and I-O provide some ideas for enhancing credibility of the sources of discrepancy feedback (Do Paço & Reis, 2012; Ilgen, Fisher, & Taylor, 1979; Jain & Kaur, 2006). Source credibility may rely more on whether people trust the source (Zhu, Xie, & Gan, 2011) than on the source's actual expertise. Answering people's implicit questions about motive sharing through appropriate emotive content of messages may play a central role here (Onwezen, et al., 2017; Palomo-Vélez, et al., 2018; Lefevre, et al., 2015).

THE ADAPTIVE CAPACITY SCORECARD

Existing Public Policy Approaches

There are also existing public policy approaches that may have important advantages, and which may be enhanced using the psychology of sustainability. In practice, stakeholder engagement in community interventions has gained considerable popularity in local politics in recent years, partly because it has been successful in creating positive change (Gabriel, Leichtling, Bolan, & Becker, 2013; Headey et al., 2006; Newson & Chalk, 2004; Selman, 2004). Engaging stakeholders with different viewpoints in a constructive discussion has also been suggested by both basic and applied researchers (Johnson et al., 2000; Swim, 2013; Ter Mors, Weenig, Ellemers, & Daamen, 2010) as a way to increase awareness and buy-in.

As yet, there is still much to know about psychological variables involved in applications of this approach to sustainability (Rogers, Simmons, Convery, & Weatherall, 2012). Obviously, conflict is very likely when people with different interests and views of the situation sit down to try to try to work together. There is some awareness among public administration professionals of the inadequacy of current approaches, but as yet not much about a role that psychologists might play in facilitating these conflict laden processes (Harrington, Curtis, & Black, 2008; Warner, 1997). There may be opportunities here for scientist-practitioners with training in group facilitation (Fisher, 1993) to provide decision support, particularly in the emotionally laden phase of discrepancy testing.

We have seen that, in addition to its practicality and effectiveness, the stakeholder engagement approach is also consistent with modern ethical principles. In fact, part of its practicality may be that the parties involved are more likely to see the actions stemming from genuine stakeholder engagement as fair. Thus, perceived fairness may be a practical component of successful implementation, as well as part of an ethical process (Eriksson, Garvill, & Nordlund, 2006).

Another viable approach to getting people to see a problem is to talk about disaster preparedness—a well funded area of policy and governance in many communities. It seems a bit ironic that problem awareness often occurs only after disasters occur. Public policies to support disaster responses have already taken counsel from applied psychologists, with considerable success (Raimi, Stern, & Maki, 2017). We will return to this.

Criterion Two: Thinking about the World and Your Identity in It

It should be very clear by now that deliberative decision making is predictable, based on individual differences in mental abilities, openness, and developmental variables. We saw in Chapters 8 and 9 that applications in education have a record of enhancing deliberativeness, given the right time and circumstances. To the extent that media target educational and developmental criteria, there are also examples where individual difference variables can be directly addressed in very broad interventions to increase deliberativeness. For example, a recent meta-analysis showed a significant enhancement in children's cognitive development, safety and health knowledge, and social development as a result of viewing the popular public television program *Sesame Street* (Mares & Pan, 2013).

Applying this approach to increase deliberativeness about sustainability seems like a promising approach, at least for children. For young adults, we have seen that targeting and social identity can affect sustainable beliefs, if not behaviors (Lee, 2008, 2011). However, current environmental education for adults appears to happen in circumstances that are removed from routine settings, such as park visits, vacations, and stand alone outdoor experiences. Finding ways to engage psychologists in developing and, more importantly, *transferring* deliberative approaches across situations seems to be a gap in the research literature. Trying to develop metacognitive skills through outdoor experiences is an example of a current practice that provides an avenue for further research into metacognitive transfer.

Joining a city? Just as advertisements have tried to get people to internalize and maintain a brand identity for such things as sports teams, cars, and other products, a few researchers have explored similar brand identities for cities (Merrilees, Miller, & Herington, 2013). Part of the idea behind this approach is to draw people to distressed areas and increase quality of life through various means—including sustainable development.

Perhaps a less obvious approach is to use marketing techniques in order to influence basic lifestyle choices. Deciding where to live, how to commute, what to wear, and other major purchase decisions are typically done more deliberatively than other choices. Inserting sustainability into these and other more deliberative decisions may be a powerful way to influence sustainability with single, large decisions. Figure 11.1 provides a few examples of more and less deliberative decisions that have environmental impact. For example, compact city growth and good public transport may be "selling points" for people seeking to relocate (see box above). Advocates of sustainability might invest greater effort into influencing these sorts of decisions by working with city chambers of commerce, real estate boards, convention and visitor bureaus, and other interested parties.

Sadly, deliberation may also be greater after people are faced with major losses, such as natural disasters and economic problems (Crompton & Kasser, 2009; Miller, 2012). Once people's immediate needs are being met, mental

Less			**More**
Brushing teeth	Choosing a vacation spot		Accepting a job
Turning on a light	Buying groceries		Deciding to relocate
Listening to music	Reading a magazine		Remodeling a kitchen
Eating a meal	Driving to work	Buying a car	Choosing a college

Figure 11.1 Some more and less deliberative decisions

Figure 11.2 Iterative steps in ethical choice

health professionals are often called to these settings to assist with periods of adjustment. These interventions may create opportunities for redirecting people's choices through deliberative prompts. Many people in these circumstances are faced with fundamental problems of identity maintenance (Crompton & Kasser, 2009; Murray & Zautra, 2012). Mental health practitioners provide opportunities for future oriented identity repair and support (Miller, 2012; Murray & Zautra, 2012), which integrate well with sustainability.

Finally, once people have taken action in public decision processes (criterion four), there may be a tendency for them to be more deliberative about their own, individual choices (Levy & Zint, 2013; Plax, Kearney, Ross, & Jolly, 2008). This is represented in the feedback loop in Figure 11.2. Encouraging people to get involved in voluntary activities in their broader communities may prove to be a powerful precursor to deliberative, long term decision making (Ascher, 2009; Jacobs & Clark, 2011). Understanding how our own motives relate to those of neighbors, political parties, advocacy groups, and others in our community is a potential source for cementing, as well as for changing our identities. There may be fewer ethical concerns with this approach than with some others.

Criterion Three: Being Willing and Able to Learn

In any case, we have seen that identity may be a critical lever for learning and change. To the extent that broad interventions lead people to see themselves as environmentally aware (or not), altruistic (or not), and deliberative (or not), they are likely to have substantial effects on behaviors across circumstances (Crompton & Kasser, 2009; Scott, 2009).

Although behavioral interventions are still possible on a broad scale, there are problems of transfer across contexts and over time. In particular, behavioral interventions tend to assume a "big brother" approach (Jackson, 2008; Schouborg, 2001). For example, mandating recycling often requires government intervention. Such government interventions have happened and will continue to happen. But, applied psychologists have taken very little part in efforts to predict and control the political processes that lead, for example, to the passage of recycling ordinances (Krosnick, 2002). There are ethical reasons for this reluctance, as we have seen.

By contrast, broad efforts to influence cognitive learning are everywhere in the media (Desmond & Carveth, 2007). To the extent that scientist-practitioners take part in these already, there are many opportunities to aid in efforts to help develop cognitive maps across large groups in the population (Levy & Zint, 2013). We have already discussed this in the CP section, but it bears repeating: visual-audio media (VAM) are pervasive, targetable, and do not rely on context to the same extent as many other kinds of interventions. Their ongoing potential for facilitating learning is enormous.

It also bears repeating that the type of learning that is desired relies partly on the emotions that accompany different discrepancy test frames (Bortree et al., 2012; Gruszczynski, Balzer, Jacobs, Smith, & Hibbing, 2013; Pettit, 2009). A better understanding of the motive sharing messages that accompany learning may enhance media effects even further.

Community based approaches have proved valuable for broad dissemination of health information and behavior change. While psychology tends to have less of a place at the public health table, these interventions have provided important research, as well as potential opportunities for broad, community level learning interventions (Campbell & Cornish, 2012).

Criterion Four: Inspiring Action

Broad interventions to prompt collective, altruistic, and inclusive action are a major frontier for sustainability psychologists ("Inspiring action," 2011). In many cases, this will require getting people to consider the idea that future inhabitants of the planet deserve a voice. Targeting will almost certainly be necessary here (Diaz-Rainey & Ashton, 2011). Targeting based on existing measures of *future orientation* may be helpful, particularly in multicultural communities (Milfont, Wilson, & Diniz, 2012). Paradoxically, since it is unlikely that efforts at inclusion will reach those who value their own interests to the exclusion of others (McCright & Dunlap, 2013), targeting for *exclusion* may reduce the costs associated with action efforts.

Going further, targeting efforts might start from a different direction than is common in current communications about sustainability (Bortree et al., 2012). As we have discussed, many of the current approaches to persuasion seem to assume that their audience believes that others' interests matter.

THE ADAPTIVE CAPACITY SCORECARD

Given the conventional moral development of a large percentage of people, targeting people who consider others' interests only to the extent that they coincide with their own social identity might be a more fruitful place to start. One way of thinking of this is that sustainability advocates currently spend more time "preaching to the choir" than they do considering legitimate interests of those who are not currently inclined toward action. In other words, advocates themselves do not understand that inclusion of others' *more narrow* interests is essential to broad collective action. Following from developmental psychology, it is important to speak to people from a perspective that they understand.

More generally, community needs assessment provides a natural, inclusive avenue for stimulating action. This involves the sort of targeting we have already discussed (e.g., Diaz-Rainey & Ashton, 2011). But, we have seen in Chapter 10 that needs assessment can go much further than this, measuring and adapting interventions to the *particular situation*. Needs assessment methodologies have been applied to community interventions for disaster relief (García-Mira, González, & Rivas, 2008; Guan et al., 2011; Silove & Bryant, 2006; Tyler & Rankin, 2012), public safety (Gittleman et al., 2010; Tyler & Rankin, 2012), public health (de Viggiani, 2012; Gustafson, Goodyear, & Keough, 2008), and international aid (Chowdhury & Mukhopadhaya, 2012). Psychologists have been involved in these, often in lead roles. The relevance of such needs assessments to managing community environmental problems is obvious, and applied psychologists almost certainly have valuable roles to play.

At very least, feedback from such needs assessment can be used to address criterion one: Discrepancies between perceptions and realities, between one group's views and another's, and between current and desired states (Tyler & Rankin, 2012). Dunlap and Van Liere (1978, 2008) provide an example of this by showing differences in perceptions of the importance of sustainability issues for citizens as compared with members of an environmental advocacy group. Situational limitations on *willingness to pay* also represent a discrepancy threshold worth considering in public needs assessment for sustainability (Hofmann, Hoelzl, & Kirchler, 2008; Wertenbroch & Skiera, 2002). Identifying discrepancies like these may uncover situational limits and opportunities and provide an "empirical mirror" for communities to work with as they take action.

As with other needs assessments, approaches to prevention in health and safety needs assessments are embodiments of criterion two: Basing decisions on actual data is itself deliberative. Needs assessment is also a deliberate, institutionally sanctioned approach to action (criterion four) in itself, and feedback from needs assessment is itself an intervention for community change (criterion three).

Resistance and Subversion

It is notable that much of the important change that has occurred historically has not been institutionally driven. Resistance and subversion have held prominent roles in some of the most notable historical changes. *Subversion* is defined as "a systematic attempt to overthrow or undermine a government or political system by persons working secretly from within" (Merriam-Webster, 2013). One component of this definition applies to many sources of psychological influence—its mechanisms and effects are not obvious even to those who have been changed by them (Cialdini, 1999). This is not to say that psychologists are themselves subversive—at least in ethical practice, they do not usually seek to undermine, but rather to build competency, identity, and other adaptive tools in individuals and groups. It might be better to describe their efforts as *crypto influences*: "People working secretly from within."

Similarly, open, nonviolent *resistance* presents important paradoxes for scientist-practitioners in sustainability. First, minority influence research (Chapter 6) has shown that solidarity may be important to effective resistance. Recall that consistent, polarized minorities may exert normative influence (Downing et al., 1992; Martin et al., 2007; Wood et al., 1994), at least on people whose emotive responses have them paying attention. To the extent that resistance groups are cohesive and "on message," the consistency of their message is retained. Within such groups, "preaching to the choir" may be a helpful way to maintain the groups' solidarity and *exclusiveness* in the face of counter-resistance. This particular influence tactic is thus inconsistent with the idea that sustainability is based on *inclusiveness*.

Second, while resistance movements are advancing one group's well-being, they may often do so at the expense of others. To the extent that this leads to constructive controversy and appropriate compromise, it may be highly functional, and may even invite psychologists into the conflict facilitation process. However, resistance movements have a way of leading to win–lose outcomes. In the case of sustainability, equitable outcomes are particularly delicate, given the tendency of actions in prosperous areas to disproportionately and negatively affect less prosperous areas (Taylor et al., 2006; Thomas & Twyman, 2005).

Third, even the basic research literature on resistance is sparse and inconclusive (Haslam & Reicher, 2012). Applied psychologists' roles in such resistance movements are therefore dubious, since science (rather than resistance) is the basis for ethical practice, under the current scientist-practitioner model. Nevertheless, there may be situations where scientist-practitioners can play an ethically appropriate role in resistance (see Haslam & Reicher, 2012). For a few examples, organizing community actions, such as boycotts and "buycotts," neighborhood purchasing of urban open spaces, and community resistance of unsustainable development (Mannarini, Roccato, Fedi,

& Rovere, 2009) provide potential venues for decision facilitation. These are also examples that could serve as test cases for future discussions of the ethics of broad psychological application.

Psychology for Motivational Support

Establishing the efficacy of community political organizing is also likely to be important to mobilizing action (Levy & Zint, 2013). As with any other action, ability and knowing what to do are not enough (Equation 4.1). People need to believe that what they will do will make a difference before they will act. This may seem obvious, but it is not easy to establish or maintain such *efficacy*. Levy and Zint (2013) provide a thorough review of some of the things that teachers, leaders, and scientist-practitioners can do to strengthen people's efficacy with respect to environmental action. For a few examples, open ended discussions of political issues, opportunities to spend time with action groups, and involvement in simulated political action may all prove helpful.

Maintaining *collective efficacy* may be an even greater challenge. It seems easy to find people who are resistant to "risky" change, but much harder to find committed advocates. Sustained *advocacy* is particularly important for sustainability, given the lack of a *present* voice for future planetary inhabitants. Other human rights movements have usually been able to muster at least a few committed voices directly from stakeholder groups whose rights were being advocated. This is not as true for sustainability. And ethically conscious, persistent, collective voices may be the best that future stakeholders can hope for.

Sustained advocacy is also particularly important once collective community action has led to *institutional action*. Once people have instigated political processes for changing policies, laws and ordinances, the selling has only begun. Getting legal reforms is also a selling process involving legislative bodies, news media, and voters. The psychological dynamics that influence consideration, passage, and acceptance of new environmental laws are not well understood (Castro, 2012). Compliance with environmental laws also presents many challenges that governments are currently facing, but that applied psychologists have done little to directly address (Jackson, 2008).

The movie *Lincoln* (directed by Spielberg, 2012) depicted the political salesmanship that went on behind the scenes in the Lincoln administration's successful effort to sell a congressional majority on the 14th Amendment to the U.S. Constitution. The many more battles for state ratification that went on after the U.S. Congress approved the measure undoubtedly shared a resemblance to what went on at the national level.

Psychologists may have much to offer in support of political salesmanship.

Criterion Five: Being Practical

It is essential for advocates to understand that, although a majority of the citizens of many countries may agree with the primary aims of sustainability, over thirty years of work have yielded slow, incremental changes in most of these same countries (Dilling & Farhar, 2007). Laws that "make it easy" to recycle, reduce emissions, and increase green spaces are major advances. Similar laws that improve the health of people's inner environments have also gradually emerged from substantial controversy and litigation (Doherty & Clayton, 2011). The engagement of applied psychologists contributed to these efforts through the many channels we have discussed. High impact decisions in organizations and consumer choices, and smaller cumulative effects of clinical and educational interventions, have proved to be highly practical means that were already in place when they were put to use.

> *More than just government.* Advocacy and resistance can be directed at other institutions than government. The results of these may be less obvious, but can also be quite broad. For one example, advocacy has led banks to change policies in order to reduce the environmental impact of their customers' actions (Rupp et al., 2010). Obviously, such advocacy is likely to make changes that are consistent with the interests of the organization. But, to the extent that they are customer driven, they may be relatively quick, when compared with other sorts of advocacy. This is probably because customer *resistance* means loss of income.

Criterion Six? Preparing to Be Practical

The difficult truth is that we are entering a period of increased natural disasters. The good news here is that *disaster response* offers another practical, existing platform for applying psychology to sustainability. Starting with the military, psychologists have taken important roles in preparing to deal with the short term after-effects of disasters for some time now (Guan et al., 2011; Silove & Bryant, 2006; Tyler & Rankin, 2012). More recently, this has included community needs assessment (Guan et al., 2011), interventions immediately and for longer periods after crises (Silove & Bryant, 2006), and follow up studies to identify key issues in effective responses (García-Mira et al., 2008).

Sadly, psychologists will probably continue to be involved in disaster response. Proactive development of education, relief infrastructure, and rapid response are all established components of applied practice in clinical, human factors engineering, and I-O (Chacón & Vecina, 2007; Cherry, 2009; Hung & Wyer, 2009; Ng et al., 2012; Nickerson, 2011; Rytwinski,

Scur, Feeny, & Youngstrom, 2013; Toyosawa, Karasawa, & Fukuwa, 2010). Psychologists play many roles here. For example, clinical psychologists help structure mental health response mobilization in hurricane prone areas. Educational psychologists develop effective preparedness interventions for weather related events. I-O psychologists help to staff and train firefighters in areas where wildfire frequency is increasing. Consumer psychologists help to encourage charitable support for areas hard hit by tsunamis.

Broad popular awareness of such institutional preparedness may serve to do more than reduce casualties in the event of disasters. Making people aware that established institutions are expending time and money on preparing for future natural disasters may increase popular acceptance of the reality of environmental problems. Although we have seen that awareness is not always a precondition for change, it may help in some circumstances (Hansla et al., 2008). Advocacy efforts might also be directed toward such visible, institutional preparation for the inconveniences (shortages, lost productivity) and catastrophes (e.g., increases in storm frequency and intensity) already set in motion by human activities. Public investment may also send the message that environmental problems are surmountable, and efforts to reduce their impact are consistent with general well-being (Thompson et al., 2013).

The Practical Reasons for Optimism

> Act as if what you do makes a difference. It does.
> William James [*]

Before arriving at any final, overall grade for our adaptive capacity, there is one final point that needs to be made. The evidence about both human action and human health is fairly clear: People need to be optimistic about the future. Trait optimism is related to health (Patton et al., 2011; Rasmussen, Scheier, & Greenhouse, 2009; Schwarzer, 1999), self-regulation (Solberg Nes, Carlson, Crofford, de Leeuw, & Segerstrom, 2011), and willingness to change (Hillbrand & Young, 2008; Sherman, Crawford, & McConnell, 2004). Its relationship to PEB is unclear (Hatfield & Job, 2000; Ojala, 2012). But, the belief that we can do something about the world is certainly a cornerstone for our willingness to give it a try (Bandura, 2012; Ojala, 2012). Maintaining an optimistic approach is thus good for us individually and, ultimately, may be very important to our planetary habitation. So, even a lower combined grade than our current $C+$ is reason to keep at it.

REFERENCES

Aaker, J. L., Brumbaugh, A. M., & Grier, S. A. (2000). Nontarget markets and viewer distinctiveness: The impact of target marketing on advertising attitudes. *Journal of Consumer Psychology, 9*(3), 127–140.

Abelson, R. P. (1981). Psychological status of the script concept. *American Psychologist, 36,* 715–729.

Abney, D. H., McBride, D. M., & Petrella, S. N. (2013). Interactive effects in transfer-appropriate processing for event-based prospective memory: The roles of effort, ongoing task, and pm cue properties. *Memory & Cognition,* doi:10.3758/s13421-013-0324-7

Aboud, F. E. (2003). The formation of in-group favoritism and out-group prejudice in young children: Are they distinct attitudes? *Developmental Psychology, 39*(1), 48–60.

Abrahamse, W., Steg, L., Vlek, C., & Rothengatter, T. (2005). A review of intervention studies aimed at household energy conservation. *Journal of Environmental Psychology, 25* (3), 273–291.

Ackerman, P. L., & Kanfer, R. (2004). Cognitive, affective, and conative aspects of adult intellect within a typical and maximal performance framework. In D. Dai & R. J. Sternberg (Eds.), *Motivation, emotion, and cognition: Integrative perspectives on intellectual functioning and development* (pp. 119–141). Mahwah, NJ: Lawrence Erlbaum Associates Publishers.

Ackerman, P. L., Kanfer, R., & Beier, M. E. (2013). Trait complex, cognitive ability, and domain knowledge predictors of baccalaureate success, STEM persistence, and gender differences. *Journal of Educational Psychology, 105*(3), 911–927.

Adams, D. (1986). *The hitchhiker's guide to the galaxy.* New York: Wings Books.

Adams, H. (1916). Holding the attention. In H. F. Adams (Ed.) *Advertising and its mental laws* (pp. 123–152). New York: MacMillan Co.

Adams, P. R., & Adams, G. R. (1984). Mount Saint Helens's ashfall: Evidence for a disaster stress reaction. *American Psychologist, 39*(3), 252–260.

Aderka, I. M., Nickerson, A., Bøe, H., & Hofmann, S. G. (2012). Sudden gains during psychological treatments of anxiety and depression: A meta-analysis. *Journal of Consulting and Clinical Psychology, 80*(1), 93–101.

Aguilera, A., Garza, M. J., & Muñoz, R. F. (2010). Group cognitive-behavioral therapy for depression in Spanish: Culture-sensitive manualized treatment in practice. *Journal of Clinical Psychology, 66*(8), 857–867.

Aguinas, H., & Glavas, A. (2013). What corporate environmental sustainability can do for industrial-organizational psychology. In A. H. Huffman & S. R. Klein (Eds.), *Green organizations: driving change with I-O psychology* (pp. 379–392). New York: Routledge.

REFERENCES

Aguinis, H., & Kraiger, K. (2009). Benefits of training and development for individuals and teams, organizations, and society. *Annual Review of Psychology, 60*, 451–474.

Aguinis, H., & Smith, M. A. (2007). Understanding the impact of test validity and bias on selection errors and adverse impact in human resource selection. *Personnel Psychology, 60*(1), 165–199.

Ajzen, I. (1991). The theory of planned behavior. *Organizational Behavior and Human Decision Processes, 50*(1), 179–211.

Ajzen, I., & Fishbein, M. (1980). *Understanding attitudes and predicting social behavior.* Englewood Cliffs, NJ: Prentice-Hall.

Albanese, R., & Van Fleet, D. D. (1985). Rational behavior in groups: The free-riding tendency. *Academy of Management Review, 10*(2), 244–255.

Albee, G. W. (1979). The next revolution: Primary prevention of psychopathology. *Clinical Psychologist, 32*(3), 16–23.

Alberto, P. A., & Troutman, A. C. (2008). *Applied behavioral analysis for teachers.* Columbus, OH: Pearson.

Albinsson, P. A., & Perera, B. (2012). Alternative marketplaces in the 21st century: Building community through sharing events. *Journal of Consumer Behaviour, 11*(4), 303–315.

Aldag, R. J., & Fuller, S. R. (1993). Beyond fiasco: A reappraisal of the groupthink phenomenon and a new model of group decision processes. *Psychological Bulletin, 113*(3), 533–552.

Alexander, S., & Ussher, S. (2012). The voluntary simplicity movement: A multi-national survey analysis in theoretical context. *Journal of Consumer Culture, 12*(1), 66–86.

Allen, J. A., Pugh, S., Grandey, A. A., & Groth, M. (2010). Following display rules in good or bad faith? Customer orientation as a moderator of the display rule-emotional labor relationship. *Human Performance, 23*(2), 101–115.

Alsem, K., & Kostelijk, E. (2008). Identity based marketing: A new balanced marketing paradigm. *European Journal of Marketing, 42*(9–10), 907–914.

Altemeyer, B. (2004). Highly dominating, highly authoritarian personalities. *The Journal of Social Psychology, 144*(4), 421–447.

Altus, D. E., & Morris, E. K. (2009). B. F. Skinner's utopian vision: Behind and beyond Walden Two. *The Behavior Analyst, 32*(2), 319–335.

Ambec, S., & Lanoie, P. (2008). Does it pay to be green? A systematic overview. *The Academy of Management Perspectives, 22*(4), 45–62.

Amel, E. L., Manning, C. M., & Scott, B. A. (2009). Mindfulness and sustainable behavior: Pondering attention and awareness as means for increasing green behavior. *Ecopsychology, 1*(1), 14–25.

American Educational Research Association (2013). www.aera.net/AboutAERA/Who WeAre/tabid/10089/Default.aspx

American Psychological Association (2013a). www.apa.org/ethics/code/index.aspx? item=12

American Psychological Association (2013b). www.apa.org/helpcenter/about-psycholo gists.aspx

American Psychological Association (2013c). www.apa.org/about/division/div15.aspx

American Psychological Association (2013d). www.apa.org/about/division/div41.aspx

Anderson, B. A., Romani, J. H., Phillips, H., Wentzel, M., & Tlabela, K. (2007). Exploring environmental perceptions, behaviors and awareness: Water and water pollution in South Africa. *Journal of Population, 28*(3), 133–161.

Anderson, J. R. (2007). *How can the human mind occur in the physical universe?* New York: Oxford University Press, doi:10.1093/acprof:oso/9780195324259.001.0001

REFERENCES

Anderson, K. B., Cooper, H., & Okamura, L. (1997). Individual differences and attitudes toward rape: A meta-analytic review. *Personality and Social Psychology Bulletin, 23* (3), 295–315.

Anderson, L., & Jones, R. G. (2000). Affective, cognitive, and behavioral acceptance of feedback: Individual difference moderators. In N. Ashkanasy, C. Hartel, & W. Zerbe (Eds.), *Emotions in organizational life* (pp. 130–140). Westport, CT: Quorum.

Andrews, D. A., & Bonta, J. (2010). Rehabilitating criminal justice policy and practice. *Psychology, Public Policy, and Law, 16*(1), 39–55.

Ano, G. G., & Vasconcelles, E. B. (2005). Religious coping and psychological adjustment to stress: A meta-analysis. *Journal of Clinical Psychology, 61*(4), 461–480.

Antonuccio, D., & Jackson, R. (2009). The science of forgiveness. In W. O'Donohue & S. R. Graybar (Eds.), *Handbook of contemporary psychotherapy: Toward an improved understanding of effective psychotherapy* (pp. 269–284). Thousand Oaks, CA: Sage Publications, Inc.

Aqueveque, C. (2006). Extrinsic cues and perceived risk: The influence of consumption situation. *Journal of Consumer Marketing, 23*(5), 237–247.

Arbuthnot, J. (1977). The roles of attitudinal and personality variables in the prediction of environmental behavior and knowledge. *Environment and Behavior, 9*(2), 217–232.

Argyris, C. (2002). Double-loop learning, teaching, and research. *Academy of Management Learning & Education, 1*(2), 206–218.

Ariely, D. (2008). *Predictably irrational: The hidden forces that shape our decisions.* New York: HarperCollins.

Armenta, M. F., Rodríguez, A. M. M., & Verdugo, V. C. (2009). Analysis of factors influencing the development of environmental norms and anti-ecological behavior. *Revista Interamericana De Psicología, 43*(2), 309–322.

Arnocky, S., Stroink, M., & De Cicco, T. (2007). Self-construal predicts environmental concern, cooperation, and conservation. *Journal of Environmental Psychology, 27*(4), 255–264.

Aronson, E. (2004). *The social animal* (9th ed.). New York: Worth Publishers.

Arthur, W., Bennett, W., Stanush, P. L., & McNelly, T. L. (1998). Factors that influence skill decay and retention: A quantitative review and analysis. *Human Performance, 11*(1), 57–101.

Arts, J. W. C., Frambach, R. T., & Bijmolt, T. H. A. (2011). Generalizations on consumer innovation adoption: A meta-analysis on drivers of intention and behavior. *International Journal of Research in Marketing, 28*(2), 134–144 (June).

Arvaniti, A., Samakouri, M., Kalamara, E., Bochtsou, V., Bikos, C., & Livaditis, M. (2009). Health service staff's attitudes towards patients with mental illness. *Social Psychiatry and Psychiatric Epidemiology, 44*(8), 658–665.

Asch, S. E. (1956). Studies of independence and conformity: I. A minority of one against a unanimous majority. *Psychological Monographs, 70*(9, Whole No. 416).

Ascher, W. (2009). *Bringing in the future: Strategies for farsightedness and sustainability in developing countries.* Chicago, IL: University of Chicago Press.

Ashby, W. R. (1956). *An introduction to cybernetics.* New York: Wiley.

Ashforth, B. E., & Humphrey, R. H. (1993). Emotional labor in service roles: The influence of identity. *The Academy of Management Review, 18*(1), 88–115.

Ashkanasy, N. M., Härtel, C. J., & Daus, C. S. (2002). Diversity and emotion: The new frontiers in organizational behavior research. *Journal of Management, 28* (3), 307–338.

Ashkanasy, N. M., & Jackson, C. A. (2002). Organizational culture and climate. In N. Anderson, D. S. Ones, H. Sinangil, & C. Viswesvaran (Eds.), *Handbook of industrial, work and organizational psychology, Volume 2: Organizational psychology* (pp. 398–415). Thousand Oaks, CA: Sage Publications, Inc.

REFERENCES

Ashton, M. C., Paunonen, S. V., Helmes, E., & Jackson, D. N. (1998). Kin altruism, reciprocal altruism, and the Big Five personality factors. *Evolution and Human Behavior, 19*(4), 243–255.

Ask, K., & Granhag, P. A. (2007). Hot cognition in investigative judgments: The differential influence of anger and sadness. *Law and Human Behavior, 31*(6), 537–551.

Åstebro, T., & Elhedhli, S. (2006). The effectiveness of simple decision heuristics: Forecasting commercial success for early-stage ventures. *Management Science, 52*(3), 395–409.

Atkinson, L. (2013). Smart shoppers? Using QR codes and "green" smartphone apps to mobilize sustainable consumption in the retail environment. *International Journal of Consumer Studies, 37*(4), 387–393.

Austerweil, J. L., & Griffiths, T. L. (2011). Seeking confirmation is rational for deterministic hypotheses. *Cognitive Science, 35*, 499–526.

Austin, J. T., Humphreys, L. G., & Hulin, C. L. (1989). Another view of dynamic criteria: A critical reanalysis of Barrett, Caldwell, and Alexander. *Personnel Psychology, 42* (3), 583–596.

Austin, J. T., & Villanova, P. (1992). The criterion problem: 1917–1992. *Journal of Applied Psychology, 77*(6), 836–874.

Baas, M., De Dreu, C. W., & Nijstad, B. A. (2008). A meta-analysis of 25 years of mood-creativity research: Hedonic tone, activation, or regulatory focus? *Psychological Bulletin, 134*(6), 779–806.

Baby, S. (2012). Development of self-concept and health. *Social Science International, 28* (2), 253–263.

Bælum, J. (1985). Response of solvent-exposed printers and unexposed controls to six-hour toluene exposure. *Scandinavian Journal of Work, Environment & Health, 11*(4), 271–280.

Bailie, C., Kuyken, W., & Sonnenberg, S. (2012). The experiences of parents in mindfulness-based cognitive therapy. *Clinical Child Psychology and Psychiatry, 17*(1), 103–119.

Baker, E. M., & Schuck, J. R. (1975). Theoretical note: Use of signal detection theory to clarify problems of evaluating performance in industry. *Organizational Behavior and Human Performance, 13*, 307–317.

Baldinger, A. L., & Rubinson, J. (1996). Brand loyalty: The link between attitude and behavior. *Journal of Advertising Research, 36*(6), 22–34.

Baldwin, J. (1895). In *Mental development in the child and the race: Method and processes* (pp. 367–430). New York: Macmillan Publishing.

Balliet, D., & Van Lange, P. A. M. (2013). Trust, conflict, and cooperation: A meta-analysis. *Psychological Bulletin, 139*, 1090–1112.

Balzer, W. K., Doherty, M. E., & O'Connor, R. (1989). Effects of cognitive feedback on performance. *Psychological Bulletin, 106*(3), 410–433.

Balzer, W. K., Hammer, L. B., Sumner, K. E., Birchenough, T. R., Martens, S., & Raymark, P. H. (1994). Effects of cognitive feedback components, display format, and elaboration on performance. *Organizational Behavior and Human Decision Processes, 58*(3), 369–385.

Balzer, W. K., Sulsky, L. M., Hammer, L. B., & Sumner, K. E. (1992). Task information, cognitive information, or functional validity information: Which components of cognitive feedback affect performance? *Organizational Behavior and Human Decision Processes, 53*(1), 35–54.

Bamberg, S., & Möser, G. (2007). Twenty years after Hines, Hungerford, and Tomera: A new meta-analysis of psycho-social determinants of pro-environmental behaviour. *Journal of Environmental Psychology, 27*(1), 14–25.

REFERENCES

Bamburg, J., & Rowledge, L. (2009). Building the Bainbridge Graduate Institute (BGI) pioneering management education for global sustainability. In C. Wankel & J. F. Stoner (Eds.), *Management education for global sustainability* (pp. 207–226). Charlotte, NC: IAP Information Age Publishing.

Bandura, A. (1969). Social learning of moral judgments. *Journal of Personality and Social Psychology, 11*(3), 275–279.

Bandura, A. (1978). The self-system in reciprocal determinism. *American Psychologist, 33*, 344–358.

Bandura, A. (1982). Self-efficacy mechanism in human agency. *American Psychologist, 37* (2), 122–147.

Bandura, A. (2005). The primacy of self-regulation in health promotion. *Applied Psychology: An International Review, 54*(2), 245–254.

Bandura, A. (2012). Social cognitive theory. In P. A. Van Lange, A. W. Kruglanski, & E. T. Higgins, (Eds.), *Handbook of theories of social psychology* (Vol. 1) (pp. 349–373). Thousand Oaks, CA: Sage Publications.

Bandura, A., & Locke, E. A. (2003). Negative self-efficacy and goal effects revisited. *Journal of Applied Psychology, 88*(1), 87–99.

Bandura, A., & Walters, R. H. (1963). *Social learning theory and personality development.* New York: Holt, Rinehart & Winston.

Banerjee, N. (2012). Prominent climate change denier now admits he was wrong. *Christian Science Monitor*, July 31.

Baron, J. (1990). Reflectiveness and rational thinking: Response to Duemler and Mayer (1988). *Journal of Educational Psychology, 82*(2), 391–392.

Baron, J. (2007). *Thinking and deciding* (4th ed.). New York: Cambridge University Press.

Barrick, M. R., & Mount, M. K. (2012). Nature and use of personality in selection. In N. Schmitt (Ed.), *The Oxford handbook of personnel assessment and selection* (p. 225–251). New York: Oxford University Press.

Barry, R. J. (1978). Conservation of number: An examination of Piaget's stage analysis. *Genetic Psychology Monographs, 97*(1), 161–178.

Barry, T. E. (1987). The development of the hierarchy of effects: An historical perspective. *Current Issues and Research in Advertising, 10*, 251–295.

Barth, M., & Thomas, I. (2012). Synthesising case-study research: Ready for the next step? *Environmental Education Research, 18*(6), 751–764.

Bartram, D. (2005). The Great Eight competencies: A criterion-centric approach to validation. *Journal of Applied Psychology, 90*(6), 1185–1203.

Bateman, T. S., O'Neill, H., & Kenworthy-U'Ren, A. (2002). A hierarchical taxonomy of top managers' goals. *Journal of Applied Psychology, 87*(6), 1134–1148.

Batson, C., Batson, J. G., Griffitt, C. A., Barrientos, S., Brandt, J., Sprengelmeyer, P., & Bayly, M. J. (1989). Negative-state relief and the empathy: Altruism hypothesis. *Journal of Personality and Social Psychology, 56*(6), 922–933.

Baum, A., Fleming, I., Israel, A., & O'Keeffe, M. K. (1992). Symptoms of chronic stress following a natural disaster and discovery of a human-made hazard. *Environment and Behavior, 24*(3), 347–365.

Baumeister, R. F. (1989). Social intelligence and the construction of meaning in life. In R. Wyer & T. K. Srull (Eds.), *Social intelligence and cognitive assessments of personality* (pp. 71–80). Hillsdale, NJ: Lawrence Erlbaum Associates, Inc.

Baumgardner, M. H., Leippe, M. R., Ronis, D. L., & Greenwald, A. G. (1983). In search of reliable persuasion effects: II. Associative interference and persistence of persuasion in a message-dense environment. *Journal of Personality and Social Psychology, 45*(3), 524–537.

Baunach, D. (2012). Changing same-sex marriage attitudes in America from 1988 through 2010. *Public Opinion Quarterly, 76*(2), 364–378.

REFERENCES

Beach, L. R. (2009). Decision making: Linking narratives and action. *Narrative Inquiry*, *19*(2), 393–414.

Bechtel, R. B. (1997). *Environment and behavior*. Thousand Oaks, CA: Sage.

Bechtoldt, M. N., Beersma, B., Rohrmann, S., & Sanchez-Burks, J. (2013). A gift that takes its toll: Emotion recognition and conflict appraisal. *European Journal of Work and Organizational Psychology*, *22*(1), 56–66.

Becker, E. A., & Gibson, C. C. (1998). Fishbein and Ajzen's theory of reasoned action: Accurate prediction of behavioral intentions for enrolling in distance education courses. *Adult Education Quarterly*, *49*(1), 43–55.

Begany, J. J., & Milburn, M. A. (2002). Psychological predictors of sexual harassment: Authoritarianism, hostile sexism, and rape myths. *Psychology of Men & Masculinity*, *3* (2), 119–126.

Beier, M. E., & Kanfer, R. (2010). Motivation in training and development: A phase perspective. In S. J. Kozlowski & E. Salas (Eds.), *Learning, training, and development in organizations* (pp. 65–97). New York: Routledge/Taylor & Francis Group.

Beilin, H. (1996). Mind and meaning: Piaget and Vygotsky on causal explanation. *Human Development*, *39*(5), 277–286.

Belk, R. (1975). Situational variables and consumer behavior. *Journal of Consumer Research*. December, *2*, 157–164.

Bell, P. A., Greene, T. C., Fisher, J. D., & Baum, A. (2001). *Environmental psychology* (5th ed.). New York: Psychology Press.

Belovicz, M. W., & Finch, F. E. (1971). A critical analysis of the "risky shift" phenomenon. *Organizational Behavior & Human Performance*, *6*(2), 150–168.

Bengtsson, F., & Agerfalk, P. J. (2011). Information technology as a change actant in sustainability innovation: Insights from Uppsala. *Journal of Strategic Information Systems*, *20*(1), 96–112.

Benish, S. G., Imel, Z. E., & Wampold, B. E. (2008). The relative efficacy of bona fide psychotherapies for treating post-traumatic stress disorder: A meta-analysis of direct comparisons. *Clinical Psychology Review*, *28*(5), 746–758.

Bereiter, C. (1995). A dispositional view of transfer. In A. McKeough, J. Lupart, & A. Marini (Eds.), *Teaching for transfer: Fostering generalization in learning* (pp. 21–34). Hillsdale, NJ and England: Lawrence Erlbaum Associates, Inc.

Berenguer, J. (2007). The effect of empathy in proenvironmental attitudes and behaviors. *Environment and Behavior*, *39*(2), 269–283.

Berenguer, J. (2010). The effect of empathy in environmental moral reasoning. *Environment and Behavior*, *42*(1), 110–134.

Berenguer, J., Corraliza, J. A., & Martín, R. (2005). Rural–urban differences in environmental concern, attitudes, and actions. *European Journal of Psychological Assessment*, *21*(2), 128–138.

Berry, M., Reichman, W., Klobas, J., MacLachlan, M., Hui, H. C., & Carr, S. C. (2011). Humanitarian work psychology: The contributions of organizational psychology to poverty reduction. *Journal of Economic Psychology*, *32*(2), 240–247.

Best, H., & Kneip, T. (2011). The impact of attitudes and behavioral costs on environmental behavior: A natural experiment on household waste recycling. *Social Science Research*, *40*(3), 917–930.

Bettenhausen, K., & Murnighan, J. K. (1985). The emergence of norms in competitive decision-making groups. *Administrative Science Quarterly*, *30*, 350–372.

Betz, N. E., & Klein, K. L. (1996). Relationships among measures of career self-efficacy, generalized self-efficacy, and global self-esteem. *Journal of Career Assessment*, *4*(3), 285–298.

Betz, N. E., & Wolfe, J. B. (2005). Measuring confidence for basic domains of vocational activity in high school students. *Journal of Career Assessment*, *13*(3), 251–270.

REFERENCES

Beuhner, M. J. (2003). Rethinking temporal contiguity and the judgement of causality: Effects of prior knowledge, experience, and reinforcement procedure. *The Quarterly Journal of Experimental Psychology A: Human Experimental Psychology, 56A*(5), 865–890.

Beutler, L. E., Harwood, T., Michelson, A., Song, X., & Holman, J. (2011). Resistance/reactance level. *Journal of Clinical Psychology, 67*(2), 133–142.

Biel, A., & Thøgersen, J. (2007). Activation of social norms in social dilemmas: A review of the evidence and reflections on the implications for environmental behaviour. *Journal of Economic Psychology, 28*(1), 93–112.

Billings, R. S., Milburn, T. W., & Schaalman, M. L. (1980). Crisis perception: A theoretical and empirical analysis. *Administrative Science Quarterly, 25*, 300–315.

Birnbaum, R., & Deutsch, R. (1996). The use of dynamic assessment and its relationship to the Code of Practice. *Educational and Child Psychology, 13*(3), 14–24.

Bisantz, A. M., & Pritchett, A. R. (2003). Measuring the fit between human judgments and automated alerting algorithms: A study of collision detection. *Human Factors, 45*(2), 266–280.

Bissing-Olson, M. J., Zacher, H., Fielding, K. S., & Iyer, A. (2012). An intraindividual perspective on pro-environmental behaviors at work. *Industrial and Organizational Psychology: Perspectives on Science and Practice, 5*(4), 500–502.

Biyalogorsky, E., Boulding, W., & Staelin, R. (2006). Stuck in the past: Why managers persist with new product failures. *Journal of Marketing, 70*, 108–121.

Black, H., & Phillips, S. (1982). An intervention program for the development of empathy in student teachers. *Journal of Psychology: Interdisciplinary and Applied, 112*(2), 159–168.

Blackwell, R. C., Miniard, P. W., & Engel, J. F. (2006). *Consumer behavior* (10th ed.). Mason, OH: Thomson/South-Western.

Blickle, G., Schlegel, A., Fassbender, P., & Klein, U. (2006). Some personality correlates of business white-collar crime. *Applied Psychology: An International Review, 55*(2), 220–233.

Blomfield, J. M., Troth, A. C., & Jordan, P. J. (2016). Emotional thresholds and change agent success in corporate sustainability. In N. M. Ashkanasy, C. E. J. Härtel, & W. J. Zerbe (Eds.), *Emotions and organizational governance* (Vol.12, pp. 191–216). Bingley: Emerald Group Publishing.

Bloom, R. W. (1993). Psychological assessment for security clearances, special access, and sensitive positions. *Military Medicine, 158*(9), 609–613.

Blume, B. D., Ford, J., Baldwin, T. T., & Huang, J. L. (2010). Transfer of training: A meta-analytic review. *Journal of Management, 36*(4), 1065–1105.

Boardley, I. D., & Kavussanu, M. (2008). The moral disengagement in sport scale–short. *Journal of Sports Sciences, 26*(14), 1507–1517.

Bobko, P., & Colella, A. (1994). Employee reactions to performance standards: A review and research propositions. *Personnel Psychology, 47*(1), 1–29.

Bock, M., & Izquierdo, S. (2006). Product placement, markengedächtnis, markenimage (1): Literaturübersicht und ein weiterführendes experiment. *Zeitschrift Für Medienpsychologie, 18*(3), 106–118.

Böcker, P., & Breuer, F. (1980). On the structure and variation of therapeutic goal statements. *Zeitschrift Für Klinische Psychologie, 9*(4), 245–265.

Boer, D., & Fischer, R. (2013). How and when do personal values guide our attitudes and socialty? Explaining cross-cultural variability in attitude-value linkages. *Psychological Bulletin, 139*, 1113–1147.

Bogacki, D. F., Armstrong, D. J., & Weiss, K. J. (2005). Reducing school violence: The Corporal Punishment Scale and its relationship to authoritarianism and pupil-control ideology. *Journal of Psychiatry & Law, 33*(3), 367–386.

REFERENCES

Boin, A., & McConnell, A. (2007). Preparing for critical infrastructure breakdowns: The limits of crisis management and the need for resilience. *Journal of Contingencies and Crisis Management, 15*(1), 50–59.

Bolter, N. D., & Weiss, M. R. (2013). Coaching behaviors and adolescent athletes' sportspersonship outcomes: Further validation of the Sportsmanship Coaching Behaviors Scale (SCBS). *Sport, Exercise, and Performance Psychology, 2*(1), 32–47.

Bonaiuto, M., Carrus, G., Martorella, H., & Bonnes, M. (2002). Local identity processes and environmental attitudes in land use changes the case of natural protected areas. *Journal of Economic Psychology, 23*, 631–653.

Bonaccio, S., Dalal, R. S., Highhouse, S., Ilgen, D. R., Mohammed, S., & Slaughter, J. E. (2010). Taking workplace decisions seriously: This conversation has been fruitful! *Industrial and Organizational Psychology: Perspectives on Science and Practice, 3* (4), 455–464.

Bonnici, J. (2006). Brain tattoos: Creating unique brands that stick in your customers' minds; profit brand: How to increase the profitability, accountability and sustainability of brands; brand sense: Build powerful brands through touch, taste, smell, sight, and sound. *Journal of Marketing Research, 43*(1), 133–134.

Booth, R. F., Bucky, S. F., & Berry, N. H. (1978). Predictors of psychiatric illness among Navy hospital corpsmen. *Journal of Clinical Psychology, 34*(2), 305–308.

Boring, E. G. (1933). The law of effect. *Science, 77*, doi:10.1126/science.77.1995.307

Borman, W. C. (1992) Job behavior, performance, and effectiveness. In M. D. Dunnette & L. Hough (Eds.), *The handbook of industrial and organizational psychology*, Vol. 2 (pp. 271–326). Palo Alto, CA: CPI.

Borman, W. C., Bryant, R. H., & Dorio, J. (2010). The measurement of task performance. Defining and measuring results of workplace behavior. In J. L. Farr & N. T. Tippins (Eds.), *Handbook of employee selection* (pp. 439–461). New York: Routledge.

Borman, W. C., & Smith, T. N. (2012). The use of objective measures as criteria in I/O psychology. In N. Schmitt (Ed.), *The Oxford handbook of personnel assessment and selection.* (pp. 532–542). New York: Oxford University Press.

Born, M. P., Bleichrodt, N., & Van der Flier, H. (1987). Cross-cultural comparison of sex-related differences on intelligence tests: A meta-analysis. *Journal of Cross-Cultural Psychology, 18*(3), 283–314.

Bornstein, B. H., & Wiener, R. L. (2010). Emotion and the law: A field whose time has come. In B. H. Bornstein & R. L. Wiener (Eds.), *Emotion and the law: Psychological perspectives* (pp. 1–12). New York: Springer Science + Business Media, 56.

Bortree, D., Ahern, L., Dou, X., & Smith, A. (2012). Framing environmental advocacy: A study of 30 years of advertising in *National Geographic Magazine. International Journal of Nonprofit and Voluntary Sector Marketing, 17*(2), 77–91.

Botelho, A., Dinar, A., Pinto, L. M. C., & Rapoport, A. (2014). Time and uncertainty in resource dilemmas: Equilibrium solutions and experimental results. *Experimental Economics, 17*(4), 649–672.

Bouton, M. E., Todd, T. P., & León, S. P. (2013). Contextual control of discriminated operant behavior. *Journal of Experimental Psychology: Animal Behavior Processes*, doi:10.1037/xan0000002

Bowman, N. A. (2010). College diversity experiences and cognitive development: A meta-analysis. *Review of Educational Research, 80*(1), 4–33.

Bowman, N. A., Brandenberger, J. W., Hill, P. L., & Lapsley, D. K. (2011). The long-term effects of college diversity experiences: Well-being and social concerns 13 years after graduation. *Journal of College Student Development, 52*(6), 729–739.

Boyle, C. L., & Lutzker, J. R. (2011). A quantitative analysis of generalization outcomes found in behavioral parent training programs for reduction of child problem behavior. *International Journal of Child and Adolescent Health, 4*(1), 7–15.

REFERENCES

Bradley, G. L., & Sparks, B. A. (2012). Antecedents and consequences of consumer value: A longitudinal study of timeshare owners. *Journal of Travel Research*, *51*(2), 191–204.

Bradu, C., Orquin, J. L., & Thøgersen, J. (2013). The mediated influence of a traceability label on consumer's willingness to buy the labelled product. *Journal Of Business Ethics*, doi:10.1007/s10551-013-1872-2

Brainerd, C. J. (1978). The stage question in cognitive-developmental theory. *Behavioral and Brain Sciences*, *1*(2), 173–213.

Branje, S. J. T., Van Lieshout, C. F. M., & Gerris, J. R. M. (2007). Big Five personality development in adolescence and adulthood. *European Journal of Personality*, *21*(1), 45–62.

Bratanova, B., Loughnan, S., & Gatersleben, B. (2012). The moral circle as a common motivational cause of cross-situational pro-environmentalism. *European Journal of Social Psychology*, *42*(5), 539–545.

Brehm, S. S., & Brehm, J. W. (1981). *Psychological reactance: A theory of freedom and control.* Cambridge, MA: Academic Press.

Brett, J. M., & Reilly, A. H. (1988). On the road again: Predicting the job transfer decision. *Journal of Applied Psychology*, *73*(4), 614–620.

Bretz, R. R., & Judge, T. A. (1998). Realistic job previews: A test of the adverse self-selection hypothesis. *Journal of Applied Psychology*, *83*(2), 330–337.

Brinkerhoff, M. B., & Jacob, J. C. (1999). Mindfulness and quasi-religious meaning systems: An empirical exploration within the context of ecological sustainability and deep ecology. *Journal for the Scientific Study of Religion*, *38*(4), 524–542.

Brinkmann, J., & Peattie, K. (2008). Consumer ethics research: Reframing the debate about consumption for good. *Electronic Journal of Business Ethics and Organization Studies*, *13*(1), 22–31.

Broberg, A., Kyttä, M., & Fagerholm, N. (2013). Child-friendly urban structures: Bullerby revisited. *Journal of Environmental Psychology*, *35*, 110–120.

Bröder, A. (2003). Decision making with the "adaptive toolbox": Influence of environmental structure, intelligence, and working memory load. *Journal of Experimental Psychology: Learning, Memory, and Cognition*, *29*(4), 611–625.

Brotheridge, C. M., & Grandey, A. A. (2002). Emotional labor and burnout: Comparing two perspectives of "people work". *Journal of Vocational Behavior*, *60*(1), 17–39.

Brown, J. W. (1989). *Innovation for excellence: The paracollege model.* New York: University Press of America.

Brown, K., & Ryan, R. M. (2003). The benefits of being present: Mindfulness and its role in psychological well-being. *Journal of Personality and Social Psychology*, *84*(4), 822–848.

Brown, S. P., Homer, P. M., & Inman, J. J. (1998). A meta-analysis of relationships between ad-evoked feelings and advertising responses. *Journal of Marketing Research*, *35* (1), 114–126.

Bruner, G. C. (1986). Problem recognition styles and search patterns: An empirical investigation. *Journal of Retailing*, *62*(3), 281–297.

Brunswik, E. (1952). *The conceptual framework of psychology.* Chicago, IL: University of Chicago Press.

Brunswik, E. (1955). Representative design and probabilistic theory in a functional psychology. *Psychological Review*, *62*(3), 193–217.

Buckley, K. W. (1982). The selling of a psychologist: John Broadus Watson and the application of behavioral techniques to advertising. *Journal of the History of the Behavioral Sciences*, *18*(3), 207–221.

Buckley, R. (2012). Sustainable tourism: Research and reality. *Annals of Tourism Research*, *39*(2), 528–546.

REFERENCES

Buenaver, L. F., McGuire, L., & Haythornthwaite, J. A. (2006). Cognitive-behavioral self-help for chronic pain. *Journal of Clinical Psychology, 62*(11), 1389–1396.

Bunting, C. J., Tolson, H., Kuhn, C., Suarez, E., & Williams, R. B. (2000). Physiological stress response of the neuroendocrine system during outdoor adventure tasks. *Journal of Leisure Research, 32*(2), 191–207.

Burke, L. A., & Hutchins, H. M. (2007). Training transfer: An integrative literature review. *Human Resource Development Review, 6*(3), 263–296.

Burke, M. J., Salvador, R. O., Smith-Crowe, K., Chan-Serafin, S., Smith, A., & Sonesh, S. (2011). The dread factor: How hazards and safety training influence learning and performance. *Journal of Applied Psychology, 96*(1), 46–70.

Burke, M. J., Sarpy, S., Smith-Crowe, K., Chan-Serafin, S., Salvador, R. O., & Islam, G. (2006). Relative effectiveness of worker safety and health training methods. *American Journal of Public Health, 96*(2), 315–324.

Burnette, J. L., O'Boyle, E. H., VanEpps, E. M., Pollack, J. M., & Finkel, E. J. (2013). Mind-sets matter: A meta-analytic review of implicit theories and self-regulation. *Psychological Bulletin, 139*(3), 655–701.

Burris, C. T., & Rempel, J. K. (2004). "It's the end of the world as we know it": Threat and the spatial-symbolic self. *Journal of Personality and Social Psychology, 86*(1), 19–42.

Business Dictionary (2013). Definition of values. www.businessdictionary.com/defin ition/values.html#ixzz2AumwYgAC

Buss, A. H. (2012). *Pathways to Individuality.* Washington, DC: American Psychological Association.

Buss, D. M., Haselton, M. G., Shackelford, T. K., Bleske, A. L., & Wakefield, J. C. (1998). Adaptations, exaptations, and spandrels. *American Psychologist, 53*, 533–548.

Byron, K., & Khazanchi, S. (2012). Rewards and creative performance: A meta-analytic test of theoretically derived hypotheses. *Psychological Bulletin, 138*(4), 809–830.

Byron, K., Khazanchi, S., & Nazarian, D. (2010). The relationship between stressors and creativity: A meta-analysis examining competing theoretical models. *Journal of Applied Psychology, 95*(1), 201–212.

Cacioppo, J. T., & Hawkley, L. C. (2012). Designed for social influence. In D. T. Kenrick, N. J. Goldstein, & S. L. Braver (Eds.), *Six degrees of social influence: Science, application, and the psychology of Robert Cialdini* (pp. 90–97). New York: Oxford University Press.

Cacioppo, J. T., Petty, R. E., Feinstein, J. A., Jarvis, W., & Blair, G. (1996). Dispositional differences in cognitive motivation: The life and times of individuals varying in need for cognition. *Psychological Bulletin, 119*(2), 197–253.

Cahill, D. J. (1997). Target marketing and segmentation: Valid and useful tools for marketing. *Management Decision, 35*(1), 10–13.

Campbell, C., & Cornish, F. (2012). How can community health programmes build enabling environments for transformative communication? Experiences from India and South Africa. *AIDS and Behavior, 16*(4), 847–857.

Campbell, D. E., Provolt, L., & Campbell, J. E. (2013). Going green: Eco-industrial and organizational psychology. In J. Olson-Buchanan, L. K. Bryan, & L. F. Thompson (Eds.), *Using industrial-organizational psychology for the greater good* (pp. 45–74). New York: Routledge.

Campbell, J. P. (1990). Modeling the performance prediction problem in I/O psychology. In M. D. Dunnette & L. Hough (Eds.), *The handbook of industrial and organizational psychology*, Vol. 1 (pp. 704–715). Palo Alto, CA: CPI.

Campbell, J. P., McCloy, R. A., Oppler, S. H., & Sager, C. E. (1993). A theory of performance. In N. Schmitt & W. Borman, and Associated (Eds.), *Personnel selection in organizations* (pp. 222–246). San Francisco, CA: Jossey-Bass.

REFERENCES

Campbell, L., Vasquez, M., Behnke, S., & Kinscherff, R. (2010). *APA ethics code commentary and case illustrations.* Washington, DC: American Psychological Association.

Canova, L., Rattazzi, A., & Webley, P. (2005). The hierarchical structure of saving motives. *Journal of Economic Psychology, 26*(1), 21–34.

Carayon, P. (2010). Human factors in patient safety as an innovation. *Applied Ergonomics, 41*(5), 657–665.

Carmeli, A., & Josman, Z. E. (2006). The relationship among emotional intelligence, task performance, and organizational citizenship behaviors. *Human Performance, 19*(4), 403–419.

Carré, J. M., Fisher, P. M., Manuck, S. B., & Hariri, A. R. (2012). Interaction between trait anxiety and trait anger predict amygdala reactivity to angry facial expressions in men but not women. *Social Cognitive and Affective Neuroscience, 7*(2), 213–221.

Carrete, L., Castaño, R., Felix, R., Centeno, E., & González, E. (2012). Green consumer behavior in an emerging economy: Confusion, credibility, and compatibility. *Journal of Consumer Marketing, 29*(7), 470–481.

Carroll, J. B. (1993). *Human cognitive abilities: A survey of factor-analytic studies.* New York: Cambridge.

Carrus, G., Passafaro, P., & Bonnes, M. (2008). Emotions, habits and rational choices in ecological behaviours: The case of recycling and use of public transportation. *Journal of Environmental Psychology, 28*(1), 51–62.

Carson, R. (1962). *Silent spring.* New York: Houghton-Mifflin, Harcourt.

Carthy, T., Horesh, N., Apter, A., & Gross, J. J. (2010). Patterns of emotional reactivity and regulation in children with anxiety disorders. *Journal of Psychopathology and Behavioral Assessment, 32*(1), 23–36.

Carver, C. S., La Voie, L., Kuhl, J., & Ganellen, R. J. (1988). Cognitive concomitants of depression: A further examination of the roles of generalization, high standards and self-criticism. *Journal of Social and Clinical Psychology, 7,* 350–365.

Carver, C. S., & Scheier, M. F. (1999). Themes and issues in the self-regulation of behavior. In R. S. Wyer (Ed.), *Perspectives on behavioral self-regulation: Advances in social cognition* (Vol. XII) (pp. 1–105). Mahwah, NJ: Lawrence Erlbaum Associates.

Carver, C. S., & Scheier, M. F. (2012a). A model of behavioral self-regulation. In P. A. Van Lange, A. W. Kruglanski, & E. T. Higgins (Eds.), *Handbook of theories of social psychology,* Vol. 1 (pp. 505–525). Thousand Oaks, CA: Sage.

Carver, C. S., & Scheier, M. F. (2012b). Cybernetic control processes and the self-regulation of behavior. In R. M. Ryan (Ed.), *The Oxford handbook of human motivation* (pp. 28–42) New York: Oxford University Press.

Cascio, W. F., & Fogli, L. (2010). The business value of employee selection. In J. L. Farr & N. T. Tippins (Eds), *Handbook of employee selection* (pp. 235–252). New York: Routledge.

Cash, T. F. (2005). The influence of sociocultural factors on body image: Searching for constructs. *Clinical Psychology: Science and Practice, 12*(4), 438–442.

Cassaday, H. J., Bloomfield, R. E., & Hayward, N. (2002). Relaxed conditions can provide memory cues in both undergraduates and primary school children. *British Journal of Educational Psychology, 72*(4), 531–547.

Castro, P. (2012). Legal innovation for social change: Exploring change and resistance to different types of sustainability laws. *Political Psychology, 33*(1), 105–121.

Cawley, B. D., Keeping, L. M., & Levy, P. E. (1998). Participation in the performance appraisal process and employee reactions: A meta-analytic review of field investigations. *Journal of Applied Psychology, 83*(4), 615–633.

Ceci, S. J., & Liker, J. K. (1986). A day at the races: A study of IQ, expertise, and cognitive complexity. *Journal of Experimental Psychology: General, 115*(3), 255–266.

REFERENCES

Cegarra-Navarro, J., Eldridge, S., & Martinez-Martinez, A. (2010). Managing environmental knowledge through unlearning in Spanish hospitality companies. *Journal of Environmental Psychology, 30*(2), 249–257.

Chacko, T. I., & McElroy, J. C. (1983). The cognitive component in Locke's theory of goal setting: Suggestive evidence for a causal attribution interpretation. *Academy of Management Journal, 26*(1), 104–118.

Chacón, F., & Vecina, M. (2007). The 2004 Madrid Terrorist attack: Organizing a large-scale psychological response. In E. K. Carll (Ed.), *Trauma psychology: Issues in violence, disaster, health, and illness, Vol. 1: Violence and disaster* (pp. 163–193). Westport, CT: Praeger Publishers/Greenwood Publishing Group.

Challenger, R., Clegg, C. W., & Shepherd, C. (2013). Function allocation in complex systems: Reframing an old problem. *Ergonomics, 56*(7), 1051–1069.

Chan, D. (2010). Values, styles, and motivational constructs. In J. L. Farr & N. T. Tippins (Eds.), *Handbook of employee selection.* (pp. 321–337). New York: Routledge/Taylor & Francis Group.

Chan, D., & Schmitt, N. (2002). Situational judgment and job performance. *Human Performance, 15*(3), 233–254.

Chang, A., Bordia, P., & Duck, J. (2003). Punctuated equilibrium and linear progression: Toward a new understanding of group development. *Academy of Management Journal, 46*(1), 106–117.

Chang, C., Ferris, D., Johnson, R. E., Rosen, C. C., & Tan, J. A. (2012). Core self-evaluations: A review and evaluation of the literature. *Journal of Management, 38* (1), 81–128.

Chang, K., Lee, I., & Hargreaves, T. (2008). Scientist versus practitioner: An abridged meta-analysis of the changing role of psychologists. *Counselling Psychology Quarterly, 21* (3), 267–291.

Charbonneau, D., & Nicol, A. A. M. (2002). Emotional intelligence and prosocial behaviors in adolescents. *Psychological Reports, 90*(2), 361–370.

Charlton, S. G. (2002). Measurement of cognitive states in test and evaluation. In S. G. Charlton & T. G. O'Brien (Eds.), *Handbook of human factors testing and evaluation* (2nd ed.) (pp. 97–126). Mahwah, NJ: Lawrence Erlbaum Associates Publishers.

Chatterjee, A., & Hunt, J. M. (2005). The relationship of character structure to persuasive communication in advertising. *Psychological Reports, 96*(1), 215–221.

Chattopadhyay, P., Glick, W. H., & Huber, G. P. (2001). Organizational actions in response to threats and opportunities. *Academy of Management Journal, 44*(5), 937–955.

Cheatwood, D. (1993). Capital punishment and the deterrence of violent crime in comparable counties. *Criminal Justice Review, 18*(2), 165–181.

Chen, J. A., & Pajares, F. (2010). Implicit theories of ability of grade 6 science students: Relation to epistemological beliefs and academic motivation and achievement in science. *Contemporary Educational Psychology, 35*(1), 75–87.

Chen, J. A., & Usher, E. L. (2013). Profiles of the sources of science self-efficacy. *Learning and Individual Differences, 24*, 11–21.

Chen, S., Hui, N. H., Bond, M., Sit, A. F., Wong, S., Chow, V. Y., ... Law, R. M. (2006). Reexamining personal, social, and cultural influences on compliance behavior in the United States, Poland, and Hong Kong. *The Journal of Social Psychology, 146* (2), 223–244.

Chen, X., Lupi, F., He, G., & Liu, J. (2009). Linking social norms to efficient conservation investment in payments for ecosystem services. *PNAS Proceedings of the National Academy of Sciences of the United States of America, 106*(28), 11812–11817.

Cheon, H., Cho, C., & Sutherland, J. (2007). A meta-analysis of studies on the determinants of standardization and localization of international marketing and advertising strategies. *Journal of International Consumer Marketing, 19*(4), 109–147.

REFERENCES

Cheon, J. (2008). Best practices in community-based prevention for youth substance reduction: Towards strengths-based positive development policy. *Journal of Community Psychology, 36*(6), 761–779.

Cherrier, H. (2009). Anti-consumption discourses and consumer-resistant identities. *Journal of Business Research, 62*(2), 181–190.

Cherry, K. E. (2009). *Lifespan perspectives on natural disasters: Coping with Katrina, Rita, and other storms.* New York: Springer Science + Business Media.

Chiaburu, D. S., Oh, I., Berry, C. M., Li, N., & Gardner, R. G. (2011). The five-factor model of personality traits and organizational citizenship behaviors: A meta-analysis. *Journal of Applied Psychology, 96*(6), 1140–1166.

Chiesa, A., & Serretti, A. (2009). Mindfulness-based stress reduction for stress management in healthy people: A review and meta-analysis. *The Journal of Alternative and Complementary Medicine, 15*(5), 593–600.

Chiesi, F., Primi, C., & Morsanyi, K. (2011). Developmental changes in probabilistic reasoning: The role of cognitive capacity, instructions, thinking styles, and relevant knowledge. *Thinking & Reasoning, 17*(3), 315–350.

Chiles, J. (2001). *Inviting disaster.* New York: HarperBusiness.

Cho, C. H., Martens, M. L., Kim, H., & Rodrigue, M. (2011). Astroturfing global warming: It isn't always greener on the other side of the fence. *Journal of Business Ethics, 104*(4), 571–587.

Chow, K., & Healey, M. (2008). Place attachment and place identity: First-year undergraduates making the transition from home to university. *Journal of Environmental Psychology, 28*(4), 362–372.

Chowdhury, T., & Mukhopadhaya, P. (2012). Limitations of the theories of nonprofits and benchmarking services delivery dimensions of poverty-reduction programs in rural Bangladesh. *Journal of Nonprofit & Public Sector Marketing, 24*(4), 325–350.

Church, A. H., Margiloff, A., & Coruzzi, C. (1995). Using surveys for change: An applied example in a pharmaceuticals organization. *Leadership & Organization Development Journal, 16*(4), 3–11.

Church, A. H., & Waclawski, J. (2008). Establishing successful client relationships. In J. W. Hedge & W. C. Borman (Eds.), *The I/O consultant: Advice and insights for building a successful career* (pp. 205–213). Washington, DC: American Psychological Association.

Cialdini, R. (1988). *Influence: Science and practice* (2nd ed.). Glenview, IL: Scott, Foresman.

Cialdini, R. (2007). *Influence: The psychology of persuasion.* New York: Collins.

Cialdini, R., Vincent, J., Lewis, S., Catalan, J., Wheeler, D., & Darby, B. (1975). Reciprocal concessions procedure for inducing compliance: The door-in-the-face technique. *Journal of Personality and Social Psychology, 31*(2), 206–215.

Cialdini, R. B. (1999). Of tricks and tumors: Some little-recognized costs of dishonest use of effective social influence. *Psychology & Marketing, 16*(2), 91–98.

Cialdini, R. B. (2003). Crafting normative messages to protect the environment. *Current Directions in Psychological Science, 12*(4), 105–109.

Cialdini, R. B. (2012). The focus theory of normative conduct. In P. M. Van Lange, A. W. Kruglanski, & E. Higgins (Eds.), *Handbook of theories of social psychology*, Vol. 2 (pp. 295–312). Thousand Oaks, CA: Sage.

Cialdini, R. B., Goldstein, N. J., & Griskevicius, V. (2011). What social psychologists can learn from evaluations of environmental interventions. In M. M. Mark, S. I. Donaldson, & B. Campbell (Eds.), *Social psychology and evaluation* (pp. 267–285). New York: Guilford Press.

Clancy, K. J., Berger, P. D., & Magliozzi, T. L. (2003). The ecological fallacy: Some fundamental research misconceptions corrected. *Journal of Advertising Research, 43*(4), 370–380.

REFERENCES

Clark, C. F., Kotchen, M. J., & Moore, M. R. (2003). Internal and external influences on pro-environmental behavior: Participation in a green electricity program. *Journal of Environmental Psychology, 23*(3), 237–246.

Clark, I. (2012). Formative assessment: Assessment is for self-regulated learning. *Educational Psychology Review, 24*(2), 205–249.

Clark, R. A. & Eddy, R. P. (2017). *Warnings.* New York: Ecco Press.

Clary, E., & Tesser, A. (1983). Reactions to unexpected events: The naive scientist and interpretive activity. *Personality and Social Psychology Bulletin, 9*(4), 609–620.

Clegg, S., Kornberger, M., & Rhodes, C. (2007). Organizational ethics, decision making, undecidability. *The Sociological Review, 55*(2), 393–409.

Cleveland & Colella (2010) Criterion validity and criterion deficiency: What we measure well and what we ignore. In J. L. Farr & N. T. Tippins (Eds), *Handbook of employee selection* (pp. 551–567). New York: Routledge.

Cleveland, M., Kalamas, M., & Laroche, M. (2005). Shades of green: Linking environmental locus of control and pro-environmental behaviors. *Journal of Consumer Marketing, 22*(4), 198–212.

Clulow, V. (2005). Futures dilemmas for marketers: Can stakeholder analysis add value? *European Journal of Marketing, 39*(9–10), 978–997.

Cohen, J. E. (1995). *How many people can the earth support?* New York: Norton.

Cohen, M. D., March, J. G., & Olsen, J. P. (1972). A garbage can model of organizational choice. *Administrative Science Quarterly 17*(1), 1–25.

Cohen-Cole, J. (2005). The reflexivity of cognitive science: The scientist as model of human nature. *History of the Human Sciences, 18*(4), 107–139.

Cohn, L. D., & Westenberg, P. (2004). Intelligence and maturity: Meta-analytic evidence for the incremental and discriminant validity of Loevinger's measure of ego development. *Journal of Personality and Social Psychology, 86*(5), 760–772.

Colby, A., Lawrence, K., Gibbs, J., & Lieberman, M. (1994). A longitudinal study of moral judgment. In B. Puka (Ed.), *New research in moral development.* (pp. 1–124). New York: Garland Publishing.

Cole, D. A., Peeke, L. G., Martin, J. M., Truglio, R., & Seroczynski, A. D. (1998). A longitudinal look at the relation between depression and anxiety in children and adolescents. *Journal of Consulting and Clinical Psychology, 66*(3), 451–460.

Cole, M., & Wertsch, J. V. (1996). Beyond the individual-social antinomy in discussions of Piaget and Vygotsky. *Human Development, 39*(5), 250–256.

Collado, S., Staats, H., & Corraliza, J. A. (2013). Experiencing nature in children's summer camps: Affective, cognitive and behavioural consequences. *Journal of Environmental Psychology, 33*, 37–44.

Collin, K. (2009). Work-related identity in individual and social learning at work. *Journal of Workplace Learning, 21*(1), 23–35.

Colquitt, J. A. (2001). On the dimensionality of organizational justice: A construct validation of a measure. *Journal of Applied psychology, 86*, 386–400.

Colquitt, J. A., LePine, J. A., & Noe, R. A. (2000). Toward an integrative theory of training motivation: A meta-analytic path analysis of 20 years of research. *Journal of Applied Psychology, 85*(5), 678–707.

Cone, J. D., & Hayes, S. C. (1980). *Environmental problems and behavioral solutions.* Belmont, CA: Wadsworth.

Connelly, B. S., Lilienfeld, S. O., & Schmeelk, K. M. (2006). Integrity Tests and Morality: Associations with Ego Development, Moral Reasoning, and Psychopathic Personality. *International Journal of Selection and Assessment, 14*(1), 82–86.

Conway, J. M., Amel, E. L., & Gerwien, D. P. (2009). Teaching and learning in the social context: A meta-analysis of service learning's effects on academic, personal, social, and citizenship outcomes. *Teaching of Psychology, 36*(4), 233–245.

REFERENCES

Cook, T. D., & Campbell, D. T. (1979). *Quasi-experimentation: Design and analysis issues for field settings*. Boston, MA: Houghton-Mifflin.

Cooper, H., & Patall, E. A. (2009). The relative benefits of meta-analysis conducted with individual participant data versus aggregated data. *Psychological Methods, 14*(2), 165–176.

Coovert, M. D., & McNelis, K. (1992). Team decision making and performance: A review and proposed modeling approach employing Petri nets. In R. W. Swezey & E. Salas (Eds.), *Teams: Their training and performance* (pp. 247–280). Westport, CT: Ablex.

Cordano, M., Welcomer, S., Scherer, R. F., Pradenas, L., & Parada, V. (2011). A cross-cultural assessment of three theories of pro-environmental behavior: A comparison between business students of Chile and the United States. *Environment and Behavior, 43*(5), 634–657.

Cordova, J. V. (2001). Acceptance in behavior therapy: Understanding the process of change. *The Behavior Analyst, 24*(2), 213–226.

Cornelissen, G., Dewitte, S., Warlop, L., & Vzerbyt, V. (2007). Whatever people say I am, that's what I am: Social labeling as a social marketing tool. *International Journal of Research in Marketing, 24*(4), 278–288.

Cornelissen, J., Christensen, L., & Kinuthia, K. (2012). Corporate brands and identity: Developing stronger theory and a call for shifting the debate. *European Journal of Marketing, 46*(7-8), 1093–1102.

Corral-Verdugo, V., Bonnes, M., Tapia-Fonllem, C., Fraijo-Sing, B., Frías-Armenta, M., & Carrus, G. (2009). Correlates of pro-sustainability orientation: The affinity towards diversity. *Journal of Environmental Psychology, 29*(1), 34–43.

Corral-Verdugo, V., Frias-Amenta, M., & Gonzalez-Lomelí, D. (2003). On the relationship between antisocial and anti-environmental behaviors: An empirical study. *Population and Environment: A Journal of Interdisciplinary Studies, 24*(3), 273–286.

Corral-Verdugo, V. V., & Pinheiro, J. Q. (2006). Sustainability, future orientation and water conservation. *European Review of Applied Psychology / Revue Européenne de Psychologie Appliquée, 56*(3), 191–198.

Corrigan, P. W., & Miller, F. E. (2004). Shame, blame, and contamination: A review of the impact of mental illness stigma on family members. *Journal of Mental Health, 13*(6), 537–548.

Costa, P. T., & McCrae, R. R. (1988). Personality in adulthood: A six-year longitudinal study of self-reports and spouse ratings on the NEO Personality Inventory. *Journal of Personality and Social Psychology, 54*, 853–863.

Costa, P. T., Jr., & McCrae, R. R. (1989). *The NEO-PI/NEO-FFI manual supplement*. Odessa, FL: Psychological Assessment Resources.

Coutanche, M. N., & Thompson-Schill, S. L. (2012). Reversal without remapping: What we can (and cannot) conclude about learned associations from training-induced behavior changes. *Perspectives on Psychological Science, 7*(2), 118–134.

Cowan, P. A., Longer, J., Heavenrich, J., & Nathanson, M. (1969). Social learning and Piaget's cognitive theory of moral development. *Journal of Personality and Social Psychology, 11*(3), 261–274.

Cox, B. D. (1997). The rediscovery of the active learner in adaptive contexts: A developmental-historical analysis of transfer of training. *Educational Psychologist, 32*(1), 41–55.

Cox, L. A. (2007). Regulatory false positives: True, false, or uncertain? *Risk Analysis, 27* (5), 1083–1086.

Cox, L. R. (2012). Community resilience and decision theory challenges for catastrophic events. *Risk Analysis, 32*(11), 1919–1934.

Cozzarelli, C., Wilkinson, A. V., & Tagler, M. J. (2001). Attitudes toward the poor and attributions for poverty. *Journal of Social Issues, 57*(2), 207–227.

REFERENCES

Crain, W. (2000). *Theories of development: Concepts and applications* (4th ed.). Upper Saddle River, NJ: Prentice-Hall.

Crandall, C. S., Eshleman, A., & O'Brien, L. (2002). Social norms and the expression and suppression of prejudice: The struggle for internalization. *Journal of Personality and Social Psychology, 82*(3), 359–378.

Crano, W. D., & Prislin, R. (1995). Components of vested interest and attitude-behavior consistency. *Basic and Applied Social Psychology, 17*(1–2), 1–21.

Cristea, I. A., Montgomery, G. H., Szamoskozi, Ş., & David, D. (2013). Key constructs in "classical" and "new wave" cognitive behavioral psychotherapies: Relationships among each other and with emotional distress. *Journal of Clinical Psychology, 69*(6), 584–599.

Crompton, T., & Kasser, T. (2009). *Meeting environmental challenges: The role of human identity.* Surrey: World Wildlife Fund UK.

Cronshaw, S. F., & Lord, R. G. (1987). Effects of categorization, attribution, and encoding processes on leadership perceptions. *Journal of Applied Psychology, 72*(1), 97–106.

Cropanzano, R., & Greenberg, J. (1997). Progress in organizational justice: Tunneling through the maze. In C. L. Cooper & I. T. Robertson (Eds.), *International review of industrial and organizational psychology* (pp. 317–372). New York: Wiley.

Cross, R., Ernst, C., & Pasmore, B. (2013). A bridge too far? How boundary spanning networks drive organizational change and effectiveness. *Organizational Dynamics, 42*(2), 81–91.

Cuijpers, P., van Straten, A., Andersson, G., & van Oppen, P. (2008). Psychotherapy for depression in adults: A meta-analysis of comparative outcome studies. *Journal of Consulting and Clinical Psychology, 76*(6), 909–922.

Cullin, J. (2005). The ethics of paradox: Cybernetic and postmodern perspectives on non-direct interventions in therapy. *Australian and New Zealand Journal of Family Therapy, 26*(3), 138–146.

Cummings, L. L., Schwab, D. P., & Rosen, M. (1971). Performance and knowledge of results as determinants of goal setting. *Journal of Applied Psychology, 55*(6), 526–530.

Cummings, R., Maddux, C. D., Cladianos, A., & Richmond, A. (2010). Moral reasoning of education students: The effects of direct instruction in moral development theory and participation in moral dilemma discussion. *Teachers College Record, 112*(3), 621–644.

Cunningham, T. R., Galloway-Williams, N., & Geller, E. S. (2010). Protecting the planet and its people: How do interventions to promote environmental sustainability and occupational safety and health overlap? *Journal of Safety Research, 41* (5), 407–416.

Cyert, R. M., Dill, W. R., & March, J. G. (1958). The role of expectations in business decision making. *Administrative Science Quarterly, 3,* 307–340.

Dacin, P. A., & Brown, T. J. (2006). Corporate Branding, Identity, and Customer Response. *Journal of the Academy of Marketing Science, 34*(2), 95–98.

Dainoff, M. J., Mark, L. S., & Gardner, D. L. (1999). Scaling problems in the design of work spaces for human use. In P. A. Hancock (Ed.), *Human performance and ergonomics* (pp. 265–290). San Diego, CA: Academic Press.

Dalal, D. K., Diab, D. L., Balzer, W. K., & Doherty, M. E. (2010). The lens model: An application of JDM methodologies to IOOB practice. *Industrial and Organizational Psychology: Perspectives on Science and Practice, 3*(4), 424–428.

Darke, P. R., Chattopadhyay, A., & Ashworth, L. (2006). The importance and functional significance of affective cues in consumer choice. *Journal of Consumer Research, 33*(3), 322–328.

REFERENCES

Daselaar, S. M., Veltman, D. J., & Witter, M. P. (2004). Common pathway in the medial temporal lobe for storage and recovery of words as revealed by event-related functional MRI. *Hippocampus*, *14*(2), 163–169.

David, A., Ghinea, C., Macavei, B., & Eva, K. (2005). A search for "hot" cognitions in a clinical and a non-clinical context: Appraisal, attributions, core relational themes, irrational beliefs, and their relations to emotion. *Journal of Cognitive and Behavioral Psychotherapies*, *5*(1), 1–42.

David, B., & Turner, J. C. (1996). Studies in self-categorization and minority conversion: Is being a member of the out-group an advantage? *British Journal of Social Psychology*, *35*(1), 179–199.

Davids, A. (1955). Some personality and intellectual correlations of intolerance of ambiguity. *The Journal of Abnormal and Social Psychology*, *51*(3), 415–420.

Davies, M. (2011). Introduction to the special issue on critical thinking in higher education. *Higher Education Research & Development*, *30*(3), 255–260.

Davis, J. A., & Plas, J. M. (1983). A lens-model approach to the evaluation of consumer experience with special education service delivery. *The Journal of Special Education*, *17* (1), 89–103.

Davis, J. L., Le, B., & Coy, A. E. (2011). Building a model of commitment to the natural environment to predict ecological behavior and willingness to sacrifice. *Journal of Environmental Psychology*, *31*(3), 257–265.

Davis, M. A. (2009). Understanding the relationship between mood and creativity: A meta-analysis. *Organizational Behavior and Human Decision Processes*, *108*(1), 25–38.

Davison, R. B., Hollenbeck, J. R., Barnes, C. M., Sleesman, D. J., & Ilgen, D. R. (2012). Coordinated action in multiteam systems. *Journal of Applied Psychology*, *97*(4), 808–824.

Dawes, R. M. (1980). Social dilemmas. *Annual Review of Psychology*, *31*, 169–193.

Dawis, R. V., & Lofquist, L. H. (1976). Personality style and the process of work adjustment. *Journal of Counseling Psychology*, *23*, 55–59.

Dawson, T. L. (2002). New tools, new insights: Kohlberg's moral judgement stages revisited. *International Journal of Behavioral Development*, *26*(2), 154–166.

de Barcellos, M., Krystallis, A., de Melo Saab, M., Kügler, J., & Grunert, K. G. (2011). Investigating the gap between citizens' sustainability attitudes and food purchasing behaviour: Empirical evidence from Brazilian pork consumers. *International Journal of Consumer Studies*, *35*(4), 391–402.

de Beuckelaer, A., Lievens, F., & Swinnen, G. (2007). Measurement equivalence in the conduct of a global organizational survey across countries in six cultural regions. *Journal of Occupational and Organizational Psychology*, *80*(4), 575–600.

de Haan, E., Duckworth, A., Birch, D., & Jones, C. (2013). Executive coaching outcome research: The contribution of common factors such as relationship, personality match, and self-efficacy. *Consulting Psychology Journal: Practice and Research*, *65*(1), 40–57.

de Hoog, N., Stroebe, W., & de Wit, J. B. F. (2007). The impact of vulnerability to and severity of a health risk on processing and acceptance of fear-arousing communications: A meta-analysis. *Review of General Psychology*, *11*(3), 258–285.

de Kwaadsteniet, E. W., van Dijk, E., Wit, A., & de Cremer, D. (2006). Social dilemmas as strong versus weak situations: Social value orientations and tacit coordination under resource size uncertainty. *Journal of Experimental Social Psychology*, *42*(4), 509–516.

de Mooij, M., & Hofstede, G. (2011). Cross-cultural consumer behavior: A review of research findings. *Journal of International Consumer Marketing*, *23*(3-4), 181–192.

de Moura, R., Abrams, G., Retter, D., Gunnarsdottir, C., & Ando, K. (2009). Identification as an organizational anchor: How identification and job satisfaction combine to predict turnover intention. *European Journal Of Social Psychology*, *39*(4), 540–557.

REFERENCES

de Viggiani, N. N. (2012). Adapting needs assessment methodologies to build integrated health pathways for people in the criminal justice system. *Public Health, 126*(9), 763–769.

De Waal, F. B. M. (2002). Evolutionary psychology: The wheat and the chaff. *Current Directions in Psychological Science, 11*(6), 187–191.

De Young, R. (2013). Environmental psychology overview. In A. H. Huffman & S. R. Klein (Eds.), *Green organizations: Driving change with I-O psychology* (pp. 17–33). New York: Routledge.

de Zavala, A. G., Cichocka, A., Eidelson, R., & Jayawickreme, N. (2009). Collective narcissism and its social consequences. *Journal of Personality and Social Psychology, 97*(6), 1074–1096.

Deary, I. J., Whalley, L. J., Lemmon, H., Crawford, J. R., & Starr, J. M. (2000). The stability of individual differences in mental ability from childhood to old age: Follow-up of the 1932 Scottish Mental Survey. *Intelligence, 28*(1), 49–55.

Decety, J., Michalska, K. J., & Kinzler, C. D. (2012). The contribution of emotion and cognition to moral sensitivity: A neurodevelopmental study. *Cerebral Cortex, 22*(1), 209–220.

DeJaeghere, J. G., & Cao, Y. (2009). Developing US teachers' intercultural competence: Does professional development matter? *International Journal of Intercultural Relations, 33*(5), 437–447.

Dekker, S. (2011). *Drift into failure: From hunting broken components to understanding complex systems*. Burlington, VT: Ashgate.

Dekker, S., & Fischer, R. (2008). Cultural differences in academic motivation goals: A meta-analysis across 13 societies. *The Journal of Educational Research, 102*(2), 99–110.

Dekker, S. A., Hancock, P. A., & Wilkin, P. (2013). Ergonomics and sustainability: Towards an embrace of complexity and emergence. *Ergonomics, 56*(3), 357–364.

DeLeon, I. G., Bullock, C. E., & Catania, A. (2013). Arranging reinforcement contingencies in applied settings: Fundamentals and implications of recent basic and applied research. In G. J. Madden, W. V. Dube, T. D. Heckenberg, G. P. Hanley, & K. A. Lattal (Eds.), *APA handbook of behavior analysis* (Vol. 2) (pp. 47–75). Washington, DC: American Psychological Association.

Delicado, A. (2012). Environmental education technologies in a social void: The case of "Greendrive". *Environmental Education Research, 18*(6), 831–843.

Delton, A. W., Nemirow, J., Robertson, T. E., Cimino, A., & Cosmides, L. (2013). Merely opting out of a public good is moralized: An error management approach to cooperation. *Journal of Personality and Social Psychology, 105*, 621–638.

DeRue, D., & Ashford, S. J. (2010). Who will lead and who will follow? A social process of leadership identity construction in organizations. *The Academy Of Management Review, 35*(4), 627–647.

DeRue, D. S., Hollenbeck, J., Ilgen, D., & Feltz, D. (2010). Efficacy dispersion in teams: Moving beyond agreement and aggregation. *Personnel Psychology, 63*(1), 1–40.

DeShon, R. P. (2013). Inferential meta-themes in organizational science research: Causal inference, system dynamics, and computational models. In N. W. Schmitt, S. Highhouse, & I. B. Weiner (Eds.), *Handbook of psychology: Industrial and organizational psychology, Vol. 12*, 2nd ed. (pp. 14–42). Hoboken, NJ: John Wiley & Sons Inc.

Desmond, R., & Carveth, R. (2007). The effects of advertising on children and adolescents: A meta-analysis. In R. W. Preiss, B. Gayle, N. Burrell, M. Allen, & J. Bryant (Eds.), *Mass media effects research: Advances through meta-analysis* (pp. 169–179). Mahwah, NJ: Lawrence Erlbaum Associates Publishers.

Devereux, E. C. (1972). Authority and moral development among German and American children: A cross-national pilot experiment. *Journal of Comparative Family Studies, 3* (1), 99–124.

REFERENCES

Devine, D. J., Clayton, L. D., Dunford, B. B., Seying, R., & Pryce, J. (2001). Jury decision making: 45 years of empirical research on deliberating groups. *Psychology, Public Policy, and Law, 7*(3), 622–727.

Devine-Wright, P. (2011). Place attachment and public acceptance of renewable energy: A tidal energy case study. *Journal of Environmental Psychology, 31*(4), 336–343.

Devine-Wright, P., & Howes, Y. (2010). Disruption to place attachment and the protection of restorative environments: A wind energy case study. *Journal of Environmental Psychology, 30*(3), 271–280.

Devlin, B. B., Daniels, M., & Roeder, K. (1997). The heritability of IQ. *Nature, 388* (6641), 468–471.

DeYoung, C. G., Peterson, J. B., & Higgins, D. M. (2002). Higher-order factors of the Big Five predict conformity: Are there neuroses of health? *Personality and Individual Differences, 33*(4), 533–552.

Diamond, B., Morris, R. G., & Barnes, J. C. (2012). Individual and group IQ predict inmate violence. *Intelligence, 40*(2), 115–122.

Diaz-Rainey, I., & Ashton, J. K. (2011). Profiling potential green electricity tariff adopters: Green consumerism as an environmental policy tool? *Business Strategy and the Environment, 20*(7), 456–470.

Dickerson, C. A., Thibodeau, R., Aronson, E., & Miller, D. (1992). Using cognitive dissonance to encourage water conservation. *Journal of Applied Social Psychology, 22*(11), 841–854.

Dickinson, J. L., Crain, R., Yalowitz, S., & Cherry, T. M. (2013). How framing climate change influences citizen scientists' intentions to do something about it. *The Journal of Environmental Education, 44*(3), 145–158.

Dierdorff, E. C., Norton, J. J., Gregory, C. M., Rivkin, D., & Lewis, P. M. (2013). O*Net's national perspective on the greening of the world of work. In A. H. Huffman & S. R. Klein (Eds.), *Green organizations: Driving change with I-O psychology* (pp. 348–378). New York: Routledge.

Dietrich, B. (2010). Environmental toxicants. In K. Yeates, M. Ris, H. Taylor, & B. F. Pennington (Eds.), *Pediatric neuropsychology: Research, theory, and practice* (2nd ed.) (pp. 211–264). New York: Guilford Press.

Digman, J. M. (1997). Higher-order factors of the Big Five. *Journal of Personality and Social Psychology, 73*(6), 1246–1256.

Dilling, L., & Farhar, B. (2007). Making it easy: Establishing energy efficiency and renewable energy as routine best practice. In S. C. Moser & L. Dilling (Eds.), *Creating a climate for change: Communicating climate change and facilitating social change* (pp. 359–382). New York: Cambridge University Press.

Dillon, L., & Beechler, M. (2010). Marital satisfaction and the impact of children in collectivist cultures: A meta-analysis. *Journal of Evolutionary Psychology, 8*(1), 7–22.

Dimitrova, R., Chasiotis, A., Bender, M., & van de Vijver, F. (2013). Collective identity and wellbeing of Roma minority adolescents in Bulgaria. *International Journal of Psychology, 48*(4), 502–513.

Do Paço, A., Alves, H., Shiel, C., & Filho, W. (2013). Development of a green consumer behaviour model. *International Journal of Consumer Studies, 37*(4), 414–421.

Do Paço, A., & Reis, R. (2012). Factors affecting skepticism toward green advertising. *Journal of Advertising, 41*(4), 147–155.

Dochy, F., Segers, M., Van den Bossche, P., & Gijbels, D. (2003). Effects of problem-based learning: A meta-analysis. *Learning and Instruction, 13*(5), 533–568.

Doherty, T. J., & Clayton, S. (2011). The psychological impacts of global climate change. *American Psychologist, 66*, 265–276.

REFERENCES

Dono, J., Webb, J., & Richardson, B. (2010). The relationship between environmental activism, pro-environmental behaviour and social identity. *Journal of Environmental Psychology, 30*(2), 178–186.

Donoho, C. L., & Swenson, M. J. (1996). Top-down versus bottom-up sales tactics effects on the presentation of a product line. *Journal of Business Research, 37*(1), 51–61.

Donovan, J. J. (2002). Work motivation. In N. Anderson, D. S. Ones, H. Sinangil, & C. Viswesvaran (Eds.), *Handbook of industrial, work and organizational psychology, Volume 2: Organizational psychology* (pp. 53–76). Thousand Oaks, CA: Sage Publications, Inc.

Donovan, J. J., & Radosevich, D. J. (1998). The moderating role of goal commitment on the goal difficulty–performance relationship: A meta-analytic review and critical reanalysis. *Journal of Applied Psychology, 83*(2), 308–315.

Dore, F. Y., & Dumas, C. (1987). Psychology of animal cognition: Piagetian studies. *Psychological Bulletin, 102*, 219–233.

Dowell, B. E. (2002). Succession planning. In J. W. Hedge & E. D. Pulakos (Eds.), *Implementing organizational interventions: Steps, processes, and best practices* (pp. 78–109). San Francisco, CA: Jossey-Bass.

Downing, J. W., Judd, C. M., & Brauer, M. (1992). Effects of repeated expressions on attitude extremity. *Journal of Personality and Social Psychology, 63*(1), 17–29.

DuBois, C. L. Z., Astakhova, M. N., & DuBois, D. A. (2013). Motivating behavior change to support organizational environmental sustainability. In A. H. Huffman & S. R. Klein (Eds.), *Green organizations: Driving change with I-O psychology* (pp. 186–207). New York: Routledge.

Duckworth, A. L., & Kern, M. L. (2011). A meta-analysis of the convergent validity of self-control measures. *Journal of Research in Personality, 45*(3), 259–268.

Duckworth, A., Quinn, P. D., Lynam, D. R., Loeber, R., & Stouthamer-Loeber, M. (2011). Role of test motivation in intelligence testing. *PNAS Proceedings of the National Academy of Sciences of the United States of America, 108*(19), 7716–7720.

Dudek, S. Z., & Dyer, G. B. (1972). A longitudinal study of Piaget's developmental stages and the concept of regression: I. *Journal of Personality Assessment, 36*(4), 380–389.

Duffy, S., & Verges, M. (2009). It matters a hole lot: Perceptual affordances of waste containers influence recycling compliance. *Environment and Behavior, 41*(5), 741–749.

Dul, J., Bruder, R., Buckle, P., Carayon, P., Falzon, P., Marras, W. S., … van der Doelen, B. (2012). A strategy for human factors/ergonomics: Developing the discipline and profession. *Ergonomics, 55*(4), 377–395.

Dunbar, R. I. M. (2003). The social brain: Mind, language, and society in evolutionary perspective. *Annual Review of Psychology, 32*, 163–181.

Dunlap, R. E. (2008). The new environmental paradigm scale: From marginality to worldwide use. *The Journal of Environmental Education, 40*(1), 3–18.

Dunlap, R. E., & Van Liere, K. D. (1978). The "new environmental paradigm": A proposed measuring instrument and preliminary results. *The Journal of Environmental Education, 9*(4), 10–19.

Dunn, D. S., Halonen, J. S., & Smith, R. A. (2008). *Teaching critical thinking in psychology: A handbook of best practices.* Hoboken, NJ: Wiley-Blackwell.

Dunsmuir, S., & Kratochwill, T. R. (2013). From research to policy and practice: Perspectives from the UK and the US on psychologists as agents of change. *Educational and Child Psychology, 30*(3), 60–71.

Durlak, J. A., Weissberg, R. P., Dymnicki, A. B., Taylor, R. D., & Schellinger, K. B. (2011). The impact of enhancing students' social and emotional learning: A meta-analysis of school-based universal interventions. *Child Development, 82*(1), 405–432.

Durso, F. T., & Drews, F. A. (2010). Health care, aviation, and ecosystems: A socio-natural systems perspective. *Current Directions in Psychological Science, 19*(2), 71–75.

REFERENCES

Duus, R. (2010). The spiritual greening of religion. *Psyccritiques*, *55*(42), doi:10.1037/a0021211

Duvarci, S., Nader, K., & LeDoux, J. E. (2008). De novo mRNA synthesis is required for both consolidation and reconsolidation of fear memories in the amygdala. *Learning & Memory*, *15*(10), 747–755.

Dweck, C. S. (2012). Implicit theories. In P. M. Van Lange, A. W. Kruglanski, & E. Higgins (Eds.), *Handbook of theories of social psychology* (Vol. 2) (pp. 43–61). Thousand Oaks, CA: Sage Publications Ltd.

Dweck, C. S., & Leggett, E. L. (1988). A social-cognitive approach to motivation and personality. *Psychological Review*, *95*, 256–273.

Dziengel, L. (2010). Advocacy coalitions and punctuated equilibrium in the same-sex marriage debate: Learning from pro-LGBT policy changes in Minneapolis and Minnesota. *Journal of Gay & Lesbian Social Services: The Quarterly Journal of Community & Clinical Practice*, *22*(1–2), 165–182.

Eagly, A. H., & Chaiken, S. (2007). The advantages of an inclusive definition of attitude. *Social Cognition*, *25*(5), 582–602.

Eberth, J., & Sedlmeier, P. (2012). The effects of mindfulness meditation: A meta-analysis. *Mindfulness*, *3*(3), 174–189.

Eccles, J. S., & Wigfield, A. (2002). Motivational beliefs, values, and goals. *Annual Review of Psychology*, *53*(1), 109–132.

Edens, J. F., Buffington-Vollum, J. K., Keilen, A., Roskamp, P., & Anthony, C. (2005). Predictions of future dangerousness in capital murder trials: Is it time to "disinvent the wheel?" *Law and Human Behavior*, *29*(1), 55–86.

Edwards, J. A., & Weary, G. (1998). Antecedents of causal uncertainty and perceived control: A prospective study. *European Journal of Personality*, *12*(2), 135–148.

Edwards, J. A., Weary, G., & Reich, D. A. (1998). Causal uncertainty: Factor structure and relations to the Big Five personality factors. *Personality and Social Psychology Bulletin*, *24*(5), 451–462.

Edwards, J. A., Wichman, A. L., & Weary, G. (2009). Casual uncertainty as a chronically accessible construct. *European Journal of Social Psychology*, *39*(5), 694–706.

Ehrenfeld, J. R. (2008). *Sustainability by design: A subversive strategy for transforming our consumer culture*. New Haven, CT: Yale University Press.

Ehrlich, P. (2002). Human natures, nature conservation, and environmental ethics. *Bio-Science 52*, 31–43.

Eisenberg, N., Duckworth, A. L., Spinrad, T. L., & Valiente, C. (2012). Conscientiousness: Origins in childhood? *Developmental Psychology*, *50*, 1331–1349.

Eisenberg, N., Hofer, C., Sulik, M. J., & Liew, J. (2013). The Development of prosocial moral reasoning and a prosocial orientation in young adulthood: Concurrent and longitudinal correlates. *Developmental Psychology*, *50*, 58–70.

Eisend, M. (2006). Two-sided advertising: A meta-analysis. *International Journal of Research in Marketing*, *23*(2), 187–198.

Eisend, M., & Stokburger-Sauer, N. E. (2013). Brand personality: A meta-analytic review of antecedents and consequences. *Marketing Letters*, doi:10.1007/s11002-013-9232-7

Eiser, J. R., Reicher, S. D., & Podpadec, T. J. (1994). Awareness of bad news, environmental attitudes, and subjective estimates of coastal pollution. *Risk Analysis*, *14*(6), 945–948.

Ekman, P. (1992). An argument for basic emotions. *Cognition and Emotion*, *6*(3–4), 169–200.

Ekman, P. (1993). Facial expression and emotion. *American Psychologist*, *48*, 384–392.

Ekman, P. (1994). Strong evidence for universals in facial expressions: A reply to Russell's mistaken critique. *Psychological Bulletin*, *115*, 268–287.

REFERENCES

Elgaaied, L. (2012). Exploring the role of anticipated guilt on pro-environmental behavior: A suggested typology of residents in France based on their recycling patterns. *Journal of Consumer Marketing, 29*(5), 369–377.

Elkington, J. (1998). *Cannibals with forks: The triple bottom line of 21st century business.* Stony Creek, CT: New Society Publishers.

Elliot, A. J., Eder, A. B., & Harmon-Jones, E. (2013). Approach–avoidance motivation and emotion: Convergence and divergence. *Emotion Review, 5*(3), 308–311.

Elms, A. C., & Milgram, S. (1966). Personality characteristics associated with obedience and defiance toward authoritative command. *Journal of Experimental Research in Personality, 1*(4), 282–289.

Endicott, L., Bock, T., & Narvaez, D. (2003). Moral reasoning, intercultural development, and multicultural experiences: Relations and cognitive underpinnings. *International Journal of Intercultural Relations, 27*(4), 403–419.

Environmental Protection Agency. (n.d.). www.epa.gov.

Eom, K., Kim, H. S., Sherman, D. K., & Ishii, K. (2016). Cultural variability in the link between environmental concern and support for environmental action. *Psychological Science, 27*(10), 1331–1339.

Epstein, M. J., & Widener, S. K. (2011). Facilitating sustainable development decisions: Measuring stakeholder reactions. *Business Strategy and the Environment, 20*(2), 107–123.

Epstein, S. (2010). Demystifying intuition: What it is, what it does, and how it does it. *Psychological Inquiry, 21*(4), 295–312.

Erdogan, M., & Tuncer, G. (2009). Evaluation of a course: "Education and Awareness for Sustainability". *International Journal of Environmental and Science Education, 4*(2), 133–146.

Erdogan, M., Uşak, M., & Bahar, M. (2013). A review of research on environmental education in non-traditional settings in Turkey, 2000 and 2011. *International Journal of Environmental and Science Education, 8*(1), 37–57.

Erez, M. (1977). Feedback: A necessary condition for the goal setting-performance relationship. *Journal of Applied Psychology, 62*(5), 624–627.

Erez, M., & Arad, R. (1986). Participative goal-setting: Social, motivational, and cognitive factors. *Journal of Applied Psychology, 71*(4), 591–597.

Erez, M., & Earley, P. C. (1987). Comparative analysis of goal-setting strategies across cultures. *Journal of Applied Psychology, 72*(4), 658–665.

Erikson, E. H. (1968). *Identity: Youth and crisis.* New York: Norton.

Eriksson, L., Garvill, J., & Nordlund, A. M. (2006). Acceptability of travel demand management measures: The importance of problem awareness, personal norm, freedom, and fairness. *Journal of Environmental Psychology, 26*(1), 15–26.

Estes, W. K. (1960). Learning theory and the new "mental chemistry" *Psychological Review, 67*(4), 207–223.

Etzioni, A. (1998). Voluntary simplicity: Characterization, select psychological implications and societal consequences. *Journal of Economic Psychology, 19*(5), 619–643.

Etzioni, A. (2004). The post affluent society. *Review of Social Economy, 62*(3), 407–420.

Eubanks, D. L., Murphy, S. T., & Mumford, M. D. (2010). Intuition as an influence on creative problem-solving: The effects of intuition, positive affect, and training. *Creativity Research Journal, 22*(2), 170–184.

Evans, A. M., Athenstaedt, U., & Krueger, J. I. (2013). The development of trust and altruism during childhood. *Journal of Economic Psychology, 36*, 82–95.

Evans, G. W., & Stecker, R. (2004). Motivational consequences of environmental stress. *Journal of Environmental Psychology, 24*(2), 143–165.

Ewing, G. (2001). Altruistic, egoistic, and normative effects on curbside recycling. *Environment and Behavior, 33*(6), 733–764.

REFERENCES

Eysenck, H. J. (1986). Inspection time and intelligence: A historical introduction. *Personality and Individual Differences, 7*(5), 603–607.

Ezekiel, R. S. (1968). The personal future and Peace Corps competence. *Journal of Personality and Social Psychology, 8*(2), 1–26.

Fabiano, G. A., Pelham, W. R., Coles, E. K., Gnagy, E. M., Chronis-Tuscano, A., & O'Connor, B. C. (2009). A meta-analysis of behavioral treatments for attention-deficit/hyperactivity disorder. *Clinical Psychology Review, 29*(2), 129–140.

Fagerstrøm, A., & Arntzen, E. (2013). On motivating operations at the point of online purchase setting. *The Psychological Record, 63*(2), 333–344.

Fang, Y.-M., & Sun, M.-S. (2016). Applying eco-visualisations of different interface formats to evoke sustainable behaviours towards household water saving. *Behaviour & Information Technology, 35*(9), 748–757.

Farmer, A., Breazeale, M., Stevens, J. L., & Waites, S. F. (2017). Eat green, get lean: Promoting sustainability reduces consumption. *Journal of Public Policy & Marketing, 36* (2), 299–312.

Farr, J. L., & Tippins, N. T. (2010). Handbook of employee selection: An introduction and overview. In J. L. Farr & N. T. Tippins (Eds.), *Handbook of employee selection* (pp. 1–6). New York: Routledge/Taylor & Francis Group.

Fearon, R., Bakermans-Kranenburg, M. J., van Ijzendoorn, M. H., Lapsley, A., & Roisman, G. I. (2010). The significance of insecure attachment and disorganization in the development of children s externalizing behavior: A meta-analytic study. *Child Development, 81*(2), 435–456.

FeldmanHall, O., Dalgleish, T., & Mobbs, D. (2013). Alexithymia decreases altruism in real social decisions. *Cortex: A Journal Devoted to the Study of the Nervous System and Behavior, 49*(3), 899–904.

Fellner, G., Güth, W., & Maciejovsky, B. (2009). Satisficing in financial decision making: A theoretical and experimental approach to bounded rationality. *Journal of Mathematical Psychology, 53*(1), 26–33.

Feng, L. (2012). Teacher and student responses to interdisciplinary aspects of sustainability education: What do we really know? *Environmental Education Research, 18*(1), 31–43.

Feng, L., & Newton, D. (2012). Some implications for moral education of the Confucian principle of harmony: Learning from sustainability education practice in China. *Journal of Moral Education, 41*(3), 341–351.

Ferris, D. L., Rosen, C. R., Johnson, R. E., Brown, D. J., Risavy, S. D., & Heller, D. (2011). Approach or avoidance (or both?): Integrating core self-evaluations within an approach/avoidance framework. *Personnel Psychology, 64*(1), 137–161.

Festinger, L. (1957). *A theory of cognitive dissonance.* Evanston, IL: Row Peterson.

Festinger, L., & Carlsmith, J. M. (1959). Cognitive consequences of forced compliance. *Journal of Abnormal and Social Psychology, 58,* 203–210.

Festinger, L., Riecken, H. W., & Schachter, S. (1964). *When prophecy fails: A social and psychological study of a modern group that predicted the destruction of the world.* Oxford: Harper Torchbooks.

Feygina, I., Goldsmith, R. E., & Jost, J. T. (2010). System justification and the disruption of environmental goal-setting: A self-regulatory perspective. In R. R. Hassin, K. N. Ochsner, & Y. Trope (Eds.), *Self control in society, mind, and brain* (pp. 490–505). New York: Oxford University Press.

Feygina, I., Jost, J. T., & Goldsmith, R. E. (2010). System justification, the denial of global warming, and the possibility of "system-sanctioned change". *Personality and Social Psychology Bulletin, 36*(3), 326–338.

Fielding, K. S., & Head, B. W. (2012). Determinants of young Australians' environmental actions: The role of responsibility attributions, locus of control, knowledge and attitudes. *Environmental Education Research, 18*(2), 171–186.

348

REFERENCES

Filo, K., Chen, N., King, C., & Funk, D. C. (2013). Sport tourists' involvement with a destination: A stage-based examination. *Journal of Hospitality & Tourism Research, 37* (1), 100–124.

Finlay, K., Marmurek, H. C., & Morton, R. (2005). Priming effects in explicit and implicit memory for textual advertisements. *Applied Psychology: An International Review, 54*(4), 442–455.

Finlay-Robinson, D. (2009). What's in it for me? The fundamental importance of stakeholder evaluation. *Journal of Management Development, 28*(4), 380–388.

Finney, P. D., & Helm, B. (1982). The actor–Observer relationship: The effect of actors' and observers' responsibility and emotion attributions. *The Journal of Social Psychology, 117*(2), 219–225.

Fischer, R., & Poortinga, Y. H. (2012). Are cultural values the same as the values of individuals? An examination of similarities in personal, social and cultural value structures. *International Journal of Cross Cultural Management, 12*(2), 157–170.

Fischer, U., Moeller, K., Cress, U., & Nuerk, H. (2013). Interventions supporting children's mathematics school success: A meta-analytic review. *European Psychologist, 18* (2), 89–113.

Fischhoff, B. (1975). Hindsight ≠ foresight: The effect of outcome knowledge on judgment under uncertainty. *Journal of Experimental Psychology. Human Perception and Performance, 1*, 288–299.

Fisher, C. D. (2002). Antecedents and consequences of real-time affective reactions at work. *Motivation and Emotion, 26*(1), 3–30.

Fisher, R. J. (1993). Developing the field of interactive conflict resolution: Issues in training, funding, and institutionalization. *Political Psychology, 14*(1), 123–138.

Fisher, S. F. (1985). Identity of two: The phenomenology of shame in borderline development and treatment. *Psychotherapy: Theory, Research, Practice, Training, 22*(1), 101–109.

Fiske, S. T. (2002). What we know about bias and intergroup conflict, the problem of the century. *Current Directions in Psychological Science, 11*(4), 123–128.

Fiske, S. T. (2004). Intent and ordinary bias: Unintended thought and social motivation create casual prejudice. *Social Justice Research, 17*(2), 117–127.

Fiske, S. T. (2012). Managing ambivalent prejudices: Smart-but-cold and warm-but-dumb stereotypes. *Annals of the American Academy of Political and Social Science, 639*(1), 33–48.

Flemming, T. M., Beran, M. J., Thompson, R. K. R., Kleider, H. M., & Washburn, D. A. (2008). What meaning means for same and different: Analogical reasoning in humans (homo sapiens), chimpanzees (pan troglodytes), and rhesus monkeys (macaca mulatta). *Journal of Comparative Psychology, 122*(2), 176–185.

Flückiger, C., Del Re, A. C., Wampold, B. E., Symonds, D., & Horvath, A. O. (2012). How central is the alliance in psychotherapy? A multilevel longitudinal meta-analysis. *Journal of Counseling Psychology, 59*(1), 10–17.

Fodor, E. M., Wick, D. P., Hartsen, K. M., & Preve, R. M. (2008). Right-wing authoritarianism in relation to proposed judicial action, electromyographic response, and affective attitudes toward a schizophrenic mother. *Journal of Applied Social Psychology, 38*(1), 215–233.

Fontes, L. (2008). *Interviewing clients across cultures: A practitioner's guide.* New York: Guilford Press.

Ford, J. (1997). Transfer of training: The criterion problem. *Applied Psychology: An International Review, 46*(4), 349–354.

Ford, J., Smith, E. M., Weissbein, D. A., Gully, S. M., & Salas, E. (1998). Relationships of goal orientation, metacognitive activity, and practice strategies with learning outcomes and transfer. *Journal of Applied Psychology, 83*(2), 218–233.

REFERENCES

Forgas, J. P. (1995). Mood and judgment: The affect infusion model (AIM). *Psychological Bulletin, 117*(1), 39–66.

Forsyth, D. R., O'Boyle, E. R., & McDaniel, M. A. (2008). East meets West: A meta-analytic investigation of cultural variations in idealism and relativism. *Journal of Business Ethics, 83*(4), 813–833.

Fox, E., & Riconscente, M. (2008). Metacognition and self-regulation in James, Piaget, and Vygotsky. *Educational Psychology Review, 20*(4), 373–389.

Fox, S., & Spector, P. E. (2000). Relations of emotional intelligence, practical intelligence, general intelligence, and trait affectivity with interview outcomes: It's not all just "G". *Journal of Organizational Behavior, 21,* 203–220.

Frank, N. (2013). The president's pleasant surprise: How LGBT advocates ended don't ask, don't tell. *Journal of Homosexuality, 60*(2–3), 159–213.

Franklin, M. B. (2000). Considerations for a psychology of experience: Heinz Werner's contribution. *Journal of Adult Development, 7*(1), 31–39.

Frewen, P. A., Dozois, D. J. A., Neufeld, R. W. J., & Lanius, R. A. (2008). Meta-analysis of alexithymia in posttraumatic stress disorder. *Journal of Traumatic Stress, 21* (2), 243–246.

Fried, M. (2000). Continuities and discontinuities of place. *Journal of Environmental Psychology, 20,* 193–205.

Friedrichsmeier, T., Matthies, E., & Klöckner, C. A. (2013). Explaining stability in travel mode choice: An empirical comparison of two concepts of habit. *Transportation Research Part F: Traffic Psychology and Behaviour, 16,* 1–13.

Frijda, N. H. (1953). The understanding of facial expression of emotion. *Acta Psychologica, 9,* 294–362.

Frijda, N. H., Kuipers, P., & Ter Schure, E. (1989). Relations among emotion, appraisal, and emotional action readiness. *Journal of Personality and Social Psychology, 57,* 212–228.

Fritsche, I., Jonas, E., Kayser, D., & Koranyi, N. (2010). Existential threat and compliance with pro-environmental norms. *Journal of Environmental Psychology, 30*(1), 67–79.

Frone, M. R. (1990). Intolerance of ambiguity as a moderator of the occupational role stress-strain relationship: A meta-analysis. *Journal of Organizational Behavior, 11*(4), 309–320.

Fujiwara, T. (2007). The role of altruistic behavior in generalized anxiety disorder and major depression among adults in the United States. *Journal of Affective Disorders, 101* (1–3), 219–225.

Funder, D. C. (1989). Accuracy in personality judgment and the dancing bear. In D. Buss & N. Cantor (Eds.), *Personality research for the 1990s* (pp. 210–223). New York: Springer-Verlag.

Gabenesch, H., & Hunt, L. L. (1971). The relative accuracy of interpersonal perception of high and low authoritarians. *Journal of Experimental Research in Personality, 5,* 43–48.

Gabriel, R. M., Leichtling, G. J., Bolan, M., & Becker, L. G. (2013). Using community surveys to inform the planning and implementation of environmental change strategies: Participatory research in 12 Washington communities. *American Journal of Community Psychology, 51*(1–2), 243–253.

Gadenne, D. L., Kennedy, J., & McKeiver, C. (2009). An empirical study of environmental awareness and practices in SMEs. *Journal of Business Ethics, 84*(1), 45–63.

Gaeta, M., Teruel, M., & Orejudo, S. (2012). Motivational, volitional and metacognitive aspects of self regulated learning. *Electronic Journal of Research in Educational Psychology, 10*(1), 73–94.

Gagné, R. M. (1962). Military training and principles of learning. *American Psychologist, 17*(2), 83–91.

REFERENCES

Gagné, R. M. (1984). Learning outcomes and their effects: Useful categories of human performance. *American Psychologist, 39*(4), 377–385.

Gagné, R. M., & Medsker, K. L. (1996). *The conditions of learning.* Fort Worth, TX: Harcourt-Brace.

Galante, J., Iribarren, S. J., & Pearce, P. F. (2013). Effects of mindfulness-based cognitive therapy on mental disorders: A systematic review and meta-analysis of randomised controlled trials. *Journal of Research in Nursing, 18*(2), 133–155.

Galinsky, A. D., Maddux, W. W., Gilin, D., & White, J. B. (2008). Why it pays to get inside the head of your opponent: The differential effects of perspective taking and empathy in negotiations. *Psychological Science, 19*(4), 378–384.

Galinsky, A. D., Magee, J. C., Gruenfeld, D., Whitson, J. A., & Liljenquist, K. A. (2008). Power reduces the press of the situation: Implications for creativity, conformity, and dissonance. *Journal of Personality and Social Psychology, 95*(6), 1450–1466.

Galinsky, A. D., & Moskowitz, G. B. (2000). Perspective-taking: Decreasing stereotype expression, stereotype accessibility, and in-group favoritism. *Journal of Personality and Social Psychology, 78*(4), 708–724.

Gallagher, C. A., Joseph, L. E., & Park, M. V. (2002). Implementing organizational change. In J. W. Hedge & E. D. Pulakos (Eds.), *Implementing organizational interventions: Steps, processes, and best practices* (pp. 12–42). San Francisco, CA: Jossey-Bass.

Ganzach, Y. (1994). Theory and configurality in expert and layperson judgment. *Journal of Applied Psychology, 79*(3), 439–448.

García-Mira, R., González, C., & Rivas, X. (2008). The social perception of the 2006 forest fires in the northwest region of Spain: Information, trust, education and participation. In K. H. Kiefer (Ed.), *Applied psychology research trends* (pp. 183–210). Hauppauge, NY: Nova Science Publishers.

Garland, H. (1984). Relation of effort-performance expectancy to performance in goal-setting experiments. *Journal of Applied Psychology, 69*(1), 79–84.

Garland, H. (1985). A cognitive mediation theory of task goals and human performance. *Motivation and Emotion, 9*(4), 345–367.

Garland, H., & Adkinson, J. H. (1987). Standards, persuasion, and performance: A test of cognitive mediation theory. *Group & Organization Studies, 12*(2), 208–220.

Gaudreau, P., Carraro, N., & Miranda, D. (2012). From goal motivation to goal progress: The mediating role of coping in the self-concordance model. *Anxiety, Stress & Coping: An International Journal, 25*(5), 507–528.

Gawronski, B. (2012). Back to the future of dissonance theory: Cognitive consistency as a core motive. *Social Cognition, 30*(6), 652–668.

Geary, D. C. (2005). General intelligence in modern society. In *The origin of mind: Evolution of brain, cognition, and general intelligence* (pp. 307–337). Washington, DC: American Psychological Association.

Gegenfurtner, A., & Vauras, M. (2012). Age-related differences in the relation between motivation to learn and transfer of training in adult continuing education. *Contemporary Educational Psychology, 37*(1), 33–46.

Gehrie, M. J. (1999). On boundaries and intimacy in psychoanalysis. In A. Goldberg (Ed.), *Pluralism in self psychology: Progress in self psychology* (Vol. 15) (pp. 83–94). Mahwah, NJ: Analytic Press.

Gelbrich, K., & Roschk, H. (2011). Do complainants appreciate overcompensation? A meta-analysis on the effect of simple compensation vs. overcompensation on post-complaint satisfaction. *Marketing Letters, 22*(1), 31–47.

Gelfand, M. J. (2012). Culture's constraints: International differences in the strength of social norms. *Current Directions in Psychological Science, 21*(6), 420–424.

REFERENCES

Geller, E. (1992). Solving environmental problems: A behavior change perspective. In S. Staub & P. Green (Eds.), *Psychology and social responsibility: Facing global challenges* (pp. 248–268). New York: New York University Press.

Geller, E. (1995). Integrating behaviorism and humanism for environmental protection. *Journal of Social Issues, 51*(4), 179–195.

Geller, E. S. (2002). The challenge of increasing proenvironmental behavior. In R. B. Bechtel & A. Churchman (Eds.), *Handbook of environmental psychology* (pp. 525–540). New York: Wiley.

Gersick, C. J. (1991). Revolutionary change theories: A multilevel exploration of the punctuated equilibrium paradigm. *The Academy of Management Review, 16*(1), 10–36.

Gibson, A., Dodds, R., Joppe, M., & Jamieson, B. (2003). Ecotourism in the city? Toronto's green tourism association. *International Journal of Contemporary Hospitality Management, 15*(6), 324–327.

Gifford, R. (2007a). *Environmental psychology: Principles and practice* (4th ed.). Colville, WA: Optimal.

Gifford, R. (2007b). Environmental psychology and sustainable development: Expansion, maturation, and challenges. *Journal of Social Issues, 63*, 199–212.

Gifford, R. (2008). Psychology's essential role in alleviating the impacts of climate change. *Canadian Psychology, 49*, 273–280.

Gifford, R. (2011). The dragons of inaction: Psychological barriers that limit climate change mitigation and adaptation. *American Psychologist, 66* (4), Special issue: Psychology and Global Climate Change, 290–302.

Gifford, R., Ng, C. F., & Wilkinson, M. (1985). Nonverbal cues in the employment interview: Links between applicant qualities and interviewer judgments. *Journal of Applied Psychology, 70*(4), 729–736.

Gifford, R., Scannell, L., Kormos, C., Smolova, L., Biel, A., Boncu, S., … Uzzell, D., (2009). Temporal pessimism and spatial optimism in environmental assessments: An 18-nation study. *Journal of Environmental Psychology, 29*(1), 1–12.

Gigerenzer, G. (2011). Moral satisficing: Rethinking moral behavior as bounded rationality. In G. Gigerenzer, R. Hertwig, & T. Pachur (Eds.), *Heuristics: The foundations of adaptive behavior* (pp. 203–221). New York: Oxford University Press.

Gijbels, D., Dochy, F., Van den Bossche, P., & Segers, M. (2005). Effects of problem-based learning: A meta-analysis from the angle of assessment. *Review of Educational Research, 75*(1), 27–61.

Gilbert, P. (2010). *Compassion focused therapy: Distinctive features.* New York: Routledge/Taylor & Francis Group.

Gilin, D., Maddux, W. W., Carpenter, J., & Galinsky, A. D. (2013). When to use your head and when to use your heart: The differential value of perspective-taking versus empathy in competitive interactions. *Personality and Social Psychology Bulletin, 39*(1), 3–16.

Gillespie, S. M., Mitchell, I. J., Fisher, D., & Beech, A. R. (2012). Treating disturbed emotional regulation in sexual offenders: The potential applications of mindful self-regulation and controlled breathing techniques. *Aggression and Violent Behavior, 17* (4), 333–343.

Gilligan, C. (1982). *In a different voice.* Cambridge: Cambridge University Press.

Gilliland, S. W., & Cherry, B. (2000). Managing "customers" of the selection process. In J. F. Kehoe (Ed.), *Managing selection in changing organizations* (p. 158–196). San Francisco, CA: Jossey-Bass.

Gingerich, W. J., Kim, J. S., Stams, G. M., & Macdonald, A. J. (2012). Solution-focused brief therapy outcome research. In C. Franklin, T. S. Trepper, W. J. Gingerich, &

REFERENCES

E. E. McCollum (Eds.), *Solution-focused brief therapy: A handbook of evidence-based practice* (pp. 95–111). New York: Oxford University Press.

Ginns, P., Martin, A. J., & Marsh, H. W. (2013). Designing instructional text in a conversational style: A meta-analysis. *Educational Psychology Review*, doi:10.1007/s10648-013-9228-0

Giordano, P. J. (1997). Establishing rapport and developing interviewing skills. In J. R. Matthews & C. Walker (Eds.), *Basic skills and professional issues in clinical psychology* (pp. 59–82). Needham Heights, MA: Allyn & Bacon.

Gittleman, J. L., Gardner, P. C., Haile, E., Sampson, J. M., Cigularov, K. P., Ermann, E. D., ... Chen, P. Y. (2010). Citycenter and cosmopolitan construction projects, Las Vegas, Nevada: Lessons learned from the use of multiple sources and mixed methods in a safety needs assessment. *Journal of Safety Research, 41*(3), 263–281.

Giuliani, M., & Scopelliti, M. (2009). Empirical research in environmental psychology: Past, present, and future. *Journal of Environmental Psychology, 29*(3), 375–386.

Gladstein, D. L., & Reilly, N. P. (1985). Group decision making under threat: The tycoon game. *Academy of Management Journal, 28*(3), 613–627.

Glasman, L. R., & Albarracín, D. (2006). Forming attitudes that predict future behavior: A meta-analysis of the attitude-behavior relation. *Psychological Bulletin, 132*(5), 778–822.

Gluck, M. A., & Myers, C. E. (2001). *Gateway to memory: An introduction to neural network modeling of the hippocampus and learning.* Cambridge, MA: MIT Press.

Gobet, F., & Simon, H. A. (1998). Expert chess memory: Revisiting the chunking hypothesis. *Memory, 6*(3), 225–255.

Gold, M. (1992). Metatheory and field theory in social psychology: Relevance or elegance? *Journal of Social Issues, 48*(2), 67–78.

Goldring, E., & Berends, M. (2009). *Leading with data: Pathways to improve your school.* Thousand Oaks, CA: Corwin Press.

Goldstein, I. L., & Ford, J. K. (2002). *Training in organizations* (4th ed.). Belmont, CA: Wadsworth.

Goldstein, N., Cialdini, R., & Griskevicius, V. (2011). *Reciprocity by proxy: Harnessing obligation for cooperation in environmental sustainability programs.* Wellington: International Association of Conflict Management (IACM).

Goldstein, N. J., Cialdini, R. B., & Griskevicius, V. (2008). A room with a viewpoint: Using social norms to motivate environmental conservation in hotels. *Journal of Consumer Research, 35*(3), 472–482.

Goldstein, N. J., Griskevicius, V., & Cialdini, R. B. (2011). Reciprocity by proxy: A novel influence strategy for stimulating cooperation. *Administrative Science Quarterly, 56*(3), 441–473.

Gontijo, P. D., & Zhang, S. (2007). The mental representation of brand names: Are brand names a class by themselves? In T. M. Lowrey (Ed.), *Psycholinguistic phenomena in marketing communications* (pp. 23–37). Mahwah, NJ: Lawrence Erlbaum Associates Publishers.

Goodman, G. S., & Melinder, A. (2007). Child witness research and forensic interviews of young children: A review. *Legal and Criminological Psychology, 12*(1), 1–19.

Gordijn, E. H., Postmes, T., & de Vries, N. K. (2001). Devil's advocate or advocate of oneself: Effects of numerical support on pro- and counterattitudinal self-persuasion. *Personality and Social Psychology Bulletin, 27*(4), 395–407.

Gottfredson, (1997). Mainstream science on intelligence: An editorial with 52 signatories, history and bibliography. *Intelligence, 24*, 13–23.

Graham, J. D., & Wiener, J. B. (2008). The precautionary principle and risk-risk trade-offs: A comment. *Journal of Risk Research, 11*(4), 465–474.

REFERENCES

Grant, L. K. (2010). Sustainability: From excess to aesthetics. *Behavior and Social Issues*, *19*, 7–47.

Grasmück, D., & Scholz, R. W. (2005). Risk perception of heavy metal soil contamination by high-exposed and low-exposed inhabitants: The role of knowledge and emotional concerns. *Risk Analysis*, *25*(3), 611–622.

Green, D. M., & Swets, J. A. (1966). *Signal detection theory and psychophysics.* New York: Wiley.

Greenberg, J. (1988). Equity and workplace status: A field experiment. *Journal of Applied Psychology*, *73*(4), 606–613.

Greene, E., Heilbrun, K., Fortune, W. H., & Nietzel, M. T. (2007). *Psychology and the legal system* (6th ed.). New York: Wadsworth.

Greenspan, A. (2008). Statement of Alan Greenspan, former chairman of the Federal Reserve Board.

Greenwald, A. G., Pratkanis, A. R., Leippe, M. R., & Baumgardner, M. H. (1986). Under what conditions does theory obstruct research progress? *Psychological Review*, *93*(2), 216–229.

Gregory, G. D., & Di Leo, M. (2003). Repeated behavior and environmental psychology: The role of personal involvement and habit formation in explaining water consumption. *Journal of Applied Social Psychology*, *33*(6), 1261–1296.

Greitemeyer, T. (2013). Beware of climate change skeptic films. *Journal of Environmental Psychology*, *35*, 105–109.

Greitemeyer, T., Schulz-Hardt, S., & Frey, D. (2009). The effects of authentic and contrived dissent on escalation of commitment in group decision making. *European Journal of Social Psychology*, *39*(4), 639–647.

Grewal, D., Kavanoor, S., Fern, E. F., Costley, C., & Barnes, J. (1997). Comparative versus noncomparative advertising: A meta-analysis. *Journal of Marketing*, *61*(4), 1–15.

Grinstein, A., & Nisan, U. (2009). Demarketing, minorities, and national attachment. *Journal of Marketing*, *73*(2), 105–122.

Gromet, D. M., & Darley, J. M. (2009). Punishment and beyond: Achieving justice through the satisfaction of multiple goals. *Law & Society Review*, *43*(1), 1–38.

Grønhøj, A., & Thøgersen, J. (2011). Feedback on household electricity consumption: Learning and social influence processes. *International Journal of Consumer Studies*, *35*(2), 138–145.

Grønhøj, A., & Thøgersen, J. (2012). Action speaks louder than words: The effect of personal attitudes and family norms on adolescents' pro-environmental behaviour. *Journal of Economic Psychology*, *33*(1), 292–302.

Grossman, P., Niemann, L., Schmidt, S., & Walach, H. (2004). Mindfulness-based stress reduction and health benefits: A meta-analysis. *Journal of Psychosomatic Research*, *57*(1), 35–43.

Gruber, A. J., & McDonald, R. J. (2012). Context, emotion, and the strategic pursuit of goals: Interactions among multiple brain systems controlling motivated behavior. *Frontiers in Behavioral Neuroscience*, *6*, doi:10.3389/fnbeh.2012.00050

Gruszczynski, M. W., Balzer, A., Jacobs, C. M., Smith, K. B., & Hibbing, J. R. (2013). The physiology of political participation. *Political Behavior*, *35*(1), 135–152.

Guagnano, G. A., Dietz, T., & Stern, P. C. (1994). Willingness to pay for public goods: A test of the contribution model. *Psychological Science*, *5*(6), 411–415.

Guan, L., Xiang, H., Wu, X., Ma, N., Wu, B., Cheng, W., … Xiao, Z. (2011). Needs assessment for the psychosocial support at the severely-affected counties after Wenchuan earthquake. *Chinese Mental Health Journal*, *25*(2), 107–112.

Guilford, J. P. (1972). Thurstone's primary mental abilities and structure-of-intellect abilities. *Psychological Bulletin*, *77*(2), 129–143.

REFERENCES

Gulas, C. S., & Weinberger, M. G. (2006). *Humor in advertising: A comprehensive review.* Armonk, NY: M. E. Sharpe.

Gully, S. M., Phillips, J. M., Castellano, W. G., Han, K., & Kim, A. (2013). A mediated moderation model of recruiting socially and environmentally responsible job applicants. *Personnel Psychology, 66*(4), 935–973.

Gupta, S., & Ogden, D. T. (2009). To buy or not to buy? A social dilemma perspective on green buying. *Journal of Consumer Marketing, 26*(6), 376–391.

Gustafson, D. L., Goodyear, L., & Keough, F. (2008). When the dragon's awake: A needs assessment of people injecting drugs in a small urban centre. *International Journal of Drug Policy, 19*(3), 189–194.

Güth, W., Levati, M. V., & Ploner, M. (2010). Satisficing in strategic environments: A theoretical approach and experimental evidence. *The Journal of Socio-Economics, 39* (5), 554–561.

Haase, C. M., Heckhausen, J., & Wrosch, C. (2013). Developmental regulation across the life span: Toward a new synthesis. *Developmental Psychology, 49*(5), 964–972.

Hackett, G., & Betz, N. E. (1989). An exploration of the mathematics self-efficacy/mathematics performance correspondence. *Journal for Research in Mathematics Education, 20*(3), 261–273.

Hakel, M. D. (2013). Commentary: *Homo Economicus*, industrial psychology, and the greater good. In J. Olson-Buchanan, L. K. Bryan, & L. F. Thompson (Eds.), *Using industrial-organizational psychology for the greater good* (pp. 559–566). New York: Routledge.

Hall, D. L., Matz, D. C., & Wood, W. (2010). Why don't we practice what we preach? A meta-analytic review of religious racism. *Personality and Social Psychology Review, 14* (1), 126–139.

Halpenny, E. A. (2010). Pro-environmental behaviours and park visitors: The effect of place attachment. *Journal of Environmental Psychology, 30*(4), 409–421.

Hamann, S., Herman, R. A., Nolan, C. L., & Wallen, K. (2004). Men and women differ in amygdala response to visual sexual stimuli. *Nature Neuroscience, 7*(4), 411–416.

Hamer, M., Taylor, A., & Steptoe, A. (2006). The effect of acute aerobic exercise on stress related blood pressure responses: A systematic review and meta-analysis. *Biological Psychology, 71*(2), 183–190.

Hammer, M. R., Bennett, M. J., & Wiseman, R. (2003). Measuring intercultural sensitivity: The Intercultural Development Inventory. *International Journal of Intercultural Relations, 27*(4), 421–443.

Hammond, K. R. (1996). Upon reflection. *Thinking and Reasoning, 2,* 239–248.

Hammond, M. M., Neff, N. L., Farr, J. L., Schwall, A. R., & Zhao, X. (2011). Predictors of individual-level innovation at work: A meta-analysis. *Psychology of Aesthetics, Creativity, and the Arts, 5*(1), 90–105.

Han, S., & Dobbins, I. G. (2008). Examining recognition criterion rigidity during testing using a biased-feedback technique: Evidence for adaptive criterion learning. *Memory & Cognition, 36*(4), 703–715.

Han, T.-I., & Stoel, L. (2017). Explaining socially responsible consumer behavior: A meta-analytic review of theory of planned behavior. *Journal of International Consumer Marketing, 29*(2), 91–103.

Hanges, P. J., Schneider, B., & Niles, K. (1990). Stability of performance: An interactionist perspective. *Journal of Applied Psychology, 75*(6), 658–667.

Hansen, S., Foss von Krauss, M. P. K., & Tickner, J. A. (2007b). Response to "Regulatory false positives: True, false, or uncertain?" *Risk Analysis, 27*(5), 1087–1089.

Hansen, S. F., von Krauss, M. P. K., & Tickner, J. A. (2007a) Categorizing mistaken false positives in regulation of human and environmental health. *Risk Analysis, 27*(1), 255–269.

REFERENCES

Hansla, A., Gamble, A., Juliusson, A., & Gärling, T. (2008). The relationships between awareness of consequences, environmental concern, and value orientations. *Journal of Environmental Psychology, 28*(1), 1–9.

Hanson, M. A. (2013). Green ergonomics: Challenges and opportunities. *Ergonomics, 56* (3), 399–408.

Hanss, D., & Böhm, G. (2013). Promoting purchases of sustainable groceries: An intervention study. *Journal of Environmental Psychology, 33*, 53–67.

Haq, S., & Zimring, C. (2003). Just down the road a piece: The development of topological knowledge of building layouts. *Environment and Behavior, 35*(1), 132–160.

Hardin, G. (1968, December 13). The tragedy of the commons. *Science, 162*, 1243–1248.

Hardin, G. (2007). The tragedy of the unmanaged commons. In D. J. Penn & I. Mysterud (Eds.), *Evolutionary perspectives on environmental problems* (pp. 105–107). Piscataway, NJ: Transaction.

Harland, P., Staats, H., & Wilke, H. A. M. (2007). Situational and personality factors as direct or personal norm mediated predictors of pro-environmental behavior: Questions derived from norm-activation theory. *Basic and Applied Social Psychology, 29* (4), 323–334.

Harmon-Jones, E., & Harmon-Jones, C. (2019). Understanding the motivation underlying dissonance effects: The action-based model. In E. Harmon-Jones (Ed.), *Cognitive dissonance: Reexamining a pivotal theory in psychology*, 2nd ed. (pp. 63–89). Washington, DC: American Psychological Association.

Harrington, C., Curtis, A., & Black, R. (2008). Locating communities in natural resource management. *Journal of Environmental Policy & Planning, 10*(2), 199–215.

Harris, K. R. (1990). Developing self-regulated learners: The role of private speech and self-instructions. *Educational Psychologist, 25*(1), 35–49.

Harris, M. D., Tetrick, L. E., & Tiegs, R. B. (1993). Cognitive ability and motivational interventions: Their effects on performance outcomes. *Current Psychology: A Journal for Diverse Perspectives on Diverse Psychological Issues, 12*(1), 57–65.

Hart, W., Albarracín, D., Eagly, A. H., Brechan, I., Lindberg, M. J., & Merrill, L. (2009). Feeling validated versus being correct: A meta-analysis of selective exposure to information. *Psychological Bulletin, 135*(4), 555–588.

Hart, W., Ottati, V. C., & Krumdick, N. D. (2011). Physical attractiveness and candidate evaluation: A model of correction. *Political Psychology, 32*(2), 181–203.

Hartig, T., & Staats, H. (2003). Guest's editors' introduction: Restorative environments. *Journal of Environmental Psychology, 23*(2), 103–107.

Hartlieb, S., & Jones, B. (2009). Humanising business through ethical labelling: Progress and paradoxes in the UK. *Journal of Business Ethics, 88*(3), 583–600.

Hartman, R. O., & Betz, N. E. (2007). The five-factor model and career self-efficacy: General and domain-specific relationships. *Journal of Career Assessment, 15*(2), 145–161.

Hartman, T. K., & Weber, C. R. (2009). Who said what? The effects of source cues in issue frames. *Political Behavior, 31*(4), 537–558.

Hartwig, M., & Bond, C. F., Jr. (2011). Why do lie-catchers fail? A lens model meta-analysis of human lie judgments. *Psychological Bulletin, 137*(4), 643–659.

Harvey, P., & Victoravich, L. M. (2009). The influence of forward-looking antecedents, uncertainty, and anticipatory emotions on project escalation. *Decision Sciences, 40*(4), 759–782.

Haslam, R., & Waterson, P. (2013). Ergonomics and sustainability. *Ergonomics, 56*(3), 343–347.

Haslam, S., & Reicher, S. D. (2012). When prisoners take over the prison: A social psychology of resistance. *Personality and Social Psychology Review, 16*(2), 154–179.

REFERENCES

Hastings, G. (2013). *The marketing matrix: How the corporation gets its power – and how we can reclaim it.* New York: Routledge.

Hastings, P. D., Zahn-Waxler, C., & McShane, K. (2006). We are, by nature, moral creatures: Biological bases of concern for others. In M. Killen & J. G. Smetana (Eds.), *Handbook of moral development* (pp. 483–516). Mahwah, NJ: Lawrence Erlbaum Associates Publishers.

Hatfield, J., & Job, R. (2000). Pro-environmental behaviour as a health behaviour I: A review of the role of environment-related optimism bias & other factors. *Journal of Applied Health Behaviour, 2*(2), 7–13.

Hatfield, J. J., & Soames, R. F. (2000). Pro-environmental behaviour as a health behaviour II: A review of the role of environment-related optimism bias & other factors. *Journal of Applied Health Behaviour, 2*(2), 14–23.

Hathcoat, J. D., & Barnes, L. L. B. (2010). Explaining the relationship among fundamentalism and authoritarianism: An epistemic connection. *International Journal for the Psychology of Religion, 20*(2), 73–84.

Hattie, J., Biggs, J., & Purdie, N. (1996). Effects of learning skills interventions on student learning: A meta-analysis. *Review of Educational Research, 66*(2), 99–136.

Hattie, J., Marsh, H. W., Neill, J. T., & Richards, G. E. (1997). Adventure education and outward bound: Out-of-class experiences that make a lasting difference. *Review of Educational Research, 67*(1), 43–87.

Hatzithomas, L., Zotos, Y., & Boutsouki, C. (2011). Humor and cultural values in print advertising: A cross-cultural study. *International Marketing Review, 28*(1), 57–80.

Haug, E. G., & Taleb, N. N. (2011). Option traders use (very) sophisticated heuristics, never the Black–Scholes–Merton formula. *Journal of Economic Behavior & Organization, 77*(2), 97–106.

Hay, R. (1998). Sense of place in developmental context. *Journal of Environmental Psychology, 18*, 5–29.

Hays-Thomas, R. (2006). Challenging the scientist-practitioner model: Question about I-O education and training. *The Industrial and Organizational Psychologist, 44*, 47–53.

Hazan, E., Agarwal, A., & Kale, S. (2007). Logarithmic regret algorithms for online convex optimization. *Machine Learning, 69*(2-3), 169–192.

He, H., & Brown, A. D. (2013). Organizational identity and organizational identification: A review of the literature and suggestions for future research. *Group & Organization Management, 38*(1), 3–35.

He, Z., Cassaday, H. J., Bonardi, C., & Bibby, P. A. (2013). Do personality traits predict individual differences in excitatory and inhibitory learning? *Frontiers in Psychology, 4*, e-journal.

Headey, A., Pirkis, J., Merner, B., VandenHeuvel, A., Mitchell, P., Robinson, J., &., … Burgess, P. (2006). A review of 156 local projects funded under Australia's National Suicide Prevention Strategy: Overview and lessons learned. *Aejamh (Australian E-Journal for the Advancement of Mental Health), 5*(3), 1–15.

Heath, C. (1995). Escalation and de-escalation of commitment in response to sunk costs: The role of budgeting in mental accounting. *Organizational Behavior and Human Decision Processes, 62*(1), 38–54.

Heath, M. T. P. and Chatzidakis, A. (2012). Blame it on marketing: Consumers views on unsustainable consumption. *International Journal of Consumer Studies, 36*, 656–667.

Heath, R. (2012). *Seducing the subconscious: The psychology of emotional influence in advertising.* Hoboken, NJ: Wiley-Blackwell, doi:10.1002/9781119967637

Heath, R., Brandt, D., & Nairn, A. (2006). Brand relationships: Strengthened by emotion, weakened by attention. *Journal of Advertising Research, 46*(4), doi:10.2501/S002184990606048X

REFERENCES

Heaton-Armstrong, A., Shepherd, E., Gudjonsson, G., & Wolchover, D. (2006). *Witness testimony: Psychological, investigative and evidential perspectives.* New York: Oxford University Press.

Heaven, P. C. L., Ciarrochi, J., & Leeson, P. (2011). Cognitive ability, right-wing authoritarianism, and social dominance orientation: A five-year longitudinal study amongst adolescents. *Intelligence, 39*(1), 15–21.

Heckhausen, J. (1997). Developmental regulation across adulthood: Primary and secondary control of age-related challenges. *Developmental Psychology, 33,* 176–187.

Heckhausen, J., Wrosch, C., & Schulz, R. (2010). A motivational theory of life-span development. *Psychological Review, 117*(1), 32–60.

Hedge, J. W., & Borman, W. C. (2008). Building and maintaining client relationships. In J. W. Hedge & W. C. Borman (Eds.), *The I/O consultant: Advice and insights for building a successful career* (pp. 183–187). Washington, DC: American Psychological Association.

Hedge, J. W., & Pulakos, E. D. (2002). Grappling with implementation: Some preliminary thoughts and relevant research. In J. W. Hedge & E. D. Pulakos (Eds.), *Implementing organizational interventions: Steps, processes, and best practices* (pp. 1–11). San Francisco, CA: Jossey-Bass.

Heft, H. (2013). Environment, cognition, and culture: Reconsidering the cognitive map. *Journal of Environmental Psychology, 33,* 14–25.

Heft, H., & Chawla, L. (2006). Children as agents in sustainable development: The ecology of competence. In C. Spencer & M. Blades (Eds.), *Children and their environments: Learning, using and designing spaces* (pp. 199–216). New York: Cambridge University Press.

Helmstadter, G. C., & Ellis, D. S. (1952). Rate of manipulative learning as a function of goal-setting techniques. *Journal of Experimental Psychology, 43*(2), 125–129.

Hendershot, C. S., Witkiewitz, K., George, W., & Marlatt, G. (2011). Relapse prevention for addictive behaviors. *Substance Abuse treatment, prevention, and Policy, 6,* doi:10.1186/1747-597X-6-17

Henry, R. A., Kmet, J., Desrosiers, E., & Landa, A. (2002). Examining the impact of interpersonal cohesiveness on group accuracy interventions: The importance of matching versus buffering. *Organizational Behavior and Human Decision Processes, 87*(1), 25–43.

Henry, R. A., Strickland, O. J., Yorges, S. L., & Ladd, D. (1996). Helping groups determine their most accurate member: The role of outcome feedback. *Journal of Applied Social Psychology, 26*(13), 1153–1170.

Hernández, B., Hidalgo, M., Salazar-Laplace, M., & Hess, S. (2007). Place attachment and place identity in natives and non-natives. *Journal of Environmental Psychology, 27*(4), 310–319.

Hernández, B., Martín, A. M., Ruiz, C., & Hidalgo, M. (2010). The role of place identity and place attachment in breaking environmental protection laws. *Journal of Environmental Psychology, 30*(3), 281–288.

Hernandez, I., & Preston, J. L. (2013) Disfluency disrupts the confirmation bias. *Journal of Experimental Social Psychology, 49*(1),178–182.

Herring, C. (2012). Pop quiz: What's the NBA's wonderlic? *Wall Street Journal,* http://online.wsj.com/article/SB10001424052702304058404577494464201742 1700.html

Hertwig, R., & Herzog, S. M. (2009). Fast and frugal heuristics: Tools of social rationality. *Social Cognition, 27*(5), 661–698.

Hidalgo, M., & Hernández, B. (2002). Attachment to the physical dimension of places. *Psychological Reports, 91*(3, Pt2), 1177–1182.

REFERENCES

Higgins, E. T. (1990). Personality, social psychology, and person-situation relations: Standards and knowledge activation as a common language. In L. A. Pervin, (Ed.), *Handbook of personality theory and research* (pp. 301–338). New York: Guilford.

Higgins, E. T. (2012). Motivational fit. In B. Gawronski & F. Strack (Eds.), *Cognitive consistency* (pp. 132–153). New York: Guilford.

Highhouse, S. (2008). Stubborn reliance on intuition and subjectivity in employee selection. *Industrial and Organizational Psychology: Perspectives on Science and Practice, 1*(3), 333–342.

Hilbert, M. (2012). Toward a synthesis of cognitive biases: How noisy information processing can bias human decision making. *Psychological Bulletin, 138*(2), 211–237.

Hilbig, B. E., Zettler, I., Leist, F., & Heydasch, T. (2013). It takes two: Honesty–humility and agreeableness differentially predict active versus reactive cooperation. *Personality and Individual Differences, 54*(5), 598–603.

Hillbrand, M., & Young, J. L. (2008). Instilling hope into forensic treatment: The antidote to despair and desperation. *Journal of the American Academy of Psychiatry and the Law, 36*(1), 90–94.

Hinds, J., & Sparks, P. (2008). Engaging with the natural environment: The role of affective connection and identity. *Journal of Environmental Psychology, 28*(2), 109–120.

Hine, D. W., Bhullar, N., Marks, A. G., Kelly, P., & Scott, J. G. (2011). Comparing the effectiveness of education and technology in reducing wood smoke pollution: A field experiment. *Journal of Environmental Psychology, 31*(4), 282–288.

Hine, D. W., Marks, A. G., Nachreiner, M., Gifford, R., & Heath, Y. (2007). Keeping the home fires burning: The affect heuristic and wood smoke pollution. *Journal of Environmental Psychology, 27*(1), 26–32.

Hine, D. W., Reser, J. P., Phillips, W. J., Cooksey, R., Marks, A. D. G., Nunn, P., … Glendon, A. I. (2013). Identifying climate change interpretive communities in a large Australian sample. *Journal of Environmental Psychology, 36*, 229–239.

Hines, J. M., Hungerford, H. R., & Tomera, A. N. (1986). Analysis and synthesis of research on responsible environmental behavior: A meta-analysis. *The Journal of Environmental Education, 18*(2), 1–8.

Hinrichs, J. R. (1991). Survey data as a catalyst for employee empowerment and organizational effectiveness. In R. J. Niehaus & K. F. Price (Eds.), *Bottom line results from strategic human resource planning* (pp. 301–308). New York: Plenum Press.

Hinsz, V. B. (2008). The social context of work motivation: A social-psychological perspective. In R. Kanfer, G. Chen, & R. D. Pritchard (Eds.), *Work motivation: Past, present, and future* (pp. 553–568). New York: Routledge/Taylor & Francis Group.

Hipp, J., & Ogunseitan, O. A. (2011). Effect of environmental conditions on perceived psychological restorativeness of coastal parks. *Journal of Environmental Psychology, 31*(4), 421–429.

Hirsh, J. B., DeYoung, C. G., & Peterson, J. B. (2009). Metatraits of the Big Five differentially predict engagement and restraint of behavior. *Journal of Personality, 77*(4), 1085–1102.

Hirsh, J. B., Kang, S. K., & Bodenhausen, G. V. (2012). Personalized persuasion: Tailoring persuasive appeals to recipients' personality traits. *Psychological Science, 23*(6), 578–581.

Hitt, M. A., & Barr, S. H. (1989). Managerial selection decision models: Examination of configural cue processing. *Journal of Applied Psychology, 74*(1), 53–61.

Hixson, E. J., McCabe, S. S., & Brown, G. (2011). Event attendance motivation and place attachment: An exploratory study of young residents in Adelaide, South Australia. *Event Management, 15*(3), 233–243.

REFERENCES

Hoch, S. J., & Loewenstein, G. F. (1989). Outcome feedback: Hindsight and information. *Journal of Experimental Psychology: Learning, Memory, and Cognition, 15*(4), 605–619.

Hodson, G., & Busseri, M. A. (2012). Bright minds and dark attitudes: Lower cognitive ability predicts greater prejudice through right-wing ideology and low intergroup contact. *Psychological Science, 23*(2), 187–195.

Hoever, I. J., Knippenberg, D. V., Ginkel, W. P. V., & Barkema, H. G. (2012). Fostering team creativity: Perspective taking as a key to unlocking diversity's potential. *Journal of Applied Psychology, 97*, 982–996.

Hoffman, M. L. (1975). Altruistic behavior and the parent–child relationship. *Journal of Personality and Social Psychology, 31*(5), 937–943.

Hofmann, E., Hoelzl, E., & Kirchler, E. (2008). Preconditions of voluntary tax compliance: Knowledge and evaluation of taxation, norms, fairness, and motivation to cooperate. *Zeitschrift Für Psychologie / Journal of Psychology, 216*(4), 209–217.

Hofstede, G. (1980). *Culture's consequences: International differences in work-related values.* Beverly Hills, CA: Sage.

Hogan, J., & Brinkmeyer, K. (1997). Bridging the gap between overt and personality-based integrity tests. *Personnel Psychology, 50*(3), 587–599.

Hogan, R. (1998). What is personality? *Psychological Inquiry, 9*, 152–153.

Hogan, R., Curphy, G. J., & Hogan, J. (1994). What we know about leadership: Effectiveness and personality. *American Psychologist, 49*(6), 493–504.

Hogan, R., & Hogan, J. (2007). *Hogan personality inventory manual* (3rd ed.). Tulsa, OK: Hogan Assessment Systems.

Hogan, R., & Roberts, B. W. (2000). A socioanalytic perspective on person–environment interaction. In W. B. Walsh & K. H. Craik (Eds.), *Person–environment psychology: New directions and perspectives,* 2nd ed. (pp. 1–23). Mahwah, NJ: Erlbaum.

Hogan, R., & Shelton, D. (1998). A socioanalytic perspective on job performance. *Human Performance, 11*, 129–144.

Hogarth, R. M. (2010). Intuition: A challenge for psychological research on decision making. *Psychological Inquiry, 21*(4), 338–353.

Hollenbeck, J. R., Ellis, A. P. J., Humphrey, S. E., Garza, A. S., & Ilgen, D. R. (2011). Asymmetry in structural adaptation: The differential impact of centralizing versus decentralizing team decision-making structures. *Organizational Behavior and Human Decision Processes, 114*(1), 64–74.

Hollenbeck, J. R., Ilgen, D. R., Sego, D. J., Hedlund, J., Major, D. A., & Phillips, J. (1995). Mutlilevel theory of team decision making: Decision performance in teams incorporating distributed expertise. *Journal of Applied Psychology, 80*(2), 292–316.

Hollenbeck, J. R., Williams, C. R., & Klein, H. J. (1989). An empirical examination of the antecedents of commitment to difficult goals. *Journal of Applied Psychology, 74*(1), 18–23.

Hollin, C. R. (2013). *Psychology and crime: An introduction to criminological psychology* (2nd ed.). New York: Routledge/Taylor & Francis Group.

Hollnagel, E., & Woods, D. D. (1999). Cognitive Systems Engineering: New wine in new bottles. *International Journal of Human-Computer Studies, 51*(2), 339–356.

Homburg, A., & Wagner, U. (2007). Factors of individual threat, efficacy and cost appraisal in the context of environmental stressors. *Zeitschrift Für Sozialpsychologie, 38*(1), 53–65.

Hong, Y., Morris, M. W., Chiu, C., & Benet-Martínez, V. (2000). Multicultural minds: A dynamic constructivist approach to culture and cognition. *American Psychologist, 55*(7), 709–720.

REFERENCES

Hornik, J., Cherian, J., Madansky, M., & Narayana, C. (1995). Determinants of recycling behavior: A synthesis of research results. *The Journal of Socio-Economics, 24*(1), 105–127.

Hornsey, M. J. & Fielding, K. S. (2017). Attitude roots and Jiu Jitsu persuasion: Understanding and overcoming the motivated rejection of science. *American Psychologist, 72* (5), 459–473.

Hothersall, D. (1995). *History of psychology.* New York: McGraw-Hill.

Hough, W. G., & O'Brien, K. P. (2005). The effect of community treatment orders on offending rates. *Psychiatry, Psychology and Law, 12*(2), 411–423.

House, R., Javidan, M., Hanges, P., & Dorfman, P. (2001). Project GLOBE: An introduction. *Applied Psychology: An International Review, 50,* 489–505.

Howard, A., & Bray, D. W. (1988). *Managerial lives in transition: Advancing age and changing times.* New York: Guilford Press.

Huang, Y., Ding, H., & Kao, M. (2009). Salient stakeholder voices: Family business and green innovation adoption. *Journal of Management & Organization, 15*(3), 309–326.

Hubbard, G. (2009). Measuring organizational performance: Beyond the triple bottom line. *Business Strategy and the Environment, 18*(3),177–191.

Huffman, A. H., & Klein, A. R. (2013). *Green organizations.* New York: Routledge.

Hughes, J. N. (2012). Teachers as managers of students' peer context. In A. M. Ryan & G. W. Ladd (Eds.), *Peer relationships and adjustment at school* (pp. 189–218). Charlotte, NC: IAP Information Age Publishing.

Hund, A. M., & Nazarczuk, S. N. (2009). The effects of sense of direction and training experience on wayfinding efficiency. *Journal of Environmental Psychology, 29*(1), 151–159.

Huneke, M. E. (2005). The face of the un-consumer: An empirical examination of the practice of voluntary simplicity in the United States. *Psychology & Marketing, 22*(7), 527–550.

Hung, I. W., & Wyer, R. R. (2009). Differences in perspective and the influence of charitable appeals: When imagining oneself as the victim is not beneficial. *Journal of Marketing Research, 46*(3), 421–434.

Hunt, N. J., Waters, K. A., & Machaalani, R. (2013). Orexin receptors in the developing piglet hypothalamus, and effects of nicotine and intermittent hypercapnic hypoxia exposures. *Brain Research, 1508,* 73–82., 73–82

Hunter, S. T., Bedell, K. E., & Mumford, M. D. (2007). Climate for creativity: A quantitative review. *Creativity Research Journal, 19*(1), 69–90.

Huppert, F. A. (2009). A new approach to reducing disorder and improving well-being. *Perspectives on Psychological Science, 4*(1), 108–111.

Hustad, E., & Bechina, A. (2012). Exploring the role of boundary spanning in distributed networks of knowledge. *Electronic Journal of Knowledge Management, 10*(2), 121–130.

Hutchins, H. M., & Burke, L. A. (2006). Has relapse prevention received a fair shake? A review and implications for future transfer research. *Human Resource Development Review, 5*(1), 8–24.

Hutchins, S. D., Wickens, C. D., Carolan, T. F., & Cumming, J. M. (2013). The influence of cognitive load on transfer with error prevention training methods: A meta-analysis. *Human Factors, 55*(4), 854–874.

Igna, R. (2011). Effectiveness of mindfulness-based interventions in chronic pain: A meta-analysis. Highlighting the effectiveness of mindfulness-based interventions in chronic pain. A meta-analytic review. *Erdélyi Pszichológiai Szemle, 12*(1), 43–57.

Ilgen, D. R., Fisher, C. D., & Taylor, M. (1979). Consequences of individual feedback on behavior in organizations. *Journal of Applied Psychology, 64*(4), 349–371.

REFERENCES

Imel, Z. E., Hubbard, R. A., Rutter, C. M., & Simon, G. (2013). Patient-rated alliance as a measure of therapist performance in two clinical settings. *Journal of Consulting and Clinical Psychology, 81*(1), 154–165.

Inspiring action: The role of psychology in environmental campaiging and activism. (2011). *Ecopsychology, 3*(2), 139–148. No authorship indicated.

Isenberg, D. J. (1986). Group polarization: A critical review and meta-analysis. *Journal of Personality and Social Psychology, 50*(6), 1141–1151.

Islam, M., Barnes, A., & Toma, L. (2013). An investigation into climate change scepticism among farmers. *Journal of Environmental Psychology, 34*, 137–150.

Izard, C. E. (1994). Innate and universal facial expressions: Evidence from developmental and cross-cultural research. *Psychological Bulletin,115*, 288–299.

Jaafar, M., & Maideen, S. (2012). Ecotourism-related products and activities, and the economic sustainability of small and medium island chalets. *Tourism Management, 33*(3), 683–691.

Jackson, L. M. (2011). Toward a wider lens: Prejudice and the natural world. In Jackson, L. M., *The psychology of prejudice: From attitudes to social action* (pp. 137–158). Washington, DC: American Psychological Association.

Jackson, S. E., & Dutton, J. E. (1988). Discerning threats and opportunities. *Administrative Science Quarterly, 33*(3), 370–387.

Jackson, T. (2008). Sustainable consumption and lifestyle change. In A. Lewis (Ed.), *The Cambridge handbook of psychology and economic behaviour* (pp. 335–362). New York: Cambridge University Press.

Jacob, J., Jovic, E., & Brinkerhoff, M. B. (2009). Personal and planetary well-being: Mindfulness meditation, pro-environmental behavior and personal quality of life in a survey from the social justice and ecological sustainability movement. *Social Indicators Research, 93*(2), 275–294.

Jacobs, K. R., & Clark, S. G. (2011). Review of "Bringing in the future: strategies for farsightedness and sustainability in developing countries". *Political Psychology, 32*(6), 1095–1098.

Jacobson, F. N., & Rettig, S. (1959). Authoritarianism and intelligence. *The Journal of Social Psychology, 50*, 213–219.

Jacobson, J. A. (2007). The relationship among causal uncertainty, reassurance seeking, and dysphoria. *Journal of Social and Clinical Psychology, 26*(8), 922–939.

Jacobson, J. A., Weary, G., & Lin, Y. S. (2008). Causal uncertainty and metacognitive inferences about goal attainment. *Cognition and Emotion, 22*(7), 1276–1305.

Jain, S. K., & Kaur, G. (2006). Role of socio-demographics in segmenting and profiling green consumers: An exploratory study of consumers in India. *Journal of International Consumer Marketing, 18*(3), 107–146.

James, L. R., & LeBreton, J. M. (2012). *Assessing the implicit personality through conditional reasoning*. Washington, DC: American Psychological Association.

James River Basin Partnership (2020). Jamesriverbasin.com

James, W. (1890). *The principles of psychology*. Cambridge, MA: Harvard University Press.

Janssens, W., & De Pelsmacker, P. (2005). Emotional or informative? Creative or boring? The effectiveness of different types of radio commercial. *International Journal of Advertising: The Quarterly Review of Marketing Communications, 24*(3), 373–394.

Järvenoja, H., Volet, S., & Järvelä, S. (2013). Regulation of emotions in socially challenging learning situations: An instrument to measure the adaptive and social nature of the regulation process. *Educational Psychology, 33*(1), 31–58.

Jarvik, M. E. (1951). Probability learning and a negative recency effect in the serial anticipation of alternative symbols. *Journal of Experimental Psychology, 41*, 291–297.

Jayawickreme, E., Forgeard, M. J. C., & Seligman, M. E. P. (2012). The engine of well-being. *Review of General Psychology, 16*(4), 327–342.

REFERENCES

Jenkins, J. O. (2010). A multi-faceted formative assessment approach: Better recognising the learning needs of students. *Assessment & Evaluation in Higher Education, 35*(5), 565–576.

Ji, M. F., & Wood, W. (2007). Purchase and consumption habits: Not necessarily what you intend. *Journal of Consumer Psychology, 17*(4), 261–276.

John, O. P., & Naumann, L. P. (2010). Surviving two critiques by Block? The resilient big five have emerged as the paradigm for personality trait psychology. *Psychological Inquiry, 21*(1), 44–49.

Johnson, B. T., & Eagly, A. H. (1989). Effects of involvement on persuasion: A meta-analysis. *Psychological Bulletin, 106*(2), 290–314.

Johnson, D. W., Johnson, R. T., & Tjosvold, D. (2000). Constructive controversy: The value of intellectual opposition. In M. Deutsch & P. T. Coleman (Eds.), *The handbook of conflict resolution: Theory and practice* (pp. 65–85). San Francisco, CA: Jossey-Bass.

Johnson, J. A., Hogan, R., Zonderman, A. B., Callens, C., & Rogolsky, S. (1981). Moral judgment, personality, and attitudes toward authority. *Journal of Personality and Social Psychology, 40*(2), 370–373.

Johnson, S. C., Dweck, C. S., Chen, F. S., Stern, H. L., Ok, S., & Barth, M. (2010). At the intersection of social and cognitive development: Internal working models of attachment in infancy. *Cognitive Science, 34*(5), 807–825.

Jones, R. G. (1997b). Statistical and methodological reasoning: A protection against media predation. *Journal of Public Affairs, 1*, 43–51.

Jones, R. G. (2012). *Nepotism in organizations.* New York: Taylor & Francis/Routledge.

Jones, R. G., & Born, M. P. (2008). Assessor constructs in use as the missing component in validation of assessment center dimensions: A critique and directions for research. *International Journal of Selection and Assessment, 16*, 229–238.

Jones, R. G., & Culbertson, S. S. (2011). Why performance management will remain broken: Authoritarian communication. *Industrial and Organizational Psychology, 4*, 179–180.

Jones, R. G., Chomiak, M., Rittman, A., & Green, T. (2006). Distinguishing motive through perception of emotions. *Psichothema, 18*, 67–71.

Jones, R. G., & Lindley, W. (1998). Issues in the transition to teams. *Journal of Business and Psychology, 13*, 31–40.

Jones, R. G., & Parameswaran, G. (2005). Predicting the human weather: How differentiation and contextual complexity affect behavior prediction. In K. Richardson (Ed.), *Managing the complex: Philosophy, theory, and applications* (pp. 183–199). Greenwich, CT: Information Age.

Jones, R. G., & Rittman, A. (2002). A model of emotional and motivational components of interpersonal interactions in organizations. In N. Ashkanasy, C. Hartel, & W. Zerbe (Eds.), *Managing emotions in the workplace.* Armonk, NY: M. E. Sharpe.

Jones, R. G., Stevens, M. J., & Fischer, D. L. (2000). Selection in team contexts. In J. F. Kehoe (Ed.), *Managing selection in changing organizations.* San Francisco, CA: Jossey-Bass.

Jones, R. G., & Wilson, K. Y. (2013). Prescription before careful diagnosis. *Industrial and Organizational Psychology, 6*, 497–500.

Jordan, P. J., Dasborough, M. T., Daus, C. S., & Ashkanasy, N. M. (2010). A call to context. *Industrial and Organizational Psychology: Perspectives on Science and Practice, 3*(2), 145–148.

Jorgensen, B. S., & Stedman, R. C. (2001). Sense of place as an attitude: Lakeshore owners' attitudes toward their properties. *Journal of Environmental Psychology, 21*, 233–248.

REFERENCES

Joseph, D. L., & Newman, D. A. (2010). Emotional intelligence: An integrative meta-analysis and cascading model. *Journal of Applied Psychology, 95*(1), 54–78.

Jost, J. T., Glaser, J., Kruglanski, A. W., & Sulloway, F. J. (2003). Political conservatism as motivated social cognition. *Psychological Bulletin, 129*(3), 339–375.

Judge, T. A. (2009). Core self-evaluations and work success. *Current Directions in Psychological Science, 18*(1), 58–62.

Judge, T. A., Higgins, C. A., Thoresen, C. J., & Barrick, M. A. (1999). The Big Five personality traits, general mental ability, and career success across the lifespan. *Personnel Psychology, 52*, 621–652.

Judge, T. A., Ilies, R., & Dimotakis, N. (2010). Are health and happiness the product of wisdom? The relationship of general mental ability to educational and occupational attainment, health, and well-being. *Journal of Applied Psychology, 95*(3), 454–468.

Jung, Y., & Kang, H. (2010). User goals in social virtual worlds: A means–end chain approach. *Computers in Human Behavior, 26*(2), 218–225.

Kadak, A. C. (2000). Intergenerational risk and decision making: A practical example. *Risk Analysis, 20*, 883–894.

Kaempf, G. L., & Orasanu, J. (1997). Current and future applications of naturalistic decision making in aviation. In C. E. Zsambok & G. Klein (Eds.), *Naturalistic decision making* (pp. 81–90). Hillsdale, NJ and England: Lawrence Erlbaum Associates, Inc.

Kagan, J. (2012). The biography of behavioral inhibition. In M. Zentner & R. L. Shiner (Eds.), *Handbook of temperament* (pp. 69–82). New York: Guilford Press.

Kahn, P. R., & Lourenço, O. (2002). Water, air, fire, and earth: A developmental study in Portugal of environmental moral reasoning. *Environment and Behavior, 34*(4), 405–430.

Kahneman, D. (2011). *Thinking, fast and slow.* New York: Farrar, Straus, and Giroux.

Kahneman, D., & Tversky, A. (1984). Choices, values, and frames. *American Psychologist, 39*(4), 341–350.

Kaiser, R. B., Hogan, R., & Craig, S. (2008). Leadership and the fate of organizations. *American Psychologist, 63*(2), 96–110.

Kalechstein, A. D., & Nowicki, S. R. (1997). A meta-analytic examination of the relationship between control expectancies and academic achievement: An 11-yr follow-up to Findley and Cooper. *Genetic, Social, and General Psychology Monographs, 123*(1), 27–56.

Kamioka, H., Tsutani, K., Mutoh, Y., Honda, T., Shiozawa, N., Okada, S., ... Handa, S. (2012). A systematic review of randomized controlled trials on curative and health enhancement effects of forest therapy. *Psychology Research and Behavior Management, 5*, 85–95.

Kane, A. A. (2010). Unlocking knowledge transfer potential: Knowledge demonstrability and superordinate social identity. *Organization Science, 21*(3), 643–660.

Kane, J. S. (1997). Assessment of the situational and individual components of job performance. *Human Performance, 10*(3), 193–226.

Kanfer, R., & Ackerman, P. L. (1996). A self-regulatory skills perspective to reducing cognitive interference. In I. G. Sarason, G. R. Pierce, & B. R. Sarason (Eds.), *Cognitive interference: Theories, methods, and findings* (pp. 153–171). Hillsdale, NJ and England: Lawrence Erlbaum Associates, Inc.

Kanfer, R., & Ackerman, P. L. (2000). Individual differences in work motivation: Further explorations of a trait framework. *Applied Psychology: An International Review, 49*(3), 470–482.

Kanfer, R., Beier, M. E., & Ackerman, P. L. (2013). Goals and motivation related to work in later adulthood: An organizing framework. *European Journal of Work and Organizational Psychology, 22*(3), 253–264.

REFERENCES

Kantola, S. J., Syme, G. J., & Nesdale, A. R. (1983). The effects of appraised severity and efficacy in promoting water conservation: An informational analysis. *Journal of Applied Social Psychology, 13*(2), 164–182.

Kantola, S. J., Syme, G. J., & Campbell, N. A. (1984). Cognitive dissonance and energy conservation. *Journal of Applied Psychology, 69*(3), 416–421.

Kaplan, B. (2013). In good humour. *The Psychologist, 26*(6), 384.

Kaplan, R. (1990). Collaboration from a cognitive perspective: Sharing models across expertise. In R. I. Selby, K. H. Anthony, J. Choi, & B. Orland (Eds.), *Coming of age* (pp. 45–51). Edmond, OK: Environmental Design Research Association.

Karau, S. J., & Williams, K. D. (1993). Social loafing: A meta-analytic review and theoretical integration. *Journal of Personality and Social Psychology, 65*(4), 681–706.

Karlin, B., Zinger, J. F., & Ford, R. (2015). The effects of feedback on energy conservation: A meta-analysis. *Psychological Bulletin, 141*(6), 1205–1227.

Karpiak, C. P., & Baril, G. L. (2008). Moral reasoning and concern for the environment. *Journal of Environmental Psychology, 28*(3), 203–208.

Kassin, S. M., & Baron, R. M. (1985). Basic determinants of attribution and social perception. In J. H. Harvey & G. Weary (Eds.), *Attribution: Basic issues and applications* (pp. 180–200). New York: Academic Press.

Katz, A., & Meiri, N. (2006). Brain-derived neurotrophic factor is critically involved in thermal-experience-dependent developmental plasticity. *The Journal of Neuroscience, 26* (15), 3899–3907.

Katz, D., & Kahn, R. L. (1978). *The social psychology of organizations* (2nd ed.). New York: Wiley.

Kaufman, S. B., DeYoung, C. G., Reis, D. L., & Gray, J. R. (2011). General intelligence predicts reasoning ability even for evolutionarily familiar content. *Intelligence, 39*(5), 311–322.

Kazantzis, N., Whittington, C., & Dattilio, F. (2010). Meta-analysis of homework effects in cognitive and behavioral therapy: A replication and extension. *Clinical Psychology: Science and Practice, 17*(2), 144–156.

Kazantzis, N., Whittington, C., Zelencich, L., Kyrios, M., Norton, P. J., & Hofmann, S. G. (2016). Quantity and quality of homework compliance: A meta-analysis of relations with outcome in cognitive behavior therapy. *Behavior Therapy, 47*(5), 755–772.

Kehoe, J. F., Mol, S. T., & Anderson, N. R. (2010). Managing sustainable selection programs. In J. L. Farr & N. T. Tippins (Eds.), *Handbook of employee selection* (pp. 213–234 pp. 22). New York: Routledge.

Kehoe, J. F., & Murphy, K. R. (2010). Current concepts of validity, validation, and generalizability. In J. L. Farr & N. T. Tippins (Eds.), *Handbook of employee selection* (pp. 99–123). New York: Routledge/Taylor & Francis Group.

Keil, M., Depledge, G., & Rai, A. (2007). Escalation: The role of problem recognition and cognitive bias. *Decision Sciences, 38*, 391–421.

Kellen, D., Klauer, K. C., & Singmann, H. (2012). On the measurement of criterion noise in signal detection theory: The case of recognition memory. *Psychological Review, 119*(3), 457–479.

Kelly, G., & Hosking, K. (2008). Nonpermanent residents, place attachment, and "sea change" communities. *Environment and Behavior, 40*(4), 575–594.

Kennedy, M. G., Felner, R. D., Cauce, A., & Primavera, J. (1988). Social problem solving and adjustment in adolescence: The influence of moral reasoning level, scoring alternatives, and family climate. *Journal of Clinical Child Psychology, 17*(1), 73–83.

Kessler, T., & Cohrs, J. C. (2008). The evolution of authoritarian processes: Fostering cooperation in large-scale groups. *Group Dynamics: Theory, Research, and Practice, 12*(1), 73–84.

REFERENCES

Ketefian, S. (2001). The relationship of education and moral reasoning to ethical practice: A meta-analysis of quantitative studies. *Scholarly Inquiry for Nursing Practice, 15*(1), 3–18.

Khalil, E. L. (2004). What is altruism? A reply to critics. *Journal of Economic Psychology, 25*(1), 141–143.

Khanna, G., Medsker, G. J., & Ginter, R. (2012). 2012 income and employment survey results for the Society for Industrial and Organizational Psychology. Technical report for the Society for I-O Psychology, Bowling Green, OH.

Kilbourne, W., & Mittelstaedt, J. (2012). From profligacy to sustainability: Can we get there from here? In D. G. Mick, S. Pettigrew, C. Pechmann, & J. L. Ozanne (Eds.), *Transformative consumer research* (pp. 283–300). New York: Routledge.

Killen, M., & Smetana, J. G. (2006). *Handbook of moral development.* Mahwah, NJ: Lawrence Erlbaum.

Kim, G., & Kwak, K. (2011). Uncertainty matters: Impact of stimulus ambiguity on infant social referencing. *Infant and Child Development, 20*(5), 449–463.

Kim, H., & Gupta, S. (2012). Investigating customer resistance to change in transaction relationship with an internet vendor. *Psychology & Marketing, 29*(4), 257–269.

Kim, J., Kim, M., & Svinicki, M. D. (2012). Situating students' motivation in cooperative learning contexts: Proposing different levels of goal orientations. *Journal of Experimental Education, 80*(4), 352–385.

Kim, K. (2008). Meta-analyses of the relationship of creative achievement to both IQ and divergent thinking test scores. *The Journal of Creative Behavior, 42*(2), 106–130.

Kim, M., & Sankey, D. (2009). Towards a dynamic systems approach to moral development and moral education: A response to the JME special issue, September 2008. *Journal of Moral Education, 38*(3), 283–298.

King, D. B., Viney, W., & Woody, W. D. (2009). *A history of psychology: Ideas and context* (4th ed.). Boston, MA: Pearson.

Kingston, N., & Nash, B. (2011). Formative assessment: A meta-analysis and a call for research. *Educational Measurement: Issues and Practice, 30*(4), 28–37.

Kirmeyer, S. L., & Dougherty, T. W. (1988). Work load, tension, and coping: Moderating effects of supervisor support. *Personnel Psychology, 41*(1), 125–139.

Kitchin, R. M. (1994). Cognitive maps: What are they and why study them? *Journal of Environmental Psychology, 14*, 1–19.

Klassen, R. M., Tze, V. C., & Hannok, W. (2013). Internalizing problems of adults with learning disabilities: A meta-analysis. *Journal of Learning Disabilities, 46*(4), 317–327.

Klein, H. J., Wesson, M. J., Hollenbeck, J. R., & Alge, B. J. (1999). Goal commitment and the goal-setting process: Conceptual clarification and empirical synthesis. *Journal of Applied Psychology, 84*(6), 885–896.

Klein, S. R., & Huffman, A. H. (2013). I-O psychology and environmental sustainability in organizations: A natural partnership. In S. R. Klein & A. H. Huffman (Eds.), *Green organizations: Driving change with I-O psychology* (pp. 3–16). New York: Routledge.

Kleingeld, A., van Mierlo, H., & Arends, L. (2011). The effect of goal setting on group performance: A meta-analysis. *Journal of Applied Psychology, 96*(6), 1289–1304.

Klimoski, R., & Brickner, M. (1987). Why do assessment centers work? The puzzle of assessment center validity. *Personnel Psychology, 40*(2), 243–260.

Klimoski, R., & Mohammed, S. (1994). Team mental model: Construct or metaphor? *Journal of Management, 20*(2), 403–437.

Klimoski, R. J., & Jones, R. G. (2008). Intuiting the selection context. *Industrial and Organizational Psychology, 1*(3), 352–354.

Kluger, A. N., & DeNisi, A. (1996). The effects of feedback interventions on performance: A historical review, a meta-analysis, and a preliminary feedback intervention theory. *Psychological Bulletin, 119*(2), 254–284.

REFERENCES

Kluger, A. N., & DeNisi, A. (1998). Feedback interventions: Toward the understanding of a double-edged sword. *Current Directions in Psychological Science, 7*(3), 67–72.

Knapp, R. J. (1976). Authoritarianism, alienation, and related variables: A correlational and factor-analytic study. *Psychological Bulletin, 83*(2), 194–212.

Knowles, E. S., & Linn, J. A. (2004). *Resistance and persuasion.* Mahwah, NJ: Lawrence Erlbaum Associates Publishers.

Knussen, C., & Yule, F. (2008). "I'm not in the habit of recycling": The role of habitual behavior in the disposal of household waste. *Environment and Behavior, 40* (5), 683–702.

Kobau, R., Seligman, M. E. P., Peterson, C., Diener, E., Zack, M. M., Chapman, D., & Thompson, W. (2011). Mental health promotion in public health: Perspectives and strategies from positive psychology. *American Journal of Public Health, 101*(8), e1–e9.

Koch, L. (2004). The student-teacher working alliance in rehabilitation counselor education. *Rehabilitation Education, 18*(4), 235–242.

Koehler, J. J., Gibbs, B. J., & Hogarth, R. M. (1994). Shattering the illusion of control: Multi-shot versus single-shot gambles. *Journal of Behavioral Decision Making, 7*(3), 183–191.

Koger, S. M., Schettler, T., & Weiss, B. (2005). Environmental toxicants and developmental disabilities: A challenge for psychologists. *American Psychologist, 60* (3), 243–255.

Koger, S. M., & Winter, D. D. N. (2010). *The psychology of environmental problems.* New York: Routledge.

Koh, G. C. H., Khoo, H. E., & Wong, M. L. (2008). The effects of problem-based learning during medical school on physician competency: A systematic review. *Canadian Medical Association Journal, 178*(1), 34–41.

Koh, P. P., & Wong, Y. D. (2013). Influence of infrastructural compatibility factors on walking and cycling route choices. *Journal of Environmental Psychology, 36*, 202–213.

Kohlberg, L., Levine, C., & Hewer, A. (1994). Moral stages: A current formulation and a response to critics: 3 Synopses of criticisms and a reply; 4 Summary and conclusion. In B. Puka (Ed.), *New research in moral development.* (pp. 126–188). New York: Garland Publishing.

Kollmuss, A., & Agyeman, J. (2002). Mind the gap: Why do people act environmentally and what are the barriers to pro-environmental behavior? *Environmental Education Research, 8*(3), 239–260.

Komarraju, M., Karau, S. J., Schmeck, R., & Avdic, A. (2011). The Big Five personality traits, learning styles, and academic achievement. *Personality and Individual Differences, 51*(4), 472–477.

Kontogiannis, T. (2011). A systems perspective of managing error recovery and tactical re-planning of operating teams in safety critical domains. *Journal of Safety Research, 42* (2), 73–85.

Koocher, G. P., & Keith-Spiegel, P. (2008). *Ethics in psychology and the mental health professions: Standards and cases* (3rd ed.). New York: Oxford University Press.

Korpela, K. M., Hartig, T., Kaiser, F. G., & Fuhrer, U. (2001). Restorative experience and self-regulation in favorite places. *Environment and Behavior, 33*(4), 572–589.

Korunka, C., Dudak, E., Molnar, M., & Hoonakker, P. (2010). Predictors of a successful implementation of an ergonomic training program. *Applied Ergonomics, 42* (1), 98–105.

Koschate-Fisther, N., Stefan, I. V., & Hoyer, W. D. (2012). Willingness to pay for cause-related marketing: The impact of donation amount and moderating effects. *Journal of Marketing Research, 49*(6), 910–927.

Košir, K. (2005). The influence of teacher's classroom management style on pupils' self-regulative behavior. *Studia Psychologica, 47*(2), 119–144.

REFERENCES

Kotler, P. (2011). Reinventing marketing to manage the environmental imperative. *Journal of Marketing, 75*(4), 132–135.

Kotrschal, A., & Taborsky, B. (2010). Environmental change enhances cognitive abilities in fish. *PLoS Biology, 8*(4), 1–7.

Kotsou, I., Nelis, D., Grégoire, J., & Mikolajczak, M. (2011). Emotional plasticity: Conditions and effects of improving emotional competence in adulthood. *Journal of Applied Psychology, 96*(4), 827–839.

Kowalik, J., Weller, J., Venter, J., & Drachman, D. (2011). Cognitive behavioral therapy for the treatment of pediatric posttraumatic stress disorder: A review and meta-analysis. *Journal of Behavior Therapy and Experimental Psychiatry, 42*(3), 405–413.

Kozinets, R. V., Belz, F., & McDonagh, P. (2012). Social media for social change: A transformative consumer research perspective. In D. Mick, S. Pettigrew, C. Pechmann, & J. L. Ozanne (Eds.), *Transformative consumer research for personal and collective well-being* (pp. 205–223). New York: Routledge/Taylor & Francis Group.

Kozlowski, S. J., Gully, S. M., Brown, K. G., Salas, E., Smith, E. M., & Nason, E. R. (2001). Effects of training goals and goal orientation traits on multidimensional training outcomes and performance adaptability. *Organizational Behavior and Human Decision Processes, 85*(1), 1–31.

Kraag, G., Zeegers, M. P., Kok, G., Hosman, C., & Abu-Saad, H. (2006). School programs targeting stress management in children and adolescents: A meta-analysis. *Journal of School Psychology, 44*(6), 449–472.

Krasner, L., & Richards, C. S. (1976). Issues in open education and environmental design. *Psychology in the Schools, 13*(1), 77–81.

Krebs, D. L., & Denton, K. (2006). Explanatory limitations of cognitive-developmental approaches to morality. *Psychological Review, 113*(3), 672–675.

Kreshel, P. J. (1990). John B. Watson at J. Walter Thompson: The legitimation of "science" in advertising. *Journal of Advertising, 19*(2), 49–59.

Krishen, A. S., Berezan, O., & Raab, C. (2019). Feelings and functionality in social networking communities: A regulatory focus perspective. *Psychology & Marketing, 36*, 675–686.

Krosnick, J. A. (2002). Is political psychology sufficiently psychological? Distinguishing political psychology from psychological political science. In J. H. Kuklinski (Ed.), *Thinking about political psychology* (pp. 187–216). New York: Cambridge University Press.

Kruglanski, A. W. (1989). The psychology of being "right": The problem of accuracy in social perception and cognition. *Psychological Bulletin, 106*(3), 395–409.

Kruglanski, A. W., Bélanger, J. J., Chen, X., Köpetz, C., Pierro, A., & Mannetti, L. (2012). The energetics of motivated cognition: A force-field analysis. *Psychological Review, 119*(1), 1–20.

Kruglanski, A. W., & Gigerenzer, G. (2011). Intuitive and deliberate judgments are based on common principles. *Psychological Review, 118*(1), 97–109.

Krynski, T. R., & Tenenbaum, J. B. (2007). The role of causality in judgment under uncertainty. *Journal of Experimental Psychology: General, 136*(3), 430–450.

Ku, G. (2008). Learning to de-escalate: The effects of regret in escalation of commitment. *Organizational Behavior and Human Decision Processes, 105*(2), 221–232.

Kudryavtsev, A., Stedman, R. C., & Krasny, M. E. (2012). Sense of place in environmental education. *Environmental Education Research, 18*(2), 229–250.

Kuhn, D. (1990). Education for thinking: What can psychology contribute? In M. Schwebel, C. A. Maher, & N. S. Fagley (Eds.), *Promoting cognitive growth over the life span* (pp. 25–45). Hillsdale, NJ: Lawrence Erlbaum Associates, Inc.

REFERENCES

Kuhn, D. (2011). What is scientific thinking and how does it develop? In U. Goswami (Ed.), *The wiley-blackwell handbook of childhood cognitive development*, 2nd ed. (pp. 497–523). Hoboken, NJ: Wiley-Blackwell.

Kuhn, D., Cheney, R., & Weinstock, M. (2000). The development of epistemological understanding. *Cognitive Development, 15*(3), 309–328.

Kuk, G. (2000). "When to speak again": Self-regulation under facilitation. *Group Dynamics: Theory, Research, and Practice, 4*(4), 291–306.

Kulik, J. A., Sledge, P., & Mahler, H. I. M. (1986). Self-confirmatory attribution, egocentrism, and the perpetuation of self-beliefs. *Journal of Personality and Social Psychology, 50*(3), 587–594.

Kumar, S., & Jagacinski, C. M. (2011). Confronting task difficulty in ego involvement: Change in performance goals. *Journal of Educational Psychology, 103*(3), 664–682.

Kumkale, G. T., & Albarracín, D. (2004). The sleeper effect in persuasion: A meta-analytic review. *Psychological Bulletin, 130*(1), 143–172.

Kuppens, S., Laurent, L., Heyvaert, M., & Onghena, P. (2012). Associations between parental psychological control and relational aggression in children and adolescents: A multilevel and sequential meta-analysis. *Developmental Psychology*, doi:10.1037/a0030740

Kyle, G., Graefe, A., Manning, R., & Bacon, J. (2004a). Effect of activity involvement and place attachment on recreationists' perceptions of setting density. *Journal of Leisure Research, 36*(2), 209–231.

Kyle, G., Graefe, A., Manning, R., & Bacon, J. (2004b). Effects of place attachment on users' perceptions of social and environmental conditions in a natural setting. *Journal of Environmental Psychology, 24*(2), 213–225.

Læssøe, J., & Ohman, J. (2010). Learning as democratic action and communication: Framing Danish and Swedish environmental and sustainability education. *Environmental Education Research, 16*(1), 1–7.

Laguna, L., Linn, A., Ward, K., & Rupslaukyte, R. (2010). An examination of authoritarian personality traits among police officers: The role of experience. *Journal of Police and Criminal Psychology, 25*(2), 99–104.

Laitala, K., Boks, C., & Klepp, I. (2011). Potential for environmental improvements in laundering. *International Journal of Consumer Studies, 35*(2), 254–264.

Laitala, K., Klepp, I. G., & Boks, C. (2012). Changing laundry habits in Norway. *International Journal of Consumer Studies, 36*(2), 228–237.

Lamm, C., & Lewis, M. D. (2010). Developmental change in the neurophysiological correlates of self-regulation in high- and low-emotion conditions. *Developmental Neuropsychology, 35*(2), 156–176.

Lanaj, K., Chang, C. H., & Johnson, R. E. (2012). Regulatory focus and work-related outcomes: A review and meta-analysis. *Psychological Bulletin, 138*(5), 998–1034.

Lang, P. J. (1995). The emotion probe: Studies of motivation and attention. *American Psychologist, 50*, 372–385.

Langevin, R., Curnoe, S., Fedoroff, P., Bennett, R., Langevin, M., Peever, C., &., … Sandhu, S. (2004). Lifetime sex offender recidivism: A 25-year follow-up study. *Canadian Journal of Criminology and Criminal Justice, 46*(5), 531–552.

Langhe, B., de van Osselaer, S. M. J., & Wierenga, B. (2011). The effects of process and outcome accountability on judgment process and performance. *Organizational Behavior and Human Decision Processes, 115*(2), 238–252.

Langley, A., DeCarlo Santiago, C., Rodríguez, A., & Zelaya, J. (2013). Improving implementation of mental health services for trauma in multicultural elementary schools: Stakeholder perspectives on parent and educator engagement. *The Journal of Behavioral Health Services & Research, 40*(3), 247–262.

REFERENCES

Langner, S., Hennigs, N., & Wiedmann, K. (2013). Social persuasion: Targeting social identities through social influencers. *Journal of Consumer Marketing, 30*(1), 31–49.

Lanzini, P., & Khan, S. A. (2017). Shedding light on the psychological and behavioral determinants of travel mode choice: A meta-analysis. *Transportation Research Part F: Traffic Psychology and Behaviour, 48*, 13–27.

Latham, G. P. (2007). *Work motivation: History, theory, research, and practice.* Thousand Oaks, CA: Sage Publications, Inc.

Latham, G. P., Erez, M., & Locke, E. A. (1988). Resolving scientific disputes by the joint design of crucial experiments by the antagonists: Application to the Erez–Latham dispute regarding participation in goal setting. *Journal of Applied Psychology, 73*(4), 753–772.

Latham, G. P., & Heslin, P. A. (2003). Training the trainee as well as the trainer: Lessons to be learned from clinical psychology. *Canadian Psychology/Psychologie Canadienne, 44*(3), 218–231.

Law, K. S., Wong, C. S., & Song, L. J. (2004). The construct and criterion validity of Emotional Intelligence and its potential utility for management studies. *Journal of Applied Psychology, 89*(3), 483–496.

Lawson, R. (1997). Consumer decision making within a goal-driven framework. *Psychology & Marketing, 14*(5), 427–449.

Lazarus, R. S. (1995). Cognition and emotion from the RET viewpoint. *Journal of Rational-Emotive and Cognitive-Behavior Therapy, 13*, 29–54.

Le Coze, J. (2013). What have we learned about learning from accidents? Post-disasters reflections. *Safety Science, 51*(1), 441–453.

Leahy, T. H. (2008). Review of "Popper, Otto Selz, and the rise of evolutionary epistemology". *Journal of the History of the Behavioral Sciences, 44*(1), 89–90.

Lebens, H., Roefs, A., Martijn, C., Houben, K., Nederkoorn, C., & Jansen, A. (2011). Making implicit measures of associations with snack foods more negative through evaluative conditioning. *Eating Behaviors, 12*(4), 249–253.

Lederbogen, F., Kirsch, P., Haddad, L., Streit, F., Tost, H., Schuch, P., … Meyer-Lindenberg, A. (2011). City living and urban upbringing affect neural social stress processing in humans. *Nature, 474*(7352), 498–501.

Lee, J. K. H., Sudhir, K., & Steckel, J. H. (2002). A multiple ideal point model: Capturing multiple preference effects from within an ideal point framework. *Journal of Marketing Research, 39*(1), 73–86.

Lee, K. (2008). Opportunities for green marketing: Young consumers. *Marketing Intelligence & Planning, 26*(6), 573–586.

Lee, K. (2011). The role of media exposure, social exposure and biospheric value orientation in the environmental attitude-intention-behavior model in adolescents. *Journal of Environmental Psychology, 31*(4), 301–308.

Lee, K., & Kim, J. (2011). Integrating suppliers into green product innovation development: An empirical case study in the semiconductor industry. *Business Strategy and the Environment, 20*(8), 527–538.

Lee, W., & Choi, S. (2005). The role of horizontal and vertical individualism and collectivism in online consumers' responses toward persuasive communication on the web. *Journal of Computer-Mediated Communication, 11*(1), 317–336.

Lee, Y., Lawton, L. J., & Weaver, D. B. (2013). Evidence for a South Korean model of ecotourism. *Journal of Travel Research, 52*(4), 520–533.

Lee, Y., & Qiu, C. (2009). When uncertainty brings pleasure: The role of prospect imageability and mental imagery. *Journal of Consumer Research, 36*(4), 624–633.

Leeson, P., Heaven, P. C. L., & Ciarrochi, J. (2012). Revisiting the link between low verbal intelligence and ideology. *Intelligence, 40*(2), 213–216.

Lefcourt, H. M., & Shepherd, R. S. (1995). Organ donation, authoritarianism, and perspective-taking humor. *Journal of Research in Personality, 29*(1), 121–138.

REFERENCES

Lefevre, C. E., de Bruin, W. B., Taylor, A. L., Dessai, S., Kovats, S., & Fischhoff, B. (2015). Heat protection behaviors and positive affect about heat during the 2013 heat wave in the United Kingdom. *Social Science & Medicine, 128*, 282–289.

Lefkowitz, J. (2008). To prosper, organizational psychology should..expand the values of organizational psychology to match the quality of its ethics. *Journal of Organizational Behavior, 29*(4), 439–453.

Lefkowitz, J. (2013). Values and ethics of a changing I-O- psychology: A call to further action. In J. Olson-Buchanan, L. K. Bryan, & L. F. Thompson (Eds.), *Using industrial-organizational psychology for the greater good* (pp. 13–42). New York: Routledge.

Leidner, D., & Elam, J. J. (1995). The impact of executive information systems on organizational design, intelligence and decision making. *Organization Science, 6*(6), 645–664.

Leiserowitz, A., Smith, N., & Marlon, J. R. (2011). *American teens' knowledge of climate change*. New Haven, CT: Yale University Yale Project on Climate Change Communication, 5.

Lent, R., & Hackett, G. (1994). Sociocognitive mechanisms of personal agency in career development: Pantheoretical prospects. In M. L. Savikas & R. Lent (Eds.), *Convergence in career development theories: Implications for science and practice* (pp. 77–101). Palo Alto, CA: CPP Books.

Lenton, A. P., Penke, L., Todd, P. M., & Fasolo, B. (2013). The heart has its reasons: Social rationality in mate choice. In R. Hertwig & U. Hoffrage (Eds.), *Simple heuristics in a social world* (pp. 433–457). New York: Oxford University Press.

León, I., & Hernández, J. A. (1998). Testing the role of attribution and appraisal in predicting own and other's emotions. *Cognition and Emotion, 12*(1), 27–43.

Let's Move (2013). https://letsmove.obamawhitehouse.archives.gov/

Leutwyler, B. (2009). Metacognitive learning strategies: Differential development patterns in high school. *Metacognition and Learning, 4*(2), 111–123.

Levin, W. E., & Unsworth, S. J. (2013). Do humans belong with nature? The influence of personal vs. abstract contexts on human–Nature categorization at different stages of development. *Journal of Environmental Psychology, 33*9–13.

Levine, J. M., & Moreland, R. L. (2012). A history of small group research. In A. W. Kruglanski & W. Stroebe (Eds.), *Handbook of the history of social psychology* (pp. 383–405). New York: Psychology Press.

Levy, B. M., & Zint, M. T. (2013). Toward fostering environmental political participation: Framing an agenda for environmental education research. *Environmental Education Research, 19*(5), 553–576.

Lévy-Leboyer, C. (1988). Success and failure in applying psychology. *American Psychologist, 43*(10), 779–785.

Levy-Leboyer, C., Bonnes, M., Chase, J., Ferreira-Marques, J., & Pawlik, K. (1996). Determinants of pro-environmental behaviors: A five-countries comparison. *European Psychologist, 1*(2), 123–129.

Levy-Leboyer, C. I. (1979). Applied psychology or the application of psychology? *International Review of Applied Psychology, 28*(2), 75–80.

Lewicka, M. (2011). Place attachment: How far have we come in the last 40 years? *Journal of Environmental Psychology, 31*(3), 207–230.

Lewin, J. E., & Donthu, N. (2005). The influence of purchase situation on buying center structure and involvement: A select meta-analysis of organizational buying behavior research. *Journal of Business Research, 58*(10), 1381–1390.

Lewin, K. (1935). *A dynamic theory of personality*. New York: McGraw-Hill.

Lewin, K. (1951). Formalization and progress in psychology. In D. Cartwright (Ed.), *Field theory in social science* (pp. 1–29). New York: Harper.

REFERENCES

Lewis, I. I., Watson, B. B., & White, K. M. (2008). An examination of message-relevant affect in road safety messages: Should road safety advertisements aim to make us feel good or bad? *Transportation Research Part F: Traffic Psychology and Behaviour, 11*(6), 403–417.

Li, W., Harris, D., & Chen, A. (2007). Eastern minds in Western cockpits: Meta-analysis of human factors in mishaps from three nations. *Aviation, Space, and Environmental Medicine, 78* (4, Sect 1), 420–425.

Li, Y., Ahlstrom, D., & Ashkanasy, N. M. (2010). A multilevel model of affect and organizational commitment. *Asia Pacific Journal of Management, 27*(2), 193–213.

Libby, R., Trotman, K. T., & Zimmer, I. (1987). Member variation, recognition of expertise, and group performance. *Journal of Applied Psychology, 72*(1), 81–87.

Liddle, H. A., Dakof, G. A., Turner, R. M., Henderson, C. E., & Greenbaum, P. E. (2008). Treating adolescent drug abuse: A randomized trial comparing multidimensional family therapy and cognitive behavior therapy. *Addiction, 103*(10), 1660–1670.

Lieberman, J. D. (2011). The utility of scientific jury selection: Still murky after 30 years. *Current Directions in Psychological Science, 20*(1), 48–52.

Lievens, F., & De Soete, B. (2011). Instrumenten om personeel te selecteren in de 21ste eeuw: Onderzoek en praktijk. *Gedrag En Organisatie, 24*(1), 18–42.

Lillie, R. (2007). Getting clients to hear: Applying principles and techniques of Kiesler's Interpersonal Communication Therapy to assessment feedback. *Psychology and Psychotherapy: Theory, Research and Practice, 80*(1), 151–163.

Lim, T., & Kim, S. (2007). Many faces of media effects. In R. W. Preiss, B. Gayle, N. Burrell, M. Allen, & J. Bryant (Eds.), *Mass media effects research: Advances through meta-analysis* (pp. 315–325). Mahwah, NJ: Lawrence Erlbaum Associates Publishers.

Lima, M. L. (2006). Predictors of attitudes towards the construction of a waste incinerator: Two case studies. *Journal of Applied Social Psychology, 36*(2), 441–466.

Linhares, A. (2005). An active symbols theory of chess intuition. *Minds and Machines, 15* (2), 131–181.

Little, B. R., & Chambers, N. C. (2004). Personal project pursuit: On human doings and well-beings. In W. Cox & E. Klinger (Eds.), *Handbook of motivational counseling: Concepts, approaches, and assessment* (pp. 65–82). New York: John Wiley & Sons Ltd.

Liu, J. H., & Sibley, C. G. (2004). Attitudes and behavior in social space: Public good interventions based on shared representations and environmental influences. *Journal of Environmental Psychology, 24*(3), 373–384.

Locke, E. A., & Latham, G. P. (2006). New directions in goal-setting theory. *Current Directions in Psychological Science, 15*(5), 265–268.

Loizzo, J. (2012). *Sustainable happiness: The mind science of well-being, altruism, and inspiration.* New York: Routledge/Taylor & Francis Group.

Lombardo, T., Schneider, S., & Bryan, L. K. (2013). Corporate leaders of sustainable organizations: Balancing planet, profit, and people. In J. Olson-Buchanan, L. K. Bryan, & L. F. Thompson (Eds.), *Using industrial-organizational psychology for the greater good* (pp. 75–109). New York: Routledge.

London, M. (1997). *Job feedback: Giving, seeking, and using feedback for performance improvement.* Hillsdale, NJ and England: Lawrence Erlbaum Associates, Inc.

London, M. (2002). *Leadership development: Paths to self-insight and professional growth.* Mahwah, NJ: Lawrence Erlbaum Associates Publishers.

Long, S., & Benton, D. (2013). Effects of vitamin and mineral supplementation on stress, mild psychiatric symptoms, and mood in nonclinical samples: A meta-analysis. *Psychosomatic Medicine, 75*(2), 144–153.

López-Mosquera, N., & Sánchez, M. (2013). Direct and indirect effects of received benefits and place attachment in willingness to pay and loyalty in suburban natural areas. *Journal of Environmental Psychology, 34*, 27–35.

REFERENCES

Lord, R. G., Diefendorff, J. M., Schmidt, A. M., & Hall, R. J. (2010). Self-regulation at work. *Annual Review of Psychology, 61*, 543–568.

Lou, Y., Abrami, P. C., & d'Apollonia, S. (2001). Small group and individual learning with technology: A meta-analysis. *Review of Educational Research, 71*(3), 449–521.

Louis, M. R., & Sutton, R. I. (1991). Switching cognitive gears: From habits of mind to active thinking. *Human Relations, 44*, 55–76.

Lourenço, O. (2012). Piaget and Vygotsky: Many resemblances, and a crucial difference. *New Ideas in Psychology, 30*(3), 281–295.

Lowman, R. L. (1998). *The ethical practice of psychology in organizations.* Washington, DC: American Psychological Association.

Lowman, R. L. (2013). Is sustainability an ethical responsibility of I-O and consulting psychologists? In A. H. Huffman & S. R. Klein (Eds.), *Green organizations: Driving change with I-O psychology* (pp. 34–54). New York: Routledge.

Lu, X. (1998). An interface between individualistic and collectivistic orientations in Chinese cultural values and social relations. *Howard Journal of Communications, 9*(2), 91–107.

Lukersmith, S., & Burgess-Limerick, R. (2013). The perceived importance and the presence of creative potential in the health professional's work environment. *Ergonomics, 56*(6), 922–934.

Luszczynska, A., Benight, C. C., & Cieslak, R. (2009). Self-efficacy and health-related outcomes of collective trauma: A systematic review. *European Psychologist, 14*(1), 51–62.

Ma, Q. G., & Wang, K. (2009).The effect of positive emotion and perceived risk on usage intention to online decision aids. *CyberPsychology and Behavior, 12*(5), 529–532.

Maani, K. E., & Maharaj, V. (2004). Links between systems thinking and complex decision making. *System Dynamics Review, 20*(1), 21–48.

Maass, A., & Clark, R. D. (1983). Internalization versus compliance: Differential processes underlying minority influence and conformity. *European Journal of Social Psychology, 13*(3), 197–215.

Mace, B. L., Corser, G. C., Zitting, L., & Denison, J. (2013). Effects of overflights on the national park experience. *Journal of Environmental Psychology, 35*, 30–39.

Macey, W. H., & Schneider, B. (2008). The meaning of employee engagement. *Industrial and Organizational Psychology: Perspectives on Science and Practice, 1*(1), 3–30.

MacKay, D. G. (1988). Under what conditions can theoretical psychology survive and prosper? Integrating the rational and empirical epistemologies. *Psychological Review, 95*(4), 559–565.

MacLaren, V. V. (2001). A quantitative review of the Guilty Knowledge Test. *Journal of Applied Psychology, 86*(4), 674–683.

Maddi, S. R. (1998). Creating meaning through making decisions. In P. P. Wong & P. S. Fry (Eds.), *The human quest for meaning: A handbook of psychological research and clinical applications* (pp. 3–26). Mahwah, NJ: Lawrence Erlbaum Associates Publishers.

Madhavan, P. P., & Gonzalez, C. C. (2010). The relationship between stimulus-response mappings and the detection of novel stimuli in a simulated luggage screening task. *Theoretical Issues in Ergonomics Science, 11*(5), 461–473.

Maeda, Y., Thoma, S. J., & Bebeau, M. J. (2009). Understanding the relationship between moral judgment development and individual characteristics: The role of educational contexts. *Journal of Educational Psychology, 101*(1), 233–247.

Mahajan, V., Muller, E., & Bass, F. M. (1990). New product diffusion models in marketing: A review and directions for research. *Journal of Marketing, 54*(1), 1–26.

Mahn, H., & John-Steiner, V. (2013). Vygotsky and sociocultural approaches to teaching and learning. In W. M. Reynolds, G. E. Miller, & I. B. Weiner (Eds.), *Handbook of psychology, Vol. 7: Educational psychology* (2nd ed.) (pp. 117–145). Hoboken, NJ: Wiley & Sons.

REFERENCES

Maibach, E. W., Leiserowitz, A., Roser-Renouf, C., & Mertz, C. K. (2011). Identifying like-minded audiences for global warming public engagement campaigns: An audience segmentation analysis and tool development. *PLoS One, 6*(3), e17571.

Maiden, R. J., Peterson, S. A., Caya, M., & Hayslip, B. (2003). Personality changes in the old-old: A longitudinal study. *Journal of Adult Development, 10*(1), 31–39.

Maier, S. F., Peterson, C., & Schwartz, B. (2000). In J. E. Gillham (Ed.), *The science of optimism and hope: Research essays in honor of Martin E. P. Seligman* (pp. 11–37). West Conshohocken, PA: Templeton Foundation Press.

Major, J. T., Johnson, W., & Bouchard, T. J., Jr. (2011). The dependability of the general factor of intelligence: Why small, single-factor models do not adequately representing. *Intelligence, 39*(5), 418–433.

Malaviya, P., Kisielius, J., & Sternthal, B. (1996). The effect of type of elaboration on advertisement processing and judgment. *Journal of Marketing Research, 33*(4), 410–421.

Malone, J. C. (2004). Modern molar behaviorism and theoretical behaviorism: Religion and science. *Journal of the Experimental Analysis of Behavior, 82*(1), 95–102.

Maloney, M. P., & Ward, M. P. (1973). Ecology: Let's hear from the people. An objective scale for the measurement of ecological attitudes and knowledge. *American Psychologist, 28*, 583–586.

Mann, K. V. (2011). Theoretical perspectives in medical education: Past experience and future possibilities. *Medical Education, 45*(1), 60–68.

Mann, S. (2007). Expectations of emotional display in the workplace: An American/ British comparative study. *Leadership & Organization Development Journal, 28*(6), 552–570.

Mannarini, T., Roccato, M., Fedi, A., & Rovere, A. (2009). Six factors fostering protest: Predicting participation in locally unwanted land uses movements. *Political Psychology, 30*(6), 895–920.

Marcus, B., Wagner, U., Poole, A., Powell, D. M., & Carswell, J. (2009). The relationship of GMA to counterproductive work behavior revisited. *European Journal of Personality, 23*(6), 489–507.

Mares, M.-L., & Pan, Z. (2013). Effects of Sesame Street: A meta-analysis of children's learning in 15 countries. *Journal of Applied Developmental Psychology, 34*(3), 140–151.

Marewski, J. N., & Mehlhorn, K. (2011). Using the ACT-R architecture to specify 39 quantitative process models of decision making. *Judgment and Decision Making, 6*(6), 439–519.

Markowitz, E. M., Goldberg, L. R., Ashton, M. C., & Lee, K. (2012). Profiling the "pro-environmental individual": A personality perspective. *Journal of Personality, 80*(1), 81–111.

Marks, J. B., & MacDougall, V. (1959). Authoritarianism, intelligence, and work effectiveness among psychiatric aides. *The Journal of Social Psychology, 49*, 237–242.

Markus, H. (1977). Self-schemata and processing information about the self. *Journal of Personality and Social Psychology, 35*, 63–78.

Markus, H., & Cross, S. (1990). The interpersonal self. In L. A. Pervin (Ed.), *Handbook of personality: Theory and research* (pp. 576–608). New York: Guilford Press.

Markus, H., & Kitayama, S. (2010). Cultures and selves: A cycle of mutual constitution. *Perspectives on Psychological Science, 5*(4), 420–430.

Markus, H., & Kunda, Z. (1986). Stability and malleability of the self-concept. *Journal of Personality and Social Psychology, 51*, 858–866.

Markus, H., & Nurius, P. (1986). Possible selves. *American Psychologist, 41*(9), 954–969.

Markus, H., & Wurf, E. (1987). The dynamic self-concept: A social psychological perspective. *Annual Review of Psychology, 39*, 299–337.

Martin, I. M., Bender, H., & Raish, C. (2007). What motivates individuals to protect themselves from risks: The case of wildland fires. *Risk Analysis, 27*(4), 887–900.

REFERENCES

Martin, K. K., Legg, S. S., & Brown, C. C. (2013). Designing for sustainability: Ergonomics—Carpe diem. *Ergonomics, 56*(3), 365–388.

Martin, M. S., Dorken, S. K., Wamboldt, A. D., & Wootten, S. E. (2012). Stopping the revolving door: A meta-analysis on the effectiveness of interventions for criminally involved individuals with major mental disorders. *Law and Human Behavior, 36*(1), 1–12.

Martin, R., Martin, P. Y., Smith, J. R., & Hewstone, M. (2007). Majority versus minority influence and prediction of behavioral intentions and behavior. *Journal of Experimental Social Psychology, 43*(5), 763–771.

Martinez, C. R., Jr., & Forgatch, M. S. (2001). Preventing problems with boys' noncompliance: Effects of a parent training intervention for divorcing mothers. *Journal of Consulting and Clinical Psychology, 69*(3), 416–428.

Marzbali, M., Abdullah, A., Razak, N. D., & Maghsoodi Tilaki, M. (2012). The influence of crime prevention through environmental design on victimisation and fear of crime. *Journal of Environmental Psychology, 32*(2), 79–88.

Marzocchi, G., Morandin, G., & Bergami, M. (2013). Brand communities: Loyal to the community or the brand? *European Journal of Marketing, 47*(1-2), 93–114.

Masnick, A. M., & Zimmerman, C. (2009) Evaluating scientific research in the context of prior belief: Hindsight bias or confirmation bias? *Journal of Psychology of Science and Technology, 2*(1), 29–36.

Masuda, A., & Visio, M. (2012). Nepotism practices and the work-family interface. In R. G. Jones (Ed.), *Nepotism in organizations* (pp. 147–170). New York: Routledge/Taylor & Francis Group.

Matsumoto, D., & Ekman, P. (1989). American-Japanese cultural differences in intensity ratings of facial expressions of emotion. *Motivation and Emotion, 13*(2), 143–157.

Matthews, J. R. (2011). Understanding the nuances of ethical behavior. *Psyccritiques, 56* (6), doi:10.1037/a0022836

Maul, A. (2011). The factor structure and cross-test convergence of the Mayer–Salovey–Caruso model of emotional intelligence. *Personality and Individual Differences, 50*(4), 457–463.

Maurer, T. J., Solamon, J. M., Andrews, K. D., & Troxtel, D. D. (2001). Interviewee coaching, preparation strategies, and response strategies in relation to performance in situational employment interviews: An extension of Maurer, Solamon, and Troxtel (1998). *Journal of Applied Psychology, 86*(4), 709–717.

Mayer, J. D. (1998). A systems framework for the field of personality. *Psychological Inquiry, 9*(2), 118–144.

Mayer, J. D., Salovey, P., & Caruso, D. R. (2004). Emotional intelligence: Theory, research, and findings. *Psychological Inquiry, 15*, 197–215.

Mayflower Group, The (2013). http://mayflowergroup.org/

Mazumdar, S., & Mazumdar, S. (2004). Religion and place attachment: A study of sacred places. *Journal of Environmental Psychology, 24*(3), 385–397.

McArthur, L. Z., & Baron, R. M. (1983). Toward an ecological theory of social perception. *Psychological Review, 90*, 215–238.

McCleary, D. F., & Williams, R. L. (2009). Sociopolitical and personality correlates of militarism in Democratic societies. *Peace and Conflict: Journal of Peace Psychology, 15*(2), 161–187.

McCourt, K., Bouchard, T. R., Lykken, D. T., Tellegen, A., & Keyes, M. (1999). Authoritarianism revisited: Genetic and environmental influences examined in twins reared apart and together. *Personality And Individual Differences, 27*(5), 985–1014.

McCright, A. M., & Dunlap, R. E. (2013). Bringing ideology in: The conservative white male effect on worry about environmental problems in the USA. *Journal of Risk Research, 16*(2), 211–226.

REFERENCES

McDaniel, M. A., Morgeson, F. P., Finnegan, E. B., Campion, M. A., & Braverman, E. P. (2001). Use of situational judgment tests to predict job performance: A clarification of the literature. *Journal of Applied Psychology, 86*(4), 730–740.

McDaniel, M. A., & Whetzel, D. L. (2005). Situational judgment test research: Informing the debate on practical intelligence theory. *Intelligence, 33*(5), 515–525.

McDonald, M. M., & Donnellan, M. (2012). Is ostracism a strong situation? The influence of personality in reactions to rejection. *Journal of Research in Personality, 46*(5), 614–618.

McDonald, S., & Oates, C. J. (2006). Sustainability: Consumer perceptions and marketing strategies. *Business Strategy and the Environment, 15*(3), 157–170.

McDonough, G. P. (2005). Moral maturity and autonomy: Appreciating the significance of Lawrence Kolhberg's Just Community. *Journal of Moral Education, 34*(2), 199–213.

McDougle, L. M., Greenspan, I., & Handy, F. (2011). Generation green: Understanding the motivations and mechanisms influencing young adults' environmental volunteering. *International Journal of Nonprofit and Voluntary Sector Marketing, 16*(4), 325–341.

McDowell, J. J. (2013). On the theoretical and empirical status of the matching law and matching theory. *Psychological Bulletin, 139*, 1000–1028.

McFillen, J. M., O'Neil, D. A., Balzer, W. K., & Varney, G. H. (2013). Organizational diagnosis: An evidence-based approach. *Journal of Change Management, 13* (2), 223–246.

McInerney, D. M., & Ali, J. (2006). Multidimensional and hierarchical assessment of school motivation: Cross-cultural validation. *Educational Psychology, 26*(6), 717–734.

McKenzie-Mohr, D. (2000). Fostering sustainable behavior through community-based social marketing. *American Psychologist, 55*(5), 531–537.

McLeod, B. D. (2011). Relation of the alliance with outcomes in youth psychotherapy: A meta-analysis. *Clinical Psychology Review, 31*(4), 603–616.

McMichael, A. J., & Butler, C. D. (2011). Promoting global population health while constraining the environmental footprint. *Annual Review of Public Health, 32*, 179–197.

McRaney, D. (2011). *You are not so smart.* New York: Gotham Books.

Meadows, D. (2008). *Thinking in systems: A primer.* Post Mills, VT: Chelsea Green.

Meadows, D. H. (2004). *The limits to growth: The 30-year update.* White River Junction, VT: Chelsea Green.

Meadows, D. H., Meadows, D. L., & Randers, J. (1992). *Beyond the limits.* Post Mills, VT: Chelsea Green.

Mehrez, A., & Steinberg, G. (1998). Rule based expert system versus novices' heuristics: A matching identification problem. *Psychological Reports, 82*, 1423–1431.

Meijers, F. F. (1998). The development of a career identity. *International Journal for the Advancement of Counselling, 20*(3), 191–207.

Meijers, M. H. C., Noordewier, M. K., Verlegh, P. W. J., Willems, W., & Smit, E. G. (2019). Paradoxical side effects of green advertising: How purchasing green products may instigate licensing effects for consumers with a weak environmental identity. *International Journal of Advertising: The Review of Marketing Communications*, e-journal

Mena, J. A., Hult, G. T. M., Ferrell, O. C., & Zhang, Y. (2019). Competing assessments of market-driven, sustainability-centered, and stakeholder-focused approaches to the customer-brand relationships and performance. *Journal of Business Research, 95*, 531–543.

Mento, A. J., Steel, R. P., & Karren, R. J. (1987). A meta-analytic study of the effects of goal setting on task performance: 1966–1984. *Organizational Behavior and Human Decision Processes, 39*(1), 52–83.

Meredith, G. P. (1927). Consciousness of method as a means of transfer of training. *Forum of Education, 5*, 37–45.

REFERENCES

Merlo, O., Lukas, B. A., & Whitwell, G. J. (2008). Heuristics revisited: Implications for marketing research and practice. *Marketing Theory*, *8*(2), 189–204.

Merriam-Webster (2013). www.merriam-webster.com/dictionary/subversion

Merrilees, B., Miller, D., & Herington, C. (2013). City branding: A facilitating framework for stressed satellite cities. *Journal of Business Research*, *66*(1), 37–44.

Meshkati, N., Tabibzadeh, M., Farshid, A., Rahimi, M., & Alhanaee, G. (2016). People-technology-ecosystem integration: A framework to ensure regional interoperability for safety, sustainability, and resilience of interdependent energy, water, and seafood sources in the (Persian) Gulf. *Human Factors*, *58*(1), 43–57.

Mesmer-Magnus, J., Glew, D. J., & Viswesvaran, C. (2012). A meta-analysis of positive humor in the workplace. *Journal of Managerial Psychology*, *27*(2), 155–190.

Meyer, J. P., Stanley, D. J., Jackson, T. A., McInnis, K. J., Maltin, E. R., & Sheppard, L. (2012). Affective, normative, and continuance commitment levels across cultures: A meta-analysis. *Journal of Vocational Behavior*, *80*(2), 225–245.

Meyer, R. D., & Dalal, R. S. (2009). Situational strength as a means of conceptualizing context. *Industrial and Organizational Psychology: Perspectives on Science and Practice*, *2*(1), 99–102.

Milfont, T. L., & Duckitt, J. (2010). The Environmental Attitudes Inventory: A valid and reliable measure to assess the structure of environmental attitudes. *Journal of Environmental Psychology*, *30*(1), 80–94.

Milfont, T. L., & Sibley, C. G. (2012). The big five personality traits and environmental engagement: Associations at the individual and societal level. *Journal of Environmental Psychology*, *32*(2), 187–195.

Milfont, T. L., Wilson, J., & Diniz, P. (2012). Time perspective and environmental engagement: A meta-analysis. *International Journal of Psychology*, *47*(5), 325–334.

Milgram, S. (1974). *Obedience to authority*. New York: Harper & Row.

Miller, D. T., Effron, D. A., & Zak, S. V. (2010). From moral outrage to social protest: The role of psychological standing. In D. Bobocel, A. C. Kay, M. P. Zanna, & J. M. Olson (Eds.), *The psychology of justice and legitimacy* (pp. 103–123). New York: Psychology Press.

Miller, J. L. (2012). *Psychosocial capacity building in response to disasters*. New York: Columbia University Press.

Miller, P. A., & Eisenberg, N. (1988). The relation of empathy to aggressive and externalizing/antisocial behavior. *Psychological Bulletin*, *103*(3), 324–344.

Miller, P. A., Kozu, J., & Davis, A. C. (2001). Social influence, empathy, and prosocial behavior in cross-cultural perspective. In W. Wosinska, R. B. Cialdini, D. W. Barrett, & J. Reykowski (Eds.), *The practice of social influence in multiple cultures* (pp. 63–77). Mahwah, NJ: Lawrence Erlbaum Associates Publishers.

Millet, K., & Dewitte, S. (2007). Altruistic behavior as a costly signal of general intelligence. *Journal of Research in Personality*, *41*(2), 316–326.

Minami, H. (2009). Commentary: Is place experience culturally specific? A commentary on Yoly Zentella's article. *Culture & Psychology*, *15*(2), 209–215.

Miner, F. C. (1984). Group versus individual decision making: An investigation of performance measures, decision strategies, and process losses/gains. *Organizational Behavior and Human Performance*, *33*, 112–124.

Minkov, M., & Hofstede, G. (2012). Hofstede's fifth dimension: New evidence from the world values survey. *Journal of Cross-Cultural Psychology*, *43*(1), 3–14.

Minton, E., Lee, C., Orth, U., Kim, C., & Kahle, L. (2012). Sustainable marketing and social media: A cross-country analysis of motives for sustainable behaviors. *Journal of Advertising*, *41*(4), 69–84.

REFERENCES

Mischel, W. (1977). The interaction of person and situation. In D. Magnusson & N. S. Endler (Eds.), *Personality at the crossroads: Current issues in interactional psychology* (pp. 333–352). Hillsdale, NJ: Lawrence Erlbaum Associates, Inc.

Mischel, W. (2004). Toward an integrative model for CBT: Encompassing behavior, cognition, affect, and process. *Behavior Therapy, 35*(1), 185–203.

Mischel, W., Ayduk, O., Berman, M. G., Casey, B. J., Gotlib, I. H., Jonides, J., &., … Shoda, Y. (2011). "Willpower" over the life span: Decomposing self-regulation. *Social Cognitive and Affective Neuroscience, 6*(2), 252–256.

Mischel, W., & Mischel, H. N. (1994). A cognitive social-learning approach to morality and self-regulation. In B. Puka (Ed.), *Defining perspectives in moral development* (pp. 186–210). New York: Garland Publishing.

Mischel, W., Shoda, Y., & Mendoza-Denton, R. (2002). Situation-behavior profiles as a locus of consistency in personality. *Current Directions in Psychological Science, 11*(2), 50–54.

Mishra, S., Mazumdar, S., & Suar, D. (2010). Place attachment and flood preparedness. *Journal of Environmental Psychology, 30*(2), 187–197.

Mitte, K. (2005). Meta-analysis of cognitive-behavioral treatments for generalized anxiety disorder: A comparison with pharmacotherapy. *Psychological Bulletin, 131*(5), 785–795.

Mohammed, S., & Dumville, B. C. (2001). Team mental models in a team knowledge framework: Expanding theory and measurement across disciplinary boundaries. *Journal of Organizational Behavior, 22*(2), 89–106.

Mohr, D. M. (1978). Development of attributes of personal identity. *Developmental Psychology, 14*(4), 427–428.

Molnar, A. (1997). *The construction of children's character.* Chicago, IL: The National Society for the Study of Education.

Molnar, T. S. (1967). *Utopia: The perennial heresy.* New York: Sheed and Ward.

Montgomery, K. C., & Chester, J. (2009). Interactive food and beverage marketing: Targeting adolescents in the digital age. *Journal of Adolescent Health, 45* (3,Suppl), S18–S29.

Moore, T. (2004). The critical thinking debate: How general are general thinking skills? *Higher Education Research & Development, 23*(1), 3–18.

Moreland, R. L., & Levine, J. M. (1991). Problem identification by groups. In S. Worchel, W. Wood, & J. A. Simpson (Eds.), *Group process and productivity* (pp. 17–47). Thousand Oaks, CA: Sage.

Morgan, J. F., & Hancock, P. A. (2011). The effect of prior task loading on mental workload: An example of hysteresis in driving. *Human Factors, 53*(1), 75–86.

Morgan, P. (2010). Towards a developmental theory of place attachment. *Journal of Environmental Psychology, 30*(1), 11–22.

Morgeson, F. P., Delaney-Klinger, K., & Hemingway, M. A. (2005). The importance of job autonomy, cognitive ability, and job-related skill for predicting role breadth and job performance. *Journal of Applied Psychology, 90*(2), 399–406.

Morgeson, F. P., Garza, A. S., & Campion, M. A. (2013). Work design. In N. W. Schmitt, S. Highhouse, & I. B. Weiner (Eds.), *Handbook of psychology, Vol. 12: Industrial and organizational psychology* (2nd ed.) (pp. 525–559). Hoboken, NJ: John Wiley & Sons Inc.

Morling, B., & Lamoreaux, M. (2008). Measuring culture outside the head: A meta-analysis of individualism-collectivism in cultural products. *Personality and Social Psychology Review, 12*(3), 199–221.

Morozov, E. (2013). *To save everything, click here.* New York: Public Affairs.

Morren, M., & Grinstein, A. (2016). Explaining environmental behavior across borders: A meta-analysis. *Journal of Environmental Psychology, 47*, 91–106.

Morrison, J. R. (1993). *The first interview: A guide for clinicians.* New York: Guilford Press.

REFERENCES

Morrow, D., Leirer, V., Altiteri, P., & Fitzsimmons, C. (1994). When expertise reduces age differences in performance. *Psychology and Aging, 9*(1), 134–148.

Moscardo, G., & Pearce, P. L. (1986). Visitor centres and environmental interpretation: An exploration of the relationships among visitor enjoyment, understanding and mindfulness. *Journal of Environmental Psychology, 6*(2), 89–108.

Moscardo, G. M. (1988). Toward a cognitive model of visitor responses in interpretive centers. *The Journal of Environmental Education, 20*(1), 29–38.

Moskowitz, G. B., & Chaiken, S. (2001). Mediators of minority social influence: Cognitive processing mechanisms revealed through a persuasion paradigm. In C. W. De Dreu & N. K. De Vries (Eds.), *Group consensus and minority influence: Implications for innovation* (pp. 60–90). Malden: Blackwell Publishing.

Mõttus, R., Allik, J., Konstabel, K., Kangro, E. M., & Pullmann, H. (2008). Beliefs about the relationships between personality and intelligence. *Personality and Individual Differences, 45*(6), 457–462.

Muchinsky, P. M. (2000). *Psychology applied to work: An introduction to industrial and organizational psychology* (6th ed.). Belmont, CA: Wadsworth/Thomson Learning.

Muchinsky, P. M. (2004). When the psychometrics of test development meets organizational realities: A conceptual framework for organizational change, examples, and recommendations. *Personnel Psychology, 57*(1), 175–209.

Muchinsky, P. M. (2013). Foreward. In A. H. Huffman & S. R. Klein (Eds.), *Green organizations: Driving change with I-O psychology*. New York: Routledge.

Mueller, V., Rosenbusch, N., & Bausch, A. (2013). Success patterns of exploratory and exploitative innovation: A meta-analysis of the influence of institutional factors. *Journal of Management, 39*(6), 1606–1636.

Mulder, L. B., & Nelissen, R. M. A. (2010). When rules really make a difference: The effect of cooperation rules and self-sacrificing leadership on moral norms in social dilemmas. *Journal of Business Ethics, 95*, 57–72.

Mullen, B., Anthony, T., Salas, E., & Driskell, J. E. (1994). Group cohesiveness and quality of decision making: An integration of tests of the groupthink hypothesis. *Small Group Research, 25*(2), 189–204.

Mullen, B., & Copper, C. (1994). The relation between group cohesiveness and performance: An integration. *Psychological Bulletin, 115*(2), 210–227.

Mullins, J. W., & Cummings, L. L. (1999). Situational strength: A framework for understanding the role of individuals in initiating proactive strategic change. *Journal of Organizational Change Management, 12*(6), 462–479.

Mumenthaler, C., & Sander, D. (2012). Social appraisal influences recognition of emotions. *Journal of Personality and Social Psychology, 102*(6), 1118–1135.

Munro, G. D. (2010). The scientific impotence excuse: Discounting belief-threatening scientific abstracts. *Journal of Applied Social Psychology, 40*(3), 579–600.

Munro, G. D., & Stansbury, J. A. (2009). The dark side of self-affirmation: Confirmation bias and illusory correlation in response to threatening information. *Personality and Social Psychology Bulletin, 35*(9), 1143–1153.

Murayama, K., Pekrun, R., Lichtenfeld, S., & Vom Hofe, R. (2013). Predicting long-term growth in students' mathematics achievement: The unique contributions of motivation and cognitive strategies. *Child Development, 84*(4), 1475–1490.

Murphy, B., Maguiness, P., Pescott, C., Wislang, S., Ma, J., & Wang, R. (2005). Stakeholder perceptions presage holistic stakeholder relationship marketing performance. *European Journal of Marketing, 39*(9-10), 1049–1059.

Murphy, D. J., Bruce, D., & Eva, K. W. (2008). Workplace-based assessment for general practitioners: Using stakeholder perception to aid blueprinting of an assessment battery. *Medical Education, 42*(1), 96–103.

REFERENCES

Murphy, K. R. & Cleveland, J. (1995). *Understanding Performance Appraisal*. Thousand Oaks, CA: Sage.

Murray, E. A., Brasted, P. J., & Wise, S. P. (2002). Arbitrary sensorimotor mapping and the life of primates. In L. R. Squire & D. L. Schacter (Eds.), *Neuropsychology of memory* (3rd ed.) (pp. 339–348). New York: Guilford Press.

Murray, K., & Zautra, A. (2012). Community resilience: Fostering recovery, sustainability, and growth. In M. Ungar (Ed.), *The social ecology of resilience: A handbook of theory and practice* (pp. 337–345). New York: Springer Science + Business Media.

Murty, V. P., LaBar, K. S., & Adcock, R. (2012). Threat of punishment motivates memory encoding via amygdala, not midbrain, interactions with the medial temporal lobe. *The Journal of Neuroscience, 32*(26), 8969–8976.

Myers, D. G. (2009). *Psychology* (9th ed.). New York: Worth.

Nadadur, G., & Parkinson, M. B. (2013). The role of anthropometry in designing for sustainability. *Ergonomics, 56*(3), 422–439.

Nakatani, Y., Matsumoto, Y., Mori, Y., Hirashima, D., Nishino, H., Arikawa, K., & Mizunami, M. (2009). Why the carrot is more effective than the stick: Different dynamics of punishment memory and reward memory and its possible biological basis. *Neurobiology of Learning and Memory, 92*(3), 370–380.

Naragon-Gainey, K. (2010). Meta-analysis of the relations of anxiety sensitivity to the depressive and anxiety disorders. *Psychological Bulletin, 136*(1), 128–150.

Nathan, B. R., & Lord, R. G. (1983). Cognitive categorization and dimensional schemata: A process approach to the study of halo in performance ratings. *Journal of Applied Psychology, 68*(1), 102–114.

National Geographic (2018). *Freshwater Crisis*. www.nationalgeographic.com/environment/freshwater/freshwater-crisis/

National Institute for Health (1979). *The Belmont Report*. www.hhs.gov/ohrp/humansubjects/guidance/belmont.html

Nature Conservancy, The (2018). *Tackling Water Shortage*. www.nature.org/ourinitiatives/regions/northamerica/areas/coloradoriver/index.htm

Needham, M. D., & Little, C. M. (2013). Voluntary environmental programs at an Alpine ski area: Visitor perceptions, attachment, value orientations, and specialization. *Tourism Management, 35*, 70–81.

Nelson, N. W., Hoelzle, J. B., Sweet, J. J., Arbisi, P. A., & Demakis, G. J. (2010). Updated meta-analysis of the MMPI-2 Symptom Validity Scale (FBS): Verified utility in forensic practice. *The Clinical Neuropsychologist, 24*(4), 701–724.

Nemeth, D. G., Hamilton, R. B., & Kuriansky, J. (2012). *Living in an environmentally traumatized world: Healing ourselves and our planet*. Santa Barbara, CA: Praeger/ABC-CLIO.

Nerb, J. (2007). Exploring the dynamics of the appraisal-emotion relationship: A constraint satisfaction model of the appraisal process. *Cognition and Emotion, 21*(7), 1382–1413.

Nestler, S., Blank, H., & von Collani, G. (2008). Hindsight bias and causal attribution: A causal model theory of creeping determinism. *Social Psychology, 39*(3), Special issue: 50 Years of Attribution Research, 182–188.

Neubert, M. J. (1998). The value of feedback and goal setting over goal setting alone and potential moderators of this effect: A meta-analysis. *Human Performance, 11*(4), 321–335.

Neuman, G. A., Edwards, J. E., & Raju, N. S. (1989). Organizational development interventions: A meta-analysis of their effects on satisfaction and other attitudes. *Personnel Psychology, 42*(3), 461–489.

Neumann, D. L. (2007). The resistance of renewal to instructions that devalue the role of contextual cues in a conditioned suppression task with humans. *Learning and Motivation, 38*(2), 105–127.

REFERENCES

Nevin, J. A. (1999). Analyzing Thorndike's Law of Effect: The question of stimulus–Response bonds. *Journal of the Experimental Analysis of Behavior, 72*(3), 447–450.

Newman, C. L., Howlett, E., Burton, S., Kozup, J. C., & Tangari, A. (2012). The influence of consumer concern about global climate change on framing effects for environmental sustainability messages. *International Journal of Advertising: The Quarterly Review of Marketing Communications, 31*(3), 511–527.

Newport, F. (2010). Four in 10 Americans believe in strict creationism. www.gallup.com/poll/145286/Four-Americans-Believe-Strict-Creationism.aspx

Newson, M., & Chalk, L. (2004). Environmental capital: An information core to public participation in strategic and operational decisions: The example of river "best practice" projects. *Journal of Environmental Planning & Management, 47*(6), 899–920.

Ng, C. K., Wong, K., & Fai, E. (2008). Emotion and organizational decision making: The roles of negative affect and anticipated regret in making decisions under escalation situations. In N. M. Ashkanasy & C. L. Cooper (Eds.), *Research companion to emotion in organizations* (pp. 45–60). Northampton, MA: Edward Elgar Publishing.

Ng, E., Chan, S., & Hui, C. (2012). Personnel psychology for disaster response and recovery. In S. C. Carr, M. MacLachlan, & A. Furnham (Eds.), *Humanitarian work psychology* (pp. 225–246). New York: Palgrave Macmillan.

Nguyen, N. C., Graham, D., Ross, H., Maani, K., & Bosch, O. (2012). Educating systems thinking for sustainability: Experience with a developing country. *Systems Research and Behavioral Science, 29*(1), 14–29.

Nichols, B. (2012). The development, validation, and implications of a measure of consumer competitive arousal (CCAr). *Journal of Economic Psychology, 33*(1), 192–205.

Nicholson, R. A., & Norwood, S. (2000). The quality of forensic psychological assessments, reports, and testimony: Acknowledging the gap between promise and practice. *Law and Human Behavior, 24*(1), 9–44.

Nickerson, R. (1998). Confirmation bias: A ubiquitous phenomenon in many guises. *Review of General Psychology, 2*(2),175–220.

Nickerson, R. S. (2011). Roles of human factors and ergonomics in meeting the challenge of terrorism. *American Psychologist, 66*(6), 555–566.

Nicol, A. A. M., Charbonneau, D., & Boies, K. (2007). Right-wing authoritarianism and social dominance orientation in a Canadian military sample. *Military Psychology, 19*(4), 239–257.

Nicol, D. (2007). Laying a foundation for lifelong learning: Case studies of e-assessment in large 1st-year classes. *British Journal of Educational Technology, 38*(4), 668–678.

Nielsen-Pincus, M., Hall, T., Force, J., & Wulfhorst, J. D. (2010). Sociodemographic effects on place bonding. *Journal of Environmental Psychology, 30*(4), 443–454.

Nigbur, D., Lyons, E., & Uzzell, D. (2010). Attitudes, norms, identity and environmental behaviour: Using an expanded theory of planned behaviour to predict participation in a kerbside recycling programme. *British Journal of Social Psychology, 49*(2), 259–284.

Nisbett, R. E., Aronson, J., Blair, C., Dickens, W., Flynn, J., Halpern, D. F., & Turkheimer, E. (2012) Intelligence: New findings and theoretical developments. *American Psychologist, 67*(2), 130–159.

Nishikawa, H., Schreier, M., & Ogawa, S. (2013). User-generated versus designer-generated products: A performance assessment at Muji. *International Journal of Research in Marketing, 30*(2), 160–167.

Nobel Prize (2013). www.nobelprize.org/nobel_prizes/economic-sciences/laureates/

Noe, R. A. (1986). Trainees' attributes and attitudes: Neglected influences on training effectiveness. *The Academy of Management Review, 11*(4), 736–749.

Noe, R. A., Tews, M. J., & Dachner, A. (2010). Learner engagement: A new perspective for enhancing our understanding of learner motivation and workplace learning. *The Academy of Management Annals, 4*(1), 279–315.

REFERENCES

Noell, G. H., Gansle, K. A., Mevers, J., Knox, R., Mintz, J., & Dahir, A. (2013). Improving treatment plan implementation in schools: A meta-analysis of single subject design studies. *Journal of Behavioral Education*, doi:10.1007/s10864-013-9177-1

Nokes, J. D., Dole, J. A., & Hacker, D. J. (2007). Teaching high school students to use heuristics while reading historical texts. *Journal of Educational Psychology*, *99*(3), 492–504.

Nollet, J., Rebolledo, C., & Popel, V. (2012). Becoming a preferred customer one step at a time. *Industrial Marketing Management*, *41*(8), 1186–1193.

Norcini, J., Anderson, B., Bollela, V., Burch, V., Costa, M., Duvivier, R., … Roberts, T. (2011). Criteria for good assessment: Consensus statement and recommendations from the Ottawa 2010 conference. *Medical Teacher*, *33*(3), 206–214.

Norcross, J. C., Krebs, P. M., & Prochaska, J. O. (2011). Stages of change. *Journal of Clinical Psychology*, *67*, 143–154.

Nordlund, A., & Garvill, J. (2002). Value structures behind proenvironmental behavior. *Environment and Behavior*, *34*(6), 740–756.

North, M. S., & Fiske, S. T. (2012). A history of social cognition. In A. Kruglanski & W. Stoebe (Eds.), *Handbook of the history of social psychology* (pp. 81–99). New York: Psychology Press.

Norton, T. R., Bogart, L. M., Cecil, H., & Pinkerton, S. D. (2005). Primacy of affect over cognition in determining adult men's condom-use behavior: A review. *Journal of Applied Social Psychology*, *35*(12), 2493–2534.

Norwich, B. (1988). Educational psychology services in LEAs: What future? In N. Jones & J. Sayer (Eds.), *Management and the psychology of schooling* (pp. 107–117). Oxford: Falmer Press/Taylor & Francis, Inc..

Nsamenang, A. (2006). Human ontogenesis: An indigenous African view on development and intelligence. *International Journal of Psychology*, *41*(4), 293–297.

O'Boyle, E. H., Jr., Humphrey, R. H., Pollack, J. M., Hawver, T. H., & Story, P. A. (2011). The relation between emotional intelligence and job performance: A meta-analysis. *Journal of Organizational Behavior*, *32*(5), 788–818.

O'Connor, P. (1952). Ethnocentrism, "intolerance of ambiguity", and abstract reasoning ability. *Journal of Abnormal and Social Psychology*, *47*, 526–530.

O'Connor, T. G., Spagnola, M., & Byrne, J. (2012). Reactive attachment disorder and severe attachment disturbances. In P. Sturmey & M. Hersen (Eds.), *Handbook of evidence-based practice in clinical psychology, Vol 1: Child and adolescent disorders* (pp. 433–453). Hoboken, NJ: John Wiley & Sons Inc.

O'Donoghue, R. (2006). Locating the environmental in environmental education research: A review of research on nature's nature, its inscription in language and recent memory work on relating to the natural world. *Environmental Education Research*, *12*(3–4), 345–357.

O'Donohue, W., & Ferguson, K. E. (2001). *The psychology of B.F. Skinner*. Thousand Oaks, CA: Sage.

O'Neill, O. A. (2009). Workplace expression of emotions and escalation of commitment. *Journal of Applied Social Psychology*, *39*(10), 2396–2424.

Oaksford, M., & Chater, N. (1992). Bounded rationality in taking risks and drawing inferences. *Theory and Psychology*, *2*(2), 225–230.

Oates, C., McDonald, S., Alevizou, P., Hwang, K., Young, W., & McMorland, L. (2008). Marketing sustainability: Use of information sources and degrees of voluntary simplicity. *Journal of Marketing Communications*, *14*(5), 351–365.

Oesterreich, D. (2005). Flight into security: A new approach and measure of the authoritarian personality. *Political Psychology*, *26*(2), 275–297.

The Office of Personnel Management (2013). www.opm.gov/

REFERENCES

Ojala, M. (2012). Hope and climate change: The importance of hope for environmental engagement among young people. *Environmental Education Research, 18*(5), 625–642.

Olatunji, B. O., & Wolitzky-Taylor, K. B. (2009). Anxiety sensitivity and the anxiety disorders: A meta-analytic review and synthesis. *Psychological Bulletin, 135*(6), 974–999.

Oldham, G. R., & Hackman, J. (2010). Not what it was and not what it will be: The future of job design research. *Journal of Organizational Behavior, 31*(2-3), 463–479.

Olson, K. R., & Dweck, C. S. (2009). Social cognitive development: A new look. *Child Development Perspectives, 3*(1), 60–65.

Oluk, S., & Özalp, I. (2007). The teaching of global environmental problems according to the constructivist approach: As a focal point of the problem and the availability of concept cartoons. *Kuram Ve Uygulamada Eğitim Bilimleri, 7*(2), 881–896.

Ones, D. S., & Dilchert, S. (2012). Environmental sustainability at work: A call to action. *Industrial and Organizational Psychology, 5*, 444–466.

Ones, D. S., & Dilchert, S. (2013). Measuring, understanding, and influencing employee green behavior. In A. H. Huffman & S. R. Klein (Eds.), *Green organizations: Driving change with I-O psychology* (pp. 115–148). New York: Routledge.

Ones, D. S., Dilchert, S., Viswesvaran, C., & Judge, T. A. (2007). In support of personality assessment in organizational settings. *Personnel Psychology, 60*(4), 995–1027.

Ones, D. S., & Viswesvaran, C. (2001). Integrity tests and other criterion-focused occupational personality scales (COPS) used in personnel selection. *International Journal of Selection and Assessment, 9*(1–2), 31–39.

Ones, D. S., Viswesvaran, C., & Dilchert, S. (2005). Cognitive ability in selection decisions. In O. Wilhelm & R. W. Engle (Eds.), *Handbook of understanding and measuring intelligence* (pp. 431–468). Thousand Oaks, CA: Sage Publications, Inc.

Onwezen, M. C., Reinders, M. J., & Sijtsema, S. J. (2017). Understanding intentions to purchase bio-based products: The role of subjective ambivalence. *Journal of Environmental Psychology, 52*, 26–36.

Ordóñez, L. D., Schweitzer, M. E., Galinsky, A. D., & Bazerman, M. H. (2009). On good scholarship, goal setting, and scholars gone wild. *The Academy of Management Perspectives, 23*(3), 82–87.

Oreskes, N., & Conway, E. M. (2010). *Merchants of doubt: How a handful of scientists obscured the truth on issues from tobacco smoke to global warming.* New York: Bloomsbury Press.

Organ, D. W., Podsakoff, P. M., & Podsakoff, N. P. (2011). Expanding the criterion domain to include organizational citizenship behavior: Implications for employee selection. In S. Zedeck (Ed.), *APA handbook of industrial and organizational psychology, Vol 2: Selecting and developing members for the organization* (pp. 281–323). Washington, DC: American Psychological Association.

Orme-Johnson, D. W. (2000). An overview of Charles Alexander's contribution to psychology: Developing higher states of consciousness in the individual and the society. *Journal of Adult Development, 7*(4), 199–215.

Orton, J. D., & Weick, K. E. (1990). Loosely coupled systems: A reconceptualization. *The Academy of Management Review, 15*(2), 203–223.

Osbaldiston, R., & Schott, J. P. (2012). Environmental sustainability and behavioral science: Meta-analysis of proenvironmental behavior experiments. *Environment and Behavior, 44*(2), 257–299.

Oskamp, S. (1995). Resource conservation and recycling: Behavior and policy. *Journal of Social Issues, 51*(4), 157–177.

Oskamp, S. (2000). A sustainable future for humanity? How can psychology help? *American Psychologist, 55*(5), 496–508.

Osman, M. (2012). The effects of self set or externally set goals on learning in an uncertain environment. *Learning and Individual Differences, 22*(5), 575–584.

REFERENCES

Ostman, R. E., & Parker, J. L. (1986). A public's environmental information sources and evaluations of mass media. *The Journal of Environmental Education, 18*(2), 9–17.

Ostrom, T. (1990). Personal communication, Ohio State University.

Ostrom, T. M., Carpenter, S. L., Sedikides, C., & Li, F. (1993). Differential processing of in-group and out-group information. *Journal of Personality and Social Psychology, 64*(1), 21–34.

Oudejans, R. R. D. (2008). Reality-based practice under pressure improves handgun shooting performance of police officers. *Ergonomics, 51*(3), 261–273.

Overstreet, R. E., Cegielski, C., & Hall, D. (2013). Predictors of the intent to adopt preventive innovations: A meta-analysis. *Journal of Applied Social Psychology, 43*(5), 936–946.

Pachur, T., Hertwig, R., & Steinmann, F. (2012). How do people judge risks: Availability heuristic, affect heuristic, or both? *Journal of Experimental Psychology: Applied, 18*, 314–340.

Pachur, T., Mata, R., & Schooler, L. J. (2009). Cognitive aging and the adaptive use of recognition in decision making. *Psychology and Aging, 24*(4), 901–915.

Painter, J., Semenik, R., & Belk, R. (1983). Is there a generalized energy conservation ethic? A comparison of the determinants of gasoline and home heating energy conservation. *Journal of Economic Psychology, 3*(3-4), 317–331.

Palomo-Vélez, G., Tybur, J. M., & van Vugt, M. (2018). Unsustainable, unhealthy, or disgusting? Comparing different persuasive messages against meat consumption. *Journal of Environmental Psychology, 58*, 63–71.

Parboteeah, K. P., Addae, H. M., & Cullen, J. B. (2012). Propensity to support sustainability initiatives: A cross-national model. *Journal of Business Ethics, 105*, 403–413.

Parboteeah, K. P., Bronson, J., & Cullen, J. B. (2005). Does national culture affect willingness to justify ethically suspect unethical behaviors? A focus on the globe national culture scheme. *International Journal of Cross-Cultural Management, 5*(2), 123–138.

Parker, J., & McDonough, M. H. (1999). Environmentalism of African Americans: An analysis of the subculture and barriers theories. *Environment and Behavior, 31*(2), 155–177.

Parker, M. R., Jordan, K. R., Kirk, E. R., Aspiranti, K. B., & Bain, S. K. (2010). Publications in four gifted education journals from 2001 to 2006: An analysis of article types and authorship characteristics. *Roeper Review: A Journal on Gifted Education, 32*(3), 207–216.

Patrick, V. M., & Hagtvedt, H. (2012). How to say "no": Conviction and identity attributions in persuasive refusal. *International Journal of Research in Marketing, 29*(4), 390–394.

Patton, G. C., Tollit, M. M., Romaniuk, H., Spence, S. H., Sheffield, J., & Sawyer, M. G. (2011). A prospective study of the effects of optimism on adolescent health risks. *Pediatrics, 127*(2), 308–316.

Pearlman, K., & Sanchez, J. I. (2010). Work analysis. In J. L. Farr, N. T. Tippins (Eds.), *Handbook of Employee Selection* (pp. 73–98). New York: Routledge/Taylor & Francis Group.

Pedersen, P. J. (2010). Assessing intercultural effectiveness outcomes in a year-long study abroad program. *International Journal of Intercultural Relations, 34*(1), 70–80.

Pelletier, L. G. (2002). A motivational analysis of self-determination for pro-environmental behaviors. In E. L. Deci & R. M. Ryan (Eds.), *Handbook of self-determination research* (pp. 205–232). Rochester, NY: University of Rochester Press.

Pelletier, L. G., Dion, S., Tuson, K., & Green-Demers, I. (1999). Why do people fail to adopt environmental protective behaviors? Toward a taxonomy of environmental amotivation. *Journal of Applied Social Psychology, 29*(12), 2481–2504.

Pelletier, L. G., Lavergne, K. J., & Sharp, E. C. (2008). Environmental psychology and sustainability: Comments on topics important for our future. *Canadian Psychology/Psychologie Canadienne, 49*(4), 304–308.

REFERENCES

Pelletier, L. G., Tuson, K. M., Green-Demers, I., Noels, K., & Beaton, A. M. (1998). Why are you doing things for the environment? The Motivation Toward the Environment Scale (MTES). *Journal of Applied Social Psychology, 28*(5), 437–468.

Penn, D. C., Holyoak, K. J., & Povinelli, D. J. (2008). Darwin's mistake: Explaining the discontinuity between human and nonhuman minds. *Behavioral and Brain Sciences, 31* (2), 109–130.

Penn, D. C., & Povinelli, D. J. (2007). Causal cognition in human and nonhuman animals: A comparative, critical review. *Annual Review of Psychology, 58*, 97–118.

Penner, L. A., Dovidio, J. F., Piliavin, J. A., & Schroeder, D. A. (2005). Prosocial behavior: Multilevel perspectives. *Annual Review of Psychology, 56*, 365–392.

Penny, J. A. (2009). Review of "Why smart companies do dumb things: Avoiding eight common mistakes in new product development". *Personnel Psychology, 62*(1), 194–196.

Permut, S. E. (1973). Cue utilization patterns in student-faculty evaluation. *Journal of Psychology: Interdisciplinary and Applied, 83*(1), 41–48.

Perowne, S., & Mansell, W. (2002). Social anxiety, self-focused attention, and the discrimination of negative, neutral and positive audience members by their non-verbal behaviours. *Behavioural and Cognitive Psychotherapy, 30*(1), 11–23.

Perrott, D. A., & Bodenhausen, G. V. (2002). The way you make me feel: Integral affective influences on interpersonal behavior. *Psychological Inquiry, 13*(1), 84–86.

Perry, V., Albeg, L., & Tung, C. (2012). Meta-analysis of single-case design research on self-regulatory interventions for academic performance. *Journal of Behavioral Education, 21*(3), 217–229.

Petersen, L. E., & Dietz, J. (2008). Employment discrimination: Authority figures' demographic preferences and followers' affective organizational commitment. *Journal of Applied Psychology, 93*(6), 1287–1300.

Peterson, B. E., & Zurbriggen, E. L. (2010). Gender, sexuality, and the authoritarian personality. *Journal of Personality, 78*(6), 1801–1826.

Peterson, R. A., Albaum, G., and Beltramini, R.F. (1985). A meta-analysis of effect sizes in consumer behavior experiments. *Journal of Consumer Research, 12*(1), 97–103.

Petitmengin, C., & Bitbol, M. (2009). The validity of first-person descriptions as authenticity and coherence. *Journal of Consciousness Studies, 16*(10–12), 363–404.

Petrovich, G. D. (2011). Learning and the motivation to eat: Forebrain circuitry. *Physiology & Behavior, 104*(4), 582–589.

Petrovich, G. D., Ross, C. A., Mody, P., Holland, P. C., & Gallagher, M. (2009). Central, but not basolateral, amygdala is critical for control of feeding by aversive learned cues. *The Journal of Neuroscience, 29*(48), 15205–15, 212.

Pettit, R. (2009). From politics to marketing: An emotional framework for advertising. *Journal of Advertising Research, 49*(1), 10–11.

Petty, R. E., & Wegener, D. T. (1998). Matching versus mismatching attitude functions: Implications for scrutiny of persuasive messages. *Personality and Social Psychology Bulletin, 24*(3), 227–240.

Petty, R. E., Wheeler, S., & Tormala, Z. L. (2013). Persuasion and attitude change. In H. Tennen, J. Suls, & I. B. Weiner (Eds.), *Handbook of psychology, Vol. 5: Personality and social psychology* (2nd ed.) (pp. 369–389). Hoboken, NJ: John Wiley & Sons Inc.

Pfeffer, J. (2010). Building sustainable organizations: The human factor. *The Academy Of Management Perspectives, 24*(1), 34–45.

Pfeffer, J., Salancik, G. R., & Leblebici, H. (1976). The effect of uncertainty on the use of social influence in organizational decision making. *Administrative Science Quarterly, 21*(2), 227–245.

REFERENCES

Phillips, B., Stukes, P., & Jenkins, P. (2012). Freedom Hill is not for sale—And neither is the Lower Ninth Ward. *Journal of Black Studies, 43*(4), 405–426.

Phillips, R. (2003). *Stakeholder theory and organizational ethics*. San Francisco, CA: Berrett-Koehler.

Piaget, J. (1970). *Structuralism*. New York: Basic Books.

Pichert, D., & Katsikopoulos, K. V. (2008). Green defaults: Information presentation and pro-environmental behaviour. *Journal of Environmental Psychology, 28*(1), 63–73.

Pidd, K. (2004). The impact of workplace support and identity on training transfer: A case study of drug and alcohol safety training in Australia. *International Journal of Training and Development, 8*(4), 274–288.

Piet, J., & Hougaard, E. (2011). The effect of mindfulness-based cognitive therapy for prevention of relapse in recurrent major depressive disorder: A systematic review and meta-analysis. *Clinical Psychology Review, 31*(6), 1032–1040.

Piet, J., Würtzen, H., & Zachariae, R. (2012). The effect of mindfulness-based therapy on symptoms of anxiety and depression in adult cancer patients and survivors: A systematic review and meta-analysis. *Journal of Consulting and Clinical Psychology, 80* (6), 1007–1020.

Pinazo, D., & Agut, S. (2008). The documentary *An Inconvenient Truth*, concerns about climate change and pro-environmental behaviours: A study on pro-environmental motivation. *Revista De Psicología Social Aplicada, 18*(2), 107–125.

Pinchot, G. (1996). *The intelligent organization: Engaging the talent and initiative of everyone in the workplace*. San Francisco, CA: Berrett-Koehler Publishers.

Pinchot, G. (1999). *Intrapreneuring in action: A handbook for business innovation*. San Francisco, CA: Berrett-Koehler.

Piron, F. (2006). China's changing culture: Rural and urban customers' favorite things. *Journal of Consumer Marketing, 23*(6), 327–334.

Pivik, J. (2010). The perspective of children and youth: How different stakeholders identify architectural barriers for inclusion in schools. *Journal of Environmental Psychology, 30*(4), 510–517.

Plassmann, H., Ramsøy, T., & Milosavljevic, M. (2012). Branding the brain: A critical review and outlook. *Journal of Consumer Psychology, 22*(1), 18–36.

Plax, T. G., Kearney, P., Ross, T. J., & Jolly, J. (2008). Assessing the link between environmental concerns and consumers' decisions to use clean-air vehicles. *Communication Education, 57*(4), 417–422.

Pleskac, T. J., Keeney, J., Merritt, S. M., Schmitt, N., & Oswald, F. L. (2011). A detection model of college withdrawal. *Organizational Behavior and Human Decision Processes, 115*(1), 85–98.

Ployhart, R. E., & Weekley, J. A. (2010). Strategy, selection, and sustained competitive advantage. In J. L. Farr & N. T. Tippins (Eds.), *Handbook of employee selection* (pp. 195–212). New York: Routledge.

Pocheptsova, A., Amir, O., Dhar, R., & Baumeister, R. F. (2009). Deciding without resources: Resource depletion and choice in context. *Journal of Marketing Research, 46* (3), 344–355

Pohl, R. F., Bender, M., & Lachmann, G. (2002). Hindsight bias around the world. *Experimental Psychology, 49*(4), 270–282.

Poropat, A. E. (2009). A meta-analysis of the five-factor model of personality and academic performance. *Psychological Bulletin, 135*, 322–338.

Portes, P. R., Sandhu, D. S., & Longwell-Grice, R. (2002). Understanding adolescent suicide: A psychosocial interpretation of developmental and contextual factors. *Adolescence, 37*(148), 805–814.

Poston, J. M., & Hanson, W. E. (2010). Meta-analysis of psychological assessment as a therapeutic intervention. *Psychological Assessment, 22*(2), 203–212.

REFERENCES

Pratkanis, A. R., & Greenwald, A. G. (1985). How shall the self be conceived? *Journal for the Theory of Social Behaviour, 15*, 311–329.

Prebble, S. C., Addis, D. R., & Tippett, L. J. (2013). Autobiographical memory and sense of self. *Psychological Bulletin, 139*, 815–840.

Premack, S. L., & Wanous, J. P. (1985). A meta-analysis of realistic job preview experiments. *Journal of Applied Psychology, 70*(4), 706–719.

Priest, S. (1992). Factor exploration and confirmation for the dimensions of an adventure experience. *Journal of Leisure Research, 24*(2), 127–139.

Prochansky, H., Fabian, A. K., & Kaminoff, R. (1983). Place identity: Physical world socialization of the self. *Journal of Environmental Psychology, 3*, 57–83.

Proctor, R. W., & Vu, K. L. (2011). Complementary contributions of basic and applied research in human factors and ergonomics. *Theoretical Issues in Ergonomics Science, 12*(5), 427–434.

Protzko, J., Aronson, J., & Blair, C. (2013). How to make a young child smarter: Evidence from the database of raising intelligence. *Perspectives on Psychological Science, 8*(1), 25–40.

Pryor, J. B., LaVite, C. M., & Stoller, L. M. (1993). A social psychological analysis of sexual harassment: The person/situation interaction. *Journal of Vocational Behavior, 42*(1), 68–83.

Pulakos, E. D., & Hedge, J. W. (2002). The role of organizational culture in implementing organizational interventions. In J. W. Hedge & E. D. Pulakos (Eds.), *Implementing organizational interventions: Steps, processes, and best practices* (pp. 297–309). San Francisco, CA: Jossey-Bass.

Pulakos, E. D., & O'Leary, R. S. (2010). Defining and measuring results of workplace behavior. In J. L. Farr & N. T. Tippins (Eds.), *Handbook of employee selection* (pp. 513–529). New York: Routledge.

Quigley, N. R., Tesluk, P. E., Locke, E. A., & Bartol, K. M. (2007). Multilevel investigation of the motivational mechanisms underlying knowledge sharing and performance. *Organization Science, 18*(1), 71–88.

Rafaeli, A., & Sutton, R. I. (1987). Expression of emotion as part of the work role. *Academy of Management Review, 12*, 23–37.

Raimi, K. T., Stern, P. C., & Maki, A. (2017). The promise and limitations of using analogies to improve decision-relevant understanding of climate change. *PLoS ONE, 12*(1), e-journal.

Ramanujam, V., Venkatraman, N. N., & Camillus, J. C. (1986). Multi-objective assessment of effectiveness of strategic planning: A discriminant analysis approach. *Academy of Management Journal, 29*(2), 347–372.

Rand, T. M., & Wexley, K. N. (1975). Demonstration of the effect, "similar to me," in simulated employment interviews. *Psychological Reports, 36*(2), 535–544.

Ranson, S. W. (1939). The hypothalamus as a thermostat regulating body temperature. *Psychosomatic Medicine, 1*, 486–495.

Rasmussen, H. N., Scheier, M. F., & Greenhouse, J. B. (2009). Optimism and physical health: A meta-analytic review. *Annals of Behavioral Medicine, 37*, 239–256.

Rauch, A., & Frese, M. (2007). Let's put the person back into entrepreneurship research: A meta-analysis on the relationship between business owners' personality traits, business creation, and success. *European Journal of Work and Organizational Psychology, 16*(4), 353–385.

Raudsepp, M. (2005). Emotional connection to nature: Its socio-psychological correlates and associations with pro-environmental attitudes and behavior. In B. Martens & A. G. Keul (Eds.), *Designing social innovation: Planning, building, evaluating* (pp. 83–91). Ashland, OH: Hogrefe & Huber.

REFERENCES

Rawsthorne, L. J., & Elliot, A. J. (1999). Achievement goals and intrinsic motivation: A meta-analytic review. *Personality and Social Psychology Review, 3*(4), 326–344.

Ray, C. L., & Subich, L. M. (1998). Staff assaults and injuries in a psychiatric hospital as a function of three attitudinal variables. *Issues in Mental Health Nursing, 19*(3), 277–289.

Raymond, C. M., Brown, G., & Robinson, G. M. (2011). The influence of place attachment, and moral and normative concerns on the conservation of native vegetation: A test of two behavioural models. *Journal of Environmental Psychology, 31*(4), 323–335.

Raymond, C. M., Brown, G., & Weber, D. (2010). The measurement of place attachment: Personal, community, and environmental connections. *Journal of Environmental Psychology, 30*(4), 422–434.

Razza, R. A., & Raymond, K. (2013). Associations among maternal behavior, delay of gratification, and school readiness across the early childhood years. *Social Development, 22*(1), 180–196.

Reagan, I. J., Bliss, J. P., Van Houten, R., & Hilton, B. W. (2013). The effects of external motivation and real-time automated feedback on speeding behavior in a naturalistic setting. *Human Factors, 55*(1), 218–230.

Reas, E. T., & Brewer, J. B. (2013). Imbalance of incidental encoding across tasks: An explanation for non-memory-related hippocampal activations? *Journal of Experimental Psychology: General*, doi:10.1037/a0033461

Reber, R. A., & Wallin, J. A. (1984). The effects of training, goal setting, and knowledge of results on safe behavior: A component analysis. *Academy of Management Journal, 27*(3), 544–560.

Reese, G. (2012). When authoritarians protect the Earth: Authoritarian submission and proenvironmental beliefs: A pilot study in Germany. *Ecopsychology, 4*(3), 232–236.

Regehr, C., Glancy, D., & Pitts, A. (2013). Interventions to reduce stress in university students: A review and meta-analysis. *Journal of Affective Disorders, 148*(1), 1–11.

Reger, R. K., & Palmer, T. B. (1996). Managerial categorization of competitors: Using old maps to navigate new environments. *Organization Science, 7*(1), 22–39.

Reicher, S. D., Haslam, S., & Smith, J. R. (2012). Working toward the experimenter: Reconceptualizing obedience within the Milgram paradigm as identification-based followership. *Perspectives on Psychological Science, 7*(4), 315–324.

Reitman, D., Currier, R. O., Hupp, S. D. A., Rhode, P. C., Murphy, M. A., & O'Callaghan, P. M. (2001). Psychometric characteristics of the Parenting Scale in a head start population. *Journal of Clinical Child Psychology, 30*(4), 514–524.

Reno, R. R., Cialdini, R. B., & Kallgren, C. A. (1993). The transsituational influence of social norms. *Journal of Personality and Social Psychology, 64*(1), 104–112.

Reser, J. P. (1980). Automobile addiction: Real or imagined? *Man-Environment Systems, 10*(5-6), 279–287.

Reser, J. P., & Swim, J. K. (2011). Adapting to and coping with the threats and impacts of climate change. *American Psychologist, 66*(4). 277–289.

Reysen, S., & Katzarska-Miller, I. (2013). A model of global citizenship: Antecedents and outcomes. *International Journal of Psychology, 48*(5), 858–870.

Rhoades, L., & Eisenberger, R. (2002). Perceived organizational support: A review of the literature. *Journal of Applied Psychology, 87*(4), 698–714.

Rhodes, M. G., & Anastasi, J. S. (2012). The own-age bias in face recognition: A meta-analytic and theoretical review. *Psychological Bulletin, 138*(1), 146–174.

Rich, A. R., & Woolever, D. K. (1988). Expectancy and self-focused attention: Experimental support for the self-regulation model of test anxiety. *Journal of Social and Clinical Psychology, 7*(2–3), 246–259.

REFERENCES

Richardson, B., Foster, V. A., & McAdams, C. (1998). Parenting attitudes and moral development of treatment foster parents: Implications for training and supervision. *Child & Youth Care Forum, 27*(6), 409–431.

Richardson, K. M., & Rothstein, H. R. (2008). Effects of occupational stress management intervention programs: A meta-analysis. *Journal of Occupational Health Psychology, 13*(1), 69–93.

Richardson, M., Abraham, C., & Bond, R. (2012). Psychological correlates of university students' academic performance: A systematic review and meta-analysis. *Psychological Bulletin, 138*(2), 353–387.

Richeson, J. A., & Ambady, N. (2003). Effects of situational power on automatic racial prejudice. *Journal of Experimental Social Psychology, 39*(2), 177–183.

Richter, C. (2011). Usage of dishwashers: Observation of consumer habits in the domestic environment. *International Journal of Consumer Studies, 35*(2), 180–186.

Rilling, M. (1996). The mystery of the vanished citations: James McConnell's forgotten 1960s quest for planarian learning, a biochemical engram, and celebrity. *American Psychologist, 51*(6), 589–598.

Rindermann, H. (2008). Relevance of education and intelligence for the political development of nations: Democracy, rule of law and political liberty. *Intelligence, 36*(4), 306–322.

Ringold, D. (1995). Social criticisms of target marketing: Process or product? *American Behavioral Scientist, 38*(4), 578–592.

Rioux, L. (2011). Promoting pro-environmental behaviour: Collection of used batteries by secondary school pupils. *Environmental Education Research, 17*(3), 353–373.

Rivlin, L. G. (2002). The ethical imperative. In R. B. Bechtel & A. Churchman (Eds.), *Handbook of environmental psychology* (pp. 15–27). New York: Wiley.

Robelia, B. A., Greenhow, C., & Burton, L. (2011). Environmental learning in online social networks: Adopting environmentally responsible behaviors. *Environmental Education Research, 17*(4), 553–575.

Roberson, L., Kulik, C. T., & Pepper, M. B. (2009). Individual and environmental factors influencing the use of transfer strategies after diversity training. *Group & Organization Management, 34*(1), 67–89.

Roberts, B. W., Walton, K. E., & Viechtbauer, W. (2006). Personality traits change in adulthood: Reply to Costa and McCrae (2006). *Psychological Bulletin, 132*(1), 29–32.

Robertson, J. L., & Barling, J. (2013). Greening organizations through leaders' influence on employees' pro-environmental behaviors. *Journal of Organizational Behavior, 34* (2), 176–194.

Robins, R. W., Spranca, M. D., & Mendelsohn, G. A. (1996). The actor-observer effect revisited: Effects of individual differences and repeated social interactions on actor and observer attributions. *Journal of Personality and Social Psychology, 71*(2), 375–389.

Robinson, V. J., Lloyd, C. A., & Rowe, K. J. (2008). The impact of leadership on student outcomes: An analysis of the differential effects of leadership types. *Educational Administration Quarterly, 44*(5), 635–674.

Rodrigues, J., Sauzéon, H., Wallet, G., & N'Kaoua, B. (2010). Transfer of spatial-knowledge from virtual to real environment: Effect of active/passive learning depending on a test-retest procedure and the type of retrieval tests. *Journal of Cybertherapy and Rehabilitation, 3*(3), 275–283.

Roemer, L., Lee, J. K., Salters-Pedneault, K., Erisman, S. M., Orsillo, S. M., & Mennin, D. S. (2009). Mindfulness and emotion regulation difficulties in generalized anxiety disorder: Preliminary evidence for independent and overlapping contributions. *Behavior Therapy, 40*(2), 142–154.

REFERENCES

Roesch, E. B., Sander, D., Mumenthaler, C., Kerzel, D., & Scherer, K. R. (2010). Psychophysics of emotion: The QUEST for emotional attention. *Journal of Vision, 10*(3), e-journal.

Rogelberg, S. G., Barnes-Farrell, J. L., & Lowe, C. A. (1992). The stepladder technique: An alternative group structure facilitating effective group decision making. *Journal of Applied Psychology, 77*(5), 730–737.

Rogelberg, S. G., & Gill, P. M. (2004). The growth of industrial and organizational psychology: Quick facts. *The Industrial-Organizational Psychologist, 42*, 25–27.

Rogelberg, S. G., O'Connor, M. S., & Sederburg, M. (2002). Using the stepladder technique to facilitate the performance of audioconferencing. *Journal of Applied Psychology, 87*(5), 994–1000.

Rogers, J. C., Simmons, E. A., Convery, I., & Weatherall, A. (2012). Social impacts of community renewable energy projects: Findings from a woodfuel case study. *Energy Policy, 42*, 239–247.

Roisman, G. I., & Grohl, A. M. (2011). Attachment theory and research in developmental psychology: An overview and appreciative critique. In M. K. Underwood & L. H. Rosen (Eds.), *Social development: relationships in infancy, childhood, and adolescence* (pp. 101–126). New York: Guilford Press.

Rolland, R. (2012). Synthesizing the evidence on classroom goal structures in middle and secondary schools: A meta-analysis and narrative review. *Review of Educational Research, 82*(4), 396–435.

Rollero, C., & De Piccoli, N. (2010). Place attachment, identification and environment perception: An empirical study. *Journal of Environmental Psychology, 30*(2), 198–205.

Rosa, J., & Spanjol, J. (2005). Micro-level product-market dynamics: Shared knowledge and its relationship to market development. *Journal of the Academy of Marketing Science, 33*(2), 197–216.

Roseman, I. J., Dhawan, N., Rettek, S. I., Naidu, R. K., & Thapa, K. (1995). Cultural differences and cross-cultural similarities in appraisals and emotional responses. *Journal of Cross-Cultural Psychology, 26*(1), 23–48.

Rosenbaum, M. S., Ward, J., Walker, B. A., & Ostrom, A. L. (2007). A cup of coffee with a dash of love: An investigation of commercial social support and third-place attachment. *Journal of Service Research, 10*(1), 43–59.

Rosenberg, S. (1980). Objectivity in psychology and philosophy. *American Psychologist, 35* (2), 219–222.

Rossano, M. J. (2008). The moral faculty: Does religion promote 'moral expertise? *International Journal for the Psychology of Religion, 18*(3), 169–194.

Rotfeld, H. (2004). The consumer as serf. *Journal of Consumer Affairs, 38*(1), 188–191.

Roth, P. L., & Huffcutt, A. I. (2013). A meta-analysis of interviews and cognitive ability: Back to the future? *Journal of Personnel Psychology, 12*(4), 157–169.

Rotter, J. B. (1966). Generalized expectancies for internal versus external control of reinforcement. *Psychological Monographs, 80*, 1–28.

Rotter, J. B. (1990). Internal versus external control of reinforcement: A case history of a variable. *American Psychologist, 45*, 489–493.

Rousseau, R., Tremblay, S., Banbury, S., Breton, R., & Guitouni, A. (2010). The role of metacognition in the relationship between objective and subjective measures of situation awareness. *Theoretical Issues in Ergonomics Science, 11*(1–2), 119–130.

Rowe, Z. O., Wilson, H. N., Dimitriu, R., Charnley, F. J., & Lastrucci, G. (2019). Pride in my past: Influencing sustainable choices through behavioral recall. *Psychology & Marketing, 36*, 276–286.

Royo-Vela, M., Aldas-Manzano, J., Küster, I., & Vila, N. (2008). Adaptation of marketing activities to cultural and social context: Gender role portrayals and sexism in Spanish commercials. *Sex Roles, 58*(5-6), 379–390.

REFERENCES

Rucker, D. D., Petty, R. E., & Briñol, P. (2008). What's in a frame anyway? A meta-cognitive analysis of the impact of one versus two sided message framing on attitude certainty. *Journal of Consumer Psychology, 18*(2), 137–149.

Rupp, D. E., Williams, C. A., & Aguilera, R. V. (2010). Increasing corporate social responsibility through stakeholder value internalization (and the catalyzing effect of new governance): An application of organizational justice, self-determination, and social influence theories. In M. Schminke (Ed.), *Managerial ethics: Managing the psychology of morality* (pp. 69–88). New York: Routledge/Taylor & Francis Group.

Russell, J. A. (1994). Is there universal recognition of emotion from facial expression? A review of the cross-cultural studies. *Psychological Bulletin, 115,* 102–141.

Russell, J. A. (1995). Facial expressions of emotion: What lies beyond minimal universality? *Psychological Bulletin, 118*(3), 379–391.

Russell, J. A., & Mehrabian, A. (1976). Environmental variables in consumer research. *Journal of Consumer Research, 3*(1), 62–63.

Rutjens, B. T., van Harreveld, F., van der Pligt, J., Kreemers, L. M., & Noordewier, M. K. (2013). Steps, stages, and structure: Finding compensatory order in scientific theories. *Journal of Experimental Psychology: General, 142*(2), 313–318.

Ryan, B., & Wilson, J. R. (2013). Ergonomics in the development and implementation of organisational strategy for sustainability. *Ergonomics, 56*(3), 541–555.

Rye, J., Landenberger, R., & Warner, T. A. (2013). Incorporating concept mapping in project-based learning: Lessons from watershed investigations. *Journal of Science Education and Technology, 22*(3), 379–392.

Ryoo, Y., Hyun, N. K., & Sung, Y. (2017). The effect of descriptive norms and construal level on consumers' sustainable behaviors. *Journal of Advertising, 46*(4), 536–549.

Rytwinski, N. K., Scur, M. D., Feeny, N. C., & Youngstrom, E. A. (2013). The co-occurrence of major depressive disorder among individuals with posttraumatic stress disorder: A meta-analysis. *Journal of Traumatic Stress, 26*(3), 299–309.

Sablynski, C. J., Lee, T. W., Mitchell, T. R., Burton, J. P., & Holtom, B. C. (2002). Turnover: An integration of Lee and Mitchell's unfolding model and job embeddedness construct with Hulin's withdrawal construct. In J. M. Brett & F. Drasgow (Eds.), *The psychology of work: Theoretically based empirical research* (pp. 189–203). Mahwah, NJ: Lawrence Erlbaum Associates Publishers.

Sackett, P. R., Burris, L. R., & Callahan, C. (1989). Integrity testing for personnel selection: An update. *Personnel Psychology, 42*(3), 491–529.

Sackett, P. R., & Wanek, J. E. (1996). New developments in the use of measures of honesty, integrity, conscientiousness, dependability, trustworthiness, and reliability for personnel selection. *Personnel Psychology, 49*(4), 787–829.

Sagarin, B. J., Cialdini, R. B., Rice, W. E., & Serna, S. B. (2002). Dispelling the illusion of invulnerability: The motivations and mechanisms of resistance to persuasion. *Journal of Personality and Social Psychology, 83*(3), 526–541.

Sahin, E., Ertepinar, H., & Teksoz, G. (2012). University students' behaviors pertaining to sustainability: A structural equation model with sustainability-related attributes. *International Journal of Environmental and Science Education, 7*(3), 459–478.

Sahley, C. L., Boulis, N. M., & Schurman, B. (1994). Associative learning modifies the shortening reflex in the semi-intact leech Hirudo medicinalis: Effects of pairing, predictability, and CS preexposure. *Behavioral Neuroscience, 108*(2), 340–346.

Saile, H. H., Burgmeier, R. R., & Schmidt, L. R. (1988). A meta-analysis of studies on psychological preparation of children facing medical procedures. *Psychology & Health, 2*(2), 107–132.

Saks, A. M., Wiesner, W. H., & Summers, R. J. (1994). Effects of job previews on self-selection and job choice. *Journal of Vocational Behavior, 44*(3), 297–316.

REFERENCES

Salancik, G. R., & Pfeffer, J. (1977). Who gets power–And how they hold on to it: A strategic-contingency model of power. *Organizational Dynamics, 5*(3), 2–21.

Salas, E., & Cannon-Bowers, J. A. (2001). Special issue preface. *Journal of Organizational Behavior, 22*(2), 87–88.

Salas, E., DiazGranados, D., Klein, C., Burke, C., Stagl, K. C., Goodwin, G. F., & Halpin, S. M. (2008). Does team training improve team performance? A meta-analysis. *Human Factors, 50*(6), 903–933.

Salas, E., Nichols, D. R., & Driskell, J. E. (2007). Testing three team training strategies in intact teams: A meta-analysis. *Small Group Research, 38*(4), 471–488.

Salas, E., Rosen, M. A., Burke, C., & Goodwin, G. F. (2009). The wisdom of collectives in organizations: An update of the teamwork competencies. In E. Salas, G. F. Goodwin, & C. Burke (Eds.), *Team effectiveness in complex organizations: Cross-disciplinary perspectives and approaches* (pp. 39–79). New York: Routledge/Taylor & Francis Group.

Salgado, J. F., & Moscoso, S. (2002). Comprehensive meta-analysis of the construct validity of the employment interview. *European Journal of Work and Organizational Psychology, 11*(3), 299–324.

Salmon, P. M., McClure, R., & Stanton, N. A. (2012). Road transport in drift? Applying contemporary systems thinking to road safety. *Safety Science, 50*(9), 1829–1838.

Salovey, P., Caruso, D., & Mayer, J. D. (2004). Emotional intelligence in practice. In P. Linley & S. Joseph (Eds.), *Positive psychology in practice* (pp. 447–463). Hoboken, NJ: John Wiley & Sons Inc.

Samson, J. E., Ojanen, T., & Hollo, A. (2012). Social goals and youth aggression: Meta-analysis of prosocial and antisocial goals. *Social Development, 21*(4), 645–666.

Samuelson, C. D., & Watrous-Rodriguez, K. M. (2010). Group discussion and cooperation in social dilemmas: Does the medium matter? In R. M. Kramer, A. E. Tenbrunsel, & M. H. Bazerman (Eds.), *Social decision making: Social dilemmas, social values, and ethical judgments* (pp. 13–46). New York: Routledge/Taylor & Francis Group.

Sanchez, J. I., & Levine, E. L. (2012). The rise and fall of job analysis and the future of work analysis. *Annual Review of Psychology, 63*, 397–425.

Sánchez-Meca, J., Rosa-Alcázar, A. I., Marín-Martínez, F., & Gómez-Conesa, A. (2010). Psychological treatment of panic disorder with or without agoraphobia: A meta-analysis. *Clinical Psychology Review, 30*(1), 37–50.

Sarter, N. B., & Woods, D. D. (1991). Situation awareness: A critical but ill-defined phenomenon. *The International Journal of Aviation Psychology, 1*(1), 45–57.

Satterfield, T. A., Mertz, C. K., & Slovic, P. (2004). Discrimination, vulnerability, and justice in the face of risk. *Risk Analysis, 24*(1), 115–129.

Sawa, K. (2009). Predictive behavior and causal learning in animals and humans. *Japanese Psychological Research, 51*(3), 222–233.

Scaini, S., Battaglia, M., Beidel, D. C., & Ogliari, A. (2012). A meta-analysis of the cross-cultural psychometric properties of the Social Phobia and Anxiety Inventory for Children (SPAI-C). *Journal of Anxiety Disorders, 26*(1), 182–188.

Scannell, L., & Gifford, R. (2010a). Defining place attachment: A tripartite organizing framework. *Journal of Environmental Psychology, 30*(1), 1–10.

Scannell, L., & Gifford, R. (2010b). The relations between natural and civic place attachment and pro-environmental behavior. *Journal of Environmental Psychology, 30*(3), 289–297.

Scannell, L., & Gifford, R. (2013). Personally relevant climate change: The role of place attachment and local versus global message framing in engagement. *Environment and Behavior, 45*(1), 60–85.

REFERENCES

Schachter, E. P., & Rich, Y. (2011). Identity education: A conceptual framework for educational researchers and practitioners. *Educational Psychologist, 46*(4), 222–238.

Schacter, D. L., Gilbert, D. T., & Wegner, D. M. (2009). *Psychology* (2nd ed.). New York: Worth.

Schaffner, D., Demarmels, S., & Juettner, U. (2015). Promoting biodiversity: Do consumers prefer feelings, facts, advice or appeals? *Journal of Consumer Marketing, 32*(4), 266–277.

Scheier, M. F., & Carver, C. S. (2003). Goals and confidence as self-regulatory elements underlying health and illness behavior. In L. D. Cameron & H. Leventhal (Eds.), *The self-regulation of health and illness behaviour* (pp. 17–41). New York: Routledge.

Scher, S. (1999). Are adaptations necessarily genetic? *American Psychologist, 54*(6), 436–437.

Schifferstein, H. J. (2010). From salad to bowl: The role of sensory analysis in product experience research. *Food Quality and Preference, 21*(8), 1059–1067.

Schippmann, J., & Newson, D. (2008). The role of the internal consultant: How internal consultants can promote successful change. In J. W. Hedge & W. C. Borman (Eds.), *The I/O consultant: Advice and Insights for building a successful career* (pp. 45–51). Washington, DC: American Psychological Association.

Schlaefli, A., Rest, J. R., & Thoma, S. J. (1985). Does moral education improve moral judgment? A meta-analysis of intervention studies using the defining issues test. *Review of Educational Research, 55*(3), 319–352.

Schlenker, B. R., Hallam, J. R., & McCown, N. E. (1983). Motives and social evaluation: Actor–Observer differences in the delineation of motives for a beneficial act. *Journal of Experimental Social Psychology, 19*(3), 254–273.

Schloss, J. P. (2000). Wisdom traditions as mechanisms for organismal integration: Evolutionary perspectives on homeostatic "laws of life". In W. S. Brown (Ed.), *Understanding wisdom: Sources, science, and society* (pp. 153–191). West Conshohocken, PA: Templeton Foundation Press.

Schmidt, F. L., & Hunter, J. E. (1993). Tacit knowledge, practical intelligence, general mental ability, and job knowledge. *Current Directions in Psychological Science, 2*(1), 8–9.

Schmidt, F. L., Hunter, J. E., & Outerbridge, A. N. (1986). Impact of job experience and ability on job knowledge, work sample performance, and supervisory ratings of job performance. *Journal of Applied Psychology, 71*(3), 432–439.

Schmidt, H. G., van der Molen, H. T., Te Winkel, W. R., & Wijnen, W. W. (2009). Constructivist, problem-based learning does work: A meta-analysis of curricular comparisons involving a single medical school. *Educational Psychologist, 44*(4), 227–249.

Schmitt, N., Gooding, R. Z., Noe, R. A., & Kirsch, M. (1984). Metaanalyses of validity studies published between 1964 and 1982 and the investigation of study characteristics. *Personnel Psychology, 37*(3), 407–422.

Schmitt, N., Schneider, J. R., & Cohen, S. A. (1990). Factors affecting validity of a regionally administered assessment center. *Personnel Psychology, 43*(1), 1–12.

Schneider, B. H., Atkinson, L., & Tardif, C. (2001). Child–Parent attachment and children's peer relations: A quantitative review. *Developmental Psychology, 37*(1), 86–100.

Schneider, M., & Andrade, H. (2013). Teachers' and administrators' use of evidence of student learning to take action: Conclusions drawn from a special issue on formative assessment. *Applied Measurement in Education, 26*(3), 159–162.

Schott, J. P., Scherer, L. D., & Lambert, A. J. (2011). Casualties of war and sunk costs: Implications for attitude change and persuasion. *Journal of Experimental Social Psychology, 47*(6), 1134–1145.

REFERENCES

Schouborg, G. (2001). Big Brother's ecological psychology. *American Psychologist, 56*(5), 458–459.

Schuelke, M. J., Day, E., McEntire, L. E., Boatman, P. R., Boatman, J., Kowollik, V., & Wang, X. (2009). Relating indices of knowledge structure coherence and accuracy to skill-based performance: Is there utility in using a combination of indices? *Journal of Applied Psychology, 94*(4), 1076–1085.

Schultz, P., & Oskamp, S. (1996, December). Effort as a moderator of the attitude-behavior relationship: General environmental concern and recycling. *Social Psychology Quarterly, 59*(4), 375–383.

Schultz, P., & Searleman, A. (2002). Rigidity of thought and behavior: 100 years of research. *genetic, social, and General Psychology Monographs, 128*(2), 165–207.

Schultze, T., Pfeiffer, F., & Schulz-Hardt, S. (2012). Biased information processing in the escalation paradigm: Information search and information evaluation as potential mediators of escalating commitment. *Journal of Applied Psychology, 97*(1), 16–32.

Schum, D. A. (1994). *Evidential foundations of probabilistic reasoning.* New York: Wiley.

Schwab, A. (2007). Incremental organizational learning from multilevel information sources: Evidence for cross-level interactions. *Organization Science, 18*(2), 233–251.

Schwartz, C., Meisenhelder, J., Ma, Y., & Reed, G. (2003). Altruistic social interest behaviors are associated with better mental health. *Psychosomatic Medicine, 65*(5), 778–785.

Schwartz, S. H. (2007). Universalism values and the inclusiveness of our moral universe. *Journal of Cross-Cultural Psychology, 38*(6), 711–728.

Schwartz, S. H., Cieciuch, J., Vecchione, M., Davidov, E., Fischer, R., Beierlein, C., … Konty, M. (2012). Refining the theory of basic individual values. *Journal of Personality and Social Psychology, 103*(4), 663–688.

Schwarzer, R. (1999). Self-regulatory processes in the adoption and maintenance of health behaviors: The role of optimism, goals, and threats. *Journal of Health Psychology, 4*(2), 115–127.

Schweiger, D. M., Sandberg, W. R., & Ragan, J. W. (1986). Group approaches for improving strategic decision making: A comparative analysis of dialectical inquiry, devil's advocacy, and consensus. *Academy of Management Journal, 29*(1), 51–71.

Schwenk, C. R., & Cosier, R. A. (1980). Effects of the expert, devil's advocate, and dialectical inquiry methods on prediction performance. *Organizational Behavior & Human Performance, 26*(3), 409–424.

Scott, B. A. (2009). Review of "Meeting environmental challenges: The role of human identity". *Journal of Environmental Psychology, 29*(4), 535–537.

Scully-Russ, E. (2012). Human resource development and sustainability: Beyond sustainable organizations. *Human Resource Development International, 15*(4), 399–415.

Seligman, M. E. P., & Csikszentmihalyi, M. (2000). Positive psychology: An introduction. *American Psychologist, 55* (1), Special issue: Positive Psychology, 5–14.

Seligman, M. E. P., Steen, T. A., Park, N., & Peterson, C. (2005). Positive psychology progress: Empirical validation of interventions. *American Psychologist, 60*(5), 410–421.

Sellmann, D., & Bogner, F. X. (2013). Effects of a 1-day environmental education intervention on environmental attitudes and connectedness with nature. *European Journal of Psychology of Education, 28*(3), 1077–1086.

Selman, P. (2004). Community participation in the planning and management of cultural landscapes. *Journal of Environmental Planning & Management, 47*(3), 365–392.

Semken, S., & Freeman, C. (2008). Sense of place in the practice and assessment of place-based science teaching. *Science Education, 92*(6), 1042–1057.

Sen, S., Gürhan-Canli, Z., & Morwitz, V. (2001). Withholding consumption: A social dilemma perspective on consumer boycotts. *Journal of Consumer Research, 28*(3), 399–417.

REFERENCES

Sevincer, A. T., Kluge, L., & Oettingen, G. (2014). Implicit theories and motivational focus: Desired future versus present reality. *Motivation and Emotion, 38*(1), 36–46.

Shaffer, J. A., & Postlethwaite, B. E. (2012). A matter of context: A meta-analytic investigation of the relative validity of contextualized and noncontextualized personality measures. *Personnel Psychology, 65,* 445–493.

Shah, A. K., & Oppenheimer, D. M. (2009). The path of least resistance: Using easy-to-access information. *Current Directions in Psychological Science, 18*(4), 232–236.

Shama, A., & Wisenblit, J. (1984). Values of voluntary simplicity: Lifestyle and motivation. *Psychological Reports, 55*(1), 231–240.

Shanahan, M. J., Hill, P. L., Roberts, B. W., Eccles, J., & Friedman, H. S. (2012). Conscientiousness, health, and aging: The life course of personality model. *Developmental Psychology, 50,* 1407–1425.

Sharf, J. C., & Jones, D. P. (2000). Employment risk management. In J. F. Kehoe (Ed.), *Managing selection in changing organizations* (pp. 271–318). San Francisco, CA: Jossey-Bass.

Sharma, P. (2010). Measuring personal cultural orientations: Scale development and validation. *Journal of the Academy of Marketing Science, 38,* 787–806.

Sharp, K. L., Williams, A. J., Rhyner, K. T., & Ilardi, S. S. (2013). The clinical interview. In K. F. Geisinger, B. A. Bracken, J. F. Carlson, J. C. Hansen, N. R. Kuncel, S. P. Reise, & M. C. Rodriguez (Eds.), *APA handbook of testing and assessment in psychology, Vol. 2: Testing and assessment in clinical and counseling psychology* (pp. 103–117). Washington, DC: American Psychological Association.

Sher, K. J., Winograd, R., & Haeny, A. M. (2013). Disorders of impulse control. In G. Stricker, T. A. Widiger, & I. B. Weiner (Eds.), *Handbook of psychology, Vol. 8: Clinical psychology* (2nd ed.) (pp. 217–239). Hoboken, NJ: John Wiley & Sons Inc.

Sherblom, S. A. (2015). A Moral Experience Feedback Loop: Modeling a system of moral self-cultivation in everyday life. *Journal of Moral Education, 44*(3), 364–381.

Sherman, R. A., Nave, C. S., & Funder, D. C. (2012). Properties of persons and situations related to overall and distinctive personality-behavior congruence. *Journal of Research in Personality, 46*(1), 87–101.

Sherman, S. J., Crawford, M. T., & McConnell, A. R. (2004). Looking ahead as a technique to reduce resistance to persuasive attempts. In E. S. Knowles & J. A. Linn (Eds.), *Resistance and persuasion* (pp. 149–174). Mahwah, NJ: Lawrence Erlbaum Associates Publishers.

Sheth, J. N., Sethia, N. K., & Srinivas, S. (2011). Mindful consumption: A customer-centric approach to sustainability. *Journal of the Academy of Marketing Science, 39*(1), 21–39.

Shibbal-Champagne, S., & Lipinska-Stachow, D. M. (1985). Alzheimer's educational/support group: Considerations for success: Awareness of family tasks, preplanning, and active professional facilitation. *Journal of Gerontological Social Work, 9*(2), 41–48.

Shimojo, S., Simion, C., Shimojo, E., & Scheier, C. (2003). Gaze bias both reflects and influences preference. *Nature Neuroscience, 6*(12), 1317–1322.

Sieber, J. E. (2010). New research domains create new ethical challenges. *Journal of Empirical Research on Human Research Ethics, 5*(1), 1–2.

Siegfried, W. D., Tedeschi, R. G., & Cann, A. (1982). The generalizability of attitudinal correlates of proenvironmental behavior. *The Journal of Social Psychology, 118*(2), 287–288.

Siegler, R. S., & Chen, Z. (2008). Differentiation and integration: Guiding principles for analyzing cognitive change. *Developmental Science, 11*(4), 433–448.

Silove, D., & Bryant, R. (2006). Rapid assessments of mental health needs after disasters. *JAMA: Journal of the American Medical Association, 296*(5), 576–578.

REFERENCES

Silverberg, S. B., Betis, S. C., Huebner, A. J., & Cota-Robles, S. (1996). Implicit beliefs about change: A theory-grounded measure applied to community organizations serving children, youth, and families. *Journal of Sociology and Social Welfare, 23*(4), 57–76.

Simunich, B. (2009). Emotion arousing message forms and personal agency arguments in persuasive messages: Motivating effects on pro-environmental behaviors. Dissertation, Ohio State University.

Singer, R. D., & Feshbach, S. (1959). Some relationships between manifest anxiety, authoritarian tendencies, and modes of reaction to frustration. *The Journal of Abnormal and Social Psychology, 59*(3), 404–408.

Singh, V. P., Hansen, K. T., & Blattberg, R. C. (2006). Market entry and consumer behavior: An investigation of a wal-mart supercenter. *Marketing Science, 25*(5), 457–476.

Sinha, A., & Verma, J. (2006). Indian value types: An empirical study. *Psychological Studies, 51*(4), 235–244.

SIOP (Society for Industrial and Organizational Psychology) (2013a). www.siop.org/history/crsppp.aspx

SIOP (2013b). www.siop.org/Media/News/hotjob.aspx

SIOP (2015) www.siop.org/Events-Education/Educators/Guidelines-Education-Training

Sitzmann, T., & Ely, K. (2011). A meta-analysis of self-regulated learning in work-related training and educational attainment: What we know and where we need to go. *Psychological Bulletin, 137*(3), 421–442.

Skowronski, J. J., & Carlston, D. E. (1992). Caught in the act: When impressions based on highly diagnostic behaviours are resistant to contradiction. *European Journal of Social Psychology, 22*(5), 435–452.

Skowronski, J. J., & Ostrom, T. M. (1992). Cognition in social behavior: Articulating the unconscious. *Psyccritiques, 37*(1), 29–30.

Slovic, P., & Peters, E. (2006). Risk perception and affect. *Current Directions in Psychological Science, 15*, 322–325.

Smetana, J. G., Jambon, M., Conry-Murray, C., & Sturge-Apple, M. L. (2012). Reciprocal associations between young children's developing moral judgments and theory of mind. *Developmental Psychology, 48*(4), 1144–1155.

Smith, A. (1776). *The wealth of nations.* Cincinnati, OH: Simon and Brown.

Smith, C. A., Haynes, K. N., Lazarus, R. S., & Pope, L. K. (1993). In search of the "hot" cognitions: Attributions, appraisals, and their relation to emotion. *Journal of Personality and Social Psychology, 65*(5), 916–929.

Smith, C. A., & Kirby, L. D. (2009). Putting appraisal in context: Toward a relational model of appraisal and emotion. *Cognition and Emotion, 23*(7), Special issue: Individual differences in emotion, 1352–1372.

Smith, C. A., & Lazarus, R. S. (1993). Appraisal components, core relational themes, and the emotions. *Cognition and Emotion, 7*, 233–269.

Smith, E. M., Ford, J., & Kozlowski, S. J. (1997). Building adaptive expertise: Implications for training design strategies. In M. A. Quiñones & A. Ehrenstein (Eds.), *Training for a rapidly changing workplace: Applications of psychological research* (pp. 89–118). Washington, DC: American Psychological Association.

Smith, J. R., Louis, W. R., Terry, D. J., Greenaway, K. H., Clarke, M. R., & Cheng, X. (2012). Congruent or conflicted? The impact of injunctive and descriptive norms on environmental intentions. *Journal of Environmental Psychology, 32*(4), 353–361.

Smith, L. (1994). The Binet-Piaget connection: Have developmentalists missed the epistemological point? *Archives De Psychologie, 62*(243), 275–285.

REFERENCES

Smith, N., & Cooper-Martin, E. (1997). Ethics and target marketing: The role of product harm and consumer vulnerability. *Journal of Marketing, 61*(3), 1–20.

Smith, R. (2002). Professional educational psychology and community relations education in Northern Ireland. *Educational Psychology in Practice, 18*(4), 275–295.

Smither, J. W., & London, M. (2009). Best practices in performance management. In J. W. Smither & M. London (Eds.), *Performance management: Putting research into action* (pp. 585–625). San Francisco, CA: Jossey-Bass.

Smith-Sebasto, N. J., & Cavern, L. (2006). Effects of pre- and posttrip activities associated with a residential environmental education experience on students' attitudes toward the environment. *The Journal of Environmental Education, 37*(4), 3–17.

Smith-Sebasto, N. J., & Obenchain, V. L. (2009). Students' perceptions of the residential environmental education program at the New Jersey School of Conservation. *The Journal of Environmental Education, 40*(2), 50–62.

Snyder, C. R., & Lopez, S. J. (2002). *Handbook of positive psychology.* New York: Oxford University Press.

Snyder, M., & Dwyer, P. C. (2013). Altruism and prosocial behavior. In H. Tennen, J. Suls, & I. B. Weiner (Eds.), *Handbook of psychology, Vol. 5: Personality and social psychology* (2nd ed., pp. 467–485). Hoboken, NJ: John Wiley & Sons Inc.

Snyder, R., Shapiro, S., & Treleaven, D. (2012). Attachment theory and mindfulness. *Journal of Child and Family Studies, 21*(5), 709–717.

Society for Consumer Psychology (2013). www.myscp.org

Solberg Nes, L., Carlson, C. R., Crofford, L. J., de Leeuw, R., & Segerstrom, S. C. (2011). Individual differences and self-regulatory fatigue: Optimism, conscientiousness, and self-consciousness. *Personality and Individual Differences, 50*(4), 475–480.

Søndergaard, H., & Harmsen, H. (2007). Using market information in product development. *Journal of Consumer Marketing, 24*(4), 194–201.

Songer, N., Kelcey, B., & Gotwals, A. (2009). How and when does complex reasoning occur? Empirically driven development of a learning progression focused on complex reasoning about biodiversity. *Journal of Research in Science Teaching, 46*(6), 610–613.

Sørensen, J. B. (2002). The strength of corporate culture and the reliability of firm performance. *Administrative Science Quarterly, 47*(1), 70–91.

Sowislo, J., & Orth, U. (2013). Does low self-esteem predict depression and anxiety? A meta-analysis of longitudinal studies. *Psychological Bulletin, 139*(1), 213–240.

Soyez, K. (2012). How national cultural values affect pro-environmental consumer behavior. *International Marketing Review, 29*(6), 623–646.

Spector, P. E., Cooper, C. L., & Sparks, K. (2001). An international study of the psychometric properties of the Hofstede Values Survey Module 1994: A comparison of individual and country/province level results. *Applied Psychology: An International Review, 50*(2), 269–281.

Speekenbrink, M., & Shanks, D. R. (2010). Learning in a changing environment. *Journal of Experimental Psychology: General, 139*(2), 266–298.

Spinrad, T. L., Stifter, C. A., Donelan-McCall, N., & Turner, L. (2004). Mothers' regulation strategies in response to toddlers' affect: Links to later emotion self-regulation. *Social Development, 13*(1), 40–55.

Sportel, B., Nauta, M. H., de Hullu, E., & de Jong, P. J. (2013). Predicting internalizing symptoms over a two year period by BIS, FFFS and attentional control. *Personality and Individual Differences, 54*(2), 236–240.

Srinivasan, S., Vanhuele, M., & Pauwels, K. (2010). Mind-set metrics in market response models: An integrative approach. *Journal of Marketing Research, 47*(4), 672–684.

REFERENCES

Srofe, L., & Waters, E. (1976). The ontogenesis of smiling and laughter: A perspective on the organization of development in infancy. *Psychological Review, 83*(3), 173–189.

Stackert, R. A., & Bursik, K. (2006). Ego development and the therapeutic goal-setting capacities of mentally ill adults. *American Journal of Psychotherapy, 60*(4), 357–371.

Stahl, G. K., & Voigt, A. (2008). Do cultural differences matter in mergers and acquisitions? A tentative model and examination. *Organization Science, 19*(1), 160–176.

Stajkovic, A. D., & Luthans, F. (1998). Self-efficacy and work-related performance: A meta-analysis. *Psychological Bulletin, 124*(2), 240–261.

Stanford, M. S., & Felthous, A. R. (2008). Introduction to this issue: Impulsivity and the law. *Behavioral Sciences and the Law, 26*(6), 671–673.

Stanger, N., Kavussanu, M., Boardley, I. D., & Ring, C. (2013). The influence of moral disengagement and negative emotion on antisocial sport behavior. *Sport, Exercise, and Performance Psychology, 2*(2), 117–129.

Stanton, N. A., Salmon, P. M., Walker, G. H., Salas, E., & Hancock, P. A. (2017). State-of-science: Situation awareness in individuals, teams and systems. *Ergonomics, 60*(4), 449–466.

Star, S. A. (1949a). Psychoneurotic symptoms in the Army. In S. A. Stouffer, A. A. Lumsdaine, et al (Eds.), *The American soldier* (Vol. II). Princeton, NJ: Princeton University Press, chapter 9.

Star, S. A. (1949b). Problems of rotation and reconversion. In S. A. Stouffer, A. A. Lumsdaine, et al (Eds.), *The American soldier* (Vol. II). Princeton, NJ: Princeton University Press, chapter 10.

Staw, B. M. (1997). The escalation of commitment: An update and appraisal. In Z. Shapira, (Ed.), *Organizational decision making* (pp. 191–215). New York: Cambridge University Press.

Steadman, H. J., Osher, F. C., Robbins, P. C., Case, B., & Samuels, S. (2009). Prevalence of serious mental illness among jail inmates. *Psychiatric Services, 60*, 761–765.

Stedman, R. C. (2006). Understanding place attachment among second home owners. *American Behavioral Scientist, 50*(2), 187–205.

Stedmon, A. W., Winslow, R., & Langley, A. (2013). Micro-generation schemes: User behaviours and attitudes towards energy consumption. *Ergonomics, 56*(3), 440–450.

Steel, P., Schmidt, J., & Shultz, J. (2008). Refining the relationship between personality and subjective well-being. *Psychological Bulletin, 134*(1), 138–161.

Steenbergen-Hu, S., & Cooper, H. (2013). A meta-analysis of the effectiveness of intelligent tutoring systems on k–12 students' mathematical learning. *Journal of Educational Psychology*, doi:10.1037/a0032447

Steg, L., Dreijerink, L., & Abrahamse, W. (2006). Why are energy policies acceptable and effective effective? *Environment and Behavior, 38*(1), 92–111.

Steg, L., & Vlek, C. (2009). Encouraging pro-environmental behaviour: An integrative review and research agenda. *Journal of Environmental Psychology, 29*(3), 309–317.

Stelzl, M., & Seligman, C. (2009). Multiplicity across cultures: Multiple national identities and multiple value systems. *Organization Studies, 30*(9), 959–973.

Stenson, H. H. (1974). The lens model with unknown cue structure. *Psychological Review, 81*(3), 257–264.

Sterman, J. D. (2006). Learning from evidence in a complex world. *American Journal of Public Health, 96*(3), 505–514.

Stern, M. J., Powell, R. B., & Ardoin, N. M. (2008). What difference does it make? Assessing outcomes from participation in a residential environmental education program. *The Journal of Environmental Education, 39*(4), 31–43.

REFERENCES

Stern, P. C. (2000). Toward a coherent theory of environmentally significant behavior. *Journal of Social Issues, 55,* 407–424.

Sternberg, R. J. (1997). The concept of intelligence and its role in lifelong learning and success. *American Psychologist, 52*(10), Special issue: Intelligence and Lifelong Learning, 1030–1037.

Sternberg, R. J. (2004). Culture and Intelligence. *American Psychologist, 59*(5), 325–338.

Stokols, D. (1978). Environmental psychology. *Annual Review of Psychology, 29,* 253–295.

Stoléru, S., Fonteille, V., Cornélis, C., Joyal, C., & Moulier, V. (2012). Functional neuroimaging studies of sexual arousal and orgasm in healthy men and women: A review and meta-analysis. *Neuroscience and Biobehavioral Reviews, 36*(6), 1481–1509.

Stone-Romero, E. F., & Stone, D. L. (2002). Cross-cultural differences in responses to feedback: Implications for individual, group, and organizational effectiveness. In G. R. Ferris & J. J. Martocchio (Eds.), *Research in personnel and human resources management* (pp. 275–331). New York: Elsevier Science/JAI Press.

Story, P. A., & Forsyth, D. R. (2008b). Watershed conservation and preservation: Environmental engagement as helping behavior. *Journal Of Environmental Psychology, 28*(4), 305–317.

Stouffer, S. A. (1949). Job assignment and job satisfaction. In S. A. Stouffer, A. A. Lumsdaine, et al (Eds.), *The American soldier* (Vol. I). Princeton, NJ: Princeton University Press, chapter 7.

Stricker, G. (1997). Are science and practice commensurable? *American Psychologist, 52*(4), 442–448.

Strickland, B. R. (1989). Internal-external control expectancies: From contingency to creativity. *American Psychologist, 44*(1), 1–12.

Strizhakova, Y., & Coulter, R. A. (2013). The "green" side of materialism in emerging BRIC and developed markets: The moderating role of global cultural identity. *International Journal of Research in Marketing, 30*(1), 69–82.

Stroebe, M. S., & Archer, J. (2013). Origins of modern ideas on love and loss: Contrasting forerunners of attachment theory. *Review of General Psychology, 17*(1), 28–39.

Sturm, R. (2008). Stemming the global obesity epidemic: What can we learn from data about social and economic trends? *Public Health, 122*(8), 739–746.

Stürmer, S., Snyder, M., & Omoto, A. M. (2005). Prosocial emotions and helping: The moderating role of group membership. *Journal of Personality and Social Psychology, 88*(3), 532–546.

Suddendorf, T., & Whiten, A. (2001). Mental evolution and development: Evidence for secondary representation in children, great apes, and other animals. *Psychological Bulletin, 127*(5), 629–650.

Suggate, S. (2010). Why what we teach depends on when: Grade and reading intervention modality moderate effect size. *Developmental Psychology, 46*(6), 1556–1579.

Suls, J., & David, J. P. (1996). Coping and personality: Third time's the charm? *Journal of Personality, 64*(4), 993–1005.

Sun, H., Zimmer, H. D., & Fu, X. (2011). The influence of expertise and of physical complexity on visual short-term memory consolidation. *The Quarterly Journal of Experimental Psychology, 64*(4), 707–729.

Sundstrom, E., Bell, P. A., Busby, P. L., & Asmus, C. (1996). Environmental psychology 1989–1994. *Annual Review of Psychology, 47,* 485–512.

Surface, E. A. (2012). Training needs assessment: Aligning learning and capability with performance requirements and organizational objectives. In M. A. Wilson, W. R. Bennett, S. G. Gibson, & G. M. Alliger (Eds.), *The handbook of work analysis: Methods, systems, applications and science of work measurement in organizations* (pp. 437–462). New York: Routledge/Taylor & Francis Group.

REFERENCES

Swami, V., Chamorro-Premuzic, T., Snelgar, R., & Furnham, A. (2010). Egoistic, altruistic, and biospheric environmental concerns: A path analytic investigation of their determinants. *Scandinavian Journal of Psychology*, *51*(2), 139–145.

Swanson, J. M., Kinsbourne, M., Nigg, J., Lanphear, B., Stefanatos, G. A., Volkow, N., & Wadhwa, P. D. (2007). Etiologic subtypes of attention-deficit/hyper-activity disorder: Brain imaging, molecular genetic and environmental factors and the dopamine hypothesis. *Neuropsychology Review*, *17*(1), 39–59.

Swim, J. K. (2013). Confronting for conservation. *Ecopsychology*, *5*(1), 1–2.

Swim, J. K., & Bloodhart, B. (2013). Portrayal of animals harmed by climate change: Motivational qualities and behavioral implications. Unpublished manuscript, Pennsylvania State University.

Swim, J. K., Clayton, S., & Howard, G. S. (2011). Human behavioral contributions to climate change: Psychological and contextual drivers. *American Psychologist*, *66*(4), 251–264.

Swim, J. K., Stern, P. C., Doherty, T. J., Clayton, S., Reser, J. P., Weber, E. U., ... Howard, G. S. (2011). Psychology's contributions to understanding and addressing global climate change. *American Psychologist*, *66*(4), 241–250.

Syme, G. J., Seligman, C., Kantola, S. J., & MacPherson, D. K. (1987). Evaluating a television campaign to promote petrol conservation. *Environment and Behavior*, *19*(4), 444–461.

Szymanski, D. M., & Henard, D. H. (2001). Customer satisfaction: A meta-analysis of the empirical evidence. *Journal of the Academy of Marketing Science*, *29*(1), 16–35.

Taatgen, N. A. (2013). The nature and transfer of cognitive skills. *Psychological Review*, *120*(3), 439–471.

Tabernero, C., & Hernández, B. (2011). Collective motivation for managing our common environment. In M. Bonaiuto, M. Bonnes, A. Nenci, & G. Carrus (Eds.), *Urban diversities: Environmental and social issues* (pp. 193–202). Cambridge, MA: Hogrefe Publishing.

Taddicken, M. (2013). Climate change from the user's perspective: The impact of mass media and internet use and individual and moderating variables on knowledge and attitudes. *Journal of Media Psychology: Theories, Methods, and Applications*, *25*(1), 39–52.

Tajfel, H. (1982). Social psychology of inter-group relations. *Annual Review of Psychology*, *33*, 1–39.

Takahashi, N. (1997). A single garbage can model and the degree of anarchy in Japanese firms. *Human Relations*, *50*(1), 91–108.

Takahashi, Y., Veríssimo, D., MacMillan, D. C., & Godbole, A. (2012). Stakeholder perceptions of potential flagship species for the sacred groves of the north Western Ghats, India. *Human Dimensions of Wildlife*, *17*(4), 257–269.

Tanes, Z., & Cho, H. (2013). Goal setting outcomes: Examining the role of goal inter-action in influencing the experience and learning outcomes of video game play for earthquake preparedness. *Computers in Human Behavior*, *29*(3), 858–869.

Tang, K., Robinson, D. A., & Harvey, M. (2011). Sustainability managers or rogue mid-managers? A typology of corporate sustainability managers. *Management Decision*, *49*(8), 1371–1394.

Tannenbaum, S. I., & Cerasoli, C. P. (2013). Do team and individual debriefs enhance performance? A meta-analysis. *Human Factors*, *55*(1), 231–245.

Taras, V., Kirkman, B. L., & Steel, P. (2010). Examining the impact of culture's consequences: A three-decade, multilevel, meta-analytic review of Hofstede's cultural value dimensions. *Journal of Applied Psychology*, *95*(3), 405–439.

Taufik, D. (2018) Prospective "warm-glow" of reducing meat consumption in China: Emotional associations with intentions for meat consumption curtailment and consumption of meat substitutes, *Journal of Environmental Psychology*, *60*, pp. 48–54.

REFERENCES

Taylor, W. C., Poston, W., Jones, L., & Kraft, M. (2006). Environmental justice: Obesity, physical activity, and healthy eating. *Journal of Physical Activity & Health, 3* (Suppl1), S30–S54.

Teachout, M. S., & Hall, C. R. (2002). Implementing training: Some practical guidelines. In J. W. Hedge & E. D. Pulakos (Eds.), *Implementing organizational interventions: Steps, processes, and best practices* (pp. 198–231). San Francisco, CA: Jossey-Bass.

Tellis, G. J., Stremersch, S., & Yin, E. (2003). The international takeoff of new products: The role of economics, culture, and country innovativeness. *Marketing Science, 22* (2), 188–208.

Tencati, A., & Zsolnai, L. (2009). The collaborative enterprise. *Journal of Business Ethics, 85*(3), 367–376.

Ter Mors, E., Weenig, M. W. H., Ellemers, N., & Daamen, D. D. L. (2010). Effective communication about complex environmental issues: Perceived quality of information about carbon dioxide capture and storage (CCS) depends on stakeholder collaboration. *Journal of Environmental Psychology, 30*(4), 347–357.

Tett, R. P., & Burnett, D. D. (2003). A personality trait-based interactionist model of job performance. *Journal of Applied Psychology, 88*(3), 500–517.

Tett, R. P., & Guterman, H. A. (2000). Situation trait relevance, trait expression, and cross-situational consistency: Testing a principle of trait activation. *Journal of Research in Personality, 34*(4), 397–423.

Thanellou, A., & Green, J. T. (2011). Spontaneous recovery but not reinstatement of the extinguished conditioned eyeblink response in the rat. *Behavioral Neuroscience, 125* (4), 613–625.

Thatcher, A. (2013). Green ergonomics: Definition and scope. *Ergonomics, 56*(3), 389–398.

Thatcher, A., & Yeow, P. H. P. (2016). A sustainable system of systems approach: A new HFE paradigm. *Ergonomics, 59*(2), 167–178.

Thayer, R. (1996). *The origin of everyday mood: Managing energy, tension, and stress.* New York: Oxford Press.

Thelen, E. (1995). Motor development: A new synthesis. *American Psychologist, 50,* 79–95.

Thierry, H. (1998). Motivation and satisfaction. In P. D. Drenth, H. Thierry, & C. J. de Wolff (Eds.), *Handbook of work and organizational psychology, Vol. 4: Organizational psychology* (2nd ed.) (pp. 253–289). Hove: Psychology Press/Erlbaum, Taylor & Francis.

Thiessen, E. D., Kronstein, A. T., & Hufnagle, D. G. (2013). The estraction and integration framework: A two-process account of statistical learning. *Psychological Bulletin, 139,* 792–814.

Thøgersen, J. (1999). spillover processes in the development of a sustainable consumption pattern. *Journal of Economic Psychology, 20*(1), 53–81.

Thøgersen, J. (2006). Norms for environmentally responsible behaviour: An extended taxonomy. *Journal of Environmental Psychology, 26*(4), 247–261.

Thøgersen, J. (2008). Social norms and cooperation in real-life social dilemmas. *Journal of Economic Psychology, 29*(4), 458–472.

Thøgersen, J. (2009). The motivational roots of norms for environmentally responsible behavior. *Basic and Applied Social Psychology, 31*(4), 348–362.

Thøgersen, J., Jørgensen, A. K., & Sandager, S. (2012). Consumer decision making regarding a "green" everyday product. *Psychology & Marketing, 29*(4), 187–197.

Thøgersen, J., & Ölander, F. (2003). Spillover of environment-friendly consumer behaviour. *Journal of Environmental Psychology, 23*(3), 225–236.

Thøgersen, J., & Ölander, F. (2006). The dynamic interaction of personal norms and environment-friendly buying behavior: A panel study. *Journal of Applied Social Psychology, 36*(7), 1758–1780.

REFERENCES

Thomas, D. G., & Twyman, C. (2005). Equity and justice in climate change adaptation amongst natural-resource-dependent societies. *Global Environmental Change Part A: Human & Policy Dimensions, 15*(2), 115–124.

Thomas, H., & Cornuel, E. (2012). Business schools in transition? Issues of impact, legitimacy, capabilities and re-invention. *Journal of Management Development, 31*(4), 329–335.

Thomas, J. P., Whitman, D. S., & Viswesvaran, C. (2010). Employee proactivity in organizations: A comparative meta-analysis of emergent proactive constructs. *Journal of Occupational and Organizational Psychology, 83*(2), 275–300.

Thomas, K. F., Laurance, H. E., Nadel, L., & Jacobs, W. (2010). Stress-induced impairment of spatial navigation in females. *South African Journal of Psychology, 40*(1), 32–43.

Thompson, S., Marks, N., & Jackson, T. (2013). Well-being and sustainable development. In S. A. David, I. Boniwell, & A. Conley Ayers (Eds.), *The Oxford handbook of happiness* (pp. 498–516). New York: Oxford University Press.

Thompson, S. A., & Sinha, R. K. (2008). Brand communities and new product adoption: The influence and limits of oppositional loyalty. *Journal of Marketing, 72*(6), 65–80.

Thompson, S. C., & Barton, M. (1994). Ecocentric and anthropocentric attitudes toward the environment. *Journal of Environmental Psychology, 14*, 149–157.

Thorkildsen, T. A. (2006). Strengthening a human connection to nature. *Psyccritiques, 51*(48), doi:10.1037/a0005842

Thorndike, E. L. (1927). The law of effect. *The American Journal of Psychology, 39*, 212–222.

Thorndike, E. L. (1933). A proof of the law of effect. *Science, 77*, 173–175.

Thornton, G. C., III, & Rupp, D. E. (2006). *Assessment centers in human resource management: Strategies for prediction, diagnosis, and development.* Mahwah, NJ: Lawrence Erlbaum Associates.

Tichy, M., Johnson, D. W., Johnson, R. T., & Roseth, C. J. (2010). The impact of constructive controversy on moral development. *Journal of Applied Social Psychology, 40*(4), 765–787.

Tideman, E., & Gustafsson, J. (2004). Age-related differentiation of cognitive abilities in ages 3-7. *Personality and Individual Differences, 36*(8), 1965–1974.

Tippins, N. T. (2002). Issue in implementing large-scale selection programs. In J. W. Hedge & E. D. Pulakos (Eds.), *Implementing organizational interventions: Steps, processes, and best practices* (pp. 232–269). San Francisco, CA: Jossey-Bass.

Tjosvold, D. (2008). Constructive controversy for management education: Developing committed, open-minded researchers. *Academy of Management Learning & Education, 7* (1), 73–85.

Tobias, R., Brügger, A., & Mosler, H. (2009). Developing strategies for waste reduction by means of tailored interventions in Santiago de Cuba. *Environment and Behavior, 41* (6), 836–865.

Tobin, S. J., & Weary, G. (2008). The effects of causal uncertainty, causal importance, and initial attitude on attention to causal persuasive arguments. *Social Cognition, 26*(1), 44–65.

Tobin, S. J., Weary, G., Brunner, R. P., Gonzalez, J., & Han, H. A. (2009). Causal uncertainty and stereotype avoidance: The role of perceived category fit. *Social Cognition, 27*(6), 917–928.

Todd, P. M., & Gigerenzer, G. (2012). What is ecological rationality? In P. M. Todd & G. Gigerenzer (Eds.), *Ecological rationality: Intelligence in the world* (pp. 3–30). New York: Oxford University Press.

Tolman, E. C. (1948). Cognitive maps in rats and men. *Psychological Review, 55*(4), 189–208.

REFERENCES

Tom, D. Y., Cooper, H., & McGraw, M. (1984). Influences of student background and teacher authoritarianism on teacher expectations. *Journal of Educational Psychology, 76* (2), 259–265.

Tosi, H. L. (1973). The effect of the interaction of leader behavior and subordinate authoritarianism. *Personnel Psychology, 26*(3), 339–350.

Totterdell, P., & Holman, D. (2003). Emotion regulation in customer service roles: Testing a model of emotional labor. *Journal of Occupational Health Psychology, 8*(1), 55–73.

Toufaily, E., Ricard, L., & Perrien, J. (2013). Customer loyalty to a commercial website: Descriptive meta-analysis of the empirical literature and proposal of an integrative model. *Journal of Business Research, 66*(9), 1436–1447.

Toyosawa, J., Karasawa, K., & Fukuwa, N. (2010). Effects of disaster education for elementary school children on their guardians' disaster preparedness action: Changes in children's affect and cognition. *Japanese Journal Of Educational Psychology, 58*(4), 480–490.

Tracey, M. D. (2005). Crafting persuasive pro-environment messages. *Monitor on Psychology, 36*(9), 44–46.

Tracy, J. L., Shariff, A. F., Zhao, W., & Henrich, J. (2013). Cross-cultural evidence that the nonverbal expression of pride is an automatic status signal. *Journal of Experimental Psychology: General, 142*(1), 163–180.

Trapero-Bertran, M. M., Mistry, H. H., Shen, J. J., & Fox-Rushby, J. J. (2013). A systematic review and meta-analysis of willingness-to-pay values: The case of malaria control interventions. *Health Economics, 22*(4), 428–450.

Trudel, R., Klein, J., Sen, S., & Dawar, N. (2019). Feeling good by doing good: A selfish motivation for ethical choice. *Journal of Business Ethics*, e-journal

Truelove, H., & Parks, C. (2012). Perceptions of behaviors that cause and mitigate global warming and intentions to perform these behaviors. *Journal of Environmental Psychology, 32*(3), 246–259.

Tryon, W. W. (2010). Learning as core of psychological science and clinical practice. *The Behavior Therapist, 33*(1), 10–12.

Tsai, M. H., & Young, M. J. (2010). Anger, fear, and escalation of commitment. *Cognition and Emotion, 24*(6), 962–973.

Tubbs, M. E. (1986). Goal setting: A meta-analytic examination of the empirical evidence. *Journal of Applied Psychology, 71*(3), 474–483.

TVB (2013). www.tvb.org/trends/4705

Tversky, A., & Kahneman, D. (1973). Availability: A heuristic for judging frequency and probability. *Cognitive Psychology, 5*, 207–232.

Tversky, A., & Kahneman, D. (1974). Judgment under uncertainty: Heuristics and biases. *Science, 185*, 1124–1131.

Tversky, A., & Kahneman, D. (1983). Extensional vs. intuitive reasoning: The conjunction fallacy in probability judgment. *Psychological Review, 90*, 293–315.

Twenge, J. M., Campbell, W., & Freeman, E. C. (2012). Generational differences in young adults' life goals, concern for others, and civic orientation, 1966–2009. *Journal of Personality and Social Psychology, 102*(5), 1045–1062.

Tyler, T. R., Orwin, R., & Schurer, L. (1982). Defensive denial and high cost prosocial behavior. *Basic and Applied Social Psychology, 3*(4), 267–281.

Tyler, T. R., & Rankin, L. E. (2012). Public attitudes and punitive policies. In J. A. Dvoskin, J. L. Skeem, R. W. Novaco, & K. S. Douglas (Eds.), *Using social science to reduce violent offending* (pp. 103–123). New York: Oxford University Press.

Tziner, A., & Murphy, K. R. (1999). Additional evidence of attitudinal influences in performance appraisal. *Journal of Business and Psychology, 13*(3), 407–419.

Uiterkamp, A., & Vlek, C. (2007). Practice and outcomes of multidisciplinary research for environmental sustainability. *Journal of Social Issues, 63*(1), 175–197.

REFERENCES

United State Geological Survey (2018). *Saline water: Desalination.* https://water.usgs.gov/edu/drinkseawater.html

Upreti, G., Liaupsin, C., & Koonce, D. (2010). Stakeholder utility: Perspectives on school-wide data for measurement, feedback, and evaluation. *Education & Treatment of Children, 33*(4), 497–511.

Uzzell, D., Pol, E., & Badenas, D. (2002). Place identification, social cohesion, and environmental sustainability. *Environment and Behavior, 34*, 26–53.

Valacich, J. S., & Schwenk, C. (1995). Devil's advocate and dialectical inquiry effects on face-to-face and computer-mediated group decision making. *Organizational Behavior and Human Decision Processes, 63*(2), 158–173.

Vallerand, R. J., Deshaies, P., Cuerrier, J. P., Pelletier, L. G., & Mongeau, C. (1992). Ajzen and Fishbein's theory of reasoned action as applied to moral behavior: A confirmatory analysis. *Journal of Personality and Social Psychology, 62*(1), 98–109.

Valor, C., Antonetti, P., & Carrero, I. (2018). Stressful sustainability: A hermeneutic analysis. *European Journal of Marketing, 52*(3–4), 550–574.

Van Cappellen, P., Corneille, O., Cols, S., & Saroglou, V. (2011). Beyond mere compliance to authoritative figures: Religious priming increases conformity to informational influence among submissive people. *International Journal for the Psychology of Religion, 21*(2), 97–105.

van Dam, Y. K., & van Trijp, H. M. (2011). Cognitive and motivational structure of sustainability. *Journal of Economic Psychology, 32*(5), 726–741.

van de Vijver, F. (1997). Meta-analysis of cross-cultural comparisons of cognitive test performance. *Journal of Cross-Cultural Psychology, 28*(6), 678–709.

van de Wetering, S., Bernstein, D. M., & Loftus, E. F. (2005). Advertising as information or misinformation? *Cognitive Technology, 10*(1), 24–28.

van der Maas, H. J., & Straatemeier, M. (2008). How to detect cognitive strategies: Commentary on "Differentiation and integration: Guiding principles for analyzing cognitive change". *Developmental Science, 11*(4), 449–453.

van der Wal, A. J., van Horen, F., & Grinstein, A. (2018). Temporal myopia in sustainable behavior under uncertainty. *International Journal of Research in Marketing, 35*, 378–393.

van Dick, R., Stellmacher, J., Wagner, U., Lemmer, G., & Tissington, P. A. (2009). Group membership salience and task performance. *Journal of Managerial Psychology, 24*(7), 609–626.

van Geert, P. (2000). The dynamics of general developmental mechanisms: From Piaget and Vygotsky to dynamic systems models. *Current Directions in Psychological Science, 9*(2), 64–68.

Van Hooft, E. J., Born, M. H., Taris, T. W., & Van der Flier, H. (2006). Ethnic and gender differences in applicants' decision-making processes: An application of the theory of reasoned action. *International Journal of Selection and Assessment, 14*(2), 156–166.

Van Ijzendoorn, M. H., & Kroonenberg, P. M. (1988). Cross-cultural patterns of attachment: A meta-analysis of the strange situation. *Child Development, 59*(1), 147–156.

van Osselaer, S. M. J., & Janiszewski, C. (2001). Two ways of learning brand associations. *Journal of Consumer Research, 28*(2), 202–223.

Van Vugt, E., Gibbs, J., Stams, G., Bijleveld, C., Hendriks, J., & van der Laan, P. (2011). Moral development and recidivism: A meta-analysis. *International Journal of Offender Therapy and Comparative Criminology, 55*(8), 1234–1250.

van Zomeren, M., & Spears, R. (2009). Metaphors of protest: A classification of motivations for collective action. *Journal of Social Issues, 65*(4), 661–679.

VandenBos, G. R., & Bryant, B. K. (1987). *Cataclysms, crises, and catastrophes: Psychology in action.* Washington, DC US: American Psychological Association.

REFERENCES

Veehof, M. M., Oskam, M., Schreurs, K. G., & Bohlmeijer, E. T. (2011). Acceptance-based interventions for the treatment of chronic pain: A systematic review and meta-analysis. *Pain, 152*(3), 533–542.

Velden, F. S., Ten Beersma, B., & De Dreu, C. K. W. (2007). Majority and minority influence in group negotiation: The moderating effects of social motivation and decision rules. *Journal of Applied Psychology, 92*(1), 259–268.

Venhoeven, L. A., Bolderdijk, J. W., & Steg, L. (2016). Why acting environmentally-friendly feels good: Exploring the role of self-image. *Frontiers in Psychology, 7.*

Verdugo, V. C. (2006). Contributions of behaviorism to the study of pro-ecological behavior. *Revista Mexicana De Análisis De La Conducta, 32*(2), 111–127.

Vernon, D. T., & Blake, R. L. (1993). Does problem-based learning work? A meta-analysis of evaluative research. *Academic Medicine, 68*(7), 550–563.

Verplanken, B., & Wood, W. (2006). Interventions to break and create consumer habits. *Journal of Public Policy & Marketing, 25*(1), 90–103.

Vinchur, A. J., & Koppes, L. L. (2011). A historical survey of research and practice in industrial and organizational psychology. In S. Zedeck (Ed.), *APA handbook of industrial and organizational psychology, Vol 1: Building and developing the organization* (pp. 3–36). Washington, DC: American Psychological Association.

Viney, W. (2001). The radical empiricism of William James and philosophy of history. *History of Psychology, 4*(3), 211–227.

Vinten, G. (2000). The stakeholder manager. *Management Decision, 38*(6), 377–383.

Virués-Ortega, J. (2010). Applied behavior analytic intervention for autism in early childhood: Meta-analysis, meta-regression and dose-response meta-analysis of multiple outcomes. *Clinical Psychology Review, 30*(4), 387–399.

Vitterso, J., Vorkinn, M., & Vistad, O. (2001). Congruence between recreational mode and actual behavior: A prerequisite for optimal experiences? *Journal of Leisure Research, 33*(2), 137–159.

Vlek, C., & Steg, L. (2007). Human behavior and environmental sustainability: Problems, driving forces, and research topics. *Journal of Social Issues, 63*, 1–19.

Volet, S., & Kimmel, K. (2012). Editorial introduction: Motivation and learning in multiple contexts. *European Journal of Psychology of Education, 27*(2), 155–160.

von der Heidt, T., & Lamberton, G. (2011). Sustainability in the undergraduate and postgraduate business curriculum of a regional university: A critical perspective. *Journal of Management & Organization, 17*(5), 670–690.

Von Stumm, S., & Ackerman, P. L. (2013). Investment and intellect: A review and meta-analysis. *Psychological Bulletin, 139*(4), 841–869.

Vorkinn, M., & Riese, H. (2001). Environmental concern in a local context: The significance of place attachment. *Environment and Behavior, 33*(2), 249–263.

Voydanoff, P. (2005). Consequences of boundary-spanning demands and resources for work-to-family conflict and perceived stress. *Journal of Occupational Health Psychology, 10*(4), 491–503.

Wade-Benzoni, K. A., Tenbrunsel, A. E., & Bazerman, M. H. (1996). Egocentric interpretations of fairness in asymmetric, environmental social dilemmas: Explaining harvesting behavior and the role of communication. *Organizational Behavior and Human Decision Processes, 67*(2), 111–126.

Walden, J. (2012). Review of "Global advertising, attitudes and audiences". *New Media & Society, 14*(5), 886–888.

Walker, L. J., Gustafson, P., & Hennig, K. H. (2001). The consolidation/transition model in moral reasoning development. *Developmental Psychology, 37*(2), 187–197.

REFERENCES

Walker, L. J., & Hennig, K. H. (1997). Moral development in the broader context of personality. In S. Hala (Ed.), *The development of social cognition* (pp. 297–327). Hove: Psychology Press/Erlbaum, Taylor & Francis.

Wallach, W. (2010). Cognitive models of moral decision making. *Topics in Cognitive Science, 2*(3), 420–429.

Walters, G. D. (2003). Predicting criminal justice outcomes with the psychopathy checklist and lifestyle criminality screening form: A meta-analytic comparison. *Behavioral Sciences & the Law, 21*(1), 89–102.

Walton, G. M., Cohen, G. L., Cwir, D., & Spencer, S. J. (2012). Mere belonging: The power of social connections. *Journal of Personality and Social Psychology, 102*(3), 513–532.

Wang, J. M., Seidler, R. D., Hall, J. L., & Preston, S. D. (2012). The neural bases of acquisitiveness: Decisions to acquire and discard everyday goods differ across frames, items, and individuals. *Neuropsychologia, 50*(5), 939–948.

Warner, M. (1997). "Consensus" participation: An example for protected areas planning. *Public Administration & Development, 17*(4), 413–432.

Watson, J. B. (1914). *Behavior: An introduction to comparative psychology.* New York: Henry Holt and Co.

Watson, J. B. (1998). *Behaviorism.* Piscataway, NJ: Transaction Publishers.

Watson, L., & Spence, M. T. (2007). Causes and consequences of emotions on consumer behaviour: A review and integrative cognitive appraisal theory. *European Journal of Marketing, 41*(5–6), 487–511.

Watson, W., Michaelsen, L. K., & Sharp, W. (1991). Member competence, group interaction, and group decision making: A longitudinal study. *Journal of Applied Psychology, 76*(6), 803–809.

Waung, M. (1995). The effects of self-regulatory coping orientation on newcomer adjustment and job survival. *Personnel Psychology, 48*(3), 633–650.

Waxman, H. C., Wang, M. C., Anderson, K. A., & Walberg, H. J. (1985). Adaptive education and student outcomes: A quantitative synthesis. *The Journal of Educational Research, 78*(4), 228–236.

Weary, G. (1985). *Attribution: Basic issues and applications.* Orlando, FL: Academic Press.

Weary, G., & Edwards, J. A. (1994). Individual differences in causal uncertainty. *Journal of Personality and Social Psychology, 67*(2), 308–318.

Weary, G., & Jacobson, J. A. (1997). Causal uncertainty beliefs and diagnostic information seeking. *Journal of Personality and Social Psychology, 73*(4), 839–848.

Weary, G., Jacobson, J. A., Edwards, J. A., & Tobin, S. J. (2001). Chronic and temporarily activated causal uncertainty beliefs and stereotype usage. *Journal of Personality and Social Psychology, 81*(2), 206–219.

Weatherford, J. M. (2004). *Genghis Khan and the making of the modern world.* New York: Three Rivers Press.

Weaver, D. B. (2005). Comprehensive and minimalist dimensions of ecotourism. *Annals of Tourism Research, 32*(2), 439–455.

Weber, R. J. (1980). Energy conservation and feedback metering for the automobile: Ideal requirements. *Bulletin of the Psychonomic Society, 16*(4), 301–302.

Webster, G. D., & Crysel, L. C. (2012). "Hit me, maybe, one more time": Brief measures of impulsivity and sensation seeking and their prediction of blackjack bets and sexual promiscuity. *Journal of Research in Personality, 46*(5), 591–598.

Weilbacher, W. M. (2003). How advertising affects consumers. *Journal of Advertising Research, 43*(2), 230–234.

Weiss, H. M., & Adler, S. (1984). Personality and organizational behavior. *Research in Organizational Behavior, 6*, 1–50.

REFERENCES

Weiss, H. M., & Cropanzano, R. (1996). Affective events theory: A theoretical discussion of the structure, causes and consequences of affective experiences at work. *Research in Organizational Behavior, 18*, 1–74.

Wells, A. (2003). Anxiety disorders, metacognition, and change. In R. L. Leahy (Ed.), *Roadblocks in cognitive-behavioral therapy: Transforming challenges into opportunities for change* (pp. 69–90). New York: Guilford Press.

Wells, A. (2009). *Metacognitive therapy for anxiety and depression.* New York: Guilford Press.

Welsch, H., & Kühling, J. (2010), Pro-environmental behavior and rational consumer choice: Evidence from surveys of life satisfaction. *Journal of Economic Psychology, 31*(3), 405–420.

Wenar, C., & Curtis, K. M. (1991). The validity of the Rorschach for assessing cognitive and affective changes. *Journal of Personality Assessment, 57*(2), 291–308.

Werner, C. M. (2013). Designing interventions that encourage permanent changes in behavior. In A. H. Huffman & S. Klein (Eds.), *Green organizations* (pp. 208–230). New York: Routledge.

Werner, C. M., Brown, B. B., & Gallimore, J. (2010). Light rail use is more likely on "walkable" blocks: Further support for using micro-level environmental audit measures. *Journal of Environmental Psychology, 30*(2), 206–214.

Werner, H. (1957). *Comparative psychology of mental development,* revised ed. Oxford: International Universities Press.

Werner, H., & Kaplan, B. (1963). *Symbol formation: An organismic developmental approach to language and the expression of thought.* New York: John Wiley.

Wertenbroch, K., & Skiera, B. (2002). Measuring consumers' willingness to pay at the point of purchase. *Journal of Marketing Research, 39*(2), 228–242.

Wharton, A. S., & Erickson, R. J. (1993). Managing emotions on the job and at home: Understanding the consequences of multiple emotional roles. *The Academy of Management Review, 18*(3), 457–486.

Winefield, H. R., & Harvey, E. J. (1996). Psychological maturity in early adulthood: Relationships between social development and identity. *The Journal of Genetic Psychology: Research and Theory on Human Development, 157*(1), 93–103.

White, K., & Simpson, B. (2013). When do (and don't) normative appeals influence sustainable consumer behaviors? *Journal of Marketing, 77*(2), 78–95.

White, M. P., Pahl, S., Ashbullby, K., Herbert, S., & Depledge, M. H. (2013). Feelings of restoration from recent nature visits. *Journal of Environmental Psychology, 35*, 40–51.

White, P. R. (2012). Enhancing the experience of connection with nature: Participants' responses to the MAPIN Strategy. *Ecopsychology, 4*(4), 345–354.

Whitmarsh, L., & O'Neill, S. (2010). Green identity, green living? The role of pro-environmental self-identity in determining consistency across diverse pro-environmental behaviours. *Journal of Environmental Psychology, 30*(3), 305–314.

Whittler, T. E. (1994). Eliciting consumer choice heuristics: Sales representives' persuasion strategies. *Journal of Personal Selling & Sales Management, 14*(4), 41–53.

Wickens, C. D. (2008). Situation awareness: Review of Mica Endsley's 1995 articles on situation awareness theory and measurement. *Human Factors, 50*(3), 397–403.

Wickens, C. D., Hutchins, S., Carolan, T., & Cumming, J. (2013). Effectiveness of part-task training and increasing-difficulty training strategies: A meta-analysis approach. *Human Factors, 55*(2), 461–470.

Widiger, T. A., & Trull, T. J. (1997). Assessment of the five-factor model of personality. *Journal of Personality Assessment, 68*(2), 228–250.

Wiebe, R. P. (2004). Delinquent behavior and the five-factor model: Hiding in the adaptive landscape? *Individual Differences Research, 2*(1), 38–62.

Wiernik, B. M., Dilchert, S., & Ones, D. S. (2016). Age and employee green behaviors: A meta-analysis. *Frontiers in Psychology, 7*, e-journal.

REFERENCES

Wildes, J. E., & Emery, R. E. (2001). The roles of ethnicity and culture in the development of eating disturbance and body dissatisfaction: A meta-analytic review. *Clinical Psychology Review, 21*(4), 521–551.

Williams, K. E., Ciarrochi, J., & Heaven, P. L. (2012). Inflexible parents, inflexible kids: A 6-year longitudinal study of parenting style and the development of psychological flexibility in adolescents. *Journal of Youth and Adolescence, 41*(8), 1053–1066.

Wilson, E. O. (2012). *The social conquest of earth.* New York: Liveright.

Winkel, G., Saegert, S., & Evans, G. W. (2009). An ecological perspective on theory, methods, and analysis in environmental psychology: Advances and challenges. *Journal of Environmental Psychology, 29*(3), 318–328.

Winkler, R. C., & Winett, R. A. (1982). Behavioral interventions in resource conservation: A systems approach based on behavioral economics. *American Psychologist, 37*(4), 421–435.

Winter, D. (2004). Shopping for sustainability: Psychological solutions to overconsumption. In T. Kasser & A. D. Kanner (Eds.), *Psychology and consumer culture: The struggle for a good life in a materialistic world* (pp. 69–87). Washington, DC: American Psychological Association.

Wiseman, M. M., & Bogner, F. X. (2003). A higher-order model of ecological values and its relationship to personality. *Personality and Individual Differences, 34*(5), 783–794.

Witherspoon, C. L., Bergner, J., Cockrell, C., & Stone, D. N. (2013). Antecedents of organizational knowledge sharing: A meta-analysis and critique. *Journal of Knowledge Management, 17*(2), 250–277.

Witmer, A. J., & Gotlib, I. H. (2013). An attentional scope model of rumination. *Psychological Bulletin, 139*, 1036–1061.

Wolf, M., & Mehl, K. (2011). Experiential learning in psychotherapy: Ropes course exposures as an adjunct to inpatient treatment. *Clinical Psychology & Psychotherapy, 18*(1), 60–74.

Wolsko, C., & Lindberg, K. (2013). Experiencing connection with nature: The matrix of psychological well-being, mindfulness, and outdoor recreation. *Ecopsychology, 5*(2), 80–91.

Wong, K. F. E., Yik, M., & Kwong, J. Y. Y. (2006). Understanding the emotional aspects of escalation of commitment: The role of negative affect. *Journal of Applied Psychology, 91*(2), 282–297.

Wonderlic, Inc. (2007). *Wonderlic personnel test normative report.* Libertyville, IL: Author.

Wood, W., Lundgren, S., Ouellette, J. A., Busceme, S., & Blackstone, T. (1994). Minority influence: A meta-analytic review of social influence processes. *Psychological Bulletin, 115*(3), 323–345.

Woodley, M. A., & Meisenberg, G. (2012). Ability differentials between nations are unlikely to disappear. *American Psychologist, 67*(6), 501–502.

Woods, C. P. (1996). Gender differences in moral development and acquisition: A review of Kohlberg's and Gilligan's models of justice and care. *Social Behavior and Personality, 24*(4), 375–384.

Woodward, W. R. (1982). The "discovery" of social behaviorism and social learning theory, 1870–1980. *American Psychologist, 37*(4), 396–410.

Woollett, K., & Maguire, E. A. (2010). The effect of navigational expertise on wayfinding in new environments. *Journal of Environmental Psychology, 30*(4), 565–573.

Wortman, P. M. 1983. Evaluation research: A methodological perspective. *Annual Review of Psychology, 34*, 223–260.

Wright, M., & MacRae, M. (2007). Bias and variability in purchase intention scales. *Journal of the Academy of Marketing Science, 35*(4), 617–624.

Wright, N. S., & Bennett, H. (2011). Business ethics, CSR, sustainability and the MBA. *Journal of Management & Organization, 17*(5), 641–655.

Wu, A. S., Tang, C. S., & Yogo, M. (2013). Death anxiety, altruism, self-efficacy, and organ donation intention among Japanese college students: A moderated mediation analysis. *Australian Journal of Psychology, 65*(2), 115–123.

REFERENCES

Wu, C.-H., & Griffin, M. A. (2012). Longitudinal relationships between core self-evaluations and job satisfaction. *Journal of Applied Psychology, 97*(2), 331–342.

Wu, J., & Lebreton, J. M. (2011). Reconsidering the dispositional basis of counterproductive work behavior: The role of aberrant personality. *Personnel Psychology, 64*(3), 593–626.

Wu, L. L., & Lin, J. Y. (2006). The quality of consumers' decision-making in the environment of e-commerce. *Psychology & Marketing, 23*(4), 297–311.

Yamamoto, S. (2010). Helping upon request in chimpanzees: Evolutionary basis for human altruism and reciprocity. *Japanese Psychological Review, 53*(3), 422–433.

Yang, S. (2013). Wisdom and good lives: A process perspective. *New Ideas in Psychology, 31*(3), 194–201.

Yeager, D., Trzesniewski, K. H., & Dweck, C. S. (2013). An implicit theories of personality intervention reduces adolescent aggression in response to victimization and exclusion. *Child Development, 84*(3), 970–988.

Yeager, D. S., Larson, S. B., Krosnick, J. A., & Tompson, T. (2011). Measuring Americans' issue priorities: A new version of the most important problem question reveals more concern about global warming and the environment. *Public Opinion Quarterly, 75*(1), 125–138.

Yechiam, E. and Hochman, G. (2013). Losses as modulators of attention: Review and analysis of the unique effects of losses over gains. *Psychological Bulletin, 139*, 497–518.

Yoon, E., Langrehr, K., & Ong, L. (2011). Content analysis of acculturation research in counseling and counseling psychology: A 22-year review. *Journal of Counseling Psychology, 58*(1), 83–96.

Zelazo, P., & Lyons, K. E. (2011). Mindfulness training in childhood. *Human Development, 54*(2), 61–65.

Zelezny, L. C. (1999). Educational interventions that improve environmental behaviors: A meta-analysis. *The Journal of Environmental Education, 31*(1), 5–14.

Zemke, R. E. (1994). Training needs assessment: The broadening focus of a simple concept. In A. Howard (Ed.), *Diagnosis for organizational change: Methods and models* (pp. 139–151). New York: Guilford Press.

Zhang, L. F. (2002). Thinking styles and cognitive development. *The Journal of Genetic Psychology: Research and Theory on Human Development, 163*(2), 179–196.

Zhang, Y., & Zuo, B. (2008). The psychological research on humor. *Chinese Journal of Clinical Psychology, 16*(4), 409–412.

Zheng, Y. (2010). Association analysis on pro-environmental behaviors and environmental consciousness in main cities of East Asia. *Behaviormetrika, 37*(1), 55–69.

Zhu, D., Xie, X., & Gan, Y. (2011). Information source and valence: How information credibility influences earthquake risk perception. *Journal of Environmental Psychology, 31*(2), 129–136.

Zimmerman, B. J. (2008). Investigating self-regulation and motivation: Historical background, methodological developments, and future prospects. *American Educational Research Journal, 45*(1), 166–183.

Zimmerman, B. J., & Moylan, A. R. (2009). Self-regulation: Where metacognition and motivation intersect. In D. J. Hacker, J. Dunlosky, & A. C. Graesser (Eds.), *Handbook of metacognition in education* (pp. 299–315). New York: Taylor & Francis.

Zoogah, D. B., & Peng, M. W. (2011). What determines the performance of strategic alliance managers? Two lens model studies. *Asia Pacific Journal of Management, 28*(3), 483–508.

Zovanyi, G. (2013). *The no-growth imperative: Creating sustainable communities under ecological limits to growth.* New York: Routledge.

Zubeltzu, J. E., Erauskin, T. A., & Heras, S. I. (2018). Shedding light on the determinants of eco-innovation: A meta-analytic study. *Business Strategy and the Environment, 27*(7), 1093–1103.

INDEX

Page locators in *italics* and **bold** refer to images and tables, respectively.

14th Amendment of the US
   Constitution 323

"abilities and other" traits (AOs) 71
ability, individual differences 71,
   76–80, 102
abstract reasoning 61, *62*
acceptance therapies 174
accidental death 234, **235**, 236
across time/context transfer of training
   problems 219–220
action *see* collective action
actor–observer difference 144
Adams, D. 306–307
Adams, J. 25–26
adaptive capacity 19–21; development
   psychology 200–201; individual
   differences 70–71
adaptive capacity scorecards 12,
   303–325; community based
   interventions 315–325; criterion
   problems 305, 307–315
adaptive education, behavioral change/
   learning 232
adaptive expertise, transfer of training
   problems 223
adaptive psychology: broad interventions
   278–279; human activities and the
   environment 8–10; scientist-
   practitioner models 38
ADHD (attention deficit/hyperactivity
   disorder) 255
adoption 287, 288, 292–293
adult identity, ontogenesis 177

advertising 205, 285–289, 290–292, 294
advocacy 323
AERA (American Educational Research
   Association) 246, 247
affect: decision-making 119–120, 124;
   heuristics 53, **54**; social contexts
   143–144
affinity toward diversity (ATD)
   192–193
affordances 244
aggregating individual responses,
   determinism 59
aggregation of individuals, levels of
   analysis 22
agreeableness 81, 99
agreed-upon criteria 40
alliances 259–260
Altemeyer, B. 87
altruism: adaptive capacity scorecards
   319–320; applied culture/social
   contexts 140–142; broad interventions
   277–278; individual differences 97;
   ontogenesis 180, 189, 193
ambivalent social attachment (patterns
   of), ontogenesis 177
American Educational Research
   Association (AERA) 246, 247
American Psychological Association
   (APA): consumer psychology 282–283;
   educational psychology 246, 247;
   ethics/precautionary principle 17;
   forensic psychology 262
amicus briefs 262
amygdala: associative learning 207–208;
   decision-making 115

INDEX

An Enquiry Concerning Human Understanding (Hume) 1
analysis of error 63–65, *65*; individual differences 83–86; *see also* bias
anchoring and adjustment 53, **54**
anger: decision-making 119, 124; forensic psychology 260–261
anthropocentric (social-altruistic) perspectives 141–142
anticipation of pleasant emotions 124
anxieties/anxiety disorders 254; forensic psychology 260–261; impracticality of action 258–259
APA *see* American Psychological Association
appraisals: associative learning 206; broad interventions 296; decision-making 105–106, 113, 114–117; theories of emotion 105–106, 114–117
approach framing: adoption 292; decision-making 115–116
archaeopteryx (genetic adaptation) 19, *20*
arid regions 5, 10
arousal: associative learning 207–208; decision-making 116, 118, 119, 124; development psychology/motivation 194; learning theories 205; *see also* emotions
artificial intelligence 107–108
"As Temperatures Keep Rising, Geoengineering Gets a Closer Look" (Basken) 106–107
Ask, K. 119
assertiveness, social contexts 138
assessment, broad interventions 269–270, **271**, 279
assessment center methods 150
assimilation 171
associations: determinism 53–54, 69; durable change/decay 208–209
associative learning 203, 205–213, 231; applications 209–213; consumer psychology 212–213; development psychology/motivation 194; durable change/decay 208–209; effort/motivation 207–208; problems 205–206; research on memory 206–207
assumptions: and environment 8–10; rational man/economics 55
ATD *see* affinity toward diversity

attachment: development psychology 199; ontogenesis 177, 180–183
attention deficit/hyperactivity disorder (ADHD) 255
attitudes: determinism 69; individual differences 74, 89–91, 92–93, 93–94, 101–102; social contexts 132–133, 156–157; theory 93–94; *see also* self-regulation
attribution error 53, **54**, 68; social contexts 131
authoritarianism: individual differences 87–88, 97; limitations of 30; ontogenesis 187
authority: determinism 50–52, **54**; ontogenesis 188–189; right and wrong 29; social contexts 133, *133*, 134, 135–136, 161, 165; target marketing/branding 291; *see also* heuristics
autism 255
automobiles: Brunswick Lens Model 121, *121*, 122; car buying decision matrices *122*; dependency 289–290; emissions 3; hybrid cars 18–19; reducing emissions 3
availability heuristics 53, **54**
avoidance framing: adoption 292; decision-making 115–116; social contexts 138
avoidance of unpleasant emotions 124
avoidant social attachment (patterns of) 177
awareness: adaptive capacity scorecards 316–317, 319–320; decision-making 129; human factor engineering 243–245; individual differences 100; morality/ontogenesis 187; social contexts 137; *see also* criterion problem

Bacon, J. 200
Balzer, W. K. 215–216
Bandura, A. 194–195
Bandura's theory 89–90
Baron, J. 55
baseline measures, broad interventions 269–270, **271**, 272–273
basic competencies, applied science and sustainability 14–48
basic emotions, decision-making 117
basic research psychology: applied psychology function 9; competence/expertise 16; individual differences 71,

76–77; overview of applied psychology 236–240

Basken, P. 106–107

Batson's negative state relief hypotheses of altruism 193

Bazerman, M. H. 160

behavioral change 46–47, 202–233; adaptive capacity scorecards 311; applied cognitive learning 213–227; applied cognitive maps 225–227; applied learning 209–211; associative learning 231; cognitive learning 214–217, 224–225, 231–232; creativity/innovation 227–229; criterion problems 229–233; decay 208–209; decision-making 128–130; determinism 66–67, 69; development psychology 194–195, 198–199, 200–201; durable change 208–209; evidence-based practice 47; individual differences 76–80, 98–99, 101–102; learning theories 204–213; problem-based learning 217–219; safety training as analogue 227; self-regulatory approaches 221–224; social contexts 163–164, 165; social learning 217–219; socio-cognitive learning 214–217; transfer of training problems 219–221; *see also* interventions

behavioral intentions: attitudes/individual differences 92–93; ontogenesis 193

behavioral psychology: applied psychology/placement 37–38; competence/expertise 16; interactionist perspective/social contexts 159–160; learning 203; social contexts 133; target marketing/branding 291

behavioral response (*R*) 204

behavioral scientists 36

behavioral targeting 285–286

behaviorist perspectives 72, 204

Bender, H. 113

benevolence, social contexts 138

Berenguer, J. 141–142

Betz, N. E. 89

bias: decision-making 114; determinism 51–53, **54**, 57, 58, 62–66, 68; *see also* heuristics

big brother approaches 320

biospheric values 140–141

BLM (Brunswick Lens Model) 64, 106, 120–127, 215

Boer, D. 160

Bogner, F. X. 248

Botelho, A. 114

boundaries: broad interventions 280; deliberative choice 257; social contexts 131–132, 143, 160–165

bowing (habitual values) 94–95

boxcar demographics 71

brand identities, broad interventions 266

branding 285, 286, 290–292

broad interventions 264–302; adaptive capacity scorecards 315; community based ethics 301–302; consumer psychology 264–265, 281–301; criterion problems 269–281, 294–299; industrial-organizational psychology 264–281, 283, 285, 299–301; needs assessment 269–281; work organizations and contexts 265–267

Brunswick Lens Model (BLM) 64, 106, 120–124, 126–127, 215

built environments 22–23

Burnett, D. D. 157–158, 159

cancers 234, **235**, 236

capacity *see* adaptive capacity

Carroll, J. B. 77

carrying capacity 21–22

cars *see* automobiles

Carson, R. 234

causal uncertainty (CU) 89, 96

causality/causation 27, 28, 30, 49–52, 55–61, 60–61, 132–133, 266–267

causes (basic research/overview) 236

causes of death indicators 234, **235**, 236

causes and facets of happiness 40

causes of problems 37–38

causes of waste 4–5

caveat emptor doctrine 213

Ceci, S. J. 79–80

cerebellum 206–207

cerebrum 206–207

certainty 26–28

change *see* behavioral change

characteristics and individual differences 71

Chattopadhyay, P. 119

Chief Executive Officers (CEOs) 40–41, 220

Chiesi, F. 67

Chiles, J. 308

INDEX

choice of criteria 43
Cialdini, R. 29, 151, 161
civic values 140–141
classroom interventions 247–249
Clayton, S. 42–43
climate change 106–107
clinical psychology: deliberative choice 255–258; discrepancy testing 253–255; forensics 253, 260–262; impracticality of action 258–259; interventions 259–260; and related subdisciplines 252–263
coaching 279
codes of ethics 17
cognition: decision-making 110; individual differences 83; ontogenesis 182–183; power of situation 132–133
cognitive approaches: decision-making 124; determinism 54–55; human factor engineering 244–245; ontogenesis 170–175, 189–190; recent associanist research 206; social contexts 151–152; *see also* decision-making
Cognitive Behavioral Therapy (CBT): applied scientific psychology 32–33; deliberative choice 256–257; development psychology 174–175, 198; ontogenesis 174–175, 178
cognitive dissonance: applied cognitive maps 226–227; decision-making 128; social contexts 156–157
cognitive inconsistency 156–157
cognitive learning 203, 206, 213–227, 231–232; adaptation/genetics 20–21; applied cognitive maps 225–227; safety training as analogue 227; self-regulatory approaches 221–224; social learning/problem-based learning 217–219; social-cognitive learning 214–217; and sustainability 224–225; transfer of training problems 219–221
cognitive load 244–245
cognitive maps 204, 220–221, 225–227
cognitive psychology, impulse control 45–46, 178
cohort learning programs 219
cold cognition, decision-making 110
collective action 46–47; adaptive capacity scorecards 311–314, 320–324; behavioral change/learning 230–231, 232; broad interventions 299; clinical psychology 258–259; decision-making

129; determinism 65–66, 67; development psychology 197–198; individual differences 100–101; social contexts 164–165
collective efficacy, adaptive capacity scorecards 323
collective narcissism, social contexts 164
collectivism, social contexts 138, 139–140
collectivist Russian culture 141–142
Colorado River Project 33–35
commitment: applied problem identification 111–112; infallible causality 56; social contexts 151
commitment and consistency 53, **54**; social contexts 151
common sense 50
commons, tragedy of 21–22
communicative functions, social contexts 145–146
community based ethics 301–302
community based interventions 315–325
community level of analysis 240
community needs assessment 321; *see also* needs assessment
community property, Native peoples of the United States 139–140
community treatment programs 261
competencies: applied science and sustainability 14–48; defining terms 16–17; ethics/precautionary principle 17; scientist-practitioners 14–15; *see also* expertise; *knowledge*
complex contingencies, knowledge of 15
complexity of the world 26–28, 29, 32, 37
computers, target marketing 285–286
Comte, A. 58
concept mapping 225–226
conditional learning 204
conditional nature of the world 29
conditional reasoning measures, ontogenesis 193
conditional relationships 30
confirmation bias 52, 53, **54**
conformity: determinism 53, **54**, 82; individual differences 99; ontogenesis 188–189; social contexts 135–136, 151–153, 161, 165
confrontation 274
congeniality bias 53, **54**
conjunction fallacy 53, **54**, 68
connectionism 203
conscientiousness 81, 90, 99, 220–221

INDEX

conscious behavioral responses 110

consent, social contexts 137, 163–164

consequences: competency/expertise 15; determinism 51

conservation ethics 290–291

consistency: applied cognitive maps 226–227; social contexts 151

Constitution of the United States 323

constraints (trait activation approach) 158

construal of emotion 145

consultants 241

consulting psychology 253

consumer behaviorists 72

consumer psychology (CP): adaptive capacity scorecards 309, 310, 316, 320; applied learning 209–210; applied problem identification 111; associative learning 212–213; behavioral change 212–213; broad interventions 264–265, 281–301; carefulness of decision-making 45; competence/expertise 17; criterion problems 294–299; deliberative choice 256, 257; determinism 69; historical perspectives 288–290; individual differences 74; intervention approaches 283–288; media and sustainability interventions 293–294; processes of applied psychology 234, 242–243; social contexts 133, 137; strategies 290–293

consumption: decision-making 119–120; overconsumption 1–2, 256; waste reduction 4–5

contextual factors (moral education) 190

contextual psychology: behavioral change 203; broad interventions 265–267, 279, 279; individual differences 100; learning theories 204; level of analysis 240; ontogenesis 177; open systems perspectives 24; transfer of training problems 219–220, 222–223; *see also* social contexts

contextual variables, controlled 204

contingencies: applied cognitive maps 225–226; associative learning 207–208; cognitive learning 214; creativity/ innovation 228–229; direct social influences 134; problem-based and social learning 219; transfer of training problems 222–223

control: carefulness of decision-making 45–46; Colorado River Project 33–35;

contextual variables 204; determinism 57; human activities 6; learning theories 204; ontogenesis 178; probabilists 32

control theory: associative learning 206; decision-making 105–106

conventional morality 185

cookies (target marketing) 285–286

coordination of group function 278–279

Copernicus 26

coping strategies 254

core competencies 15, *18*

Corraliza, J. A. 141–142

cost of switching (consumer choice) 299

Costa, P. T. 81

counseling psychology 253

counter-resistance 322

CP *see* consumer psychology

creativity 227–229

creeping determinism 52

criminal profiling 71–72

criterion definition 210

criterion problems 10, 45–47; adaptive capacity scorecards 305, 307–315; applied cognitive learning 213–214; applied learning 210–211; applied science and sustainability 39–47; behavioral change/learning 229–233; broad interventions 269–281, 294–299; decision-making 124–130; determinism 62–68; development psychology 196–199; individual differences 83–84, *84*, 95–103; processes of applied psychology 253–259, 262–263; psychology of sustainability 41–43; social contexts 160–165; transfer of training problems 220

critical thinking, individual differences 76–80

Crompton, T. 195

crypto influences 322

CU (causal uncertainty) 89, 96

cue validity: decision-making 123; transfer of training problems 222–223

culture: broad interventions 272; direct social influences 136; individual differences 94–95; internalized social contexts 137–142; level of analysis 240; problem-based and social learning 219; social contexts 165

cybernetic models 105–109

414

INDEX

dancing bear (Funder/abstract reasoning) 61, *62*

Darfur region 5, 10

Darwin, C. 19, 20–21, 303

De Dreu, C. K. W. 160

decay 208–209

decision facilitators 266–267

decision level sustainability solutions 243

decision-making 104–124; adaptive capacity scorecards 307, 309–310; applied Brunswick Lens Model 123–124; applied emotion 119–120; applied measurement/individual differences 82; applied problem identification 111–112; appraisal theories of emotion 114–117; basic emotions 117; behavioral change/learning 230–231; Brunswick Lens Model 120–124, 126–127; cognitive learning 216; criterion problems 124–130; decision helpers/facilitators 236–237, 266–267; determinism 55, 58–61, 62–68, *65*; development psychology 197–198; discrepancy tests 107–111, 113–114, 129; emotions 117–120; emotive perception model 105–106; expected events/states 107, 108; individual differences 77–78, 82, 97–98; marketing 285–289, 290–292, 294; mood 117–118; problem identification 107–111; situational judgment tests 77–78; social contexts 134–135, 151–154, 162–163, 165; social emotions 117; thumbnail description 105–106, *106*; to sustainability 112–114; *see also* criterion problems

Declaration of Independence 25–26

declarative memory 206–207

delay of gratification 178

deliberative approaches 110, 127–128; adaptive capacity scorecards 309–310, 318, 319–320; broad interventions 269–273, **271**, 277–278, 294–298; clinical psychology 255–258; social contexts 165

deliberativeness 45

demands of the consumer 284

demographic characteristics, individual differences 70–71

demonstrations of limits to ability 54–55

DeNisi, A. 216

depression 258–259

descriptive statistics 27–28

design and implementation of interventions 269–270, **271**, 274–280

determinism 35–36, 49–69; bias 51–53, **54**, 57, 58, 62–66, 68; criterion problem 62–68; decision-making 58–61, 62–68; fallacies 53–55, **54**, 58, 59; heuristics 51–55, **54**, 57, 63–66; infallible causality 55–58; neocortex 61, *62*; rational notions *27*, 28, 29

development psychology 46, 166–201; adaptive capacity scorecards 307; applied cognitive development 172–174; applied socio-emotional development 177–179; behavioral change/learning 229–230; broad interventions 267–268, 279, 280; cognitive development 169, 171–175, 189–190; educational psychology 248–249; and implementation 246; individual differences 76–80; key issues 167–168; moral development 183–192; motivation 194–196; ontogenesis 168–193; other cognitive traits 174–175; psychology of sustainability 42; social contexts 137; socio-emotional development 175–180

devil's advocacy 162

dichotomies (either/or categories) 81–83; *see also* otherness

Dickinson, J. L. 296

differences among people *see* individual differences

differentiation: ontogenesis 169, 177, 191; social contexts 147

diffusion of innovation over time 287, *287*

direct causality, determinism 49

direct input, social contexts 132

direct social influences 134–151

directive approach, discrepancy testing 255

disaster responses 324

disconfirming of bias 52

discrepancy tests 107–111; adaptive capacity scorecards 308–309, 321; associative learning 206; broad interventions 271–272, 294–298; clinical psychology 253–255; decision-making 113–114, 129

disfluency, decision-making 128–129

415

INDEX

display rules, social contexts 147–148
displaying of emotions, social contexts 144–145
distancing 170
distractors (trait activation approach) 158
distributive justice 43
divergent thinking 228–229
Doherty, T. J. 42–43
dragons of inaction (Gifford) 67
drugs 257
dual relationships, views of psychologist's roles 241
durability, cognitive learning 217
durable change 208–209
Dweck, C. S. 194–195, 196
dynamism, development psychology 168

eating 31, 194
eating/problem of hunger 31
ecocentric values perspectives, social contexts 141–142
eco-innovation 306
ecological fallacies, determinism 59
ecological perspectives 24
ecotourism 249, 295
education, ontogenesis 190–191
educational psychology 246–252; basic research/overview 239–240; behavioral change/learning 232; cognitive learning 225, 226; current limitations 251–252; determinism 51; development psychology/motivation 196; interventions 250–251; ontogenesis 190–191; *see also* cognitive approaches
EEO (Equal Employment Opportunity) 277
efficacy: adaptive capacity scorecards 323; discrepancy testing 254; green 229–230; individual differences 89, 98–99
effort, learning theory 207–208
egalitarianism, social contexts 138
egotistical values, applied culture/social contexts 140–141
either/or categories 81–83; *see also* otherness
elder hostels 249
emissions reductions 3
emotional disfluency, decision-making 129

emotional intelligence (EI): individual differences 79, 90; social contexts 148, 150
emotions: applied socio-emotional development 177–179; broad interventions 270; decision-making 114–120, 124, 127–128; and mood 117–118; social contexts 142, 143–147, 149; socio-emotional development 175–180; stability 81, 83, 99
emotive appraisals: associative learning 206; broad interventions 296
emotive decision-making 110
Emotive Perception model (EPM) 105–106, 110, 145, 148, *148*, 149
emotive response: ontogenesis 182–183; *see also* emotions
emotive stimuli, learning theories 205
empirical systems *27*, 28–29; black boxes 104; decision-making 47; evaluation 246
employee engagement, broad interventions 269
employment relationship process 276, *276*
entity implicit theories 200
Environmental Education journal 201
Environmental Education Research journal 246–247
Environmental Protection Agency (EPA) 25
environmental psychology 1–13, 22–23; assumptions 8–10; broad interventions 273, *273*; cognitive learning 225; creativity/innovation 229; decision-making 106–108, 119–120; determinism 69; educational psychology 246–248, 251; Nature Conservancy 3–4, 33–35, 153–154; precursors 23; psychology of sustainability 42–43; stressors/impracticality of action 258–259; and systems 23–25; target marketing/branding 291; *see also* pro-environmental behaviors
Eom, K. 142
episodic emotions 117–118
epistemology, science and certainty 26, 29
EPM (Emotive Perception model) 105–106, 110, 145, 148, *148*, 149

INDEX

Equal Employment Opportunity (EEO) 277

equilibrium 198–199

ergonomics 243

error: application of individual differences 83–86; cognitive development/ontogenesis 171–172; decision-making 120–123; determinism 53–55, **54**, 58, 59, 63–64, 68; individual differences 102; social contexts 131; *see also* bias; *heuristics*

escalation of commitment 111–112

establishing rapport 259–260

ethics: adaptive capacity scorecards 314; applied psychology uses 7–8; broad interventions 301–302; choice 319, *319*; competence/expertise 17; of consumption 285; scientist-practitioner models 38; *see also* heuristics; *morality*

ethnocentric/ethnorelative orientations in socio-emotional development 179–180

European settlers 139–140

evaluation and feedback, broad interventions 269–270, **271**

evaluation research 238; reality checks 269–270, **271**, 281

evaluative dispositions 92

evidence-based practice 47

evolution 19–21

executives, broad interventions 268–269, 280

experience of emotion: social contexts 145; *see also* emotions

experiential openness 81

expertise 15–39; adaptive capacity 19–21; basic research/overview 236–237; broad interventions 278–279; carrying capacity 21–23; creativity/innovation 228–229; defining terms 16–17; determinism 35–36, 53, **54**; environment and systems 23–25; ethics/precautionary principle 17; expert only models 242; individual differences 74, 100–101, 102–103; levels of analysis 21–23; ontogenesis 171–172, 173, 176, 191; open systems perspectives 24; probabilists 32; science and certainty 26–28; scientific approach 25–28; scientific psychology application 32–35; scientist-practitioner models 38–39; situational knowledge 162–163; social contexts

143–147, 149; sustainability 25; transfer of training problems 223

exploration arousal 207–208

external characteristics of place 42

external learned stimuli 194

external strong situational social contexts 138

extroversion 81, 83, 99

facial emotional displays 144

facilitated approaches to socio-emotional development 179

facilitated process, broad interventions 273

facilitators 158, 266–267

factor analysis 54, 81

fair trade 291

fallacies, determinism 53–55, **54**, 58, 59

false negatives/positives: determinism/heuristics 64–65; individual differences 84–85

fear response 118, 124, 207

feedback: adaptive capacity scorecards 316; applied cognitive maps 226–227; basic research/overview 235, 237, 238; broad interventions 266–268, 269–270, **271**, 273–274, 279, 281; cognitive learning 215–216; decision-making 108; deliberative choice 257; development psychology/motivation 194; educational psychology 250–251; infallible causality 56–57; interventions/applied learning 209–210; learning theories 205; open systems perspectives 24; problem-based and social learning 219; socio-emotional development/non-clinical populations 179–180

Feedback Intervention Theory (FIT) 216

feel good experience, ontogenesis 182

Field Theory, social contexts 142

Fischer, R. 160

Fisher, C. 119

Five Factor Model (FFM) 80–87, 88

fixed action patterns, decision-making 110, 115

Flint, Michigan 10

following orders 51

Ford, J. 223

forensic psychology 253, 260–263; decision-making 123; individual

INDEX

differences 71–72; moral development 191–192

formal operational thinking, ontogenesis 171

formalized deliberations 269–270, **271**

formative assessment 251

Franklin, B. 25–26

free market economics 55, 212, 213, 289, 312

freezing (fixed action patterns) 115

fresh water, carrying capacity 21–22

Frijda, N. H. 117

frustration, decision-making 124

functional feedback, cognitive learning 216

fundamental attribution error, individual differences 102

Funder, D. 61, *62*

future orientation 138, 139, 320

future stakeholders 315

Gadenne, D. L. 125–126

Galton, F. 19, 20–21, 70–71

Gambler's fallacy 53, **54**

gang enforcers 164

Geary, D. C. 76–77

gender: associative learning/consumer psychology 212; social contexts 138

general mental ability 76

generalized self-efficacy, individual differences 89, 98–99

genetics, evolution 19–21

Genghis Kahn 188–189

Genovese, K. 162

geo-engineering 106–107

Gifford, R. 67, 113–114

Gilligan, C. 185

Glick, W. H. 119

global climate change 106–107

GLOBE study 141

goal setting: cognitive learning 214–215; infallible causality 56–57

gold rushes 139–140

Gore, A. 125

government spending 106–107

Graefe, A. 200

Granhag, P. A. 119

gratification (delay of) 178

green efficacy 229–230

Greenpeace 153–154

Griffin, M. A. 90

Grinstein, A. 165

group dynamics: conformity 53, **54**, 82, 99, 135–136, 151–153, 161, 165, 188–189; determinism 59, 67–68; development psychology 137; levels of analysis 22, 240; pressures 151–152; process interventions 161–162; social contexts 133; *see also* collective action; *social contexts*

habit formation 244

habitual values, individual differences 94

habituation, decision-making 110

hand-shaking (habitual values) 94–95

happiness, criterion problem 40

hard work versus innate talent 169–170

Hartman, R. O. 89

Haslam, R. 151–152

health psychology and health habits 42–43, 45–46, 178, 291

heart disease 234, **235**, 236

Heckhausen, J. 194

hereditary intelligence, development psychology 200–201

Hernandez, I. 128

heuristics: adaptive capacity scorecards 307; decision-making 114, 119, 127–128; determinism 51–55, **54**, 57, 63–68; individual differences 78

HFE (human factor engineering) 234, **235**, 236, 242–246

Hilbert, M. 58

hindsight bias 52–53, **54**

hippocampus, associative learning 206–207

The Hitchhiker's Guide to the Galaxy (Adams) 306–307

Hofstede, G. 138

Hogan, R. 157–158

Hollenbeck, J. R. 60

homeostasis 108

homework 258

homicides 234, **235**, 236

Hoover, H. 35

hospitality industries 226

hostels 249

hot cognition, decision-making 110

Huber, G. P. 119

Huffman, A. H. 43

human activities 2, *3*, 6, 8–10; *see also* environment

human factor engineering (HFE) 234, **235**, 236, 242–246

418

INDEX

human health, psychology of sustainability 42–43, 45–46, 178, 291
humane orientation, social contexts 138
humble assumption of error 85–86
Hume, D. 1, 58
humor 252, 254
hunger 31, 194
Hurricane Sandy 106–107
hybrid cars 18–19
hypotheses, science and certainty 27

ideal states, decision-making 107–108
identification: important outcomes 236; social 151–152
identity: adaptive capacity scorecards 317–319; behavioral change/learning 230–231; branding 285, 286; broad interventions 265–266; development psychology 195–196, 199; ontogenesis 170, 176; psychology of sustainability 42; social contexts 142–143; target marketing/branding 291–292; *see also* development psychology
Ilgen, D. R. 60
illusion of control, determinism 57
implicit theory, development psychology/ motivation 194–195
impracticality of action, clinical psychology 258–259
impulse, broad interventions 294–298
impulse control 45–46; ontogenesis 178
impulsive consumption 257
inaction, determinism 67
inclinations, individual differences 80–82
inclusion: educational psychology 247–248; social contexts 132–133, 149; *see also* motive sharing
An Inconvenient Truth (Al Gore) 125
individual differences 70–103; ability 76–80, 102; actor–observer difference 144; adaptive capacity scorecards 304, 307; applied attitudes 93–94; applied authoritarianism 88; applied measurement 82–86; applied psychology 71–75; applied self-regulation 90–92; attitudes 89–91, 92–94, 101–102; authoritarian personality 87–88; authoritarianism 97; automotive emissions 3; basic research/overview 240; behavioral change 76–80; behavioral change/ learning 232; consumer psychology

282; critical thinking 76–80; determinism 59, 63–64; development 76–80; error in application 83–86; evaluative dispositions toward place 42; evolution 19–21; inclinations 80–82; intelligence 79–80, 101–102; learning 76–80; measures 71; motivations 80–82, 95; ontogenesis 179, 187–189; other important trait like characteristics 86–95; personality 74, 80–82, 87–88, 90–91; predictive psychology 73–75; self-regulation 89–92; *Signal Detection Theory* 83–84, *84*; social contexts 132–138, 141–142, 144, 155–156; species-level survival problems 1–2; sustainability criteria 95–103; transfer of training problems 220–221; values 74, 92–95, 101–102, 103; *see also* bias
individual identity, ontogenesis 170
industrial-organizational (I-O) psychology: adaptive capacity scorecards 309, 316, 324–325; applied scientific psychology 32–33; broad interventions 264–281, 283, 285, 299–301; competence/expertise 17, 18–19; decision-making 119, 123; development psychology/motivation 195–196; individual differences 72–73; processes of applied psychology 234, 239–242; social contexts 137, 150, 155; transfer of training problems 220
infallibility: causality/determinism 55–58; definitions 49
inferential statistics 27–28
informed consent, social contexts 137, 163–164
in-group collectivism, social contexts 138, 139–140
initial feedback, broad interventions 269–270, **271**
innate talent 169–170
innovation 227–229; adaptive capacity scorecards 306; diffusion over time 287, *287*
inputs (causal variables) 60–61; broad interventions 266–267; social contexts 132–133
instability *see* stability
instability, broad interventions 268
institutional action 323
insufficient justification 53, **54**, 157

INDEX

integrating displays, social contexts 147
integration, ontogenesis 169
integration of self, ontogenesis 176
integrative processes, ontogenesis 171
integrity testing (moral education) 190–191
intelligence: determinism 51, 57; development psychology 200–201; evolution 19; individual differences 77–78, 79–80, 97, 101–102; ontogenesis 173; *see also* emotional intelligence
intelligent organizations, broad interventions 277–278
intentions: attitudes/individual differences 92–93; ontogenesis 193
interaction effect, social contexts 154–159
interactionist perspective, social contexts 159–160
intercultural development/sensitivity 179–180
interest arousal, associative learning 207–208
internal consultants 241
internal environments: clinical psychology 253; target marketing/branding 291
internal learned feedback, development psychology/motivation 194
internal signals, emotions/mood 118
internal, subcortical feedback, development psychology/motivation 194
internalization, problem-based and social learning 219
internalization problems, ontogenesis 177
internalization of social contexts, ontogenesis 176–177
internalized characteristics, social contexts 138
internalized contextual contingencies, transfer of training problems 222–223
internalized motivational social contexts 149–151
internalized rules, values and individual differences 94–95
internalized situational characteristics, social contexts 159
internalized social contexts 162–164; culture 137–142; identity 142–143; life space 142–143; situational expertise 143–147

internalizing of brand situation 286
International Journal of Environmental and Science Education 246–247
interventions: adaptive capacity scorecards 315–325; applied learning 209–210; clinical psychology 253, 259–260; cognitive learning 216, 224–225, 226; development psychology 168; development psychology/motivation 195–196; discrepancy testing 254; educational psychology 247–251; scientist-practitioner models 38; self-regulation/individual differences 90; social context 161–162; *see also* broad interventions
interviews 276
intra-individual approaches: determinism 59; individual differences 83
introversion 81
Inviting Disaster (Chiles) 308
Ishii, K. 142
iterative models of the scientific process 27, *27*

James River Basin Partnership (JRBP) 237–238
James, W. 325
Japan 141
Japanese culture 94–95
Jefferson, T. 25–26, 35
job demands (trait activation approach) 158
Jordan, P. J. 150
Journal of Environmental Education 246–247
justice 43

Kahneman, D. 55, 289
Kaplan, B. 170
Kasser, T. 195
Katsikopoulos, K. V. 69
Kennedy, J. 125–126
Kim, H. S. 142
King, Jr., M. L. 104, 152–153
Klein, S. 43
Kluger, A. N. 216
knowledge 220–221; associative learning/consumer psychology 213; authoritarianism 30; broad interventions 277–278; changeability 31; of complex contingencies 15; decision-making 113; individual differences 71, 73–74, 77–78, *77*, 100,

420

102–103; infallible causality 56–57; social contexts 143–147, 162–164; waste reduction 4; *see also* expertise

knowledge and skill (KS) dimensions 71, 73

Kohlberg's stages, ontogenesis 184–187

KSAO models: broad interventions 272, 283; cognitive learning 227; individual differences 90

Kühling, J. 127

Kyle, G. 200

laissez-faire doctrine (free market economics) 55, 212, 213, 289, 312

land rushes 139–140

law, individual differences 70

Law of Effect (Thorndike) 208, 209–210

leadership: broad interventions 279–280; development psychology/motivation 195–196; social contexts 132–133, 137

learned feedback, development psychology/motivation 194

learned stimuli, development psychology/ motivation 194

learning 46; adaptive capacity scorecards 307, 319–320; applied cognitive learning 213–227; applied cognitive maps 225–227; applied learning 209–211; associative learning 203, 205–213, 231; broad interventions 269–270, **271**, 273–274, 277–278, 285, 298; clinical psychology 253; cognitive learning 213–227, 231–232; consumer psychology 212–213; creativity/innovation 227–229; criterion problems 229–233; decay 208–209; decision-making 124; durable change 208–209; educational psychology 246–252; effort 207–208; evolution 19–21; individual differences 76–80; motivation 207–208; problem-based learning 217–219, 225–226; recent associanist research 206–207; safety training as analogue 227; self-regulatory approaches 221–224; social learning 217–219; socio-cognitive learning 214–217; and sustainability 224–225; theories 204–213; transfer of training problems 219–221; *see also* behavioral change; *cognitive approaches*

"Let's Move!" campaign 257

levels of analysis 21–23, 240–241, 261–262; number of people 22

Lewin, K. 142

LGBT rights 248

Libby, R. 149–150

life space, social contexts 142–143

likemindedness 59, 67–68; *see also* group dynamics

Liker, J. K. 79–80

limbic system, decision-making 115

Lincoln (Spielberg) 323

loafing, social 152

loyalty of consumers 285

Maani, K. E. 63

McCrae, R. R. 81

McDowell, J. J. 304

Machiavelli, N. 32

McKeiver, C. 125–126

McRaney, D. 55

Maharaj, V. 63

managers, broad interventions 269

mandated community treatment programs 261

manipulations of context 137

manipulations of social contexts 133

Manning, R. 200

Marine training, social contexts 157

market contexts of level of analysis 240

market creation 285, 287–288

marketing 285–289, 290–292, 294

Markowitz, E. M. 84, 85–86

Martin, I. M. 113

Martin, R. 141–142

matching law of choice (McDowell) 304

maturation, ontogenesis 175–176

Maya 26

MCPL (multiple cue probability learning) 215, 216

Meadows, D. 24

measurable characteristics 70–71; evolution 19–21; *see also* individual differences

measurement, individual differences 82–86

measures: broad interventions 269–270, **271**; individual differences 71

mediation 77; individual differences 100–101; model of human effects on environment 2, *3*

INDEX

mediator variables, target marketing/
branding 291
Meisenberg, G. 98
memory: recent associanist research
206–207; *see also* behavioral change
mental abilities measures 277–278
mental ability *see* intelligence
meta-analysis, individual differences
90–91
metacognition 174
meta-emotive facilitation 270
meta-traits, individual differences 83
military 29–30, 50–53, 51–53,
188–189, 213
mindfulness: deliberative choice 257–258;
discrepancy testing 254; ontogenesis
174, 178, 182–183, 193
minority/majority influence, social
contexts 132–133, 152–154
modeling, adaptation/genetics 20–21
moderate difficulty of goals 56
moderated relationships: social contexts
155–156, *155*; *see also* interaction effect
moral circles 247–248
morality: applied psychology uses 7;
broad interventions 280; decision-
making 197–198; forensic psychology
191–192; ontogenesis 183–193; *see also*
heuristics
Morozov, E. 245
Morsanyi, K. 67
motivations/motives 220–221; adaptive
capacity scorecards 322; applied
culture/social contexts 140–141;
associative learning/consumer
psychology 212; behavioral change/
learning 203, 204, 207–208, 212,
216–217, 229–230; branding/identity
286; cognitive learning 216–217;
decision-making 115, *115*, 116, **116**;
development psychology 194–196,
198–199; individual differences 74–77,
80–82, 95, 102–103; learning theories
204–205; ontogenesis 173–174,
176–177; problem-based and social
learning 219; readiness theories of
emotion 115, *115*, 116, **116**; social
contexts 145, *146*, 149–151; waste
reduction 4
motive sharing: adoption 292–293; social
contexts 147–149
motor memory 206–207

multiple cue probability learning (MCPL)
215, 216
multiple stakeholder engagement 261
multisource feedback 279
multivariate nature of the world 29,
30–31

narcissism, social contexts 164
National Geographic 5
Native peoples of the United States
139–140
Nature Conservancy 3–4, 33–35,
153–154
nature–nurture debates 168–170
need for cognition, individual
differences 83
needs assessment: adaptive capacity
scorecards 321; broad interventions
269–281; processes in applied
psychology 250
negative emotions, social contexts 142
negative state relief hypotheses of
altruism (Batson) 193
neocortex: determinism 61, *62*; genetic
adaptation 20
nepotism 275–276
neural processes, recent associanist
research 206
neurocognitive systems 203
neuroticism 81, 83, 98–99
Nigbur, D. 160
Nisan, U. 165
Nisbett, R. E. 98
non-compensatory psychological
models 73
non-display of emotions 145
nonviolent resistance 322
norms: decision-making 128;
enforcement 164; individual differences
74, 92–93; problem-based and social
learning 219; social contexts 135–136,
149, 152–154, 161–165
North American history 139–140
number of people, levels of analysis 22

obedience to authority 53, **54**
obesity 257
objectivity: determinism 57–58, 61; *see
also* bias
observable behaviors, applied learning
210–211
observed behaviors 204

INDEX

observers, social contexts 145–147, *146*
OE (organizational effectiveness) 264, 268
Old Testament 29–30
ontogenesis 168–193; altruism 180, 189, 193; applied attachment 180–183; applied cognitive development 172–174; applied moral development 189–191; applied moral reasoning 192–193; applied socio-emotional development 177–179; attachment 180–183; cognitive development 172–174; individual differences 187–189; Kohlberg's stages 184–187; moral development 183–192; moral education 190–191; moral reasoning 192–193; non-clinical populations 179–180; place attachment 180–181, *181*, 182–183; socio-emotional development 175–180; Werner's principle 169
open systems 24, 60, *60*, 108
openness: creativity/innovation 228–229; determinism 59; individual differences 81, 83–84, *84*, 99
operant learning 204
opportunities appraisals/framing: behavioral change/learning 229; decision-making 108–113, 125–126
optimism bias, determinism 62
optimizing, applied Brunswick Lens Model 123–124
organizational change, broad interventions 268
organizational decision processes 119
organizational effectiveness (OE) 264, 268
organizational learning, broad interventions 269–270, **271**, 273–274
organizational level of analysis 240
organizational psychology: applied problem identification 111–112; *see also* industrial-organizational (I-O) psychology
orientation 138, 139, 320; *see also* individual differences
Orwin, R. 161
Osbaldiston, R. 258
Oskamp, S. 25
otherness: determinism 67–68; development psychology 197
outcomes (basic research/overview) 236, 269–270, **271**

outputs of common decision processes 55
outsiders: development psychology 197; *see also* otherness
overconsumption 1–2, 256
overview of applied psychology areas 236–240

Paracollege program of St. Olaf College (1969) 221–222
PEBs *see* pro-environmental behaviors
peer influence 291
people (triple bottom line) 43
perceived events/states, decision-making 107–108
perceived situation, social contexts 143–144
perception psychology 104, 105–106; applied psychology uses 7; discrepancy testing 254–255; ontogenesis 171; social contexts 132–133, 137, 144; target marketing/branding 291
performance measures: broad interventions 277–278; situational knowledge/individual differences 77–78, *77*; social contexts 138
person analyses, broad interventions 272
person by situation interactions 154–159
person perception *see* perception psychology
person variables, consumer psychology 282
personal identity: ontogenesis 176; *see also* identity
personal responsibility *see* responsibility
personal and shared meanings associated with place 42
personality: authoritarian 87–88; individual differences 74, 80–82, 87–88, 90–91; measures 71; social contexts 133, *133*
personnel psychology: broad interventions 267–268; individual differences 72–73
person–situation analyses: broad interventions 272, 274–276; social contexts 157–159
perspectives: behaviorist 204; broad interventions 266–267, *266*; decision-making/determinism 60, *60*; development psychology/ motivation 195–196; learning theories 204; open systems 24, 60, *60*, 108;

INDEX

psychologist's roles 241–243; social contexts 141–142; *see also* values
persuasion: decision-making 124; determinism 69; social contexts 150–151, 156
pessimism, decision-making 113–114
physical environments, adaptation/genetics 19–21
physical precursors 23
physical stimuli, applied learning 209
Piaget, J. 171, 172–173
Pichert, D. 69
pilot study definitions 27–28
place attachment: development psychology 197; ontogenesis 180–181, *181*, 182–183; psychology of sustainability 42; social contexts 139
planet (triple bottom line) 43
plans of action, broad interventions 273
plasticity 83, 99
pleasant emotions 124
poker playing 147–149
policy capturing, decision-making 121
policy makers/making: broad interventions 268–269; determinism 35
political interventions 315–325
positive emotions, social contexts 142
positive psychology: criterion problem 40; processes of applied psychology 242
postconventional morality, ontogenesis 185
posttraumatic stress disorder (PTSD) 52–53, 254
potential interventions, broad interventions 269–270, **271**
power, social contexts 160
power distance, social contexts 138
power of situation, social contexts 132–133
practical intelligence, individual differences 77–78
practical knowledge, broad interventions 277–278
practicality criteria, adaptive capacity scorecards 314, 324–325
precautionary principle, competence/expertise 17
pre-conscious appraisals, decision-making 113
preconventional morality, ontogenesis 184–185
predictive psychology: applied psychology uses 6; carrying capacity/levels of

analysis 22–23; Colorado River Project 33–35; and control decisions 122–123; decision-making 124, 126; determinism 59; human activities 6; individual differences 71–72, 73–75, 84; probabilists 32; social contexts 134, 160–165; target marketing/branding 291; waste reduction 4
prejudice: determinism 67–68; social contexts 132–133
premature applications of science 15
preoperational cognitive development 171
preparatory coping 254
pressures, social 135–136, 151–152
Preston, J. L. 128
preticive psychology, determinism 52–53
pride 147
Primi, C. 67
principle of ontogenetic development (Werner) 169
probabilistic nature of the world 26–28, 29, 32, 37
probability learning, multiple cue 215
problem identification 111–112; decision-making 107–112; determinism 55
problem-based learning 217–219, 225–226
problems (basic research/overview) 236–237
procedural justice 43
procedural memory 206–207
process psychology 234–263; clinical psychology 252–263; competence/expertise 16; consumer psychology 284, *284*; criterion problems 253–259; definitions 4; educational psychology 246–252; human factor engineering 234, **235**, 236, 242–246; levels of analysis 240–241, 261–262; loss/social contexts 152; social contexts 132–133; views of psychologist's roles 241–243
product development 287
pro-environmental behaviors (PEBs): adaptive capacity scorecards 310; applied learning 211; broad interventions 277–278, 282–283, 291; carefulness of decision-making 45; decision-making 119–120; deliberative choice 258; educational psychology 247; individual differences 97, 98–99; ontogenesis 189; psychology of

424

INDEX

sustainability 41–42; social contexts 140–141, 159–161
profiling 71–72
profit (triple bottom line) 43
progress reports, science and certainty 26, 28
proof, social contexts 151
property, social contexts 139–140
proximity maintaining, ontogenesis 180–181
psychographics 112
psychologist's roles 241–243
psychometrics 269
PTSD (posttraumatic stress disorder) 52–53, 254
public policy approaches, adaptive capacity scorecards 317
punctuated equilibrium, development psychology 198–199
purchasing choices 285
purpose fulfillment, ontogenesis 180–181

quality of water 10

Raish, C. 113
rational choice 289
"rational man" assumptions in economics 55
rational systems *27*, 28, 104, 105–106
reactance, discrepancy testing 255
readiness, development psychology/ motivation 196
realities: discrepancy testing 254–255; evaluation research criteria 269–270, **271**, 281
reasoning: abstract 61, *62*; ontogenesis 192–193
rebate programs, applied learning 209–210
reciprocity 53, **54**, 151
recognition of expertise 278–279
reducing automotive emissions 3
referencing, social 134, 135
Reicher, S. D. 151–152
reinforcement: applied learning 209; learning theories 205
relationships: basic research/overview 236–237; broad interventions 276, 284; causal/conditionality of 30; competencies 18–19; social contexts 155; views of psychologist's roles 241–243

relaxation techniques 254
relaxed states of mind 207–208
releasers (trait activation approach) 158
religion 254
requisite variety, adaptive capacity 21
research methods, science and certainty 27
resistance: adaptive capacity scorecards 322–323; discrepancy testing 255
resource set points, decision-making 113
responses, applied psychology uses 7
responsibility: decision-making 129; individual differences 74
restorative experiences: applied cognitive maps 226; natural settings/applied learning 209; outdoor settings 259
retail firms 283
Rhazes 26
Richardson, M. 98
Riley, J. W. 131
Rioux, L. 41–42
risk: aversion 53, **54**; decision-making 119–120; target marketing/branding 291
risk management: human factor engineering 246; processes of applied psychology 242, 246
rivers, Colorado River Project 33–35
role expectations 74, 241–243
Roosevelt, T. 35
rules of behavior: individual differences 94–95; *see also* values
Russian culture, social contexts 141–142

Sabatini, R. 49
safe states of mind 207–208
safety 243; training as analogue 227
St. Olaf College (1969) 221–222
sample size, levels of analysis 22
Sandy, Hurricane 106–107
satisficing 123–124
scaled measures 27
Scaramouche (Sabatini) 49
schemas, development psychology/ motivation 194
Schmidt, H. G. 218–219
school psychology 253
Schott, J. P. 258
Schurer, L. 161
scientific psychology application 32–35
scientist-practitioner models: adaptive capacity scorecards 306, 310, 312, 314;

INDEX

applied science and sustainability 14–15, 38–39; broad interventions 264–265, 272, 281, 300–301; processes in applied psychology 241, 250–252, 254, 260, 261

scorecards of adaptive capacity 12, 303–325

scripts, decision-making 116–117

SDT (*Signal Detection Theory*) 64, *65*, 83–84, *84*, 106, 120–121, 122

secure social attachment (patterns of), ontogenesis 177

self-conscious emotions 117, 147

self-control, ontogenesis 178

self-determination, individual differences 98–99

self-efficacy: discrepancy testing 254; individual differences 89, 98–99

self-organizing systems 169

self-regulation: cognitive learning 221–224; discrepancy testing 254; individual differences 82, 89–92; ontogenesis 175–176, 178–179, 191–192

self-reported behavioral intentions 193

self-schemas 194

sell sustainability, efforts to 281

Sellmann, D. 248

"*Semper Fidelis*" (forever faithful) 157

sense of place 42

Sesame Street 317–318

set point (discrepancy thresholds), decision-making 107–108

shaking hands (habitual values) 94–95

shame 147

shared meanings of place 42

shared motives: applied culture/social contexts 140–141; problem-based and social learning 219

Sherman, D. K. 142

shortages of water 5

shortcuts, decision-making 127

Signal Detection Theory (SDT) 64, *65*, 83–84, *84*, 106, 120–121, 122

signaling functions, social contexts 145

similar-to-me bias 53, **54**

simultaneous evaluations of decision-making in determinism 60

single case studies, transfer of training problems 222

SIOP (Society for Industrial and Organizational Psychology) *18*, 72–73

SIT (Social Identity Theory) 142–143

situation specificity, social contexts 136–137

situational analyses, broad interventions 272

situational awareness, human factor engineering 243–245

situational boundaries, social contexts 131–132

situational contingencies: creativity/ innovation 228–229; problem-based and social learning 219

situational expertise: creativity/ innovation 228–229; individual differences 74, 100–101, 102–103; ontogenesis 173, 176, 191; situational knowledge 162–163; social contexts 143–147

situational judgment tests (SJT) 77–78

situational knowledge: individual differences 77–78, *77*; social contexts 162–164

situational power 132–133

situational specificity: broad interventions 285, 286; development psychology/ motivation 194

situational strength: decision-making 115–116; direct social influences 134

situational variables, consumer psychology 282

Skinner Box 204

smartphones, target marketing 285–286

smells, development psychology/ motivation 194

SMEs (subject matter experts) 272

Smith, J. R. 151–152

social adjustment 254

social causes of water shortages 5

social cognition, power of situation 132–133

social contexts 131–165; actual situations 143–144; applied culture 140–142; applied group decision processes 152–154; applied person–situation complexity 157–159; applying of 136–137; attitudes 156–157; behavioral change 163–164, 165; boundaries 143, 160–165; collective action 164–165; criterion problem 160–165; culture 137–142; decision-making 134–135, 151–154, 162–163, 165; direct influences 134–151; identity

INDEX

142–143; individual differences 132–138, 141–142, 144, 156; interactionist perspective 159–160; internalized 137–151, 162–163; life space 142–143; motive sharing 147–149; ontogenesis 176–177; person by situation interactions 154–159; power of situation 132–133; predictive psychology 160–165; situational expertise 143–147; situational knowledge 162–163; Venn diagrams 133, *133*
social development, decision-making 197–198
social dilemmas, decision-making 114, 127
social emotions 117, 147
social environments, adaptation/genetics 20–21
Social Identity Theory (SIT) 142–143
social identity/identification 142–143, 151–152, 176, 285, 286, 291; *see also* identity
social inclusion 147–149, 292–293
social influences, adaptive capacity scorecards 307
social learning 217–219
social loafing 152
social marketing, adoption 294
social norms: individual differences 74; *see also* norms
social orientation 83
social philosophy/psychology 7
social pressures 135–136
social proof 151
social referencing 53, 54–55, **54**, 134, 135
social-altruistic perspectives 141–142
social-altruistic values, applied culture/social contexts 140–141
socially dominant forms of authoritarianism 87
societal collectivism 138
societal stakeholders 191
Society for Industrial and Organizational Psychology (SIOP) *18*, 72–73
socio-cognitive learning 214–217
socioeconomic status, determinism 51
socio-emotional development 175–177; non-clinical populations 179–180; ontogenesis 189–190
soldiers *see* military

solutionism 306
solutions (basic research/overview) 236–237
sounds, development psychology/motivation 194
Spanish hospitality industry 226
species-level adaptive capacity analyses/scorecards 304
species-level survival 1–2, 19–21
specificity: attitude object/individual differences 92–93; development psychology/motivation 194; goals/infallible causality 56
Spielberg, S. 323
spontaneous recovery 208–209
Srofe, L. 175
stability: broad interventions 268; emotional 81, 83, 99
stage approach to cognitive development (Piaget) 171–172
stakeholders: adaptive capacity scorecards 306, 315, 317; broad interventions 268; criterion problem 40, 43; decision-making 124–125; development psychology/motivation 195–196; educational psychology 250; ethics/precautionary principle 17; forensic psychology 261; ontogenesis 191; scientist-practitioner models 38; social contexts 149, 163–164
Stanton, F. 212, 290
stereotyping, determinism 67–68
Sternberg, R. J. 76–77
stimulus events, learning theories 204–205
strategic planning, broad interventions 271–272
street sense 51
strength of attitude 92–93
stress/stressors 254, 288–289; illnesses 234, **235**, 236; impracticality of action 258–259; PTSD 52–53, 254
strong arousals, decision-making 117–118
strong situations: decision-making 115; social contexts 138
structured interviews 276
subcortical feedback, development psychology/motivation 194
subject matter experts (SMEs) 272
submissive forms of authoritarianism 87
substantive processing, decision-making 110

INDEX

subversion 255, 322–323

succession planning, broad interventions 279

suicide 234, **235**, 236

sunk costs problem 111–112

supervisors, broad interventions 269

surface indicators, determinism 54

survival 1–2, 19–21; criterion problem 40–41

sweating (fixed action patterns) 115

sympathetic arousal: anger/frustration 119, 124, 260–261; decision-making 119, 124; fear response 118, 124, 207

sympathetic nervous system 115

Syria 5

systems approaches: broad interventions 266–267, *266*, 273; decision-making/determinism 60, *60*; determinism 63; and environment 23–25; target marketing/branding 291; *see also* development psychology

talent 169–170

target marketing 285–286, 290–292

taxonomies 80

team training, broad interventions 278–279

temperature: decision-making 112–113; global climate change 106–107

Ten Beersma, B. 160

Tenbrunsel, A. E. 160

Tett, R. P. 157–158, 159

theoretical formulation 246

theoretical problems 93–94

therapeutic alliances 259–260

therapeutic approaches to trauma 254

thermostats 108, 112–113

thirst, development psychology/ motivation 194

Thomas, J. P. 91

Thorndike, E. L. 208, 209–210

threat appraisals/framing: decision-making 108–113, 125–126; determinism 55; discrepancy testing 254; rigidity hypotheses 119, 124

thumbnail models: broad interventions 273, 295, *295*; decision-making 105–106, *106*, 110

time: and social dilemmas 114; transfer of training problems 219–220

To Save Everything, Click Here (Morozov) 245

Tolman, E. C. 204, 206

tough-mindedness 81

tourism 181–182, 249, 295

tradition 94–95; *see also* values

tragedy of the commons 21–22

training: applied cognitive learning 213; associative learning 206; broad interventions 267–268, 278–279; cognitive learning 219–221; educational psychology 252; safety as analogue 227; social contexts 157

traits 71, 80–95; activation approach/ social contexts 157–159; cognitive development/ontogenesis 169–175; facilitators/activation 158; *see also* individual differences

transfer of deliberative approaches 318

transfer of insight 258–259

transfer of learning: broad interventions 285; clinical psychology 253

transfer problems, deliberative choice 257

transfer of training 219–221; associative learning 206; broad interventions 278; educational psychology 252

trauma 52–53, 254

treatments 253; *see also* interventions

trial-and-error learning 19, 20–21

triple bottom line 43

Trotman, K. T. 149–150

true negatives/positives: Brunswick Lens Model 122; determinism/heuristics 64–65; individual differences 84–85

trust in authorities 291

Trzesniewski, K. H. 196

turnover 269

Tversky, A. 55

Tyler, T. R. 161

ultimate criteria, transfer of training problems 220

uncertainty 89, 96, 138, 221

underlying factors/surface indicators 54

understanding: probabilists 32; *see also* knowledge; *learning*

United States: 14th Amendment to Consitution 323; automobile dependency 289–290; causes of death indicators 234, **235**, 236; Declaration of Independence 25–26; Flint Michigan water 10; geological surveys 5; *An Inconvenient Truth* 125; military/ applied cognitive learning 213; Native

INDEX

peoples 139–140; Paracollege program of St. Olaf College 221–222
units of analysis, determinism 58–59
universal recognition of facial emotional displays 144
universalism, social contexts 138, 139
unpleasant emotions, decision-making 124
urban designers, social contexts 137
us/them dichotomy 67–68, 197
usability 243
utilities CEOs, criterion problem 40–41
utopian fallacy 36

validity: decision-making 123; transfer of training problems 222–223
Valor, C. 127
values: applied culture/social contexts 140–141; broad interventions 272; direct social influences 136; individual differences 74, 92–95, 101–102, 103; science and certainty 27; social contexts 141–142; target marketing/branding 291; *see also* culture; *norms*
VAM (visual-audio media) 293–294, 320
variables: attitudes/individual differences 93–94; broad interventions 266–267; causality/inputs 60–61, 132–133, 266–267; consumer psychology 282; decision-making/determinism 60–61; definitions 31; individual differences 71, 77, 100–101; learning theories 204; mediation 77; social contexts 132–133; target marketing/branding 291
Velden, F. S. 160
Venn diagrams, social contexts 133, *133*
viability, adaptive capacity 21
views of psychologist's roles 241–243
visual indicators, decision-making/emotions 117
visual-audio media (VAM) 293–294, 320

Viswesvaran, C. 91
voluntary simplicity 291–292

Wade-Benzoni, K. A. 160
Wall Street Journal 106–107
"War on Drugs" 257
warfare 29–30, 50–53, 188–189
waste reduction 4–5
water: carrying capacity 21–22; Colorado River Project 33–35; consumption/applied learning 209–210; quality 10; shortages 5
Waters, E. 175
Watson, J. B. 118, 290
wayfinding 225
weak situations: direct social influences 134; situational expertise/social context 146–147
well-being: Oskamp & sustainability 25; psychology of sustainability 42–43
Wells, H. G. 202, 231–232
Welsch, H. 127
Werner, H. 169, 170
Western European culture 94–95
Whitman, D. S. 91
Winett, R. A. 225
Winkler, R. C. 225
Woodley, M. A. 98
work analysis 277
work versus talent 169–170
World War II 29–30, 50–53
Wu, C.-H. 90

Yeager, D. 196
You Are Not So Smart (McRaney) 55

Zelezny, L. C. 247, 249–250
Zimmer, I. 149–150

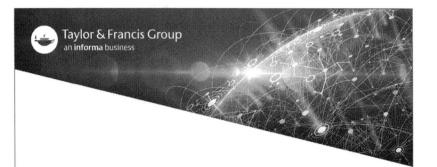